Lecture Notes in Computer Science 14597

Founding Editors

Gerhard Goos
Juris Hartmanis

The series Lecture Notes in Computer Science (LNCS), including its subseries Lecture Notes in Artificial Intelligence (LNAI) and Lecture Notes in Bioinformatics (LNBI), has established itself as a medium for the publication of new developments in computer science and information technology research, teaching, and education.

LNCS enjoys close cooperation with the computer science R & D community, the series counts many renowned academics among its volume editors and paper authors, and collaborates with prestigious societies. Its mission is to serve this international community by providing an invaluable service, mainly focused on the publication of conference and workshop proceedings and postproceedings. LNCS commenced publication in 1973.

Isaac Sserwanga · Hideo Joho · Jie Ma ·
Preben Hansen · Dan Wu · Masanori Koizumi ·
Anne J. Gilliland
Editors

Wisdom, Well-Being, Win-Win

19th International Conference, iConference 2024
Changchun, China, April 15–26, 2024
Proceedings, Part II

 Springer

Editors
Isaac Sserwanga
iSchool organization
Berlin, Germany

Hideo Joho
University of Tsukuba
Tsukuba, Japan

Jie Ma
Jilin University
Changchun, China

Preben Hansen
Stockholm University
Stockholm, Sweden

Dan Wu
Wuhan University
Wuhan, China

Masanori Koizumi
University of Tsukuba
Tsukuba, Japan

Anne J. Gilliland
University of California
Los Angeles, CA, USA

ISSN 0302-9743   ISSN 1611-3349 (electronic)
Lecture Notes in Computer Science
ISBN 978-3-031-57859-5   ISBN 978-3-031-57860-1 (eBook)
https://doi.org/10.1007/978-3-031-57860-1

This Springer imprint is published by the registered company Springer Nature Switzerland AG
The registered company address is: Gewerbestrasse 11, 6330 Cham, Switzerland

Paper in this product is recyclable.

Preface

As we embark on the proceedings of iConference 2024, we reflect upon the changes since the iConference of 2023. This annual gathering represents a symbol of the resilience, adaptability, and innovation of the information community. Emerging from the challenges posed by the global COVID-19 pandemic, the iSchools community navigated the remote conference landscape, laying the foundation for a new normal where technology became the bridge connecting minds, ideas, and aspirations.

The success of the iSchools conference of 2023 reaffirmed the pivotal role of information technologies in fostering engagement and collaboration. It set the stage for the overarching theme of the 19th iConference: "Wisdom, Well-being, and Win-win." This theme encapsulates our commitment to exploring synergies, nurturing shared goals, and leveraging the power of information to enhance the well-being of individuals and communities. As we delve into the proceedings, we invite readers to witness the culmination of efforts aimed at not only advancing scholarly discourse but also contributing to the broader landscape of wisdom-driven innovation.

The virtual iConference 2024 took place from April 15–18, 2024 before the physical conference on April 22–26, 2024 at Changchun, China. Its hosts included Jilin University, China, and University of Tsukuba, Japan.

The conference theme attracted a total of 218 submissions with 109 Full Research Papers and 109 Short Research Papers.

In a double-blind review process by 319 internationally renowned experts, 91 entries were approved, including 36 Full Research Papers and 55 Short Research Papers. The approval rate was 33% for the Full Research Papers and 50.46% for the Short Research Papers. Additional submissions were selected for the Workshops and Panels, the Doctoral Colloquium, the Early Career Colloquium, the Student Symposium, Posters, and the Spanish-Portuguese and Chinese language paper sessions.

The Full and Short Research papers are published for the ninth time in Springer's *Lecture Notes in Computer Science* (LNCS). These proceedings are sorted into the following eighteen categories, reflecting the diversity of the information research areas: "Archives and Information Sustainability", "Behavioral Research", "AI and Machine Learning", "Information Science and Data Science", "Information and Digital Literacy", "Digital Humanities", "Intellectual Property Issues", "Social Media and Digital Networks", "Disinformation and Misinformation", "Libraries, Bibliometrics and Metadata", "Knowledge Management", "Information Science Education", "Information Governance and Ethics", "Health Informatics", "Human-AI Collaboration", "Information Retrieval", "Community Informatics" and "Scholarly, Communication and Open Access".

We greatly appreciate the reviewers for their expertise and valuable review work and the track chairs for their relentless effort and vast expert knowledge. We wish to extend our gratitude to the chairs and volume editors; Full Research Papers chairs, Hideo Joho from University of Tsukuba, Jie Ma from Jilin University, and Preben Hansen from

Stockholm University; Short Research Papers chairs, Dan Wu from Wuhan University, Masanori Koizumi from University of Tsukuba, and Anne J. Gilliland from University of California, Los Angeles.

The iConference lived up to its global representation of iSchools to harness the synergy of research and teaching in the field of information and complementary areas of sustainability.

February 2024

Isaac Sserwanga
Hideo Joho
Jie Ma
Preben Hansen
Dan Wu
Masanori Koizumi
Anne J. Gilliland

Organization

Organizer

Jilin University, People's Republic of China
University of Tsukuba, Japan

Conference Chairs

Yingtong Guo	Jilin University, People's Republic of China
Atsushi Toshimori	University of Tsukuba, Japan
Atsuyuki Morishima	University of Tsukuba, Japan
Jun Deng	Jilin University, People's Republic of China

Program Chairs

Local Arrangement Chairs

Yingtong Guo	Jilin University, People's Republic of China
Jun Deng	Jilin University, People's Republic of China

Proceedings Chair

Isaac Sserwanga	Humboldt-Universität zu Berlin (iSchools Organisation), Germany

Full Research Paper Chairs

Hideo Joho	University of Tsukuba, Japan
Jie Ma	Jilin University, People's Republic of China
Preben Hansen	Stockholm University, Sweden

Short Research Paper Chairs

Dan Wu	Wuhan University, People's Republic of China
Masanori Koizumi	University of Tsukuba, Japan
Anne J. Gilliland	University of California, Los Angeles, USA

Poster Chairs

Alex Poole	Drexel University, USA
Lei Pei	Nanjing University, People's Republic of China
Ellie Sayyad Abdi	Curtin University, Australia

Spanish - Portuguese Papers Chairs

Sara Martínez Cardama	Universidad Carlos III de Madrid, Spain
Josep Cobarsí Morales	Universidad Carlos III de Madrid, Spain
Alan César Belo Angeluci	Universidade de São Paulo, Brazil
Diana Lucio Arias	Pontificia Universidad Javeriana, Colombia

Chinese Paper Chairs

Xiwei Wang	Jilin University, People's Republic of China
Yang Zhang	Sun Yat-sen University, People's Republic of China
Gaohui Cao	Central China Normal University, People's Republic of China

Workshops and Panel Chairs

Ina Fourie	University of Pretoria, South Africa
Chengzhi Zhang	Nanjing University, People's Republic of China
Wonsik Jeff Shim	Sungkyunkwan University, South Korea

Student Symposium Chairs

Hui Yan	Renmin University of China, People's Republic of China
Elizabeth Eikey	University of California, USA
Romain Herault	Linnaeus University, Sweden

Early Career Colloquium Chairs

Charles Senteio	Rutgers University, USA
Jiangping Chen	University of North Texas, USA
Debbie Meharg	Edinburgh Napier University, UK
YuXiang Zhao	Nanjing University, People's Republic of China

Doctoral Colloquium Chairs

Widad Mustafa El Hadi	University of Lille, France
Howard Rosenbaum	Indiana University Bloomington, USA
Tina Du	Charles Sturt University, Australia

Doctoral Dissertation Award Chair

Pengyi Zhang	Peking University, People's Republic of China

Conference Coordinators

Michael Seadle	iSchools Organization
Slava Sterzer	iSchools Organization
Katharina Gudat	iSchools Organization
Ulrike Liebner	iSchools Organization
Isaac Sserwanga	iSchools Organization
Wei Feng	iSchools Organization

Reviewers Full and Short Papers iConference 2024 (319)

Jacob Abbott
Naresh Kumar Agarwal
Daniel Agbaji
Aharony Noa Aharony
Farhan Ahmad Ahmad
Isola Ajiferuke
Mahir Akgun
Nicole D. Alemanne
Daniel Gelaw Alemneh
Lilach Alon
Misita Anwar
Tatjana Aparac-Jelusic
Rhea Rowena Ubana Apolinario
Lateef Ayinde
Dmitriy Babichenko
Ananth Balashankar
Sarah Barriage
Ofer Bergman
Arpita Bhattacharya
Jianxin Bi
Toine Bogers

Isak De Villiers {Diffie} Bosman
Theo J. D. Bothma
Guillaume Boutard
Sarah Elaine Bratt
Paulina Bressel
Jenny Bronstein
Leonard D. Brown
Yi Bu
Sarah A. Buchanan
Charles Bugre
Julia Bullard
Frada Burstein
Yu-Wei Chang
Haihua Chen
Hsin-liang Chen
Jiangping Chen
Xiaoyu Chen
Yi-Yun Cheng
Wonchan Choi
Yujin Choi
Yunseon Choi

Miyoung Chong
Josep Cobarsí-Morales
Isabella L. Corieri
Julian D. Cortes
Andrew Cox
Amber L. Cushing
Mats Dahlstrom
Gabriel David
Nilou Davoudi
Jun Deng
Sanhong Deng
Shengli Deng
Leyla Dewitz
Junhua Ding
Karsten Donnay
Philip Doty
Liz Dowthwaite
Yunfei Du
Zhenjia Fan
Bruce Ferwerda
Rachel Fleming-May
Ina Fourie
Rebecca D. Frank
Viviane Frings-Hessami
Hengyi Fu
Yaming Fu
Jonathan Furner
Henry Alexis Gabb
Maria Gäde
Abdullah Gadi
Chunmei Gan
Yubao Gao
Zheng Gao
Stanislava Gardasevic
Emmanouel Garoufallou
Diane Gill
Fausto Giunchiglia
Dion Goh
Patrick Thomas Golden
Liliana Gonzalez Perez
Anne Goulding
Christopher Graziul
Elke Greifeneder
Jenifer Daiane Grieger
Melissa Gross

Ece Gumusel
Qiuyan Guo
Vibhor Gupta
Ayse Gursoy
Hazel Hall
Ruohua Han
Yue Hao
Noriko Hara
Jenna Hartel
Bruce Hartpence
Stefanie Havelka
Alison Hicks
Liang Hong
Lingzi Hong
Md Khalid Hossain
Jingrui Hou
Amanda Hovious
Xinhui Hu
Yuerong Hu
Zhan Hu
Ying Huang
Shezin Waziha Hussain
Isto Huvila
Aylin Imeri (Ilhan)
Sharon Ince
Jonathan Isip
Hiroyoshi Ito
Corey Jackson
Eunmi Jeong
Jie Jiang
Michael Jones
Heidi Julien
Nicolas Jullien
Jaap Kamps
Ijay Kaz-Onyeakazi
Mat Kelly
Rebecca Kelly
Heikki Keskustalo
Mahmood Khosrowjerdi
Jiro Kikkawa
Heejun Kim
Jeonghyun Kim
Kyungwon Koh
Masanori Koizumi
Kushwanth Koya

Adam Kriesberg
Maja Krtalic
Bill Kules
Mucahid Kutlu
Sucheta Lahiri
Glen Layne-Worthey
Chengyi Le
Gregory Leazer
Deborah Lee
Kijung Lee
Lo Lee
Tae Hee Lee
Wan-Chen Lee
Kai Li
Lei Li
Muyan Li
Ying Li
Yingya Li
Yuan Li
Shaobo Liang
Chern Li Liew
Louise Limberg
Zack Lischer-Katz
Chang Liu
Jieli Liu
Annemaree Lloyd
Kun Lu
Ana Lucic
Zhuoran Luo
Lai Ma
Linqing Ma
Shutian Ma
Xiaoyue Ma
Emily Maemura
Sara Martínez-Cardama
Matthew Mayernik
Diane McAdie
Kate McDowell
Claire McGuinness
Pamela Ann McKinney
David McMenemy
Debbie Meharg
Jonas Ferrigolo Melo
Shuyuan Metcalfe
Anika Meyer

Eric Meyer
A. J. Million
J. Elizabeth Mills
Yue Ming
Lorri Mon
Atsuyuki Morishima
Heather Moulaison-Sandy
Widad Mustafa El Hadi/Prunier
Hyeong Suk Na
Maayan Nakash
Ha Quang Thinh Ngo
Huyen Nguyen
Sarah Nguyễn
David M. Nichols
Kathleen Obille
Lydia Oladapo
Gillian Oliver
Felipe Ortega
Giulia Osti
Kathleen Padova
Nayana Pampapura Madali
Hyoungjoo Park
Jinkyung Park
Min Sook Park
William Christopher Payne
Lei Pei
Olivia Pestana
Alina Petrushka
Leonor Gaspar Pinto
Alex H. Poole
Widiatmoko Adi Putranto
Xin Qian
Rahmi Rahmi
Priya Rajasagi
Arcot Rajasekar
Alexandria Rayburn
Gabby Resch
Jorge Revez
Fernanda Ribeiro
Cristian Roman Palacios
Milly Romeijn-Stout
Vassilis Routsis
Carsten Rudolph
Sarah Elizabeth Ryan
Özhan Sağlık

Songlak Sakulwichitsintu
Liliana Salas
Rachel Salzano
Madelyn Rose Sanfilippo
Vitor Santos
Ellie Sayyad Abdi
Kirsten Schlebbe
Michael Seadle
Subhasree Sengupta
Charles Senteio
Qingong Shi
Kristina Shiroma
Yan Shvartzshnaider
Luanne Sinnamon
Stephen C. Slota
Annique Smith
Vitaliy Snytyuk
António Lucas Soares
Amanda H. Sorensen
Clay Spinuzzi
Beth St. Jean
Rebecca Stallworth
Hrvoje Stancic
Ian Stockwell
Besiki Stvilia
Honglei Lia Sun
SeoYoon Sung
Jennifer Yoon Sunoo
Tokinori Suzuki
Tanja Svarre
Sue Yeon Syn
Masao Takaku
Anna Maria Tammaro
Rong Tang
Yi Tang
Zehra Taşkın
Paula Telo
Tien-I Tsai
Denise Tsunoda
Zhifang Tu
Rachel Tunis
Michael Twidale

Berthilde Uwamwezi
Neville Vakharia
Diego Vallejo-Huanga
Martie van Deventer
Brenda Van Wyk
Merce Væzquez
Travis L. Wagner
Yi Wan
Di Wang
June Wang
Ke-Rou Wang
Lin Wang
Linxu Wang
Peiling Wang
Shengang Wang
Yi-yu Wang
Zhongyi Wang
Xiaofei Wei
Brian Wentz
Namtip Wipawin
Christa Womser-Hacker
Jian Wu
Peng Wu
Peng Xiao
Iris Xie
Sherry Xie
Huimin Xu
Jian Xu
Xiao Xue
Erjia Yan
Hui Yan
Pu Yan
Feng Yang
Yuyu Yang
Ziruo Yi
Ayoung Yoon
JungWon Yoon
Sarah Young
Fei Yu
Vyacheslav I. Zavalin
Xianjin Zha
Yujia Zhai

Contents – Part II

Social Media and Digital Networks

Disinformation and Misinformation

Libraries, Bibliometrics and Metadata

Digital Humanities

Evaluation of Ancient Chinese Natural Language Understanding in Large Language Models Based on ACHNLU

Die Hu⬛, Guangyao Sun⬛, Liu Liu⬛, Chang Liu⬛, and Dongbo Wang(✉)⬛

College of Information Management, Nanjing Agricultural University, Nanjing 210095, China
2022114012@stu.njau.edu.cn

Abstract. The remarkable performance of large language models (LLMs) has garnered widespread attention across multiple research domains. The field of ancient Chinese information processing also requires the incorporation of cutting-edge technologies to meet the substantial demands for data processing. To facilitate the application of large language models in the context of ancient Chinese text processing, this study introduces the Ancient Chinese Natural Language Understanding (ACHNLU) benchmark. The benchmark includes a comprehensive evaluation mechanism for assessing the performance of LLMs in 6 typical tasks related to natural language understanding of ancient Chinese. With its high level of comprehensiveness and granularity, the system also demonstrates good scalability, offering a solid evaluation framework for related research. Based on this benchmark, the study evaluates the ancient Chinese understanding capabilities of 13 mainstream LLMs. It was found that while LLMs perform well in tasks such as sentence segmentation and punctuation, they still face significant challenges in word segmentation, part-of-speech tagging, and named entity recognition for ancient Chinese. Among all evaluated models, GPT-4 outperformed the rest. In the realm of open-source LLMs, Ziya-LLaMA-13B-v1.1 and Baichuan-13B performed relatively well, although they still lag behind highly optimized, closed-source LLMs. The LLMs evaluation based on ACHNLU provides empirical support for model selection in the domain of ancient Chinese information processing and offers valuable insights for subsequent research and practical applications.

Keywords: Large Language Models · Ancient Chinese Natural Language Understanding · Competency Evaluation

1 Introduction

The voluminous corpus of ancient Chinese books is a treasure trove for the Chinese nation, encompassing invaluable history, culture, and wisdom. Thorough understanding and effective utilization of these classical resources are crucial for the inheritance and promotion of Chinese culture. Recent years have witnessed substantial achievements in the digitization of ancient Chinese books, both in terms of scale and quality, laying the foundational conditions for their in-depth utilization [1]. The ongoing advancements in

I. Sserwanga et al. (Eds.): iConference 2024, LNCS 14597, pp. 3–18, 2024.
https://doi.org/10.1007/978-3-031-57860-1_1

information technology have expanded the range of technological options available for text mining of ancient books, propelling the field towards intelligent information processing [2]. One of the key challenges facing ancient Chinese text information processing is how to effectively leverage these advanced technologies to enhance the intelligence level of text processing tasks.

The impressive performance and automation capabilities of large language models (LLMs) have infused new hope into the domain of ancient Chinese text processing. Since the launch of ChatGPT [3], its exceptional capabilities have attracted considerable attention, leading to a surge of LLMs both domestically and internationally. To effectively foster the application of LLMs in specific domains, it is particularly important to evaluate their actual capabilities scientifically. However, most current research focused on evaluating the performance of LLMs is primarily oriented towards their understanding and processing of modern texts, with relatively less emphasis on ancient Chinese text information processing. Against this backdrop, exploring the performance of existing LLMs on ancient Chinese text tasks is a pivotal step for advancing the field into a new phase.

The ability of models to understand ancient Chinese serves as the basis for realizing ancient Chinese text information processing. Drawing on existing related studies, this paper constructs the Ancient Chinese Natural Language Understanding (ACHNLU) benchmark. This benchmark conducts a comprehensive evaluation of models' abilities to understand ancient Chinese through 6 representative ancient Chinese text understanding tasks. For this study, 13 mainstream LLMs were chosen for evaluation against this benchmark. By investigating their specific performance across different tasks and contexts, this study aims to better understand the strengths and limitations of these models when dealing with ancient Chinese texts. The evaluation benchmark and corresponding results proposed in this study can provide useful references for research in the field of ancient Chinese text information processing, thereby fostering the further development and application of LLMs in this area.

2   Related Work

The prompt-based learning approaches using LLMs open new possibilities for zero-shot and few-shot tasks. However, selecting an appropriate LLM and utilizing it effectively have become key challenges in practical applications. In light of this, scientific evaluation of the performance of LLMs becomes an imperative step.

The core task of LLMs is to enhance the performance of Natural Language Processing (NLP), which can be divided into Natural Language Understanding (NLU) and Natural Language Generation (NLG) tasks. Accordingly, most evaluations revolve around these two aspects. NLU tasks aim to enable the model to understand the syntax and semantics of natural language text and to capture implicit information within the text. In contrast, NLG tasks focus on transforming abstract data into human-readable natural language text.

Existing research on the performance evaluation of LLMs is predominantly conducted in an English context, with ChatGPT being the primary object of investigation. For example, studies by Jahan et al.[4] have explored the performance of ChatGPT in

NLU tasks such as relationship extraction and document classification, as well as in NLG tasks such as question answering and summarization with 0-shot. The study indicated that ChatGPT has significant application value in the biomedical field. Research by Bang et al. [5] demonstrated ChatGPT's high performance in NLP tasks like summarization, translation, and sentiment analysis. Further, Qin et al. [6] aimed to determine if ChatGPT is a general-purpose NLP task solver, finding that while ChatGPT excels in dialogue tasks, it still faces challenges in sequence labeling tasks like Named Entity Recognition(NER).

Moreover, some studies have delved into the performance of LLMs in low-resource languages. For instance, Kadaoui et al. [7] conducted a comprehensive evaluation of Bard and ChatGPT in machine translation tasks involving ten different types of Arabic languages. Alyafeai et al. [8]evaluated ChatGPT on seven different NLP tasks in Arabic, including part-of-speech tagging and sentiment analysis. Additionally, Adelani et al.[9] developed a news topic classification dataset for African languages and demonstrated ChatGPT's potential in topic classification tasks for 16 African languages.

Relatively speaking, research focusing on the evaluation of LLMs in a Chinese context is limited. Representative research for NLU includes studies by Bao et al.[10], which evaluated ChatGPT's performance in Chinese NER, relationship extraction, and event extraction. The study found that ChatGPT performs well in NER and event extraction but falls behind in relationship extraction compared to Chinese pre-trained models. For NLG, representative research includes studies by Zhang et al.[11], which evaluated the performance of LLMs like ChatGPT in generative tasks like summarization and reading comprehension. Shi et al. [12] employed content analysis and manual scoring to compare the answers generated by ChatGPT with manually generated answers on Zhihu in terms of external features, content features, emotion, and cognition. Representative research on the evaluation of LLMs in NLP performance is shown in Table 1.

Table 1. Representative studies of LLMs evaluation on NLP tasks which including Text Classification (TC), Relationship Extraction (RE), Event Extraction (EE), sentiment analysis (SA), Part-of-speech Tagging (PT), Named Entity Recognition (NER), Summarization (Summ.), Translation (Trans.), Question Answering (QA).

Evaluation Study	NLU						NLG			Language
	TC	RE	EE	SA	PT	NER	Summ	Trans	QA	
Jahan et al	√	√					√		√	English
Bang et al				√			√	√	√	English
Labrak et al.[13]	√				√				√	English
Belal et al.[14]				√						English
Han et al.[15]		√	√	√		√				English
Qin et al				√		√	√		√	English
Sun et al.[16]		√	√	√	√	√			√	English

(continued)

Table 1. (*continued*)

Evaluation Study	NLU						NLG			Language
	TC	RE	EE	SA	PT	NER	Summ	Trans	QA	
Zhang et al.[17]						✓				English
Kadaoui et al								✓		Arabic
Alyafeai et al				✓	✓		✓	✓		Arabic
Adelani et al	✓									African
Bao et al		✓	✓			✓				Modern Chinese
Zhang et al				✓			✓		✓	Modern Chinese
Shi et al									✓	Modern Chinese

Overall, numerous studies already exist that evaluate the performance of LLMs on multilingual text processing tasks from the perspectives of NLU and NLG. Ancient Chinese has its unique characteristics at the syntactic, lexical, and semantic levels. The field of ancient text information processing urgently requires higher levels of data processing capabilities to reconcile the contradiction between the overload of ancient texts awaiting processing and the lack of large-scale, high-quality annotated data. However, there is still a lack of research evaluating the performance of LLMs in the field of ancient text information processing. To address this gap, our study introduces ACHNLU benchmark and selects mainstream LLMs for evaluation.

3   ACHNLU Benchmark

3.1   Evaluation Tasks and Dataset

ACHNLU includes 6 representative knowledge annotation tasks based on ancient Chinese text comprehension, which can be categorized into Sentence-level and Word-level tasks. The classification system of this study is based on the granularity of knowledge labeling results. Among the ACHNLU tasks, event extraction mainly concerns the understanding and extraction of war names and war terms, and is therefore considered a Word-level task. In addition, ACHNLU set up multiple controlled experiments for each task with a given number of examples, depending on the task's difficulty.

The dataset used by ACHNLU includes hand-annotated Pre-Qin texts from 25 different works, sourced from the Language Technology Research Institute at Nanjing Normal University [18]. The corpus for event extraction related to war events is based on the *Chun Qiu Zuo Zhuan War Table* and is extracted from sentences corresponding to war events in the full text of the *Zuo Zhuan* [19]. Information on the evaluation tasks and their corresponding datasets are shown in Table 2.

From the above-mentioned corresponding datasets, 50 pieces of data were randomly selected for each task as the official evaluation dataset for ACHNLU, with additional example data selected for tasks that have examples. Pre-experimental results obtained using datasets of different sizes indicated that the model's performance rankings

Table 2. Evaluation Tasks and Dataset.

Task ID	Task Category	Task Name	Prompt	Dataset
1	Sentence-level	Sentence Segmentation	0-shot 1-shot 5-shot	264,761 Pre-Qin Dynasty Corpus
2		Punctuation	0-shot 1-shot 5-shot	
3	Word-level	Word Segmentation	1-shot 5-shot	
4		Part-of-Speech Tagging	1-shot 5-shot	
5		Named Entity Recognition	1-shot 5-shot	
6		Event Extraction	1-shot 5-shot	738 *Zuo Zhuan* War Event Corpus

remained consistent whether using 50 or 500 pieces of data. Moreover, an examination of model outputs showed that 50 test data points were sufficient to adequately demonstrate the strengths and weaknesses of different LLMs in each task. Therefore, by selecting 50 pieces of data for each evaluation task, ACHNLU can provide a comprehensive assessment of LLMs' capabilities in tasks related to ancient Chinese natural language understanding.

3.2 Evaluation Metrics

All the evaluation tasks in ACHNLU are closed-ended questions with standard answers. Therefore, metrics like Precision (P), Recall (R), and F1-score (F1) can be used for evaluation. The specific formulas for calculating these metrics are as follows.

$$P = \frac{TP}{TP + FP} \times 100\% \tag{1}$$

$$R = \frac{TP}{TP + FN} \times 100\% \tag{2}$$

$$F_1 = \frac{2 \times P \times R}{P + R} \times 100\% \tag{3}$$

In the aforementioned formulas, TP, FP, and FN represent the number of true positives. The F1 score is employed as the primary metric for evaluating the performance of the model in the task under study, as it offers a comprehensive measure that takes both P and R into account. Since the range for F1 metrics is between 0 and 1, to make comparisons between different models clearer, it will be presented in percentage form and will be rounded to two decimal places in the experiments.

3.3   Score Calculation

ACHNLU evaluates the overall natural language understanding capabilities of LLMs on ancient Chinese texts by calculating evaluation scores. These scores are obtained by taking the arithmetic mean of the F1-score across all tasks. The specific calculation formula is as follows.

$$S_n = \frac{100}{N} \sum_{i=1}^{N} F_i \tag{4}$$

$$S_{\text{Sentence}} = \frac{1}{2}(S_1 + S_2) \tag{5}$$

$$S_{\text{Word}} = \frac{1}{4}(S_3 + S_4 + S_5 + S_6) \tag{6}$$

$$S_{\text{Comprehensive}} = \frac{1}{2}(S_{\text{Sentence}} + S_{\text{Word}}) \tag{7}$$

In the formula mentioned above, S_n represents the score of the model in the n-th task, where n corresponds to the task number. N stands for the number of experimental rounds given different numbers of examples for the corresponding task, and Fi represents the F1 -score of the model in the i-th round of the experiment. S_{Sentence}, S_{Word}, and $S_{\text{Comprehensive}}$ represent the model's Sentence-level understanding score, Word-level understanding score, and comprehensive understanding score for ancient texts, respectively, which are calculated based on the scores in the corresponding tasks.

4   Research Process and Result Analysis

4.1   Sentence-Level Tasks

Sentence-level tasks primarily encompass sentence segmentation and punctuation. The task of ancient Chinese sentence segmentation is to divide the continuous text in ancient Chinese into logically complete and independent sentence units, in order to better under-stand the text's grammatical and semantic structure. And the task of punctuating ancient Chinese sentences requires the model to correctly segment sentences and mark the appro-priate punctuation symbols. During the evaluation process, this study attempts to extract and process the answers generated by LLMs in accordance with certain rules and based on the characteristics of the tasks at hand. For example, given that some models employ punctuation marks in English format, the study treats English-format punctuation as equivalent to their corresponding Chinese-format counterparts in the computation of performance metrics. That is to say, the placement of either a Chinese comma ("，") or an English comma (",") by the model is considered correct for the purpose of this evaluation.

Table 3 provides an example of the prompt information given for the ancient Chi-nese sentence segmentation task, along with randomly selected examples of model input and output. By comparing the standard answers with the model's processing results, the performance of different models in the task of ancient Chinese sentence segmentation can be intuitively observed: ERNIE-Bot's sentence segmentation result is completely

Table 3. 1-shot Example in Sentence Segmentation.

Evaluation Element		Content
Prompt Template		请使用斜杠（/）为下面的古汉语句子断句，输出断句后的结果，不要输出其他内容。
		(Please use slashes (/) to segment the following ancient Chinese sentence into individual sentences. Output only the segmented result, do not output any other content.)
		句子：(Sentence:)歲餘會皇太子所愛幸司馬良娣病且死謂太子曰妾死非天命乃諸娣妾良人更祝詛殺我太子憐之且以爲然
		断句结果：(Segmentation Result:)歲餘/會皇太子所愛幸司馬良娣病/且死/謂太子曰/妾死非天命/乃諸娣妾良人更祝詛殺我/太子憐之/且以爲然/
		句子：{输入语料}
		(Sentence: {Input Text})
		断句结果：
		(Segmentation Result:)
Input Text		正月上曰農天下之本其開籍田朕親率耕以給宗廟粢盛
Standard Answer		正月/上曰/農/天下之本/其開籍田/朕親率耕/以給宗廟粢盛/
Model Answer	GPT-4	正月上曰/農/天下之本/其開籍田/朕親率耕/以給宗廟粢盛/
	GPT-3.5-turbo	正月/上曰/農天下之本/其開籍田/朕親率耕/以給宗廟粢盛/
	ERNIE-Bot	正月/上曰/农/天下之本/其開籍田/朕親率耕/以給宗廟粢盛/
	ChatGLM-6B	正月上曰/農天下之本/其開籍田/朕親率耕以給宗廟粢盛/
	ChatGLM2-6B	正月上曰/農天下之本/其開籍田/朕親率耕/以給宗廟粢盛/
	MOSS-moon-003-sft	正月上說/農天下之本/其開籍田/朕親率耕/以給宗廟粢盛/
	Baichuan-13B	正月上曰/農天下之本/其開籍田/朕親率耕/以給宗廟粢盛/
	Phoenix-inst-chat-7b	正月上/曰/謂/農天下之本/其開籍/田/朕親率耕以給宗廟粢盛
	AquilaChat-7B	正月上曰/農天下之本/其開籍田/朕親率耕以/給宗廟粢盛/
	Ziya-LLaMA-13B-v1.1	正月上曰/農天下之本/其開籍田朕親率耕以給宗廟粢盛/
	Chinese-LLaMA-Alpaca-7B	正月上曰/衆山大帝/君王元皇帝/御笔字題匾額于/崇聖寺/殿堂内/
	Chinese-LLaMA-Alpaca-13B	正月上曰/农天下之本其开籍田朕亲率耕以供宗庙丰盛/
	Chinese-LLaMA-Alpaca-33B	正月上/曰/農天地之基礎/其開籍田/吾親率耕/為給宗

correct, but it converts the traditional character "農" to the simplified "农". The results for GPT-3.5-turbo, ChatGLM2-6B, and Baichuan-13B are identical, each displaying no errors in sentence segmentation but lacking two correct segmentations. In comparison to the aforementioned models, ChatGLM-6B and AquilaChat-7B exhibit greater inaccuracies and omissions. Additionally, MOSS-moon-003-sft and Phoenix-inst-chat-7b not only display errors and omissions, but also introduce modifications to specific words in the input sentence. The Chinese-LLaMA-Alpaca series of models output more chaotic results, mixing irrelevant content and partial sentence translations, resulting in poorer sentence segmentation performance.

As shown in Table 4, the performance of LLMs on the tasks of sentence segmentation and punctuation in ancient texts is displayed. It is evident that, across multiple experimental setups, an increase in the number of examples effectively improves the performance metrics for most models. Overall, ERNIE-Bot achieves the best performance in both tasks, reaching an F1 score of over 80% in each. GPT-4 follows closely behind, also demonstrating superior processing capabilities. Among the open-source models, Baichuan-13B excels at the sentence-level tasks in classical texts, achieving results comparable to those of GPT-3.5-turbo. In contrast, other models do not stand out in the task of sentence segmentation in ancient Chinese texts.

Table4. F1 Score (%) in the Evaluation of Sentence-level Tasks.

Model	Sentence Segmentation			Punctuation		
	0-shot	1-shot	5-shot	0-shot	1-shot	5-shot
GPT-4	81.60	84.12	85.53	71.96	73.96	76.33
GPT-3.5-turbo	77.45	80.71	81.77	64.81	72.03	71.56
ERNIE-Bot	81.80	86.25	**87.39**	69.84	77.37	**80.67**
ChatGLM-6B	65.01	68.76	74.91	57.02	61.11	65.94
ChatGLM2-6B	51.53	59.46	65.68	45.49	45.71	53.28
MOSS-moon-003-sft	41.74	58.78	58.28	33.17	50.89	52.83
Baichuan-13B	76.76	80.48	80.55	62.64	66.09	68.94
Phoenix-inst-chat-7b	30.41	39.42	26.46	19.67	28.15	24.93
AquilaChat-7B	41.18	31.06	22.16	36.90	27.95	21.65
Ziya-LLaMA-13B-v1.1	57.91	54.75	70.27	53.95	48.87	58.71
Chinese-LLaMA-Alpaca-7B	1.07	13.49	15.79	4.80	8.83	15.20
Chinese-LLaMA-Alpaca-13B	10.43	27.07	19.37	7.36	19.89	16.52
Chinese-LLaMA-Alpaca-33B	18.18	18.29	20.35	9.37	14.93	17.54

4.2   Word-Level Tasks

Word segmentation, part-of-speech tagging, and named entity recognition are representative Word-level sequence labeling tasks. Specifically, word segmentation refers to

Table 5. 1-shot Example in Part-of-Speech Tagging.

Evaluation Element		Content
Prompt Template		对下列古汉语句子进行词性标注，不要输出其他任何内容，已知词性与符号对应关系为：n，普通名词；nx，特殊名词；nr，人名姓氏；ns，地名；v，动词；w，标点；d，副词；r，代词；p，介词；c，连词；u，助词；m，数词；t，时间名词；y，语气词；a，形容词；f，方位词；q，量词；j，兼词；x，其他语素；gv，古代动词；s，拟声词
		（Perform part-of-speech tagging on the following ancient Chinese sentence without outputting any other content. The known parts-of-speech and their corresponding symbols are as follows: n, common noun; nx, special noun; nr, personal name or surname; ns, place name; v, verb; w, punctuation; d, adverb; r, pronoun; p, preposition; c, conjunction; u, auxiliary word; m, numeral; t, time noun; y, mood particle; a, adjective; f, directional word; q, measure word; j, co-verb; x, other morpheme; gv, ancient verb; s, onomatopoeic word.）
		句子：（Sentence:）丁奉字承淵，廬江安豐人也。
		标注结果：（Tagging Result:）丁奉/nr 字/n 承淵/nr，/w 廬江/ns 安豐/ns 人/n 也/u。/w
		句子：{输入语料}
		(Sentence: {Input Text})
		标注结果：
		(Tagging result:)
Input Text		太祖義之，舉為茂才。
Standard Answer		太祖/nr 義/v 之/r，/w 舉/v 為/v 茂才/nx。/w
Model Answer	GPT-4	太祖/nr 義/v 之/u，/w 舉/v 為/p 茂才/n。/w
	GPT-3.5-turbo	太祖/nr 義/n 之/u，/w 舉/v 為/p 茂才/n。/w
	ERNIE-Bot	太祖/n 義之/v，/w 舉/v 为/p 茂才/n。/w
	ChatGLM-6B	太祖/p 義/p 之/p,/舉/p 為/p 茂才/p。
	ChatGLM2-6B	太祖/n 義之/nr，/w 太祖/nr 舉/v 為/n 茂才/n 才/n。/w
	MOSS-moon-003-sft	太祖/n 義之/v，/w 舉/v 為/v 茂才/n。/w
	Baichuan-13B	太祖义之，举为茂才。
	Phoenix-inst-chat-7b	太祖義之/v 舉/v 為/v 茂才/v。/w
	AquilaChat-7B	太祖義之/nr，举为茂才/w

(continued)

Table 5. (*continued*)

Ziya-LLaMA-13B-v1.1	太祖/nr 義/a 之/m，/w 舉/v 為/v 茂才/ns。/w
Chinese-LLaMA-Alpaca-7B	{输出无关内容}
Chinese-LLaMA-Alpaca-13B	{输出无关内容}
Chinese-LLaMA-Alpaca-33B	太祖义之，/w 举/v 为/v 茂才/n .

the process of dividing continuous character sequences into meaningful words or phrase units. Part-of-speech tagging further annotates the grammatical role of each word, reflecting its lexical function within a sentence. Named entity recognition requires the model to identify named entities and subsequently determine their entity type. These three tasks play an integral role in the deep understanding and utilization of ancient Chinese. The event extraction task requires models to extract relevant elements of events from input sentences according to specified criteria. The corpus used for the event extraction task designed in this study consists of ancient Chinese sentences describing war events. LLMs are expected to output the names and terms related to wars, following the patterns provided in the prompt information. War terms are phrases in the original sentence that narrate the war, and can be directly extracted from the corpus. However, most sentences about wars do not directly include the name of the war. As a result, LLMs must deeply comprehend the input material before summarizing the name of the war based on key lexical elements like the principal entities of the war. This places high demands on the model's ability to understand ancient texts. The following will use part-of-speech tagging and event extraction as examples to illustrate the testing process for Word-level tasks.

As can be observed in Table 5, all models underperformed in part-of-speech tagging for the given sentence. Firstly, "太祖" in the sentence refers to a specific individual rather than merely a temple name; it should be tagged as a proper noun. Only GPT-4, GPT-3.5-turbo, and Ziya-LLaMA-13B-v1.1 correctly tagged it as such. Secondly, "義 之" translates to "consider him honorable" and should be tagged as a verb and pronoun, respectively; no model correctly annotated this. Lastly, "舉為茂才" means "elevate him to the status of a talented person"; here, "為" should be tagged as a verb, and "茂 才" should be tagged as a special noun as it typically refers to a candidate who has passed the local exams, serving as a specific title. Only Ziya-LLaMA-13B-v1.1 correctly tagged "為" and no models correctly tagged "茂才". These findings suggest that models need to possess both strong contextual understanding capabilities and a certain level of knowledge of ancient history to effectively perform tasks related to understanding ancient Chinese sentences. Deficiencies in either area can compromise the model's performance in specific tasks.

Unlike word-level sequence labeling tasks that have standard answers, the event extraction task adheres to distinct evaluation criteria. This study stipulates that a war's name is considered correct as long as it accurately encompasses the principal entities of the war, without reversing their active and passive relationships. As for terms related

Table 6. 1-shot Example in Event Extraction.

Evaluation Element		Content
Prompt Template		给定战争事件 scheme{'战争事件': ['战争名称','战争词']}，以 json 格式输出整个战争事件。 （Given the war event scheme {'War Event': ['War Name','War Term']}, output the entire war event in JSON format.） 句子：(Sentence:)春二月，衞寧喜、右宰穀伐孫氏，不克，複攻，克之，殺子叔及太子角 输出：{"战争名称": "衞內戰", "战争词": "伐攻殺"} (Output: {"War Name": "衞內戰", "War Term": "伐攻殺"}) 句子：{输入语料} (Sentence: {Input Text}) 输出： (Output:)
Input Text		冬，衞人助公孫滑伐鄭，取廩延。
Standard Answer		{"战争名称":"衞伐鄭","战争词":"伐取" }
Model Answer	GPT-4	{"战争名称": "衞鄭之戰", "战争词": "助伐取"}
	GPT-3.5-turbo	{"战争名称": "衞鄭战争", "战争词": "伐取"}
	ERNIE-Bot	{"战争名称": "鄭衞戰", "战争词": "伐取"}
	ChatGLM-6B	{"战争事件": ["冬", "衞人助公孫滑伐鄭"], "战争词": "伐鄭取廩延"}
	ChatGLM2-6B	{"战争名称": "卫国内战", "战争词": "伐攻殺", "时间": "春二月"}
	MOSS-moon-003-sft	{"战争名称": "廩延之役", "战争词": "伐取廩延"}
	Baichuan-13B	{"战争名称": "衞-鄭戰爭", "战争词": "伐攻取"}
	Phoenix-inst-chat-7b	{"战争名称": "衞郑战争", "战争词": "援兵"}
	AquilaChat-7B	{输出无关内容}
	Ziya-LLaMA-13B-v1.1	{"战争名称": "衞內戰", "战争词": "伐攻"}

(continued)

Table 6. (*continued*)

Chinese-LLaMA-Alpaca-7B	{"战争名称":"衞外陷","战争词":"劫夺"}
Chinese-LLaMA-Alpaca-13B	{"战争名称":"衞内之战","战争词":"夺庁"}
Chinese-LLaMA-Alpaca-33B	{"战争名称":"齐伐卫","战争词":"伐"}

to the war, they must be directly extracted from the original text and must match the standard answer to be deemed correct.

The specific evaluation process for the event extraction task is shown in Table 6. As can be seen, apart from AquilaChat-7B, all other models have output the elements of war events in a standardized format. Compared to the standard answer, GPT-4, GPT-3.5-turbo, ERNIE-Bot, Baichuan-13B, and Phoenix-inst-chat-7b can all be considered to have correctly summarized the name of the war. However, only GPT-3.5-turbo and ERNIE-Bot have accurately extracted the war terms.

The performance of LLMs in Word-level tasks is illustrated in Table 7. It is evident that GPT-4 demonstrates a distinct advantage across all tasks, particularly in named entity recognition and event extraction, where it leads other models by over 15 percentage points. Overall, the performance of LLMs at the Word -level tasks is subpar, especially in part-of-speech tagging and named entity recognition, with only three proprietary models showing relatively satisfactory results. However, it is worth noting that Ziya also achieves relatively good performance in part-of-speech tagging.

Table 7. F1 Score (%) in the Evaluation of Word -level Tasks which including WS(Word Segmentation),PT(Part-of-speech Tagging),NER(Named Entity Recognition),EE(Event Extraction).

Model	WS		PT		NER		EE	
	1-shot	5-shot	1-shot	5-shot	1-shot	5-shot	1-shot	5-shot
GPT-4	61.78	**63.35**	64.32	**66.91**	49.51	**65.42**	73.00	**84.00**
GPT-3.5-turbo	53.93	57.65	57.94	61.08	32.18	50.26	47.47	63.00
ERNIE-Bot	62.38	63.06	54.56	57.91	10.26	32.77	44.00	57.00
ChatGLM-6B	39.46	49.88	4.13	17.20	7.75	12.07	31.00	48.00
ChatGLM2-6B	28.10	34.78	7.47	18.96	5.16	14.72	34.00	52.00
MOSS-moon-003-sft	26.14	29.46	9.08	20.86	4.29	10.10	23.00	41.41
Baichuan-13B	35.53	31.68	26.43	32.79	8.28	13.43	42.00	58.00

(*continued*)

Table 7. (*continued*)

Model	WS		PT		NER		EE	
	1-shot	5-shot	1-shot	5-shot	1-shot	5-shot	1-shot	5-shot
Phoenix-inst-chat-7b	21.93	30.55	4.05	14.00	1.64	12.00	25.00	54.00
AquilaChat-7B	24.29	28.46	20.47	17.08	6.40	7.08	24.00	52.00
Ziya-LLaMA-13B-v1.1	45.12	42.14	44.87	50.65	20.69	23.29	22.00	52.00
Chinese-LLaMA-Alpaca-7B	4.21	7.00	2.21	3.37	1.74	1.79	5.05	24.00
Chinese-LLaMA-Alpaca-13B	1.10	5.15	1.14	3.81	1.83	3.70	17.35	34.02
Chinese-LLaMA-Alpaca-33B	5.81	15.96	8.46	4.13	4.55	7.84	18.60	9.86

5   Research Conclusions

Based on the score calculation formulas of ACHNLU, we can obtain the ranking of the LLMs' ability to understand ancient Chinese, as shown in Table 8.

Table 8. Comprehensive Evaluation of LLMs' Ancient Chinese NLU.

Ranking	Model	Sentence-level	Word-level	Comprehensive
1	GPT-4	78.92	66.04	72.48
2	ERNIE-Bot	80.55	47.74	64.15
3	GPT-3.5-turbo	74.72	52.94	63.83
4	Baichuan-13B	72.58	31.02	51.80
5	Ziya-LLaMA-13B-v1.1	57.41	37.60	47.50
6	ChatGLM-6B	65.46	26.19	45.82
7	ChatGLM2-6B	53.53	24.40	38.96
8	MOSS-moon-003-sft	49.28	20.54	34.91
9	AquilaChat-7B	30.15	22.47	26.31
10	Phoenix-inst-chat-7b	28.17	20.40	24.28
11	Chinese-LLaMA-Alpaca-33B	16.44	9.40	12.92
12	Chinese-LLaMA-Alpaca-13B	16.77	8.51	12.64
13	Chinese-LLaMA-Alpaca-7B	9.86	6.17	8.02

According to the evaluation scores and the actual performance of LLMs in six specific tasks, this study can draw several conclusions:

(1) LLMs generally perform well on sentence-level tasks, but still face significant challenges at the word level. According to the evaluation results, most models are able to produce fairly accurate results in sentence segmentation and punctuation tasks even

in 0-shot experiments. Most models scored above 50 points at the sentence level, with four models exceeding 70 points. However, at the word level, only GPT-4 scored above 60 points, while most of the other models were around 30 points. Particularly in part-of-speech tagging and NER tasks, the optimal F1 values for most models hovered around 20%. This suggests that word-level tasks are more challenging and can better test the model's understanding of ancient Chinese.

(2) Proprietary LLMs have a significant advantage in understanding ancient Chinese. GPT-4, ERNIE-Bot, and GPT-3.5-turbo led the evaluation results in each task. Furthermore, GPT-4 significantly outperformed ERNIE-Bot and GPT-3.5-turbo in the overall score, showing outstanding performance in understanding ancient text. In terms of their performance in specific tasks, ERNIE-Bot excels at sentence-level understanding tasks, while GPT-4 performs better at the word level. Among open-source models, Baichuan-13B and Ziya-LLaMA-13B-v1.1 performed relatively consistently but still lagged behind proprietary models. Notably, Baichuan-13B excelled in sentence segmentation and punctuation tasks.

(3) Current LLMs exhibit issues with understanding ancient Chinese texts, including altering the input text and producing outputs in Simplified Chinese with English punctuation. Modifying the content of the input directly results in invalid responses, which is a manifestation of these models' limited capability in understanding ancient Chinese. Observing the outputs in this study, it can be discerned that models such as Baichuan-13B, the Chinese-LLaMA-Alpaca series, and MOSS-moon-003-sft occasionally auto-convert inputted Traditional Chinese classical texts to Simplified Chinese and use English punctuation. Such behavior presents challenges for processing ancient texts that demand a high degree of standardization.

(4) For LLMs that have stable output, performance improves significantly when given examples. The study found that performance metrics of models with strong instruction-following abilities improve gradually with an increase in the number of examples provided. However, for models that have difficulty understanding both instructions and ancient text, providing examples can actually confuse them, leading to more chaotic outputs without achieving any improvement.

6 Summary and Outlook

This study introduced ACHNLU, a benchmark for evaluating the ability of large language models to understand ancient Chinese text. The benchmark was applied to evaluate the performance of mainstream LLMs on tasks related to understanding ancient Chinese, demonstrating its validity. Based on the findings, this paper provides reliable evaluation and model selection methods for applying LLMs in the ancient Chinese domain, as well as useful insights for their specific usage. In practical applications, it is necessary to select an appropriate LLMs based on real-world needs and to design suitable prompts to achieve optimal results. Additionally, care should be taken regarding potential issues like the model's automatic conversion between simplified and traditional Chinese characters.

Further, the results indicate that LLMs can offer viable text processing methods in the ancient Chinese field, where annotated data is scarce. However, due to the lack of fine-tuning data specific to ancient Chinese and sufficient reserves of classical Chinese knowledge, even proprietary LLMs struggle to perform well across all tasks, while open-source models generally have not demonstrated outstanding capabilities in this domain. In the meantime, the cost of accessing high-performing proprietary models must also be considered, which means that current LLMs are not sufficient to sustain ongoing research in the classical Chinese field.

Therefore, the paper suggests that it is essential to develop LLMs specifically tailored for the ancient Chinese domain. These can be achieved through domain-specific pre-training and fine-tuning to enhance their linguistic and domain expertise. Well-performing open-source models from this study, such as the Baichuan and Ziya series, could serve as baseline models for training on large-scale electronic classical Chinese resources.

Future research will further optimize the proposed benchmark by adding more representative tasks, increasing the level of automation, etc. Updated LLMs will also be evaluated to provide ongoing references for the application of such models in the ancient Chinese information processing domain.

Acknowledgements. This study is supported by the National Social Science Foundation of China (Grant No.21&ZD331) and the National Natural Science Foundation of China (Grant No. 72004095).

References

1. Huang, S.Q., Wang, D.B.: Review and trend of research on ancient chinese character information processing. Library Inform. Serv. **61**, 43–49 (2017)
2. Lin, L.T., Wang, D.B.: A survey of ancient book text mining technology. Sci. Technol. Inform. Res. **5**, 78–91 (2023)
3. Introducing ChatGPT, https://openai.com/blog/chatgpt, (Accessed 28 July 2023)
4. Jahan, I., Laskar, M.T.R., Peng, C., Huang, J.: Evaluation of ChatGPT on Biomedical Tasks: A Zero-Shot Comparison with Fine-Tuned Generative Transformers (2023). http://arxiv.org/abs/2306.04504,
5. Bang, Y., et al.: A Multitask, Multilingual, Multimodal Evaluation of ChatGPT on Reasoning, Hallucination, and Interactivity (2023). http://arxiv.org/abs/2302.04023,
6. Qin, C., Zhang, A., Zhang, Z., Chen, J., Yasunaga, M., Yang, D.: Is ChatGPT a General-Purpose Natural Language Processing Task Solver? (2023). http://arxiv.org/abs/2302.06476,
7. Kadaoui, K., et al.: TARJAMAT: Evaluation of Bard and ChatGPT on Machine Translation of Ten Arabic Varieties (2023). http://arxiv.org/abs/2308.03051,
8. Alyafeai, Z., Alshaibani, M.S., AlKhamissi, B., Luqman, H., Alareqi, E., Fadel, A.: Taqyim: Evaluating Arabic NLP Tasks Using ChatGPT Models, https://arxiv.org/abs/2306.16322v1, (Accessed 31 Aug 2023)
9. Adelani, D.I., et al.: MasakhaNEWS: News Topic Classification for African languages, https://arxiv.org/abs/2304.09972v1, (Accessed 31 Aug 2023)
10. Bao, T., Zhang, C.Z.: Performance evaluation of ChatGPT on Chinese information extraction ——an empirical study by three typical extraction tasks. Data Anal. Knowl. Dis. 1–16
11. Zhang, H.P., et al.: ChatGPT performance evaluation on chinese language and risk measure. Data Anal. Knowl. Dis. **7**, 16–25 (2023)
12. Shi, Y.L., Xu, X.: Comparison of ChatGPT's Machine Responses and Zhihu's Manual Responses. Library Tribune, pp. 1–10

13. Labrak, Y., Rouvier, M., Dufour, R.: A Zero-shot and Few-shot Study of Instruction-Finetuned Large Language Models Applied to Clinical and Biomedical Tasks (2023). http://arxiv.org/abs/2307.12114

14. Belal, M., She, J., Wong, S.: Leveraging ChatGPT As Text Annotation Tool For Sentiment Analysis, https://arxiv.org/abs/2306.17177v1, (Accessed 31 Aug 2023)

15. Han, R., Peng, T., Yang, C., Wang, B., Liu, L., Wan, X.: Is Information Extraction Solved by ChatGPT? An Analysis of Performance, Evaluation Criteria, Robustness and Errors, https://arxiv.org/abs/2305.14450v1, (Accessed 31 Aug 2023)

16. Sun, X., et al.: Pushing the Limits of ChatGPT on NLP Tasks, https://arxiv.org/abs/2306.09719v1, (Accessed 31 Aug 2023)

17. Zhang, Y.Y., Zhang, C.Z., Zhou, Y., Chen, B.K.: ChatGPT-based scientific paper entity recognition on multiple perspectives: performance measurement and availability research. Data Anal. Knowl. Dis., 1–18

18. Chen, X.H.: Information Processing of Pre-Qin Literature. World Book Publishing Company (2013)

19. Fan, W.J., et al.: A research on the visualization and metric analysis of war in Zuo Zhuan based on social network analysis. Library Inform. Serv. **64**, 90–99 (2020)

A Problematic Dichotomy in the Perspective of Field Theory: Hermeneutics and Quantitative Qnalysis in Distant Reading

Mozhuo Chen[✉]

Fudan University, Shanghai, China
rimblec1326@gmail.com

Abstract. Moretti's "distant reading" is regarded as a pioneer and an exemplar of computational literary studies. "Distant reading" puts forward a strict boundary between hermeneutics and quantitative analysis. The relationship between the two and the nature of quantitative analysis in literary studies are key issues in the theory of computational literary studies. This paper analyzes the claims and issues behind Moretti's dichotomy, and introduces Bourdieu's field theory perspective, pointing out that the nature of quantitative analysis must be understood in relation to the larger disciplinary discursive practices in which it is embedded.

Keywords: Distant Reading · Quantitative analysis · Computational Literary Studies

1 Introduction

What exactly is the relationship between the hermeneutic tradition as the traditional paradigm of literary studies and quantitative analysis as the core methodology of computational literary studies (CLS)? This relates to the epistemological construction of CLS, which is in dire need of such theoretical reflection. Therefore, the nature of quantitative analysis in literary studies needs to be clarified, so that we can theoretically grasp the way in which quantitative analysis encounters literary studies: is it a heterogeneous transplantation or intrusion, or is it a specific interaction and intersection within mutual differences?

The nature of quantitative analysis in literary studies is a controversial topic. Some researchers imply its scientificity, objectivity and validity, and consider it one of the core advantages that quantitative analysis brings to traditional literary studies that value subjectivity [10]. Conversely, some researchers highlight that quantitative analysis is equally susceptible to subjective intervention [6, 26]. In this context, the theory of "distant reading" proposed by Moretti deserves particular attention. Acknowledged as a pioneer and exemplar of CLS, "distant reading" was initially coined as a method to study world literature. It involves handling vast amounts of texts across time and space using a variety of quantitative methods, aiming to attain a macroscopic perspective of the broader history of literature and explore more universal literary patterns [12].

I. Sserwanga et al. (Eds.): iConference 2024, LNCS 14597, pp. 19–26, 2024.
https://doi.org/10.1007/978-3-031-57860-1_2

In the series of theories and practices constructed around "distant reading," Moretti borrows the concept of "hermeneutics" to distinguish between the traditional literary studies paradigm grounded in hermeneutics and the CLS paradigm centered around quantitative analysis. He insists on the heterogeneity of these two, and attributes different natures, functions, and expectations to each. In this framework, quantitative analysis is always linked to science, especially natural science. Moretti's view of separating interpretation and quantitative analysis is quite representative in computational literary studies [1, 10, 22].

This paper begins by analyzing Moretti's demarcation between quantitative analysis and hermeneutics, pointing out that there are two contradictory expectations and pursuits underpinning this demarcation: (1) the pursuit of historical materialist literary studies as a kind of social critique and (2) the pursuit of scientific and objective literary studies. Moretti's misinterpretation of quantitative analysis leads to the inability of the two pursuits to coexist, which will bring a series of negative consequences. Building on this, the paper introduces the perspective of Bourdieu's field theory, asserting that understanding the essence of quantitative analysis necessitates considering its integration within broader practices of disciplinary discourse.

2   The Construction of the Opposition

Moretti has always treated the relationship between hermeneutics and quantitative analysis as an "either/or" choice. However, the connotations of this opposition have subtly changed. In his early works such as *The Atlas of European Novel* and *Distant Reading*, the dichotomy is expressed as "explanation vs. interpretation" [11, 12]. In later treatises such as *Falso Movimento*, this opposition is expressed as quantitative analysis vs. hermeneutics [13]. In the conceptual shift, the most crucial attribute has not changed. Both 'explanation' and 'quantitative analysis' refer to literary research that employs a great deal of quantitative methods and is scientific and objective, while interpretation and hermeneutics refer to literary studies centered on hermeneutics and emphasizing the subjective element. However, there is a change in the connection with social history. In the former period, explanation emphasized the causal relationship between the text and external forces, while interpretation focused on the relationship between meaning and meaning within the textual network. In the later period, hermeneutics became a method of unraveling the connection between form and the world, while quantitative methods were confined to the interior of the textual network, turning it into an internal formal study.

This shift requires an examination within the broader framework of Moretti's entire body of work, in which we can find two central pursuits in his study of literature. Firstly, Moretti strives for a historical-materialist literary criticism, intertwined with socio-cultural critique. He sees form as the battleground of social forces, employing the study of form to unveil the disharmony within the world [15]. Secondly, Moretti pursues the scientificization of literary studies. He integrates theories and methods from natural and social sciences into literary studies, including Darwin's theory of evolution and Wallerstein's world-system theory, and the use of tree diagrams, maps, social networks. More importantly, he believes that literature can learn from the objectivity of science, leading to a more rational literary history [11, 12, 14].

Early on, Moretti was dissatisfied with hermeneutic studies' detachment from socio-historical contexts. In response, he proposed with a heterogeneous quantitative paradigm proposed to counterbalance this. Here, his expectations for quantitative methods combined the two aforementioned pursuits, aiming to explore the ways in which texts are embedded in wider literary and cultural dialogues through quantitatively analysis.

But these two demands seem contradictory: how can the scientific qualities of objectivity and neutrality achieve critique of value? It should be noted that Moretti's pursuit of objectivity primarily refers to a set of paradigms and value orientations established around natural sciences [14]. Objectivity is crucial for science, and many issues in the philosophy of science revolve around objectivity, such as problems of verification and induction, scientific explanation, experimentation, measurement and quantification, statistical evidence, repeatability, and more [21]—all of which Moretti consistently emphasizes. Yet, a fundamental aspect of this objectivity is the value-free ideal, suggesting that in scientific practice, any contextual values should ideally be minimized or at least confined within certain limits [21].

Moretti's pursuit of an objective ideal clashes with critiques emphasizing subjective intervention and human agency. Some critics also criticized the lack of humanistic concerns and the power to intervene in reality in Moretti's "distant reading" practice [2, 23]. However, all this ignores the aim of "distant reading" is to subvert the canon-centered model of literary history, which is filtered and constructed by hegemonic ideologies. Moretti actually adopts an anti-hegemonic ideological stance. Despite this, Moretti ultimately categorizes his research into two distinct types: quantitative research and social critique, claiming that these two approaches are challenging to integrate, which implies that he fails to achieve social critique in the projects of quantitative formalism [8].

Expanding on this failure, Moretti carefully constructed the opposition between hermeneutics and quantitative analysis in a theoretical approach. He states that hermeneutics and quantitative analysis are completely heterogeneous, and that the two cannot be conducted simultaneously, nor can a conceptual unity be reached [16].

In terms of conceptual unify, Moretti cites Aby Warburg's "pathosformel," Bourdieu's "field," and Schwarz's "foreign debt" from the theories of literary history and believes that they have successfully "established conceptual bridges between distant disciplines [16]." Can there be such a bridge between quantitative analysis and hermeneutics? Moretti eventually expresses serious skepticism about such a synthesis.

But we cannot help but ask, is this failure stemming from the use of quantitative methods, or from a misunderstanding of quantitative methods? We have in fact seen examples of quantitative studies serving as an effective cultural criticism, such as Ted Underwood's proposal of perspectival modeling, which allows computational modeling to simulate established cultural perspectives, and explore their premises and biases [25]. This method has been used for solid social critique. For example, Richard Jean So utilizes machine modeling to identify the white cultural perspective in texts, revealing its oppression on people of color [24]. This prompts us to question Moretti's views on the value-free nature of quantitative methods.

3   The Problem and Flaws in the Dichotomy

A closer look at the theoretical logic underlying this dichotomy reveals Moretti's misunderstanding of the nature of quantitative analysis in literary studies. Simultaneously, he narrows and elevates its scope, and thus overlooks alternative ways of integrating quantitative analysis with hermeneutics besides a conceptual unity.

On the one hand, Moretti confines quantitative analysis to pure computational operations—seemingly involving only numbers and neutral machines operations—and emphasizes its scientific and objective nature, yet ignores the hermeneutic dimensions inherent in data, code, algorithms, and models. This leads him to view it as purely objective and limits quantitative analysis to a description of form: "...and the 'vertical' link between the text and the world is replaced by a 'horizontal' one among texts that are all on the same plane [16]."

In response to Moretti's viewpoint, Joris J. van Zundert perhaps hits the nail on the head when he asserts that conversations between the digital humanities and hermeneutics cannot simply set up a disjunction between the quantitative and the qualitative, and reduces hermeneutics to qualitative interpretations of data as if those data carry no value or interpretation [26].

Moretti's neglect of the hermeneutics of computation itself may lead to a series of negative consequences. Firstly, confining quantitative analysis to the scientific study of forms can limit its potential, failing to see the ways in which quantitative literary studies can play a critical role, just as Moretti explicitly divides social critique and quantitative analysis into two distinct categories. In fact, even Moretti's own quantitative research carries the same inherent critical dimension and pursuit of value. For example, while aiming for a more equitable literary history through distant reading, Moretti in fact exposes the mechanisms of hegemonic operation, in effect hinting at possible modes of innovation and change with their zones of occurrence.

Moreover, in literary studies where the subjectivity of interpreters and the contextual nature of reading practices are heavily emphasized, the belief that purely descriptive and objective steps in research might exist could lead to the naturalization and veiling of latent ideologies, thereby aiding in the shaping and deepening of cultural hegemony. Additionally, the hermeneutics of computation, to a large extent, is left to professionals in software design and computer science, where the problem-solving paradigm of computer science threatens to replace the problematizing paradigm of literary studies. The former tends to be inductive and seeks universal conclusions, while the latter tends to be the opposite, favoring multiple perspectives and heterogeneity, treating problematizing as a means to create knowledge [26]. All of these factors may jeopardize the foundational principles of computational literary studies, and leads to computation outweighing literary studies.

On the other hand, by juxtaposing it with hermeneutics, which is not only methodological, but also epistemological and ontological for literary studies, Moretti anticipates an external synthesis, while failing to see that, because of their theoretical disparities, the integration of the two is more likely to take place within the hermeneutic tradition, that is, quantitative analysis as a methodology and to some extent a epistemology enters into hermeneutics as ontology.

It is obvious that Moretti seeks a unity of quantitative analysis and hermeneutics through categories and concepts. He believes that categories such as Bourdieu's "field" and Schwarz's "debt" achieve this kind of conceptual unity, serving as bridges between different disciplines [16]. Examining the examples Moretti provides, two noteworthy aspects emerge. For one thing, the synthesis of quantitative analysis and hermeneutics bears the nature of linking different disciplines, presupposing disciplinary boundaries, and assigning disciplinary attributes to both. The fallacy of this presupposition will be analyzed in the next section. For another, in discussing this conceptual unity, quantitative research and hermeneutics are placed on the same level, implying that both belong to the methodological domain. But it has to be taken into account that hermeneutics itself is much more than just a method, but an epistemology and ontology of literary studies with a rather long academic tradition and theoretical thickness. While quantitative analysis is, according to Moretti's definition, a relatively independent technical method that lacks the theoretical depth required for theoretical construction because it lacks meaning, value, and critique. Therefore, the "conceptual unity" is more likely to occur within hermeneutic tradition rather than outside it. In other words, quantitative analysis enters hermeneutic tradition, interacts with it, and gradually integrates with it. This is what is actually happening, as Stephen Ramsay puts it, "The computer revolutionizes, not because it proposes an alternative to the basic hermeneutical procedure, but because it reimagines that procedure at new scales, with new speeds, and among new sets of conditions [20]."

4   A Perspective from Field Theory: Problem and Flaws in the Dichotomy

In this context, adopting Bourdieu's field theory perspective facilitates a more comprehensive understanding of the complex relationship between quantitative analysis and hermeneutics. Bourdieu conceptualizes field as a network or a structure of objective relations between positions constructed by specific practice. Society consisted of a variety of fields such as economic, political, and literary fields. He emphasizes that each field possesses a certain degree of autonomy, with its own rules and operational mechanism. External factors must be transformed by the logic of the field into structural elements inherent to the field before they are able to influence its internal dynamics [3].

Each disciplinary field has its own boundaries, norms and rules of operation and constitutes a relatively independent realm. When comprehending a specific quantitative analysis or study and the embedded quantitative methods, it is crucial to consider the broader disciplinary discursive practices they are inserted in. Quantitative methods are derived from and closely integrated with natural sciences and are therefore often tacitly recognized as sharing a set of values and standards with them. Humanists' expectations of quantitative methods stem from this association, such as the emphasis on objectivity. In contrast, when quantitative methods are transplanted into literary studies, they inevitably undergo reshaping influenced by disciplinary traditions, research subjects, and the subjects of study, and hence acquire different rules, values, purposes, and expectations than those in their original context. In this process, they interact with the discourse of literary studies, which deserves great attention.

From one perspective, the rules of the literary field significantly influence the nature of quantitative analysis. Firstly, the study of literature has always emphasized the history of the text itself, such as the historical changes of its material forms, editions, and interpretations. Also, the meaning of a text is not only influenced by the metaphorical quality of literary language, which is often not definitive, but ambiguous and polysemous, but also related to the fact that a text is a complex system with lots of layers, in which meaning is not self-evident, but always calls for interpretation by the subject [27]. As a result, the digitization and computation of texts always call for a great deal of human agency. In addition, the researchers exist in specific historical context, holding specific feelings, positions, values and demands, which will greatly shape the whole studies.

From another perspective, the characteristics of quantitative analysis magnify an inherent problem in literary studies. Stanley Fish describes this problem as an arbitrary leap from description of forms to meaning [7]. This is also the challenge of "generalization" mentioned by Andrew Piper, "'Generalization' is the rhetorical strategy whereby we move from partial evidence to knowledge claims about some larger group or category [19]." The disconnect between form and meaning constitutes the most vehement criticism against CLS [5]. In this regard, the characteristics of quantitative analysis themselves amplify the existence of this problem in CLS. Because quantitative analysis initially involves breaking down the object into manageable small units [17], in some cases, they can become really abstract, like the frequency of punctuation marks [19]. This process increases the distance between formal features and meaning, making the interpretive leap more adventurous. This also means that the further the distance from the form constituted by such units to the meaning, the more adventurous the leap. This is also the distance from quantitative evidence to qualitative interpretation: "How to move from this kind of evidence and object to qualitative arguments and insights about humanistic subjects—culture, literature, art, etc.—is not clear [9]."

The gap between quantitative results and meaning is in fact dependent on external factors to fill in, including additions from relevant contexts (social, historical, literary, historical interpretations, etc.) and the researcher's interpretations and inferences. Since this issue is prevalent in literary studies, the criteria for evaluating CLS in this regard should not necessarily be stricter than for other types of literary studies.

We have also seen that uncertainty and subjectivity in quantitative research do not equate to flaws. Because literary studies do not seek certainty and scientific truth but encourages another kind of literary truth that is open, rich, and pluralistic [4]. With a clear sense of this, the subjectivity of quantitative analysis can also serve as critique of value.

5   Conclusion

Through an in-depth exploration of Moretti's dichotomy of hermeneutics and quantitative analysis, this paper analyzes Moretti's misconceptions about the nature of quantitative analysis in literary studies and its detrimental effects. Introducing the perspective of field theory aids in understanding how the disciplinary discursive practices in which quantitative analysis is embedded can impact its nature. From a theoretical standpoint, it comprehensively grasps the specific ways in which quantitative analysis and hermeneutics interpenetrate and interact. This helps establish a reflective theory for CLS and highlights the potential for social critique that quantitative analysis can fully exert within this interaction.

References

1. Archer, D.: Data mining and word frequency analysis. In: Griffin, G., Hayle, M. (eds). Research methods for reading digital data in the digital humanities. Edinburgh University Press, Edinburgh (2016)
2. Bennett, T.: Counting and seeing the social action of literary form: Franco Moretti and the sociology of literature. Cultural Sociol. 3(2), 277–297 (2009). https://doi.org/10.1177/174 9975509105535
3. Bourdieu, P.: Les Règles de l'art: Genèse et structure du champ littéraire, Seuil, Pairs (1992)
4. Chambers, E.: Computers in humanities teaching and research. Comput. Humanities 34(3): 245–254 (2000). https://www.jstor.org/stable/30204817
5. Da, N.Z.: The computational case against computational literary studies. Crit. Inq. 45(3), 601–639 (2019). https://doi.org/10.1086/702594
6. Dobson, J.E.: Critical digital humanities: the search for a methodology. University of Illinois Press, Champaign (2019)
7. Fish, S.E.: What is stylistics and why are they saying such terrible things about it?. Boundary 2 8(1), 129–146 (2019). https://doi.org/10.2307/303144
8. Hackler, R.M., Kirsten, G.: Distant reading, computational criticism, and social critique: an interview with Franco Moretti (2016). https://www.zora.uzh.ch/id/eprint/135683/1/Franco_Moretti_Interview.pdf
9. Heuser, R., Le-Khac, L.: Stanford Literary Lab Pamphlet 4: A Quantitative Literary History Method of 2,958 Nineteenth-Century British Novels: The Semantic Cohort, Stanford Literary Lab (2012). https://litlab.stanford.edu/assets/pdf/LiteraryLabPamphlet4.pdf
10. Jockers, M.L.: Macroanalysis: Digital methods and literary history. University of Illinois Press, Champaign (2013)
11. Moretti, F.: Atlas of the European novel: 1800–1900. Verso, London (1999)
12. Moretti, F.: Distant reading. Verso, London (2013)
13. Moretti, F.: Falso movimento, La svolta quantitativa nello studio della letteratura. nottetempo, Milan (2022)
14. Moretti, F.: Graphs, maps, trees: abstract models for a literary history. Verso, London (2005)
15. Moretti, F.: Signs taken for wonders: on the sociology of literary forms. Verso, London (2005)
16. Moretti, F.: The Roads to Rome. New Left Rev. 124, 125–136 (2020). https://newleftreview.org/issues/ii124/articles/franco-moretti-the-roads-to-rome
17. Paul Eve, M.: The Digital Humanities and Literary Studies. Oxford University Press, London (2022)
18. Piper, A.: Can we be wrong? The Problem of Textual evidence in a Time of Data. Cambridge University Press, Cambridge (2020)
19. Piper, A.: Enumerations: data and literary study. University of Chicago Press, Chicago (2019)
20. Ramsay, S.: Reading Machines: Toward an Algorithmic Criticism. University of Illinois Press, Champaign (2011)
21. Reiss, J., Jan, S.: Scientific objectivity. In: Zalta, E. (eds). The Stanford Encyclopedia of Philosophy (2014). https://plato.stanford.edu/entries/scientific-objectivity/
22. Rockwell, G., Sinclair, S.: Hermeneutica: Computer-assisted interpretation in the humanities. MIT Press, Cambridge (2022)

23. Serlen, R.: The distant future? Reading franco moretti. Literature Compass **7**(3), 214–225 (2010). https://doi.org/10.1111/j.1741-4113.2009.00669.x

24. So, R.J.: Redlining culture: a data history of racial inequality and postwar fiction. Columbia University Press, New York (2021)

25. Underwood, T.: Distant Horizons: Digital Evidence and Literary Change. The University of Chicago Press, Chicago (2019)

26. Van Zundert, J.J.: Screwmeneutics and hermenumericals: the computationality of hermeneutics. A New Companion Digital Humanities, 331–347 (2015). https://doi.org/10.1002/978111 8680605.ch23

27. Wellek, R., Warren, A.: Theory of Literature. Harcourt, Brace & World, Orlando (1962)

An Exploratory Study to Identify Research Interests and Analysis Approaches in German Art History with a Potential for Digital Support

Cindy Kröber(✉) (iD)

Friedrich-Schiller-Universität Jena, Jena, Germany
cindy.kroeber@uni-jena.de

Abstract. This paper presents a qualitative analysis of scholarly abstracts from art history. The abstracts support insight into current research interests and analysis approaches for the discipline. Digital humanities is involved in creating technology for art historical research; with the growing amount of digitized data available, research without any technological support becomes almost impossible. There are many research scenarios in art history which can benefit from technological advancements. Libraries, archives, and museums are the institutions that develop and adapt their platforms, features, and data to ensure the needs and requirements of scholars are met. A list of research approaches and steps is a good starting point to see where developments can be helpful.

Keywords: Digital Humanities · Art History Research · Qualitative Data Analysis

1 Introduction

Artificial intelligence (AI) has been in the news and on people' minds for months. Some watch the developments with skepticism while others get excited by the prospects of AI taking over tasks and helping to reduce workload significantly. Right now, the potential is hard to grasp. But there is hope that technological advancements will help to tackle tedious and time-consuming analysis or facilitate the investigation of large amounts of data. However, scholars' general research questions and interests will probably be affected by the innovations, too. Especially, their resources and analysis approaches will turn digital. In art history, digital innovations opened up a whole new subfield called digital art history. The development of computational tools, the creation of visualizations and reconstructions, digital publishing and machine learning methods [1] can all contribute to digital art history. The collecting institutions providing the digitized data and a variety of tools include museums, libraries, archives, and repositories. They need to monitor advances and make sure that their data and tools meet necessary requirements. With research facilities, these institutions are usually involved in the development of new research tools and platforms that are meant to support their users, including both digital and mainstream art historians. Knowing more about potential research scenarios and connected tasks or steps can therefore help to expand the set of solutions suitable for art history research.

I. Sserwanga et al. (Eds.): iConference 2024, LNCS 14597, pp. 27–42, 2024.
https://doi.org/10.1007/978-3-031-57860-1_3

The aim of this paper is to comprehensibly investigate research approaches and tasks in art history, with specific examples, to provide insight into the potential for applying new technology. Art historians themselves rather tend to discuss and critically question [2] the developments.

2 State of the Art

Art historians study the development of paintings, sculptures, and other visual arts. Art history research increasingly relies on technology to both access and analyze artworks. Many museums, galleries, and libraries create and maintain digital archives that allow researchers to access high-quality images and information from anywhere in the world. This has greatly expanded the scope of art history research, as scholars can now consider and access artworks that may have been previously unavailable to them [3].

Other means of investigation and analysis have made their way into art history, allowing researchers to collect additional data that supports investigation on a new level. Various sensing techniques – e.g., spectroscopy, UV-induced visible fluorescence analysis, reflectography, and x-ray scanning – are based on different physical principles and capture different and often complementary information on paintings. Many investigations concerned with assessment of the conservation state, knowledge of the realization techniques, evaluation of a historical period and attribution of the painting, and tracing any modification or changes of the artwork, depend on different modalities that must be combined to draw reliable conclusions. The use of signal and image processing techniques [4, 5] as well as remote sensing like stripe light projection [6] can be used to monitor changes and creation of faithful reproductions of an artwork. Another application of image processing is virtual reconstruction. The highly detailed analysis of color in a painting can be used to digitally modify an image, removing cracks to improve readability, and virtually clean the image to show what the painting looked like for the artist or how an actual cleaning will alter its appearance [4, 7]. For instance, Moran et al. use electromagnetic radiation for an evaluation concerned with forgery and restoration [8].

A different category of technology focuses on computer vision, approaches using machine learning, and multimedia feature extraction, for instance to automatically classify digital or digitized pictures of paintings by artistic style, improving the structure of large digital collections and supporting automatic recommendations [9]. These digital analysis tools can be used to identify objects and figures depicted in artworks [10] and automatically annotate images in museums to improve image retrieval [11] or analyze patterns and styles in larger collections [12]. Sigaki et al. use quantitative analysis of art to show that different artistic styles have a distinct average degree of entropy and complexity, thus allowing a hierarchical organization and clustering of styles [13]. Feature extraction is an approach that can support the recognition of artistic styles and movement in portrait paintings [14]. To support comparison of paintings and the identification of relations between them, pre-trained convolutional neural networks have potential to retrieve common visual patterns shared by a series of paintings [15]. Li and Wang use a stochastic model for a similar attempt to analyze painting styles and possible connections among artists or periods in the history of art [16]. A fractal analysis of artist's patterns has potential to be used for authenticity research [17]. An approach using a convolutional neural network classifier has been used to recognize the iconography of artworks [18]. This is very promising for iconographic studies and automatic artwork annotation, helping researchers with interpretation of meaning, investigation of the origin and diffusion (in time and space) of representations, and the study of influences across artists and artworks.

It is also worth mentioning a category concerned with the perception of art. Technology like eye tracking can be used to study how a beholder observes an artwork [19] complementing any literature review on its perception. Other approaches use computer vision and image processing to analyze aesthetic judgment of paintings and photographs [20] even considering image composition [21].

3D modeling technologies have allowed art historians to create virtual models of artworks, which can be used for analysis and educational purposes [22]. Data visualization technologies allow them to analyze large amounts of data and present it visually to emphasize argumentation like network visualization [23]. Virtual and augmented reality technologies take this one step further and can be used to create immersive experiences that allow viewers to explore artworks and historical sites in a new way. For example, virtual reality can be used to recreate lost or destroyed artworks [24], while augmented reality can be used to overlay information about artworks onto real-world settings [25].

Social media platforms such as X (formerly Twitter) and Instagram have enabled art historians to connect with each other and share research in real time. These platforms have also made it easier to inform and involve the general public [26].

All of these approaches show that digital technologies make it possible to investigate and consider the larger amount of data or images that are now available due to the digitization efforts of the last decades. New data can be incorporated more easily into the analysis keeping it up-to-date and relevant. Besides combining complementary data, digital technologies allow for reproducibility, objectivity, and impartiality within the analysis.

This overview of technological developments relevant for art history research shows a large number of approaches dealing with images and visuals, whereas support working with textual resources is less prominent. Even though written documents and texts are incredibly important for art history research, there have not been as many approaches addressing this. Computer linguistics certainly has potential to support art historians, but first it is important to find out what solutions these scholars find useful and what their requirements for new tools and platforms are. In order to get useful results through the automatic analysis it is necessary to carefully consider the traditional approaches and related quality criteria and to adapt them for digital processing. This translation process with the relevant aspects can best be illustrated with an example: the creation of a database for analyzing drinking glasses.

The database is built on an existing information platform called WissKI (Wissenschaftliche Kommunikations-Infrastruktur, or Scientific Communication Infrastructure) which will be adapted to the requirements of the object of investigation. The approach differs fundamentally from the usual methods in art history analysis. Instead of slowly approaching the object based on literature and examples, the development of a suitable set of instruments requires very precise knowledge of the object of investigation from the very beginning. The object needs to be segmented into its individual parts and features. A conceptual design of the database as well as a system of technical terms is developed. The aim is to find criteria that distinguish a good glass from an inferior glass. The drinking glass itself is therefore the goal and starting point of the project and must be precisely analyzed, schematized, and brought into a suitable classification system [27].

The example clearly highlights the initial issues connected to technological advancements. The whole research into the properties of the object must be done before setting up the database because the necessary information is only available after extensive analysis. So, in this case the technological advancement will only pay off when the database is used again for larger amounts of similar data.

3   Research Questions

This study aims to identify research interests and approaches relevant to art historians. These approaches can be evaluated to identify possible digital solutions to improve the scholar's work. Improvement usually comes in the form of time efficiency or better reproducibility, objectivity, and impartiality of investigation. Information on common analysis approaches will help to recognize data requirements and estimate the effort connected to the analysis. A look at approaches that already rely on digital technologies may uncover necessary adaptations of digital processing. The research questions are:

- What sources do art historians use in their research?
- What are common research interests and methods of analysis in art history?
- How can certain research approaches and steps be supported by technological solutions?

The outcome can help libraries, archives, and repositories to evaluate their sources and tools, e.g., concerning presentation, access, data formats and quality criteria, to better support art historians who use them. This allows institutions to determine next steps to improve their services and create tools that help researchers to completely process certain steps within their portfolio. Solutions for certain data visualizations, annotations, or data conversion are better offered by institutions that adhere to scientific standards.

4   Research Design

This is an exploratory qualitative analysis of a selection of scholarly articles by art historians. Hence, it is important to find a well-received publication that includes many different topics and foci to achieve maximum variation sampling. The aim was to consider a larger number of short articles in English or German from the last decade. The choice fell on the proceedings of the Deutscher Kunsthistorikertag (or German art historians' day, renamed Deutscher Kongress für Kunstgeschichte/German Congress for Art History in 2022) since it is a well-recognized congress for art history. Since 1948 the congress has been held about every two years in a city in Germany. The proceedings are freely available online (through www.arthistoricum.net). Six volumes of the proceedings from 2011 to 2022 were considered for this investigation (see Table 1). Ten to twelve sections in a volume cluster multiple abstracts by introducing their common genre, era, geographic area, or theme. The abstracts range in length from half a page to two pages and are written in German or English. Another nine to eighteen panels are introduced through descriptions on either the very general topic, the participants, or a controversial issue. The congress is well known in the German-speaking countries and attracts many contributors.

Table 1. Sample for qualitative analysis: List of proceedings of the German Art Historian's Day, 2011–2022.

Reference	Year	Location	Theme	Abstracts
Tagungsband XXXI. Deutscher Kunsthistorikertag, Würzburg – Genius Loci, 2011 [28]	2011	Würzburg, Germany	Genius Loci (Latin, Spirit of a Place)	12 sections with a total of 65 abstracts
Tagungsband XXXII. Deutscher Kunsthistorikertag, Greifwald – Ohne Grenzen, 2013 [29]	2013	Greifswald, Germany	Ohne Grenzen (German, Without Borders)	12 sections with a total of 60 abstracts
Tagungsband, XXXIII. Deutscher Kunsthistorikertag, Mainz – Der Wert der Kunst, 2015 [30]	2015	Mainz, Germany	Der Wert der Kunst (German, The Value of Art)	12 sections with a total of 60 abstracts
Tagungsband, XXXIV. Deutscher Kunsthistorikertag, Dresden – Kunst lokal – Kunst global, 2017 [31]	2017	Dresden, Germany	Kunst local – Kunst global (German, Art Locally – Art Globally)	12 sections with a total of 60 abstracts
Tagungsband, XXXV. Deutscher Kunsthistorikertag, Göttingen – Zu den Dingen!, 2019 [27]	2019	Göttingen, Germany	Zu den Dingen! (German, About Things!)	10 sections with a total of 50 abstracts
Tagungsband, XXXVI. Deutscher Kunsthistorikertag, Stuttgart – Form Fragen, 2022 [32]	2022	Stuttgart, Germany	Form Fragen (German, Form Issues)	11 sections with a total of 55 abstracts

The findings are derived from a qualitative analysis of 350 abstracts from the congress proceedings. This includes all contributions in the sections. No panels were included because the descriptions were too general and did not necessarily include research as the focus was on introducing a topic for discussion. The six volumes analyzed for this paper are highly diverse concerning topics, genres, and eras; therefore, they cover a wide spectrum of art history subjects and research. Sections deal with Baroque palace buildings, art critique, religious context, specific cities or areas, object digitization and design, just to name a few. Since the congress focuses on art history exclusively, research is in depth and timely. The variety of topics and approaches makes this congress highly interesting for the intended investigation.

4.1 Data Analysis

Thematic analysis was applied to identify and report themes within the scholarly articles [33]. The abstracts were analyzed through coding using the software MaxQDA. Coding helped to identify patterns in each of the abstracts [34–36] that were connected to one of the two main topics of this paper: research questions or interests and analysis approaches. The open and inductive coding allowed for multiple codes [37] which led to the themes discussed here.

The initial analysis was done in German and any terms and quotes within the findings were translated into English by the author of this paper.

The study has some limitations. All coding was done by one person leaving room for bias. Even though the sample consists of some 350 abstracts, this does not provide an exhaustive list of recent topics in art history. But it is a compilation of topics that art historians deem relevant enough to be presented at their congress. The proceedings mostly deal with topics relevant to research in Germany by German speakers. Additionally, this contribution only considers current research interests. Technological solutions for analysis may make it possible to investigate larger amounts of data which will probably also have an effect on research interests.

This approach is documented and scientifically replicable and was chosen to analyze the data and get familiar with the sample. Especially for the analysis of scholarly abstracts and their distinctive nature this approach is well suited. Considering the proposed use of technological solutions to analyze larger amounts of data, the intention is to use natural language processing techniques and large language models [38, 39] on the same sample and compare the results. If this proves satisfactory, the technologically supported approach will help to study a larger sample and potentially create a more time-efficient and partly automated workflow for repositories, archives, and libraries to monitor users and their needs.

5 Findings

In order to investigate the scope of art history research it is important to understand the subjects being researched. All abstracts dealt with at least one of the following subjects (see Fig. 1):

- artwork(s): genre, material, style, form, topic, iconography, provenance studies
- artist(s): oeuvre, biography
- beholder(s): observation, reception, perception
- ordering party or collectors: intention
- context: time, place, social & cultural circumstances

- literature (e.g., art critique, articles on connected topics, contributions from previous research).

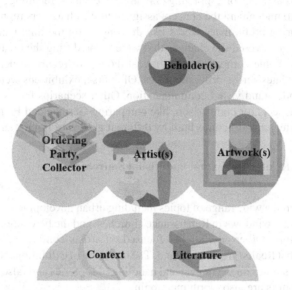

Fig. 1. Schematic representation of the mentioned research subjects.

At the beginning, it is necessary to distinguish between relevant sources. This will later help assign possible technological solutions. The sources mentioned in the abstracts were textual sources like stories and anecdotes, letters, press releases and travel accounts, bills, inventories, and archival documents, as well as descriptions. Visual sources include images, frescos, murals, tapestries, drawings, paintings, portraits, illustrations, engravings, photographs and aerial images, maps, and architectural plans.

Findings related to analysis and research approaches were condensed into twenty-one categories which are further elaborated below. Some authors did not provide any information on their approaches to analysis and merely presented a discussion on a topic. Therefore, not every abstract has a label connected to analysis. Other authors relied on a combination of approaches which were then considered in two or more categories.

5.1 Categories Related to Visual Sources

Comparison

Comparison is mentioned several times when discussing two or more art pieces. A procedure referred to as comparative analysis (German, Vergleichendes Sehen) is used for style analysis. This method involves comparing and contrasting artworks from different time periods, regions, or cultures in order to reveal similarities and differences in style, technique, and subject matter.

Often, two or more art pieces were compared, e.g., frescos from different periods, drawings by an artist, paintings of the same period, engravings in a series, or commissioned work by different artists for the same client. Different genres were compared like architectural plans and the corresponding drawings, to estimate the impact of sculptures or paintings and to understand the concept assigned to the characters represented in the artworks. Comparing preliminary works like drawings with the final painting or, e.g., copper engraving uncovered the changes that were made during the creation by either artists or artisans. Some comparisons did reveal the use of recurring details based on sketches and templates across different pieces. Of course, exhibitions were subjects for comparison to understand visual communication. Other scenarios focused on regional or geographical aspects for comparison, like comparing German and French Romantic paintings or architectural structures built by different groups of immigrants.

5.2   Categories Related to Textual and Visual Sources

Case Studies

Case studies covered a wide range of topics including urban development, design, use of castles, stained glass windows in Renaissance churches, and the perception of culturally relevant architecture. Other case studies focused on artists confronted with aesthetic shifts or on Socialist Realist artists in Poland. The reception of exhibitions was mentioned a few times. Case studies on the impact and handling of forgeries and false identification of authors/art creators are also worth mentioning.

Iconography and Iconology

This analysis is concerned with the meaning, symbolism, cultural and historical context of images. Investigations deal with the detection and interpretation of allegories, the identification of depicted people and accompanying figures, e.g., from mythology, that illustrate attributes. Mentioned symbols and themes include the gesture of the oath or judicial hand, which is fundamental to the act of jurisdiction, or oriental motifs. Analysis was applied to portraits, murals, illustrations, paintings, tapestries, drawings, and furnishings of churches.

Style Analysis and Style Criticism

Art historians often analyze the techniques and styles used by artists in different periods and regions. They may also study the evolution of these styles and techniques over time. By analyzing the style it is possible to date an artwork or to assign it to an artist by identifying certain features. Examples in the sample focused on sculptures and tombs. The evolution of styles and techniques over time as well as the deliberate choices for a certain style were subject to analysis. Style analysis of handwriting was mentioned to identify the artist involved in book illustrations.

Analyzing Architecture

Analysis of architecture was more specific and therefore deserved separate consideration. It calls for distinct solutions like excavation, investigation of architectural design (in German, Gestaltung), building research (Bauforschung), and conservation restoration (Konservierungs-Restaurierung). Research interests were related to life in and around buildings. Functional and hierarchical aspects were examined in more detail considering furnishings, space, and layout. A church is spatially divided and accommodates individual functions such as representation and memorial, demanding analysis of relations in more detail. In a castle, artistic decoration of the stately rooms and their ceremonial use were considered, as were plans and layouts to identify water supply and room disposition important for everyday use and maintenance.

Conservation and Preservation

Art historians are involved in the conservation and preservation of artworks, examining issues such as deterioration, restoration, and the ethical considerations involved in these processes. Investigations were done on reasoning, significance, and impact of declaring buildings a landmark and values connected to preservation.

Culture

Inquiries into culture focused on history, contexts, transfer, and cultural heritage.

5.3 Categories Related to Textual Sources

Reception

This method involved examining ways in which an artwork has been received and interpreted over time through analyzing its public reception. Examples include deformed pearls as grotesque valuables; the reception from people at court and connections to the historical context for monastery buildings; a new way of looking at paintings that seems to appear around the middle of the seventeenth century; changing reception of collections in the museum in Mumbai, India; the reception of Mediterranean ivory horns. Some tried to investigate the psychology behind reception or asked for values to explain a negative reception of new buildings. A different project dealt with women entering the male-dominated field of art and how their work and carriers were received.

Perception

The focus here is on who perceived what. Who refers to contemporary observers, locally and internationally, while what addresses objects and topics which can be as specific as the waterfront, cities with a diverse heritage, video installations or landscapes. Sculptures and architectural structures were among the objects investigated for viewing aspects and angles, which were photographed, documented, and analyzed. In paintings and drawings, the digitized version based on digital images was different from the reality; the perception always lies with the observer and the connected circumstances.

Object Biography

An object biography traces all steps and information related to an artwork such as the artists, period, place and process of creation, and materials used. It also investigates social, political, and cultural contexts in which an artwork was created. This may include an analysis of the artist's biography and oeuvre, the patronage or commissioning of the artwork, and the historical events and cultural movements of the time. Dating an artwork heavily relies on style analysis. Sometimes, other methods must be considered like the analysis of textual sources or preliminary work like drawings of concepts. One research project considered the influence that clients had on the artwork, especially when several different people were involved, and funding was not divided evenly among the contributors.

Artists
Several research scenarios were connected to artists but did not use to one of the distinct analysis methods. Artist biographies were not always created during object biographies. Sometimes the focus was only on the artist themselves and how their training, experiences, and travels shaped their oeuvre or even influenced the art of whole countries. Artists were interviewed on their views concerning artistic transformation. An attempt was also made to identify factors in the success of certain artists.

Network Analysis
The analysis of networks focused on the relations among and between artists as well as clients spanning different workshops, cities, regions, countries and even continents.

Reconstruction
Architecture is often related to reconstruction in the sense that damaged or destroyed buildings are reconstructed either physically or virtually. This can focus on the exterior, interior, and furnishings. The relations between them help researchers to understand or reconstruct concepts of the use of rooms as well as ceremonial aspects. Other types of reconstruction were also used; trading routes was reconstructed to investigate connections between cities and the distribution of goods and styles.

Digitization
The material dealt with digitization in several ways: the creation and use of data bases, digitization and processing of images, photographs of frescos, and digitized copper engravings as well as 2D and 3D visualizations of objects. Digital images were automatically analyzed for colors. Digital image processing helped to make inscriptions readable whereas image analysis methods were used to investigate architectural perception. Collections were digitized to be placed in online knowledge repositories to which further information could be added and linked.

5.4 Miscellaneous

A variety of approaches was briefly named and remain unrelated to the approaches above:

- Discourse analysis on aesthetic education and development of taste.
- Distant viewing to make connections between objects and space due to similar shapes.
- Investigating materials of objects like minerals using techniques from science. Analyzing paint and canvas helped researchers reach a more in-depth understanding of how a painting was created.
- Eye tracking systems to examine and understand perception and reception of art.
- Translation of a performance into drawings for investigation and interpretation.
- Translating watercolor images into contour drawings to interpret color and brush gradients.
- The analysis of video installations like video games for reception.

6 Discussion

It is important to mention that publications in art history usually focus on presenting knowledge about an object or topic through interpretation and argumentation. Interdisciplinary projects emphasize methodology and technology more, whereas articles by an art historian might only briefly mention the analysis approach or methodology if it is special or out of the ordinary.

More advanced technologies like AI or more specifically computer vision, neural networks and deep learning were not mentioned in any of the abstracts, which was expected since these technologies are relatively new. Some of the abstracts mentioned the use of four digital technologies that art historians have adopted a while ago: digitization, visualization, 3D modeling and image processing. What all these scenarios for applying digital tools have in common is that they support fast access to and analysis of data or enable the investigation of much larger amounts of data than would otherwise be possible. The most important feature is the availability of digital or digitized images for analysis or processing. As presented earlier, all four technology-driven approaches or methods are regularly used within art history research. Processes and requirements are well known and further developments can be expected with technological advancements.

The analysis of the sample of congress abstracts helped to identify a set of scenarios and approaches in art history research that can benefit greatly from digital solutions. Approaches like comparison, iconography and iconology, style analysis and style criticism as well as research related to reception and perception all rely on an initial description of the visual. A thorough image description includes a deep look into the form, structure, colors, style, and content of what is depicted. This image description is a translation of the visual into words, naming exactly what is seen in the picture. The focus is on the composition, foreground, middle ground, and background; figures, color and color application, light, and shadow; the observer and their ways of viewing an image including eye tracking and perspective; identifying the image edge or image center to explain where elements are located. This survey or inventory of the visual calls for observation of the artwork separately from interpretation and assessment. It therefore has potential for digital support. As some investigations deal with a large number of visual images, descriptions and visualizations can hardly be done traditionally for every image with the necessary extent and care. A tool for image description may be able to ensure that the results are objective, reproducible, and verifiable. AI can be used to identify similarities and differences between artworks or analyze patterns and trends in the use of color, composition, or other elements. The output can be a list with relevant terms and topics together with segmented and annotated images that can be used for visual argumentation in a publication. It is important that one tool can process visuals in different media (e.g., images, frescos, murals, tapestries, drawings, paintings, portraits, illustrations, engravings, photographs and aerial images, maps, and architectural plans) as scholars often compare and analyze artworks across a variety of media.

Another requirement for digital art history is to avoid creating a black box solution. Researchers always want to verify their results. Providing the processed and segmented images including information on reliability of the segmented areas as well as the matched terms will increase scholars' trust in the tools. Approaches that rely on computer vision and deep learning now come close to offering a suitable solution. However, more training data that is specific to art history is probably required. Even though many investigations in this area have been done, a lot of the relevant publications come in the form of long texts with images either placed throughout the text or left out due to copyright issues. Therefore, currently available digital publications often do not fit the requirements for machine-readable training data. Institutions like libraries, archives and museums can help to provide training data by digitizing and preparing older textual resources and images and setting new standards for the publication of articles they make available. Especially in art history, older contributions never lose their appeal, and it is essential to find the first mention of an idea or hypothesis.

Once an image description with a list of relevant items and topics or a segmented and annotated image is available it can be used for comparison or style analysis, looking for certain visual patterns connected to style, technique, and subject matter. Neural networks can potentially help to quantify any similarities or differences between certain images, to retrieve more candidates for comparison in larger repositories, or to date an artwork based on style and features. Analyzing similarities can be especially helpful in detecting the reuse of templates for certain features or estimating how similar a preliminary drawing is to the final artwork.

For iconography, iconology, style analysis and the other identified approaches, art historians need to consider not only visual but also textual resources. Therefore, any detected figures, elements, and symbols in a segmented image of an artwork need to be defined with the corresponding terminology to uncover related information and meaning. The automatic retrieval of search terms and key words will only enter a Google search if it is not possible to search the relevant texts and articles in the archives. It is thus essential to digitize older texts making them machine-readable and accessible. Computer aided textual analysis has not been used for long in art history research, but it has great potential to help with style analysis and criticism. Computer linguistics can be used to analyze written texts related to artworks, such as artist biographies, exhibition catalogs, and critical reviews. This can help to identify patterns and themes in the language used to describe artworks, providing insight into how they were received and interpreted. Further, computer linguistics offers many approaches to analyzing text, which can provide annotations on language, tone, and rhetoric to identify potential biases, agendas, or underlying motivations of the authors as well as omissions, contradictions, or exaggerations that may influence the interpretation. Natural language processing is a subset of computer linguistics that focuses on the interaction between computers and human language. It can be used to analyze large collections of written texts related to art history, identifying key themes and topics, and providing insight into the way that language is used to discuss artworks.

The use of AI and deep learning to help with multimodal access to data by recognizing textual passages and related images can significantly improve the retrieval of sources. Considering automatic analysis of visual and textual information for research, it is important to combine both entities into multimodal data. This can be achieved using annotations or labels for text and images [40]. Annotations can provide links or associations between different modalities, allowing researchers to establish connections, explore relationships between them, and make use of complementary information. Furthermore, annotations and labels can be visualized alongside multimodal data to enhance the presentation and argumentation and support comprehension. Concerning provenance research, the connection of multimodal data through annotations makes it easier to trace or track an object or document. For images, the qualities of a reproduction need to be certified and a link made between the original and the copy, in order to understand the path taken from the creator or client of a photographed image to its inclusion on a repository or site. Scholars share knowledge and data; annotations can promote collaboration for researchers working with multimodal data. By sharing annotated data sets, scholars can contribute to a collective pool of knowledge adding their peer-reviewed relevant publications and data, exchanging insights, and building upon each other's research.

Libraries, archives, and museums as well as digital humanities scholars can help to connect and prepare art history researchers with the necessary skills to create and improve research solutions that deploy new technologies [41]. Digital humanities scholars have a thorough insight into the relevant resources and data that needs to be processed and can take an active role in shaping digitization, processing, and access to sources [42, 43]. Libraries, archives, and museums have the infrastructure needed to disseminate and communicate about new tools and provide users with the necessary access and training.

7 Conclusion

This paper provided a glimpse into the research scope of art history to show that currently, support for the analysis of visual data is becoming more common in art history and even more approaches are possible. On the one hand, approaches dealing with textual resources rely on AI and deep learning, which currently does not offer as many ready-to-use solutions as image processing. On the other hand, any approaches that remain a black box are unlikely to be used by art historians.

The use of AI to prepare image descriptions is sensible. Once more training data can help to improve results and reliability to a degree that art historians deem trustworthy.

Multimodal data access might be the next hot thing for libraries, archives, and museums to focus on. AI and deep learning have the potential to enhance data, images, and texts through labels and annotations in order to link them. This will help tremendously with retrieval and contextualization of information.

The role of libraries, archives, museums, and repositories as keepers of knowledge and data is key in the coming developments in technology for research. These are the institutions that can help build up reference and training data and get users accustomed to new technologies and the mindset necessary to adapt the solutions for their benefit. They also have the power to advocate for scientific integrity in new approaches and solutions.

Acknowledgments. The research upon which this paper is based is part of the research project HistKI (History Infrastructure applying AI), which has received funding from the German Federal Ministry of Education and Research (BMBF) under grant identifier 01UG2120A.

Disclosure of Interests. The author has no competing interests to declare that are relevant to the content of this article.

References

1. Näslund Dahlgren, A., Wasielewski, A.: Cultures of digitization: a historiographic perspective on digital art history. Vis. Resour. **36**(4), 339–359 (2021). https://doi.org/10.1080/01973762. 2021.1928864
2. Rodriguez-Ortega, N.: Digital art history: the questions that need to be asked. Vis. Resour. **35**(1–2), 6–20 (2019). https://doi.org/10.1080/01973762.2019.1553832
3. Drucker, J.: Is there a "digital" art history? Vis. Resour. **29**(1–2), 5–13 (2013). https://doi.org/ 10.1080/01973762.2013.761106
4. Barni, M., Pelagotti, A., Piva, A.: Image processing for the analysis and conservation of paintings: opportunities and challenges. IEEE Signal Process. Mag. **22**(5), 141–144 (2005). https://doi.org/10.1109/MSP.2005.1511835
5. De Boer, J.V.A.: Infrared reflectography: a method for the examination of paintings. Appl. Opt. **7**(9), 1711–1714 (1968). https://doi.org/10.1364/AO.7.001711
6. Heinemann, C.: Evaluation der Streifenprojektion zur Zustandsanalyse und zum Monitoring von Veränderungsprozessen bei Gemälden. (2023). https://doi.org/10.11588/artdok.000 08137
7. Pouli, P., et al.: Recent studies of laser science in paintings conservation and research. Acc. Chem. Res. **43**(6), 771–781 (2010). https://doi.org/10.1021/ar900224n
8. Moran, T.C., et al.: The roles of X rays and other types of electromagnetic radiation in evaluating paintings for forgery and restoration. J. Forensic Radiol. Imaging **5**, 38–46 (2016). https://doi.org/10.1016/j.jofri.2016.02.001
9. Zujovic, J., et al.: Classifying paintings by artistic genre: an analysis of features & classifiers. In: 2009 IEEE International Workshop on Multimedia Signal Processing. IEEE (2009). https://doi.org/10.1109/MMSP.2009.5293271
10. Madhu, P., et al.: Recognizing characters in art history using deep learning. In: Proceedings of the 1st Workshop on Structuring and Understanding of Multimedia heritAge Contents. (2019). https://doi.org/10.1145/3347317.3357242
11. Surapaneni, S., Syed, S., Lee, L.Y.: Exploring themes and bias in art using machine learning image analysis. In: 2020 Systems and Information Engineering Design Symposium (SIEDS). IEEE (2020). https://doi.org/10.1109/SIEDS49339.2020.9106656
12. Castellano, G., Vessio, G.: Deep learning approaches to pattern extraction and recognition in paintings and drawings: an overview. Neural Comput. Appl. **33**(19), 12263–12282 (2021). https://doi.org/10.1007/s00521-021-05893-z
13. Sigaki, H.Y., Perc, M., Ribeiro, H.V.: History of art paintings through the lens of entropy and complexity. Proc. Natl. Acad. Sci. **115**(37), E8585–E8594 (2018). https://doi.org/10.1073/ pnas.1800083115
14. Liu, S., et al.: Novel features for art movement classification of portrait paintings. Image Vis. Comput. **108**, 104121 (2021)
15. Seguin, B., Striolo, C., diLenardo, I., Kaplan, F.: Visual link retrieval in a database of paintings. In: Hua, G., Jégou, H. (eds.) ECCV 2016. LNCS, vol. 9913, pp. 753–767. Springer, Cham (2016). https://doi.org/10.1007/978-3-319-46604-0_52
16. Li, J., Wang, J.Z.: Studying digital imagery of ancient paintings by mixtures of stochastic models. IEEE Trans. Image Process. **13**(3), 340–353 (2004). https://doi.org/10.1109/TIP. 2003.821349
17. Taylor, R.P., et al.: Authenticating Pollock paintings using fractal geometry. Pattern Recogn. Lett. **28**(6), 695–702 (2007). https://doi.org/10.1016/j.patrec.2006.08.012
18. Milani, F., Fraternali, P.: A dataset and a convolutional model for iconography classification in paintings. J. Comput. Cultural Heritage (JOCCH) **14**(4), 1–18 (2021). https://doi.org/10. 1145/3458885

19. Rosenberg, R., Klein, C.: The moving eye of the beholder: eye tracking and the perception of paintings (2015). https://doi.org/10.1093/acprof:oso/9780199670000.003.0005
20. Amirshahi, S.A., Hayn-Leichsenring, G.U., Denzler, J., Redies, C.: Jenaesthetics subjective dataset: analyzing paintings by subjective scores. In: Agapito, L., Bronstein, M.M., Rother, C. (eds.) ECCV 2014. LNCS, vol. 8925, pp. 3–19. Springer, Cham (2015). https://doi.org/10.1007/978-3-319-16178-5_1
21. Amirshahi, S.A., et al.: Evaluating the rule of thirds in photographs and paintings. Art & Perception 2(1–2), 163–182 (2014). https://doi.org/10.1163/22134913-00002024
22. Münster, S., Friedrichs, K., Hegel, W.: 3D Reconstruction Techniques as a Cultural Shift in Art History? Inter. J. Digital Art History: Issue 3, 2018: Digital Space and Architect. 3, 39 (2019)
23. Porras, S.: Keeping our eyes open: Visualizing networks and art history. Artl@ s Bull. 6(3), 3 (2017)
24. Hutson, J. and T. Olsen, Digital humanities and virtual reality: a review of theories and best practices for art history. Inter. J. Technol. Educ. (IJTE) 4(3), 491–500 (2021). https://doi.org/10.46328/ijte.150
25. Panciroli, C., Macauda, A., Russo, V.: Educating about art by augmented reality: new didactic mediation perspectives at school and in museums. In: Proceedings, MDPI (2018). https://doi.org/10.3390/proceedings1091107
26. Krö, C.: German art history students' use of digital repositories: an insight. In: Toeppe, K., Yan, H., Chu, S.K.W. (eds.) iConference 2021. LNCS, vol. 12646, pp. 176–192. Springer, Cham (2021). https://doi.org/10.1007/978-3-030-71305-8_14
27. Tagungsband, XXXV. Deutscher Kunsthistorikertag: Göttingen - Zu den Dingen! Deutscher Kunsthistorikertag. In: Kirschbaum, C., Gaeta, M. (eds.), Bonn: Verband Deutscher Kunsthistoriker e.V., vol. 35 (2019). https://archiv.ub.uni-heidelberg.de/artdok/6644/
28. Tagungsband XXXI. Deutscher Kunsthistorikertag, Würzburg - Genius Loci. Deutscher Kunsthistorikertag. In: Gaeta, M., Kleines, C. (eds.) Bonn: Verband Deutscher Kunsthistoriker e., vol. 31 (2011). https://archiv.ub.uni-heidelberg.de/artdok/2105/
29. Tagungsband XXXII. Deutscher Kunsthistorikertag, Greifwald - Ohne Grenzen. Deutscher Kunsthistorikertag. In: Gaeta, M. (ed.) Bonn: Verband Deutscher Kunsthistoriker e.V., vol. 32. (2013) https://archiv.ub.uni-heidelberg.de/artdok/2762/
30. Tagungsband, XXXIII. Deutscher Kunsthistorikertag, Mainz - Der Wert der Kunst. Deutscher Kunsthistorikertag. In: Gaeta, M., Kirschbaum, C. (eds.) Bonn: Verband Deutscher Kunsthistoriker e.V., vol. 33 (2015). https://archiv.ub.uni-heidelberg.de/artdok/3303/
31. Tagungsband, XXXIV. Deutscher Kunsthistorikertag, Dresden - Kunst lokar - Kunst global. In: Kunsthistorikertag, D., Kirschbaum, C. (eds.) Bonn: Verband Deutscher Kunsthistorik e.V., vol. 34 (2017). https://archiv.ub.uni-heidelberg.de/artdok/5245/
32. Tagungsband, XXXVI. Deutscher Kunsthistorikertag, Stuttgart - Form Fragen. Deutscher Kunsthistorikertag, ed. M. Gaeta and C. Kirschbaum. Vol. 36. 2022, Bonn: Verband Deutscher Kunsthistoriker e.V. Available from: https://archiv.ub.uni-heidelberg.de/artdok/7909/
33. Braun, V., Clarke, V.: Thematic analysis (2012). https://doi.org/10.1037/13620-004
34. Kuckartz, U., Rädiker, S.: Analyzing qualitative data with MAXQDA. Springer (2019). https://doi.org/10.1007/978-3-030-15671-8
35. Vaismoradi, M., Turunen, H., Bondas, T.: Content analysis and thematic analysis: Implications for conducting a qualitative descriptive study. Nurs. Health Sci. 15(3), 398–405 (2013). https://doi.org/10.1111/nhs.12048
36. Aronson, J.: A pragmatic view of thematic analysis. Qualitative Report 2(1), 1–3 (1995). https://doi.org/10.46743/2160-3715/1995.2069
37. Saldaña, J.: The coding manual for qualitative researchers. Sage (2015)
38. Zhang, H., et al.: QualiGPT: GPT as an easy-to-use tool for qualitative coding. arXiv preprint arXiv:2310.07061, (2023). https://doi.org/10.48550/arXiv.2310.07061

39. Gamieldien, Y., Case, J.M., Katz, A.: Advancing Qualitative Analysis: An Exploration of the Potential of Generative AI and NLP in Thematic Coding. Available at SSRN 4487768 (2023). https://doi.org/10.2139/ssrn.4487768

40. Bruschke, J., et al.: Towards querying multimodal annotations using graphs. In: Workshop on Research and Education in Urban History in the Age of Digital Libraries. Springer (2023). https://doi.org/10.1007/978-3-031-38871-2_16

41. Kamposiori, C.: The role of Research Libraries in the creation, archiving, curation, and preservation of tools for the Digital Humanities, pp. 1–38. Research Libraries UK (2017)

42. Mattmann, B., Regenass, N.: Eine neue Form der Recherche in Bibliotheken. Bibliothek Forschung und Praxis **45**(2), 304–316 (2021). https://doi.org/10.1515/bfp-2021-0010

43. Liang, S., He, D., Wu, D., Hu, H.: Challenges and opportunities of acm digital library: a preliminary survey on different users. In: Sundqvist, A., Berget, G., Nolin, J., Skjerdingstad, K.I. (eds.) iConference 2020. LNCS, vol. 12051, pp. 278–287. Springer, Cham (2020). https://doi.org/10.1007/978-3-030-43687-2_22

To Impress an Algorithm: Minoritized Applicants' Perceptions of Fairness in AI Hiring Systems

Antonio E. Girona[(✉)] [iD] and Lynette Yarger[iD]

Pennsylvania State University, University Park, PA 16802, USA
{agirona,lmk12}@psu.edu

Abstract. Technology firms increasingly leverage artificial intelligence (AI) to enhance human decision-making processes in the rapidly evolving talent acquisition landscape. However, the ramifications of these advancements on workforce diversity remain a topic of intense debate. Drawing upon Gilliland's procedural justice framework, we explore how IT job candidates interpret the fairness of AI-driven recruitment systems. Gilliland's model posits that an organization's adherence to specific fairness principles, such as *honesty* and the *opportunity to perform*, profoundly shapes candidates' self-perceptions, their judgments of the recruitment system's equity, and the overall attractiveness of the organization. Using focus groups and interviews, we interacted with 47 women, Black and Latinx or Hispanic undergraduates specializing in computer and information science to discern how gender, race, and ethnicity influence attitudes toward AI in hiring. Three procedural justice rules, *consistency of administration, job-relatedness,* and *selection information,* emerged as critical in shaping participants' fairness perceptions. Although discussed less frequently, *the propriety of questions* held significant resonance for Black and Latinx or Hispanic participants. Our study underscores the critical role of fairness evaluations for organizations, especially those striving to diversify the tech workforce.

Keywords: Algorithms · Hiring · Bias

1 Introduction

Recent studies in information sciences note a rapid shift in decision-making from humans to algorithms in talent acquisition, a trend further supported by human-computer interaction (HCI) research [46, 80, 86]. Organizations are turning to AI-driven platforms like HireVue, Textio, and Ideal for intelligent automation of various talent acquisition tasks, from job advertising and resume evaluation to candidate selection and interviewing [1]. These platforms scrutinize candidates' gestures, linguistic choices, and vocal nuances, comparing them against benchmarks set by other applicants for similar roles to generate "employability scores." The software can sift through vast stacks of resumes and harness disparate data sources to predictively match candidates with suitable positions, refine job descriptions by rectifying inherent biases in language, and deploy bots for interview scheduling [13].

© The Author(s), under exclusive license to Springer Nature Switzerland AG 2024
I. Sserwanga et al. (Eds.): iConference 2024, LNCS 14597, pp. 43–61, 2024.
https://doi.org/10.1007/978-3-031-57860-1_4

A 2020 CompTIA survey [95] involving 400 h professionals and corporate officials in the US revealed that 32% have already integrated AI tools for candidate assessment, while 80% anticipate AI significantly reshaping talent acquisition, management, and development. The purported objectivity of these tools, however, is contested by scholars who point to their potential to perpetuate or introduce new biases [12, 41, 62].

Algorithmic biases have profound implications, specifically for historically minoritized groups [62, 65]. We use the term "minoritized" to acknowledge the longstanding marginalization of tech professionals identifying as women, Black or African American, and Hispanic or Latinx. Minoritized underscores the individual agency and resilience while acknowledging the oppressive systems that have shaped their work experiences [15]. According to 2020 data from the USBureau of Labor Statistics [92], the US workforce was predominantly white (78%), followed by Black (12%) and Asian (6%) workers. Latinx or Hispanic individuals, who could belong to any racial category, constituted 18% of the workforce. Women made up nearly half (47%) of the total workforce. However, workforce demographics in the computing and mathematics sectors show greater underrepresentation of women (25%), Black (9%), and Latinx or Hispanic (8%) workers [92].

The urgency to diversify the tech workforce increases with the pervasive influence of AI. West et al. [81] argue AI systems are fundamentally classification technologies designed to differentiate, rank, and categorize. However, the consequences of these classifications are not uniform and often mirror the entrenched societal inequalities. The underrepresentation of technologists from minoritized groups in the design and development process may result in AI systems inadequately trained to discern the nuances of women and people of color [81]. Thus, the tech industry's diversity challenges may be inextricably linked to biases in the AI systems being engineered and deployed.

Our study explores how AI-driven hiring platforms can perpetuate disadvantages for job seekers with minoritized identities. Motivated by the evolving discourse on algorithmic decision-making and fairness, our research is anchored in procedural justice principles, which emphasize the perceived fairness of decision-making processes [9, 27, 45, 73]. Through this lens, we discern the fairness of AI-driven hiring platforms from the vantage point of minoritized undergraduate job seekers in computing majors. Guided by Gilliland's [27] empirical model, which juxtaposes procedural and distributive justice against perceived fairness in hiring procedures, we conducted focus groups and interviews to address two research questions:

1. What factors influence minoritized job aspirants' perceptions of fairness vis-à-vis algorithmic and human decision-making during their job search?
2. How are perceptions of fairness translated into procedural justice rules by minoritized job aspirants?

Understanding the intersection of historical disparities in tech workforce diversity and the potential pitfalls of AI-driven hiring platforms is essential for steering equitable recruitment policies, identifying the inherent biases in algorithmic decision-making, and discerning the implications of AI recruitment on historically marginalized groups [87].

2   Background

The intricate interplay between organizational decision-making processes and individuals' perceptions of these processes has been the subject of extensive scholarly attention, particularly in procedural justice. Seminal works by Thibaut, Walker, Leventhal, and Gilliland provide a foundational understanding of how individuals perceive fairness within organizational contexts. This section presents these foundational theories to provide a theoretical backdrop for our study and underscore the enduring significance of fairness perceptions in organizational contexts.

2.1   From Procedural Fairness to Procedural Justice

Thibaut and Walker [73] were among the early scholars to theorize about an organizational procedure's perceived fairness. Their work underscored the significance of an individual's "voice" or ability to exert control within fairness determinations. They posited that when individuals could influence or provide input into a decision, they were more likely to perceive the process as equitable. This initial perspective mainly focused on the fairness of the decision-making processes; a concept referred to as procedural fairness.

Marking the transition from procedural fairness to procedural justice is the expanded focus on the fairness of the processes and the outcomes and interactions within them. Leventhal's [45] seminal work intertwined procedural justice with equity theory, which birthed the concept of procedural fairness. He constructed six procedural rules: *consistency, bias-suppression, accuracy, correctability, representativeness,* and *ethicality* [27]. Each rule identifies reward allocation methods and an individual's perception of fairness within a given scenario.

Building on these foundational theories, Bies and Moag [8] introduced the concept of interactional justice. This concept focuses on an individual's ability to assimilate and communicate information throughout decision-making processes and emphasizes the decision-maker's behavior during the execution of procedures. This model highlights how individuals perceive treatment throughout these organizational processes [8]. Subsequent research highlights that when individuals confront unfavorable outcomes, providing comprehensive rationales for such decisions can potentially temper the adverse reactions [27, 28].

Through this evolution from Thibaut and Walker's emphasis on the fairness of decision-making processes to Leventhal's integration of outcomes and further to Bies and Moag's focus on interactional aspects, the concept of procedural fairness has broadened into procedural justice. This shift occurred because of a deeper understanding of the myriad factors contributing to individuals' perceptions of justice in organizational contexts, recognizing that fairness extends beyond mere processes to encompass outcomes and interpersonal interactions.

2.2   Gilliland's Procedural Justice Rules

Gilliland's framework connects procedural fairness theories to the foundational elements of well-established organizational justice research. This research encompasses studies on managerial fairness [68], the nuances of communication fairness during recruitment processes [9], the intricacies of allocation decisions [45], the dynamics of performance appraisals [28], and the norms governing interactional justice [78]. Drawing from these theories, Gilliland distills ten procedural justice rules, which are further grouped into three overarching categories: formal characteristics of procedures, the explanations provided during these procedures, and the interpersonal treatment experienced by individuals. For a detailed list of these rules and their associations with organizational justice theories, refer to Table 1. The subsequent sections describe these categories and their associated rules.

Formal Characteristics capture the foundational aspects of the hiring process, including:

1. **Job Relatedness**: The relevance of a selection test in assessing an applicant's knowledge pertinent to the job [45].
2. **Opportunity to Perform**: The chance for an applicant to provide input or showcase competencies, influencing their perception of the process's fairness [63].
3. **Reconsideration Opportunity**: Providing a second chance for applicants to influence decision-making, thereby enhancing perceived fairness [28, 62, 68].
4. **Consistency of Administration**: Ensuring uniformity in the selection mechanism or assessment across candidates, promoting equitable outcomes [50, 57, 62].

Explanation delves into the clarity and transparency of the hiring process. This domain comprises:

1. **Feedback**: The significance of providing candidates with feedback on their performance, which influences their overall perception of the process [50, 57].
2. **Selection Information**: The clarity and validity of the information provided to candidates about the selection process, which is rooted in interactional justice literature [28, 62].
3. **Honesty**: The importance of sincerity and truthfulness in the hiring process is especially crucial given the proprietary nature of many AI algorithms [9].

Interpersonal Treatment focuses on the human aspect of the hiring process, emphasizing:

1. **Interpersonal Effectiveness of Administrator**: Treating candidates with warmth and respect influences their overall perception of the organization and the process [23].
2. **Two-way Communication**: The significance of allowing candidates to provide input is especially relevant in AI-driven interviews [48].
3. **Propriety of Questions**: The importance of ensuring questions are appropriate and devoid of discriminatory overtones, maintaining the integrity of the process [2].

Lastly, Gilliland hints at **Potential Additional Procedural Rules** that might not strictly fit within traditional organizational justice literature but are relevant in the modern context. These include the ease with which candidates can fake answers during interviews [27] and concerns about the invasiveness of questions or procedures [2, 27, 86]. This comprehensive categorization offers a structured lens to evaluate the fairness of AI-driven hiring processes, ensuring they align with established principles of procedural justice. These perceptions of fairness can significantly influence an applicant's interview experience, skills assessment, and subsequent hiring decisions.

Table 1. Relationships Among Procedural Rules and Organizational Justice Theories

Procedural Rule	Organizational Justice Theory
Formal Characteristics	
Job relatedness	Accuracy rule [45], Representativeness [68]
Opportunity to perform	Voice [73], Soliciting input [28], Resource [68]
Reconsideration opportunity	Ability to modify rule [45], Ability to correct [68], Ability to challenge [28]
Consistency of administration	Consistency rule or standard [28, 45, 68, 77]
Explanation	
Feedback	Timely feedback [77], Timeliness [68]
Selection information	Information [68], Communication [68], Explanation [77]
Honesty	Truthfulness [10]
Interpersonal Treatment	
Interpersonal effectiveness	Respect [10]
Two-way communication	Two-way communication [28], Consider views [77]
Propriety of questions	Propriety of questions [10], Personal bias [45], Bias suppression [68, 77]

2.3 Procedural Justice and Algorithmic Fairness in Hiring

The landscape of employment selection has evolved significantly with the advent of technology, leading to many studies examining job applicants' reactions to these technology-enabled methods [5, 7, 16, 31, 40, 42, 61, 71, 72]. A comprehensive review of over 145 studies reveals that applicants' responses are pivotal in shaping their beliefs, intentions, and subsequent behaviors [49]. These responses offer invaluable insights into the facets of the talent acquisition process that might influence perceptions of fairness [72]. However, with the rise of AI-driven talent acquisition tools, there is a pressing need to apply these established models and techniques in empirical studies.

For example, how individuals perceive algorithmic decisions compared to human judgments remains an area ripe for exploration [44]. Scholars posit that the unique capabilities of AI-driven hiring tools might establish a hierarchy of justice attributes. Understanding this hierarchy could be instrumental in designing HR practices and technologies that champion fairness [19]. Furthermore, specific task factors might shape individuals' perceptions of fairness, reactions, and trust in algorithmic decision-making [44].

While fairness, trustworthiness, transparency, and bias have become focal points in procedural justice research [37, 43, 44], the voices of communities that may experience the most significant harm must be included, understood, and valued. Companies' increasing reliance on algorithms, driven by the allure of cost savings, task automation, and remote decision-making capabilities, necessitates a deeper understanding of potentially disparate impacts on minoritized groups [37, 43]. Lee [44]'s investigation into decision-making tasks, whether executed by algorithms or managers, offers an initial understanding. While participants perceived both entities as fair in mechanical tasks, the algorithm's judgments on more human-centric tasks were deemed less trustworthy and fair compared to human managers [44]. However, additional studies have found that participants are more inclined to accept algorithmic decisions when provided with transparent insights into the decision-making process [43].

Furthermore, AI hiring platforms are adept at integrating conventional employment data, such as resumes and performance metrics, with multifaceted data streams like audio, video, text, and even social media posts. This amalgamation facilitates the creation of comprehensive psychological profiles of candidates. A looming concern arises when algorithmically generated profiles are used as benchmarks to gauge organizational fit or predict a candidate's potential job performance. There is a tangible risk that individuals from diverse cultural backgrounds might find themselves at a systemic disadvantage, potentially perpetuating biases rather than mitigating them [87].

3   Methodology

In this study, we conducted focus groups and interviews with participants from a US university, specifically targeting undergraduate students pursuing majors in computer and information sciences. Our recruitment strategy aimed to engage students who identified as minoritized by race and/or gender. Of the students approached, 47 agreed to participate in our study. Most participants were nearing the end of their undergraduate journey, with 51.1% (n = 24) in their third to fifth years. While no students identified with non-binary gender identities, 78.7% identified as female, and 21.3% identified as male. In terms of ethnicity, the majority identified as African American or Black (46.8%), followed by White (36.2%), Asian (12.8%), and Latinx or Hispanic (4.3%).

3.1   Focus Groups

The 47 participants were divided into two sessions: one with 23 participants and the other with 24. Focus group sessions, spanning 75 to 90 min, were audio-recorded and transcribed to preserve participants' genuine sentiments and perspectives. Two researchers oversaw both sessions to ensure comprehensive data collection and observation.

To establish a common foundational understanding, we began each session by providing participants with a definition of algorithms, framing them as "processes or sets of rules that a computer follows in calculations or other problem-solving operations." Next, participants were shown a video detailing the workings of AI hiring software. This video served as a primer, explaining how such software operates, its potential applications, the spectrum of businesses leveraging this technology, and a deep dive into a specific AI hiring platform, Hirevue.

Post-video, participants were presented with one of two scenarios:

1. An individual seeks a programming position, and an algorithm curates a list of job opportunities based on the search criteria. Or,
2. An individual pursuing a programming role presents their resume to a manager at a college career fair. The manager then outlines the available positions aligning with the individual's qualifications.

Upon reflecting on their respective scenarios, participants completed a questionnaire. The session concluded with a group discussion where participants shared their responses to the scenarios. The questionnaire and discussion prompts were designed to elicit participants' perceptions of fairness, as exhibited by both the algorithm and the manager, and to elucidate the rationale behind their responses.

3.2 Interviews

After the focus group sessions, we embarked on a series of follow-up interviews with a subset of ten participants. These interviews, which ranged from 22 to 35 min, were semi-structured. The primary objective was to investigate participants' perceptions and firsthand experiences concerning algorithmic hiring. The structure allowed for pre-determined questions and the flexibility to explore emergent themes and insights.

3.3 Analysis

We employed an inductive approach to analyze the transcripts from focus groups and interviews. Thematic coding allowed us to extract meaningful themes aligned with critical areas of research interest: participants' familiarity with AI hiring platforms, their sentiments towards these systems, preferences between traditional and AI-driven interviews, their grasp of the underlying mechanisms of AI hiring tools, and discussions surrounding accent, cultural nuances, skin tone, and personal identity. We also identified participants' strategies for enhancing their performance in AI-mediated interviews and their perceptions of companies that leverage such algorithmic hiring tools. Analyzing the transcripts, we iteratively refined and organized themes into categories. A significant aspect of our analysis was identifying procedural justice rules, as articulated by our participants.

4 Findings

This section presents five themes from our data analysis and the procedural justice rules participants identified as significant throughout the recruitment process. To differentiate between the data sources, we have used the abbreviations "FG" for focus group sessions and "I" for interviews, followed by the respective participant numbers (e.g., FGP01 and IP01).

4.1 Theme 1: Previous Interactions with AI Recruitment Systems

Most participants in their third, fourth, and fifth year of study had encountered AI-driven recruitment platforms, encompassing tools for resume screening, video interview recording, and coding challenges. Despite availing themselves of the professional development resources offered by the university's career coaches, participants reported that the training was limited because they encountered a variety of hiring platforms and inconsistent hiring procedures. This variation was particularly evident in the guidance given to applicants before the interview and the interview protocols that facilitate the applicant's engagement with AI hiring platforms.

For instance, unclear pre-interview instructions compelled participants to devise strategies for interfacing with the platform during their interview. One participant, IP01, shared their experience with HireVue: "So for HireVue, they just gave me a link, and then I went to the link…I did a demo recording, made sure that everything was fine, and then after that, they gave me some kind of prompt, kind of like questions, and I had to record my answers. So I think it was around like two minutes each for each of those questions…".

The interview's duration and format varied among participants, making it difficult to develop strategies to navigate these platforms. IP01 further elaborated on the time constraints of their interview, stating, "I think it was probably being like 15 to 20 min in total…".

In contrast, FGP14 experienced a variety of interview structures: "My interview had two different types of video recordings that you would do. Some of the questions were timed, and you only had a specific amount of time to answer a question, and then there were some which you had an unlimited number of attempts…" This variation in interview structure underscores the need for flexible strategies when preparing for AI-based interviews.

IP02 experienced a longer interview duration: "The interview session lasted…about 40 min or so, and I had to answer 15 questions." This response highlights the potential for significant differences in the time commitment required by different AI interview platforms.

Most participants encountered two or three hiring platforms during their job search. IP08, for example, shared their experience where the AI tool served as a conversational partner: "…they also sent me one where it was like, it was like a phone screen, but I'm talking to an automated bot instead of another person." This example illustrates the diverse ways in which AI is integrated into the hiring process.

4.2 Theme 2: Fairness of Resume Screening

Most participants agreed that the fairness of resume evaluation is comparable, whether conducted by a human or an algorithm, when discussing automated resume reviews. FGP07, for instance, posited, "I actually thought that the resume review might be the same either way, based on the fact that I think most companies are just looking for some pretty basic information from your resume…" Other participants perceived the automated resume screening process as advantageous, enabling organizations to review more resumes and potentially enhancing their employment prospects. IP01 elaborated on this point, stating, "...I would be like, [to be] called to give an interview, let's say essentially, they were screening, let's say five, people without this tool, maybe now they can scale to 10. So, I would get like more opportunity to... express...[my] views and answers."

Other participants echoed this sentiment. IP07 noted, "So... if this platform allows me to get more interviews in the future... because they see it as a good option too... as like a screening tool, I'm okay with that because it gives me more chances." Participants attributed the source of these additional opportunities provided by AI platforms to keyword identification in resumes. As IP03 explained, "I might use some AI... to pick out keywords from resumes..." This quote highlights the potential for AI to enhance the efficiency and breadth of the resume screening process.

4.3 Theme 3: Possibility of Bias

The topics of race, culture, and identity were prominent throughout the focus groups and interviews. Many of our participants expressed apprehensions about the possibility of bias influencing their prospects of securing a particular role. IP03, for instance, raised concerns about the system favoring homogeneous candidates: "Um, but then you also have candidates who are strong in technical skills but not great with these online video platforms. Um, so it really biases the system towards people who are able to fit the mold, um, just because it's what the system looks for rather than prioritizing kind of the best candidates for the company itself."

FGP08 highlighted the potential for overlooking valuable soft skills that may not be immediately evident in written form: "So, sometimes a person may not come with the right written things, but if I'm talking, you can pick up on different soft skills that they might have that you didn't think that your company needed, so they could be overlooked because it wasn't like you said, those small dimensions being filled."

During virtual interviews, participants also raised concerns about potential bias related to the lighting conditions or the background of a workspace. FGP06 stated, "So, the thing is, I feel there's a lot you have to consider when doing a virtual interview or something like that. You need to consider lighting, what you're wearing, the background, things that are in the background, and it's more that you have to take into consideration."

However, not all participants believed that AI hiring platforms inherently favor bias. Some saw the potential for these platforms to alleviate bias concerns. IP02 suggested, "An interviewer that has some...racial bias might not be prone to hiring certain people, representatives of, [a] certain races or same thing with gender...That could be a problem. And, those interview tools, I think, could help."

While this viewpoint was not widely shared among our participants, it underscores the complexity surrounding the use of AI in hiring platforms. The potential for bias, whether mitigated or exacerbated by AI, remains critical in these tools' ongoing development and deployment.

Racial, Cultural, and Identity Bias

Participants expressed apprehension about potential racial, cultural, and identity biases that could hinder their interview progression. Specific personal attributes were high-lighted as potential issues, with several individuals citing their unique skin tones and speech patterns as possible variables the algorithm could misinterpret. FGP01, for instance, expressed concerns about skin tone: "…I have a different skin tone than the guy that was on the screen, so my emotions may not show the same that the algorithm is looking for if that makes sense." FGP03 expanded on this, pointing to cultural dif-ferences: "Yeah, in addition to facial recognition, I also think that if you come from a different society, cultural background, your reactions aren't the same as what they are probably measuring…".

Participants of color further noted how racial differences require attention to prepare for AI-based interviews adequately. IP03, for instance, shared a common struggle: "I found it challenging to ensure my face was clearly visible and well-lit in the video. Setting up the right lighting conditions was often a struggle." This quote highlights the unique challenges posed by video-based AI interview platforms, which require considerations beyond traditional interview preparation. IP09 voiced concerns about the potential for bias in AI systems, citing specific examples: "I think over-reliance on these tools can be detrimental as they can introduce a certain level of bias. I have read articles about how Amazon's facial recognition has shown bias towards people of color…".

Participants also expressed concerns about the potential for unique characteristics to be overlooked by an algorithm not designed to recognize such diversity. FGP08 noted, "I think algorithms also miss out on uniqueness." Personal experiences became particularly relevant to these concerns, especially when individuals were compared with other candidates. The lack of transparency in how these comparisons are made was frustrating. FGP10 questioned the objectivity of these comparisons: "..I did interview with a company that used HireVue, and particularly when you were talking, it made me think about things, about the way you say that the algorithms are comparing the candidate to the people that might be experts or ideal candidates in that profession, it becomes objective because it's like, 'What is the perfect candidate?'".

4.4 Theme 4: Necessity for Human Interaction

The dialogue comparing human interviews with AI interviews predominantly under-scored the necessity for human interaction. Participants also expressed concerns about the algorithm's autonomy in decision-making without human oversight or intervention. The reasons for preferring in-person interviews over AI varied among our participants, ranging from the potential for personal connection, the opportunity to glean crucial infor-mation about the organization during an in-person interview, and assessing workplace compatibility. FGP21 encapsulated this sentiment: "But I don't really like the idea that it can all be the machine, and the human gets zero say in it."

Preference for In-Person Interviews
Our participants overwhelmingly favored some form of human or in-person interviews. They frequently discussed the potential to increase their chances of success by showcas-ing their personality and establishing a rapport with the interviewer, a connection they felt could not be formed with an algorithm.

IP03, for instance, stated, "I really do like a company that values human interaction, where they value being able to talk to you face-to-face... Kind of get to know you as a person." Similarly, IP08 expressed, "...but on the other hand, I do miss out on that face-to-face interaction, which I think I perform better at." IP02 added, "...when you're talking to a person, you get to see their interviewer's mentality and...you can frame your answers in a way that would be better suited for that particular person."

During the interviews and focus groups, most participants agreed that human interaction was necessary if an organization utilizes algorithms during talent acquisition. They also mentioned the value of receiving information from the interviewer that could aid their decision-making. FGP03 noted, "...managers ideally have the best information when it comes to what their company's culture is looking for and how that person might fit into your company. That's something you may not be able to tell straight off an algorithm...".

Trust in the Algorithm
Only a few participants pointed to a trust issue they could not overcome. They voiced their concerns about the proprietary or "black box" technology and the lack of transparency in the algorithm's decision-making process. FGP05 expressed, "...You just can't trust them... I think that there still needs to be some type of human interaction." IP10 added, "I don't totally trust them. I do have some trust beforehand, but then that trust is limited...".

While only a small number of our participants addressed this issue of trust, it may become more prominent as AI continues to permeate other industries.

4.5 Theme 5: Necessity for Training

Participants underscored the importance of disseminating knowledge about these algorithms across academic institutions. Despite their active engagement with career counselors and regular participation in professional development activities offered by career services and corporate partners, they expressed uncertainty about their preparedness for AI hiring systems. Overall, participants agreed that training would be beneficial, as would the opportunity to practice AI interviews, like preparing for an in-person interview. Participants recommended three additional areas for career preparation:

1. IP02 suggested the development of training modules: "I think it would be helpful... I'm sure this 'black box' technology will continue to develop, and there will likely be online training modules offered to people to practice..."
2. FGP09 pointed out the need to understand what the algorithms are looking for: "...If you haven't done enough video interviews and don't understand what they're looking for, such as facial movements, an algorithm isn't taking that into account when searching for the right applicant for the job."
3. Participants also felt that career counselors needed additional training on algorithmic hiring processes. IP03 stated, "I do think that career offices definitely need to stay up-to-date with how recruiting happens in the real world. If there were sessions about how to navigate and succeed with these video platforms, I would have definitely attended."

4.6 Significance of Procedural Justice

Consistency of administration and *job-relatedness* were the two procedural justice rules most positively associated with participants' perceptions of fairness in AI hiring. Participants' understanding of job-relatedness was based on their experiences with LinkedIn, where the algorithm analyzes skillsets and resumes and recommends suitable job opportunities. FG12 noted, "The algorithm could be super spot on or suggest a job that has nothing to do with your field." While "algorithms could be a bit off" (IP04) in their job recommendations, they mitigate the risk of human biases in job referral networks where job leads "depend on who you know" (IP07). Skills assessments via an algorithm were generally considered fair because "you either know how to code or you don't" (FG03). In contrast, the *opportunity for reconsideration* was consistently viewed as unfair when decisions were made solely by algorithms without human oversight.

The explanation category of procedural justice rules, *Selection Information, Honesty, and Feedback,* was mentioned frequently and viewed negatively by participants when delivered from an automated system. As IP10 noted, "It does not feel as great to be rejected by a computer based on code - it is cut and dry to find out the results." Similarly, positive feedback from an algorithm was not well received. FGP20 explained, "...it would be more meaningful...hearing that from an individual who wants you in that environment, versus pretty much saying that you ticked all the boxes." These quotes may also explain why procedural justice rules in *Interpersonal Treatment*, like *two-way communication* and *interpersonal effectiveness of the administration*, were viewed negatively and discussed with the least frequency.

The *propriety of questions* was particularly salient for Black and Latinx/Hispanic participants considering potential harm during automated video interviews. These participants discussed how exclusions in training data sets led to unfair outcomes. Thus, an automated video interview "adds an extra layer of things you have to do" (FG06) because "in most cases when they make these programs, minorities are most likely not the default" (IP09). As FG07 noted, "We are being compared to people who we are nothing like."

5 Discussion

5.1 Conceptual Implications: Bridging Procedural and Distributive Justice

The landscape of AI-driven hiring is rapidly evolving, and our study offers a fresh perspective by focusing on the perceptions of aspiring technology professionals from historically underrepresented groups. This emphasis on women, Black, and Latinx or Hispanic undergraduate students in computing fields provides a richer understanding of the complexities surrounding the fairness of AI hiring systems, especially when viewed through the lens of procedural justice rules.

Our findings resonate with the broader literature on procedural justice, which has long been concerned with the fairness of decision-making processes [80, 82, 84]. However, our research introduces a novel dimension by emphasizing the intricate interplay between procedural and distributive justice. Distributive justice, as defined, revolves around the perceived fairness of allocations or, in this context, the outcomes of hiring decisions. When participants evaluate AI hiring systems, they assess the fairness of the process (procedural justice) and the fairness of the outcomes (distributive justice). Their concerns about discrimination and performance expectations, rooted in racial and gender stereotypes, can reflect their perceptions about the fairness of the outcomes they anticipate from these systems.

The role of identity emerges as a pivotal factor in shaping these perceptions. While procedural justice rules provide a framework for understanding fairness, our participants' lived experiences and identities add depth. The intersection of identity with procedural and distributive justice nuances the discourse and suggests that fairness perceptions are multifaceted and deeply personal. Algorithmic biases, as highlighted by our participants, further complicate this narrative. While algorithms designed with an emphasis on learning about underrepresented groups can potentially lead to more equitable outcomes, as Li et al. [46] suggested, the perceived fairness of these algorithms is contingent upon their transparency and adaptability. This observation underscores the importance of exploration in the hiring process, ensuring that AI systems are technically fair and perceived as such by diverse job seekers.

As expressed by our participants, the indispensable role of human interaction in the hiring process offers another layer of complexity. While AI systems can efficiently match candidates to job opportunities, the human element—characterized by empathy, understanding, and personal connection—remains irreplaceable. This sentiment aligns with the broader discourse on the limitations of AI and the enduring value of human judgment and interaction.

Our empirical findings underscore that fairness perceptions oscillate across the talent acquisition process. While algorithmic decision-making was perceived as advantageous during job sourcing and skills assessment, AI-mediated interviews were overwhelmingly deemed problematic and unjust. A yearning for human interaction emerged, with a pronounced preference for traditional face-to-face interviews over their AI counterparts. Notably, three procedural justice rules, *consistency of administration*, *job-relatedness*, and *selection information*, emerged as critical in shaping participants' fairness perceptions. Though less frequently cited, the *propriety of questions* held significant resonance for Black and Latinx/Hispanic participants.

In synthesizing these insights, our study beckons a deeper exploration into the theoretical underpinnings of AI hiring. It calls for a holistic understanding that integrates procedural justice, distributive justice, and the unique experiences of underrepresented groups, ensuring that the development and deployment of AI hiring systems are both fair and perceived as such.

5.2 Operational Insights: Navigating AI in Modern Recruitment

The insights derived from our study have profound practical ramifications for the evolving landscape of hiring practices in the age of AI-driven recruitment. The apprehensions voiced by participants about the fairness of AI hiring mechanisms underscore the pressing need for clarity in their deployment. Organizations must take the initiative to elucidate the inner workings of these systems, detailing the decision-making processes. Organizations can foster trust and assuage concerns about potential biases or unfairness by demystifying the role of AI, the criteria it employs, and the extent of human intervention.

Our participants' preference for human interaction in the interviewing process signals a clear message to organizations. While AI can streamline certain aspects of recruitment, the human element remains irreplaceable. A balanced approach might see AI tools handling preliminary screening, with human recruiters stepping in during the more nuanced stages of recruitment. This hybrid model could address both efficiency and the innate human desire for connection.

The study underscores a glaring gap in the current preparation of job seekers, especially those from underrepresented backgrounds, to navigate the intricacies of AI-driven hiring. Academic institutions, in collaboration with industry partners, should spearhead initiatives like workshops on AI interview preparedness or strategies for effective self-presentation in automated settings.

Feedback from our participants points towards the necessity of a more inclusive design philosophy for AI hiring tools that actively seek diverse input, rigorous testing of algorithms against varied datasets, and a commitment to elucidating decision-making processes for end-users.

6 Conclusion

By employing Gilliland's procedural justice rules, we understand the perceptions of fairness in hiring, particularly from the vantage point of minoritized undergraduates pursuing degrees in computer and information sciences. Our study underscores the critical role of fairness evaluations for organizations, especially those striving to achieve diversity benchmarks. To truly champion diversity, equity, and inclusion, algorithms must transcend traditional assessments of fit. Instead, they should recognize and value diverse job-seekers' talents and merits. Such a shift would align with the professed commitments of tech firms to inclusivity and foster a more equitable hiring landscape. Furthermore, it is incumbent upon university career services to evolve, offering tailored guidance on navigating the intricacies of AI-based talent acquisition platforms. Such training would better equip and enhance the marketability of minoritized job-seekers in an increasingly algorithmic hiring ecosystem.

Acknowledgment. This material is based upon work supported by the National Science Foundation under Grant Number 1841368. Any opinions, findings, and conclusions or recommendations expressed in this material are those of the author(s) and do not necessarily reflect the views of the National Science Foundation.

References

1. Anderson, N.: Applicant and Recruiter reactions to new technology in selection: a critical review and agenda for future research. Int. J. Sel. Assess. **11**(2–3), 121–136 (2003). https://doi.org/10.1111/1468-2389.00235
2. Arvey, R.D., Sackett, P.R.: Fairness in selection: Current developments and perspectives. In: Schmitt, N. and Borman, W. (eds.) Personnel Selection. Jossey-Bass, San Francisco, CA (1993)

3. Assarroudi, A., et al.: Directed qualitative content analysis: the description and elaboration of its underpinning methods and data analysis process. J. Res. Nurs. **23**(1), 42–55 (2018). https://doi.org/10.1177/1744987117741667
4. Barocas, S. et al.: Big Data, Data Science, and Civil Rights. arXiv:1706.03102 [cs]. (2017)
5. Bauer, T.N., et al.: Applicant reactions to different selection technology: face-to-face, interactive voice response, and computer-assisted telephone screening interviews. Int. J. Sel. Assess. **12**(1–2), 135–148 (2004). https://doi.org/10.1111/j.0965-075X.2004.00269.x
6. Bauer, T.N., et al.: Applicant reactions to selection: development of the selection procedural justice scale (spjs). Pers. Psychol. **54**(2), 387–419 (2001). https://doi.org/10.1111/j.1744-6570.2001.tb00097.x
7. Bauer, T.N. et al.: Applicant reactions to technology-based selection: what we know so far. In: Technology-Enhanced Assessment of Talent, pp. 190–223. John Wiley & Sons, Ltd. (2011). https://doi.org/10.1002/9781118256022.ch6
8. Bies, R.J.: Beyond formal procedures: the interpersonal context of procedural justice. In: Carroll, J.S. (ed.) Organizational Settings, vol. 88, p. 98 Erlbaum, Hillsdale, NJ (1990)
9. Bies, R.J.: Interactional justice: Communication criteria of fairness. Res. Negotiat. Organiz. **1**, 43–55 (1986)
10. Bies, R.J., Shapiro, D.L.: Voice and justification: their influence on procedural fairness judgments. Acad. Manag. J. **31**(3), 676–685 (1988)
11. Brockner, J.: Making sense of procedural fairness: how high procedural fairness can reduce or heighten the influence of outcome favorability. AMR. **27**(1), 58–76 (2002). https://doi.org/10.5465/amr.2002.5922363
12. Buyl, M. et al.: Tackling algorithmic disability discrimination in the hiring process: an ethical, legal and technical analysis. In: 2022 ACM Conference on Fairness, Accountability, and Transparency, pp. 1071–1082 Association for Computing Machinery, New York (2022). https://doi.org/10.1145/3531146.3533169
13. Celani, A., et al.: In justice we trust: A model of the role of trust in the organization in applicant reactions to the selection process. Hum. Resour. Manag. Rev. **18**(2), 63–76 (2008). https://doi.org/10.1016/j.hrmr.2008.04.002
14. Chambers, B.A.: Applicant reactions and their consequences: review, advice, and recommendations for future research. Int. J. Manag. Rev. **4**(4), 317–333 (2002). https://doi.org/10.1111/1468-2370.00090
15. Cooper, J.: A Call for a Language Shift: From Covert Oppression to Overt Empowerment, https://education.uconn.edu/2016/12/07/a-call-for-a-language-shift-from-covert-oppression-to-overt-empowerment/ (Accessed 21 Jan 2022)
16. Danieli, O., et al.: How to hire with algorithms. Harvard Bus. Rev. 17 (2016)
17. De Vries, R.E., Van Gelder, J.-L.: Explaining workplace delinquency: the role of Honesty-Humility, ethical culture, and employee surveillance. Personality Individ. Differ. **86**, 112–116 (2015). https://doi.org/10.1016/j.paid.2015.06.008
18. Denzin, N.K., Ryan, K.E.: Qualitative methodology (including focus groups). In: The SAGE Handbook of Social Science Methodology, pp. 578–594 SAGE Publications Ltd, 1 Oliver's Yard, 55 City Road, London England EC1Y 1SP United Kingdom (2007). https://doi.org/10.4135/9781848607958.n32
19. Dineen, B.R., et al.: Perceived fairness of web-based applicant screening procedures: Weighing the rules of justice and the role of individual differences. Hum. Resour. Manage. **43**(2–3), 127–145 (2004). https://doi.org/10.1002/hrm.20011
20. Elo, S., Kyngäs, H.: The qualitative content analysis process. J. Adv. Nurs. **62**(1), 107–115 (2008). https://doi.org/10.1111/j.1365-2648.2007.04569.x
21. Florentine, S.: How artificial intelligence can eliminate bias in hiring. CIO Mag. (2016)
22. Folger, R., Greenberg, J.: Procedural justice: An interpretive analysis of personnel systems. Res. Pers. Hum. Resour. Manag. **3**(1), 141–183 (1985)

23. Fried, I.: Exclusive: Many tech workers would quit if employer recorded them. https://www.axios.com/2022/05/31/tech-workers-quit-employer-recorded-surveillance (Accessed 20 June 2022)

24. Frith, H.: Focusing on sex: using focus groups in sex research. Sexualities **3**(3), 275–297 (2000). https://doi.org/10.1177/136346000003003001

25. Gilliland, S.: The tails of justice: a critical examination of the dimensionality of organizational justice constructs. Hum. Resour. Manag. Rev. **18**(4), 271–281 (2008). https://doi.org/10.1016/j.hrmr.2008.08.001

26. Gilliland, S.W.: Effects of procedural and distributive justice on reactions to a selection system. J. Appl. Psychol. **79**(5), 691–701 (1994). https://doi.org/10.1037/0021-9010.79.5.691

27. Gilliland, S.W.: The perceived fairness of selection systems: an organizational justice perspective. AMR. **18**(4), 694–734 (1993). https://doi.org/10.5465/amr.1993.9402210155

28. Greenberg, J.: Determinants of perceived fairness of performance evaluations. J. Appli. Psychol. **71**, 2, 340 (1986)

29. Hsieh, H.-F., Shannon, S.E.: Three Approaches to qualitative content analysis. Qual. Health Res. **15**(9), 1277–1288 (2005). https://doi.org/10.1177/1049732305276687

30. Iles, P.A., Robertson, I.T.: The impact of personnel selection procedures on candidates. Assessment Select. Organiz., 257–271 (1989)

31. Jansen, B.J., et al.: Using the web to look for work: Implications for online job seeking and recruiting. Internet Res. **15**(1), 49–66 (2005). https://doi.org/10.1108/10662240510577068

32. Kanara, K.: Council Post: Accelerating Through The Curve: How Value Creation Teams Help PE Firms Weather Economic Storms, https://www.forbes.com/sites/forbeshumanresourcescouncil/2020/05/21/accelerating-through-the-curve-how-value-creation-teams-help-pe-firms-weather-economic-storms/ (Accessed 19 Jan 2022)

33. Kim, P.T.: Data-driven discrimination at work. Wm. & Mary L. Rev. **58**(3), 857–936 (2016)

34. Kirat, T. et al.: Fairness and Explainability in Automatic Decision-Making Systems. A challenge for computer science and law. (2022)

35. Kirkpatrick, K.: Battling algorithmic bias: how do we ensure algorithms treat us fairly? Commun. ACM **59**(10), 16–17 (2016). https://doi.org/10.1145/2983270

36. Kitzinger, J.: The methodology of Focus Groups: the importance of interaction between research participants. Sociol. Health Illn. **16**(1), 103–121 (1994). https://doi.org/10.1111/1467-9566.ep11347023

37. Köchling, A., Wehner, M.C.: Discriminated by an algorithm: a systematic review of discrimination and fairness by algorithmic decision-making in the context of HR recruitment and HR development. Bus. Res. **13**(3), 795–848 (2020). https://doi.org/10.1007/s40685-020-00134-w

38. Konradt, U., et al.: Fairness Perceptions in Web-based Selection: Impact on applicants' pursuit intentions, recommendation intentions, and intentions to reapply. Int. J. Sel. Assess. **21**(2), 155–169 (2013). https://doi.org/10.1111/ijsa.12026

39. Konradt, U., et al.: Patterns of change in fairness perceptions during the hiring process. Int. J. Sel. Assess. **24**(3), 246–259 (2016). https://doi.org/10.1111/ijsa.12144

40. Kulkarni, S., Che, X.: Intelligent software tools for recruiting. J. Inter. Technol. Inform. Manag. **28**(2), 2–16 (2019)

41. Langer, M., et al.: Highly automated job interviews: acceptance under the influence of stakes. Int. J. Sel. Assess. **27**(3), 217–234 (2019). https://doi.org/10.1111/ijsa.12246

42. Langer, M., et al.: Information as a double-edged sword: the role of computer experience and information on applicant reactions towards novel technologies for personnel selection. Comput. Hum. Behav. **81**, 19–30 (2018). https://doi.org/10.1016/j.chb.2017.11.036

43. Lee, M.K. et al.: Procedural justice in algorithmic fairness: leveraging transparency and outcome control for fair algorithmic mediation. In: Proceedings of ACM Human-Computer Interaction, CSCW, vol. 3, pp. 182:1–182:26 (2019). https://doi.org/10.1145/3359284

44. Lee, M.K.: Understanding perception of algorithmic decisions: fairness, trust, and emotion in response to algorithmic management. Big Data Soc. **5**(1), 2053951718756684 (2018). https://doi.org/10.1177/2053951718756684

45. Leventhal, G.S.: What should be done with equity theory? In: Social Exchange, pp. 27–55 Springer. US (1980). https://doi.org/10.1007/978-1-4613-3087-5_2

46. Li, D. et al.: Hiring as Exploration (2020). https://papers.ssrn.com/abstract=3630630, https://doi.org/10.2139/ssrn.3630630.

47. Mann, G., O'Neil, C.: Hiring algorithms are not neutral. Harv. Bus. Rev. **9**, 2016 (2016)

48. Martin, C.L., Nagao, D.H.: Some effects of computerized interviewing on job applicant responses. J. Appl. Psychol. **74**(1), 72–80 (1989). https://doi.org/10.1037/0021-9010.74.1.72

49. McCarthy, J.M., et al.: Applicant perspectives during selection: a review addressing "so what?", "what's new?", and "where to next?" J. Manag. **43**(6), 1693–1725 (2017). https://doi.org/10.1177/0149206316681846

50. Miller, C.C.: Can an algorithm hire better than a human, vol. 25. The New York Times (2015)

51. Nyagadza, B., et al.: Emotions influence on customers' e-banking satisfaction evaluation in e-service failure and e-service recovery circumstances. Soc. Sci. Humanities Open. **6**, 1–14 (2022). https://doi.org/10.1016/j.ssaho.2022.100292

52. Oates, C.: Research training for social scientists. Presented at the, London January 11 (2022). https://doi.org/10.4135/9780857028051

53. O'Neil, C.: Weapons of Math Destruction: How Big Data Increases Inequality and Threatens Democracy, Crown (2016)

54. Otterbacher, J. et al.: Competent men and warm women: gender stereotypes and backlash in image search results. In: Proceedings of the 2017 CHI Conference on Human Factors in Computing Systems, pp. 6620–6631 Association for Computing Machinery, New York (2017). https://doi.org/10.1145/3025453.3025727

55. Powell, R.A., Single, H.M.: Focus Groups. Inter. J. Quality Health Care **8**(5), 499–504 (1996). https://doi.org/10.1093/intqhc/8.5.499

56. Quillian, L., et al.: Meta-analysis of field experiments shows no change in racial discrimination in hiring over time. PNAS **114**(41), 10870–10875 (2017). https://doi.org/10.1073/pnas.1706255114

57. Raub, M.: Bots, bias and big data: artificial intelligence, algorithmic bias and disparate impact liability in hiring practices comment. Ark. L. Rev. **71**(2), 529–570 (2018)

58. Rooney, K., Khorram, Y.: Tech companies say they value diversity but reports show little change in last six years. CNBC (2020)

59. Rosenbaum, S., et al.: Focus groups in HCI. Presented at the CHI 2002 Extended Abstracts on Human Factors in Computing Systems - CHI 2002 (2002). https://doi.org/10.1145/506443.506554

60. Roth, P.L., et al.: Ethnic group differences in measures of job performance: a new meta-analysis. J. Appl. Psychol. **88**(4), 694–706 (2003). https://doi.org/10.1037/0021-9010.88.4.694

61. RoyChowdhury, T., Srimannarayana, M.: Applicants' perceptions on online recruitment procedures. Manag. Labour Stud. **38**(3), 185–199 (2013). https://doi.org/10.1177/0258042X13509737

62. Ryan, A.M., Huth, M.: Not much more than platitudes? a critical look at the utility of applicant reactions research. Hum. Resour. Manag. Rev. **18**(3), 119–132 (2008). https://doi.org/10.1016/j.hrmr.2008.07.004

63. Rynes, S.L., et al.: The importance of recruitment in job choice: a different way of looking. Pers. Psychol. **44**(3), 487–521 (1991). https://doi.org/10.1111/j.1744-6570.1991.tb02402.x

64. Rynes, S.L.: Barber, AE: applicant attraction strategies: an organizational perspective. AMR. **15**(2), 286–310 (1990). https://doi.org/10.5465/amr.1990.4308158

65. Sandvig, C., et al.: Auditing algorithms: Research methods for detecting discrimination on internet platforms. Data a Discriminat. Converting Critic. Concerns Productive Inquiry. **22**, 4349–4357 (2014)
66. Schinkel, S., et al.: Selection fairness and outcomes: a field study of interactive effects on applicant reactions. Int. J. Sel. Assess. **21**(1), 22–31 (2013). https://doi.org/10.1111/ijsa.12014
67. Schuler, H.: Social validity of selection situations: a concept and some empirical results (1993)
68. Sheppard, B.H., Lewicki, R.J.: Toward general principles of managerial fairness. Soc Just Res. **1**(2), 161–176 (1987). https://doi.org/10.1007/BF01048014
69. Smithson, J.: Using and analysing focus groups: limitations and possibilities. Int. J. Soc. Res. Methodol. **3**(2), 103–119 (2000). https://doi.org/10.1080/136455700405172
70. Stanton, J.M., Stam, K.R.: The visible employee: using workplace monitoring and surveillance to protect information assets--without compromising employee privacy or trust. Information Today, Medford, N.J (2006)
71. Stone, D.L., et al.: The influence of technology on the future of human resource management. Hum. Resour. Manag. Rev. **25**(2), 216–231 (2015). https://doi.org/10.1016/j.hrmr.2015.01.002
72. Strohmeier, S.: Research in e-HRM: review and implications. Hum. Resour. Manag. Rev. **17**(1), 19–37 (2007). https://doi.org/10.1016/j.hrmr.2006.11.002
73. Thibaut, J.W., Walker, L.: Procedural justice: a psychological analysis. L. Erlbaum Associates (1975)
74. Thielsch, M.T., et al.: E-recruiting and fairness: the applicant's point of view. Inf. Technol. Manag. **13**(2), 59–67 (2012). https://doi.org/10.1007/s10799-012-0117-x
75. Truxillo, D.M., et al.: Selection fairness information and applicant reactions: a longitudinal field study. J. Appl. Psychol. **87**(6), 1020–1031 (2002). https://doi.org/10.1037/0021-9010.87.6.1020
76. Truxillo, D.M., et al.: The importance of organizational justice in personnel selection: defining when selection fairness really matters. Int. J. Sel. Assess. **12**(1–2), 39–53 (2004). https://doi.org/10.1111/j.0965-075X.2004.00262.x
77. Tyler, T., Bies, R.J.: Applied social psychology and organizational settings. Beyond formal procedures: the interpersonal context of procedural justice, pp. 77–98 (1990)
78. Vaughn, S. et al.: Why use focus group interviews in educational and psychological research. Focus Group Interv. Educ. Psychol., 12–21 (1996)
79. Walker, H.J., et al.: Watch what you say: job applicants' justice perceptions from initial organizational correspondence. Hum. Resour. Manage. **54**(6), 999–1011 (2015). https://doi.org/10.1002/hrm.21655
80. Wang, R. et al.: Factors influencing perceived fairness in algorithmic decision-making: algorithm outcomes, development procedures, and individual differences. In: Proceedings of the 2020 CHI Conference on Human Factors in Computing Systems. pp. 1–14 Association for Computing Machinery, New York (2020). https://doi.org/10.1145/3313831.3376813
81. West, S.M., et al.: Discriminating systems. AI Now (2019)
82. Wiechmann, D., Ryan, A.M.: Reactions to computerized testing in selection contexts. Int. J. Sel. Assess. **11**(2–3), 215–229 (2003). https://doi.org/10.1111/1468-2389.00245
83. Willard, G., et al.: Some evidence for the nonverbal contagion of racial bias. Organ. Behav. Hum. Decis. Process. **128**, 96–107 (2015). https://doi.org/10.1016/j.obhdp.2015.04.002
84. Williams, B.A., et al.: How Algorithms discriminate based on data they lack: challenges, solutions, and policy implications. J. Inf. Policy **8**, 78–115 (2018). https://doi.org/10.5325/jinfopoli.8.2018.0078
85. Wilson, C.. et al.: Building and auditing fair algorithms: a case study in candidate screening. In: Proceedings of the 2021 ACM Conference on Fairness, Accountability, and Transparency, pp. 666–677. Association for Computing Machinery, New York (2021). https://doi.org/10.1145/3442188.3445928

86. Woodruff, A. et al.: A qualitative exploration of perceptions of algorithmic fairness. In: Proceedings of the 2018 CHI Conference on Human Factors in Computing Systems, pp. 1–14 Association for Computing Machinery, New York (2018)

87. Yarger, L.K., et al.: Algorithmic equity in the hiring of underrepresented IT job candidates. Online Inf. Rev. (2020). https://doi.org/10.1108/oir-10-2018-0334

88. Zhang, L., Yencha, C.: Examining perceptions towards hiring algorithms. Technol. Soc. **68**, 101848 (2022). https://doi.org/10.1016/j.techsoc.2021.101848

89. Zhang, T., et al.: Working from home: small business performance and the COVID-19 pandemic. Small Bus. Econ. **58**(2), 611–636 (2022). https://doi.org/10.1007/s11187-021-004 93-6

90. Zorn, T.E., et al.: Focus groups as sites of influential interaction: building communicative self-efficacy and effecting attitudinal change in discussing controversial topics. J. Appl. Commun. Res. **34**(2), 115–140 (2006). https://doi.org/10.1080/00909880600573965

91. Zou, J., Schiebinger, L.: AI can be sexist and racist — it's time to make it fair. Nature **559**(7714), 324–326 (2018). https://doi.org/10.1038/d41586-018-05707-8

92. 2021 home : US Bureau of Labor Statistics. https://www.bls.gov/opub/mlr/2021/home.htm, (Accessed 21 Jan 2022)

93. The postpandemic workforce: Responses to a McKinsey global survey of 800 executives | McKinsey. https://www.mckinsey.com/featured-insights/future-of-work/what-800-exe cutives-envision-for-the-postpandemic-workforce, (Accessed 19 Jan 2022)

94. Workforce and Learning Trends 2021 | IT Workforce | CompTIA. https://connect.comptia. org/content/research//workforce-learning-trends-2021, l(Accessed 19 Jan 2022)

Information Needs of and Information Sources Used by Individuals with Social Anxiety Disorder

Leyla Dewitz[⊠] [iD]

Humboldt-Universität zu Berlin, 10099 Berlin, Germany
leyla.dewitz@hu-berlin.de

Abstract. Social Anxiety Disorder (SAD) is a globally significant mental health concern as it is one of the most prevalent psychological disorders. It is characterized by an intense fear of social situations and a persistent worry about being judged or embarrassed in public settings. Individuals with SAD tend to avoid social encounters, limiting their access to health information. This study fills a gap by addressing the information needs of and information sources used by individuals with SAD. Semi-structured online interviews and one written interview were conducted in Germany with 22 participants (15 females; 7 males) aged 18 to 65. The interviews incorporated visual participatory elements through the virtual whiteboard Miro, enabling participants to construct personalized health information infrastructures that reveal information needs and used information sources. Information needs and sources/channels were identified through inductive coding. Further, thematic analysis was applied, covering the interrelations of information needs and information sources used. Notably, intrapersonal health information needs emerged prominently in the data, highlighting the personal and introspective nature of SAD-related information. The most mentioned information sources are interpersonal channels such as psychotherapists, self-help groups, friends, and relatives. In addition, the findings indicated a preference for media channels such as social media and self-help books. Moreover, it became apparent that digital peer-to-peer support is essential for exchanging information and satisfying the need for social connections. Further, digital health apps (e.g., VR) for psychoeducation are integral information sources. This article is the first to address SAD within the context of information behavior in the LIS field.

Keywords: Health Information Behavior · Social Anxiety Disorder · Information Needs · Information Sources · Information Channels

1 Introduction

Anxiety is a crucial human emotion that serves to alert individuals to potential threats or perceptions of danger, whether of a physical or psychological nature. However, anxiety can become pathological when it leads to persistent anxious behavior in everyday situations, causing individuals to avoid specific situations out of fear [1].

I. Sserwanga et al. (Eds.): iConference 2024, LNCS 14597, pp. 62–81, 2024.
https://doi.org/10.1007/978-3-031-57860-1_5

Previous studies have shown that individuals with SAD tend to avoid social encounters, limiting their access to health information sources to fulfill potential information needs. This limitation in access to health information is a unique characteristic and could lead to an information barrier and respective unmet information needs [2]. In contrast, there is consensus in research that information is essential for recovery [3]. Contradictions arise from the fact that no studies to date have focused on the subjective perception of information needs and information sources used by SAD-affected individuals, indicating a lack of knowledge for specialized information services.

This study aims to identify the information needs, channels, and sources used by individuals with SAD. Therefore, semi-structured online interviews and one written interview were conducted with 22 participants *(N = 22)* aged 18 to 65. The research questions that guide this study are as follows:

- *RQ1:* What types of information needs do individuals affected by SAD have?
- *RQ2:* What types of information sources do individuals affected by SAD use?
- *RQ3:* What patterns exist between information needs of, and information sources used by individuals affected by SAD?

To answer the research questions, this article is structured as follows: Sect. 2 presents a literature review on Social Anxiety Disorder (SAD) and (mental) health information needs, channels, and sources. Furthermore, the research design is described in Sect. 3. Section 4 presents the study's results, starting with the clustered information needs and channels/sources, followed by the analysis of their respective interrelations. Section 5 discusses the study's findings, and conclusions are drawn in Sect. 6.

2 Literature Review

2.1 Social Anxiety Disorder (SAD)

SAD (ICD-11, 6B04) presents a public health concern, as it is one of the most prevalent psychological disorders, affecting approximately 2.7% of the German population within a 12-month period, with women disproportionately affected in comparison to men [1]. Researchers anticipate a rise in mental disorders, including SAD, due to the COVID-19 pandemic [4]. SAD commonly arises in childhood and teenage years, manifests as a pathological dimension in adulthood, and is often comorbid with other mental conditions, such as autism [5], attention deficit (hyperactivity) disorder (ADD, ADHD), and depression [6]. Individuals affected by SAD are susceptible to external stimuli, leading to avoiding situations in which they might be the center of attention [7]. They are also highly sensitive to internal stimuli related to their psychopathological fears, such as sensed emotions as well as self-beliefs, self-image, and conditional beliefs [8]. Symptoms of SAD can be physical (blushing, avoiding eye contact, sweating, heart racing, etc.) or mental (continuing dysfunctional thought) [9]. For those affected, these symptoms lead to significant impairment in personal, family, social, occupational, or other important areas of functioning [10]. SAD is typically treated with cognitive behavioral therapy approaches and sometimes psychopharmacological interventions [11].

2.2 Health Information Needs and Information Sources

Information needs include the recognition of an existing knowledge gap and emerge from stimuli [12]. Information needs are the initial stage preceding information-seeking [13]. However, a need for information does not always translate into action, such as actively seeking information through interactions like searching [14]. Health issues and threats can influence information behavior, particularly information needs [15]. Information needs may lead to acquiring information sources (e.g., interpersonal channels, e.g., friends; media channels, e.g., websites; institutional channels, e.g., self-help organizations). Information sources can thus be any entity, whether a person, a specific digital or physical artifact, or any other means to obtain or access information [16, 17].

2.3 Mental Health Information Needs and Information Sources

Providing essential information can significantly impact various aspects of an individual's well-being and mental health concerning decision-making and acceptance of illness. Therefore, providing information on social anxiety, e.g., in the form of psychoeducation, is crucial for the recovery process [3]. In general, decision-making is intertwined with selecting the right source of specific health information to better understand oneself or one's condition [18, 19]. Further, the quantity and quality of people's information about themselves can improve their well-being [20]. Conversely, unmet (information) needs could impede or exacerbate the recovery process and result in a sense of loss of control [21]. A scoping review by Mayrand and Bartlett [22] summarizes that individuals with mental health disorders have distinct and, therefore, specific illness-related information needs.

Olfson et al. [2] found that uncertainty about where to seek treatment was found to be the most frequently mentioned reason for not seeking therapy. Furthermore, SAD is seen as a distinct disorder (e.g., differs from other anxiety disorders), which has unique characteristics in that individuals with SAD tend to avoid social encounters, limiting their access to information [2].

A scoping review [23] examined 23 studies regarding the information needs of and information sources used by individuals with anxiety disorders in general. Regarding information needs, results show that general facts about anxiety (e.g., symptoms, diagnosis, etiology), treatment (e.g., treatment options, side effects of treatment options, available information on medication), lived experience (e.g., other people's experience of anxiety, medication, recovery), healthcare services, coping and self-management strategies, and financial and legal information, were most mentioned. Information sources most mentioned included health professionals, written materials (e.g., patient information leaflets), media (e.g., the internet), interpersonal sources (e.g., friends and relatives, self-help, or support groups), and organizational sources.

In an interview study [24] involving individuals with mental health issues and their information needs *(N = 36),* findings reveal that participants often independently explore their conditions but also experience a significant influence of stigma, which affects their information-seeking behavior. Furthermore, the study shows the sharing of personal experiences among individuals with mental health problems to be a source of information. Subsequently, an online survey involving 224 university students to explore their information needs and seeking behaviors when experiencing anxiety or depression symptoms [25]. The results indicated the internet as the most frequently mentioned source for mental health information. Additionally, many participants turned to friends, while fewer sought assistance from counselors/therapists, parents, or siblings [25]. A study that analyzed 901 tweets and 796 Instagram posts tagged the hashtag #anxiety [26] discovered that individuals experiencing anxiety use social media to share highly personal information about their recovery and therapy journeys as well as to seek peer-to-peer and self-help information through these platforms. Supplementing this, studies found that individuals with SAD intensively use digital technologies to avoid resorting to physical interactions [27, 28]. In addition, recent studies show that digital health applications (e.g., personal sensing, digital phenotyping), AI tools, like chatbots [29], and virtual reality applications [30] could significantly change the treatment of mental disorders, such as SAD.

In summary, individuals with mental health disorders have distinct and, therefore, specific illness-related information needs [22]. In contrast, studies focusing specifically on SAD are missing. The most relevant study on anxiety-specific (not SAD-specific) information needs and sources resides within a medical perspective and is based on an extensive scoping review [23]. Studies on information needs and information sources of specific mental disorders lack in-depth contextual integration to LIS [e.g., 23, 2]. This study aims to further investigate SAD in terms of information needs and sources, emphasizing SAD participants' perspectives through an inductive approach.

3   Research Design

3.1   Pretest, Recruitment, and Sample

The first pretest involved a psychologist assessing the interview guidelines' feasibility and psycho-ethical considerations, sensitizing the interviewer to potentially difficult study situations. The second pretest, conducted with an individual affected by SAD, aimed to gather feedback on question design, the practicality of using the virtual whiteboard Miro and its interactive-participative elements, and the perceived mental load during the interview. Both pretests highlighted the need for more explicit task and question formulations to avoid overwhelming participants. Subsequent adjustments were made to enhance interview flow and procedural cohesion.

Recruitment criteria included being affected by SAD (self-reported; no formal diagnoses required) and being of legal age (18 years or older). The study included 22 participants ($N = 22$) from Germany (15 females; 7 males), aged between 18 and 65 years (9 participants aged 18–28, 9 participants aged 29–39, and 4 participants aged 40–65). The sample exhibits gender imbalance. The overrepresentation of women aligns with current data indicating a higher prevalence of SAD among women than men [1].

3.2   Data Collection

In total, 22 semi-structured interviews were conducted between June and November 2022. Monetary incentives of 20 euros were provided to participants as compensation. All participants provided informed consent before participation. Interviews were conducted online using the video conferencing platform Zoom, except for one participant. Due to the severity of their SAD symptoms, SP09 chose to participate in a written interview containing the same questions and tasks as in the online interview. The duration of the interviews ranged from 53 to 111 min (average length: 83 min). All interviews were conducted in German, and quotes were translated into English after the analysis for publication. The virtual whiteboard Miro was used to map information interactions in the context of SAD in two interactive–participative parts of the interview. For a detailed explanation of the methodology employed, refer to Dewitz [31]. Figure 1 visualizes the procedure and objectives of the respective interview phases; data from phase II was not considered for the article and is therefore marked in gray.

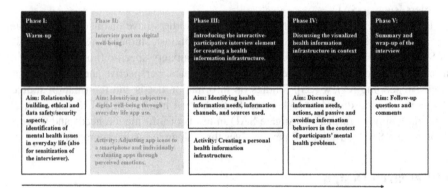

Fig. 1. Interview procedure with 5 phases and their respective aims.

To actively engage them in the interview, participants were encouraged to verbalize the information needs and sources/channels they use to answer mental health questions. This technique was inspired by the concepts of information horizons [32] and information world maps [33] and allowed for a creative and visual representation of the participants' interactions with information. A prearranged board with a few potential sources served as a starting point to stimulate participants to think about used health information sources and information needs (Fig. 2). The whiteboard was presented to the participants via screen sharing during the online interview to in situ visualize the participants' verbalizations. The researcher visualized the verbal input and moderated the Miro board to prevent pressuring participants with an unfamiliar platform and its functions.

The resulting personalized information infrastructure served as a reference point for conversation during the interviews and steered the discussion toward detailed and insightful input. Each map exhibited distinct characteristics of the participants' individual health information infrastructure, which were indicative of their explanations (Fig. 3). Throughout the research procedure, all stages were planned and executed under the guidance and supervision of trained psychologists. Continuous support for participants was ensured in case they encountered difficulties during the interview or follow-up stages.

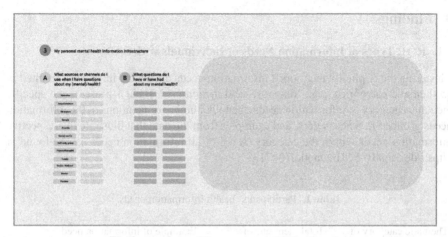

Fig. 2. Example of the pre-arranged Miro-Board.

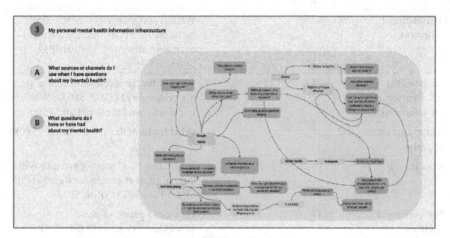

Fig. 3. Example of the personal health information infrastructure of participant SP05.

3.3 Data Analysis

After data collection, the transcribed material, including the written interview transcript of SP09, was organized, and analyzed using the qualitative data analysis software MAXQDA Plus 2022. All transcripts and the respective individual Miro-Boards were coded inductively, focusing on first in vivo and then descriptive coding techniques [34] for identifying information needs and information sources to answer RQ1 and RQ2. Afterward, information needs and information sources were transferred to an Excel spreadsheet to be clustered (Table 1, 2). To answer RQ3, information needs, used sources/channels, and their contexts were identified by applying thematic analysis [35]. During the analytical phases, inductive coding and constant comparison were employed to identify patterns in the data, resulting in the exploration and definition of themes.

4 Findings

4.1 RQ1. Types of Information Needs of Individuals with SAD

Clustering the explicitly mentioned information needs during the interviews resulted in 15 thematic categories, e.g., 'diagnosis and symptoms.' Table 1 presents the specific thematic category of information needs, the total number of mentions of the information needs grouped in this category, and examples from the data that illustrate the respective information needs within the category. A list of all information needs can be found at https://doi.org/10.5281/zenodo.10471357.

Table 1. Participants' health information needs.

Thematic category of information need	Total mentions of information needs per category	Example of information need from the data
Diagnosis and symptoms	30	What is social anxiety? (SP05, SP06, SP10, SP16, SP08); Are my anxieties normal/or abnormal? (SP10, SP12, SP03, SP04)
Intrapersonal, self-discovery, and self-awareness	25	Is it just me, or is it my disorder or just my personality? (SP08, SP18); Who am I, and why am I the way I am? (SP03)
Therapy, treatment, and recovery	21	What forms of therapy are there? (SP08)
Support	18	Where can I find support groups? What kind of support groups are there? (SP05, SP4, SP16, SP23, SP14, SP24)
Well-being and health practices	17	How can I get rid of panic attacks/anxiety attacks? (SP05, SP19)
Community	15	Are there tips/experiences from other affected people? (SP12, SP14, SP11, SP13, SP05, SP16, SP09, SP14, SP06, SP03, SP08, SP10)
Stigmatization and external perception	15	Will I be accepted, laughed at/understood? (SP12, SP18); Do other people notice that I have SAD? (SP03, SP06)
Work, education, and study	14	What would be the best strategy to deal with social anxiety at work? (SP06)
Comorbid mental disorders	12	How closely related are my depression and my social anxiety? (SP06, SP12)

(*continued*)

Table 1. (*continued*)

Thematic category of information need	Total mentions of information needs per category	Example of information need from the data
Social	9	How can people with depression or anxiety disorders date? (SP01)
(Digital) media	9	Where can I find podcasts (SP14), software (SP01), or books (SP14, SP20) on social anxiety?
Mental health concerns	7	Why is assisted suicide not permitted in Germany for mental illnesses? (SP09)
Day structuring and organization	4	How can I plan my purchases? (SP02); How can I learn to leave the house? (SP04)
Emergency	4	What can I do in case of an emergency? (SP06)
Day structuring and organization	4	How can I plan my purchases? (SP02); How can I learn to leave the house? (SP04)
Medical	3	What medications are available for my condition? (SP20)

Table 1 illustrates the prevalence of various information needs among participants. 'Diagnosis and symptoms' are the most frequently mentioned category, comprising 30 specific information needs. This is followed by 25 information needs related to 'intrapersonal, self-discovery, and self-awareness.' Additionally, 18 information needs pertain to 'support needs,' while 17 focus on 'well-being and health practices.' Furthermore, 21 information needs relate to 'therapy, treatment, and recovery.' Information needs related to the mental health 'community' covered 15 information needs; also, 15 information needs covered information needs concerning 'stigmatization and external perceptions.' Further types of information needs include (mentions in parentheses behind): work, education, and study-related information needs (14), information needs on comorbid mental disorders (12), social information needs (9), (digital) media information needs (9), information needs on mental health concerns (7), day structuring and organizational information needs (4), emergency-related (4) and medical information needs (3).

4.2 RQ2. Types of Information Channels and Sources Used by Individuals with SAD

Table 2 contains the information sources and the mentions of the source by the participants (one count per person). Furthermore, the information sources are classified as interpersonal, institutional, or media information channels.

Table 2. Participants used (health) information channels and sources.

Channel	Health information source	Total mentions of health information source (one count per person)
Interpersonal channels	Psychotherapists/psychotherapy	17
	Self-help group	15
	Friends	15
	Family	11
	Partner	6
	People in mental health online forums	6
	Acquaintances	3
	General practitioners	3
	Psychiatrists	3
	Oneself	2
	Strangers (via the Internet)	2
Media channels	Books (psychology, reference, guidebooks, and self-help books)	18
	Google	17
	Websites/Internet	16
	Social media (Facebook, Instagram, YouTube, TikTok, Twitter)	15
	Podcast	7
	Trade journals/articles or studies	4
	Wikipedia	4
	Digital Health Applications (DiGAS, only available on prescription), Chatbots	3
Institutional channels	Self-help associations	8
	Counseling centers	7
	Crisis services	2
	Libraries	2

Information sources grouped as interpersonal and media channels are most mentioned; institutional channels are relatively lagging. Regarding interpersonal channels, 17 participants mentioned psychotherapists, which makes them the most frequently used information source. Further interpersonal channels cover (mentions in parentheses): self-help groups (15), friends (15), the family (11), partners (6), online forums (6), acquaintances (3), general practitioners (3), psychiatrists (3), oneself (2) and strangers, i.e., via the internet (2). Media channels mentioned cover psychology-, reference-, guide- and self-help books (18), specific websites/the internet (16), Google (17), social media (15), podcasts (7), trade journals/articles or studies (4), Wikipedia (4), and digital health apps/chatbots (3). Institutional channels mentioned cover self-help associations (8), counseling centers (7), crisis services (2), and libraries (2).

4.3 RQ3. Patterns Between Information Needs and Information Sources Used by Individuals with SAD

Through thematic analysis, seven key themes emerged that contextualize information needs and information sources. These themes are explored below.

Finding Orientation in the SAD is Accompanied by Information Needs
All participants mentioned information needs regarding SAD, except SP13, who stated that they perceived the search for information as distressing and, therefore, avoided even thinking about information needs in connection with their condition. In contrast, all other participants *(n = 21)* reported a high need for information. SP04 stated that internet research helped to become familiar with their condition, marking their initial exposure to relevant information:

> "So just at the very beginning, when I didn't know all this stuff about social phobia and stuff like that, I researched on the internet what could be going on with me, and that's where I got the first information." (SP04).

Participants mentioned *(n = 15)* that their information needs varied according to the progression and stage of their condition. Further, nine participants reported that before becoming aware of being affected by SAD, they wanted to gain basic information on specific diagnoses of diverse mental disorders that could be related to the symptoms they felt. For example, SP05 needed information on whether extreme shyness and SP12 on whether fear of people was a clinical sign to determine if there was an illness related to the emotions they were experiencing. SP08 researched self-tests on the internet to figure out what condition they could have or whether a pathology existed that covered these symptoms. Furthermore, four participants mentioned that they needed to know whether their disorder was "normal" or "abnormal," aiming to gauge the extent to which the fears they experienced in social situations were common. In addition, participants mentioned feeling unsure about their diagnosis, mainly because of the comorbidity of their mental illness, leading to information needs that questioned the diagnosis, e.g., "Am I just introverted, or do I really have social anxiety?" (SP18), or "Is it just my personality that developed that way?" (SP08). In addition, participants expressed uncertainty about the correlations and differences between the diagnoses and their condition due to comorbidities with other illnesses, thus showing information needs regarding SAD and depression (SP06, SP12), SAD and autism (SP12), and SAD and ADHD/ADD (SP14). Due to the susceptibility to mental illnesses and multi-diagnoses received, information needs occurred at all stages of becoming aware, living, handling, and treating the participants' mental conditions.

For example, before and during the stage of becoming aware of being affected, participants expressed the need to learn more about the chances for healing and treatment (SP05, SP13), the duration of recovery (SP06, SP18), and specific treatment methods (SP08, SP16, SP19), e.g., depth psychology–based psychotherapy or cognitive behavioral therapy. Further, information covering support information needs came into focus, e.g., "where/how can I find a psychotherapist?" (SP16, SP24, SP08) or "where can I find support groups, and which support groups are there?" (SP05, SP4, SP16, SP23, SP14, SP24). However, the need for information for orientation with SAD remains consistent during the phase before and after the (potential) diagnosis. Awareness of a disease or cause of suffering goes hand in hand with setting the infrastructure for a possible facilitation or illness acceptance and recovery process (SP12, SP10).

Information is Crucial for Navigating Through the SAD Mental Health Journey and for the SAD Recovery Process
SP12 reported that many information needs were no longer present at the advanced stage of their illness because the most prominent information needs had already been resolved after diagnosis. In contrast, SP10 mentioned phases of self-acceptance related to their SAD condition, which were related to their evolving need for information over time:

> "The phases where I had panic attacks last year. I completely shut down. Because I was still in this phase of self-acceptance. Now I'm absolutely in the phase where I say: Hey, I want as much information as possible. That's why I try to gather as much information as possible so that I can then pull my own package out of it." (SP10).

Furthermore, SP08, SP04, and SP03 emphasized the importance of information for self-reflection, a vital aspect of the recovery process. Additionally, SP10 underscored the need for information as an empowering tool to combat passivity in dealing with one's illness:

> "Only when I do something for myself, then it can make a difference. You have to inform yourself sometimes. Of course, going to a psychotherapist when you get a place is always great. But if something like that doesn't happen for another six months, then you can't just go on for six months as you are now. And then you have to inform yourself on your own." (SP10).

Social anxiety can also lead to emergency and crisis information needs that occur in any stage of illness (before and during recovery). For all participants, dealing with SAD is the only option due to its chronic nature. SP06, SP09, and SP24 mentioned emergency information needs, such as what to do in a crisis situation or what support is available when one is in distress due to SAD. Perhaps partly due to the written form of the interview, SP09 was the only participant to express information needs in the context of suicide and assisted suicide. However, the need for information on SAD remains consistent during the participants' mental health journey.

Intrapersonal Information Needs and Oneself as an Information Source
Participants addressed information needs of an intrapersonal nature, i.e., questions they asked themselves and wanted to process internally and clarify through therapy. SP01 highlighted that their information needs regarding mental health issues were notably distinct from their other information needs and, therefore, only addressable in therapy:

> "Sure, I always google. But that helps relatively little, especially with psycho issues, because these are often very personal topics that have very personal causes and

therefore need very, very personal [...] solutions or courses of action. That's why it's often not so helpful [to search Google for information needs]. So sure, you can. You might find something where you can get help or something, but you don't find solutions on websites, in my opinion, but in therapy." (SP01).

Ten participants expressed primarily self-directed information needs, covering intrapersonal needs, e.g., questions for self-discovery or self-awareness. However, some of these information needs remain unresolved or unsolvable. For example, SP05 described the most crucial internal need: *"So actually, the question that I'm most concerned with is 'will it go away?' but there can be no answer to that".*

These types of information needs highlight the introspective nature of SAD and the fact that many information needs are highly individual and must be worked out individually, primarily through self-reflection or in collaboration with a psychotherapist. Related to this, SP18 and SP19 mentioned themselves as the most critical information source:

"Before, I was so in my head. Just reading, reading, reading. Gathering information. Reading books. And nowadays, I notice that I am my biggest information source; it is within me, and when I tap into that source, I connect with myself." (SP19).

In addition, 15 participants stated that they repetitively need information about how they are perceived from the outside. As confirmed by SP08, SP03, and SP06, SAD symptoms entail both fearing external judgment and requiring external validation to evaluate one's self-image. According to SP08, receiving feedback on how others perceive themselves helps with self-reflection because individuals with SAD often misjudge themselves. Explicit questions about their persona are, for example: "Am I behaving oddly?" (SP03) or "Am I okay the way I am?" (SP04).

Furthermore, information needs relating to external perception can also be associated with stigma that seems to be internalized, e.g., the need to find out whether others laugh at them or accept them concerning their illness (SP18, SP12), whether others notice their condition (SP03, SP06), or whether it is appropriate or inappropriate to disclose or reveal the mental illness to others (SP03). Besides oneself as an information source, participants primarily mentioned interpersonal sources such as close friends, specific family members, and partners as necessary in satisfying information needs related to external perception.

Experiences from Other SAD-Affected Individuals as a Constructive and Destructive Information Source

In the context of well-being and health practices, information needs on practical guidance occur, e.g., how to manage panic or anxiety attacks (SP05, SP19). These information needs are mainly discussed via self-help groups *(n = 15)*. Building on the importance of the community, for most participants *(n = 15)*, self-help groups are their primary information source. SP05 and SP07 maintain contact in group chats via communication apps with fellow SAD-affected individuals they know from self-help groups, exchanging information about experiences and the status quo of their mental health.

Fifteen participants mentioned experience reports as a crucial source for information on how other individuals deal with SAD. In addition, experience reports were mentioned by twelve participants as information need, e.g., how to find them and which sources to use best. Experience reports represent the most prevalent pattern among all information needs and information sources mentioned in this study. Participants state that learning how others cope with or manage SAD helps them understand their problems better. Identifying overlaps in symptoms between their condition and those affected helps them accept themselves and their illness.

Regarding how others deal with SAD, information needs were directed towards various digital or non-digital media channels. Information sources containing experience reports are found in self-help guides, leaflets and books (SP04, SP14, SP16, SP19, SP24, SP07), YouTube videos (SP14, SP20), Twitter/X (SP01, SP04), Instagram (SP03, SP05, SP19, SP22, SP12), TikTok (SP04, SP16), Facebook (SP09), and podcasts (SP14, SP09, SP16, SP20, SP22, SP06, SP07).

Other affected, even if they are strangers, are crucial information sources to contact when information is needed. The community is perceived as a genuine information source, as the experiences of others affected seem to help the most. SP01 found a psychotherapist via recommendations through the Twitter/X community:

"Information on Twitter. Looking for a therapy place kept me very, very busy. I wrote a lot about it on Twitter, expressed myself a lot, and then people sent me things, and I also sent things to people who basically had similar problems finding something." (SP01).

Six participants mentioned mental health online forums as a source for seeking, receiving, and exchanging information with other people suffering from SAD or comorbid conditions. SP08 uses an online forum as an information source for obtaining recommendations for psychotherapists and psychotherapy methods. However, SP04, while using online forums, mentions that reading about others and their problems sometimes has the opposite effect, lowering their mood instead of providing stability. Additionally, SP20 stated that using forums makes them feel like they are helping others more than finding answers to their own questions. SP20 framed online forums as potentially destructive because those affected tend to reinforce each other's suffering. The SAD community and their experiences seem to be significant information sources; besides constructive community feedback, they also bear potential dangers. Overall, online forums can have positive and negative outcomes for consumers and producers of SAD-related health information.

Social Belonging and Trust-Based Personal Rapport are Essential for Expressing Information Needs and Turning to Information Sources

Most participants mention personal connection or rapport with the information source as essential to address information needs *(n = 15)*. They perceive mental health information differently in nature to other information, as it is highly personal and sometimes needs to be kept secret because of the stigma attached to it (SP9, SP12, SP16). Requesting information sources in a psychologically vulnerable situation requires trust in the information source *(n = 15)*. SP10 highlights trust as a basis for revealing oneself to others in the support group and asking for information. In the context of psychotherapists, trust in the source is also seen as fundamental to being able to confide in them:

"Psychotherapist, simply because I know, from this person, I would get a scientifically sound answer that I can also trust." (SP10).

Most participants consider close personal contacts one of the most critical interpersonal information sources, with friends being mentioned 15 times, family members eleven times, and partners six times. It is noticeable that some individuals highlighted specific friends and family members. For example, SP12 mentioned their best friend, SP09 stated close friends, and SP03 reported longtime friends. Additionally, S07 and SP14 mention friends who have similar psychological issues; SP14 mentioned their grandfather, who has similar mental health problems; SP04 and SP07 their children; SP12 and SP16 mentioned their sisters (SP12, SP16); and SP20 mentioned their mother.

Furthermore, information needs concerning social questions highlight the importance of social belonging for the participants and are also described as unsolvable due to social anxiety symptoms. For example, SP20 expresses an information need regarding how they could find friends. SP01 expresses the information need on how people with SAD could go about dating.

Participants feel a high need for social belonging precisely because they are partially socially excluded. Due to anxieties and stigmatization (internalized and external), trust-based personal rapport is essential for expressing information needs and turning to information sources.

The (Unmet) Information Need for Individualized Sources for SAD Life Management

Information needs related to work, education, and study occurred prominent in the data *(n = 14)*. For example, individuals needed information about appropriate workplace behavior concerning SAD, e.g., whether they should disclose their illness and what consequences this could have (SP06, SP03, SP19, SP12). Many participants mentioned a need for practical guidance on strategically navigating their work in connection with their condition or finding a feasible job with SAD, e.g., working from home (SP12, SP19, SP06). SP01, SP10, SP12, and SP19 see practical guidance on life management, especially about vital issues such as work, out-of-home appointments (e.g., shopping, doctor's appointments), finances, and partnership, as partly not covered by conventional SAD information sources (e.g., websites, leaflets, and books about SAD). Participants mentioned self-help associations, counseling centers, and self-help groups as the primary sources to address these information needs. Moreover, one self-help association provides digital and non-digital guidebooks for various practical life tasks, which four participants were aware of but only one participant actively used.

Social Media and Digital Media are Crucial SAD Information Sources for Information Needs Regarding Self-help, Self-reflection, and Psychoeducation

In total, 15 participants reported using social media as an information source. SP03, SP04, SP19, and SP22 mention using these platforms for self-reflection. SP22 and SP04 are using Instagram, particularly in the context of specific information related to SAD, self-reflection, and self-help:

"I use it to follow people, for example, who have social anxiety [...], to see that I'm not alone with the problem. I think it helps me. I also follow psychologists;

they always give helpful tips. [...] to get encouragement, again and again, you can work on social anxieties." (SP22).

"Strangers on Twitter and TikTok, which also talk about such topics. This is where I learned a lot about myself, too. Other affected people who talk about themselves, and I can understand myself better through that." (SP04).

SP05 specifically used hashtags such as #socialanxiety or #anxiety to access information for self-help through the community. SP01 also mentioned using mental health share pics on Instagram, as they provide information on recommended health practices and mental health facts. Furthermore, SP01 emphasizes their strong connection with the mental health community on Twitter as central to information access:

"One of these tips was very good and helped me a lot – an online appointment service for a psychological emergency. I got this tip via Twitter and also passed it on via Twitter." (SP01).

Further, SP04 and SP22 use the prescription-based digital health application Invirto. The virtual reality (VR) application provides psychoeducation by offering basic SAD information and exposure therapy content. Both participants described the VR app as a helpful information source. In addition, SP04 uses two chatbots for self-reflection:

"I have two chatbot apps; one is called Woebot, and the other is Wysa. These are AIs that do check-ins to see how you're doing. And if you say that you're not doing so well, they have specific processes for asking questions to deconstruct destructive thought patterns." (SP04).

5   Discussion

5.1   Types of Information Needs

First, an inductive approach was applied to identify information needs accompanying SAD. The analysis of information needs resulted in 15 thematic categories (Table 1).

The vast majority of categories could be confirmed by comparing them with results from [23]. For example, 'diagnosis and symptoms' are the most mentioned types of information needs in this study, indicating high overlap with the category of "general facts about anxiety (e.g., symptoms, diagnosis, etiology)" outlined by [23]. The same applies to the categories 'therapy, treatment, and recovery' and 'medical' information needs found in this study, which are comparable with information needs covering the category "treatment (e.g., treatment options, side effects of treatment options, available information on medication)" found in [23]. Moreover, the categories mentioned in [23], such as "lived experience (e.g., other people's experience of anxiety, medication, recovery)", "healthcare services", "coping and self-management strategies", and "financial and legal information", show similarities in information needs regarding 'support,' 'community,' 'well-being and health practices,' 'work, education, and study,' and 'day structuring and organization' found in this study.

Although some types of information needs mentioned in both studies overlap, the inductive analysis in this study also indicates unique insights into information needs regarding SAD. First, the second most mentioned information needs, containing questions of 'intrapersonal, self-discovery, and self-awareness' nature, could not be found in any other study. Information needs respective these thematic groups show the introspective nature of information needs for dealing with oneself and circulating thoughts probably caused by the SAD disorder. This thematic category of information needs seems highly relevant for SAD information behavior, which is also confirmed by the relatively high amount of information needs that could be assigned to this thematic category (25 needs allocated to this thematic category). In addition, the information needs, summarized in the thematic category 'stigmatization and external perception,' show examples of internalized stigmatization and the need for feedback about the self by the outside world. Stigma is thought to influence information-seeking behavior [24]. This study can add that internalized stigma also seems to impact information needs.

This study identified specific information needs arising from the comorbidity of SAD with other co-occurring mental conditions. While the reciprocal connections between SAD and other mental conditions have been confirmed in psychological literature [5, 6], the need for information concerning the comorbidity of SAD has not been addressed in previous studies. In addition, the categories 'emergencies' and 'mental health concerns' are not covered by comparable studies but show the vital need for information to avert severe and life-threatening situations. Further, information needs covering '(digital) media' (e.g., software, podcasts) seem to show a high need for specialized digital information services, which is also not mentioned in other studies concerning information needs.

5.2 Types of Information Sources

The inductive analysis revealed a wide array of information sources employed by individuals, as presented in Table 2, including interpersonal (11), media (8), and institutional channels (4). The distribution of information sources mentioned in this study indicates that interpersonal and media information sources appear to be the most mentioned for SAD mental health information.

This study's most mentioned information channels are interpersonal, which contain information sources like self-help groups, friends, family, partners, people in mental health online forums, acquaintances, general practitioners, and psychiatrists. The primary information source mentioned is psychotherapists. This is confirmed by the results of previous studies, which mention health professionals as the most relevant information source besides relatives, self-help, support groups [23], or friends [23, 25]. Besides this, two salient information sources mentioned in this study are 'oneself' and 'strangers (via the internet),' which could not be found by any other study. In line with previous research [see 27, 28], participants show an affinity for digital information sources, explicitly mentioning strangers being contacted via the internet. This indicates that it may be easier for SAD-affected to socially connect with interpersonal information sources digitally to exchange information.

Further, all studies highlighted the internet [25] and social media [23, 26] as necessary for mental health and SAD-related information sources. This study found evidence that besides interpersonal channels, media channels play a pivotal role in SAD-related information behavior as participants turn to the internet (e.g., Google, Wikipedia, specific websites) and nearly all social media platforms, digital health applications, podcasts, and books. In sum, this study complements previous studies [23–26] by showing evidence that both interpersonal and media information sources are most relevant for SAD-related mental health information. The unique finding of this study is the importance of digital media channels (e.g., social media and digital health applications) for individuals with SAD.

5.3   Information Needs and Information Sources

Through thematic analysis, seven themes emerged that enabled the joint analysis of information needs and sources used by individuals with SAD.

Finding orientation with a mental illness like SAD, as well as navigating through the SAD mental health journey, is accompanied by information needs. This study found that identifying and finding information sources is an initial and salient exposure to becoming familiar with SAD. In sum, information plays a crucial role in SAD recovery, which adds to previous mental health research [3, 21].

Further, the study showed that intrapersonal information is somehow connected to SAD but has not yet been studied in LIS research. However, better self-understanding regarding the quantity and quality of information people have about themselves can improve overall well-being [3, 20]. Additionally, participants identify themselves as information source through the wealth of experience they gained in dealing with themselves and illness. To date, no other study mentions the introspective nature of information, which could be framed as one protruding aspect regarding SAD-specific information behavior. Related to this, participants address information needs to themselves. These internal information needs often remain unmet, causing the participants to suffer. Thus, internal information needs could be framed as informational problems that mainly cannot be adequately solved. Unmet information needs could impede or exacerbate the recovery process and can result in a sense of loss of control [21]. These internal information needs may arise due to internal stimuli related to the psychopathological condition, such as insecure self-beliefs, self-image, and conditional beliefs [8].

According to the study, social belonging and trust-based personal rapport are essential for expressing information needs and turning to information sources. As also evident in previous studies, people tend to use interpersonal sources to address information needs [23, 25]. In addition to the findings of earlier studies, close people who make SAD-affected individuals feel understood and empathized are the most frequently addressed sources of information. Thus, social belonging and trust-based personal rapport are pivotal in choosing interpersonal information sources for SAD-related information needs.

Information needs for life management with SAD, such as structuring and planning life to navigate the challenges posed by the severity of symptoms, align with findings from [23]. In addition, this study identified the prominent need for information sources for SAD life management as these often remain unmet.

The findings of this study show that experiences from other SAD-affected individuals are one of the most crucial information sources, albeit this kind of information is also described as sometimes destructive to participants' well-being. Findings from this study show that participants consider the community the best source of information as they turn to social media and online forums to ask for advice. Thus, experience reports from other affected individuals seem to be the most essential information source, retrieved from digital and non-digital media. There appears to be an intrinsic need for information on how other affected people handle their condition [23–26].

As previous research identified [26], social media is pivotal for the mental health community. To accomplish this, digital media is crucial for accessing SAD information regarding self-help, self-reflection, and psychoeducation. Previous studies confirm that SAD-affected tend to use digital sources, as physical sources are difficult to reach [27, 28]. Participants in the sample use digital health apps (VR tools) and chatbots that encourage self-reflection—aligning with contemporary trends in SAD treatment [29, 30]. None of the studies that examined information needs and sources included digital services like digital health apps or chatbots as information sources used by affected individuals [e.g., 23].

6 Conclusion

This study employed 22 semi-structured interviews with an interactive-participative visual mapping approach. To address the research question, the types of information sources indicate a preference for interpersonal (e.g., psychotherapists) and media channels (e.g., social media). Findings show that SAD-affected individuals have SAD-specific information needs during the recovery from or the acceptance of the (chronic) illness. Notably, intrapersonal health information needs emerge prominently in the data, highlighting the personal and introspective nature of SAD-related information behavior. Moreover, it became apparent that digital and non-digital peer-to-peer support is essential, satisfying the need for social connections and exchanging information, regardless of the evidence-based nature of the information.

The study does not claim completeness as it does not include individuals affected in the early stages of SAD. This is because this group requires special protection. It must be considered that the information landscape of SAD-affected people may differ between stages of illnesses and experiences.

However, the findings offer a comprehensive overview for enhancing tailored information services for those affected by SAD. The target group needs community-inclusive and, at the same time, evidence-based information while incorporating digital information services to reach the target group. Technology-based information services, such as health and well-being apps, virtual reality, chatbots, and digital information in general, play an essential role in providing access to vital information for people suffering from SAD. Technology-based information services must consider users' digital well-being, particularly in the realm of health. Consequently, future research will examine the digital well-being of individuals with SAD in relation to used digital information sources.

References

1. Jacobi, F., et al.: Psychische Störungen in der Allgemeinbevölkerung: Studie zur Gesundheit Erwachsener in Deutschland und ihr Zusatzmodul Psychische Gesundheit (DEGS1-MH). Nervenarzt **85**(1), 77–87 (2014). https://doi.org/10.1007/s00115-013-3961-y

2. Olfson, M., Guardino, M., Struening, E., Schneier, F.R., Hellman, F., Klein, D.F.: Barriers to treating Social Anxiety. Am. J. Psychiatry **157**(4), 521–527 (2000). https://doi.org/10.1176/appi.ajp.157.4.521

3. Nordmo, M., Sinding, A.I., Carlbring, P., Andersson, G., Havik, O.E., Nordgreen, T.: Internet-delivered cognitive behavioural therapy with and without an initial face-to-face psychoeducation session for social anxiety disorder: a pilot randomized controlled trial. Internet Interv. **2**(4), 429–436 (2015). https://doi.org/10.1016/j.invent.2015.10.003

4. Winkler, P., et al.: Prevalence of current mental disorders before and during the second wave of COVID-19 pandemic: an analysis of repeated nationwide cross-sectional surveys. J. Psychiatr. Res. **139**, 167–171 (2021). https://doi.org/10.1016/j.jpsychires.2021.05.032

5. Spain, D., Sin, J., Linder, K.B., McMahon, J., Happé, F.: Social anxiety in autism spectrum disorder: a systematic review. Research in Autism Spectrum Disorders **52**, 51–68 (2018). https://doi.org/10.1016/j.rasd.2018.04.007

6. Koyuncu, A., İnce, E., Ertekin, E., Tükel, R.: Comorbidity in social anxiety disorder: diagnostic and therapeutic challenges. Drugs in Context **8**, 1–13 (2019). https://doi.org/10.7573/dic.212573

7. Renneberg, B., Ströhle, A.: Soziale Angststörungen. Nervenarzt **77**(9), 1123–1132 (2006). https://doi.org/10.1007/s00115-006-2087-x

8. Peschard, V., Philippot, P.: Social anxiety, and information processing biases: an integrated theoretical perspective. Cogn. Emot. **30**(4), 762–777 (2016). https://doi.org/10.1080/02699931.2015.1028335

9. Schmitz, J., Hoyer, J. Soziale Angststörung. In: Schnell, T., Schnell, K. (Hrsg.), Handbuch Klinische Psychologie, pp. 1–21. Springer, Berlin (2019). https://doi.org/10.1007/978-3-662-45995-9_4-1

10. World Health Organization. ICD-11: International classification of diseases (11th revision) (2022)

11. Gould, R.A., Buckminster, S., Pollack, M.H., Otto, M.W., Yap, L.: Cognitive-behavioral and pharmacological treatment for social phobia: a meta-analysis. Clin. Psychol. Sci. Pract. **4**(4), 291–306 (1997). https://doi.org/10.1111/j.1468-2850.1997.tb00123.x

12. Belkin, N.J.: Anomalous states of knowledge as a basis for information retrieval. Canadian J. Inform. Sci. **5**, 133–143 (1980)

13. Dervin, B.: An overview of sense-making research: concepts, methods, and results. Paper Presentation at the International Communication Association Annual Meeting, Dallas, Texas, USA (1983)

14. Schlebbe, K., Greifeneder, E.: Information Need, Informationsbedarf und -bedürfnis. In: Kuhlen, R., Lewandowski, D., Semar, W., Womser-Hacker, C. (eds.) Grundlagen der Informationswissenschaft, pp. 543–552. De Gruyter, Berlin (2022). https://doi.org/10.1515/9783110769043-047

15. Lambert, S.D., Loiselle, C.G.: Health information seeking behavior. Qual. Health Res. **17**(8), 1006–1019 (2007). https://doi.org/10.1177/1049732307305199

16. Johnson, J.D., Case, D.O.: Health information seeking. Peter Lang, Frankfurt (2012)

17. Zhang, Y.: Beyond quality and accessibility: source selection in consumer health information searching: beyond quality and accessibility: source selections in consumer health information searching. J. Am. Soc. Inf. Sci. **65**(5), 911–927 (2014). https://doi.org/10.1002/asi.23023

18. Laugharne, R., Priebe, S.: Trust, choice, and power in mental health: a literature review. Soc. Psychiatry Psychiatr. Epidemiol. **41**(11), 843–852 (2006). https://doi.org/10.1007/s00127-006-0123-6

19. Dewitz, L.: Positioning digital well-being in health information behaviour. In: Proceedings of ISIC: The Information Behaviour Conference, Berlin, Germany, 26–29 September 2022. Information Research, vol. 27 (2022). https://doi.org/10.47989/irisic2224

20. Carlson, E.N.: Overcoming the barriers to self-knowledge: mindfulness as a path to seeing yourself as you really are. Perspect. Psychol. Sci. **8**(2), 173–186 (2013). https://doi.org/10.1177/1745691612462584

21. Stevenson, W., et al.: A multi-center randomized controlled trial to reduce unmet needs, depression, and anxiety among hematological cancer patients and their support persons. J. Psychosoc. Oncol. **38**(3), 272–292 (2020). https://doi.org/10.1080/07347332.2019.1692991

22. Mayrand, J., Bartlett, J.C.: Mental health in library and information science research: preliminary results of a literature review focusing on information behavior: proceedings of the american society for. Inf. Sci. Technol. **50**(1), 1–4 (2013). https://doi.org/10.1002/meet.14505001149

23. Chan, F.H.F., Lin, X., Griva, K., Subramaniam, M., Ćelić, I., Tudor Car, L.: Information needs and sources of information among people with depression and anxiety: a scoping review. BMC Psychiatry **22**(1), 1–18 (2022). https://doi.org/10.1186/s12888-022-04146-0

24. Powell, J., Clarke, A.: Information in mental health: qualitative study of mental health service users. Health Expect. **9**(4), 359–365 (2006). https://doi.org/10.1111/j.1369-7625.2006.00403.x

25. Oh, C.Y., Kornfield, R., Lattie, E.G., Mohr, D.C., Reddy, M.: University students' information behavior when experiencing mental health symptoms. Proc. Associat. Inform. Sci. Technol. **57**(1), 1–4 (2020). https://doi.org/10.1002/pra2.417

26. Dewitz, L., Ackermann, J.: Anxiety-Related Content on Instagram, and Twitter: A Mixed Methods Analysis of Mental Health Communication and Information Sharing, pp. 1–18. University of Applied Sciences Potsdam, Germany (2023). https://doi.org/10.34678/OPUS4-3220

27. Lee, B.W., Stapinski, L.A.: (2012) Seeking safety on the internet: relationship between social anxiety and problematic internet use. J. Anxiety Disorders **26**(1), 197–205 (2022). https://doi.org/10.1016/j.janxdis.2011.11.001

28. Prizant-Passal, S., Shechner, T., Aderka, I.M.: Social anxiety and internet use – a meta-analysis: what do we know? what are we missing? Comput. Hum. Behav. **62**, 221–229 (2016). https://doi.org/10.1016/j.chb.2016.04.003

29. D'Alfonso, S.: AI in mental health. Curr. Opin. Psychol. **36**, 112–117 (2020). https://doi.org/10.1016/j.copsyc.2020.04.005

30. Caponnetto, P., Triscari, S., Maglia, M., Quattropani, M.C.: The simulation game—virtual reality therapy for the treatment of social anxiety disorder: a systematic review. Int. J. Environ. Res. Public Health **18**(24), 13209 (2021). https://doi.org/10.3390/ijerph182413209

31. Dewitz, L.: Engaging Participants in Online Interviews: Lessons Learned from Implementing a Participatory Visual Approach in Two Explorative Health Information Behavior Studies. In: Proceedings of the 86th Annual Meeting of the Association for Information Science & Technology, London, 27–31 Oct 2023, pp. 98–110 (2023). https://doi.org/10.1002/pra2.772

32. Sonnenwald, D.H., Wildemuth, B.M.: Investigating information seeking behavior using the concept of information horizons. University of North Carolina, Chapel Hill, NC (2001). https://sils.unc.edu/sites/default/files/general/research/TR-2001-01.pdf, (Accessed 17 Sep 2023)

33. Greyson, D.: Information world mapping: a participatory, visual, elicitation activity for information practice interviews. Proc. Am. Soc. Inform. Sci. Technol. **50**(1), 1–4 (2013). https://doi.org/10.1002/meet.14505001104

34. Saldaña, J.: The Coding Manual for Qualitative Researchers. SAGE, Thousand Oaks (2013)

35. Braun, V., & Clarke, V. Thematic analysis: A practical guide. SAGE, Thousand Oaks (2021)

Exploring Virtual Reality Through Ihde's Instrumental Realism

He Zhang$^{(\boxtimes)}$ ⓘ and John M. Carroll ⓘ

Pennsylvania State University, University Park, State College, PA 16802, USA
{hpz5211,jmc56}@psu.edu

Abstract. Based on Ihde's theory, this paper explores the relationship between virtual reality (VR) as an instrument and phenomenology. It reviews the "technological revolution" spurred by the development of VR technology and discusses how VR has been used to study subjective experience, explore perception and embodiment, enhance empathy and perspective, and investigate altered states of consciousness. The paper emphasizes the role of VR as an instrumental technology, particularly its ability to expand human perception and cognition. Reflecting on this in conjunction with the work of Husserl and Ihde, among others, it revisits the potential of VR to provide new avenues for scientific inquiry and experience and to transform our understanding of the world through VR.

Keywords: Realism · Philosophy · Phenomenology · Instruments · Virtual Reality

1 Introduction

Virtual Reality (VR) was invented by Ivan Edward Sutherland in 1965 [54], and the technology is considered a window into the virtual world. This technology allows users to immerse themselves in a (virtual) world through a head-mounted display (HMD). VR has evolved from a lab product to a consumer-grade market over the decades and has become a widely popular technology. The high presence (immersion or realism) and ability to break the boundaries of reality that VR environments possess have received widespread popularity. In the industrial world, many companies have been involved in the development of VR devices and applications, the most representative ones being Meta (Oculus), HTC, Sony, Pico, etc. According to Market Research Report 2022 [28], the global VR market is expected to grow from $16.67 billion in 2022 to around $227.34 billion in 2029. VR applications show extraordinary promise in various fields [31], including but not limited to entertainment [4], education [49], healthcare [17], and creativity [64].

In this article, we will focus on the content and theory of Ihde's book *"Instrumental realism: The interface between philosophy of science and philosophy of technology"* [25] to explore how VR as an instrument extends the boundaries of science. By examining the content and theory of Ihde's work, this paper aims

I. Sserwanga et al. (Eds.): iConference 2024, LNCS 14597, pp. 82–93, 2024.
https://doi.org/10.1007/978-3-031-57860-1_6

to shed light on the implications of VR for human-computer interaction (HCI), phenomenology, and scientific instruments. Specifically, we will discuss Ihde's instrumental realism and its implications for VR technology. Firstly, we will discuss the role of VR as a technologically revolutionary scientific instrument and introduce the paradigm shift triggered by VR in different fields. Then, we will introduce VR in relation to the phenomenology of perception and further discuss the paradigm shift in the context of interactive that VR technology provokes. Finally, we will discuss how to understand and how to use VR for friendly interaction.

2   Technological Revolution

Advances in VR technology have transformed the way we interact with and understand the world around us. With VR devices, people can create a new space or world with their thought. Similar to how other breakthrough technologies, such as telescopes and microscopes, have changed our perception of reality, VR has helped define the boundaries of our experience through its immersive, createable capabilities that complement our understanding of the world or self-created world.

Specifically, VR technology can open up new possibilities for scientific inquiry and experimentation by immersing users in virtual environments to experience or experience rich content that breaks the limits of the real world [35].

Ihde [25] discusses Kuhn and Foucault's views on paradigm shifts and scientific revolutions. For Kuhn, a new paradigm represents a rare phenomenon, which he terms a "revolution". In contrast, Foucault perceives this as an ongoing process, suggesting that paradigms are in a state of continuous evolution. We refer to the paradigm shift associated with VR as a technological revolution rather than a mere paradigm shift for two reasons. First, even though the concept of VR has been around for decades, it has been "constructed" in juxtaposition to the natural sciences; it doesn't simply exist in nature waiting to be observed. Second, VR extends the realm of human behavior. In essence, individuals utilize VR to engage in activities previously unimaginable. VR has already had a major impact on many aspects of real life and has truly changed the paradigm [21]. Here are a few examples.

Enhanced Communication: VR allows us to connect with others more immersive and engagingly. It breaks down geographic barriers and allows people to interact with each other in shared virtual spaces, fostering collaboration and social connection. Communication through VR allows attendees to be in the same (virtual) space [48] beyond the original concept of smartphones and instant messaging [27]. VR technology has changed the paradigm of online communication. Before the advent of VR, our online communication was limited to text-based messages, phone calls, and video chats. While these tools have helped us stay connected, they still lack the immersive and engaging experience like VR. Through VR, we can see and hear others as if they were in the same space and even manipulate virtual objects collaboratively. This level of immersion and interactivity has transformed how we collaborate, learn, and socialize online. It has significant implications for personal relationships and professional teamwork, as VR enables us to communicate and collaborate more naturally, fostering social connections and significantly strengthening players' social closeness in particular [58].

Immersive Education and Training: VR is changing the way people learn and develop skills by providing highly interactive and immersive learning experiences. In a virtual environment, learners can better understand the subject matter by interacting "closer up" with the content [23,59]. At the same time, through VR, learners can continuously practice skills to improve performance in a "real", safe, and controlled environment. This approach avoids potential injury to learners during real-world training while effectively reducing costs. Compared to traditional teaching methods, which rely on textbooks, lectures, and memorization in a tedious and unattractive format, VR technology offers a more engaging, interactive, and lower-cost learning method [1,18,36].

Entertainment and Gaming: The entertainment industry is significantly impacted by VR technology today. On the one hand, the way of participating in games has been changed because of VR [53]. In the virtual environment, the gaming experience is not even lower than in the real world [43]. Instead, because of more flexible controls and a higher degree of freedom in VR, most users' gaming experience has been improved [67]. Taking traditional video games as an example, it usually requires players to stay in front of a monitor with a controller or keyboard [65,69]. VR does not have any limitations like that way. VR is not only able to let users get into a "real" virtual world but also gives a more immersive and interactive experience. As well as, with the development of VR, it has become possible to drop the controller away in the virtual environment completely [39,60,68]. On the other hand, with the development and lower cost of VR technology, it has become less expensive to immerse in a game environment for an impressive experience. For example, VR can replace the costly and complex maintenance of escape rooms or flight simulator cockpits. VR has greatly improved the accessibility of content for the general user.

It is fair to say that VR has greatly improved the accessibility of content for the general user and expanded creative expression and entertainment possibilities, providing users with a more engaging and immersive experience.

Professional Industries: VR technology has changed the paradigm of how professionals work in multiple industries. For examples, architects and engineers can use VR to visualize and manipulate their designs in three-dimensional space, enabling better decision-making and problem-solving [2,46]. Medical professionals can utilize VR for surgical simulations and therapy [14,29], while businesses can leverage VR for marketing, product demonstrations, and employee training [6].

3 VR as an Instrument in Phenomenology, Perception, and Practice

In Ihde's book "Instrumental Realism", he emphasizes the vital relationship between science and technology, specifically focusing on the role of instruments in scientific practice [25]. Ihde's instrumental realism posits that instruments are not merely passive tools but actively shape and extend human perception and understanding of the world. They are deeply embedded in knowledge production and serve as mediators between humans and their environment. Ihde applied Latour's approach and the concept of "technoscience", where science and technology are intertwined and cannot be separated, to recognize the practical (phenomenological) significance of science, the "sociogical epoche".

In this section, we will discuss the role and relationships between VR technology and phenomenology, perception, and practice.

3.1 VR and Phenomenology

Phenomenology [24] is a philosophy initiated by Edmund Husserl at the beginning of the twentieth century. Phenomenology, as a presuppositionless science and a philosophical approach, emphasizes the study of human experience and the way things appear in our consciousness, specifically, the human experience of an object or about an object [16,41].

Ihde highlights the ways in which individuals perceive and engage with the world. In his phenomenological analysis, "embodiment relations" is an important concept, i.e., embodiment, hermeneutic, alterity, and background relations. He uses this concept to describe how technology affects our perception and experience of the world, which is referred to in his other book, "Bodies in Technology" [26].

VR technology can provide a unique platform for phenomenological investigation, allowing researchers to study human experience in a controlled and simulated environment. For example, VR can be used to study how individuals perceive and interpret their surroundings, or to explore the nature of perception, embodiment, and agency in virtual environments. By placing users in immersive, interactive, and often novel environments, VR technologies can help reveal the fundamental structure of human experience, potentially contributing to our understanding of consciousness and subjective reality.

In the context of VR, phenomenology can exist in several ways:

Understanding Subjective Experiences: VR technology can provide a unique platform for studying the human experience in immersive and interactive environments. By placing users in various "real" virtual situations, researchers can study their subjective experiences [32], emotions [10,71], and reactions [44] in a controlled environment, which can reveal the fundamental structure of human experience and contribute to our understanding of consciousness and subjective reality [19].

Exploring Perception and Embodiment: VR can be used to explore the nature of perception, embodiment, and agency in virtual environments. For example, researchers can study how users perceive and interpret their virtual environments, how they feel a sense of presence or immersion [8], and how they interact with virtual objects and characters [22,30]. These investigations can provide valuable insights into the interplay of perception, cognition, and action in virtual and real-world contexts.

Enhancing Empathy and Perspective-Taking: VR has been proven to be an effective tool for developing empathy and perspective by allowing users to experience situations from the perspective of others [61]. Through immersive and interactive narratives, VR can help individuals better understand the experiences and emotions of people from different backgrounds and cultures [15]. These studies can contribute to the phenomenological study of empathy and intersubjectivity.

Investigating Altered States of Consciousness: VR can simulate altered states of consciousness or create environments that challenge our perceptual expectations, such as simulated dreaming [56]. Also, VR can provide a way for researchers to study the nature of consciousness and the boundaries of human experience in a controlled and safe manner, such as for the study of hallucinations [57].

3.2   VR and Perception

"If the 'world' changes in a paradigm shift, the object of reference of perception within its entire field changes: it reflexively implies a change of some kind in the perceiver" [25].

When paradigms change, it changes everything about how science views and explains different scenarios. Agian, when the science community discovers something new compared to the original paradigm, a paradigm shift also occurs [37]. For example, the Ancient Greeks' Perception of the Earth was to believe the earth is flat. But once Aristotle first recognized that the earth is a round sphere, a 'paradigm shift' occurred in the scientific community [62]. In the context of VR, Ihde's instrumental realism offers valuable insights into the way VR functions as an instrument that extends human perception and cognition. As a technology that allows users to experience immersive and interactive environments, VR has the potential to transform our understanding of the world by presenting new possibilities for observing, experimenting, and learning. VR environments can provide scientists with new ways of investigating phenomena that were previously inaccessible or difficult to study, thus expanding the boundaries of scientific inquiry [3].

The illusionary mechanisms provided by VR allow users to react realistically to VR scenes, effectively providing an immersive experience. The first is the place illusion (PI), also known as 'being there' or 'presence', which refers to a sense of being in a real place. The second is the plausibility illusion (PSI), an illusion that the events being portrayed are actually happening [52]. VR makes users believe they are in the environment of the game (PI) experiencing the scene as it is happening (PSI) [34]. With advances in VR technology, this illusionary mechanism is achieved primarily through head-mounted displays combined with precise motion tracking systems, allowing the user to experience an interactive 3D virtual environment [9]. One example is that players who play horror games through VR experience a much stronger sense of fear and anxiety than those playing in 2D video mode [42].

"In Husserl's case, what is fundamental is a kind of ordinary human praxis and perception, the world of the human interaction among material things and others. Its openness toward the other is sensory, and this relation is focally perceptual" [25].

VR can significantly change human perception by providing an immersive and interactive experience that changes the way we process and interpret information about our surroundings. When people are in a virtual environment, this "fake" scenario brings people a real experience.

Also, in Markham's book [38], "Life Online: Researching Real Experience in Virtual Space", she discusses how reality is defined or experienced in virtual space and the relationship between the virtual and the "body". Markham emphasizes the importance of the "real" experiences and emotions that individuals experience in virtual spaces, i.e., the experiences they have in virtual spaces are as important and influential as the interactive experiences they have in the real world.

In the VR environment, the body interacts in the virtual space and also perceives the world around it, and this virtual space is able to transcend the limitations of the real world effortlessly.

3.3   VR as an Instrument

"Led by a new paradigm, scientists adopt new instruments and look in new places" [25]. In fact, VR is an instrumental technology, not only because it is inherently device-dependent (a combination of HMD and sensors) but also because VR is a "readable technology [20]" that allows people to use the instrument to observe and experience the virtual world [13].

Moreover, we would like to emphasize the importance of VR, a scientific instrument, as a medium. VR serves as an intermediary between the real and virtual worlds, allowing for tracing features in virtual space and real life. This expands the boundaries of the real world in a sense, while giving extreme freedom. In other words, the restrictions for the virtual world are greatly reduced compared to those in the real world.

On the one hand, thanks to the immersion, interactivity, scalability, and accessibility that VR offers, conducting scientific research in a virtual environment has practical implications for real life.

On the other hand, in Ihde's view [25], *"'micro-technologies' of early physics were not yet capable of manipulation of natural phenomena in any powerful or significant way. The larger the macrophenomenon and the smaller the instrument, the more limited one is to the mere 'observational' model."* But, VR as an instrument makes it possible to manipulate phenomena in an "arbitrary" way in virtual space [45]. At the same time, the empathetic experience of the VR environment allows perception beyond the limits of "observation" [11].

In essence, we believe that VR technology has become an advanced scientific instrument and has the potential to grow even more. This is consistent with Ihde's view [25], *"...that contemporary science is more than accidentally-it is essentially-embodied technologically in its instrumentation"*, which emphasizes that contemporary science is fundamentally embodied in its technological tools and that VR is a prime example of this embodiment. As we progress, the combination of VR and scientific exploration will likely deepen, leading to discoveries and innovations that will further expand our understanding of the natural and virtual worlds.

4   Counterarguments, Counterexamples, and Challenges

Although people have become aware of the uses and potential possibilities of VR, the VR environment also comes with some risks, especially in terms of its impact on the real world. Firstly, in a highly simulated world, distinguishing between reality and simulation becomes difficult, leading to a loss of meaning in the "real" world [5]. Secondly, an overemphasis on technology (such as VR) in understanding human experience can lead to a deterministic viewpoint, where technology is seen as shaping everything, thereby undermining human agency [7]. Concerns about VR leading to escapism, loss of genuine interpersonal relationships, or issues with privacy and data security challenge the unbridled optimism surrounding VR technology [50,55,63].

In the face of these challenges, the use of phenomenology to focus on subjective experience is crucial for designing more immersive, intuitive, and meaningful user-centered VR technologies. This includes paying attention to embodied cognition [12] (the interaction between the body and the world), media theory [40] (medium - message), replacing reality [51], and the effects of other technological developments on VR, such as Large Language Models [47,72], virtual society [66], Internet of Things [33], and digital twins [70].

5   Conclusion

Focusing broadly, our emphasis should remain rooted in the practice of science. VR emerges not merely as a novelty but as an influential instrument that has the potential to redefine our perceptions and interactions with the world, enhancing the very essence of scientific practice.

From a research vantage point, VR can be envisioned as a modern-day extension of our perceptual and cognitive faculties. This opens up fresh avenues for detailed observation, inventive experimentation, and profound learning. These are foundational for the effective implementation of phenomenological methods and understanding. The unique potential of VR to craft, manipulate, and correlate phenomena across the real and simulated realms stands to revolutionize scientific research and, by extension, our daily interactions and experiences.

To conclude, when viewed through the intricate lenses of phenomenology and Ihde's Instrumental Realism, VR emerges as a profound contributor to our comprehension of the human journey. As it blurs the lines between tools and perception, and as phenomenological insights weave new definitions of consciousness, VR finds itself at a pivotal juncture. This juncture teems with prospects of new discoveries, deep self-reflection, and growth.

References

1. Aïm, F., Lonjon, G., Hannouche, D., Nizard, R.: Effectiveness of virtual reality training in orthopaedic surgery. Arthrosc. J. Arthrosc. Relat. Surg. **32**(1), 224–232 (2016)
2. Alsafouri, S., Ayer, S.K.: Mobile augmented reality to influence design and constructability review sessions. J. Archit. Eng. **25**(3), 04019016 (2019)
3. Bainbridge, W.S.: The scientific research potential of virtual worlds. Science **317**(5837), 472–476 (2007)
4. Bates, J.: Virtual reality, art, and entertainment. Presence Teleoper. Virtual Environ. **1**(1), 133–138 (1992)
5. Baudrillard, J.: Simulacra and Simulation. Body, in theory, University of Michigan Press (1994). https://books.google.com/books?id=9Z9biHaoLZIC
6. Boyd, D.E., Koles, B.: An introduction to the special issue "virtual reality in marketing": definition, theory and practice (2019)
7. Brey, P., Søraker, J.H.: Philosophy of computing and information technology. In: Philosophy of Technology and Engineering Sciences, pp. 1341–1407. Elsevier (2009). https://doi.org/10.1016/B978-0-444-51667-1.50051-3
8. Cummings, J.J., Bailenson, J.N.: How immersive is enough? a meta-analysis of the effect of immersive technology on user presence. Media Psychol. **19**(2), 272–309 (2016)
9. Davis, A., Murphy, J., Owens, D., Khazanchi, D., Zigurs, I.: Avatars, people, and virtual worlds: foundations for research in metaverses. J. Assoc. Inf. Syst. **10**(2), 1 (2009)
10. Diemer, J., Alpers, G.W., Peperkorn, H.M., Shiban, Y., Mühlberger, A.: The impact of perception and presence on emotional reactions: a review of research in virtual reality. Front. Psychol. **6**, 26 (2015)
11. El Beheiry, M., Doutreligne, S., Caporal, C., Ostertag, C., Dahan, M., Masson, J.B.: Virtual reality: beyond visualization. J. Mol. Biol. **431**(7), 1315–1321 (2019)
12. Foglia, L., Wilson, R.A.: Embodied cognition. Wiley Interdisc. Rev. Cogn. Sci. **4**(3), 319–325 (2013). https://doi.org/10.1002/wcs.1226
13. Frontoni, E., Loncarski, J., Pierdicca, R., Bernardini, M., Sasso, M.: Cyber physical systems for Industry 4.0: towards real time virtual reality in smart manufacturing. In: De Paolis, L.T., Bourdot, P. (eds.) AVR 2018. LNCS, vol. 10851, pp. 422–434. Springer, Cham (2018). https://doi.org/10.1007/978-3-319-95282-6_31
14. Gallagher, A.G., et al.: Virtual reality simulation for the operating room: proficiency-based training as a paradigm shift in surgical skills training. Ann. Surg. **241**(2), 364 (2005)

15. Georgiadou, A.: Equality inclusion and diversity through virtual reality. In: The Palgrave Handbook of Corporate Sustainability in the Digital Era, pp. 181–193 (2021)
16. Giorgi, A., Giorgi, B.: Phenomenology. Sage Publications, Inc., Thousand Oaks (2003)
17. Halbig, A., Babu, S.K., Gatter, S., Latoschik, M.E., Brukamp, K., von Mammen, S.: Opportunities and challenges of virtual reality in healthcare-a domain experts inquiry. Front. Virtual Real. 3, 837616 (2022)
18. Haque, S., Srinivasan, S.: A meta-analysis of the training effectiveness of virtual reality surgical simulators. IEEE Trans. Inf. Technol. Biomed. 10(1), 51–58 (2006)
19. Heater, C.: Being there: the subjective experience of presence. Presence Teleoper. Virtual Environ. 1(2), 262–271 (1992)
20. Heelan, P.: Natural science as a hermeneutic of instrumentation. Phil. Sci. 50(2), 181–204 (1983)
21. Heim, M.: The metaphysics of virtual reality. Oxford University Press on Demand (1993)
22. Hoffman, H.G., Hollander, A., Schroder, K., Rousseau, S., Furness, T.: Physically touching and tasting virtual objects enhances the realism of virtual experiences. Virt. Real. 3, 226–234 (1998)
23. Hudson, J., et al.: Using virtual experiences of older age: exploring pedagogical and psychological experiences of students. In: Proceedings of the Virtual and Augmented Reality to Enhance Learning and Teaching in Higher Education Conference 2018, pp. 61–72. IM Publications Open (2018)
24. Husserl, E.: Ideas: General Introduction to Pure Phenomenology. Routledge, Abingdon (2012)
25. Ihde, D.: Instrumental Realism: The Interface Between Philosophy of Science and Philosophy of Technology, vol. 626. Indiana University Press, Bloomington (1991)
26. Ihde, D.: Bodies in Technology, vol. 5. U of Minnesota Press, Minneapolis (2002)
27. Ingram, A.L., Hathorn, L.G., Evans, A.: Beyond chat on the internet. Comput. Educ. 35(1), 21–35 (2000)
28. Insights, F.B.: Virtual reality market size, share & covid-19 impact analysis (2022). https://www.fortunebusinessinsights.com/industry-reports/virtual-reality-market-101378
29. Javaid, M., Haleem, A.: Virtual reality applications toward medical field. Clin. Epidemiol. Glob. Health 8(2), 600–605 (2020)
30. Kang, H.J., Shin, J.H., Ponto, K.: A comparative analysis of 3d user interaction: how to move virtual objects in mixed reality. In: 2020 IEEE Conference on Virtual Reality and 3D User Interfaces (VR), pp. 275–284. IEEE (2020)
31. Kim, K.: Is virtual reality (VR) becoming an effective application for the market opportunity in health care, manufacturing, and entertainment industry? Eur. Sci. J. 12(9), (2016)
32. Kim, Y.M., Rhiu, I., Yun, M.H.: A systematic review of a virtual reality system from the perspective of user experience. Int. J. Human-Comput. Interact. 36(10), 893–910 (2020)
33. Li, K., et al.: When internet of things meets metaverse: convergence of physical and cyber worlds. IEEE Internet Things J. 10(5), 4148–4173 (2023). https://doi.org/10.1109/JIOT.2022.3232845
34. Lin, J.H.T.: Fear in virtual reality (VR): fear elements, coping reactions, immediate and next-day fright responses toward a survival horror zombie virtual reality game. Comput. Human Behav. 72, 350–361 (2017). https://doi.org/10.1016/j.chb.2017.02.057

35. Lv, Z.: Virtual reality in the context of internet of things. Neural Comput. Appl. **32**(13), 9593–9602 (2020)
36. Mao, R.Q., et al.: Immersive virtual reality for surgical training: a systematic review. J. Surg. Res. **268**, 40–58 (2021)
37. Margolis, H.: Paradigms and Barriers: How Habits of Mind Govern Scientific Beliefs. University of Chicago Press, Chicago (1993)
38. Markham, A.N.: Life Online: Researching Real Experience in Virtual Space, vol. 6. Rowman Altamira (1998)
39. Masurovsky, A., Chojecki, P., Runde, D., Lafci, M., Przewozny, D., Gaebler, M.: Controller-free hand tracking for grab-and-place tasks in immersive virtual reality: design elements and their empirical study. Multimodal Technol. Interact. **4**(4), 91 (2020)
40. McLuhan, M.: The medium is the message. In: Communication Theory, pp. 390–402. Routledge (2017)
41. Moran, D.: Introduction to Phenomenology. Routledge, Abingdon (2002)
42. Pallavicini, F., Ferrari, A., Pepe, A., Garcea, G., Zanacchi, A., Mantovani, F.: Effectiveness of virtual reality survival horror games for the emotional elicitation: preliminary insights using resident evil 7: biohazard. In: Antona, M., Stephanidis, C. (eds.) UAHCI 2018. LNCS, vol. 10908, pp. 87–101. Springer, Cham (2018). https://doi.org/10.1007/978-3-319-92052-8_8
43. Pastel, S., Chen, C.H., Martin, L., Naujoks, M., Petri, K., Witte, K.: Comparison of gaze accuracy and precision in real-world and virtual reality. Virt. Real. **25**, 175–189 (2021)
44. Peperkorn, H.M., Diemer, J.E., Alpers, G.W., Mühlberger, A.: Representation of patients' hand modulates fear reactions of patients with spider phobia in virtual reality. Front. Psychol. **7**, 268 (2016)
45. Pirok, G., Máté, N., Varga, J., Szegezdi, J., Vargyas, M., Dóránt, S., Csizmadia, F.: Making "real" molecules in virtual space. J. Chem. Inf. Model. **46**(2), 563–568 (2006)
46. Portman, M.E., Natapov, A., Fisher-Gewirtzman, D.: To go where no man has gone before: virtual reality in architecture, landscape architecture and environmental planning. Comput. Environ. Urban Syst. **54**, 376–384 (2015)
47. Qin, H.X., Hui, P.: Empowering the metaverse with generative AI: survey and future directions. In: 2023 IEEE 43rd International Conference on Distributed Computing Systems Workshops (ICDCSW), pp. 85–90 (2023). https://doi.org/10.1109/ICDCSW60045.2023.00022
48. Rogers, S.L., Broadbent, R., Brown, J., Fraser, A., Speelman, C.P.: Realistic motion avatars are the future for social interaction in virtual reality. Front. Virt. Real. **2**, 163 (2022)
49. Rojas-Sánchez, M.A., Palos-Sánchez, P.R., Folgado-Fernández, J.A.: Systematic literature review and bibliometric analysis on virtual reality and education. Educ. Inf. Technol. **28**(1), 155–192 (2023)
50. Rushkoff, D.: Survival of the Richest: Escape Fantasies of the Tech Billionaires. W. W. Norton (2022). https://books.google.com/books?id=v_NhEAAAQBAJ
51. Ryan, M.L.: Narrative as virtual reality. In: Immersion and Interactivity in Literature, pp. 357–359 (2001). http://www.movingimages.info/class/wp-content/uploads/2010/06/RyNarr.pdf
52. Slater, M.: Place illusion and plausibility can lead to realistic behaviour in immersive virtual environments. Phil. Trans. Royal Soc. B: Biol. Sci. **364**(1535), 3549–3557 (2009). https://doi.org/10.1098/rstb.2009.0138

53. Squire, K.D., et al.: Wherever you go, there you are: place-based augmented reality games for learning. In: The Design and Use of Simulation Computer Games in Education, pp. 273–304. Brill (2007)
54. Stark, R., Stark, R.: Major technology 7: Virtual reality-vr. In: Virtual Product Creation in Industry: The Difficult Transformation from IT Enabler Technology to Core Engineering Competence, pp. 305–326 (2022)
55. Stephanidis, C., et al.: Seven HCI grand challenges. Int. J. Human-Comput. Interact. **35**(14), 1229–1269 (2019). https://doi.org/10.1080/10447318.2019.1619259
56. Suzuki, K., Roseboom, W., Schwartzman, D.J., Seth, A.K.: A deep-dream virtual reality platform for studying altered perceptual phenomenology. Sci. Rep. **7**(1), 1–11 (2017)
57. Suzuki, K., Roseboom, W., Schwartzman, D.J., Seth, A.K.: Hallucination machine: simulating altered perceptual phenomenology with a deep-dream virtual reality platform. In: Artificial Life Conference Proceedings, pp. 111–112. MIT Press, Cambridge (2018)
58. Sykownik, P., Karaosmanoglu, S., Emmerich, K., Steinicke, F., Masuch, M.: VR almost there: simulating co-located multiplayer experiences in social virtual reality. In: Proceedings of the 2023 CHI Conference on Human Factors in Computing Systems, CHI 2023. Association for Computing Machinery, New York (2023). https://doi.org/10.1145/3544548.3581230
59. Takeuchi, L.: Kids closer up: playing, learning, and growing with digital media. Int. J. Learn. Media **3**(2), 1–23 (2011)
60. Thomasset, V., Caron, S., Weistroffer, V.: Lower body control of a semi-autonomous avatar in virtual reality: balance and locomotion of a 3D bipedal model. In: Proceedings of the 25th ACM Symposium on Virtual Reality Software and Technology, VRST 2019. Association for Computing Machinery, New York (2019). https://doi.org/10.1145/3359996.3364240
61. Van Loon, A., Bailenson, J., Zaki, J., Bostick, J., Willer, R.: Virtual reality perspective-taking increases cognitive empathy for specific others. PLoS ONE **13**(8), e0202442 (2018)
62. Vosniadou, S., Brewer, W.F.: Mental models of the earth: a study of conceptual change in childhood. Cogn. Psychol. **24**(4), 535–585 (1992)
63. Wang, H.: A survey on the metaverse: the state-of-the-art, technologies, applications, and challenges. IEEE Internet Things J. **10**(16), 14671–14688 (2023). https://doi.org/10.1109/JIOT.2023.3278329
64. Wiseman, R., Watt, C.: Experiencing the impossible and creativity: a targeted literature review. PeerJ **10**, e13755 (2022)
65. Wolf, M.J.: 1 the video game as a medium. In: The Medium of the Video Game, pp. 13–34. University of Texas Press (2002)
66. Wu, D., Yang, Z., Zhang, P., Wang, R., Yang, B., Ma, X.: Virtual-reality inter-promotion technology for metaverse: a survey. IEEE Internet Things J. **10**(18), 15788–15809 (2023). https://doi.org/10.1109/JIOT.2023.3265848
67. Yang, J.J., Holz, C., Ofek, E., Wilson, A.D.: Dreamwalker: substituting real-world walking experiences with a virtual reality. In: Proceedings of the 32nd Annual ACM Symposium on User Interface Software and Technology, UIST 2019, pp. 1093–1107. Association for Computing Machinery, New York (2019). https://doi.org/10.1145/3332165.3347875
68. Yang, L., Huang, J., Feng, T., Hong-An, W., Guo-Zhong, D.: Gesture interaction in virtual reality. Virt. Real. Intell. Hardware **1**(1), 84–112 (2019)
69. Yuan, B., Folmer, E., Harris, F.C.: Game accessibility: a survey. Univ. Access Inf. Soc. **10**, 81–100 (2011)

70. Zhang, H., et al.: Multi-channel sensor network construction, data fusion and challenges for smart home (2023)
71. Zhang, H., Li, X., Qiu, C., Fu, X.: Decoding fear: exploring user experiences in virtual reality horror games (2023). https://arxiv.org/abs/2312.15582
72. Zhang, H., Wu, C., Xie, J., Lyu, Y., Cai, J., Carroll, J.M.: Redefining qualitative analysis in the AI era: utilizing chatgpt for efficient thematic analysis (2023). https://arxiv.org/abs/2309.10771

Libraries as Partners for Emergency Preparedness and Response in Times of Crisis: Survey Design and Development

Kelda Habing[(✉)] and Lian Ruan

University of Illinois, Urbana-Champaign, IL 61820, USA
khabing2@illinois.edu

Abstract. *Libraries as Partners for Emergency Preparedness and Response in Times of Crisis* is a preliminary investigation into partnerships between libraries and emergency response groups during crises. While libraries have proven themselves as providers during emergencies, little systematic work has been conducted to explore if library partnerships with emergency responders exist and the scope, nature, and role of libraries in these partnerships. This paper will explore the design and development of the project's first step in gaining an initial understanding of library-community partnerships during emergencies: a survey of Illinois multi-type libraries. The survey's creation was guided by key factors including focus on its target population, use of Participatory Design, and development of lines of inquiry which correspond to the frameworks of Targeted Universalism and Team Cognitive Work Analysis. While the survey has not yet been released at the time of writing this paper, the survey's design and development described herein will address the paper's research questions: How can a survey be developed for a large and diverse target population with multiple stakeholders, and how can such a survey's results be relevant at an even larger scale? Anticipated results of the survey include discovery and promotion of the essential role that libraries take on during emergencies and with emergency response partners, and the increased safety and resiliency of diverse communities.

Keywords: Libraries · Emergency Management · Community Partnership

1 Introduction

This paper describes the design and development of a forthcoming survey targeting multi-type Illinois libraries. The survey is the first major activity of *Libraries as Partners for Emergency Preparedness and Response in Times of Crisis*, a two-year Institute of Museum and Library Services planning grant project which is a preliminary investigation into library partnerships with emergency response groups during community crises. In the past, libraries of all types have proven themselves as providers during emergencies; however, traditional emergency response groups may not be aware of or recognize the role that libraries can take on during crises. Therefore, the overarching research questions of the *Libraries as Partners* project as a whole are:

I. Sserwanga et al. (Eds.): iConference 2024, LNCS 14597, pp. 94–101, 2024.
https://doi.org/10.1007/978-3-031-57860-1_7

1. What types of emergencies do libraries respond to (currently or in the past)?
2. What types of partnership were present during these emergencies?
3. If partnerships were not present, what was the reason for this?
4. If partnerships were present, what was the extent and scope of the partnerships and the role of libraries in these partnerships?

To begin to answer these questions, the project's first activity is a survey targeting multi-type Illinois libraries (academic, public, school, and special), taking Illinois libraries as a microcosm of the national library community across the United States. Their survey responses will establish a baseline understanding of the current state of library-community partnerships and lay the foundation for future research that will discover and promote the essential role that libraries play in community safety and well-being, serving as a conversation starter for future collaborations and conversations on library-community partnerships during emergencies.

While the survey is forthcoming at the time of writing this paper, this paper may serve as an example for others creating similar surveys as the survey's design and development as described herein will address the paper's research questions: How can a survey be developed for a large and diverse target population with multiple stakeholders, and how can such a survey's results be relevant at an even larger scale?

2 Background

Libraries of all types have a history of providing services to their communities during different types of emergencies and are often cited as information hubs during emergencies for enhancing resiliency and post-disaster recovery efforts [1]. Libraries have consistently proven their ability as providers during a myriad of public crises including but not limited to the COVID-19 Pandemic [2], Uvalde school shooting [3], California wildfires [4], opioid crisis [5], destructive hurricanes [1], and many others. In fact, libraries are listed by the U.S. government in the Stafford Act 2011 as essential organizations alongside fire protection, police, EMS, education, and utilities as a priority to get "up and running" after a disaster [1], and the Federal Emergency Management Agency (FEMA) has recognized libraries as essential organizations as well [6]. This recognition by the federal government gives official weight to libraries' importance for aiding community recovery during and following emergencies [7].

Despite libraries' successful work during emergencies and recognition, many key emergency response organizations such as the fire service, EMS, health departments, and other emergency management groups do not recognize libraries as equal emergency preparedness and response partners [8] or are not aware of the role that libraries can take on before, during, and after emergencies [9]. Additionally, there is a literature gap on library-community partnerships during emergencies, with little systematic research conducted on the scope and nature of library partnerships with community emergency response organizations or the role that libraries play in these partnerships if partnerships do exist, as well as the different types of library-community partnerships and library partnership roles that may stem from different types of emergencies. While there have been some successful cases of libraries joining forces with community partners during emergencies (ex. Delaware Libraries and Disasters Summit, resulting in the Delaware

Libraries and Disasters Initiative [10], medical libraries' collaborations with partners during COVID-19 [11]), the combination of lack of available literature on and practice between libraries and community emergency response groups alongside little to no knowledge by these groups of the role of libraries indicates that libraries are rarely included in emergency planning and response. If library-community partnerships during emergencies do exist, there is little to no baseline research available on these partnerships in the areas of how emergency type effects partnerships, the scope and nature of partnerships, and the role of libraries in partnerships, information which would increase libraries' ability to provide services during crises.

The gap in research on library-community partnerships during emergencies necessitates the creation of the survey whose design and development is described in this paper, as well as the two-year planning project that it is a part of. The survey and the *Libraries as Partners* project as a whole will aid in deepening and expanding knowledge of these partnerships and the possibilities for libraries to help their communities even more than they already are during crises.

3   Methodology

To begin to answer the *Libraries as Partners'* four research questions, an online survey using the survey software Qualtrics was designed and developed. To ensure the survey's relevancy to respondents and the utility of its eventual findings to a large and diverse audience, three key factors were applied to the survey's creation: target population, Participatory Design, and the frameworks of Targeted Universalism and Team Cognitive Work Analysis (TeamCWA).

3.1   Target Population: Multi-type Illinois Libraries

The survey's target population is the multi-type libraries of Illinois. Illinois libraries include 158 academic, 639 public, 788 school, and 224 special libraries, and vary greatly in geographic location, number of users, and types of communities they serve. 22% of Illinois public libraries serve an area with 2,500 or less, while 64.5% serve populations that range between 2,500 and 50,000. 6.1% of Illinois public libraries serve areas with a population between 50,000 and 250,000 while only 0.2% serve areas with populations of 1,000,000 or more [12]. The Chicago Public Library is the fifth largest library service area in the U.S., serving 2.7 million [13]. Due to the amount and diversity of Illinois libraries, Illinois libraries may serve as a microcosm of the national library community. As a preliminary survey intended to provide initial understanding into the state of library-community partnerships during emergencies, the survey intends to collect as much data from as many libraries as possible regardless of type. Therefore, the broad range of Illinois' libraries and their differences had to be considered during the survey design.

3.2   Participatory Design

Participatory Design is a method which involves all stakeholders in a design process to better meet their needs. While it was not possible to include every Illinois library in the survey design process, their voices were included through the project team's collaboration with a State Advisory Committee and a National Advisory Board.

The State Advisory Committee included representatives from seven Illinois library organizations, including the Illinois State Library, three regional library systems, and three professional library organizations. These state advisors served as the voices of the Illinois library communities that they represent, guiding the survey to ensure its relevancy to Illinois multi-type libraries. Additionally, the State Advisory Committee included representatives from six Illinois emergency response organizations. These Illinois emergency response advisors helped guide the survey to ensure that the emergency response topics included in the survey were correctly described and matched the experiences and concerns of emergency responders. Collaboration with state advisors is also key to the survey's distribution, as they will assist with reaching out to their library communities to increase survey response.

While the survey's target population are the multi-type libraries of Illinois, its findings should be relevant libraries across the U.S. Therefore, a National Advisory Board was convened of representatives from nine national library organizations. National advisors critiqued the survey to ensure that it was not too specific to Illinois libraries so that its findings would be relevant to libraries across the U.S. National advisors will continue to provide a national perspective during analysis of survey findings.

3.3 Team Cognitive Work Analysis and Targeted Universalism

Two frameworks which will be used during the survey data analysis were kept in mind during the survey design. Team Cognitive Work Analysis (TeamCWA) is an analytical approach for examining collaborations in a complex socio-technical system across sectors. Leveraging successful use of TeamCWA to analyze multiple-stakeholder environments [14], results from the survey will be analyzed to identify factors in shared decision-making among multiple different community partners that contribute to effective partnerships and intended shared outcomes. Due to the complexity of emergency situations, understanding how libraries work with varied groups to prepare for and respond to emergencies will be key to suggesting best practices for sustaining library partnerships during emergencies.

Targeted Universalism is a framework which sets universal goals and achieves these goals through targeted processes. The universal goals are set for all groups that exist within a larger community, while the targeted processes are set depending on each groups' situation within their community's structure, culture, and geography to acknowledge the differences between groups [15]. Incorporation of Targeted Universalism into the survey design will begin to establish the targeted processes needed for different groups, especially underserved populations and those shown to be at higher risk during emergencies through use of the social vulnerability index [16], so that the universal goal of equitable service in library-partner crises response will be achieved across communities.

4 Survey

Taking into consideration the target population of Illinois multi-type libraries, collaboration with state and national advisors through Participatory Design, and the frameworks of TeamCWA and Targeted Universalism, the survey was created on Qualtrics. The survey will be completely anonymous unless respondents choose to provide their contact information for follow-up questions. It is intended to last 30 to 60 min, and this time will vary depending on participants' choices as some responses will prompt further details while others will not. The survey includes four sections: About You, Emergencies, Scope and Nature of Partnership, and Role of Libraries in Partnership.

4.1 About You

The "About You" section includes nine questions and gathers background data about the respondents and their library, including their primary job responsibilities and time working in libraries, and type of library work in and size of user-community served. Three questions are included in this section which were created with Targeted Universalism in mind to begin to identify the varied communities that libraries serve and how libraries interact with them:

- Please describe the diversity of your user community in your own words.
- How often do you collaborate with your user community to create library policies?
- How often do you collaborate with your user community to create library programming?

4.2 Emergencies

The "Emergencies" section includes ten primary questions with potential for follow-up questions based on responses chosen. For example, respondents can choose multiple provided emergency types in response to "Has your library responded to any of the following emergency events and long-term or ongoing crises?" For each emergency that respondents mark, they will be prompted for further details about their library's response. Many of these follow-up questions align with TeamCWA as they begin to identify partners and how libraries work with partners especially through communication:

- During the emergency, who did you contact or seek partnership with?
- What information technologies did you use to contact other partners or gather information?
- What information did you request from an external partner? Which partner?

Questions included which address Targeted Universalism continue to identify the different communities that libraries serve during emergencies:

- To what degree does your library provide services to the following groups (followed by a list of groups such as historically marginalized/underserved communities, homeless patrons, non-English speakers, etc.)
- When planning for emergencies, my library factors in the varying needs of different groups.

4.3 Scope and Nature of Partnership

The "Scope and Nature of Partnership" section begins with the question "How do you define partnership?" and followed by "Does your library have established partnerships with emergency response groups?" Depending on an affirmative or negative response, the number of questions in this section is variable. Negative responses will only be asked two other questions: why partnerships do not exist and if they plan to establish partnerships in the future. Affirmative responses will be asked ten other questions for more details on who their community partners are and how they work with them. Because of the section's focus on partners and collaboration, several questions were added that align with TeamCWA:

- In what ways does your library communicate with and share information with community partners (email, phone, in-person, etc.)?
- What is the nature of that communication? (unidirectional, bidirectional, transdirectional)?
- List and describe strategies and actions that might enhance or build sustainable partnerships with partners. Describe any barriers to enacting these strategies.

4.4 Role of Libraries in Partnership

The "Role of Libraries in Partnerships" section includes ten questions. Affirmative responses to the previous section's question on if partnerships answer all ten, while negative responses only answer two. Their shared questions are:

- What do you believe is the role of libraries during emergencies?
- What future roles would you like your library to take with community partners during emergencies?

The questions that respondents who answered affirmatively to partnerships answer provide more details on the services that they provide in partnership with emergency response groups and the benefits these partnerships bring to their communities. Three questions may uncover shared decision-making for TeamCWA, as libraries and partners may collaborate to develop common goals for emergency partnership:

- How does your library's role before, during, and after emergencies benefit your community emergency response partners?
- When you build partnerships, you have intended outcomes in mind (Strongly Agree to Strongly Disagree)
- How do you evaluate levels of intended outcomes related to partnerships for emergency management and response?

5 Discussion

As the survey progressed through multiple versions, the use of Participatory Design to collaborate with state and national advisors was the driving force behind the survey's development. Their guidance will surely contribute to the survey's relevance to the large and diverse Illinois library community as well as its relevance at the national level. Advisors' critique of the survey provided a fresh and knowledgeable perspective, inspiring the addition of new questions and changes. For example, an advisor asked, what if libraries are unable to respond to an emergency due to the building being compromised (ex. flooding, electricity outage, bomb threats)? This led to a question addition in the Emergencies section "What challenges have prevented your library from responding to emergencies?" Other advisors had experiences responding to emergencies in libraries that the project team had not considered, such as energy crises, migration, or water shortages, and these were added to the survey. Some advisors' comments led to rethinking of parts of the survey, such clarification comment the difference between single event of ongoing emergencies, with the example of the August 2023 Maui fire where the event of the fire may have passed but the emergency was still ongoing after the fire was extinguished. This comment led to the rephrasing of several questions to clarify that the survey was interested in both single events and ongoing crises. Advisors also played a role in ensuring that the survey's language would be inclusive of the whole target audience, allowing different library types to complete the survey. The advisors' contributions make it possible for the survey to reach a large and diverse target population and will increase the possibility for its results to have an impact nationally.

Keeping in mind Targeted Universalism and TeamCWA during survey design may also contribute to survey results' relevancy at a national level. As the survey is a preliminary survey to develop initial understanding of this topic, analysis of questions that align with these frameworks will provide paths of future inquiry. From these future paths, targeted processes to serve diverse groups during emergencies and suggestions for best practices for shared decision-making between libraries and emergency response groups have the possibility to increase community safety and resiliency.

6 Conclusion

The *Libraries as Partners* survey design and development is a strong example of how collaboration, knowledge of a target population, and use of frameworks can contribute to a survey's relevance to a large and diverse target population and relevancy on the national level. While the survey data collection is ongoing, findings will directly inform the second year of the project: a national discussion on library-community partnerships during emergencies. This initial survey will lay the groundwork for future research and practice, with the ultimate goal of deepening the bond and strength of community networks and increasing libraries' capacity for constituency support in times of crisis.

References

1. Stricker, M.: Ports in a storm: the role of the public library in times of crisis. Collab. Librariansh. **11**(1), 11–16 (2019)
2. Zalusky, S.: 2021 State of America's Libraries Special Report: COVID-19. American Library Association (2021)
3. Hendrick, G.: Library of hope and healing: Uvalde. LibLime (2022). https://liblime.com/2022/10/13/library-of-hope-healing-uvalde/. Accessed 15 Sept 2023
4. Peet, L.: California libraries reopen, respond to wildfires. Library J. (2018). https://www.libraryjournal.com/story/181121CAWildfires. Accessed 15 Sept 2023

5. Allen, S., et al.: Public libraries respond to opioid crisis with their communities: summary report. In: OCLC (2019)
6. Hagar, C.: Public library response to natural disasters: a 'whole community' approach. San José State University School of Information (2013). https://ischool.sjsu.edu/ciri-blog/public-library-response-natural-disasters-whole-community-approach. Accessed 15 Sept 2023
7. Patin, B.: What is essential?: understanding community resiliency and public libraries in the United States during disasters. Proc. Assoc. Inf. Sci. Technol. **57**(1) (2020)
8. Smith, M.: Top ten challenges facing public libraries. Publ. Libr. Quart. **38**(3), 241–247 (2019)
9. Hagar, C.: Public library partnerships with local agencies to meet community disasters preparedness and response needs. In: 12th International Conference of the Information Systems for Crisis Response and Management (2015)
10. Young, P.: Libraries as public health partners in times of crisis. Delaware J. Publ. Health **6**(4), 24–25 (2020)
11. Charney, R., Spencer, A., Tao, D.: A novel partnership between physicians and medical librarians during the COVID-19 pandemic. Med. Ref. Serv. Q. **40**(1), 48–55 (2021)
12. Institute of Museum and Library Services. Public libraries survey (2019). https://www.imls.gov/research-evaluation/data-collection/public-libraries-survey. Accessed 15 Sept 2023
13. American Library Association. Library statistics and figures: the nation's largest public libraries (2023). https://libguides.ala.org/librarystatistics/largest-public-libs. Accessed 15 Sept 2023
14. Ashoori, A., Burns, C.: Team cognitive work analysis: structure and control tasks. J. Cognit. Eng. Decis. Making **7**(2), 123–140 (2013)
15. Powell, J., Menendian, S., Ake, W.: Targeted Universalism: Policy & Practice. Othering & Belonging Institute at the University of California Berkeley (2022)
16. Flanagan, B., et al.: A social vulnerability index for disaster management. J. Homeland Secur. Emerg. Manag. **8**(1) (2011)

Intellectual Property Issues

Exploring Technology Evolution Pathways Based on Link Prediction on Multiplex Network: Illustrated as CRISPR

Zizuo Cheng[1], Juan Tang[1], Jiaqi Yang[1], and Ying Huang[1,2]✉

[1] School of Information Management, Wuhan University, Wuhan 430072, China
ying.huang@whu.edu.cn
[2] Centre for R&D Monitoring (ECOOM), Department of MSI, KU Leuven, 3000 Leuven, Belgium

Abstract. Exploring technology evolution pathways is essential since one can capture the best opportunity in a particular domain. Researchers attempt to exploit the critical trajectory from a historical perspective; however, only some steps forward to forecasting the future direction. This study proposes a new research framework to make reasonable predictions. Based on patents retrieved from DII, we construct a multiplex network consisting of co-citation and semantic layers. Specifically, we utilize the citation relationships between patents and extract technology topics with the Combined Topic Model(CTM), a powerful topic recognition tool. Subsequently, we employ the link prediction method to obtain future links and assemble them into a new co-citation network. We get credible predictions of future evolution trends by analyzing topics. To validate our framework, we take CRISPR, an emerging technology in gene editing, as a case study. Our experiments show that link prediction performs well in detecting future co-citation links, and the semantic layer further improves the prediction accuracy. We finally summarize seven potential directions and validate our predictions.

Keywords: CRISPR · Technology Evolution Pathways · Link Prediction · Topic Modeling

1 Introduction

Recently, Chat GPT has become popular worldwide, showcasing its remarkable capabilities. Its underlying technology, the Large Language Model, was not an overnight achievement. It resulted from continuous advancement, including the refinement of neural network models such as Transformer and the enhancements in computing devices like GPUs. Generally, technology evolution demonstrates path dependence [1]; new emerging technologies often stand on the shoulders of their predecessors. Moreover, the milestones in such a process wield tremendous influence, enabling us to decipher the main trajectory within specific domains. By discerning the critical evolutionary pathways of emerging technologies, one can formulate rational strategies to seize the best opportunities.

I. Sserwanga et al. (Eds.): iConference 2024, LNCS 14597, pp. 105–121, 2024.
https://doi.org/10.1007/978-3-031-57860-1_8

Current research has yielded fruitful results with patent analysis [2–4]. Patents have a structured format with multiple fields, allowing researchers to analyze from various perspectives. By building reasonable retrieval strategies, researchers can obtain a panorama of the latest technological developments. To get the most out of patent information, researchers often adopt two techniques: main path analysis(MPA) and text mining. MPA emphasizes citation information, while text mining focuses on semantic information. MPA attempts to mine critical trajectories in the citation network, representing knowledge diffusion between documents [5,6]. In terms of text mining, techniques like the LDA model [7,8], Word2Vec [9,10] and BERT model [11,12] are in use to identify topics and map the evolution of the technology domain. Figure 1 provides simple examples of the two approaches.

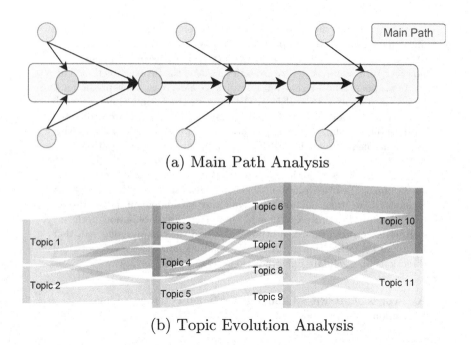

(a) Main Path Analysis

(b) Topic Evolution Analysis

Fig. 1. Examples of two methods in patent analysis. (a) Main path analysis attempts to identify crucial pathways in the citation network. (b) Topic evolution analysis extracts technology topics in patent texts and determines the evolution relationships.

In addition, several empirical studies conducted with the approaches above in different fields, like lithium iron phosphate battery [13] and biomass power generation [14], proved the validity and robustness of the applied methods.

However, there still exists research gaps. The studies above only analyze the current status of the specific domain but fail to provide further predictions about how it will evolve. Nevertheless, in the fierce market competition, providing a reasonable forecast is vital for the strategy maker, since the insight into the future is relevant to the enterprise's prospects.

In this context, the ordinary citation analysis tool becomes not applicable since it can only reflect past development and is determined once a patent gets authorized. Therefore, we switch to patent co-citation analysis to overcome such defects since it can represent knowledge diffusion and evolve dynamically. In other words, a citation relationship between two documents will not change in the future, but co-citation relationships may happen or strengthen. It is time to review this method since pioneer research has proved the effectiveness of probing future knowledge flow [15]. Regarding the text mining approaches, compared to identifying topics for a specific period, anticipating future ones becomes challenging since we cannot access patents that have yet appeared.

To this end, we can combine co-citation analysis and text mining approaches through the topic relevance between the citing documents and the co-cited ones. Although we are not able to acquire the citation relationships between existing patents and future ones, link prediction can be applicable to solve this problem. It attempts to estimate the likelihood of a connection between a pair of nodes [16], which is consistent with our purpose. Then we collect patents with emerging links and utilize the topic model to analyze future topics. In this study, we only attempt to trace the future topic nodes rather than determine the evolution lines since previous research has provided various effective methods.

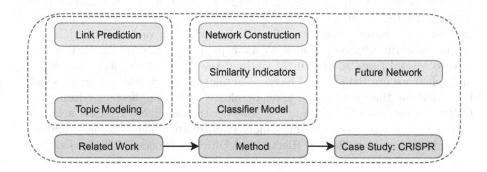

Fig. 2. The framework of this study

Figure 2 shows the framework of this study. First, we provide a short overview of related literature, including brief introductions to link prediction and topic modeling. Then we elaborate on the complete research framework in detail. We choose CRISPR, an emerging technology in the gene editing field, as a case to validate our framework. Finally, we illustrate a comprehensive discussion of the results and disclose the limitations of this study.

2   Related Work

2.1   Link Prediction

In brief, link prediction attempts to identify missing links or predict future links in a network [16,17]. In the early stages, scientists follow the rule that if pair nodes have similar features in topological structures, they are more likely to connect [18]. A classic example is to count the common neighbors between node pairs. Subsequently, as machine learning progresses, whether the pair nodes have links can be treated as a binary classification problem [19,20].

The same entities often have various relationships [21]. For instance, students in a class might form discrepant social networks on Facebook and YouTube due to their preferences. Scientists explored the interaction among the relations [22] and proposed new indicators to measure inter-layer relations, extending link prediction from single layer to multiplex [23–25].

Some scientists applied link prediction to the citation network since it is a powerful tool to characterize knowledge diffusion [26,27]. However, the studies above seldom provided specific application scenarios. Therefore, we attempt to fill the research gap.

2.2   Topic Modeling

Current studies [28–30] often choose Latent Dirichlet Allocation(LDA) [31] to identify the topics buried in the patent texts. Nevertheless, determining the optimal topic number becomes difficult when applying such a method. There are two generic solutions. One is to set a predefined interval and repeat the process several times to obtain the optimal result. In this scenario, perplexity and coherence are the classical metrics. Perplexity reflects the degree to which the model fits the corpus, with lower perplexity indicating better performance. Coherence measures the relevance of words within a topic; therefore, a higher coherence score means the result is more interpretable. The other is to employ the enhanced version like the Hierarchical Dirichlet Process(HDP) model [32], which can automatically generate the best results.

Furthermore, the traditional LDA model has other limitations. It ignores the sequential order of words, making it hard to capture the contextual relations between terms. Since the BERT model [33] demonstrates a robust contextual understanding that can well compensate for the defects of the LDA, Bianchi [34] proposed the Combined Topic Model(CTM). This powerful tool fully utilizes the Prod LDA [35] and BERT to recognize topics. Therefore, we choose CTM to extract semantic information in patent texts.

3   Methods

In this section, we elaborate on our research framework in detail, shown in Fig. 3.

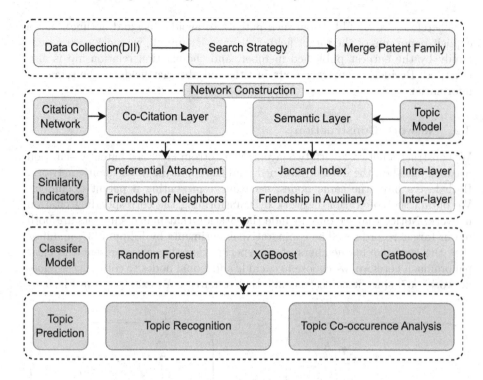

Fig. 3. The skeleton of the proposed method

3.1 Data Collection

We choose Derwent Innovations Index(DII) as the database. After obtaining the original dataset with a reasonable retrieval strategy, however, patents in the same family exist. A patent family is a collection of closely related patents derived from the same core technology but issued by authorities in different countries [36] (Fig. 4).

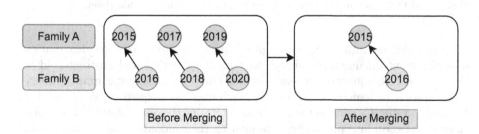

Fig. 4. An example of merging patent family. We select the earliest patent to represent each patent family, and the citation relationships should be combined.

Therefore, we should merge such patents to avoid noise and outline a more explicit panorama of the target field. Following Huang [2], we mark each patent family by the earliest published member, and the citation relationship is also inherited. Besides, we extract texts in title and abstract fields as the semantic information.

3.2   Network Construction

We construct a network with two layers. The bottom layer is a patent co-citation network based on the dataset obtained, and the top layer is a semantic network. Both layers have the same nodes, each one representing a patent document. We obtain the co-citation network by transforming the corresponding citation network. Notice that we only include the citation that pair documents are both in our target record set. The comparative experiments by Filippin [37] manifest that the core patent members of the specific domain can represent the clear panorama. Therefore, we choose to exclude additional nodes to construct a "close network" [37] since it can save computing resources. An example is in Fig. 5.

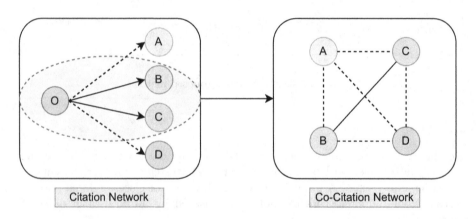

Fig. 5. An example of conversion from citation network to co-citation network. Note that A and D are not in the record collection, so we should exclude them.

As for the semantic layer, we adopt CTM to determine the topic distribution of each patent document. In detail, we combine the title and abstract field as the corpus. Subsequently, we conduct necessary pre-processing from sentence segmentation to removal of words with high and low frequency. We choose the Coherence value(Cv) [38] as the metric to determine the optimal number of topics since it·has good interpretability. Considering the randomness of the algorithm, we repeat the training process for ten rounds and calculate the average score as the final result. We choose the one with the highest Cv score and then obtain the topic distribution of patent documents as a matrix.

3.3 Link Prediction

Before our illustration, some important notations [24,39] are in Table 1.

Table 1. A summary of notations in link prediction

Notations	Explanation
$G(G_1, G_2, \cdots, G_i)$	Multiplex network with i layers
$G_i = (V_i, E_i)$	The network of layer i
V_i	Set of nodes in G_i
E_i	Set of edges in G_i
α	The target layer of the multiplex network (co-citation layer)
β	The auxiliary layer of the multiplex network (semantic layer)
U_α	Set of all possible edges in α
E_α	Set of all existing edges in α
$\overline{E_\alpha}$	Set of all unconnected edges in α
U_α^{Tr}	Training set
U_α^{Te}	Testing set
U_α^{P}	Predicting set

We will divide U_α into three subsets according to the time distribution of the co-cited patents. For example, if a patent dataset covers N years from Y_1 to Y_n, and we choose the dividing year Y_p and Y_q, then we obtain three time intervals. Subsequently, for each time interval, we collect the co-citation information and generate the corresponding subset for training, testing, and predicting.

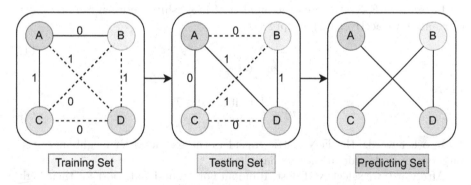

Fig. 6. A toy example of link prediction. The label of each node pair depends on the linkage in the subsequent period. In the training set, for example, A and C are connected and have an edge in the testing set, resulting in a label of 1 for the AC pair. Similarly, even though B and D have no link in the training set, they have one in the testing set, and hence a label of 1. This principle applies to all other pairs as well.

Our purpose is to make predictions about evolution; therefore, the existence of a link in U_α^{Tr} depends on whether it appears in the next period, i.e., U_α^{Te} [40]. The principle is the same for those in U_α^{Te} and the predicting set is free from the procedure. Figure 6 illustrates our labeling strategy. Because of the imbalance between the two parts, we should make adjustments and randomly sample them for the final training and testing set to perform better.

Subsequently, we need to choose some indicators as features of pair nodes. In general, we do not select ones that are time-consuming to compute since our network contains two layers and is relatively complex. Since both layers are undirected, classical indicators are applicable.

First, we choose preferential attachment(PA) as the baseline indicator [15]. PA is effective because it's consistent with the intuition that the rich get richer, which also exists in the patent co-citation network. For the PA [16] index, it can be obtained by

$$PA = k(x) \cdot k(y) \tag{1}$$

where $k(i)$ is the degree of node i.

Next, we will focus on the semantic layer. As the auxiliary layer, it can provide additional information and enhance the prediction accuracy. Here we choose Jaccard Index(JI) for its simiplicity and efficiency [16]:

$$JI = \frac{|\Gamma_x \cap \Gamma_y|}{|\Gamma_x \cup \Gamma_y|} \tag{2}$$

where Γ_i is the neighbor of node i.

We also consider the interlayer relationship. Following Shan [24], we choose Friendship in Auxiliary Layer(FAL) and Friendship of Neighbors(FoN). For each node pair (x, y) chosen, FAL is defined as

$$FAL = \begin{cases} 1, & \text{if } (x,y) \in E_\beta \\ 0, & \text{if } (x,y) \notin E_\beta \end{cases} \tag{3}$$

In terms of FoN, it counts the number of friendships between the neighbors of x and y, respectively. The expression is

$$FoN = \sum_{u \in \Gamma_i(x)} \sum_{v \in \Gamma_i(y)} e(u, v) \tag{4}$$

where

$$e(u, v) = \begin{cases} 1, & \text{if } (x,y) \in E_\beta \\ 0, & \text{if } (x,y) \notin E_\beta \end{cases} \tag{5}$$

In other words, the FoN metric considers the second-order neighbors of the target layer node pair in the auxiliary layer.

Afterward, we select XGBoost, Random Forest, and CatBoost for their high classification efficiency. We choose Area Under Curve(AUC) and Precision(PR) to evaluate our results because they are practical and accessible indicators. Then we can obtain the best-performed model for predicting the future links in the network. Finally, we will generate a new patent co-citation network to analyze potential topics.

4 Case Study: CRISPR

In brief, CRISPR is a powerful genome editing technology that can modify DNA efficiently. Researchers find it effective to discover disease mechanisms and provide medical treatment. They also utilize it in agriculture to improve crop yields. In 2020, Emmanuelle Charpentier and Jennifer A. Doudna won the Nobel Prize in Chemistry for their momentous research on CRISPR. Therefore, we select it to conduct an empirical study.

4.1 Data Collection

We adopt the same retrieval strategy as Zhang [8] since it is valid. In detail, we use "ABD = ("Clustered Regularly Interspaced Short Palindromic Repeat*" OR CRISPR) OR TID = ("Clustered Regularly Interspaced Short Palindromic Repeat*" OR CRISPR) AND PY> = (2002) AND PY< = (2021)" and fetch 7544 patent records. The distribution over time is in Fig. 7.

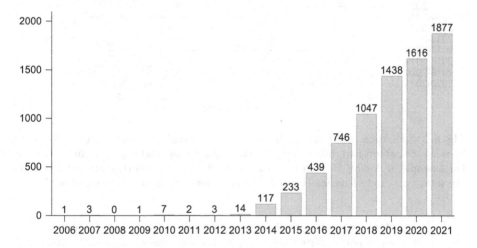

Fig. 7. Year distribution of CRISPR-related patents (2006–2021)

We can observe that the growth of CRISPR-related technology has two parts. From 2006 to 2013, it was in a period of exploration. Since 2014, the number of related patents has shown a blowout trend. The panorama is consistent with the development trend of CRISPR. Specifically, scientists' research on CRISPR has three stages. In the late 1980s to early 1990s, they observed CRISPR with iconic achievements [41,42]. From 2005 to 2012, research in this field made steady progress, and scientists discovered the universal defense function of CRISPR. Subsequently, two landmark achievements in CRISPR-Cas9 [43,44] were released, attracting wide social attention. Much investment poured into the market, and the number of patents steadily increased.

4.2 Network Construction

In terms of the co-citation layer, we set different time intervals to reveal the characteristics of knowledge flow in the network. We choose to focus on patents between 2014 and 2021, as there are very few published prior to 2014. In detail, we set the time span to 1 year and 2 years. For each time interval, we select the corresponding patents, trace their citation relationships, and construct the target co-citation network. Finally, we consider the time distribution of nodes in co-citation networks. In other words, we explore whether patents tend to cite the latest ones. The results are in Fig. 8.

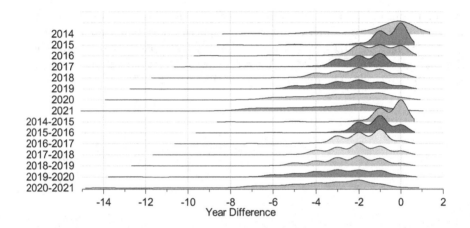

Fig. 8. Distribution of patents in the co-citation network. We set the year difference between the patents and their citing ones as the horizontal axis to align the distribution. For example, if A cites B, then 0 on the horizontal axis means they are published in the same year, and −1 means B is published one year earlier than A, and so on.

It is apparent that patents during the specified time period referenced a greater number of patents from the last 1 to 3 years, suggesting a rapid diffusion of knowledge in the CRISPR field. This outcome aligns with the conclusion [15] that more recent patents are more frequently cited. This temporal attribute provides a strong basis for our upcoming link prediction.

For the semantic layer, we employ the CTM for topic recognition after text pre-processing. Since CRISPR falls under the biomedical domain, we select a specialized PubMed BERT pre-training model [45] to improve efficiency.

The final results are in Fig. 9. Therefore, we set 12 as the topic number, then we can obtain the document-topic matrix and calculate the cosine similarity of each patent document pair. We set the similarity threshold at the top 2% to ensure closely related patent documents. We obtain a similar number of edges to the co-citation network. The auxiliary layer network can enhance link prediction, but too few or too many edges can be unhelpful or introduce noise. Then we proceed with link prediction.

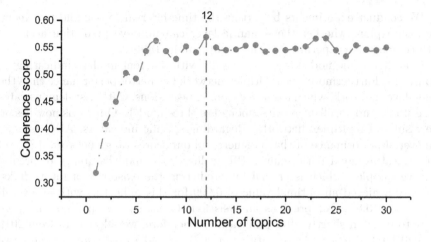

Fig. 9. Coherence score of each topic number

4.3   Link Prediction

Table 2. The results of link prediction

Train	Test	Model	Single Layer Network		Multiplex Network	
			AUC	PR	AUC	PR
2015	2016	RF	0.633	0.604	**0.883**	**0.945**
		XG	0.561	0.555	0.880	0.938
		CAT	0.668	0.624	0.877	0.936
2016	2017	RF	0.688	0.715	0.743	0.771
		XG	0.701	0.761	0.753	0.795
		CAT	0.700	0.789	**0.758**	**0.820**
2017	2018	RF	0.739	0.780	0.777	0.827
		XG	0.763	0.805	0.803	0.859
		CAT	0.776	0.826	**0.808**	**0.858**
2018	2019	RF	0.727	0.766	0.787	0.820
		XG	0.778	0.802	0.817	0.831
		CAT	0.784	0.818	**0.823**	**0.845**
2019	2020	RF	0.835	0.807	0.813	0.825
		XG	0.857	0.808	0.887	0.853
		CAT	0.866	0.804	**0.912**	**0.872**
2014–2015	2016–2017	RF	0.687	0.684	**0.781**	0.797
		XG	0.726	0.741	0.773	0.784
		CAT	0.737	0.755	0.706	**0.994**
2015–2016	2017–2018	RF	0.725	0.758	0.772	0.798
		XG	0.779	0.850	**0.830**	0.897
		CAT	0.780	0.899	0.829	**0.927**
2016–2017	2018–2019	RF	0.783	0.875	0.824	0.901
		XG	0.794	0.886	0.834	0.924
		CAT	0.794	0.894	**0.835**	**0.923**

RF = Random Forest, XG = XGBoost, CAT = CatBoost

We conduct experiments by setting the time interval to one and two years. We also explore whether the semantic layer can improve prediction accuracy with comparative experiments. The results are in Table 2.

Overall, our method shows good results with different models, indicating its robustness. Furthermore, the multiplex network has better performance than the single-layer network, which aligns with our expectations. CatBoost demonstrates more stable and excellent results among the three models. Our focus now lies on the results of multiplex networks. Regarding specific indicators, AUC assesses the overall performance of the classifier, and our scores range between 0.75 and 0.9, indicating good performance. PR evaluates the model's ability to predict positive samples, which is crucial for predicting the existence of future links. We have achieved an optimal value of 0.999 for this indicator, with an overall score above 0.85. Our previous analysis found that specific patents are more likely to be cited shortly after publication. Therefore, we select data from 2019 to 2020 for training and use data from 2021 to make predictions. Finally, we obtain 44,050 future edges with 664 nodes. Then, we extract them to construct the future network for analysis.

4.4   Topic Analysis

First, we conduct topic recognition again for the patents in the future network. The best topic number is 7, and we name each one according to its feature words. We put each patent into its most likely category, and the distribution results are in Fig. 10.

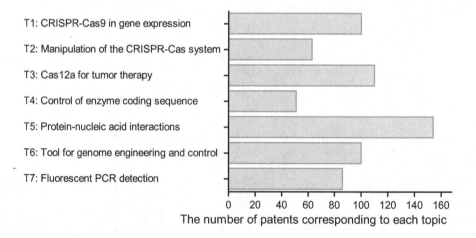

Fig. 10. The topic distribution in the future network

We can see that Topic 5 stands out. Protein-nucleic acid interactions are essential for several fundamental biological processes involving replication and transcription [46]. CRISPR systems are modular proteins that can be engineered to bind specific nucleic sequences [47]. Without such interactions, CRISPR can not perform its gene editing function. Therefore, this research direction deserves continuous investment. We also observe that Cas9 and Cas12a have a good prospect of application. Many diseases are often accompanied by deleterious genes during the course of development, and measures to inhibit this activation or restore the expression of protective genes are important for targeting certain chronic diseases [48]. Therefore, designing a modified form of Cas9 like dCas9 to regulate the expression of target genes is a potential. Compared to Cas9, Cas12a is more flexible in targeting specific gene sequences. It can play an important role in detecting circulating tumor DNA in complex microenvironments. Overall, our results are consistent with the current academic hot spots in CRISPR research (Fig. 11).

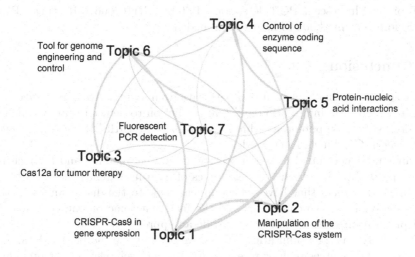

Fig. 11. Topic co-occurrence in the future network

Then, we explore the topic of co-occurrence relations. Topic 1, Topic 2, and Topic 5 are closely related. Analyzing these three subjects may provide valuable technical insights. Conversely, Topic 7 weakly connects to other topics, indicating its relative independence and numerous self-loops. Therefore, researchers may explore potential opportunities for technology convergence in this area.

Finally, we conduct a simple experiment to validate our results. We retrieve the CRISPR-related patents in 2022 and 2023 with the same strategy and fetch 3002 records. For each topic, we show a typical representative as evidence. Since the patent titles are too long, we choose to make a brief description.

Topic 1 (CRISPR-Cas9 in gene expression): Patent CN116875580-B utilizes Cas9 to perform site-directed mutations in the corn genome to obtain corn male sterile lines with different mutation types.

Topic 2 (Manipulation of the CRISPR-Cas system): Patent KR2500873-B1 utilizes CRISPR to design a gene manipulation technique for NK cells, which can help cancer therapy.

Topic 3 (Cas12a for tumor therapy): Patent JP2023546158-W utilizes Cas12a protein to generate a new composition for treating cancer.

Topic 4 (Control of enzyme coding sequence): Patent US11359187-B1 utilizes information in nucleic acid sequence to provide a system for identifying cells having genome that is rationally edited.

Topic 5 (Protein-nucleic acid interactions): Patent CN114934031-B utilizes Cas9 protein and guide RNA to generate CRISPR-CAS complex, which can be useful in preparing reagents for modifying target nucleic acid sequence.

Topic 6 (Tool for genome engineering and control): Patent CN114574516-B provides a method that is useful for stably integrating Cas9-based yeast genome in preparing yeast genetically engineered bacterium.

Topic 7 (Fluorescent PCR detection): Patent CN116790676-B utilizes PCR and Fluorescent methods to help screen medicine.

5 Conclusion

We explore the technology evolution pathways from a predictive perspective. We combine co-citation information and link prediction to detect future knowledge diffusion. We obtain potential technology topics in the CRISPR domain through the powerful Combined Topic Model.

Our study relies on the topic associations between patents and their citing counterparts. In other words, we use topics of existing patent collections to fit the topics of patents that have yet to appear. Due to the discrepancies in the topics between the two collections and the fact that some patents are cited in their publication year, we can only provide an approximate result.

Our study has some limitations. First, we only utilize the patent data, and including other sources such as research articles and web news might provide a more comprehensive understanding of the specific technology. However, adopting multi-resource data also means that our proposed methods require adjustments. When applying the framework to another technology field and the network is sparse, traditional indicators may not be practical because a sparse network might provide inadequate information. In this situation, deep learning methods like graph neural network may be more applicable. Finally, we do not mention the evolution relationship between the existing and potential topics. One could combine Zhang [8] and our study to for a complete analysis.

Acknowledgments. We appreciate the anonymous reviewers' careful examination of the manuscript and helpful comments. We appreciate Yihe Zhu, Yuanda Zhang, and Elysia Valentina for their help. We acknowledge support from the National Natural Science Foundation of China (Grant 72004169).

Disclosure of Interests. The authors have no competing interests to declare that are relevant to the content of this article.

References

1. Dosi, G.: Technological paradigms and technological trajectories: a suggested interpretation of the determinants and directions of technical change. Res. Policy **11**(3), 147–162 (1982). https://doi.org/10.1016/0048-7333(82)90016-6

2. Huang, Y., et al.: A hybrid method to trace technology evolution pathways: a case study of 3D printing. Scientometrics **111**(1), 185–204 (2017). https://doi.org/10.1007/s11192-017-2271-8

3. Huang, Y., Zhu, F., Porter, A.L., Zhang, Y., Zhu, D., Guo, Y.: Exploring technology evolution pathways to facilitate technology management: from a technology life cycle perspective. IEEE Trans. Eng. Manag. **68**(5), 1347–1359 (2021). https://doi.org/10.1109/TEM.2020.2966171

4. Chen, L., Xu, S., Zhu, L., Zhang, J., Xu, H., Yang, G.: A semantic main path analysis method to identify multiple developmental trajectories. J. Informet. **16**(2), 101281 (2022). https://doi.org/10.1016/j.joi.2022.101281

5. Hummon, N.P., Dereian, P.: Connectivity in a citation network: the development of DNA theory. Social Netw. **11**(1), 39–63 (1989)

6. Batagelj, V.: Efficient algorithms for citation network analysis (2003)

7. Liu, H., Chen, Z., Tang, J., Zhou, Y., Liu, S.: Mapping the technology evolution path: a novel model for dynamic topic detection and tracking. Scientometrics **125**(3), 2043–2090 (2020). https://doi.org/10.1007/s11192-020-03700-5

8. Zhang, Y., Xu, S., Yang, Y., Huang, Y.: Topic evolution analysis based on optimized combined topic model: illustrated as crispr technology. In: Sserwanga, I., et al. (eds.) Information for a Better World: Normality, Virtuality, Physicality, Inclusivity, vol. 13972, pp. 47–64. Springer, Cham (2023). https://doi.org/10.1007/978-3-031-28032-0_4

9. Gao, Q., Huang, X., Dong, K., Liang, Z., Wu, J.: Semantic-enhanced topic evolution analysis: a combination of the dynamic topic model and word2vec. Scientometrics **127**(3), 1543–1563 (2022). https://doi.org/10.1007/s11192-022-04275-z

10. Huang, L., Chen, X., Zhang, Y., Wang, C., Cao, X., Liu, J.: Identification of topic evolution: network analytics with piecewise linear representation and word embedding. Scientometrics **127**(9), 5353–5383 (2022). https://doi.org/10.1007/s11192-022-04273-1

11. Puccetti, G., Giordano, V., Spada, I., Chiarello, F., Fantoni, G.: Technology identification from patent texts: a novel named entity recognition method. Technol. Forecast. Social Change **186**, 122160 (2023). https://doi.org/10.1016/j.techfore.2022.122160. https://www.sciencedirect.com/science/article/pii/S0040162522006813

12. Wei, T., Jiang, T., Feng, D., Xiong, J.: Exploring the evolution of core technologies in agricultural machinery: a patent-based semantic mining analysis. Electronics **12**(20) (2023). https://doi.org/10.3390/electronics12204277. https://www.mdpi.com/2079-9292/12/20/4277

13. Hung, S.C., Liu, J.S., Lu, L.Y.Y., Tseng, Y.C.: Technological change in lithium iron phosphate battery: the key-route main path analysis. Scientometrics **100**(1), 97–120 (2014). https://doi.org/10.1007/s11192-014-1276-9

14. Li, M., Xu, X.: Tracing technological evolution and trajectory of biomass power generation: a patent-based analysis. Environ. Sci. Pollut. Res. **30**(12), 32814–32826 (2022). https://doi.org/10.1007/s11356-022-24339-0

15. Smojver, V., Štorga, M., Zovak, G.: Exploring knowledge flow within a technology domain by conducting a dynamic analysis of a patent co-citation network. J. Knowl. Manag. **25**(2), 433–453 (2021). https://doi.org/10.1108/JKM-01-2020-0079

16. Lü, L., Zhou, T.: Link prediction in complex networks: a survey. Phys. A **390**(6), 1150–1170 (2011). https://doi.org/10.1016/j.physa.2010.11.027
17. Zhou, T.: Progresses and challenges in link prediction. iScience **24**(11), 103217 (2021). https://doi.org/10.1016/j.isci.2021.103217
18. Wang, P., Xu, B., Wu, Y., Zhou, X.: Link prediction in social networks: the state-of-the-art. Sci. China Inf. Sci. **58**(1), 1–38 (2014). https://doi.org/10.1007/s11432-014-5237-y
19. Wu, H., Song, C., Ge, Y., Ge, T.: Link prediction on complex networks: an experimental survey. Data Sci. Eng. **7**(3), 253–278 (2022). https://doi.org/10.1007/s41019-022-00188-2
20. Shibata, N., Kajikawa, Y., Sakata, I.: Link prediction in citation networks. J. Am. Soc. Inf. Sci. Technol. **63**(1), 78–85 (2012). https://doi.org/10.1002/asi.21664
21. Cardillo, A., et al.: Emergence of network features from multiplexity. Sci. Rep. **3**(1), 1344 (2013). https://doi.org/10.1038/srep01344
22. Granell, C., Gómez, S., Arenas, A.: Dynamical interplay between awareness and epidemic spreading in multiplex networks. Phys. Rev. Lett. **111**(12), 128701 (2013). https://doi.org/10.1103/PhysRevLett.111.128701
23. Yao, Y., et al.: Link prediction via layer relevance of multiplex networks. Int. J. Mod. Phys. C **28**(8), 1750101 (2017). https://doi.org/10.1142/s0129183117501017
24. Shan, N., Li, L., Zhang, Y., Bai, S., Chen, X.: Supervised link prediction in multiplex networks. Knowl.-Based Syst. **203**, 106168 (2020). https://doi.org/10.1016/j.knosys.2020.106168
25. Bai, S., Zhang, Y., Li, L., Shan, N., Chen, X.: Effective link prediction in multiplex networks: a topsis method. Expert Syst. Appl. **177**, 114973 (2021). https://doi.org/10.1016/j.eswa.2021.114973
26. Yoon, B., Kim, S., Kim, S., Seol, H.: Doc2vec-based link prediction approach using SAO structures: application to patent network. Scientometrics **127**(9), 5385–5414 (2022). https://doi.org/10.1007/s11192-021-04187-4
27. Vital, A., Amancio, D.R.: A comparative analysis of local similarity metrics and machine learning approaches: application to link prediction in author citation networks. Scientometrics **127**(10), 6011–6028 (2022). https://doi.org/10.1007/s11192-022-04484-6
28. Song, B., Suh, Y.: Identifying convergence fields and technologies for industrial safety: LDA-based network analysis. Technol. Forecast. Soc. Chang. **138**, 115–126 (2019). https://doi.org/10.1016/j.techfore.2018.08.013
29. Qiu, Z., Wang, Z.: Technology forecasting based on semantic and citation analysis of patents: a case of robotics domain. IEEE Trans. Eng. Manag. **69**(4), 1216–1236 (2022). https://doi.org/10.1109/TEM.2020.2978849
30. Liu, Y., Chen, M.: The knowledge structure and development trend in artificial intelligence based on latent feature topic model. IEEE Trans. Eng. Manag. 1–12 (2023). https://doi.org/10.1109/TEM.2022.3232178
31. Blei, D.M., Ng, A.Y., Jordan, M.I.: Latent Dirichlet allocation. J. Mach. Learn. Res. **3**, 993–1022 (2003)
32. Teh, Y.W., Jordan, M.I., Beal, M.J., Blei, D.M.: Hierarchical Dirichlet processes. J. Am. Stat. Assoc. **101**(476), 1566–1581 (2006). https://doi.org/10.1198/016214506000000302
33. Devlin, J., Chang, M.W., Lee, K., Toutanova, K.: Bert: pre-training of deep bidirectional transformers for language understanding (2019)
34. Bianchi, F., Terragni, S., Hovy, D.: Pre-training is a hot topic: contextualized document embeddings improve topic coherence (2021)

35. Srivastava, A., Sutton, C.: Autoencoding variational inference for topic models (2017)
36. OuYang, K., Weng, C.S.: A new comprehensive patent analysis approach for new product design in mechanical engineering. Technol. Forecast. Soc. Chang. **78**(7), 1183–1199 (2011). https://doi.org/10.1016/j.techfore.2011.02.012
37. Filippin, F.: Do main paths reflect technological trajectories? applying main path analysis to the semiconductor manufacturing industry. Scientometrics **126**(8), 6443–6477 (2021). https://doi.org/10.1007/s11192-021-04023-9
38. Röder, M., Both, A., Hinneburg, A.: Exploring the space of topic coherence measures. In: Proceedings of the Eighth ACM International Conference on Web Search and Data Mining, pp. 399–408. ACM, Shanghai (2015). https://doi.org/10.1145/2684822.2685324
39. Boccaletti, S., et al.: The structure and dynamics of multilayer networks. Phys. Rep. **544**(1), 1–122 (2014). https://doi.org/10.1016/j.physrep.2014.07.001
40. Huang, L., Chen, X., Ni, X., Liu, J., Cao, X., Wang, C.: Tracking the dynamics of co-word networks for emerging topic identification. Technol. Forecast. Soc. Chang. **170**, 120944 (2021). https://doi.org/10.1016/j.techfore.2021.120944
41. Ishino, Y., Shinagawa, H., Makino, K., Amemura, M., Nakata, A.: Nucleotide sequence of the iap gene, responsible for alkaline phosphatase isozyme conversion in escherichia coli, and identification of the gene product. J. Bacteriol. **169**(12), 5429–5433 (1987). https://doi.org/10.1128/jb.169.12.5429-5433.1987
42. Mojica, F.J.M., Juez, G., Rodriguez-Valera, F.: Transcription at different salinities of haloferax mediterranei sequences adjacent to partially modified psti sites. Mol. Microbiol. **9**(3), 613–621 (1993). https://doi.org/10.1111/j.1365-2958.1993.tb01721.x
43. Jinek, M., Chylinski, K., Fonfara, I., Hauer, M., Doudna, J.A., Charpentier, E.: A programmable dual-rna–guided dna endonuclease in adaptive bacterial immunity. Science **337**(6096), 816–821 (2012). https://doi.org/10.1126/science.1225829
44. Cong, L.: Multiplex genome engineering using crispr/cas systems. Science **339**(6121), 819–823 (2013). https://doi.org/10.1126/science.1231143
45. Gu, Y., et al.: Domain-specific language model pretraining for biomedical natural language processing. ACM Trans. Comput. Healthcare **3**(1), 1–23 (2022). https://doi.org/10.1145/3458754
46. Zhang, X., Mei, L., Gao, Y., Hao, G., Song, B.: Web tools support predicting protein-nucleic acid complexes stability with affinity changes. WIREs RNA **14**(5) (2023). https://doi.org/10.1002/wrna.1781
47. Pickar-Oliver, A., Gersbach, C.A.: The next generation of crispr-cas technologies and applications. Nat. Rev. Molecu. Cell Biol. **20**(8), 490–507 (2019). https://doi.org/10.1038/s41580-019-0131-5
48. Li, T., et al.: Crispr/cas9 therapeutics: progress and prospects. Signal Transd. Target. Therapy **8**(1) (2023). https://doi.org/10.1038/s41392-023-01309-7

Matching Patent and Research Field Classifications Using Lexical Similarity and Bipartite Network—Evidence from Colombia

Julián D. Cortés[1,2]([✉]) [ID] and María Catalina Ramírez-Cajiao[2] [ID]

[1] School of Management and Business, Universidad del Rosario, Bogotá, Colombia
julian.cortess@urosario.edu.co
[2] Engineering School, Universidad de Los Andes, Bogotá, Colombia

Abstract. Patentometrics in middle and low-income countries is an emergent field. Here, we propose a methodological appraisal which combines text mining (lexical similarity) and network science (bipartite network) to associate the inventive structure of research and patents by matching classification standards in a middle-income country, Colombia, as a pilot study. We sourced and processed a sample of 2900+ patents and 42,800+ research articles. First, we matched two research and patenting classification standards using lexical similarity and modeled their connections using a bi-partite network. Based on this matching, we identified frequent correspondence between the research fields and the patent sections. Then, we estimated the correlation between research and patenting output-proxy as a national inventive and scientific capacity. There is no overall significant relationship between inventive and scientific capacities. Global and local factors, such as the growth of knowledge specialization or bypassing the path dependency of science and inventive capacities, shed light on this misalignment.

Keywords: Patents · Patentometrics · Bibliometrics · Network science · Text mining

1 Introduction

The study of the inventive structure in middle and low-income countries is a field with barely any fruit trees. We define an inventive structure as an abstract-information-based network that emerged from the inter-relationship between the standard classification assigned to patents [16, 41, 45]. There is a well-established research agenda on the inventive structure, production, and impact of patents in high-income countries [4, 7, 20, 30]. However, implementing these methodological and theoretical frameworks in middle and low-income regions, such as Latin America and the Caribbean (LAC), has not gone further than descriptive statistics; concrete insights on collaboration networks and fields (e.g., immunology); econometric growth models; and text mining on historical patent data [1, 5–7, 27, 31].

© The Author(s), under exclusive license to Springer Nature Switzerland AG 2024
I. Sserwanga et al. (Eds.): iConference 2024, LNCS 14597, pp. 122–130, 2024.
https://doi.org/10.1007/978-3-031-57860-1_9

This research in progress explores the relationship between the inventive structure of patents and research by matching patent and research classification standards in Colombia as a pilot study. Our contribution is threefold. First, we provide an outlook of the matching capacities and output of both inventive and research agendas, a vital assessment in countries with scarce R&D (Research and Development) investment and limited scientific human capital [38, 39]. Second, it expands the LAC-Colombian patentometrics and bibliometrics research through a novel approach to patent semantic analysis [3, 19]. And third, our findings add to a growing interest in examining country level case—particularly, middle-low-income regions [11–14, 23, 29].

2   Data and Methodology

2.1   Classification Standards and Databases

Patents and Research Field. We considered two classification systems, namely the International Patent Classification (IPC) and the All-Science Journals Classification (ASJC). First, the IPC is the international standard for patents retrieval and inventive non-obviousness assessment, classified into eight sections: A-Human necessities; B-performing operations, transporting; C-chemistry, metallurgy; D-textiles, paper; E-fixed constructions; F-mechanical engineering, lighting, heating, weapons, blasting; G-physics; and H-electricity [41]. Second, the ASJC is a standard system designed by experts at Elsevier's Scopus to assign a journal a single or multiple fields, classified into five areas namely physical sciences, life sciences, health sciences, social sciences & humanities, and multidisciplinary [34]. With these two well-established classification standards, we matched plausive similarities between inventive sections and research fields. On a minor note, there are concerns and discussions about how reliable are patents to study innovation or inventiveness dynamics in a country [32]. While such a wider discussion is not aimed to be solved in this study, patents are still being used in the study of innovation disruption and technological improvement rates [37, 44].

Patents and Scientific Publications Databases. We replicated the search query for Colombian patents used by Cortés and Ramírez-Cajiao [16] in PATENTSCOPE, the World Intellectual Property Organization (WIPO) database with over 107 million patent documents [42]. This query sourced patents in which the: i) applicant address country; or ii) applicant nationality; or iii) applicant residence; or iv) inventor nationality, was Colombia(n). We sourced 2916 patents between 1983 and 2021. Regarding scientific publications, we used Scopus [33]. Scopus has 77 million items authored from 16 million authors affiliated with 70,000+ institutions [35]. We replicated the search query used by Cortés and Ramírez-Cajiao [15] to source 42,800+ research articles published by at least one author affiliated with a Colombian institution and limited to journals with at least 50 articles between 1996–2022 (i.e., ~2 articles publish by an author with Colombian affiliation every year in such a journal). The latter restriction aims to source research output with demonstrable national maturity and research capacities.

2.2 Methods

We implemented techniques from patentometrics, text mining and network science. Patentometrics study patents and citations through methods deriving from bibliometrics [21]. Text mining applies statistical techniques methods to analyze large-scale textual sources, finding complex patterns and meanings [25]. From network science, we used the bipartite network approach [24, 28].

Patents Semantic and Text Mining Analysis. We used patents semantic instead of a citation appraisal [22]. Our main reason for this is the high citations concentration in high-income countries. For instance, there is no Latin-American institution ranked among the Top 100 Global Innovators report, which considers both patents and research citation indicators [40]. Therefore, we consider instead patents and scientific output, not their impact by high-income countries' standards. Such an appraisal is being used elsewhere to run comprehensive examinations of middle and low-income countries' structure of research, University-Industry research fronts, and disciplinary consensus [8–11].

We matched patent and research field classifications via a lexical similarity approach. The technique applied was the *soundex* algorithm [26]. This algorithm identifies similar-sounding strings. For instance, the algorithm scored a higher similarity between IPC-class A01: *agriculture; forestry; animal husbandry; hunting; trapping; fishing*, and ASJC-field 1100: *general agricultural and biological sciences*. We defined a comparable number of IPC and ASJC sub-classifications. The IPC is way more refined with 79,000+ subclasses, compared to 334 ASJC-fields. Therefore, we applied the lexical similarity approach to 132 IPC-classes and 334 ASJC-fields. Multiple ASJC could be assigned to one IPC-class. We hand-curated the matching to add missing processed IPC-classes and ASJC-fields.

Bipartite Network. Bipartite networks are suitable for examining and represent diverse and real world mutualistic networks, from transportation systems, epidemiology or trade, to the World Wide Web [24, 36]. This type of network comprises two distinct types of nodes, with links only between different nodes [24]. Here, type-1 nodes are IPC-classes and type-2 are ASJC-fields. An undirected link is created between a node of type-1 and a node type-2 if a high lexical similarity was detected. Multiple links between a single type-1 node and several type-2 nodes could be assigned. At the node level, we computed the degree: a standard indicator on the number of links the node has to other nodes,

$$C_D(p_k) = \sum_{i=1}^{n} a(p_i, p_k) \tag{1}$$

where n is the number of nodes and $a(p_i, p_k) = 1$ if and only if the node i and k are linked; $a(p_i, p_k) = 0$ otherwise [28]. We shared a file with the network edge list, node features, and Fig. 1 in high-quality format in the following link: http://bit.ly/3mUkBd5.

3 Results

The automated and hand-curated method for lexical similarity method proposed matched 113 (85%) IPC-classes with 105 (31%) of the ASJC-fields. Multiple IPC-classes found no match in ASJC-fields considering that research-related activities that might not include (useful) arts (e.g., footwear, hand cutting tools, cutting, writing, or drawing implements, bureau accessories severing, among others). In this process, we identified unexplored ASJC-fields with no frequency, particularly in physical science (26 fields, such as applied mathematics, artificial intelligence, or automotive engineering), health sciences (six fields, such as emergency medical services, food animals, or health informatics), and social sciences and humanities (five fields, such as developmental and educational psychology, information systems and management, or life-span and life-course studies).

Figure 1 displays the bipartite network. The network has 218 nodes and 293 links. Most of the matched IPC-classes nodes (type-1 nodes connected at least once with a type-2 nodes) were from B-performing operations, transporting section (~16%), followed by C-chemistry, metallurgy (~9%), and F-mechanical engineering, lighting, heating, weapons, blasting (~8%). Most of the matched ASJC-fields were from physical sciences (~29%), followed by social sciences & humanities (~8%) and life sciences (~7%). IPC nodes with high degree indicators (i.e., over 6), were from the G-physics and H-electricity sections (e.g., information and communication technology specially adapted for specific application fields; information storage; and generation, conversion, or distribution of electric power). Those from the ASJC (i.e., degree over 11), were similarly from the physical sciences (e.g., industrial and manufacturing engineering, mechanics of materials, and general materials science).

As a proxy variable for productivity, we calculated the frequency of IPC-class by patent and ASJC-fields by journal where each article was published. The most frequent IPC-classes were A6-medical or veterinary science; hygiene (1798 times); followed by A01-agriculture; forestry; animal husbandry; hunting; trapping; fishing (440 times); and C12-biochemistry; beer; spirits; wine; vinegar; microbiology; enzymology; mutation or genetic engineering (439 times). The most frequent ASJC-fields were general engineering (3824 times), followed by animal science and zoology (2672 times), and general agricultural and biological sciences (2401 times).

There are cases of high co-occurrence between IPC-classes and ASJC-fields. However, those are not systematically correlated. For instance, both IPC-class: agriculture, forestry, animal husbandry, hunting, trapping, fishing; and ASJC-field: animal science and zoology, are lexically linked and highly frequent. Another case is that of the IPC-class: biochemistry, beer, spirits, wine, vinegar, microbiology; enzymology, mutation; and ASJC-field: genetic engineering, and general chemistry. In sum, there is no correlation between IPC-class and ASJC-fields frequency in Colombia, $r(292) = .06, p > .5; 95\% conf.interval : [-.04; .18]$. Therefore, our findings do not support a matching national capacity between inventive and scientific production.

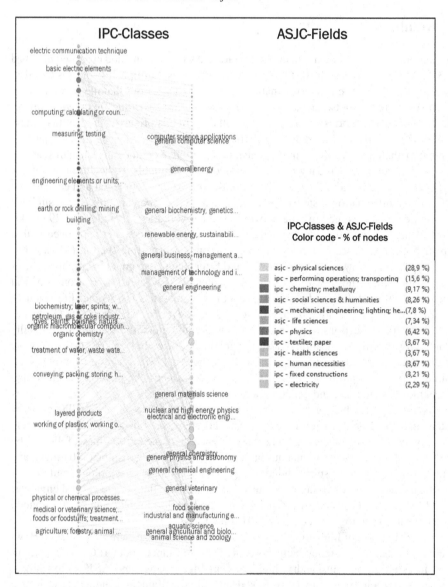

Fig. 1. Bipartite network of matching results between IPC-classes and ASJC-fields. Note: visible labels only for top-20 most frequent IPC-class and ASJC-fields. Node size is proportional to its degree. Source: Scopus & WIPO [34, 41]; network layout using Gephi [2].

4   Discussion and Conclusion

We aimed to explore the relationship between the inventive structure of patents and research by matching patents and research fields' classification standards in Colombia as a pilot study. In countries with few resources and human capacities for R&D, our results can inform decision-making practices in the private or public sectors to visualize the alignment between basic and applied research and inventive capacities, drawing paths between both sources of knowledge.

One study on historical data on Colombian patents between 1930 and 2000 found a high quantity of patents classified in the IPC-section A-human necessities, followed by B-performing operations, transporting, and E-fixed constructions [7]. Our results updated and contrasted those findings since there was a shift to other sections, such as C-chemistry, metallurgy and F-mechanical engineering, lighting, heating, weapons, blasting. High-income countries are publishing large volumes of patents in energy-related technologies (e.g., fuel cell technology, wind energy, geothermal energy), which are concentrated in sections such as H-electricity and F-mechanical engineering, lighting [43].

The relevance of the F-Section is also important at the structural level. One study on the inventive structure of Colombia, computed the betweenness centrality (i.e., an indicator at the node level that unveils the capacity of nodes to interlink inventive characteristics between central and peripheral nodes) of IPC-subclasses [16]. This study found that Section-F subclass: *"machines or engines for liquids; wind, spring, or weight motors; producing mechanical power or a reactive propulsive thrust, not otherwise provided for,"* has the highest betweenness.

The mismatch between inventive and research capacities adds to a stream of evidence which points towards an atomization and disconnection between Science, Technology and Innovation Policies (STIP); and the scientific workforce, national research fronts, and research path dependency in Colombia [14, 15, 17, 18]. Multiple factors might explain this misalignment, such as the growth of knowledge specialization; international collaboration; time-lag between STIP implementation and impact; and bypassing path dependency of science and inventive capacities, among others [15].

Studies on scientific-technological innovation in higher income regions could shed light on the innovation dynamics in different country-based contexts. A study conducted in the US [37] aimed to predict the yearly performance improvement rates for various technology domains. It found that technological domains such as *Dynamic information exchange and support systems integrating multiple channels* exhibited the highest improvement rate, compared to the *Mechanical Skin treatment- Hair Removal and wrinkles,* which showed the lowest improvement rate. Also, it was found that fast improving domains, such as software and algorithm-driven innovations, are concentrated in a few technological areas. Meanwhile, here we found that the most frequent IPC-classes and ASJC-fields were associated with agriculture, animal science, and general engineering. The lack of correlation between IPC-class and ASJC-fields frequency in Colombia further highlights the complexities of measuring and interpreting patterns of scientific and technological innovation in developing countries. The brief discussion of both approaches underscores the need for a multifaceted approach to understanding and measuring technological innovation in middle-low-income countries.

Partly virtue, partly limitation of our study is the in-depth focus in a single country and the exclusive use of Scopus as a bibliographic database. The lexical similarity applied to IPC-classes can be more comprehensive by including subsequent hierarchies (i.e., such as subclasses and groups) and using wider science/research classification systems. In further stages of the project, the scope to other middle and low-income can be expanded. More diverse and robust network indicators and methodologies (e.g., multilayer networks) can be implemented. Concerning the limitation of Scopus, further stages could integrate further bibliographic databases (e.g., OpenAlex, Dimensions) or additional variables related to inventive and scientific workforce-stock and mobility could be included.

References

1. Agüero Aguilar, C.E.: Redes de colaboración y producción de patentes en universidades de la Comunidad Andina de Naciones (UCANS) 2005–2015. Rev. Española Doc. Científica. **40**(2 SE-Estudios), e172 (2017). https://doi.org/10.3989/redc.2017.2.1401
2. Bastian, M., et al.: Gephi: an open source software for exploring and manipulating networks. In: International AAAI Conference on Weblogs and Social Media (2009)
3. Bergeaud, A., et al.: Classifying patents based on their semantic content. PLoS ONE **12**, 4 (2017). https://doi.org/10.1371/journal.pone.0176310
4. Bettencourt, L.M.A., et al.: Urban scaling and its deviations: Revealing the structure of wealth, innovation and crime across cities. PLoS ONE **5**(11), 1–9 (2010). https://doi.org/10.1371/jou rnal.pone.0013541
5. Campo Robledo, J., Herrera Saavedra, J.P.: Patentes y crecimiento económico: innovación de residentes o no residentes? Rev. Desarro. y Soc. **76**, 243–272 (2016). https://doi.org/10.13043/dys.76.6
6. Campos Jiménez, E., Campos Ferrer, A.: Análisis biotecnológico de Latinoamérica a través de las patentes en Inmunología. Rev. Cuba. Inf. en Ciencias la Salud. **25**(2), 172–182 (2014)
7. Cortés-Sánchez, J.D.: Patents for all: a content analysis of an open-access dataset of Colombian patents 1930–2000. In: Pardo Martínez, C.I., et al. (eds.) Analysis of Science, Technology, and Innovation in Emerging Economies, pp. 65–93. Springer, Cham (2019). https://doi.org/10.1007/978-3-030-13578-2_4
8. Cortés, J.D.: Dissension or consensus? Management and business research in Latin America and the Caribbean. In: Glänzel, W., et al. (eds.) 18th International Conference on Scientometrics and Informetrics, ISSI 2021, pp. 293–298. International Society for Scientometrics and Informetrics, Leuven (2021)
9. Cortés, J.D.: Identifying the dissension in management and business research in Latin America and the Caribbean via co-word analysis. Scientometrics **127**(12), 7111–7125 (2022). https://doi.org/10.1007/s11192-021-04259-5
10. Cortés, J.D.: Industry-research fronts – Private sector collaboration with research institutions in Latin America and the Caribbean. J. Inf. Sci. In press. 016555152211317 (2023). https://doi.org/10.1177/01655515221131796
11. Cortés, J.D., et al.: Innovation for sustainability in the Global South: bibliometric findings from management & business and STEM (science, technology, engineering and mathematics) fields in developing countries. Heliyon. **7**(8), e07809 (2021). https://doi.org/10.1016/j.hel iyon.2021.e07809
12. Cortés, J.D., Andrade, D.A.: The Colombian scientific elite—Science mapping and a comparison with Nobel Prize laureates using a composite citation indicator. PLoS One. **17**(5), e0269116 (2022). https://doi.org/10.1371/journal.pone.0269116
13. Cortés, J.D., Andrade, D.A.: Winners and runners-up alike?—a comparison between awardees and special mention recipients of the most reputable science award in Colombia via a composite citation indicator. Humanit. Soc. Sci. Commun. **9**(1), 217 (2022). https://doi.org/10.1057/s41599-022-01241-1
14. Cortés, J.D., Ramirez-Cajiao, M.C.: The Missing Linkage Between Science Technology and Innovation Policy and the Scientific Workforce — Evidence from Colombia. Submitted (2023)

15. Cortés, J.D., Ramírez-Cajiao, M.C.: Is Science Technology and Innovation Policy related to National Research Fronts? Submitted (2023)

16. Cortés, J.D., Ramírez-Cajiao, M.C.: Mapping the inventive structure in middle-low income countries — The patent network of Colombia. Submitted (2023)

17. Cortés, J.D., Ramírez-Cajiao, M.C.: The Content Structure of Science Technology and Innovation Policy — Applying co-word analysis to funding calls in Colombia. In: Sserwanga, I., et al. (eds.) Lecture Notes in Computer Science (including subseries Lecture Notes in Artificial Intelligence and Lecture Notes in Bioinformatics), vol. 2, pp. 187–196. Springer, Cham (2023)

18. Cortés, J.D., Ramírez-Cajiao, M.C.: The Policy is Dead, Long Live the Policy — Unveiling Science Technology and Innovation Policy Priorities and Government Transitions via Network Analysis. Submitted (2023)

19. Gerken, J.M., Moehrle, M.G.: A new instrument for technology monitoring: novelty in patents measured by semantic patent analysis. Scientometrics **91**(3), 645–670 (2012). https://doi.org/10.1007/s11192-012-0635-7

20. Hall, B.H., et al.: Market value and patent citations. RAND J. Econ. **36**(1), 16–38 (2005)

21. Hammarfelt, B.: Linking science to technology: the "patent paper citation" and the rise of patentometrics in the 1980s. J. Doc. **77**(6), 1413–1429 (2021). https://doi.org/10.1108/JD-12-2020-0218

22. Hung, W.C.: Measuring the use of public research in firm R&D in the Hsinchu Science Park. Scientometrics **92**(1), 63–73 (2012). https://doi.org/10.1007/s11192-012-0726-5

23. Khanna, S., et al.: Recalibrating the scope of scholarly publishing: a modest step in a vast decolonization process. Quant. Sci. Stud. 1–19 (2023). https://doi.org/10.1162/QSS_A_00228

24. Liew, C.Y. et al.: A methodology framework for bipartite network modeling. Appl. Netw. Sci. **8**(1), 6 (2023). https://doi.org/10.1007/s41109-023-00533-y

25. Macanovic, A.: Text mining for social science – The state and the future of computational text analysis in sociology. Soc. Sci. Res. **108**, 102784 (2022). https://doi.org/10.1016/j.ssresearch.2022.102784

26. National Archives: Soundex System. https://www.archives.gov/research/census/soundex. Accessed 07 Feb 2023

27. OCyT. Tableros CTeI 2020 – Portal de datos 2021. https://portal.ocyt.org.co/tableros-ctei-2020/. Accessed 19 Sept 2022

28. Opsahl, T., et al.: Node centrality in weighted networks: generalizing degree and shortest paths. Soc. Netw. **32**(3), 245–251 (2010). https://doi.org/10.1016/j.socnet.2010.03.006

29. Rodríguez-Navarro, A., Brito, R.: The link between countries' economic and scientific wealth has a complex dependence on technological activity and research policy. Scientometrics **127**(5), 2871–2896 (2022). https://doi.org/10.1007/s11192-022-04313-w

30. Rodríguez-Salvador, M., et al.: Scientometric and patentometric analyses to determine the knowledge landscape in innovative technologies: the case of 3D bioprinting. PLoS ONE **12**(6), 1–22 (2017). https://doi.org/10.1371/journal.pone.0180375

31. Sánchez, J.M., et al.: Publicación internacional de patentes por organizaciones e inventores de origen colombiano. Cuad. Econ. **26**(47), 249–270 (2007)

32. Schwall, A., Wagner, J.: The persistence of worthless patents? World Pat. Inf. **72**, 102179 (2023). https://doi.org/10.1016/j.wpi.2023.102179

33. Scopus. Scopus - Document Search. https://bit.ly/3KhKoDn. Accessed 01 June 2020

34. Scopus. What is the complete list of Scopus Subject Areas and All Science Journal Classification Codes (ASJC)? https://service.elsevier.com/app/answers/detail/a_id/15181/supporthub/scopus/. Accessed 10 Dec 2021

35. Scopus - Research Intelligence. Content Coverage Guide (2020)

36. Scott, J.: Social Network Analysis - A Handbook. SAGE Publications Ltd, London (2009)
37. Singh, A., et al.: Technological improvement rate predictions for all technologies: use of patent data and an extended domain description. Res. Policy **50**(9), 104294 (2021). https://doi.org/10.1016/j.respol.2021.104294
38. The World Bank. Data: Research and development expenditure (% of GDP). https://bit.ly/3qzhwia. Accessed 18 Jan 2022
39. UNESCO. UIS Statistics. http://data.uis.unesco.org/Index.aspx. Accessed 22 Sept 2022
40. White, E., Hanganu, M.: Top 100 Global Innovators (2023)
41. WIPO. Guide to the International Patent Classification (2022)
42. WIPO. PATENTSCOPE. https://patentscope.wipo.int/search/es/search.jsf. Accessed 19 Sept 2022
43. WIPO: World Intellectual Property Indicators 2020. (2020). https://doi.org/10.34667/TIND.42184
44. Wu, L., et al.: Large teams develop and small teams disrupt science and technology. Nature **566**(7744), 378–382 (2019). https://doi.org/10.1038/s41586-019-0941-9
45. Yan, E., Ding, Y.: Scholarly network similarities: how bibliographic coupling networks, citation networks, cocitation networks, topical networks, coauthorship networks, and coword networks relate to each other. J. Am. Soc. Inf. Sci. Technol. **63**(7), 1313–1326 (2012). https://doi.org/10.1002/asi.22680

Mapping the Inventive Structure in Middle-Low Income Countries—The Patent Network of Colombia

Julián D. Cortés[1,2]([✉]) [iD] and María Catalina Ramírez-Cajiao[2] [iD]

[1] School of Management and Business, Universidad del Rosario, Bogotá, Colombia
julian.cortess@urosario.edu.co
[2] Engineering School, Universidad de Los Andes, Bogotá, Colombia

Abstract. Patentometrics studies in middle-low-income countries is an emergent field. This study aims to unveil the inventive structure of Colombia from 1983–2021 as a pilot case. Applying the co-word analysis network analysis to the IPC (International Patent Classification) subclasses of +2,900 patents granted to inventors/applicants with Colombian affiliation/origin, we constructed the inventive network for three periods 1983–2000, 2001–2010, 2011–2021, and detected highly strategic IPC subclasses. Furthermore, we identify the structural changes by IPC sections and highlight the clustering properties of IPC sections for Colombia, such as C-Chemistry, metallurgy; A-Human necessities; B-Performing operations, transporting; G-Physics; and F-mechanical engineering, lighting, heating, weapons, blasting.

Keywords: Patents · Patentometrics · Bibliometrics · Network science · Text mining

1 Introduction

Patentometrics is an emerging field that studies patent production and citations via methods from bibliometrics [10]. It studies the production (e.g., number of patents per million inhabitants), structure (e.g., patents co-inventors or co-applicant networks; gender roles), and impact (e.g., research articles cited in patents, patents cited in patents) of national, regional, or organizational inventive capacities [2, 6, 9, 14].

There was a global patent application increase despite the COVID-19 pandemic economic downturn. Out of 3.3 million patent applications in 2020—an increase of 1.6% compared to 2019—1.6% was generated from LAC offices [18]. Besides full-counting, descriptive statistics, and specific insights on collaboration networks between universities, econometric growth models, immunology patenting, and text mining on historical patent data, the stream of research on the inventive structure of Latin-America & Caribbean (LAC) is still ongoing work [1, 4–6, 11, 15].

This research in progress aims to unveil the inventive structure of Colombia from 1983–2021 as a pilot case using patentometrics techniques. We define an inventive structure as an abstract-information-based network that emerged from the inter-relationship

I. Sserwanga et al. (Eds.): iConference 2024, LNCS 14597, pp. 131–137, 2024.
https://doi.org/10.1007/978-3-031-57860-1_10

between the standard classification assigned to patents [16, 20]. The preliminary insights presented here are part of a Ph.D. project to study similar phenomena in LAC and other middle-low-income countries. Our contribution expands the LAC-Colombian patento-metrics research stream by introducing the bibliometric-science mapping technique of co-word analysis to unveil the inventive structure of patents granted to inventors or appli-cants in Colombia as a pilot case. Furthermore, identifying strategic patent classes can enlighten private or public sector policies on dimensions of growth and interconnec-tion of the inventive activity. After this introduction, we describe the source material and methods. Then, we present our results. Finally, we outline the discussion and conclusion.

2 Methodology

2.1 Materials

We source patent data from PATENTSCOPE: the open WIPO database to International Patent Cooperation Treaty (PCT) applications which holds data on 107 million patent documents [19]. Our search equation was: AADC: (CO) OR ANA: (CO) OR ARE: (CO) OR IADC: (CO). It returned patents in which the: i) applicant address country; or ii) applicant nationality; or iii) applicant residence; or iv) inventor nationality, was Colombia(n). We source a total of 2,916 patents from 1983–2021.

2.2 Methods

We focused our analysis on the International Patent Classification (IPC) assigned to each patent to build a patent network applying co-word analysis. The IPC is the uniform international classification of patent documents established in 1971. It aims to institute an effective search tool for the retrieval of patent documents, thus facilitating the evaluation of inventive steps or non-obviousness of technical disclosures in patent applications [16]. The IPC is divided into four hierarchy levels: i) section; ii) class; iii) subclass; and iv) group. There are eight sections, with their correspondent capital letters A through H: A-Human necessities; B-performing operations; transporting; C-chemistry; metallurgy; D-textiles, paper; E-fixed constructions; F-mechanical engineering, lighting, heating, weapons, blasting; G-physics; and H-electricity [16]. A well-known exemplary patent could be "Lasers" with the IPC: H01S 3/00. It reads as follows: i) section "H": electricity; ii) class "01": basic electric elements; iii) subclass "S": "devices using the process of light amplification by stimulated emission of radiation [laser] to amplify or generate light"; and iv) groups "3/00": lasers.

There are patents assigned to multiple IPC. It applies when invention information relates to multiple inventive things that can be classified into different groups [16]. Therefore, a patent could be an invention connecting multiple areas in the IPC body of knowledge. Such is the case of the patent *"Method for real-time detection of power transmission lines using unmanned aerial vehicles,"* which has six IPC classifications from sections B, G, and H. Therefore, we restricted our analysis to the IPC subclass for a medium-level granularity of patents with more than two IPC classifications (i.e., IPC triads). Since we follow a structural approach, triadic configurations are the basis for network theoretical and empirical structural features [7]. Therefore, the patents with one or two IPC subclasses were excluded and will be part of further analyses, such as those related to net-output or textual analysis of the complete corpus. Also, since we maintain the established classification of the IPC subclasses to group patents, we did not apply any additional cut-off or cluster algorithm.

We used co-word analysis considering the relational nature of the IPC data. This approach establishes the connection between words (i.e., concepts, problems, ideas) and combines network analysis techniques to unveil their underlying structure [3]. Table 1 presents an example of how to build an undirected weighted co-word network with the IPC data of each patent based on the example mentioned above. We built an edge list based on 8,654 unchained IPC subclasses per patent. We computed the betweenness centrality to identify relevant IPC subclass, i.e., nodes. Nodes with high betweenness can link different IPC subclass clusters and the inventive characteristics between central and peripheral nodes in the network [8]. Equation 1 shows how to calculate a node's betweenness [13].

$$C_B(p_k) = \sum_{i<j}^{n} \frac{g_{ij}(p_k)}{g_{ij}}; i \neq j \neq k \tag{1}$$

where gij is the shorter path that links nodes pi and $gij(pk)$ is the shorter path that links nodes pi and $pjpk$. The higher the value, the higher its betweenness. We also divided our analysis into three periods 1983–2000, 2001–2010, and 2011–2021. IPC subclass year was anchored to the first year a patent with that IPC subclass assigned was published. We implemented the circular layout algorithm for network visualization.

Table 1. IPC subclass network example based on co-word network analysis.

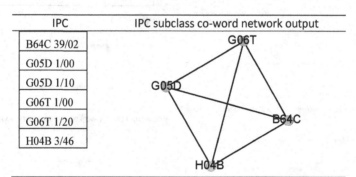

IPC	IPC subclass co-word network output
B64C 39/02	
G05D 1/00	
G05D 1/10	
G06T 1/00	
G06T 1/20	
H04B 3/46	

3   Results

The following temporary link provides open access to the network indicators https://bit.ly/3S3a6ij. A permanent link will be provided in the research article version of this ongoing research. For the 1983–2000 network (Fig. 1), the structure of Colombian inventive was composed of 65 unique IPC subclasses, primarily clustered in the C-Chemistry, metallurgy section, followed by A-Human necessities, and B-Performing operations, transporting. The IPC subclass with the highest betweenness was B- "working of plastics; working of substances in a plastic state in general."

The 2001–2010 network (Fig. 2) was composed of 215 unique IPC subclasses. Section G-Physics climbed to the top three clusters, along with sections B and A, and displacing section C. However, section B holds the IPC subclass with the highest betweenness: *"physical or chemical processes or apparatus in general."*

The 2011–2021 network (Fig. 3) was composed of 128 unique IPC subclasses. Section F-mechanical engineering, lighting, heating, weapons, blasting, climbed to the top three clusters, displacing section A. Also, Section F placed the IPC subclass with the highest betweenness: *"machines or engines for liquids; wind, spring, or weight motors; producing mechanical power or a reactive propulsive thrust, not otherwise provided for."*

Besides identifying highly strategic and clustered IPC subclasses and sections, we noticed peripherical sections. Common IPC sections with lower cluster composition in all periods were D-Textile, paper; and E-Fixed constructions. However, this interpretation should be taken cautiously since individual IPC subclasses in such sections exhibit higher betweenness. For the 2011–2021 network, the IPC subclass D- *"treatment of textiles or the like; laundering; flexible materials not otherwise provided for"* ranked among the top-5 with higher betweenness. A supporting point for calculating betweenness centrality for all nodes in the networks.

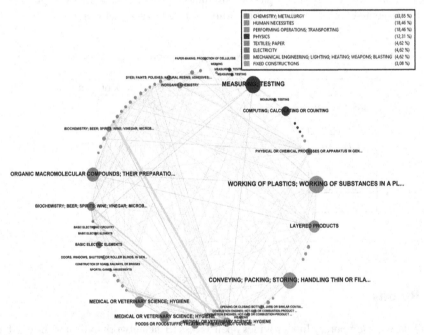

Fig. 1. IPC subclass network 1983–2000. Source: WIPO [19]. Note: visible nodes according to top-5 higher betweenness by IPC section.

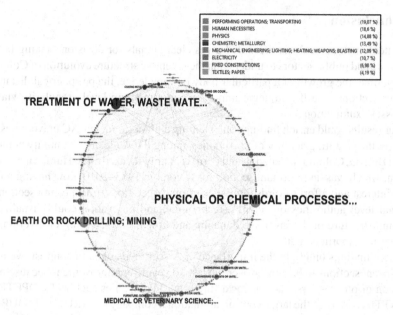

Fig. 2. IPC subclass network 2001–2010. Source: WIPO [19]. Note: visible nodes according to top-5 higher betweenness by IPC section.

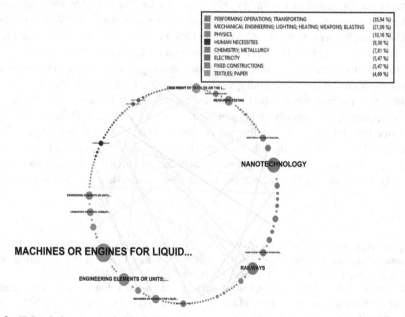

Fig. 3. IPC subclass network 2011–2021. Source: WIPO [19]. Note: visible nodes according to top-5 higher betweenness by IPC section.

4   Conclusion

The patentometrics analysis presented gives clear signals for decision-making both in the private and public sectors to understand the inventive structure evolution of Colombia through time, the growth of a particular body of knowledge, the peripherical distancing of other sections, and the strategic importance at a medium level granularity via IPC subclasses examination.

Our results could enrich findings on patenting collaboration in LAC universities. For instance, the patenting activity of universities among the Andean Community countries (CAN: Bolivia, Colombia, Ecuador, and Peru) is mainly focused on A-Human necessities section, which was an important section for Colombia 1983–2010, now having a more active interest and effort towards the B-Performing operations, transporting section [1]. National level authorities on science, technology, and innovation could visualize the changing structure of the inventive dynamic and how it is converging or diverging the regional-neighborhood path.

These findings highlight the importance of A-section patents. In contrast, we found other patent sections to be denser over the last 10 years; an improvement because of the inclusion of other actors, such as local (important) companies such as ECOPETROL-ESENTTIA S.A. (i.e., the largest petroleum/national company) or ARGOS GROUP (i.e., one of the largest cements/energy conglomerates), besides universities (e.g., Pontificia Universidad Javeriana, Universidad de Los Andes, Universidad Nacional), which are the top patent applicants in Colombia [17]. Also, our insight provides additional resolution to the descriptive and investment-related approach provided by WIPO regional reports or national reports by the Colombian Observatory of Science and Technology (*Observatorio Colombiano de Ciencia y Tecnología*—OCyT) [11, 18].

Future inclusion of these findings into policy-making and practice can be promoted to stakeholders by sharing key findings effectively (e.g., publishing scientific communication notes, business-related press releases, corporate-public dialogue) and building a transdisciplinary community (e.g., generating research agenda collaboratively with knowledge transfer office or intellectual property office) [12]. Further stages of the project could extend the geographical scope to other LAC, African, and Asian (i.e., global south countries), including patent-citation data or other text-mining techniques to identify textual similarities between national innovation systems at the regional level.

References

1. Agüero Aguilar, C.E.: Redes de colaboración y producción de patentes en universidades de la Comunidad Andina de Naciones (UCANS) 2005–2015. Rev. Española Doc. Científica. **40**(2 SE-Estudios), e172 (2017). https://doi.org/10.3989/redc.2017.2.1401
2. Bettencourt, L.M.A., et al.: Urban scaling and its deviations: revealing the structure of wealth, innovation and crime across cities. PLoS One. **5**(11), 1–9 (2010). https://doi.org/10.1371/jou rnal.pone.0013541
3. Callon, M., et al.: From translations to problematic networks: an introduction to co-word analysis. Soc. Sci. Inf. **22**(2), 191–235 (1983). https://doi.org/10.1177/053901883022002003
4. Campo Robledo, J., Herrera Saavedra, J.P.: Patentes y crecimiento económico: ¿innovación de residentes o no residentes? Rev. Desarro. y Soc. **76**, 243–272 (2016). https://doi.org/10.13043/dys.76.6

5. Campos Jiménez, E., Campos Ferrer, A.: Análisis biotecnológico de Latinoamérica a través de las patentes en Inmunología. Rev. Cuba. Inf. en Ciencias la Salud. **25**(2), 172–182 (2014)

6. Cortés-Sánchez, J.D.: Patents for all: a content analysis of an open-access dataset of Colombian patents 1930–2000. In: Pardo Martínez, C.I., et al. (eds.) Analysis of Science, Technology, and Innovation in Emerging Economies, pp. 65–93. Springer, Cham (2019). https://doi.org/10.1007/978-3-030-13578-2_4

7. Faust, K.: A puzzle concerning triads in social networks: graph constraints and the triad census. Soc. Netw. **32**(3), 221–233 (2010). https://doi.org/10.1016/j.socnet.2010.03.004

8. Freeman, L.C.: A set of measures of centrality based on betweenness. Sociometry. **40**(1), 35–41 (1977). https://doi.org/10.2307/3033543

9. Hall, B.H., et al.: Market value and patent citations. RAND J. Econ. **36**(1), 16–38 (2005)

10. Hammarfelt, B.: Linking science to technology: the "patent paper citation" and the rise of patentometrics in the 1980s. J. Doc. **77**(6), 1413–1429 (2021). https://doi.org/10.1108/JD-12-2020-0218

11. OCyT: Tableros CTeI 2020 – Portal de datos 2021. https://portal.ocyt.org.co/tableros-ctei-2020/. Accessed 19 Sept 2022

12. Oliver, K., Boaz, A.: Transforming evidence for policy and practice: creating space for new conversations. Palgrave Commun. **5**(1), 60 (2019). https://doi.org/10.1057/s41599-019-0266-1

13. Opsahl, T., et al.: Node centrality in weighted networks: generalizing degree and shortest paths. Soc. Netw. **32**(3), 245–251 (2010). https://doi.org/10.1016/j.socnet.2010.03.006

14. Rodríguez-Salvador, M., et al.: Scientometric and patentometric analyses to determine the knowledge landscape in innovative technologies: the case of 3D bioprinting. PLoS One. **12**(6), 1–22 (2017). https://doi.org/10.1371/journal.pone.0180375

15. Sánchez, J.M., et al.: Publicación internacional de patentes por organizaciones e inventores de origen colombiano. Cuad. Econ. **26**(47), 249–270 (2007)

16. WIPO: Guide to the International Patent Classification. (2022)

17. WIPO: Information by Country: Colombia. https://www.wipo.int/directory/en/details.jsp?country_code=CO. Accessed 20 Nov 2023

18. WIPO: IP Facts and Figures 2021. Geneva (2021). https://doi.org/10.34667/tind.44650

19. WIPO. PATENTSCOPE. https://patentscope.wipo.int/search/es/search.jsf. Accessed 19 Sept 2022

20. Yan, E., Ding, Y.: Scholarly network similarities: how bibliographic coupling networks, citation networks, cocitation networks, topical networks, coauthorship networks, and coword networks relate to each other. J. Am. Soc. Inf. Sci. Technol. **63**(7), 1313–1326 (2012). https://doi.org/10.1002/asi.22680

Social Media and Digital Networks

Evolving Definitions of Hate Speech: The Impact of a Lack of Standardized Definitions

Seul Lee(✉) and Anne Gilliland

University of California, Los Angeles, Los Angeles, CA 90095, USA
seul@g.ucla.edu, gilliland@gseis.ucla.edu

Abstract. Although studies in many fields have highlighted growing concern surrounding online hate speech, standardized definitions for what is considered to be hate speech are still lacking. This poses challenges for research studies and applied efforts to combat hate speech. This research conducted a three-pronged study to better understand the reasons behind this lack of consensus and to propose more effective ways of operationalizing hate speech. Reporting on this study, the existing literature on hate speech is scrutinized across various disciplines, examining scholarly perspectives and those of legal bodies. Subsequently, an analysis is conducted on the perspectives of social media platforms. Thirdly, this research presents examples of insights provided by adolescents who participated in the survey and focus groups conducted by Social Media and the Spread of Hate: Examining Exposure and Impact (SMASH), a research project collaborating with middle and high school students and their schools in the United States. Based on these inputs, this research concludes that while more closely defining hate speech is important, solely focusing on how to define hate speech in social media contexts is insufficient. To foster a healthier online environment, promote knowledge shaped by reliable information, and safeguard the well-being of adolescents, it is also necessary to identify how the various and evolving features of social media contribute to the promotion of hate speech and related behaviors.

Keywords: Online Hate Speech · Social Media Studies · Internet Regulation · Definitional Challenges · Youth Online Safety

1 Introduction

Numerous studies have identified hate speech on social media as a growing concern. What is considered to be hate speech remains inadequately defined, however, making the concept difficult to operationalize in research studies and counter-hate speech programming. This three-pronged study sought to understand better why hate speech has been variously defined and to examine how hate speech could be more effectively operationalized. This paper first presents the results of an analysis of existing literature published by scholars in different fields and legislative bodies pertaining to "hate speech," identifying a range of definitions of hate speech. Moving the concept of hate speech into the digital realm, the paper then discusses the perspectives of social media platforms regarding

© The Author(s), under exclusive license to Springer Nature Switzerland AG 2024
I. Sserwanga et al. (Eds.): iConference 2024, LNCS 14597, pp. 141–156, 2024.
https://doi.org/10.1007/978-3-031-57860-1_11

their transformative impact on the dynamic digital landscape. Thirdly, the paper provides examples of insights provided by teenagers who participated in surveys and focus groups conducted by SMASH.[1] It then briefly reflects on the repercussions of the lack of standardized definitions and outlines the next steps being taken by SMASH. It concludes that while clearer definitions are beneficial in a variety of ways, it is also necessary to consider how the evolving characteristics of social media continually contribute to the nature of hate speech on social media and associated behaviors.

1.1 Research Background

American adolescents typically receive their first mobile device during their transition into adolescence [1, 2]. A recent investigation [3] that compared media activities among "tweens" (8- to 12-year-olds) and teens (13- to 18-year-olds) in 2019 and 2021, shows that 42 percent of 10-year-olds own a smartphone, as do approximately three in 10 of all 8 and 9-year-olds, while nearly half of US children are engaging with social media platforms by the age of 12. The study [3] specifically highlights a rise in social media use by tweens. A 2018 survey [4] by the Pew Research Center (2018) found that 95% of teenagers have access to smartphones, with 45% of teens reporting that they were online "almost constantly." The survey [4] further found that a majority of American teenagers reported using social media, with 85% using YouTube, 72% using Instagram, 69% using Snapchat, and approximately 51% using Facebook as their primary social media platform. A 2022 report [5] by the Pew Research Center highlights that the more adolescents use social media, the harder it becomes for them to give it up. Data from surveys conducted by our partner, the Organization for Social Media Safety (OFSMS), obtained directly from students using personal digital clicker devices during school assemblies across the US, also show similar results. During the 2022-23 school year of 7,982 students participating in the OFSMS surveys, approximately 39% reported spending between 7 and 11+ h per day using social media, while 16% reported spending 11+ h per day. On average, the participants spent 6.7 h per day on social media.

Part of the widespread appeal of social media platforms can be attributed to their heavy reliance on user-generated content (UGC), which significantly influences users' trends, preferences, purchasing choices, and perceptions [6, 7]. Research has shown that social media platforms activate similar neural pathways to those activated by gambling and recreational drugs to maximize user engagement with their products [8]. Furthermore, studies conducted by scholars investigating the impact of social media on the

---

[1] SMASH is funded by the University of California, Los Angeles' Initiative for the Study of Hate. SMASH is a collaboration of academic researchers in the UCLA School of Education & Information Studies and the Organization for Social Media Safety (OFSMS). OFSMS, established in 2019, is a national nonprofit organization dedicated to promoting social media safety, with a specific focus on addressing hate speech and cyberbullying among students. SMASH is studying the perceptions of, exposure to, and educational impact of hate speech on social media among US students in grades 5 to 12 in order to develop and implement strategies in schools that can effectively counter social media-based hate speech and cyberbullying targeting students. The study reported here is an initial step in the project's efforts to address the lack of standardized definitions of hate speech and to develop a conceptual framework that can enhance the understanding and operationalization of this term.

human brain have revealed that while individuals tend to talk about themselves at a rate of approximately 30 to 40% in face-to-face interactions, this proportion significantly increases to 80% on social media platforms [9]. This heightened self-focused behavior is driven by the anticipation of positive social validation, which in turn triggers the release of dopamine in the brain as a reward mechanism, thereby reinforcing and perpetuating the habit of using social media. The incomplete development of the prefrontal cortex in children also makes them more susceptible to adopting harmful behaviors, hindering their ability to exercise self-control and effectively manage their social media usage [10]. Consequently, there has been an observed correlation between the impact of social media content and a noticeable increase in mental health problems[2] among children nationwide [8].

In recent years, there has been a notable increase in the prevalence of offensive, hate speech, and violent content in user-generated social media posts [11]. Lupu et al. [12] conducted a study examining six popular social media platforms[3] between June 2019 and December 2020, revealing a noticeable upward trend in the overall volume of posts containing hate speech during this period. The study specifically observed a 250% surge in racial hate speech following the murder of George Floyd on May 25, 2020. In a study conducted by the youth charity Ditch the Label in 2022 [13, 17], an analysis of 263 million social media conversations in the UK and US between 2019 and mid-2021 revealed a 20% increase in online hate speech in both countries since the start of the pandemic. During significant events,[4] the report found that 50.1 million conversations involved racist hate speech. In a 2021 study [14] conducted by the UK's communications regulator, Ofcom, a sample of over 2,000 participants was surveyed about their experiences using online video platforms during the preceding three months. Approximately one-third of the study participants reported encountering hate speech during this time frame.

Increasing volumes of UGC that contain offensive and hate speech have resulted in greater exposure of youth to such content [15]. An online survey[5] conducted by the Pew Research Center [16] over a three-week period, from April 14 to May 4, 2022, found that nearly half of U.S. teens aged 13 to 17 (46%) have experienced online harassment or bullying.[6] The results [16] also indicate that teenagers who claim to be online almost constantly are not only more likely to have encountered online harassment compared to those who spend less time online, but they are also more likely to have experienced a variety of forms of online abusive behaviors. As a result, it is not surprising that a substantial proportion of adolescents are familiar with the term "hate speech" and have

---

[2] These symptoms include anxiety, unease, and emotional turmoil.

[3] Facebook, VKontakte, Instagram, Gab, Telegram, and 4chan.

[4] These include the World Health Organization (WHO)'s declaration of the Covid-19 outbreaks as a pandemic in March 2020, the Black Lives Matter protests in June 2020, and the murder of Sarah Everard in March 2021.

[5] This report also highlights that the majority of teenagers believe that teachers, social media companies, and politicians are not adequately addressing the online harassment or bullying issues.

[6] These include physical threats, false rumors, offensive name-calling, unsolicited explicit images, or non-consensual sharing of explicit images.

encountered instances of it. For instance, OFSMS's 2022–23 survey found that 81% of student respondents reported witnessing hate speech on social media in the past month, and that the odds of witnessing hate speech increased with higher grade levels and with more hours spent using social media. However, further research is necessary to ascertain the frequency and specific contexts in which these encounters occur.

As this prior discussion indicates, although the issue of young people's exposure to hate speech on social media is widely recognized as a significant problem, and students are frequently reporting encountering hate speech when using social media, there is a lack of clarity regarding what actually comprises hate speech across different stakeholders, including researchers, policy makers, and social media platforms, as well as schools and parents. In essence, there is a lack of consensus or standardized understanding among practitioners and scholars regarding the precise definition of hate speech [18]. It also remains unclear the extent to which how researchers understand the concept aligns with the understandings of young people at different developmental stages, thus running the methodological risk that what researchers think they are studying and what students are reporting are not always the same thing. This lack of definitional clarity poses challenges in conducting research studies as well as developing policy and modifying the design of social media platforms to try to lessen hate speech and its effects.

2   The Intricacies of Hate Speech Definitions

2.1   Definitions by Scholars

In scholarly discourse, the concept of hate speech has been the subject to a range of nuanced definitions, each offering distinct yet interconnected perspectives. Allport (1954), an American psychologist renowned for developing a measure of prejudice and discrimination, sought to elucidate hate speech by articulating several fundamental elements contributing to its role in escalating violence, with one of these prerequisites being the presence of prolonged and intense verbal hostility [21]. His analysis not only shed light on the cognitive underpinnings of hate speech but also highlighted the emotional aspects, characterized by feelings of hatred, intolerance, prejudice, bigotry, or stereotyping. Allport [21] also emphasized a common tendency among individuals to make hasty generalizations about all members of a specific outgroup based on single experiences with a member of that group. Asante [60] emphasized the emotional content conveyed through hate speech, defining it as a form of verbal aggression that conveys sentiments of hatred, contempt, ridicule, or intimidation toward a specific group or category of people. Asante [60] also highlighted the role of hate speech in serving as a means of articulating derogatory sentiments to misrepresent the historical narratives of specific groups, to diminish the autonomy of these groups, and to perpetuate negative cultural, racial, and ethnic stereotypes about them. Delgado and Stefancic [22], proponents of Critical Race Theory, defined hate speech as a conscious and willful public statement intended to denigrate a particular group of people, emphasizing the intention behind hate speech as a deliberate act aimed at demeaning a particular group. Simpson [23], who studies social and political philosophy related to freedom of speech, delineated hate speech as discourse that seeks to stigmatize and demonize groups based on perceived negative traits or inherent inferiority [23, 24]. According to the definition offered by Matsuda

[25], an American lawyer, activist, and law professor who studies hate speech and discrimination, in order for speech to be considered actionable, it must explicitly deny the personhood of targeted individuals in terms of the group to which they belong and regard all members of that group as both similar and inferior. Moran [26], another legal scholar, focused on speech intended to foment hatred against traditionally disadvantaged groups.

Kinney [59] provided various examples of hate speech, including ethnophaulisms, racial slurs and epithets, sexist comments, and homophobic speech, and delved into the contentious issue of regulating hate speech in democratic societies by examining the justifications for such regulation, including its potential impacts on social and racial cohesion. Brown [61] also raised the issue of the prevalent approach among scholars to define hate speech by listing specific characteristics, statuses, or identities,[7] pointing out that the existing lists are typically illustrative or suggestive, often lacking clarification regarding the common underlying feature or essential nature shared by all the enumerated characteristics.

In recent years, there has been a growing interest among scholars in the study of online hate speech. For instance, in the context of social media, Mondal, Silva, and Benevenuto [27] analyzed hate speech as offensive posts motivated by bias against a particular group. They proposed a method for identifying hate speech based on sentence structure and found that the targeted hate groups varied by geography. Uyheng and Carley [28] presented a methodological pipeline for assessing the links between hate speech and bot-driven activity, employing a combination of machine learning and network science techniques to analyze Twitter discussions pertaining to the pandemic in the United States and the Philippines. In a different approach, Gao, and Huang [29] introduced two distinct models for detecting hate speech that integrate contextual information: a logistic regression model with context features and a neural network model with learning components for context analysis. Each of these scholars offered a unique lens through which to understand and define the multifaceted concept of hate speech.

However, despite the abundance of literature on the causes, consequences, and countermeasures of hate speech, as pointed out by Sellers [30], there is a lack of scholarly efforts to provide a comprehensive or operationalizable definition of hate speech. As Sellars points out, depending on the context, various content might or might not meet a definition of hate speech. For instance, as Delgado pointed out, the use of language that includes epithets may not always be perceived as hate speech by the individual uttering it or targeted recipient. Siegel [32] observed that Delgado's proposed tort for racist speech [31] requires the plaintiff to prove intent, impact, and the objective perception of demeaning language based on race. In contrast, as highlighted by Parekh et al. [33], the use of more subtle language to attack a specific outgroup may not immediately register as hate speech to casual observers, yet it can wield a palpable influence on individuals and the interrelationships among diverse social groups.

While common themes emerge across these definitions of hate speech, such as targeting and degrading specific groups, the intent and impact of hate speech, and the promotion of hatred, the complexity of hate speech lies in its context-dependent nature, making it challenging to grapple with theoretically and methodologically. Speech may

---

[7] Such as race, ethnicity, religion, nationality, gender or gender identity, sexual orientation, and disability.

be interpreted as hateful or not, depending on the context in which it occurs and the perceptions of the targeted group, other parties, or the general public. This variability also poses challenges in establishing uniform and universally applicable definitions and underscores the need for nuanced and context-specific approaches to effectively address hate speech.

2.2 Legislative Definitions

The historical roots of hate speech regulation, particularly in relation to racially and religiously offensive speech, can be traced back to the 1940s and 50s, a period heavily influenced by the response of American civil rights organizations to the atrocities witnessed during World War II [19, 20]. Although very little legislation was enacted in the end [19], the concept has since been elaborated in many different ways. Building upon the varied definitions of hate speech proposed by scholars, Jeremy Waldron, an American legal philosopher, brought a distinct perspective to the discourse from his field [34]. Waldron's perspective illuminated the regulatory landscape surrounding this phenomenon, shedding light on how hate speech is addressed in practice, particularly within the context of maintaining public order.[8] Waldron [34] broadened the scope of protection to include not only racial and ethnic groups but also religious categories. Waldron [34] also underscored a significant divergence between the United States and Western liberal democracies such as Canada, Britain, Denmark, Germany, and New Zealand, where the latter have legal provisions to prohibit public statements that incite hatred against identifiable groups. Waldron highlighted that hate speech is not legally defined under U.S. law and is not subject to direct regulation by the government or indeed any explicit limiting legislation, but rather is protected by the constitutional right to freedom of speech [43, 44].

While legal definitions and approaches to hate speech vary widely across countries, they share certain commonalities. In his book [34], Waldron provided a comprehensive analysis of varying perspectives on hate speech across different nations. For instance, in the United Kingdom, hate speech was defined within the framework of the Public Order Act of 1986 [35]. According to Section 18 of this legislation [35], employing language or conduct that is threatening, abusive, or insulting with the explicit intention of inciting racial hatred or where there is a reasonable likelihood of such hatred being provoked, is considered a criminal offense. In Canada,[9] hate speech is addressed in the Criminal Code [36] (Section 319), which specifically prohibits public incitement of hatred against any identifiable group[10] if such incitement is likely to result in a breach of the peace. Similarly, the German Criminal Code [37] (Section 130) addressed hate speech and hate

---

[8] Delgado (1982) [31] also advocated for the imposition of legal restrictions on hate speech and argued that tackling defamation alone is insufficient to effectively address the issue of hate speech.

[9] Crimes falling under section 318, which pertains to the act of advocating genocide, are classified as straight indictable offenses. The prescribed maximum punishment for such offenses is a period of imprisonment not to exceed five years.

[10] The definition of an identifiable group encompasses categories such as color, race, religion, ethnic origin, sexual orientation, gender identity or expression, as well as mental or physical disability.

crimes by prohibiting incitement to hatred against segments of the population based on race, ethnicity, religion, or nationality. Meanwhile, in France, provisions against hate speech were enshrined within the Act of 1881 on Freedom of the Press [38], which seeks to find a balance between countering racist propaganda and safeguarding freedom of opinion and expression. Specifically, Article 24 of the 1881 Act [38] established criminal consequences for individuals who, through the methods outlined in Article 23, encourage hatred or violence towards an individual or group based on their ethnic background, nationality, race, religion, sexual orientation, or gender identity, whether real or perceived. The intention behind such incitement must be to prompt discriminatory actions against individuals who are protected under this law.

The 2019 United Nations Strategy and Plan of Action on Hate Speech [39] offered a broader perspective by defining hate speech as any form of communication that employs discriminatory or pejorative language directed at an individual or group based on characteristics such as religion, ethnicity, nationality, race, color, descent, gender, or other identity factors. This definition encompasses various forms of expression, including images, symbols, and online content, and is relevant both offline and online. While international human rights law does not yet have a universally accepted definition of hate speech, the UN's approach highlights the multi-dimensional nature of this phenomenon. Hate speech is not limited to incitement to discrimination, hostility, or violence; it encompasses language that belittles, demeans, or stigmatizes based on identity factors. However, a distinction is made between hate speech directed at individuals or groups and discourse involving states, religious leaders, symbols, or public officials.

In recent legislative developments, Ireland has introduced a new approach to defining and addressing hate speech [40]. The 2022 Criminal Justice (Incitement to Violence or Hatred and Hate Offences) Bill introduced strict measures against hate speech, while also including provisions to safeguard legitimate forms of expression. The statute explicitly prohibits behaviors that condone, deny, or trivialize genocide, war crimes, crimes against humanity, and crimes against peace. This legislative change [40] signifies a significant shift in the legal landscape regarding hate speech, driven by recognition of the need to combat hate speech more effectively and to balance freedom of expression with safeguarding vulnerable groups. Due to its troubled history, hate speech had previously been indirectly addressed in Northern Ireland's legal framework, where enhanced sentences were possible if hostility toward protected characteristics such as race, religion, sexual orientation, and disability could be proven. The new Irish legislation explicitly outlines offenses related to hate speech and violence incitement [40, 41]. Possessing material with the potential to incite hate against individuals based on attributes such as "non-binary" gender identities, sexuality, or national origin could result in a prison sentence of up to two years, while communicating such material to others could lead to imprisonment for five years. The jurisdiction of this legislation extends beyond physical borders; accessing "hateful material" hosted offshore by Irish information systems could render an individual liable for prosecution, regardless of their geographic location [40–42].

In South Africa, the recently proposed Prevention and Combating of Hate Crimes and Hate Speech Bill [45, 46] has precipitated a range of conflicting perspectives. The proposed legislation, currently under consideration in Parliament, contains provisions aimed at defining hate speech. Section 10 of the Bill outlines hate speech as a deliberate intention to cause harm, incite harm, or promote and propagate hatred based on various protected characteristics, including race, gender, sex, ethnic or social origin, color, sexual orientation, religion, belief, culture, language, birth, disability, HIV status, nationality, gender identity, albinism, or occupation or trade [45, 46].

East Asian countries vary in their approaches. South Korea does not have a specific ban on expressions of hatred towards individuals or groups, unless they are considered defamatory [47, 48]. Since South Korea primarily relies on laws related to defamation to address hate speech, this situation leads to ongoing debates about the laws' practical effectiveness [47, 48]. Although Japan has implemented the Hate Speech Act of 2016, the Act does not explicitly prohibit hate speech, nor does it establish penalties for its commission [49]. In China, censorship is primarily enforced through the appointment of censors in various media sectors, with editors and webmasters being held accountable for any questionable content, including hate speech [50]. Although laws often reflect the unique cultural and historical contexts of individual countries, thus accounting for variations in legal language and approaches, collectively such regulations draw attention to the potential consequences of hate speech for victims and society at large. They also underscore its criminal intent, defining hate speech as language or conduct explicitly intended to incite hatred, violence, or discrimination against individuals or groups, or the actual and perceived attributes of individuals or groups.

2.3 Content Moderation Decisions by Platforms

Many social media platforms, including Meta, Instagram, X (formerly known as Twitter), YouTube, and TikTok, have taken measures to tackle the recent surge in violent and hateful content on their platforms. There is a widespread consensus among these platforms regarding the definition of hate speech, which is acknowledged as content that promotes or condones violence, discrimination, disparagement, or incitement of hatred against individuals or groups based on specific characteristics [51].[11] These platforms also acknowledge the pivotal role of context when evaluating content. This acknowledgment of context, in addition to content, is significant as it underscores the platforms' commitment to a more nuanced and discerning approach to content moderation by monitoring and managing user-generated content to ensure compliance with community standards, guidelines, and regulations.

Meta and Instagram [52–54] define hate speech as a form of explicit aggression directed towards individuals, rather than abstract ideas or organizations, based on certain attributes that are considered to be protected characteristics.[12] They also extend protections to refugees, migrants, immigrants, and asylum seekers, which may not be explicitly included by other platforms. However, according to their policies, they do allow the use of specific slurs or hate speech under certain circumstances, such as for

---

[11] These "protected characteristics" encompass a wide array of attributes, such as race, ethnicity, religion, disability, age, nationality, sexual orientation, gender, gender identity, caste, and others associated with systemic discrimination.

[12] These attributes include race, ethnicity, national origin, disability, religious affiliation, caste, sexual orientation, sex, gender identity, and serious disease.

denouncing or promoting awareness, as long as the intention behind such usage is evident. To enforce these policies, they employ global review teams comprising thousands of human reviewers who assess content based on factors such as severity, virality, and the likelihood of policy violations. Google [55] and YouTube [56] highlight the importance of systemic discrimination or marginalization when evaluating characteristics, broadening the scope beyond explicitly listed attributes. According to their definitions, hate speech refers to any form of expression that advocates or approves of violence, prejudice, or derogation, or primarily aims to provoke animosity towards an individual or a collective based on their protected attributes[13] or any other characteristic that is linked to systemic discrimination or marginalization. They also place importance on context in their enforcement approach, recognizing that certain discussions might discuss or criticize hate speech without promoting it.

X [57] employs the term, "hateful conduct" to encapsulate behaviors that promote violence against or directly attack or threaten other people based on race, ethnicity, national origin, caste, sexual orientation, gender, gender identity, religious affiliation, age, disability, or serious disease. TikTok [58] maintains a zero-tolerance stance towards organized hate groups and ideologies, explicitly denouncing associations with white supremacy, male supremacy, anti-Semitism, and other hate-based beliefs. Notably, TikTok recently expanded its definition of hate speech to encompass actions like deadnaming and misgendering. This alteration is part of a comprehensive update to the community guidelines of the video-sharing platform, with the aim of eradicating transphobic and other detrimental behaviors. The decision to incorporate these specific forms of discrimination into the guidelines is based on the input and recommendations provided by its content creators and by civil society organizations, who emphasized the significance of clearly outlining acceptable conduct within the community. X also emphasizes incorporating its users' perspectives into its content moderation processes, allowing targeted individuals to provide context and information to aid in enforcement decisions. Although all these platforms collectively contribute to the intricate landscape of addressing online hate speech by engaging with their communities to refine their definitions and combat hate speech more effectively, the variations in their strategies show the complexities of maintaining a fair and inclusive online atmosphere while supporting freedom of speech, and alarming high proportion of adolescents still report encountering hate speech when using these platforms.

2.4 Youth Perceptions of Hate Speech

The surveys of students' experiences with social media, conducted using personal digital clicker devices at school assemblies by OFSMS at middle and high schools across the US, have yielded substantial quantitative data. However, to obtain qualitative insights into what students perceive to be hate speech and the nature of their experiences with it on social media, SMASH researchers have recently begun conducting volunteer student focus groups. An example from an initial focus group comprising three students provides interesting and potentially confirmatory glimpses into why young people may find participating in online hate speech alluring.

---

[13] See footnote 12.

All the student participants in this focus group highlighted behavioral and platform design factors that contribute to the addictive nature of engaging in online hate speech. They noted that anonymity, particularly through the ability to create new profiles or accounts, contributes to the temptation to engage in hate speech online. For instance, "They're left anonymous at the time when they make a whole new profile... that can be addictive." The student emphasized the sense of freedom and self-expression that social media provides. They also noted that messaging friends and engaging in private conversations without revealing their identities can foster addictive behavior and enhance the appeal of online interactions, including the propagation of hate speech.

They mentioned that these platforms allow individuals to comment and express themselves without facing significant consequences. The student said, "Why do we think it is okay to do it? Because there is not much consequence online. Usually, in person, they are obviously not going to share their hate speech."

Furthermore, the students pointed out that although online hate speech and cyber-bullying are common among their peers, they believe that many students who witness or are victims of such incidents would be hesitant to report them because not everyone is willing to openly discuss their experiences with cyberbullying or hate speech, even under conditions of anonymity. As one student put it, "I feel like not everyone is going to speak about it. Even if it is anonymous, I don't feel like everyone feels comfortable admitting that they've been cyberbullied although a lot of students have actually been cyberbullied."

Another recurring theme was the use of humor. They pointed out that some people employ hate speech disguised as humor, leading many to initially dismiss it as harmless. However, the students were aware that such content could still have serious consequences for the targeted students. One student mentioned that some individuals may dismiss hate speech as jokes and label those who take offense as oversensitive. They viewed this dismissal as a form of hate speech in itself, however, since it diminishes and undermines the emotions experienced by individuals who are affected by online hate.

They also observed that hate speech is often targeted toward specific groups. While the targets could vary, racial groups were frequently mentioned as victims. They noted that hate speech tends to be directed toward identifiable communities or groups, some-times through subtle or indirect means such as backhanded comments or indirect ref-erences. They emphasized that intent plays a significant role in determining whether content qualifies as hate speech, recognizing that different people may interpret content differently based on their perspectives.

Students expressed a willingness to report online hateful content that they encoun-tered, but they also acknowledged the limitations of reporting mechanisms. They men-tioned that it may require a collective effort of many users to have a video or content com-pletely removed, as creators can easily circumvent penalties by creating new accounts and uploading such content again.

Finally, the students noted that the prevalence of hateful content on social media can lead to desensitization. They opined that many students, including themselves, may gradually become indifferent to online hate, simply scrolling past it without significant consideration. Such normalization of hate speech is a concerning trend among young people. Overall, the insights from this and ongoing focus groups are helping to shed light on the multifaceted nature of youth perceptions of online hate speech, including such aspects as the allure of anonymity, the role of humor as camouflage, and the intricacies of both platform and school reporting systems.

3 Discussion

The examination of various inputs on hate speech revealed an apparent gap in the current discourse, especially in the understanding of hate speech as perceived by school-aged children and adolescents, who are particularly susceptible to online hate speech. Our as yet limited insights into adolescent participants' perceptions of hate speech suggest that students are cognizant of the addictive nature of online interactions, particularly due to anonymity and how these are encouraged by platforms affordances, as well as young people's related behavior patterns such as the role of humor in disguising hate speech, and the hesitancy to report incidents. This knowledge gap highlights a crucial inadequacy in addressing the issues that school-aged children and adolescents encounter in relation to hate speech.

The issue of hate speech is widely discussed in both public discourse and academic circles, with varying perspectives on its definition being expressed and debated. Looking across these three inputs, the prevailing consensus appears to be that hate speech is widely understood as an act that endorses or tolerates violence, discrimination, disparagement, or incitement of hatred against individuals and groups with protected characteristic.[14] Another shared aspect is the acknowledgement of the importance of considering context and intent when evaluating hate speech, due to the often intricate and nuanced nature of speech. Within such consensus, scholars present diverse viewpoints and foci regarding hate speech, focusing on cognitive aspects, its group-based nature, the emotional content conveyed, or various forms it can take. Legal definitions and interpretations of hate speech vary across different jurisdictions. Several countries have explicit definitions and laws that criminalize hate speech, whereas others place a higher emphasis on safeguarding freedom of expression while indirectly addressing specific elements of hate speech. Social media platforms have their own nuanced definitions of hate speech and vary in the attributes each considers to be protected and the extent to which context is examined during content moderation processes.

Despite shared perspectives on the definition and interpretation of hate speech, there is a lack of an overarching definition. Legislative approaches to hate speech vary widely across countries, resulting in variances in legal language and enforcement strategies. Social media platforms also differ in their policies and enforcement mechanisms, such as which attributes they consider protected and when they permit the use of slurs. These divergent platform responses not only pose challenges for researchers and parents in understanding adolescents' experiences with online hate speech on these platforms, but also may lead adolescent users to believe that their efforts to report online hate speech are ineffective and unsustainable. Moreover, normalization of hate speech and desensitization may occur due to its prevalence on social media or increasing exposure. This study therefore highlights the need for nuanced approaches that consider not only

---

[14] These characteristics include but are not limited to race, ethnicity, religion, disability, gender, gender identity, and other similar attributes.

technological but also cognitive, educational, cultural, legal, and societal factors when defining and addressing online hate speech.

Similarly, while it is clear that the issue of young people's exposure to hate speech on social media is a significant problem, it is less clear what they, or indeed researchers, policymakers, social media platforms, schools, or parents, understand or perceive to be hate speech. This lack of definitional clarity coupled with the rapidly evolving capabilities of and dynamic adolescent preferences for certain social media platforms make studying hate speech challenging to operationalize in research studies. It also makes it slippery to describe for policy development purposes, or to characterize and target in social media platform design. Scholars who have attempted to delineate hate speech among children and young people through empirical data have theorized that there is an overlap between hate speech and bullying, including cyberbullying. However, their definitions of hate speech and their assessment instruments have still been heterogeneous. Since there is a lack of consensus or standardized understanding among practitioners and scholars regarding the precise definition of hate speech [18], they have employed a variety of criteria to identify and assess instances of hate speech. Furthermore, it is not clear to what extent the understandings of researchers correspond with those of young people at different developmental levels.

This study suggests that exclusively focusing on how to define hate speech in social media contexts is insufficient, and researchers should also consider how the affordances of the social media platforms may promote hate speech and related behaviors among school-aged students. Those affordances need to be modified accordingly, and flexible guidelines need to be implemented to recognize the intent, contextual nuances, and potential impact of hate speech. Continuous review of these measures is necessary as the digital environment and social contexts of use can shift quickly and in unanticipated ways. Moving forward on each front will require collaborative work between scholars, social media platforms, governments, policymakers, educators, and adolescents. To gain a deeper understanding of what constitutes hate speech, it is important to incorporate the perspectives of individuals who have encountered it, consider the specific contexts in which it is encountered, and understand its impact on various groups.

It is also crucial to develop definitions that are specifically tailored to the youth population by actively involving young individuals from diverse backgrounds. This can be achieved through the establishment of forums such as focus groups and workshops to explore their perspectives on hate speech and assess whether their understanding aligns with established definitions and existing solutions. Additionally, longitudinal studies that monitor adolescents' evolving understanding of hate speech can be beneficial in identifying whether or when their perceptions might align with legal or academic definitions as they progress in maturity and years of exposure to social media. To enhance the efficacy of mitigation, educational programs can raise awareness of the harmful effects of online hate speech and teach digital literacy and social media responsibility. Adopting such approaches that prioritize cultural sensitivity, contextual analysis, platform accountability and transparency regarding their content moderation policies and practices, and education for adolescents can effectively mitigate online hate speech on social media. Establishing more nuanced and comprehensive definitions that encompass the perspectives of scholars, legislative bodies, platforms, adolescents, and other users can be a foundational step in this direction. In addition to implementing qualitative data gathering, SMASH researchers have, therefore, reviewed the questions and students' responses used in the school assembly surveys to decide whether and how they might be revised for use in the new rounds of surveys based on students' responses.

Acknowledgements. This work was funded through a grant from the University of California, Los Angeles Initiative to Study Hate. We would like to express our sincere gratitude to Arif Amlani and Christine Ong for their invaluable contributions in refining the content of this paper. Special thanks to Mark Hansen, Marc Berkman, and Sarah Krongard for their insightful suggestions, which greatly enhanced the quality of our work in their respective fields.

References

1. Pew Research Center. Parenting children in the age of screens. https://www.pewresearch.org/internet/2020/07/28/parenting-children-in-the-age-of-screens/. Accessed 27 Dec 2023
2. Clark, S.J., Schultz, S.L., Gebremariam, A., Singer, D.C., Freed, G.L.: Sharing too soon? Children and social media apps. In: C.S. Mott Children's Hospital National Poll on Children's Health, vol. 39, no. 4. University of Michigan (2021). https://mottpoll.org/reports/sharing-too-soon-children-and-social-media-apps. Accessed 27 Dec 2023
3. Rideout, V., Peebles, A., Mann, S., Robb, M.B.: Common sense census: media use by tweens and teens 2021. In: Common Sense, San Francisco (2022). https://www.commonsensemedia.org/sites/default/files/research/report/8-18-census-integrated-report-final-web_0.pdf. Accessed 27 Dec 2023
4. Pew Research Center. Teens, social media & technology 2018. https://www.pewresearch.org/internet/2018/05/31/teens-social-media-technology-2018/. Accessed 27 Dec 2023
5. Pew Research Center. Teens, social media & technology 2022. https://www.pewresearch.org/internet/2022/08/10/teens-social-media-and-technology-2022/
6. Nosto. Stackla survey finds authenticity drives brand affinity and consumer-created content influences purchases. https://www.nosto.com/blog/consumer-content-report-influence-in-the-digital-age/. Accessed 27 Dec 2023
7. Wertz, J.: 4 Ways user generated content helps e-commerce businesses increase sales. Forbes (2020). https://www.forbes.com/sites/jiawertz/2020/03/23/four-ways-user-generated-content-helps-ecommerce-businesses-increase-sales/?sh=70078ce86b87. Accessed 27 Dec 2023
8. Bila, J.: YouTube's dark side could be affecting your child's mental health. CNBC (2018). https://www.cnbc.com/2018/02/13/youtube-is-causing-stress-and-sexualization-in-young-children.html. Accessed 27 Dec 2023
9. Addiction Center. Social media addiction: Recognizing the signs. https://www.addictioncenter.com/drugs/social-media-addiction/. Accessed 27 Dec 2023
10. Gugushvili, N., Täht, K., Ruiter, R., Verduyn, P.: Facebook use intensity and depressive symptoms: a moderated mediation model of problematic Facebook use, age, neuroticism, and extraversion. BMC Psychology **10**(279) (2022). https://doi.org/10.1186/s40359-022-00990-7
11. Statistia. Actioned violence and graphic content items on Facebook worldwide from 4th quarter 2017 to 1st quarter 2023. https://www.statista.com/statistics/1013880/facebook-violence-and-graphic-content-removal-quarter/. Accessed 27 Dec 2023
12. Lupu, Y., et al.: Offline events and online hate. PLoS ONE **18**(1), e0278511 (2023). https://doi.org/10.1371/journal.pone.0278511

13. Ditch the Label. Report cyberbullying and online abuse. https://www.ditchthelabel.org/report. Accessed 27 Dec 2023

14. Ofcom. One in three video-sharing users find hate speech. https://www.ofcom.org.uk/news-centre/2021/one-in-three-video-sharing-users-find-hate-speech. Accessed 27 Dec 2023

15. American Academy of Child and Adolescent Psychiatry. Social media and teens. https://www.aacap.org/AACAP/Families_and_Youth/Facts_for_Families/FFF-Guide/Social-Media-and-Teens-100.aspx. Accessed 27 Dec 2023

16. Pew Research Center. Teens and cyberbullying 2022. https://www.pewresearch.org/internet/2022/12/15/teens-and-cyberbullying-2022/. Accessed 27 Dec 2023

17. Brandwatch. Ditch the Label announce findings of report into cyberbullying and hate speech online. https://www.brandwatch.com/press/press-releases/ditch-label-announce-findings-report-cyberbullying-hate-speech-online/. Accessed 27 Dec 2023

18. Kansok-Dusche, J., et al.: A systematic review on hate speech among children and adolescents: definitions, prevalence, and overlap with related phenomenon. Trauma Violence Abuse **24**(4), 2598–2615 (2022). https://doi.org/10.1177/15248380221108070

19. Walker, S.: Hate Speech: The History of An American Controversy. University of Nebraska Press, Lincoln, Nebraska (1994)

20. White, S.: Civil rights, World War II, and U.S. public opinion. Stud. Am. Politic. Develop. **30**(1), 38–61 (2016). https://doi.org/10.1017/S0898588X16000055

21. Allport, G.W.: The Nature of Prejudice (Abridged). Doubleday, Garden (1954). Allport, G.W.: The Nature of Prejudice. Addison-Wesley, Reading (1954)

22. Delgado, R., Stefancic, J.: Images of the outsider in American law and culture: can free expression remedy systemic social ills? In: Delgado, R. (ed.), Critical Race Theory: The Cutting Edge, pp. 217–227. Temple University, Philadelphia (1995)

23. Simpson, R.M.: Dignity, harm, and hate. Speech Law Philos. **32**(6), 701–728 (2013)

24. Simpson, R.M.: 'Won't somebody please think of the children?' Hate speech, harm, and childhood. Law Philos. **38**(1), 79–108 (2019)

25. Matsuda, M.J.: Public response to racist speech: considering the victim's story, 87 Mich. L. Rev. 2320. Matsuda, supra note 7, at 2323 (1989)

26. Moran, M.: Talking about hate speech: a rhetorical analysis of American and Canadian approaches to the regulation of hate speech, 1994 Wisc. L. Rev. 1425, 1452 n.113. Moran, supra note 98 (1994)

27. Mondal, M., Silva, L.A., Benevenuto, F.: A measurement study of hate speech in social media. In: Proceedings of the 28th ACM Conference on Hypertext and Social Media, pp. 85–94 (2017)

28. Uyheng, J., Carley, K.M.: Bots and online hate during the COVID-19 pandemic: case studies in the United States and the Philippines. J. Comput. Soc. Sci. **3**, 445–468 (2020). https://doi.org/10.1007/s42001-020-00087-4

29. Gao, L., Huang, R.: Detecting online hate speech using context aware models. arXiv preprint arXiv:1710.07395 (2018)

30. Sellars, A.: Defining hate speech, Berkman Klein Center Research Publication, 2016–2020, Boston University School of Law, Public Law Research Paper No. 16–48 (2016). https://ssrn.com/abstract=2882244 or https://doi.org/10.2139/ssrn.2882244

31. Delgado, R.: Words that wound: A tort action for racial insults, epithets, and name-calling, 17 Harv. C.R.–C.L. L. Rev. 133 (1982)

32. Siegel, A.: Online hate speech. In: Persily, N., Tucker, J. (eds.) Social Media and Democracy: The State of the Field, Prospects for Reform (SSRC Anxieties of Democracy), pp. 56–88. Cambridge University Press, Cambridge (2020)

33. Parekh, B.: Is there a case for banning hate speech? In: Herz, M., Molnar, P. (eds.) The Content and Context of Hate Speech: Rethinking Regulation and Responses, pp. 37–56. Cambridge University Press, Cambridge (2012)

34. Waldron, J.: The Harm in Hate Speech. Harvard University Press, Cambridge (2012). 35. United Kingdom. Public Order Act 1986. Section 18(1)
35. United Kingdom. The Criminal Justice and Public Order Act 1994. Section 4A
36. Canada. Criminal Code 1985. Section 319
37. Germany. German Criminal Code 1871. Section 130
38. France. Loi sur la liberté de la presse du 29 juillet 1881 (Freedom Act of the French Re public. 1881)
39. United Nations. United Nations strategy and plan of action on hate speech (2019). https://www.un.org/en/genocideprevention/documents/UN%20Strategy%20and%20Plan%20of%20Action%20on%20Hate%20Speech%2018%20June%20SYNOPSIS.pdf
40. An Bille um Cheartas Coiriúil (Gríosú chun Foréigin nó Fuatha agus Cionta Fuatha), 2022 Criminal Justice (Incitement to Violence or Hatred and Hate Offences) Bill (2022). https://data.oireachtas.ie/ie/oireachtas/bill/2022/105/eng/memo/b10522d-memo.pdf
41. BBC. Hate crime definition in NI should include gender and age. BBC (2020). https://www.bbc.com/news/uk-northern-ireland-55137721
42. Kula, A.: What is in Ireland's new so-called 'thought crime' bill, how many years in jail can you get, and which parties are backing it? Newsletter (2023). https://www.newsletter.co.uk/news/politics/what-is-in-irelands-new-so-called-thought-crime-bill-how-many-years-in-jail-can-you-get-and-which-parties-are-backing-it-4126844
43. Stanford Encyclopedia of Philosophy: Freedom of Speech (2002). https://plato.stanford.edu/entries/freedom-speech/. Accessed 10 Sept 2023
44. American Library Association. Hate speech and hate crime (2017). https://www.ala.org/advocacy/intfreedom/hate#FN%201. Accessed 10 Sept 2023
45. South African Human Rights Commission. Hate speech information sheet (2017). https://www.sahrc.org.za/home/21/files/Hate%20Speech%20Information%20Sheet-%20print%20ready-.pdf
46. Staff writer: New hate speech laws face pushback in South Africa. BusinessTech (2023). https://businesstech.co.za/news/government/689199/new-hate-speech-laws-face-pushback-in-south-africa/
47. Min-sik, Y.: Anti-Moon protests give impetus to hate speech ban in Korea. The Korea Herald (2022). https://www.koreaherald.com/view.php?ud=20220608000860
48. Park, M.S., Choo, J.H.: Study of hate speech and its responsive maneuvers, Korean Institute of Criminology and Justice (2017). https://www.kicj.re.kr/board.es?mid=a20201000000&bid=0029&list_no=12448&act=view
49. Library of Congress: Japan. New act targets hate speech against persons from outside Japan (2016). https://www.loc.gov/item/global-legal-monitor/2016-08-31/japan-new-act-targets-hate-speech-against-persons-from-outside-japan/
50. Fu, H.: China's hate speech conundrum (n.d.). https://www.ohchr.org/sites/default/files/Documents/Issues/Expression/ICCPR/Bangkok/FuHualing.pdf
51. Ward, K.: Free speech and the development of liberal virtues: An examination of the controversies involving flag-burning and hate speech, 52 U. Miami L. Rev. 733 (1998). https://repository.law.miami.edu/umlr/vol52/iss3/4/. Accessed 05 Sept 2023
52. Meta. Hate speech (n.d.). https://transparency.fb.com/policies/community-standards/hatespeech/. Accessed 07 Sept 2023
53. Meta. How Meta enforces its policies (n.d.). https://transparency.fb.com/enforcement/. Accessed 07 Sept 2023
54. Allen, R.: Hard questions: who should decide what is hate speech in an online global community? Meta (2017). https://about.fb.com/news/2017/06/hard-questions-hate-speech/
55. Google. Hate speech (n.d.). https://support.google.com/contributionpolicy/answer/11412392?hl=en&sjid=15123418514938027351-NC. Accessed 07 Sept 2023

56. YouTube. Hate speech policy (n.d.). https://support.google.com/youtube/answer/2801939?
    hl=en#:~:text=Don't%20post%20content%20on,for%20violence%20as%20real%20threats.
    Accessed 07 Sept 2023
57. X. Hateful conduct (2023). https://help.twitter.com/en/rules-and-policies/hateful-conduct-
    policy. Accessed 07 Sept 2023
58. Ghaffary, S.: How TikTok's hate speech detection tool set off a debate about racial bias on
    the app. Vox (2021). https://www.vox.com/recode/2021/7/7/22566017/tiktok-black-creators-
    ziggi-tyler-debate-about-black-lives-matter-racial-bias-social-media
59. Kinney, T.A.: Hate speech and ethnophaulisms. The International Encyclopedia of Com-
    munication (2003). https://doi.org/10.1002/9781405186407.wbiech004. https://communica
    tion.iresearchnet.com/intercultural-and-intergroup-communication/hate-speech-and-ethnop
    haulisms/. Accessed 27 Dec 2023
60. Asante, M.K.: Identifying racist language: Linguistic acts and signs. In: Hecht, M. (ed.)
    Communicating Prejudice, pp. 87–98. Sage, Thousand Oaks (1998)
61. Brown, A.: What is hate speech? Part 1: the myth of hate. Law Philos. **36**, 419–468 (2017).
    https://doi.org/10.1007/s10982-017-9297-1

Understanding the Motivations Behind Knowingly Spreading Rumors on Social Media Using Q Methodology

Xiao-Liang Shen[1]([✉]) [iD], Qianwen Qian[1] [iD], and You Wu[2] [iD]

[1] School of Information Management, Wuhan University, Wuhan 430072, China
xlshen@whu.edu.cn

[2] Economics and Management School, Wuhan University, Wuhan 430072, China

Abstract. "Knowingly spreading rumors" has become an increasingly prevalent and seriously damaging phenomenon, yet existing research failed to provide enough theoretical explanations and empirical investigations of this issue. To bridge this research gap, this study utilizes the Q-methodology, which combines qualitative and quantitative approaches, to comprehensively explore the underlying core motivations and individual differences among social media users who knowingly spread rumors. By collecting, screening, and validating statements that encompass various reasons for knowingly spreading rumors on social media, we constructed a Q-set consisting of 44 statements. Subsequently, we invited 275 P-samples (in Q-methodology research, "P-samples" refer to the participants) to perform Q-sorting. Through factor analysis, we identified four types of motivations for knowingly spreading rumors on social media: Personal Involvement Type, Social Status Seeking Type, Entertainment Value Enhancement Type, and Uncertainty Reduction Type. Furthermore, our exploration delved into the unique relationships between these motivation types and demographic variables. The findings of this study not only broaden the boundaries of research within the realm of rumor spreading but also inspire further scholarly investigations into this underexamined behavior. This study also offers practical guidance for social media platforms, debunking organizations, and educational institutions, empowering them to develop effective strategies for preventing and intervening in the knowingly spread of rumors.

Keywords: Unverified Rumors · Knowingly Spread Rumors · Social Media · Q Methodology

1 Introduction

Unverified rumors often circulate for a long time before receiving official validation [1], and their spread rate is much faster than information already verified as true or false [1]. This leads to a notably higher quantity of unverified rumors spreading across social media [2]. For instance, Wang et al. [2] revealed that official authorities verified only 33.8% of rumors in Taiwan. Consequently, social media users frequently find themselves overwhelmed by a vast number of unverified rumors [3].

I. Sserwanga et al. (Eds.): iConference 2024, LNCS 14597, pp. 157–174, 2024.
https://doi.org/10.1007/978-3-031-57860-1_12

While information literacy education, designed to combat rumors, can enhance critical thinking skills [4, 5] and sometimes make individuals aware of unverified rumors, knowing the absence of authenticity in the information does not hinder people from spreading it [6, 7]. An increasingly prevalent but perplexing phenomenon is that even when individuals are aware that certain information has not been officially verified, they still spread unverified rumors on social media [7, 8]. This phenomenon of knowingly spreading rumors can cause severe harm, particularly during emergencies, disasters, or critical situations. During these crucial moments, people often recklessly disseminate unverified rumors about uncertain events on social media [9], leading to the rapid proliferation of numerous unverified rumors and ultimately resulting in an "infodemic" [10, 11].

Furthermore, due to the higher quantity [2] and faster dissemination rate [1, 12] of unverified rumors, combined with the increased intent and purposefulness of knowingly spreading rumors, and the enhanced dissemination capabilities of social media platforms [13], the harms caused by the knowingly spreading unverified rumors exhibit a cumulative, explosive, and exponential growth pattern. This not only has negative implications at the individual level, such as misleading the public and jeopardizing health, but also poses numerous challenges across various societal and political dimensions [14–16]. Therefore, understanding the reasons why people knowingly spread rumors is essential for developing effective strategies to counter the significant harms and challenges caused by this behavior.

While exploring the motivations behind knowingly spreading rumors is crucial, most existing literature primarily examines the reasons for behaviors like rumor spreading [17–20], rumor sharing [12, 21–28], and rumor forwarding [29, 30]. It is important to note that many of these studies have investigated the motivations for spreading rumors by measuring motivations for spreading information (meaning participants were not explicitly informed that the information they were spreading was a rumor) [12, 19, 22, 23, 25–30]. Therefore, there has been insufficient attention given to the behavior of knowingly spreading rumors in existing research. As a result, existing interventions aimed at curbing rumor dissemination, such as enhancing individuals' digital media literacy and reducing their susceptibility to rumors, may likely be ineffective strategies against knowingly spreading rumors [8]. Additionally, existing research primarily employs quantitative methods. However, the act of spreading rumors is influenced by multiple factors. This complexity makes it challenging to develop generalized models and hypotheses, rendering sole reliance on quantitative methods inadequate for fully understanding the motivations behind rumor spreading.

To address the aforementioned gaps, this paper focuses on knowingly spreading rumors and employs the Q-methodology, which is well-suited for addressing subjective and complex issues [31–33], to comprehensively and systematically explore the core motivations and individual differences among general social media users who knowingly spread rumors. In terms of theoretical implications, the research findings deepen the academic understanding of knowingly spreading rumors, expand the current scientific inquiries within the field of rumor spreading, and inspire LIS scholars to further explore this interesting and important phenomenon. In practical terms, the results can assist various stakeholders in developing more effective strategies for preventing, intervening in, and managing the behavior of knowingly spreading rumors.

2 Related Work

Rumor is defined as "unverified information" [34], which later can be proven to be true or false [35]. Social media platforms have revolutionized the way people access and disseminate information [36], resulting in faster rumor sharing, wider reach [13], and greater challenges in controlling the spread of rumors [37, 38].

Currently, a significant amount of research has explored the reasons behind rumor spreading [17–20], rumor sharing [12, 21–28], and rumor forwarding [29, 30]. These studies have found that individuals engage in spreading rumors on social media due to various reasons, including the characteristics of the rumor (credibility, relevance, content, rumor type), individual motivations (trust, fact-checking, enhancing social relationships, self-enhancement), and personal traits (health literacy, cognitive beliefs, age).

While research on rumor-related behaviors has been steadily growing in recent years, the majority of existing studies have not explicitly informed participants that the information they saw and disseminated were rumors [12, 19, 22, 23, 25–30]. Instead, participants often perceived that they were sharing general information or interesting stories. Thus, existing research fundamentally measures the motives for "unknowingly spreading rumors" by exploring the motivations for general information dissemination, lacking an analysis of the crucial behavior of "knowingly spreading rumors". Very limited research has also touched upon the topic of knowingly spreading rumors, revealing that people consciously share rumors for entertainment value [7] or to establish positive social connections [7, 39, 40]. However, existing studies have failed to provide a comprehensive and in-depth understanding of the users' motivations for the knowingly spread rumors behavior.

Furthermore, existing research heavily relies on quantitative methods such as the structural equation model [12, 25, 26, 30], experiments [19, 21, 23], numerical simulations [18, 20], questionnaire surveys, and regression analysis [22, 27] to investigate the reasons behind rumor dissemination. Quantitative methods primarily focus on quantitative analysis and empirical validation of specific research models or hypotheses, but these methods encounter difficulty in providing a comprehensive and systematic exploration of the underlying causes of a particular behavior, especially when there is limited knowledge about a specific topic, as in the case of "knowingly spreading rumors" addressed in this paper.

In this regard, Q Methodology, developed from factor analysis theory in the 1930s, offers a suitable approach to explore the motivations behind knowingly spreading rumors on social media. Q Methodology combines the strengths of quantitative and qualitative research methods and is capable of comprehensively and systematically revealing individuals' beliefs and opinions on specific issues [41, 42]. What is more, Q Methodology is exploratory in nature, particularly suitable for investigating complex and under-examined questions [31], and ultimately identifies the core viewpoints and major types related to the research topic [43], rather than solely confirming existing theories and hypotheses.

Given the unique advantages of Q Methodology, this study employs it to analyze the motivations behind the knowingly spreading rumors behavior on social media. Specifically, this study aims to address the following two research questions:

RQ1: What are the core types of motivations that drive individuals to knowingly spread rumors on social media, and what are the characteristics of these types?
RQ2: What is the relationship between the types of motivations for knowingly spreading rumors on social media and the demographic variables of social media users?

3 Methods

3.1 Research Design

This study rigorously followed the standard procedure of the Q methodology (see Fig. 1) to investigate the types of motivations behind knowingly spreading rumors on social media.

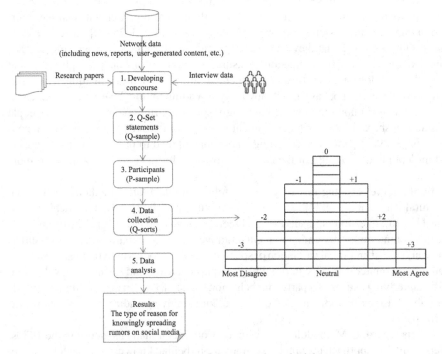

Fig. 1. Overview of the research methodology.

Developing Concourse. The first stage involved developing the concourse, which is a comprehensive collection of statements related to the specific issue under investigation [44]. To overcome the limitation of a single data source, we focused on the motivations behind knowingly spreading rumors and collected statements from diverse channels including academic literature, semi-structured interviews, news reports, and user-generated content on the internet. Following saturation criteria, we gathered a total of 252 preliminary statements, forming the concourse.

Q-Set Statements (Q-Sample). The second phase involved refining the statement collection from the concourse, resulting in a Q-sample for subsequent Q-sorting. Initially, 52 statements were distilled through two rounds of manual coding. Then, three graduate students assessed the comprehensiveness, distinctiveness, and clarity of the statements, leading to further refinement into 50 statements. Finally, we distributed expert surveys to six experts in the fields of rumor management and user information behavior to validate the statements and provide suggestions for modifications. In the end, a Q-set comprising 44 statements was finalized (see Table 2), which aligns with the recommended range of 40–80 statements [45].

Participants (P-Sample). The next stage involved selecting the P-sample, which are participants responsible for Q-sorting and answering additional questions. These participants needed to be stakeholders in the research topic. Therefore, we employed a "snowball" recruitment approach to enlist participants who had knowingly spread rumors on social media within the past six months. Specifically, we initially recruited the first group of participants through various channels such as WeChat, Sina Weibo, and QQ. We then encouraged these participants to attract more eligible individuals to participate in the survey through sharing recruitment information. To minimize potential reluctance to participate the survey due to the term "knowingly spread rumors", which may be considered undesirable behavior and many people may be unwilling to admit, this study implemented the following measures: 1) Providing a neutral and objective definition of "knowingly spread rumors": It refers to the act of individuals disseminating unverified information while knowing that this information has not been officially validated. 2) Strictly adhering to research ethical principles, including ensuring informed consent, protecting the anonymity of participants, maintaining data security, and encouraging voluntary participation in the study, among other considerations. We ultimately recruited 275 participants. This sample size was deemed adequate for Q-methodology, which excels in discerning core viewpoints within small samples [46]. The P-sample consisted of 58.55% males and 41.45% females, representing a heterogeneous group in terms of age, education level, and monthly income.

Data Collection (Q-Sorts). The Q-sort task involves the P-sample participants sorting the statements related to the reasons for knowingly spreading rumors from the Q-sample. To efficiently survey a heterogeneous sample, we used the Q-sorting platform (Q-sortware) and the survey platform (Credemo) to design an online Q-sorting survey task. The formal questionnaire was then developed based on the results of the pretest to ensure its effectiveness and reliability.

The P-sample was required to cognitively read the informed consent form and related concept analysis before formally starting the research task. The process involved five steps: First, participants were required to recall their experiences of knowingly spreading unverified rumors on social media in the past six months. Second, participants read the Q-sorting operational instructions and confirmed their understanding of all research tasks. Third, participants clicked on a webpage link to access the Q-sorting page and sorted the 44 pre-collected statements related to knowingly spreading rumors. The Q-sorting was divided into two rounds, where participants initially sorted all statements into three categories: Disagree, Neutral, and Agree. They then further categorized them into seven cells, ranging from −3 (Strongly Disagree) to + 3 (Strongly Agree) (see Fig. 1). This is a table depicting a normal distribution, which aligns with the requirements of the Q-method. Fourth, they are expected to provide the statement numbers and reasons for both the statement they most agree with and the statement they most disagree with. Finally, participants answered demographic questions. Upon careful completion of the entire research process and passing attention checks, P-sample participants received a compensation of ¥10 (Chinese Yuan). The estimated duration for each participant to complete the survey was between 25–55 min, and the research period lasted from July 10, 2023, to August 30, 2023.

Data Analysis. In the Q-methodology, participant sorting results are subjected to factor analysis to classify core viewpoints [31]. We input the 275 sets of Q-sort data into Ken-Q, a specialized application designed for Q-sort analysis.

When determining the number of factor rotation, an acceptable level of explained variance is considered to be 35%–40% or above [47]. The initial results of the viewpoint analysis indicate that the explained variance for three factors is 37%, and for four factors, it is 40%. Therefore, this study should consider at least four factors. Furthermore, after comparing the results of factor rotations for different numbers of factors based on the criteria of simplicity, clarity, low correlations, and stability outlined by Webler et al. [48], it was found that the four-factor solution is the most ideal one (it involves the fewest number of factors, exhibits low inter-factor correlations, has a relatively higher number of P samples loading onto each factor, and offers the best explanatory power for each factor). Consequently, we have decided to proceed with the factor rotation and factor analysis using four factors.

3.2   Results

The factor rotation results reveal that the four factors account for 41% of the variance, with a total of 180 participants primarily loading onto a single factor (see Table 1). The remaining participants primarily exhibit two scenarios: 1) having approximately equal loadings on multiple factors (e.g., participant 11), implying agreement with mixed view-points from two or more factors, or 2) displaying lower factor loadings (e.g., participant 4), signifying a lack of commonality with all four factors. Consequently, participants falling into these two scenarios were excluded from further analysis [33].

RQ1: What are the Core Types of Motivations that Drive Individuals to Know-ingly Spread Rumors on Social Media, and What are the Characteristics of These Types? Following previous studies [49, 50], this study adopts the following approach: 1) identifying the most agreeable and disagreeable statements, and 2) distinguishing statements to label and expound upon each factor (see Table 2). In Q methodology, a distinguishing statement refers to a statement where its score on a particular factor significantly differs from its scores on any other factors [51].

Specifically, in line with Q methodology practices [49, 50], this study named each type based on the distinguishing statements with the highest Z-scores and used all distinguishing statements to elucidate the meaning of each type. For instance, the distinguishing statement with the highest Z-score for Type 3 is Q13 - "I knowingly spread rumors on social media, because of the entertainment value of the rumor." Therefore, Type 3 is named "Entertainment Value Enhancement Type". Additionally, this paper employs all the distinguishing statements of Type 3 to interpret its meaning (see Table 2).

Table 1. Factor loadings.

Participant ID	Factor 1	Factor 2	Factor 3	Factor 4
1	0.3412	0.383	0.3734	0.0503
2	0.2828	0.1242	**0.4009X**	0.2506
3	0.1694	0.1096	0.1776	−0.0881
4	−0.21	0.2426	0.0958	−0.0001
5	**0.4779X**	0.0725	0.3713	0.1219
6	**0.5698X**	0.3134	0.21	−0.0192
7	**0.5905X**	0.2736	0.3542	0.0532
8	0.5027	0.3894	0.3206	−0.0264
9	0.0986	0.1141	0.0685	−0.2401
10	0.2528	**0.4904X**	0.1372	0.1536
11	0.4753	0.369	0.3639	0.1694
...	...	...	...	...
275	−0.0907	0.0948	−0.1121	**0.6769X**
The number of participants	57	68	45	10
% Explained Variance	12	16	10	3

Note: X represents the factor where the participant falls, and the preceding number indicates the proportion of explained variance in the rotated factor.

Type 1: Personal Involvement Type. 57 participants strongly support Type 1, accounting for 12% of the variance. This category is referred to as the "Personal Involvement Type" (see Table 2). This category of participants is eager to knowingly share rumors because the information is highly relevant to their personal lives and holds great importance, even if they are aware that this information is a rumor not verified by official sources (Q6, Q4). Their dissemination behavior is rooted in trust psychology (Q17), as they tend to believe that information aligning with their values, cognition, and beliefs is true (Q26). It is worth noting that these participants are often motivated to spread rumors due to the intrinsic appeal of the information itself, both in terms of content and emotion (Q7), especially in environments characterized by freedom of speech (Q34). Furthermore, this category of participants places great emphasis on the value of objective information

Table 2. Z-scores of the statements for each factor.

Statement (Q-Set) I knowingly spread rumors on social media...	Type 1	Type 2	Type 3	Type 4
1......because the source credibility of the rumor is high	1.14	−0.23	1.07	−0.66
2......because the content of the rumor is highly credible	1.54	1.10	1.09	1.14
3......because the rumor is the most recent and highly timely news	−0.76	−0.71	0.53	0.19
4......because the rumor pertains to highly important issues	**1.86**	1.16	**0.54**	1.12
5......because the rumor has a strong influence and garners extensive discussion	0.41	0.49	0.57	**1.03**
6......because the rumor is highly relevant to me	**2.00**	**0.80**	**0.32**	**−1.74**
7......because of the rumor's compelling content or strong emotional appeal	**0.43**	1.49	1.06	1.35
8......because the rumor's content is highly uncertain, leaving me filled with doubt	**0.14**	**1.16**	**−0.36**	2.10
9......because of altruistic motives	1.57	1.77	1.49	**0.32**
10......because of malevolent motives	−2.62	**−2.21**	−2.74	**−1.44**
11......because of the herd mentality	−0.69	**1.01**	−0.46	**−1.52**
12......because of the motive of managing social relationships	−1.37	**0.49**	**−0.19**	−1.3
13......because of the entertainment value of the rumor	**−0.87**	**−1.92**	1.63	**−0.09**
14......because I want to alleviate intense emotions	**−0.71**	−0.4	**0.93**	−0.20
15......because I want to safeguard my personal image	**−0.38**	**0.85**	**−0.06**	−1.13
16......because I want to pursue social status	−1.32	**1.26**	**0.38**	−0.84
17......because I genuinely believe the rumor is true	**1.57**	0.51	0.69	**−0.16**
18......because the content mentioned in the rumor is too significant to ignore, adhering to a "better safe than sorry" mindset	0.99	0.90	0.72	**−1.09**
19......because I don't believe the rumor and want to debunk it	**−0.02**	1.54	1.17	1.15
20......because I have doubts about the rumor and want to seek more information	0.67	**0.21**	0.48	**1.88**
21......because I recognize the difficulties in verifying rumors, so I authenticate them through sharing	−0.36	−1.12	−0.56	−0.78
22......because I am not aware of the adverse consequences or consider them insignificant	0.14	**−0.57**	**−1.39**	0.12
23......because I want to address the societal issues inherent in the rumors by sharing	0.61	0.74	0.52	0.85

(continued)

Table 2. (*continued*)

Statement (Q-Set) I knowingly spread rumors on social media...	Type 1	Type 2	Type 3	Type 4
24......because I have some specific intentions such as creating social chaos or engaging in competitive business practices	−2.47	−2.01	−2.16	**0.04**
25......because I want to seek help in discerning the rumors through sharing	0.16	**−1.16**	**−0.63**	0.51
26......because the rumor aligns with my values, inherent cognition, and own beliefs	**0.81**	1.20	1.10	**−0.69**
27......because the anonymity feature allows me to conceal my true identity	0.07	0.06	**−1.67**	**−2.37**
28......because recommendation algorithm technology repeatedly exposes me to previously viewed or supported rumors	**0.18**	−0.81	−0.12	−0.45
29......because the content presentation features of media platforms facilitate my access to and browsing of rumors	0.05	**−0.66**	0.26	**0.97**
30......because the content creation features of media platforms make it easy for me to edit and modify rumors	−0.33	−1.01	−0.82	−0.39
31......because the social features of media platforms facilitate discussions with others about rumors	0.52	**−0.23**	**0.80**	0.27
32......because the distribution features of media platforms enable me to quickly and widely share rumors	0.70	0.60	0.52	0.77
33......because I am influenced by the post-truth era, where emotions and beliefs outweigh facts	**−1.05**	−0.82	−0.57	−0.39
34......because I am in an environment of relatively unrestricted freedom of speech	**0.38**	−0.13	**0.96**	−0.07
35......because it has become more challenging for official institutions to timely clarify the truth in the age of information overload	−0.28	**−1.22**	−0.28	**0.25**
36......because the credibility of official media or government has declined, and I trust my judgment over official verification	−0.11	−0.31	−0.96	−1.20
37......because, on interest-driven social media platforms, rumors often gain more exposure due to their strong appeal	**−1.15**	−0.53	−0.31	−0.02
38......because I am easily influenced by online public opinion, which widely accepts and spreads rumors	−0.20	**−0.63**	−0.37	**0.32**
39......because of the diverse perspectives the online public holds regarding rumors	0.36	0.42	0.13	**1.17**

(*continued*)

Table 2. (*continued*)

Statement (Q-Set) I knowingly spread rumors on social media...	Type 1	Type 2	Type 3	Type 4
40......because other social media users have limited ability to discern and evaluate rumors, and these rumors have already widely spread online, thus I am eager to obtain the truth by sharing the rumors	−0.01	−0.34	−0.23	0.32
41......because I am influenced by family members and friends who widely accept and spread rumors	−0.17	0.53	−0.10	0.40
42......because my family and friends are more tolerant of my sharing and discussing rumors	**0.09**	−0.41	**0.51**	**−1.08**
43......because the widespread spreading of rumors reduces my concerns about the consequences and responsibilities of doing so	**−0.72**	**−1.13**	**−1.51**	**0.35**
44......because of the relatively weak penalties from official and non-official regulatory institutions for spreading rumors	**−0.79**	**0.25**	**−1.97**	**1.02**

Note: Z-scores are indicators of the priority level for each statement, showing the extent of agreement among all participants regarding various statements. The bolded notes indicate that the z-scores are significantly different from others ($p < 0.01$), representing distinct statements within that factor.

characteristics and does not knowingly spread rumors for specific purposes (Q24) or to pursue personal status (Q16).

Participants of this type provided the following qualitative comments: "Because relevant and important information is closely related to my interests, I do not pay attention to their veracity" (Participant 30, Type 1). "The rumors not verified by official sources I spread are closely tied to my own life" (Participant 147, Type 1).

Type 2: Social Status Seeking Type. 68 participants significantly supported Type 2, accounting for 16% of the variance. This type is referred to as the "Social Status Seeking Type" (see Table 2). Participants of this type knowingly spread rumors not verified by official sources to satisfy their desire for social status-seeking (Q16). They believe that enhancing relationships with others is a core motivator and often engage in rumor-sharing due to a herd mentality (Q11). They selectively spread rumors that benefit their image and interests (Q15) to strengthen social relationships, conform to their social group, and avoid isolation (Q12). Additionally, they knowingly spread rumors because of the uncertainty of the rumor and its high relevance to themselves (Q6, Q8). It is noteworthy that participants of this type of highly value social status-seeking. They strongly disapprove of motives that harm social relationships, such as damaging others' reputations, provoking others, or causing harm (Q10). Additionally, they do not engage in spreading rumors for self-amusement purposes (Q13).

Participants of this type provided the following qualitative comments: "I knowingly spread rumors in hopes of getting more views, likes, and followers on social media"

(Participant 37, Type 2). "I knowingly spread rumors to satisfy my social presence" (Participant 97, Type 2).

Type 3: Entertainment Value Enhancement Type. 45 participants significantly supported Type 3, explaining 10% of the variance. This type can be referred to as the "Entertainment Value Enhancement Type" (see Table 2), where these participants view knowingly spreading rumors as a means of seeking enjoyment, passing the time, or self-entertainment (Q13). Additionally, they may knowingly spread rumors because they want to alleviate their polarized emotions (Q14). Furthermore, in an environment characterized by freedom of speech (Q34), the interactive and discussion features of social media platforms accelerate the act of knowingly spreading rumors (Q31). It is worth noting that these participants are aware of potential penalties from relevant authorities (Q44). They believe that even with anonymity and shared responsibility protection, they still need to bear the consequences and responsibility for spreading rumors (Q27, Q43, Q22). Nevertheless, they choose to knowingly spread rumors due to a strong motivation to derive entertainment and emotional value.

Participants of this type provided the following qualitative comments: "The primary purpose of disseminating information is for entertainment and passing the time" (participant 31, Type 3). "I hope to find emotional resonance by spreading rumors" (participant 111, Type 3).

Type 4: Uncertainty Reduction Type. 10 participants significantly supported Type 4, explaining 3% of the variance. This type is referred to as the "Uncertainty Reduction Type" (see Table 2). These participants typically focus on the uncertainty of information content and have a strong desire to seek the latest information (Q8), as a result, they knowingly spread rumors. They attempt to explore the truth and dispel doubts by knowingly spreading rumors, even though they are aware that these rumors have not been officially confirmed (Q20, Q39). Of course, they may also spread rumors due to the rumors' strong impact (Q5). These individuals believe that the regulatory penalties from both official and unofficial institutions are relatively weak (Q44). Furthermore, they are less concerned about the consequences and responsibilities of rumor spreading because of the high circulation of rumors (Q43). It is noteworthy that even though they are aware that anonymity does not exempt them from the responsibility and consequences of spreading rumors (Q27), and despite the rumors not being highly relevant to them (Q6), these participants engage in knowingly spreading unverified rumors due to their strong motivation to reduce uncertainty.

Participants of this type provided the following qualitative comments: "I knowingly spread rumors to reduce uncertainty" (Participant 257, Type 4). "The strong uncertainty made me full of doubts, so I spread rumors" (Participant 206, Type 4).

RQ2: What is the Relationship Between the Types of Motivations for Knowingly Spreading Rumors on Social Media and the Demographic Variables of Social Media Users? As Q-methodology is oriented towards heterogeneity, it is necessary to examine the associations between the types of motivations and demographic variables of social media users.

This study employed a chi-square test to examine the relationships between the four types of motivations behind knowingly spreading rumors and demographic variables.

Table 3. Association between four types of motivations and demographic variables.

Title	Category	Motivation Type (%)				Total	χ2	p
		Type 1 Personal Involvement Type	Type 2 Social Status Seeking Type	Type 3 Entertainment Value Enhancement Type	Type 4 Uncertainty Reduction Type			
Gender	Female	35(61.40)	15(22.06)	22(48.89)	7(70.00)	79(43.89)	23.48	***
	Male	22(38.60)	53(77.94)	23(51.11)	3(30.00)	101(56.11)		
Age	<18	3(5.26)	3(4.41)	6(13.33)	2(20.00)	14(7.78)	48.11	***
	18–25	32(56.14)	22(32.35)	31(68.89)	0(0.00)	85(47.22)		
	26–35	8(14.04)	11(16.18)	3(6.67)	2(20.00)	24(13.33)		
	36–45	10(17.54)	8(11.76)	3(6.67)	4(40.00)	25(13.89)		
	>45	4(7.02)	24(35.29)	2(4.44)	2(20.00)	32(17.78)		
Education Level	≤Junior college	17(29.82)	45(66.17)	11(24.44)	6(60.00)	79(43.89)	41.85	***
	Undergraduate	31(54.39)	10(14.71)	30(66.67)	1(10.00)	72(40.00)		
	Postgraduate	9(15.79)	13(19.12)	4(8.89)	3(30.00)	29(16.11)		
Monthly Income	≤¥2,000	24(42.11)	12(17.65)	17(37.78)	0(0.00)	53(29.44)	28.83	***
	¥2,001-¥5,000	18(31.58)	27(39.71)	18(40.00)	1(10.00)	64(35.56)		
	¥5,001-¥10,000	9(15.79)	18(26.47)	7(15.56)	4(40.00)	38(21.11)		
	>¥10,000	6(10.52)	11(16.17)	3(6.66)	5(50.00)	25(13.89)		

$* p < 0.05; ** p < 0.01; *** p < 0.001$

Table 3 reports significant differential distributions ($p < 0.001$) of demographic variables across the different types of motivations. Based on these findings, users' demographic profiles associated with each type of motivation were developed (see Fig. 2).

Type 1: Personal Involvement Type 1. Females 2. Young adults (18-25 years old) 3. Undergraduate 4. Low income level (monthly income less than ¥2,000)	**Type 2: Social Status Seeking Type** 1. Males 2. Middle-aged to elderly adults (aged over 45 years old) 3. Moderate income level (monthly income ranging from ¥5,001 to ¥10,000)
Type 3: Entertainment Value Enhancement Type 1. Young adults (18-25 years old) 2. Undergraduate 3. Low income level (monthly income less than ¥2,000)	**Type 4: Uncertainty Reduction Type** 1. Females 2. Middle-aged adults (26-45 years old) 3. Postgraduate (Master's or Ph.D. degrees) or Junior college education and below 4. Moderate income level (monthly income ranging from ¥5,001 to ¥10,000)

Fig. 2. Demographic profiles of four motivation types

4 General Discussion

4.1 Summary of Findings

Utilizing Q-methodology, this study identified four types of motivations: Personal Involvement Type, Social Status Seeking Type, Entertainment Value Enhancement Type, and Uncertainty Reduction Type, to explain why individuals knowingly spread unverified rumors on social media.

In particular, this paper focuses on a less-explored issue, and some notable findings have emerged. Firstly, the Personal Involvement Type confirms that information that is highly relevant to oneself and perceived as important will accelerate rumor-spreading behaviors [19, 21]. Due to these rumors being closely aligned with the interests or benefits of individuals, social media users tend to spread them even when they know these are unverified rumors.

The Social Status Seeking Type illustrates that people knowingly spread rumors to gain the respect of others or seek social status within a group. Previous research on information sharing has highlighted the importance of establishing and maintaining social relationships [52, 53]. However, knowingly spreading rumors for the sake of enhancing social status possesses its uniqueness. In the context of this study, knowingly spreading unverified rumors to others presents an attempt to express concern for others or to indicate that they know something others do not, thereby maintaining social relationships and enhancing social status.

The Entertainment Value Enhancement Type represents an unexpected yet interesting finding, which also echoes previous research on online rumor dissemination [19]. In an increasingly liberalized online communication landscape, particularly among Generation Z, spreading rumors might not be perceived as a serious concern. Instead, sharing interesting but unverified rumors with family or friends can serve as a means to alleviate work and life pressures. It is worth noting that the entertainment value of rumors remains an exceedingly overlooked research topic.

The Uncertainty Reduction Type indicates that individuals knowingly spread rumors in hopes of acquiring more information from others to reduce uncertainty. Prior research has also suggested that individuals engage in rumor dissemination as a means of fact-checking [19, 34] to alleviate the anxiety stemming from uncertainty [54, 55]. This also implies that due to the delay in clarifying the truth or the lack of widespread dissemination of rumor rebuttals, individuals may resort to spreading rumors to obtain the truth they seek.

Furthermore, this study further explores the relationship between the identified motivation types and demographic variables, thus unveiling potential user profiles associated with each motivation. Specifically, those motivated by personal involvement are predominantly young women with undergraduate degrees, typically having lower incomes. Individuals driven by social status-seeking motivation are mainly middle-aged to elderly men, with middle-level incomes. Users motivated by entertainment value enhancement are primarily from Generation Z, a cohort raised alongside the Internet. They are exposed to a more liberal online environment, possess more open-minded thoughts, and are more inclined to pursue the entertainment value of rumors. Users motivated by uncertainty reduction are predominantly middle-aged women. Interestingly, this demographic, whether highly educated (holding postgraduate degrees) or less educated (junior college and below), tends to spread rumors to seek external information support, thereby mitigating their perceived uncertainty.

4.2 Theoretical Implications

This paper contributes to the existing literature in three ways. Firstly, it introduces an important yet underexplored research question - knowingly spreading rumors behavior, thus expanding the current academic discussion within the field of rumor spreading. Although previous research has examined rumor spreading behaviors [17–20], or other related behaviors, such as rumor sharing [12, 21–28] and rumor forwarding [29, 30], the act of spreading rumors unconsciously (or unknowingly) is fundamentally similar to general information dissemination behavior. Consequently, the motivations identified for unknowingly rumor spreading behaviors tend to be more aligned with the motives for general information sharing. This paper bridges the research gap by delving into the phenomenon of knowingly spreading rumors and exploring the core motivations behind this interesting and unique phenomenon.

Secondly, this study employs Q methodology, which merges both quantitative and qualitative approaches, to identify the underlying motivations. As a result, four main motivational types behind knowingly spreading rumors on social media have emerged: Personal Involvement Type, Social Status Seeking Type, Entertainment Value Enhancement Type, and Uncertainty Reduction Type. A comprehensive and systematic investigation of the reasons why people knowingly spread rumors on social media not only enriches the current understanding of disseminating unverified rumors but also provides a validated theoretical framework for further examining the psychological mechanisms underlying the behavior of knowingly spreading rumors.

Thirdly, this study investigates the profiles of users who knowingly spread rumors, providing valuable insights to unveil the dissemination motivations across various demographic groups. Starting from basic demographic characteristics such as gender, age, education level, and monthly income, this paper discovers that young women, middle-aged and elderly men, Generation Z, and middle-aged women each emphasize different dissemination motivations in the process of knowingly spreading rumors, thereby illustrating significant individual differences. Therefore, this paper contributes to a deeper understanding of unverified rumor spreading by profiling social media users with different dissemination motivations.

4.3 Practical Implications

This study provides actionable suggestions for effectively governing the behavior of knowingly spreading rumors. Firstly, knowingly spreading rumors is a pervasive and highly detrimental phenomenon, which should attract the attention of social media platforms and relevant regulatory agencies. In terms of specific measures, regulatory agencies can start from the four types of motivations identified in this paper and adopt targeted preventive and intervention strategies. For example, for the Personal Involvement Type motivation, authoritative institutions should promptly clarify rumors that are closely related to the general public. This is because even when people are aware that these are rumors, they might still spread them due to personal interests. Therefore, timely clarification of the facts becomes especially important. For the Social Status Seeking Type motivation, efforts should be made to create a public climate where spreading unverified information is detrimental to one's social image. Regarding the Entertainment Value Enhancement Type motivation, it is necessary to make people aware of the harmful consequences of spreading rumors, increase the penalties for rumor dissemination, enhance public social responsibility, and provide alternative means to alleviate intense emotions, thereby decreasing the demand for spreading rumors as a source of entertainment. For the Uncertainty Reduction Type motivation, providing additional reliable information sources and resources for authenticity verification can meet individuals' needs for achieving accurate information, thereby reducing the inclination to rely on spreading rumors to alleviate uncertainty. Additionally, information literacy education and training can be provided to help individuals better understand and evaluate the credibility and authenticity of information.

Secondly, this paper creates user profiles for the four motivations behind knowingly spreading rumors, thereby aiding regulatory agencies in effectively identifying potential rumor spreaders and implementing targeted intervention measures. This study reveals distinct motivational differences among young women, middle-aged and elderly men, Generation Z, and middle-aged women when they engage in knowingly spreading rumors. Therefore, social media platforms and regulatory agencies should tailor their approaches, by considering the characteristics of different populations, to develop customized debunking strategies and prevent rumor spreading. For instance, for Generation Z users, it is necessary to employ various methods such as online campaigns and real-life examples, to underscore the adverse consequences associated with spreading rumors.

4.4 Limitations and Directions for Future Research

While this study contributes to both academia and industry, some limitations can be addressed in future research. Firstly, the data were collected from participants in China, which is characterized as collectivistic culture and implicit communication. Therefore, caution should be exercised when generalizing the findings to other cultural contexts. Future research could further validate the four motivation types for knowingly spreading rumors by collecting data from other countries. Secondly, although the Q-methodology combines qualitative and quantitative methods and allows for a comprehensive and systematic understanding of a particular phenomenon, this method is exploratory in nature and not reliant on existing theories. Consequently, the findings of this study can be used as a basis for future empirical research to formulate theories and test hypotheses.

5 Conclusions

This study extends previous research on rumor spreading by addressing the behavior of knowingly spreading rumors on social media and identifying the primary motivations behind this behavior, as well as the distinct user profiles associated with each motivation. By employing Q-methodology, the study reveals that social media users engage in knowingly spreading rumors due to four core types of motivations: Personal

Involvement, Social Status Seeking, Entertainment Value Enhancement, and Uncertainty Reduction. Furthermore, through chi-square analysis, this paper further establishes the relationships between motivation types and demographic variables, thereby creating user profiles aligned with each motive type. In summary, this study advances the current academic understanding of the motivations driving knowingly spreading rumors on social media and offers practical insights to effectively intervene and manage such behavior.

Acknowledgements. The work described in this paper was partially supported by grants from the National Natural Science Foundation of China (Project No. 72274144, 72311540158), and the Humanities and Social Sciences Foundation of the Ministry of Education, China (Project No. 22YJA870013).

References

1. Zubiaga, A., Liakata, M., Procter, R., Wong Sak Hoi, G., Tolmie, P.: Analysing how people orient to and spread rumors in social media by looking at conversational threads. PloS One **11**(3), e0150989 (2016)
2. Wang, A.W., Lan, J.Y., Wang, M.H., Yu, C.: The evolution of rumors on a closed social networking platform during COVID-19: algorithm development and content study. JMIR Med. Inform. **9**(11), e30467 (2021)
3. Kumar, A., Nayar, K.R.: COVID 19 and its mental health consequences. J. Ment. Health **30**(1), 1–2 (2021)
4. Grafstein, A.: A discipline-based approach to information literacy. J. Acad. Librariansh. **28**(4), 197–204 (2002)
5. Igbinovia, M.O., Okuonghae, O., Adebayo, J.O.: Information literacy competence in curtailing fake news about the COVID-19 pandemic among undergraduates in Nigeria. Ref. Serv. Rev. **49**(1), 3–18 (2021)
6. Barthel, M., Mitchell, A., Holcomb, J.: Many Americans believe fake news is sowing confusion (2016)
7. Aditya, S., Darke, P.R.: Role of entertainment, social goals, and accuracy concerns in knowingly spreading questionable brand rumors. J. Assoc. Consum. Res. **5**(2), 220–237 (2020)
8. Buchanan, T.: Why do people spread false information online? The effects of message and viewer characteristics on self-reported likelihood of sharing social media disinformation. PLoS ONE **15**(10), e0239666 (2020)
9. Tasnim, S., Hossain, M.M., Mazumder, H.: Impact of rumors and misinformation on COVID-19 in social media. J. Prev. Med. Public Health **53**(3), 171–174 (2020)
10. Zhang, C., Lin, Z., Jin, S.: What else besides war: deliberate metaphors framing COVID-19 in Chinese online newspaper editorials. Metaphor. Symb. **37**(2), 114–126 (2022)
11. Apuke, O.D., Omar, B.: User motivation in fake news sharing during the COVID-19 pandemic: an application of the uses and gratification theory. Online Inf. Rev. **45**(1), 220–239 (2021)
12. Luo, P., Wang, C., Guo, F., Luo, L.: Factors affecting individual online rumor sharing behavior in the COVID-19 pandemic. Comput. Hum. Behav. **125**, 106968 (2021)
13. Meel, P., Vishwakarma, D.K.: Fake news, rumor, information pollution in social media and web: a contemporary survey of state-of-the-arts, challenges and opportunities. Expert Syst. Appl. **153**, 112986 (2020)
14. Walsh, J.P.: Social media and moral panics: assessing the effects of technological change on societal reaction. Int. J. Cult. Stud. **23**(6), 840–859 (2020)

15. Ferrara, E., Chang, H., Chen, E., Muric, G., Patel, J.: Characterizing social media manipulation in the 2020 US presidential election. First Monday (2020)
16. Zhang, L., Chen, K., Jiang, H., Zhao, J.: How the health rumor misleads people's perception in a public health emergency: lessons from a purchase craze during the COVID-19 outbreak in China. Int. J. Environ. Res. Public Health **17**(19), 7213 (2020)
17. Lee, H., Kim, J., Kim, J.N.: Mechanics of rumor mills and epistemic motivational processes of food-related rumor spread: Interplay between attitude and issue motivation. Health Commun. **36**(6), 722–730 (2021)
18. Chen, X., Wang, N.: Rumor spreading model considering rumor credibility, correlation and crowd classification based on personality. Sci. Rep. **10**(1), 5887 (2020)
19. Shen, Y.C., Lee, C.T., Pan, L.Y., Lee, C.Y.: Why people spread rumors on social media: developing and validating a multi-attribute model of online rumor dissemination. Online Inf. Rev. **45**(7), 1227–1246 (2021)
20. Hosni, A.I.E., Li, K., Ahmad, S.: Analysis of the impact of online social networks addiction on the propagation of rumors. Physica A **542**, 123456 (2020)
21. Oh, H.J., Lee, H.: When do people verify and share health rumors on social media? The effects of message importance, health anxiety, and health literacy. J. Health Commun. **24**(11), 837–847 (2019)
22. Kwon, K.H., Rao, H.R.: Cyber-rumor sharing under a homeland security threat in the context of government Internet surveillance: the case of South-North Korea conflict. Gov. Inf. Q. **34**(2), 307–316 (2017)
23. Chua, A.Y., Banerjee, S.: Intentions to trust and share online health rumors: an experiment with medical professionals. Comput. Hum. Behav. **87**, 1–9 (2018)
24. Sudhir, S., Unnithan, A.B.: Role of affect in marketplace rumor propagation. Mark. Intell. Plan. **37**(6), 631–644 (2019)
25. Liu, J., Liu, X., Lai, K.H., Zhang, X., Ma, X.: Exploring rumor behavior during the COVID-19 pandemic through an information processing perspective: the moderating role of critical thinking. Comput. Hum. Behav. **147**, 107842 (2023)
26. Guo, F., Zhou, A., Zhang, X., Xu, X., Liu, X.: Fighting rumors to fight COVID-19: investigating rumor belief and sharing on social media during the pandemic. Comput. Hum. Behav. **139**, 107521 (2023)
27. He, L., Yang, H., Xiong, X., Lai, K.: Online rumor transmission among younger and older adults. SAGE Open **9**(3), 2158244019876273 (2019)
28. Chua, A.Y., Banerjee, S.: To share or not to share: the role of epistemic belief in online health rumors. Int. J. Med. Informatics **108**, 36–41 (2017)
29. Kim, J.W.: Rumor has it: the effects of virality metrics on rumor believability and transmission on Twitter. New Media Soc. **20**(12), 4807–4825 (2018)
30. Lin, T.C., Huang, S.L., Liao, W.X.: Examining the antecedents of everyday rumor retransmission. Inf. Technol. People **35**(4), 1326–1345 (2022)
31. Kim, J.Y.: A study of social media users' perceptional typologies and relationships to self-identity and personality. Internet Res. **28**(3), 767–784 (2018)
32. Nunnally, J.C.: Psychometric Theory, 2nd edn. McGraw Hill, New York (1978)
33. Brown, S.: Political Subjectivity: Applications of Q Methodology in Political Science. Yale University Press, New Haven (1980)
34. DiFonzo, N., Bordia, P.: Rumor, gossip and urban legends. Diogenes **54**(1), 19–35 (2007)
35. Alkhodair, S.A., Ding, S.H., Fung, B.C., Liu, J.: Detecting breaking news rumors of emerging topics in social media. Inf. Process. Manage. **57**(2), 102018 (2020)
36. Dhir, A., Yossatorn, Y., Kaur, P., Chen, S.: Online social media fatigue and psychological wellbeing—a study of compulsive use, fear of missing out, fatigue, anxiety and depression. Int. J. Inf. Manage. **40**, 141–152 (2018)

37. Ozturk, P., Li, H., Sakamoto, Y.: Combating rumor spread on social media: the effectiveness of refutation and warning. In: 2015 48th Hawaii International Conference on System Sciences, pp. 2406–2414. IEEE (2015)
38. Stieglitz, S., Dang-Xuan, L.: Emotions and information diffusion in social media—sentiment of microblogs and sharing behavior. J. Manag. Inf. Syst. **29**(4), 217–248 (2013)
39. DePaulo, B.M., Kashy, D.A.: Everyday lies in close and casual relationships. J. Pers. Soc. Psychol. **74**(1), 63 (1998)
40. Hickman, T., Ward, J.: The dark side of brand community: inter-group stereotyping, trash talk, and schadenfreude. ACR North American Advances (2007)
41. Zheng, Y., Lu, X., Ren, W.: Tracking the evolution of Chinese learners' multilingual motivation through a longitudinal Q methodology. Mod. Lang. J. **104**(4), 781–803 (2020)
42. Brown, S.R., Durning, D.W., Selden, S.: Q Methodology. In: Miller, G.J., Whicker, M.L. (eds.) Handbook of Research Methods in Public Administration, pp. 599–637. Marcel Dekker, New York (1999)
43. Brown, S.R.: A primer on Q methodology. Operant Subjectivity **16**, 91–138 (1993)
44. Stephenson, W.: Protoconcursus: the concourse theory of communication: I. Operant Subjectivity **9**(2), 37–58 (1986)
45. Shinebourne, P.: Using Q method in qualitative research. Int. J. Qual. Methods **8**(1), 93–97 (2009)
46. Rajé, F.: Using Q methodology to develop more perceptive insights on transport and social inclusion. Transp. Policy **14**(6), 467–477 (2007)
47. Kline, P.: An Easy Guide to Factor Analysis. Routledge (1994)
48. Webler, T., Danielson, S., Tuler, S.: Using Q Method to reveal social perspectives in environmental research. Greenfield, MA: Soc. Environ. Res. Inst. **54**, 1–45 (2009)
49. Selvanathan, H.P., Uluğ, Ö.M., Burrows, B.: What should allies do? Identifying activist perspectives on the role of white allies in the struggle for racial justice in the United States. Eur. J. Soc. Psychol. **53**(1), 43–60 (2023)
50. VanScoy, A.: Using Q methodology to understand conflicting conceptualizations of reference and information service. Libr. Inf. Sci. Res. **43**(3), 101107 (2021)
51. Akhtar-Danesh, N., Baumann, A., Cordingley, L.: Q-methodology in nursing research: a promising method for the study of subjectivity. West. J. Nurs. Res. **30**(6), 759–773 (2008)
52. Lee, C.S., Ma, L.: News sharing in social media: the effect of gratifications and prior experience. Comput. Hum. Behav. **28**(2), 331–339 (2012)
53. Park, N., Kee, K.F., Valenzuela, S.: Being immersed in social networking environment: Facebook groups, uses and gratifications, and social outcomes. Cyberpsychol. Behav. **12**(6), 729–733 (2009)
54. Ashford, S.J., Black, J.S.: Proactivity during organizational entry: the role of desire for control. J. Appl. Psychol. **81**(2), 199 (1996)
55. Bordia, P., DiFonzo, N.: Psychological motivations in rumor spread. In: Rumor Mills, pp. 87–102. Routledge (2017)

Spatial Analysis of Social Media's Proxies for Human Emotion and Cognition

Anthony J. Corso(✉) [iD], Nicolas C. Disanto[iD], Nathan A. Corso[iD], and Esther Lee[iD]

California Baptist University, Riverside, CA 92504, USA
{acorso,nicolasc.disanto,nathan.corso,elee}@calbaptist.edu

Abstract. Apparent and latent knowledge claims made by social media authors are uncovered via Natural Language Processing tools and techniques. This phenomenon presents several fundamental issues as researchers distinguish correlation factors between an author's endogenous self-described and self-validated data disclosure and exogenous relationships. While social media processing protocols produce near-instantaneous analysis of a social dataset, studies examining such tools often overlook the strength of the correlation relationship. In addition, they frequently neglect to report an assessment of the normality of data distribution, disregard the rationale for choosing Pearson's or Spearman's test of correlations, and sometimes even use contrasting interpretations of correlation coefficients. This study proffers a correlation study research approach via direct inquiry that strengthens the theoretical foundation for identifying the relationship among social media emotion, sentiment, and cognition across diverse locations concerning real-world events. It attempts to answer the main research question: Does any relationship exist between social media's sentiment and cognition variables? It constructs a robust research-based analysis to validate the main question and fill the gap that other projects fail to address. Furthermore, it presents and discusses methods for investigating and interpreting correlation matrices and scatterplots. Moreover, it answers the research question and attempts to prove spatial relationships among variables. Last, it guides and describes future work of a predictive artifact that will input, process, and visualize a spatiotemporal, NLP processed, social media dataset and its integration with Pearson's and Spearman's correlations, and visual data constructs.

Keywords: Social Media · Location Analytics · Natural Language Processing

1 Introduction

Daily engagement on social media platforms results in the generation of extensive social, emotional, and cognitive data. The ongoing revolution is facilitated by the prevalence of smartphones and the widespread practice of texting behavior [1]. These data reflect personal experiences, provide dynamic commentary observed in real-time physical events, and enable researchers to study individuals in both the virtual realm and physical environment [2]. Current research in this area yields valuable insights for stakeholders utilizing

© The Author(s), under exclusive license to Springer Nature Switzerland AG 2024
I. Sserwanga et al. (Eds.): iConference 2024, LNCS 14597, pp. 175–185, 2024.
https://doi.org/10.1007/978-3-031-57860-1_13

social media-based Geographic Information Systems (GIS) and provides a unique spatiotemporal perspective on contemporary events. It taps into vast, real-time data sources that represent a human author and their interconnectedness with the world [3, 4]. However, researchers in this thread face many challenges when attempting to distinguish factors between an author's self-described and self-validated emotion and a connected exogenous event [5]. Challenges include authenticating an author's emotion, assessing its potential social influence, verifying correlations with self-described events, and confirming if real-world events were externally authored and simply forwarded on social media.

Social media processing protocols, e.g., Natural Language Processing (NLP), allow for rapid mining of the endogenous content of a social media post [6]. This extends social media-based GIS artifacts and facilitates the identification and prediction of real-world events via analysis of social media's structure. For example, social media feature engineering readily operationalizes a social dataset's textual content and therefore can represent specific locations, demographics, emotions, cognition, etc. and offer analytical insights that are instrumental for strategic information systems [7, 8]. As a result, stakeholders have access to near-real-time (NRT) decision support (DS) dashboards that draw insight from social media's endogenous and exogenous dataspace [9].

Beyond the hidden patterns NLP feature engineering extracts from social media, Social Network Analysis (SNA) dives deep into the underlying structures, tracing the intricate threads of relationships that bind individuals. Informed by diverse theories, SNA researchers leverage rich network datasets to unveil how interconnectedness shapes individual behaviors and attributes [10]. The correlations they disclose between variables associated with network members are not mere suggestions but concrete evidence of social influence in action [11]. Accordingly, SNA differs significantly from an NLP approach, and neither holds absolute dominance in deciphering the complex interplay of social media, individual traits, human emotion, and cognition.

This investigation reveals a research gap where a deeper understanding of social media variables could enhance both NLP and SNA. It illuminates the under-explored environment by utilizing an interdisciplinary perspective. Three probing questions guide the exploration of this landscape and its potential to advance both fields.

- Question 1) Does any relationship exist between social media's sentiment and cognitive variables?
- Question 2) Does any relationship exist between location and social media's sentiment and cognitive variables?
- Question 3) Given the extreme subjectiveness of social media; Is the measurement of social media's human behavior and cognitive variables robust and scalable?

1.1 Project Overview

This research seeks to refine the theoretical foundations related to identifying and estimating relationships among specifically crafted features designed to characterize social media, i.e., emotion, sentiment, and cognition, and an author's observance of a real-world event. It also demonstrates the value of a correlation study by developing a robust framework that adheres to meta-analytical guidelines, presenting a clearly defined research approach and results that substantiate and answer the research questions [12–14]. NLP unlocks features derived from social media platforms [15] and allows for a comprehensive examination of the latent dynamics encompassing human behavior. The study extends prior research emphasizing long-term trust in correlated variables through comparative analysis and attempts to uncover generalizable patterns.

The progression of this study involves an initial literature review, succeeded by a section detailing the research approach, which formalizes the project's deductive research plan. Following this is an explanation of data, results, discussion, and the acknowledgment of project limitations. The study concludes with a final section covering the conclusion and outlining avenues for future work.

2 Literature Review

2.1 Social Media Protocols

Research of sparse text social media classification explores the NLP continuum from simple keyword event extraction to parsing the frequency of obscure bigrams used to identify structural relationships between words [16]. Tokenization, serving as a unit of measure for a block of text-based content, is a crucial element in sparse text classification. It is a massive endeavor to provide comprehensive insights into this discipline's theoretical, practical, and evaluative aspects [17, 18]. Certain research domains must explore this arena to capture broad attention; various communities can derive substantial benefits by delving into the foundational aspects of unstructured social media analysis. The scholarly contributions of Hirst and Feiguina [19], Phan et al. [20], Sriram et al. [18], and Piao and Whittle [17] share several noteworthy traits. Each builds robust learning models by identifying NLP features of common domain artifacts and implements these features to label short text corpora. Additionally, all of them establish a baseline for their respective project's corpus by selecting features that best suit the linguistic components of unit analysis. All four researchers use subject matter expert analysis and additional machine-based statistical analysis to evaluate their proposed models. Piao and Whittle [17] are instrumental because their work extends Frantzi et al. [21] in calculating automatic recognition of n-grams based on the c-value metric and developed an evaluation metric based on linguistic and statistical analysis. In the context of this research, handling short texts poses a challenge in NLP pipelines [19] and is a crucial issue that needs addressing.

Natural language processing methodologies exist that mitigate tweet noise; thus, normalizing a sparse tweet corpus and preparing it for examination. Two customary methods include spell-checking, as implemented by Choudhury et al. [22] and Mays et al. [23], and more currently, normalization via noisy channel methods [24]. The latter scrutinizes a sparse corpus using an unsupervised text normalization approach, and on a set of 303 text messages, they achieved 59% overall accuracy. Thus, the latent features within can be explored, e.g., via NLP [25, 26] and various other techniques [27].

2.2 Social Media Location Analytics

Location analytics spans many applications, from marketing to manufacturing to monitoring outbreaks through social media platforms like Twitter. Spatial analytics plays a meaningful role in enhancing the immersion experience for shopping in digital market-places [28, 29]. Still, others propose a method to predict locations based on patterns of frequent trajectories and demonstrate its effectiveness and efficiency in manufacturing [32]. Last, research shows that flu-related social media trends lag actual flu trends, uti-lizing spatial and temporal metrics and feature-engineered variables that use temporal, spatial, and textual content to spatially correlate tweets with flu outbreaks [33].

3   Research Approach

3.1   Correlation Study

A correlation research design offers a comprehensive framework for investigating and measuring relationships between variables. This approach involves assessing the strength and direction of association between two or more variables, aiming to determine if changes in one variable correspond to changes in another. The categories of this method-ology are based on the number of variables under consideration and the necessity to control the influence of additional factors.

Although its simplicity and strong statistical foundation make it an attractive option, this approach is infrequently applied in developing social media information systems, especially when dealing with the complex interplay of location, social media as a proxy for human emotion and cognition, and the analysis of texting as a fundamental human behavior. This hesitation could be attributed to the initial research stages, where evident relationships between variables might not be immediately discernable.

To harness the potential of correlation analysis and reveal connections among various social media concepts, it is imperative to precisely define high-level human behaviors, such as emotion, sentiment, and cognition—each is relevant to this study. Table 1 pro-vides a comprehensive structure for dissecting various aspects of social media content. It delineates three overarching social media concepts related to human behavior, and is accompanied by detailed descriptions. Notably, the last column in the table underscores the distinct measurement levels for each high-level social media concept, serving as the focal point for evaluating relationship strength. Additionally, the column specifies the source code variables utilized to represent each measurement.

The measurement variables are pivotal in revealing both unique and common patterns among social media authors, enabling predictions about reported events.

Selecting the appropriate correlation method is paramount for any study, with height-ened significance in social media information systems. The choice between Pearson's and Spearman's correlation methods can shape or undermine a study. Pearson's is a preferred option for assessing linear relationships between variables, e.g., it proves very effective in scenarios like measuring the strength of correlation between positive tweets and follower count. Conversely, Spearman's offers greater flexibility by not assuming linearity. It explores monotonic relationships, whereas one variable increases, the other follows suit (or decreases), but not necessarily in a straight line. This is advantageous when dealing with nuanced relationships, such as those involving emotions.

Table 1. Measures of NLP-Processed Social Media Content

High-level Social Media Concept	Description	Levels of Measure [Source Code Variables]
Emotion	Measure of subjective response or feeling expressed in a piece of text	Happy, Neutral, Sad [HapEm, NeuEm, SadEm]
Sentiment (Polarity)	Measure of subjective stance or opinion expressed in a piece of text	Positive, Neutral, Negative [PosPol, NeuPol, NegPol]
Cognition	Measure of binary emotional perception shaped by the cognitive processes	Yes (perceived event) No (no perceived event) [YesCog, NoCog]

3.2 Data Collection and Processing

Naturalistic observation serves as the primary process for social media data collection and involves the observation of tweet authors in the setting of a baseball game. The dataset, also referred to as a corpus, considers approximately 1,512,000 tweets. It was collected via the Twitter stream between March 2016 and December 2019 using the standard Twitter v1.1 API endpoints. Figure 1 (left image) displays the thirty (30) U.S. Major League Baseball sites where data were collected. The collection process concentrated on tweets originating within specific geographic areas, each delineated by a virtual bounding box using latitude and longitude coordinates, Fig. 1 (right image).

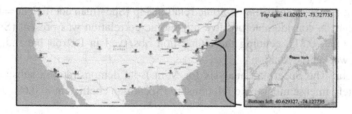

Fig. 1. Data Collection Sites

To ensure direct relevance, analyzed tweets were confined to specified locations of interest. Java libraries parsed Twitter's JSON data, extracting key elements: posting time, coordinates, and text. Data integrity was maintained by removing duplicates, posts from official sources, and poorly formed tweets. Sample units, individual tweets within a bounding box on a team's home game day, were chosen for analysis. Each unit's text underwent NLP processing, and measurement variables from Table 1 were appropriately updated and saved for later analysis.

3.3 Results

This study investigated the intricate relationships between `YesCog` (perceived event) and `PosPol` (positive polarity) in three distinct geographical locations: Detroit, San Diego, and Minnesota. These measures were treated as proxy indicators for human cognition and sentiment and extracted from the realm of social media. Figures 2 and 3 depict the results through Pearson's and Spearman's correlation; each is shown below.

- Detroit: A remarkably strong positive linear relationship was observed (Pearson coefficient = 0.93), indicating a close alignment between `PosPol` and `YesCog`.
- San Diego: A substantial positive linear relationship was present (Pearson coefficient = 0.85), suggesting a noteworthy but slightly weaker association than Detroit.
- Minnesota: A significant but moderately intense linear association was found (Pearson coefficient = 0.64), indicating a weaker connection compared to the other sites.

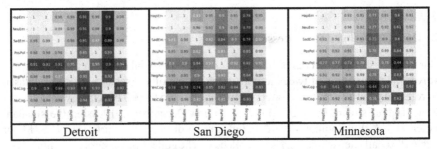

Fig. 2. Pearson's Correlation Matrices

- Detroit: The Spearman correlation reinforced the findings of Pearson's analysis, revealing a robust positive monotonic relationship (Spearman coefficient = 0.89).
- San Diego: A considerable positive monotonic correlation was present (Spearman coefficient = 0.81), echoing the connection observed in Detroit but indicating a slightly weaker association.
- Minnesota: The Spearman analysis for Minnesota demonstrated a substantial yet moderately intense monotonic relationship (Spearman coefficient = 0.60).

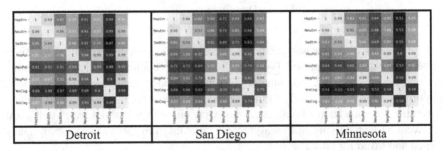

Fig. 3. Spearman's Correlation Matrices

A scatterplot visually represents data points in a two-dimensional space, indicating relationships between two variables. Positive correlation is suggested by an upward trend, while a downward trend implies negative correlation. Figure 4 shows scatterplot results.

| Detroit | San Diego | Minnesota |

Fig. 4. Scatterplots of YesCog and PosPol

The scatterplot for Detroit vividly illustrates a strong positive relationship between YesCog and PosPol, with data points forming a discernible upward trend. This aligns seamlessly with the robust positive linear relationship indicated by both Pearson's and Spearman's correlation coefficients. In San Diego's scatterplot, a clear positive relationship is evident, as YesCog and PosPol data points exhibit an upward trend. This visual representation substantiates the positive linear association observed through both Pearson's and Spearman's correlation analyses. Minnesota's scatterplot also portrays a positive relationship between YesCog and PosPol, with data points forming a discernible trend.

As illustrated in Fig. 5, this analysis, a component of location analytics, confirms the positive relationships between YesCog and PosPol across diverse locations, again reinforcing confidence in the results from Pearson's and Spearman's analyses.

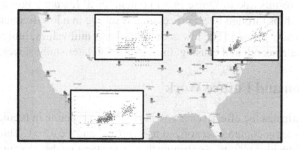

Fig. 5. Location Analytics

3.4 Discussion

The investigation robustly answers the first research question by affirming a positive relationship between social media sentiment (PosPol) and cognitive variables (YesCog). Across diverse locations, both Pearson and Spearman correlation analyses consistently revealed statistically significant associations. This signifies that elevated positive sentiment on social media tends to coincide with a heightened perception of events, suggesting a nuanced interplay possibly influenced by shared experiences or emotional contagion.

Addressing the second research question, findings indicate location-specific differences in the strength of the PosPol and YesCog association. Detroit exhibited the highest correlation coefficients, followed by San Diego and Minnesota. This implies that geographical context and local factors play a role in shaping how sentiments and perceived events interact on social media. The observed variations invite further exploration into cultural characteristics, community demographics, or unique events contributing to these differences.

Concerning the third research question, the study underscores the robust and scalable measurement of PosPol and YesCog using correlation analysis despite the inherent subjectivity of social media posts. Significant and consistent findings across diverse locations suggest that these measures capture meaningful patterns in social media data.

This study contributes valuable insights into the intricate interplay of social media emotion and cognition, addressing research questions while inspiring further exploration of collective behaviors and online community dynamics. The identified positive relationship between PosPol and YesCog prompts consideration of causal directions, urging future studies to broaden emotional and cognitive exploration. As research in this domain evolves, ethical considerations will continue to be of paramount importance.

3.5 Limitations

Corpus collection, tokenization, and feature identification are challenges, and each pos error risks. Obtaining a representative sample from Twitter's vast stream via the standard REST API results in a smaller dataset than the Firehose API. Further challenges arise with user location preferences, requiring the researcher to determine exact tweet origins. For feature identification, tweet tokenization and part-of-speech tagging are used, potentially impacting results due to sparse tweet content. NLP feature engineering explores variable relationships through tweet processing, resulting in a low-frequency count due to stringent inclusion criteria. The low count introduces null values, limiting regression analysis in future research and causing discrepancies in later study stages.

4 Conclusion and Future Work

This study investigates the effectiveness of an innovative pipeline in predicting the relevance of social media content categorized as YesCog and PosPol. The correlational analysis yielded positive results, confirming that understanding the structured framework in a sparse text social media corpus efficiently allows for extracting meaningful content while excluding irrelevant structures. Furthermore, this approach unveils a captivating and unexplored aspect of sparse and acronym-based short message content, highlighting its potential as a valuable source for identifying real-time events. This study uniquely innovates by emphasizing the need for enhanced grammar-based, feature-engineered, NLP treatments explicitly designed for sparse-text social media corpora. This generates more meaningful and efficient results and is a stride toward comprehending and extracting valuable insights from social media communication.

Future research endeavors should enrich the current study by delving into more intricate details facilitated by NLP capabilities. A more sophisticated grammatical tagging of a tweet corpus employed at a very fine grain level will perform well in contrast to a chance-based baseline or an expert-tagged social media corpus. The key element underlying this concept tests the interplay between social media and grammar while maintaining control over levels of grammatical tagging. A positive outcome in this exploration is the creation of an artifact with enhanced capabilities to predict functional or comparative tweets grounded in their grammatical correctness. This research is a foundational step for subsequent social media processing initiatives, including social media as an orthogonal variable in a GIS artifact within the sharing economy context.

References

1. Greenwood, M.A., Aswani, N., Bontcheva, K.: Reputation Profiling with GATE, p. 7 (2012)
2. McMinn, A.J., Moshfeghi, Y., Jose, J.M.: Building a large-scale corpus for evaluating event detection on twitter. In: Proceedings of the 22nd ACM International Conference on Information & Knowledge Management - CIKM 2013, pp. 409–418. ACM Press, San Francisco, California, USA (2013)
3. Fan, W., Gordon, M.: The power of social media analytics. Commun. ACM 57, 74–81 (2014). https://doi.org/10.1145/2602574
4. Zhu, Y.-Q., Chen, H.-G.: Social media and human need satisfaction: implications for social media marketing. Bus. Horiz. 58, 335–345 (2015). https://doi.org/10.1016/j.bushor.2015.01.006
5. Ng, K.W., Horawalavithana, S., Iamnitchi, A.: Forecasting topic activity with exogenous and endogenous information signals in twitter. In: Proceedings of the 2021 IEEE/ACM International Conference on Advances in Social Networks Analysis and Mining. pp. 95–98. ACM, Virtual Event Netherlands (2021)
6. Genc, Y., Sakamoto, Y., Nickerson, J.V.: Discovering context: classifying Tweets through a semantic transform based on Wikipedia. In: Schmorrow, D.D., Fidopiastis, C.M. (eds.) Foundations of Augmented Cognition. Directing the Future of Adaptive Systems, pp. 484–492. Springer, Cham (2011). https://doi.org/10.1007/978-3-642-21852-1_55
7. Wijeratne, S., et al.: Feature engineering for twitter-based applications. In: Dong, G. (ed.) Feature Engineering for Machine Learning and Data Analytics, pp. 359–393. CRC Press (2018)
8. De Francisci Morales, G., Gionis, A., Lucchese, C.: From chatter to headlines: harnessing the real-time web for personalized news recommendation. In: Proceedings of the Fifth ACM International Conference on Web Search and Data Mining, pp. 153–162. ACM, Seattle, Washington, USA (2012)
9. Wakamiya, S., Lee, R., Sumiya, K.: Urban area characterization based on semantics of crowd activities in twitter. In: Claramunt, C., Levashkin, S., Bertolotto, M. (eds.) GeoSpatial Semantics, pp. 108–123. Springer, Heidelberg (2011). https://doi.org/10.1007/978-3-642-20630-6_7
10. Tabassum, S., Pereira, F.S.F., Fernandes, S., Gama, J.: Social network analysis: an overview. WIREs Data Min. Knowl. Discov. 8, e1256 (2018). https://doi.org/10.1002/widm.1256

11. Baumann, F., Lorenz-Spreen, P., Sokolov, I.M., Starnini, M.: Modeling echo chambers and polarization dynamics in social networks. Phys. Rev. Lett. **124**, 048301 (2020). https://doi.org/10.1103/PhysRevLett.124.048301

12. Creswell, J.W.: Research Design: Qualitative, Quantitative, and Mixed Methods Approaches. SAGE Publications, Thousand Oaks (2014)

13. Bryman, A.: Social Research Methods. Oxford University Press, Oxford, New York (2012)

14. Robson, C.: Real World Research. Blackwell, Oxford, Cambridge (1993)

15. Zhang, X., Fuehres, H., Gloor, P.A.: Predicting stock market indicators through twitter "I hope it is not as bad as I fear." Procedia - Soc. Behav. Sci. **26**, 55–62 (2011). https://doi.org/10.1016/j.sbspro.2011.10.562

16. Jurafsky, D.: Speech and Language Processing. Pearson Education India, New Delhi (2000)

17. Piao, S., Whittle, J.: A feasibility study on extracting twitter users' interests using NLP tools for serendipitous connections. In: 2011 IEEE Third International Conference on Privacy, Security, Risk and Trust and 2011 IEEE Third International Conference on Social Computing, pp. 910–915. IEEE, Boston, MA, USA (2011)

18. Sriram, B., Fuhry, D., Demir, E., Ferhatosmanoglu, H., Demirbas, M.: Short text classification in twitter to improve information filtering. In: Proceedings of the 33rd International ACM SIGIR Conference on Research and Development in Information Retrieval, pp. 841–842. ACM, Geneva, Switzerland (2010)

19. Hirst, G., Feiguina, O.: Bigrams of syntactic labels for authorship discrimination of short texts. Lit. Linguist. Comput. **22**, 405–417 (2007). https://doi.org/10.1093/llc/fqm023

20. Phan, X.-H., Nguyen, L.-M., Horiguchi, S.: Learning to classify short and sparse text & web with hidden topics from large-scale data collections. In: Proceedings of the 17th International Conference on World Wide Web, pp. 91–100. Association for Computing Machinery, New York, NY, USA (2008)

21. Frantzi, K., Ananiadou, S., Mima, H.: Automatic recognition of multi-word terms: the C-value/NC-value method. Int. J. Digit. Libr. **3**, 115–130 (2000). https://doi.org/10.1007/s007999900023

22. Choudhury, S., Breslin, J.G.: Extracting semantic entities and events from sports tweets, p. 12 (2011)

23. Castillo, A., Benitez, J., Liorens, J., Braojos, J.: Impact of social media on the firm's knowledge exploration and knowledge exploitation: the role of business analytics talent. J. Assoc. Inf. Syst. **22**, 1472–1508 (2021). https://doi.org/10.17705/1jais.00700

24. Cook, P., Stevenson, S.: An unsupervised model for text message normalization. In: Proceedings of the Workshop on Computational Approaches to Linguistic Creativity - CALC 2009, pp. 71–78. Association for Computational Linguistics, Boulder, Colorado (2009)

25. Yue, L., Chen, W., Li, X., Zuo, W., Yin, M.: A survey of sentiment analysis in social media. Knowl. Inf. Syst. **60**, 617–663 (2019). https://doi.org/10.1007/s10115-018-1236-4

26. Corso, A.J., Alsudais, A.: GIS investigation of crime prediction with an operationalized tweet corpus. In: Free and Open Source Software for Geospatial (FOSS4G) Conference Proceedings, p. 21 (2017)

27. Volkova, S., Bachrach, Y., Armstrong, M., Sharma, V.: Inferring latent user properties from texts published in social media. Proc. AAAI Conf. Artif. Intell. **29** (2015)

28. Almarzouqi, A., Aburayya, A., Salloum, S.A.: Prediction of user's intention to use metaverse system in medical education: a hybrid SEM-ML learning approach. IEEE Access **10**, 43421–43434 (2022). https://doi.org/10.1109/ACCESS.2022.3169285

29. Elawady, M., Sarhan, A., Alshewimy, M.A.M.: Toward a mixed reality domain model for time-sensitive applications using IoE infrastructure and edge computing (MRIoEF). J. Supercomput. **78**, 10656–10689 (2022). https://doi.org/10.1007/s11227-022-04307-8

30. Jang, S.H., et al.: Synthesis and characterisation of triphenylmethine dyes for colour conversion layer of the virtual and augmented reality display. Dyes Pigments **204**, 110419 (2022). https://doi.org/10.1016/j.dyepig.2022.110419
31. Li, T., Wu, Y., Zhang, Y.: Twitter hash tag prediction algorithm, p. 5 (2012)
32. Cai, H., Guo, Y., Lu, K.: A location prediction method for work-in-process based on frequent trajectory patterns. Proc. Inst. Mech. Eng. Part B J. Eng. Manuf. **233**, 306–320 (2019). https://doi.org/10.1177/0954405417708222
33. Abazari Kia, M., Ebrahimi Khaksefidi, F.: Twitter flu trend: a hybrid deep neural network for tweet analysis. In: Bramer, M., Stahl, F. (eds.) Artificial Intelligence XXXIX, pp. 37–50. Springer, Cham (2022). https://doi.org/10.1007/978-3-031-21441-7_3

Exploring Influential Factors in Expert Advice Adoption on Social Media: Insights from Weibo Trending Topics

Jiaqi Liao[✉] [ID]

School of Information Management, Sun Yat-sen University, Guangzhou 510000, China
liaojq7@mail2.sysu.edu.cn

Abstract. Social media has long served as a platform for discussions on public agendas. However, the dissemination of expert advice on social media is facing a crisis of public trust. To explore the factors influencing the adoption of expert advice on social media, this paper focuses on 326 Weibo trending topics related to expert advice and user comments. Drawing upon theories related to information adoption, professional opinion leadership, and science communication, this study examines the impact of factors at the expert level, media level, and information level on user information adoption behavior. The results indicate that factors including the expert's field, the expert's academic affiliation, media type, topic type, use of multimedia, level of detail, information framing, and narrative style have an impact on user information adoption. This study expands the theory of science communication on social media and provides guidance for social media platforms and media entities on how to effectively disseminate expert advice.

Keywords: Information Adoption · Expert Advice · Social media · Science Communication · Trending topics

1 Introduction and Background

Social media has become an increasingly popular source of news information for online users. According to social media users, Weibo has shown significant advantages in disseminating news and comments [1].

"Weibo Trending" on Sina Weibo is a key section that displays real-time updates on hot news topics. It plays roles in policy promotion and trending topic marketing. This section serves as a crucial channel for users to access news on Weibo [2].

Experts are people with expertise in a particular field, usually appearing as scientists, scholars, or senior practitioners [3]. In social media and public opinion, experts are using these platforms to share professional content and scientific insights. They have become influential opinion leaders, providing timely and reasoned guidance to the public [4–7].

In May 2022, a trending topic on Weibo emerged with the title "We advise experts not to give advice." This topic garnered significant attention, with users expressing skepticism and rejection of expert advice on social media. Users cited various reasons,

I. Sserwanga et al. (Eds.): iConference 2024, LNCS 14597, pp. 186–197, 2024.
https://doi.org/10.1007/978-3-031-57860-1_14

including perceived lack of authority, scientific credibility, etc. [8]. These voices point to the problem of information adoption on Weibo. Theoretically, expert advice information is characterized by high quality and reliability. However, the abundance of information producers, a low threshold for publication, and challenges in maintaining quality control on social media have led to a crisis of public trust, even in information labeled as expert advice.

The study approaches the issue from an empirical perspective. It examines the impact of experts, media, and information factors on user information adoption, using trending topics related to expert advice as the research subject. The research expands the theoretical understanding of scientific communication and expert advice in the context of social media. In practice, it provides insights into shaping the public agenda of expert advice on social media effectively.

2   Literature Review

2.1   Information Adoption Behavior in Social Media

The Information Adoption Theory (IAT) posits that argument quality and source credibility have a positive influence on information usefulness, which in turn positively affects the degree of information adoption. The foundation of this theory draws from the Elaboration Likelihood Model (ELM) [9], the Technology Acceptance Model (TAM) [10], and the Theory of Reasoned Action (TRA) [11], each contributing from aspects of information features, information system usage, and behavioral intentions [12].

In social media information adoption research, topics focus on consumer behavior, health information, and travel decision-making. The Information Acceptance Model (IACM) extends the IAT in consumer studies, considering factors like information needs and attitudes [13]. Health information adoption research explores the relationship between themes, narratives, media characteristics, and user adoption [14, 15]. In travel decision-making, information richness and vividness impact adoption [16]. While these studies form a theoretical foundation, more targeted research is required on expert advice information adoption.

2.2   Information Influence of Professional Opinion Leaders in Social Media

Opinion leaders are individuals who provide specialized or insightful insights and garner attention in a particular field or on a public issue. Traditional opinion leaders acquire information from the media and subsequently disseminate their opinions through these channels. In contrast, professional opinion leaders primarily draw upon their research or industry experience to express their views, which they then convey through traditional media or social media platforms, with the media serving as intermediaries [6, 17, 18]. Different types of media and account characteristics can influence the effectiveness of information dissemination. Professional opinion leaders should aim to simplify complex information to facilitate understanding among the public [19]. They typically maintain connections with the media, and their reputation and media exposure impact discussions on topics and public responses. Social media users are influenced by opinion leaders through actions such as likes, comments, and shares, with comments often reflecting deeper engagement [20, 21].

2.3 Science Communication in Social Media

Science communication aims to convey scientific information from professionals to non-expert audiences [22]. Traditional science communication relies on media or decision-making institutions as intermediaries, which is a multi-trusted approach. However, social media has altered the way information is exchanged, breaking the fixed flow of information. Scientists, decision-makers, media platforms, and the public can process and exchange information through social media [3]. This new model can potentially lead to the sensationalization of hot topics and intense debates, disrupting the public's trust in scientific information [23]. Therefore, professional communicators need to adopt new methods, such as presenting statistical data or logical reasoning, to build trust and use multimedia formats effectively [24].

In terms of communication elements, research indicates that content creators, content themes, and text formats influence the effectiveness of science communication. The use of information framing may also affect the construction of scientific communication discourse [25]. Media information creators may prioritize highlighting certain aspects of information to resonate with the public. For instance, the gain-loss framework is a common information framing, where emphasizing loss may be more persuasive than emphasizing gain. Moreover, vague, and unprofessional language can lead to a decrease in trust [26, 27].

3 Research Hypotheses

Drawing from literature, we posit that expert, media, and information factors on social media may impact user information adoption (UIA) of expert advice. The paper presents three groups of research hypotheses, the multitude of hypotheses is intended to capture the multifaceted nature of social media dynamics and the various elements that could potentially influence UIA.

H1 to H4 are expert-level factors.

H1: There will be differences in UIA among experts from different fields.

H2: There will be differences in UIA based on whether experts are affiliated with academic or research institutions.

H3: Experts' media influence will positively affect UIA.

H4: Whether the expert has a personal social media account will make a difference in UIA.

H5 to H6 are media-level factors.

H5: There will be differences in UIA of expert advice based on different media types.

H6: There will be a negative correlation between media communication effectiveness and the degree of UIA.

H7 to H11 are information-level factors.

H7: There are differences in UIA based on different types of trending topics.

H8: There will be differences in UIA when expert advice is presented with video, pictures, full article links or pure texts.

H9: There will be differences in UIA based on the degree of detail in expert advice tweets.

H10: There will be differences in UIA based on the information framework in expert advice tweets.

H11: There will be a difference in UIA whether the expert advice is presented with factual information or logical reasoning.

4 Methods

We collected and crawled trending search entries related to "expert advice" on the Weibo trending search engine [28] from May 2020 to August 2023[1]. Regarding entries about expert advice, Weibo trending topics typically start with the phrase "Expert Advice". We initially used "expert" as the search keyword, retrieving a total of 459 trending search entries. After manual screening, we excluded entries unrelated to expert advice and those with invalid links. Finally, we retained 326 entries with valid information. This information includes entry names, topic types, media coverage, and original article links. Based on this, we accessed the original topics of each trending search entry and collected a total of 48,664 valid comments as the data source. We categorized the collected data into expert-level, media-level, and information-level, and use them as explanatory variables. The dependent variable is the degree of UIA, which is measured using sentiment analysis values to characterize it. These sentiment values are computed using NLP models applied to user comments. Table 1 illustrates the source and acquisition of data.

Table 1. Source and acquisition of data

Variables	Data	Measurement	Source
Expert-level	Expert's field	1. STEM 2. Medical science 3. Social Science/Management 4. Humanities and arts	Retrieve expert background information from the original text or search engine
	Academic employment	Check whether the expert is affiliated with an academic institution	Retrieve expert background information from the original text or search engine
	Media influence	Media Coverage Frequency	Retrieve expert names from WiseSearch[a] to obtain the frequency of news reports
	Personal account	Check whether experts have publicly verified personal accounts	Weibo
Media-level	Media types	1. Official media 2. Mainstream media 3. Self-media	Introduction on the Weibo media homepage
	Media communication effectiveness	The propagation popularity index of hot search terms	WiseSearch

(continued)

---

[1] The earliest data available from the trending search engine is May 2020.

Table 1. (*continued*)

Variables	Data	Measurement	Source
Information-level	Topic	Weibo trending topic categories: 1. Society[b] 2. Science and Technology[c] 3. Politics[d] 4. Epidemic[e] 5. Health[f] 6. Finance[g] 7. Nature[h] 8. Lifestyle[i] 9. Entertainment[j]	Trending topic homepage/posts
	Multimedia	Check whether expert advice is presented with: 1. Video 2. Images 3. Full article links 4. Pure texts	Trending topic homepage/posts
	Degree of detail	1. Less than 100 words 2. 101 to 200 words 3. More than 201 words	Character count statistics for posts
	Information framework	1. Gain Frame 2. Loss Frame 3. Neither	Trending topic homepage/posts
	Factual information or logical reasoning	1. Adopted 2. Not Adopted	Trending topic homepage/posts
User information adoption	Sentiment values	The sentiment value of the comments was tested through Baidu Sentiment Analysis Open API	48,664 comments

[a]WiseSearch is a comprehensive media big data platform. Through this database, one can access news coverage and related data about events.
[b]Social issues, law, and policy.
[c]Scientific phenomena and technology.
[d]Diplomacy, international situations, military.
[e]COVID-19, smallpox, avian flu, and other infectious diseases.
[f]Medical issues (excluding epidemics).
[g]Economic and financial issues.
[h]Environment and biology.
[i]Daily life.
[j]Cultural industry and gaming

The independent variables include binary variables, categorical variables, and continuous variables. The dependent variable is continuous. The statistical analysis methods involved include t-tests, one-way analysis of variance, correlation analysis, and regression analysis. SPSS 27 is a tool for conducting statistical hypothesis testing.

5   Results

5.1   Descriptive Statistics

Expert-Level Data. Figures 1, 2 and 3 depict experts' expertise fields, affiliations with academic institutions, and possession of personal accounts. Notably, among Weibo's trending hot searches experts, nearly half (40%) are from the medical field, while the humanities and arts field contribute the fewest. 77% of experts are affiliated with academic institutions, and 72% either lack or cannot be found with public accounts. Regarding media influence, the experts' maximum value is 99,955, averaging 12,053.22.

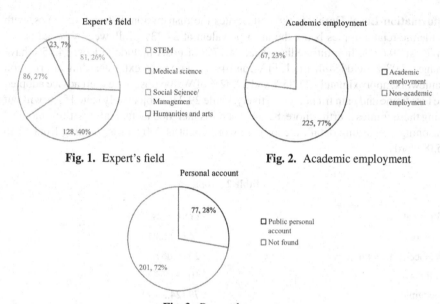

Fig. 1. Expert's field

Fig. 2. Academic employment

Fig. 3. Personal account

Media-Level Data. Figure 4 displays media type distribution among publishing entities, with 51% from mainstream media, 34% from official outlets like CCTV News, and only 15% from self-media. Regarding media communication effectiveness in all relevant posts, the average is 732,790.35, ranging from a minimum of 8,423 to a maximum of 6,033,443.

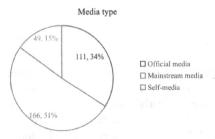

Fig. 4. Media type

Information-Level Data. Table 2 illustrates the distribution of trending topics, with Epidemic-related topics being the most prevalent at 24.23%, followed by social issues topics at 19.63%. In multimedia usage, 74.77% of posts include videos, 14.15% have images, 7.08% include full article links, and 4% contain only text. Regarding information framework, approximately 37.85% and 32.92% of Weibo posts on expert advice adopted the loss frame and gain frame, respectively, while 29.23% objectively stated facts without using these frames. Furthermore, 81.54% of posts included factual information or logical reasoning. Regarding detail, the average word count is 260 words, ranging from 65 to 3538 words.

Table 2. Topic

Topic category	Frequency (%)
Society	64 (19.63%)
Science and Technology	23 (7.06%)
Politics	10 (3.07%)
Epidemic	79 (24.23%)
Health	39 (11.96%)
Finance	39 (11.96%)
Nature	34 (10.43%)
Lifestyle	30 (9.20%)
Entertainment	8 (2.45%)

User Information Adoption. The average UIA rate is 0.48, with a standard deviation of 0.18. The maximum adoption rate is 0.96, while the minimum is 0.10. Overall, Weibo users do not have a high overall adoption rate of expert advice.

5.2   Inferential Statistical Analysis

As shown in Table 3, the data analysis results indicate that out of the eleven hypotheses, eight were supported, while three were not.

Table 3. Inferential statistical analysis and hypothesis testing results

Hypothesis	Statistical method	Reporting data	Hypothesis testing results
H1	ANOVA	$F = 18.123$ $p < 0.001$	Supported
H2	T-test	$t = 3.388$ $p = 0.001$	Supported
H3	Linear regression	$F = 2.206$ $p = 0.139 > 0.05$	Not Supported
H4	T-test	$t = 1.740$ $p = 0.083 > 0.05$	Not Supported
H5	ANOVA	$F = 11.973$ $p < 0.001$	Supported
H6	Correlation	$p = 0.513 > 0.05$	Not Supported
H7	ANOVA	$F = 9.537$ $p < 0.001$	Supported
H8	ANOVA	$F = 4.045$ $p = 0.008$	Supported
H9	ANOVA	$F = 4.295$ $p = 0.014$	Supported
H10	ANOVA	$F = 3.244$ $p = 0.040$	Supported
H11	T-test	$t = 6.360$ $p < 0.001$	Supported

Supported hypotheses were visually explained using charts and graphs to highlight differences. Figure 5 demonstrates that samples from different expert fields exhibit significant differences in user information adoption. Hypothesis 1 is supported. Experts from the STEM field have the highest UIA rate, while those from the social sciences and management fields show the opposite trend. Figure 6 displays a significant difference in adoption rates based on whether experts are affiliated with academic or research institutions.

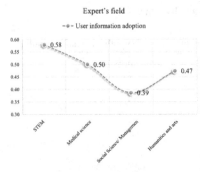

Fig. 5. UIA in different expert's field

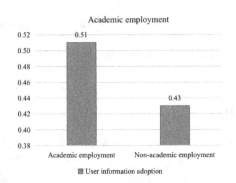

Fig. 6. UIA in different employment

Figure 7 shows a significant decreasing trend in the adoption rates of expert advice information from official media, mainstream media, and self-media. Figure 8 displays trending topics in different fields, revealing differences in user adoption rates. Among these, topics related to Finance (0.35) and Society (0.42) have relatively lower adoption rates.

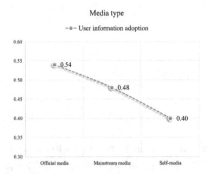

Fig. 7. UIA in different media type

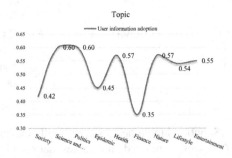

Fig. 8. UIA in different trending topic

At the information level, all hypotheses find support. Figure 9 shows that including full article links in posts with expert advice results in a relatively lower adoption rate (0.38), while posts with videos (0.50) or pure text (0.51) have higher adoption rates. Figure 10 reveals a distinct adoption rate (0.52) for Weibo trending posts with word counts between 101 and 200, compared to the other two categories. In Fig. 11, posts without any information frame show the highest adoption rate (0.52), followed by those using the loss frame (0.49), slightly higher than the gain frame (0.45). Figure 12 indicates that in expert advice-related posts, the adoption rate (0.51) significantly increases when factual information or logical reasoning is used.

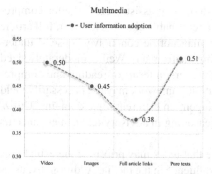

Fig. 9. UIA in different multimedia use

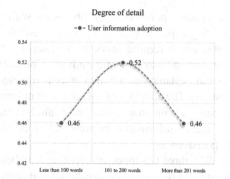

Fig. 10. UIA in different degree detail

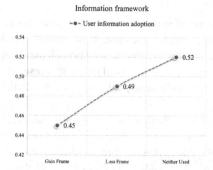

Fig. 11. UIA in different information framework

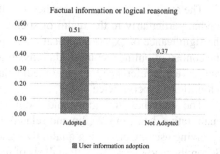

Fig. 12. UIA in different statement mode

6 Discussions and Conclusion

This study conducted specific content extraction from 326 Weibo trending topics related to expert advice and performed sentiment analysis on 48,664 corresponding comments. It explored the influence of factors at the expert, media, and information levels on user adoption of expert advice on social media. The study proposed eleven hypotheses, of which eight hypotheses received support.

Over the last three years, pandemic-related expert advice, particularly from medical experts, has been prominent on Weibo. However, negative online sentiments during the pandemic may have influenced people's willingness to adopt expert advice. In fields like science and technology, STEM experts have contributed valuable recommendations, resulting in higher information adoption. Conversely, in social and political topics, advice from social sciences or management experts has faced lower user adoption. This implies that social science dissemination on social media may diverge from traditional communication theories, and some media outlets may selectively highlight social topics to increase exposure and stimulate debates.

From the perspective of experts and the media, increasing the academic credentials of interviewed experts and ensuring the media's adherence to standards and professionalism may contribute to the effective dissemination of advisory information. From the

information perspective, Weibo posts with videos may assist users in better comprehending expert advice, and pure texts are also a reasonable choice. However, full article
links, which require users to click separately, may not be conducive to users' understanding and adoption of the advice. Considering the format of Weibo, moderately sized
textual explanations are also more favorable for users in terms of reading and comprehension. The adoption of a gain or loss information framework may not necessarily yield
superior results in all cases and could be contingent on different topic domains. Utilizing factual information or presenting logical reasoning in advisory text can enhance its
persuasiveness.

The three unsupported hypotheses indicate that users may prioritize the actual professional expertise of experts rather than their influence in the media. Additionally, users
may place more emphasis on professionalism and content quality rather than whether an
expert has a personal account. In certain situations, even efficient media communication
does not guarantee user adoption of expert advice.

The study has broadened the theoretical scope of science communication on social
media, particularly in the realm of social science communication. It has underscored
the significance of expert qualifications, media credibility, and information elements in
the context of online recommendations on social media. In practical terms, this research
can serve as a reference for social media platforms and media publishers to enhance the
adoption of expert advice.

The study has limitations and room for improvement. Firstly, it mainly relied on
quantitative data from Weibo and related databases, lacking direct qualitative analysis
involving users. Conducting qualitative research can supplement research conclusions.
Secondly, machine sentiment analysis of natural language text has limitations, as users'
online language is complex, and sentiment analysis may not fully capture their adoption
attitudes. Exploring more precise representation methods is anticipated.

References

1. An, S., Li, H.: China social media users' usage behavior research report 2020–2021. In: Hu, Z., Huang, C., Wu, X. (eds.) Annual Report on the Development of New Media in China, pp. 119–138. Social Science Literature Press, Beijing (2022)
2. Lei, L.: Weibo's, "trending list" and the regulation of Internet information services. Journalist 10, 81–87 (2019)
3. Hardoš, P.: Who exactly is an expert? On the problem of defining and recognizing expertise. Sociológia-Slovak Sociol. Rev. 50(3), 268–288 (2018)
4. Wang, Y.: From celebrity to "micro celebrity": a study on the identity change and influence of opinion leaders in the mobile social era. Shanghai Journalism Rev. 457(03), 27–39 (2021)
5. Meng, S., Shang, J., Zhang, F., Yang, F., Liu, M.: Research on the impact of COVID-19 science information dissemination on social media and the factors influencing the choice of crisis coping strategies: an empirical analysis based on popular micro-blog texts of scientists' groups. Libr. Inf. Serv. 66(13), 91–101 (2022)
6. Liu, Y., Zhan, J.: Voices of the National "Great Gods of Life": dominant roles and multi-identities of the medical opinion leaders during the COVID-19 pandemic. Journalism Mass Commun. Monthly 05, 44–56 (2020)
7. Kuang, W., Fang, Y.: Multi-subject participation model of science communication in public health emergencies——an analysis based on six scientific issues of COVID-19. J. Northwest Normal Univ. (Soc. Sci.) 59(05), 56–64 (2022)

8. Workers' Daily. "Advise experts not to advise" is to expect experts to speak properly (2022). https://m.thepaper.cn/baijiahao_18278985

9. Petty, R., Cacippo, J.: Communication and Persuasion: Central and Peripheral Routes to Attitude Change. Springer, New York (1986)

10. Davis, F.D.: Perceived usefulness, perceived ease of use, and user acceptance of information technology. MIS Q. **13**(3), 319–340 (1989)

11. Ajzen, I., Fishbein, M.: Understanding Attitudes and Predicting Social Behavior, p. 278, Englewood Cliffs (1980)

12. Sussman, S.W., Siegal, W.S.: Informational influence in organizations: an integrated approach to knowledge adoption. Inf. Syst. Res. **14**(1), 47–65 (2003)

13. Erkan, I., Evans, C.: The influence of eWOM in social media on consumers' purchase intentions: an extended approach to information adoption. Comput. Hum. Behav. **61**, 47–55 (2016)

14. Huo, C., Zhang, M., Ma, F.: Factors influencing people's health knowledge adoption in social media: the mediating effect of trust and the moderating effect of health threat. Library Hi Tech **36**(1), 129–151 (2018)

15. Wang, Z., Sun, Z.: Can the adoption of health information on social media be predicted by information characteristics? Aslib J. Inf. Manag. **73**(1), 80–100 (2021)

16. Zhang, J., Ito, N., Wu, W., Li, Z.: "Don't Let Me Think!" Chinese adoption of travel information on social media: moderating effects of self-disclosure. In: Schegg, R., Stangl, B. (eds.) Information and Communication Technologies in Tourism 2017, pp. 639–653. Springer, Cham (2017). https://doi.org/10.1007/978-3-319-51168-9_46

17. Katz, E.: The two-step flow of communication: an up-to-date report on an hypothesis. Public Opin. Q. **21**(1), 61–78 (1957)

18. Xu, Q., Yu, N., Song, Y.: User engagement in public discourse on genetically modified organisms: the role of opinion leaders on social media. Sci. Commun. **40**(6), 691–717 (2018)

19. Leißner, L., Stehr, P., Rössler, P., Döringer, E., Morsbach, M., Simon, L.: Parasocial opinion leadership: media personalities' influence within parasocial relations: theoretical conceptualization and preliminary results. Publizistik **59**, 247–267 (2014)

20. Napoli, P.M.: Audience Evolution: New Technologies and the Transformation of Media Audiences. Columbia University Press, New York (2011)

21. Cho, M., Schweickart, T., Haase, A.: Public engagement with nonprofit organizations on Facebook. Public Relat. Rev. **40**(3), 565–567 (2014)

22. Burns, T.W., O'Connor, D.J., Stocklmayer, S.M.: Science communication: contemporary definition. Public Underst. Sci. **12**(2), 183–202 (2003)

23. Dahlgren, P.: Media, knowledge, and trust: the deepening epistemic crisis of democracy. Javnost-The Public **25**(1–2), 20–27 (2018)

24. Van Dijck, J., Alinejad, D.: Social media and trust in scientific expertise: debating the Covid-19 pandemic in the Netherlands. Soc. Media+ Soc. **6**(4), 2056305120981057 (2020)

25. Rothman, A.J., Bartels, R.D., Wlaschin, J., Salovey, P.: The strategic use of gain-and loss-framed messages to promote healthy behavior: how theory can inform practice. J. Commun. **56**(suppl_1), S202–S220 (2006)

26. Shoemaker, P.J., Reese, S.D.: Mediating the Message, pp. 781–795. Longman, White Plains (1996)

27. Rothman, A.J., Salovey, P.: Shaping perceptions to motivate healthy behavior: the role of message framing. Psychol. Bull. **121**(1), 3 (1997)

28. Weibo trending search engine homepage. https://weibo.zhaoyizhe.com/. Accessed 2 Sept 2023

From Stickers to Personas: Utilizing Instant Messaging Stickers for Impression Management by Gen Z

Haoran Qiu[1]([✉]), Dion Hoe-Lian Goh[1], Ruoxi Liu[1], and Peter J. Schulz[1,2]

[1] Nanyang Technological University, 31 Nanyang Link, Singapore 637718, Singapore
{haoran004,ruoxi001}@e.ntu.edu.sg, {ashlgoh,
peterj.schulz}@ntu.edu.sg
[2] University of Lugano, Via Buffi 13, 6900 Lugano, Switzerland

Abstract. The present study investigated how and why Generation Z (Gen Z) individuals utilize stickers for impression management in instant messaging (IM) applications, as well as the impacts on interpersonal interactions. Through 30 semi-structured online interviews, five typical sticker types and their corresponding personas that are typically constructed were uncovered. Furthermore, we identified four primary motivations that drive Gen Z's utilization of IM stickers for impression management purposes, including creating personal tags, gaining group identity, acknowledging authority, and fostering a communicative atmosphere. In terms of the impacts on interpersonal interactions, we discovered that Gen Z individuals were highly adept at utilizing IM stickers to construct their personas, which helps them to reduce online interpersonal distance with others and enhance their socializing abilities in various contexts. However, online social anxiety is a potential risk to their interpersonal relationships. Based on the findings, practical and theoretical insights were discussed.

Keywords: Generation Z · Instant Messaging · Stickers · Impression Management · Interpersonal Interactions

1 Introduction

Instant messaging (IM) stickers have gained immense popularity among younger-generation users in recent years. Stickers are often considered a kind of visual expression that has evolved from emojis, and refer to "larger, more elaborate, character-driven illustrations or animations to which text is sometimes attached" [7]. Stickers are also customizable and emotionally expressive, empowering users with a stronger online social presence.

Impression management is a prevalent interpersonal interaction behavior. It is the process where people attempt to influence others' perceptions of themselves [6, 9, 10]. With the popularity of IM, many Internet users, especially younger ones, are highly skilled at managing their images online [1, 13]. Online communication facilitates users

I. Sserwanga et al. (Eds.): iConference 2024, LNCS 14597, pp. 198–207, 2024.
https://doi.org/10.1007/978-3-031-57860-1_15

to intentionally construct and project desirable personas for various audiences [14, 15], with stickers being an important graphicon tool and visual language [11].

Generation Z (Gen Z), comprising individuals born from the mid-1990s to the late-2000s, represents the youngest and increasingly influential segment entering the workforce and consumer market [5]. As "digital natives" that grow up with the Internet [5], Gen Z have been influenced by digitalization in every way and demonstrate a stronger acceptance of digitized social engagement compared to others [12]. Within this context, they have developed their own way of self-presentation and personal branding on social media, influencing various aspects of their lives, such as job searching, online dating, and intergenerational communication [4, 8, 20]. The utilization of graphicon, such as stickers on social media, has emerged as a popular social strategy of interpersonal interactions among Gen Z. Initially a subcultural trend, this practice has now evolved into a mainstream phenomenon in the online context [11].

Although prior scholars have attempted to explore people's social media graphicon usage behavior through the interpersonal relationship perspectives [17, 21], there is insufficient research on how IM users, especially younger generation like Gen Z, manage their impressions through stickers, and what their motivations are. Additionally, there is also little knowledge about how this affects their interpersonal interactions. Currently, over 342 million active Internet users in China are Gen Zs [18], representing a huge user population holding significant sway in digital trends.

Addressing the abovementioned gaps within the context of China helps us further understand people's interpersonal interactions in the digital era and provides practical insights for the digital marketing and internet industries focused on young consumers in China. Moreover, there is limited work investigating individuals' utilization of stickers from the perspective of impression management. Delving into this area may contribute to the extension of impression management theory in graphicon expression and IM settings.

Hence, the present study aims to answer the following questions in the Chinese context: RQ1: How do Gen Z individuals engage in impression management utilizing IM stickers? RQ2: What motivations drive Gen Z's utilization of IM stickers for impression management purposes? RQ3: What are the impacts of utilizing IM stickers for impression management on Gen Z's interpersonal interaction?

2 Methodology

We conducted online semi-structured interviews for data collection. A total of 30 Gen Z participants from China, with ages between 21 to 27, were recruited through convenience and snowball sampling. The participants were either students or working adults, including 15 males and 15 females. All of them used IM applications like WeChat, WhatsApp, or QQ daily.

2.1 Data Collection

Two trained researchers conducted semi-structured interviews according to an interview protocol (see Appendix A). The average duration of each interview was about 1 h. During the interviews, some questions were rephrased as needed to improve comprehension. Context-based situational questions were added to maintain participant engagement.

All participants were first asked about their demographic information, IM application usage, frequently used sticker types, and reasons. Subsequent questions inquired whether and how they utilized those stickers for impression management purposes in IM. Participants were also requested to display some example stickers they utilized to shape or influence others' impressions of themselves and to share the usage scenarios and motivations. Follow-up questions delved into participants' perspectives on the impact of impression management through IM stickers on interpersonal interactions, both for themselves and others.

2.2 Data Analysis

All interviews were video-recorded and transcribed into text for analysis. We adopted Braun and Clarke's [2] approach for thematic analysis: (1) familiarizing with the data; (2) generating initial codes; (3) searching for themes; (4) reviewing potential themes; (5) defining and naming themes; and (6) producing the report.

To ensure reliability, two coders were employed to conduct the analysis with a constant comparative method. This refers to "comparing data applicable to each code and modifying code definitions so as to fit new data" [19]. First, the two coders independently completed line-by-line coding for all the transcripts. Then, they discussed and adjusted the codes to generate a unified codebook with initial themes and codes. Subsequently, the two coders reviewed the transcripts and constantly adjusted the codebook until reaching code saturation. Codes with fewer than three occurrences were deleted at this stage. Finally, according to the codebook, the two coders reviewed and defined all the themes.

3 Findings

3.1 Typical Sticker Types, Persona Construction, and Usage Scenarios

Firstly, we found that all participants had experiences of attempting to utilize IM Stickers to construct personas or influence others' impressions of themselves. Five typical sticker types that were employed by Gen Zs for impression management purposes were identified, namely (1) cute animals; (2) cartoons or comics; (3) funny memes; (4) organizational identity; and (5) individual identity. These sticker types are not mutually exclusive, as a sticker may belong to multiple types, for example, funny meme stickers of anime characters. Figure 1 shows some examples that were displayed by the participants during interviews, while Fig. 2 illustrates their usage and comparisons between each type.

According to Fig. 2, stickers with cute animals and cartoon or comic characters were the two most frequently utilized types. Following closely were the funny meme stickers. Stickers highlighting identity attributes were the least utilized type, with those representing organizational identity seeing more usage compared to those reflecting personal identity.

Fig. 1. Examples of sticker types for impression management purposes

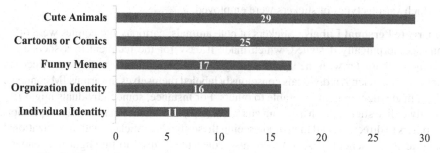

Fig. 2. Usage of sticker types for impression management purposes by Gen Z

Cute Animals. Stickers with cute animals were the most frequent-utilized type, with anthropomorphic features usually embedded. Most Gen Z individuals utilized them for constructing friendly, approachable, or communicative personas. These stickers were widely applicable in most usage scenarios and were particularly favored in unfamiliar relationships and public contexts to soften the sense of distance.

Cartoons or Comics. Stickers sourced from comics or anime works were also popular among Gen Z in IM. These personalized cartoon characters were popular, helping them present a youthful, optimistic image. At the same time, the shared cultural elements made these stickers bring like-minded people closer together. These types of stickers were mostly seen in communication between friends.

Funny Memes. These stickers typically had funny and entertaining features, which are made by Internet users based on popular memes or Internet trends. Gen Z individuals utilized them for humorous and character-driven persona-building. Because funny memes could be easily misunderstood, stickers of funny memes were mainly utilized privately among friends, instead of in formal or public settings.

Organizational Identity. Stickers with organizational identity (e.g., logos or mascots) were intentionally utilized by Gen Z to demonstrate belonging and loyalty within specific organizations, such as companies or schools. These stickers were effective in building group identity and pleasing superiors. However, they were rarely used outside the organization context, as Gen Zs felt it was pointless and contrived.

Individual Identity. Some Gen Z individuals self-made stickers based on their portraits. These stickers commonly showed beautified portraits and carried strong intimacy and emotional expressions. People mainly utilize them in intimate relationships to show a sincere, romantic, or affectionate image towards their significant other.

3.2 Motivations for Impression Management in Sticker Utilization

We uncovered four primary motivations for Gen Z's utilization of IM stickers for impression management purposes. Additionally, we mapped these motivations with scenarios in which various types of stickers were employed.

To Create Personal Labels. Stickers of cute animals, cartoons and comics were often anthropomorphically designed, which made it easy for the recipient to associate the graphicon character with the sender's image. Through the heavy utilization of certain stickers, many Gen Z individuals consciously labeled themselves in various IM contexts, which made them more memorable to others. For instance, some individuals might frequently utilize stickers with a certain character (e.g., Doraemon) in group chats, prompting others to directly recall them upon seeing these stickers. Stickers with organizational identities (e.g., school mascots) were also consistently used to highlight the sender's organizational affiliation.

To Foster an Atmosphere of Communication. Many Gen Z individuals believed that text-only communication in IM was serious, cold, and even impersonal. Crafting online personas through stickers facilitates communication. In unfamiliar or awkward situations, this could help to alleviate tension. For instance, many individuals indicated that intentionally utilizing animal or cartoon stickers in conversations with new friends or in new group chats can quickly establish closeness. Simultaneously, within intimate relationships like couples, sticker-based personas could develop a unique shared visual language, thereby facilitating emotional expression. Many couples created and used personalized stickers that reflected their unique identities. They believed these stickers not only facilitated communication but also served as a testament to their relationships.

To Gain Group Identity. Demonstrating loyalty and belonging to the organization was a key driver of many Gen Z individuals' utilization of stickers with organizational identities. This helped them to better integrate into the group and be recognized by other members. Many individuals believe that utilizing their organization's stickers when communicating with members within the same organization helped reduce the guardedness of others. Moreover, Gen Z individuals also utilized funny memes stickers with shared cultural elements to resonate with each other. For example, Cantonese people intentionally utilized stickers with Cantonese-style memes among themselves to evoke regional identity.

To Acknowledge Authority. Unlike the other usage scenarios, most Gen Zs did not proactively utilize stickers when addressing authoritative figures, such as superiors or teachers, to avoid misunderstandings and show respect. Instead, they observed, probed, and imitated authority figures' sticker utilization to present a persona that better matched the target's expectations. This also showed their respect and recognition of hierarchical relationships, which made it easier to catch the authoritative figures' attention and facilitate their work.

3.3 Impacts on Interpersonal Interactions

We further discovered that utilizing stickers for impression management in IM had both positive and negative impacts on interpersonal interactions. On the positive side, it reduced the interpersonal distance in online engagements and enhanced individuals' socializing abilities. However, the heavy utilization of stickers might also increase people's online social anxiety.

Reduction of Online Interpersonal Distance. As many stickers come with friendly and anthropomorphic visual settings, utilizing stickers for impression management reduced the psychological barriers with others in the online environment. A digitized sticker-based persona reduced mutual caution and facilitated a more congenial chatting environment, in which potential misunderstandings or negative emotions could be easily diffused. Some people in workplaces claimed that an approachable persona could be effectively constructed by stickers, making it easier to present opposing views to others with a low risk of the deterioration of relationships.

Enhancement of Individual's Socializing Abilities. IM stickers offered people a vehicle to show diverse traits that might not be apparent in in-person interactions. A digitized persona with multiple flexible traits made Gen Z individuals become more adept at socializing with various audiences and thus helping them have a stronger social presence. For example, some individuals were introverted in real life and were afraid to speak in public. However, they were able to tactically utilize stickers to become talkative and humorous in IM group chats, which made it easier for them to gain the attention and recognition of others than in real life. In addition, Gen Z did not consider this practice as deceptive or embarrassing; on the contrary, they regarded it as appropriate and normative, as they believed that a digitized persona was also part of their identity.

Risk of Online Social Anxiety. However, heavy utilization of stickers might also put a strain on interpersonal interactions. As sticker utilization becomes a customary etiquette, people's cost of communication in IM has increased. Many participants indicated that they struggled with what stickers to use in simple chats, even when it was not necessary. In addition, the same sticker might have various interpretations in different contexts. Most Gen Z individuals had experiences of misunderstanding or being misunderstood about sticker utilization, particularly in intergenerational conversations, sometimes leading to financial or customer-related repercussions. For instance, a participant working in an educational consulting sector mentioned that he had been questioned by a client about his competence due to improper sticker utilization. Gen Z individuals thus were often caught in the dilemma of deciding when and when not to utilize stickers, resulting in increasing online social anxiety.

4 Discussion

Gen Z individuals are highly adept at using IM stickers for impression management in various contexts. They can switch personas by utilizing different stickers to facilitate their interpersonal interaction in various scenarios. Stickers with cute animals, cartoonish, or comic characters are mostly utilized for friendly persona construction. These stickers are applicable in almost all scenarios. Funny memes stickers are popular in familiar settings, which help Gen Z individuals both show their individuality and be less likely to be misinterpreted by others. Stickers with identity elements, such as organizational and individual identity, tend to be used only in specific groups or contractual relationships. Specifically, stickers with organizational identity are mostly used for intra-organizational communication, whereas those with personal identity are restricted to intimate relationships.

The varied utilization of stickers also reflects different impression management motivations. In formal or public settings, Gen Z's motivations are usually related to self-enhancement and utilitarian purposes, such as pleasing their superiors or gaining recognition from the group. In these scenarios, their impression management tactics through stickers are often defensive and sometimes deceptive. Thus, generic, and unambiguous stickers are preferred. In contrast, in informal or private settings, they usually boldly and authentically develop personas instead of intentionally building a glorified image with stickers. Most of them tend to exhibit unique traits and assert their individuality, which helps them better express emotions and enhance closeness with others. Surprisingly, we also found that Chinese Gen Zs tend to empathetically utilize stickers. They embraced others' sticker usage and responded with similar ones (even if they personally disliked them) to construct appropriate personas and facilitate communication. These findings have not been extensively mentioned in previous studies within the Western context or perspectives. A plausible explanation is that, influenced by collectivist values, Chinese individuals tend to emphasize harmony in their social interactions [16], prioritizing the maintenance of interpersonal relationships or *guanxi* [3]. This may lead Chinese Gen Zs to focus intensely on constructing personas in online communications, whether deceptive or authentic, to ensure their presentations and interactions conforms to the norms within various context. In this process, stickers play a vital role as a graphicon tool and visual language [11].

It is worth noting that utilizing stickers for impression management is a double-edged sword. While it brings convenience to Gen Z's interpersonal interactions, it also adds to the social pressure they experience at the same time. On the one hand, the affordance of stickers allows people to better showcase their multifaceted personalities, and the personified design of these stickers can significantly soften the sense of distance and enhance their socializing abilities in online interaction, thus facilitating relationships with others. On the other hand, with increasing habitual usage, stickers have gradually evolved into a non-universal symbolized language among Gen Z. People also worry about the risk of being misunderstood when utilizing stickers, which potentially impact their reputations and relationships. Further, it may increase their online social anxiety and fatigue in IM.

5 Conclusion

In conclusion, the present study provides preliminary findings on how and why Gen Z individuals utilize IM stickers for impression management, with the impact on interpersonal interaction further explored. According to the findings, we offer the following practical implications. First, the general findings benefit digital marketing and other practitioners who focus on topics related to Gen Z's digitalized personas, IM usage, and interpersonal interactions. The impression management strategies identified in this study can help in refining the strategies of online customer relationship management. In addition, the study's findings on Gen Z's preferences and motivations for sticker utilization also inform organizational and brand communication, especially in sticker design and promotion. Finally, as we found that sticker utilization affects people's social anxiety, mental well-being practitioners who focus on the domain of social phobia, social media fatigue, and interpersonal relationships may also build upon the findings of this study.

In terms of theoretical implications, we suggest potential influential factors for individuals' online impression management: (1) self-promotion desire; (2) the target's degree of familiarity; (3) the target's social hierarchy; (4) empathic tendencies. We further explored the impacts of impression management through stickers on interpersonal relationships, encompassing both positive and negative sides. These findings provide insights into constructing research frameworks and developing impression management theories in the domains of instant messaging and graphicon expression.

There are also limitations in this study that may offer guidance for future research. First, due to the nature of the qualitative methods used, our findings lack generalizability. However, our results can inform subsequent quantitative studies to verify the proposed motivations and impacts of Gen Z's impression management through stickers. Second, as this study only focused on Gen Zs in China, future work could compare our outcomes across different countries and age groups.

Appendix A: Semi-structured Interview Protocol

Part 1: Demographic Information and IM Sticker Usage

1. **Demographic Information**
    1.1 What is your age?
    1.2. What is your gender?
    1.3 What is your educational background?
    1.4 What is your occupation?
2. IM Applications Usage
    2.1. Which instant messaging (IM) applications are you currently utilizing?
    2.2 Could you specify the frequency of your usage for these IM applications?
3. Sticker Preferences

3.1 Which stickers do you commonly utilize in IM applications? Could you show me some examples?

3.2 What are your reasons for preferring these specific stickers?

Part 2: Sticker Utilization for Impression Management

4. **Impression Construction**

4.1 Have you ever attempted to construct or sustain a specific persona or impression by utilizing these IM stickers? If so, could you elaborate on what kind of personas or impressions you want to build?

4.2 How did you employ these IM stickers to achieve your intended personas or impressions? Could you provide specific examples or strategies you used?

5. Motivations

5.1 Could you describe specific instances or scenarios where you have used IM stickers to manage your impression on others? Could you provide detailed examples?

5.2 Why do you choose to construct certain personas through the utilization of IM stickers? What motivates this choice?

Part 3: Impact on Interpersonal Interactions

6. **Perception**

6.1 How do you perceive the role of impression management by IM stickers in social relationship dynamics? Could you share your experiences and observations regarding this phenomenon?

7. **Interpersonal Interaction Dynamics**

7.1 In what ways does the use of IM stickers for impression management influence your interpersonal interactions? Could you provide specific examples, either personally or in the context of others' experiences?

8. **Follow-Up Questions**

8.1 Are there any additional significant responses or unique insights you would like to elaborate on?

References

1. Bareket-Bojmel, L., et al.: Strategic self-presentation on Facebook: personal motives and audience response to online behavior. Comput. Hum. Behav. **55**, 788–795 (2016). https://doi.org/10.1016/j.chb.2015.10.033
2. Braun, V., Clarke, V.: Thematic analysis. In: APA Handbook of Research Methods in Psychology, Research Designs: Quantitative, Qualitative, Neuropsychological, and Biological, vol. 2, pp. 57–71 American Psychological Association, Washington, DC, US (2012). https://doi.org/10.1037/13620-004
3. Chen, C.C., et al.: Chinese *Guanxi* : an integrative review and new directions for future research. Manag. Organ. Rev. **9**(1), 167–207 (2013). https://doi.org/10.1111/more.12010

4. Gala, J., Ghadiyali, N.N.: Romantic memes and beliefs: influence on relationship satisfaction. Psychol. Stud. **65**(4), 394–407 (2020). https://doi.org/10.1007/s12646-020-00585-5

5. Gentina, E., Parry, E.: The New Generation Z in Asia: Dynamics, Differences, Digitalisation. Emerald Publishing Limited, Bingley (2020)

6. Goffman, E.: The Presentation of Self in Everyday Life. Doubleday, Oxford (1959)

7. Konrad, A., et al.: Sticker and emoji use in Facebook messenger: implications for graphicon change. J. Comput.-Mediat. Commun. **25**(3), 217–235 (2020). https://doi.org/10.1093/jcmc/zmaa003

8. Labrecque, L.I., et al.: Online personal branding: processes, challenges, and implications. J. Interact. Mark. **25**(1), 37–50 (2011). https://doi.org/10.1016/j.intmar.2010.09.002

9. Leary, M.R.: Self-presentation: Impression Management and Interpersonal Behavior. Routledge, London (2019)

10. Leary, M.R., Kowalski, R.M.: Impression management: a literature review and two-component model. Psychol. Bull. **107**, 34–47 (1990)

11. Liu, R.: WeChat online visual language among Chinese Gen Z: virtual gift, aesthetic identity, and affection language. Front. Commun. **8** (2023)

12. Mason, M.C., et al.: Glued to your phone? Generation Z's smartphone addiction and online compulsive buying. Comput. Hum. Behav. **136**, 107404 (2022). https://doi.org/10.1016/j.chb.2022.107404

13. Ranzini, G., Hoek, E.: To you who (I think) are listening: imaginary audience and impression management on Facebook. Comput. Hum. Behav. **75**, 228–235 (2017). https://doi.org/10.1016/j.chb.2017.04.047

14. Schlosser, A.E.: Self-disclosure versus self-presentation on social media. Curr. Opin. Psychol. **31**, 1–6 (2020). https://doi.org/10.1016/j.copsyc.2019.06.025

15. Siibak, A.: Constructing the self through the photo selection: visual impression management on social networking websites. Cyberpsychology **3**, 1–9 (2009)

16. Tam, B.K.Y., Bond, M.H.: Interpersonal behaviors and friendship in a Chinese culture. Asian J. Social Psycho. **5**(1), 63–74 (2002). https://doi.org/10.1111/1467-839X.00094

17. Tang, Y., Hew, K.F.: Emoticon, emoji, and sticker use in computer-mediated communication: a review of theories and research findings. Int. J. Commun. **13**, 27 (2019)

18. Thomala, L.L.: China: Gen Z active internet users 2022. https://www.statista.com.remotexs.ntu.edu.sg/statistics/1199305/china-number-of-genz-active-internet-users/. Accessed 25 Aug 2023

19. Tracy, S.J.: Qualitative Research Methods. Wiley-Blackwell, Chichester (2013)

20. Wang, X.: Social Media in Industrial China. UCL Press, London (2016)

21. Wang, Y., et al.: Culturally-embedded visual literacy: a study of impression management via emoticon, emoji, sticker, and meme on social media in China. Proc. ACM Human-Computer Interact. **3**(CSCW), 1–24 (2019)

Disinformation and Misinformation

Arguing About Controversial Science in the News: Does Epistemic Uncertainty Contribute to Information Disorder?

Heng Zheng[✉][iD], Theodore Dreyfus Ledford[iD], and Jodi Schneider[✉][iD]

School of Information Sciences, University of Illinois Urbana-Champaign,
Champaign, IL, USA
{zhenghz,tledfo2,jodi}@illinois.edu

Abstract. News informs the public, especially in crisis situations. The news significantly impacted the public's beliefs about COVID-19. Handling uncertainty in scientific evidence production is a particular challenge. The public controversy in the United States over mask mandates and the effectiveness of masks to prevent COVID-19 was reignited by a controversial scientific review article that Cochrane published in early 2023, which concluded "There is uncertainty about the effects of masks." The current paper presents a case study of 58 news articles that linked to the review article according to Altmetric.com; news articles were published from February 1, 2023 to March 9, 2023 (inclusive). We use an argument mapping approach called polylogue analysis to diagram the players and positions covered in the news. We find that news articles citing the Cochrane Review took contradictory positions such as "masks work" and "masks don't work," neither of which was falsified by the conclusions of the review article. However, these positions require further contextualization. We argue that current definitions of information disorder, which focus on misinformation, disinformation, and malinformation, cannot adequately account for the challenges associated with conveying scientific information. In particular, due to epistemic uncertainty, multiple contradictory positions can coexist as credible. Future work on information disorder in science needs to consider not only the intention to harm but also the risks associated with oversimplification or decontextualization of current scientific evidence.

Keywords: Altmetrics · Argument mapping · Epistemic uncertainty · Masks for COVID-19 · Scientific controversies

1 Introduction

News informs the public, especially in crisis situations. The news significantly impacted the public's beliefs about COVID-19 [11,24,43,50]. However, informing the public is more difficult with the disruption of traditional print news and a concomitant increase in online news, which have decreased the number of full-time science journalists working for major news outlets [23,56].

The original version of the chapter has been revised. The third author has been labelled as corresponding author. In addition, some minor changes have been made to the main text and the references. A correction to this chapter can be found at
https://doi.org/10.1007/978-3-031-57860-1_29

I. Sserwanga et al. (Eds.): iConference 2024, LNCS 14597, pp. 211–235, 2024.
https://doi.org/10.1007/978-3-031-57860-1_16

Handling uncertainty in scientific evidence production [23] is a particular challenge. News about scientific controversies may be reported with dramatization; a common problem is reporting a "false balance" that distorts scientific consensus instead of "making clear what the relative positions mean in relation to the current scientific understanding" [23]. Journalists' simplification of science is essential to ensure that the public can understand scientific information, but it can lead to challenges due to the contrast between the institutional logics used by the media (e.g., meeting standards of newsworthiness) and in science (e.g., embracing the complexity of scientific information) [34].

Whether mask-wearing can reduce or prevent the spread of coronavirus was the subject of continuous debate since the beginning of the COVID-19 pandemic. The public controversy in the United States over mask mandates and the effectiveness of masks for preventing COVID-19 was reignited by a controversial scientific review article that Cochrane published on January 30, 2023, called "Physical interventions to interrupt or reduce the spread of respiratory viruses" [33]. That review article includes phrases such as "little to no difference" and "uncertainty of the effects," which were often cited in US news.

Here we present a case study that analyzes altmetric news data using an argument mapping approach called polylogue analysis to explore how scientists, public health officials, and others reacted to the review article. In the rest of the paper, we first present the background and introduce our case study. We then describe our methodology and present our results. We discuss our findings, limitations, and future work before concluding the paper.

2   Background

Next we discuss background in five areas: how news consumption impacted Americans' understanding of COVID-19; the relationship between information disorder, trust in science, and COVID-19; epistemic uncertainty; altmetrics; and argument mapping and polylogue analysis.

2.1   How News Consumption Impacted Americans' Understanding of COVID-19

News media, particularly cable news, is heavily polarized in America. Based on a nationally representative survey of the US conducted in March 2020, watching ABC News, CBS News, or NBC News correlated with "accurate beliefs" about protection from infection, while watching Fox and other conservative news correlated with the belief that the US Centers for Disease Control and Prevention (CDC) was overplaying the virus to undermine Donald Trump's presidency [24]. News sources influenced viewers' worry over perceived threat of COVID-19 and adherence to guidelines, according to Mechanical Turk surveys conducted in July and August 2020 [43]. Viewers of conservative media and Trump briefings were less likely to perceive COVID-19 as a serious threat; they doubted the efficacy of mitigation efforts and had lower intentions to adopt preventive behavior, according to a June 2020 survey [11]. Greater consumption of Fox News had a causal increase on vaccine hesitancy reflected in lower vaccination rates at the county level, even after controlling for "self-reported Republican and conservative affiliation from Gallup" based on nationwide cable news viewership statistics in April-June 2021; CNN and MSNBC viewership had no impact [50]. Households exposed to online left-wing news such as CNN, *Huffington Post*, and *The Guardian* were less likely to have a positive COVID-19 test in a nationally representative survey of the US conducted from August to November 2021 [59].

2.2 Trust in Science, COVID-19, and Information Disorder

People reason about and act on COVID-19 knowledge differently based on their trust in science [65], drawing not only on the science but also on social, economic, and moral aspects [16].

A number of different factors contribute to how well informed Americans are about science [54]. Simplification of science for the news, while essential [34], is not politically neutral [26]. Journalists' own views and the interests of their audiences impact the extent to which they amplify claims about what is not known in science [61]. How news stories cover "claims intended to amplify scientific unknowns and uncertainties" impacts the public understanding of science and science-based policymaking [62]. News articles contain an amalgamation of facts and sources compiled by their authors. Articles may contain outdated facts when journalists do not use standardized verification methods [69] or lack access to people who can be relevant sources [25].

Information disorder refers to misinformation ("content that is false but not intended to harm"), disinformation ("content that is false and intended to harm"), and malinformation ("truthful information that is intended to harm") [70]. A small amount of misinformation can have an outsized effect, due to personalization of information and peoples' propensity to seek out confirmatory information [54]. A study selecting 100 news articles about vaccines for COVID-19 from June 2021 detected that only 3.2% contained misinformation, whether included as primary information, fact-checking errors, or references made to other misinformation [41]. However, visitor traffic to web pages with articles containing misinformation was proportionally larger than traffic to other articles [41].

2.3 Epistemic Uncertainty

Gaps or disconnects within and between bodies of research should be expected, yet people are averse to accepting uncertainty [8]. Crises demand urgent action from policymakers to determine the most reliable information available [15]. Pressure for scientists to "speak in one voice" to simplify scientific discussion and minimize epistemic uncertainty [29] can backfire: Overconfidence in science can undermine public trust in scientific expertise [72]. Policymakers often need to make decisions in the absence of scientific evidence, or with suboptimal evidence [4]. One common consideration is the *precautionary principle*: minimize risks in the face of uncertainty [22]. Another consideration is that absence of evidence is not evidence of absence [4]. Accepting scientific uncertainty, recognizing the different speeds of science and politics, and separating the technical and political contributions to decision-making, could have improved early COVID-19 pandemic decision-making [15].

2.4 Altmetrics

Altmetrics measures the online attention to scientific research [52], extending traditional bibliometrics. Altmetrics data is available through a number of commercial and non-commercial data providers [48].

Altmetric Explorer is a user-friendly platform provided by Altmetric.com that allows users to retrieve altmetrics data. While news data from Altmetric.com is "a relatively reliable source" [18], the data has shortcomings [73]. Altmetric.com's composite metric which simply adds together the number of mentions in news articles, blogs, Wikipedia, and social media has been criticized for its uninterpretability [63, page 5].

We briefly review a few studies that incorporated altmetrics of COVID-19-related publications. Fleerackers et al. [19] examined how news articles described COVID-19 preprints' publication status when mentioning or linking to preprints; they identified four types of uncertainty frames which were sometimes, but not consistently, used in news stories to discuss added uncertainty associated with sharing science before peer review and formal publication. Two studies used data from Altmetric.com to analyze public argumentation about mask science [10,21]: data for both studies consisted of a corpus of 4775 tweets from January to April 2020 from Altmetric.com that referred to 6 research publications on cloth masks. Altmetrics data has also been used to study how COVID-19 biomedical research was used by policy documents [49]. Recently a preprint by Alperin et al. [3] noted that social media was more likely to link to news articles discussing COVID-19 research ("second-order citations") than directly to the research articles.

2.5 Argument Mapping and Polylogue Analysis

People put forth arguments to communicate ideas, make decisions, and check that reasoning is sound. The multidisciplinary field that analyzes arguments is known as argumentation theory [14]. One powerful technique is argumentation analysis, which identifies and analyzes support and attack relationships between different positions.

The computer-supported collaborative work community has used software tools for argumentation to support sense-making and group deliberation in educational and organizational contexts [35]. Argument mapping can help clarify a group's understanding of a disagreement [20] and can be used to visualize web-scale debates [27]. In the past 15 years, technologists have also sought to develop an Argument Web, combining an interchange-focused ontology with a series of tools, systems and services [53]. For instance, chatbots to increase critical thinking have built on knowledge bases and dialogue engines [46] among other applications [38].

While argumentation is often simplified to two-position settings, such as the pro and con sides of a debate or the plaintiffs and defendants in courts, recently attention has been focused on complex, multi-party communication, described as a "polylogue" [39]. In an early demonstration of polylogue analysis Aakhus and Lewiński analyzed a single *New York Times* article on the fracking controversy to demonstrate the practical application of polylogue analysis [2]. Polylogue analysis mainly concerns players, positions, and places. Players are individuals or groups of individuals (e.g., government agencies, scientific research teams) who share their positions in particular venues, the places. In the fracking controversy, the players included local citizens, industry groups, and US federal regulators [39]. A *player* (local citizen) puts forth a *position* ("fracking makes our community unsafe") in a *place* (an informal public encounter in a local restaurant) [2]. In general, polylogue analysis considers the players, positions, and places where arguments occur.

3   Introducing Our Case Study

We apply polylogue analysis to describe how news articles mentioned a controversial scientific review article about the effectiveness of mask-wearing in the first 5 weeks after its publication.

3.1   The Cochrane Review: A Widely Discussed Article from Highly Regarded Producers of Medical Reviews

Cochrane, as a review producer, is highly regarded and often considered the "gold standard" in medical literature reviews [36]. Their review "Physical interventions to interrupt or reduce the spread of respiratory viruses," published on January 30, 2023, focuses on masks, handwashing, and similar physical interventions [33]. It is the fifth version of the review, with previous versions published in 2007, 2010, 2011, and November 2020. A protocol for this series of reviews was published in 2006. We use the term "Cochrane Review" to refer to the 2023 version of the review [33], not the whole series.

The Cochrane Review reviewed Randomized Controlled Trials about the effectiveness of mask-wearing, and its conclusions report considerable uncertainty, especially at the start of a 2-page plain language summary shown in Fig. 1. Its heading lists two "Key messages" [33]: "We are uncertain whether wearing masks or N95/P2 respirators helps to slow the spread of respiratory viruses based on the studies we assessed. Hand hygiene programmes may help to slow the spread of respiratory viruses."

The Cochrane Review as a whole delivered positions such as:

1. "The high risk of bias in the trials, variation in outcome measurement, and relatively low adherence with the interventions during the studies hampers drawing firm conclusions." [33]

of medical/surgical masks compared with N95/P2 respirators in healthcare workers when used in routine care to reduce respiratory viral infection. Hand hygiene is likely to modestly reduce the burden of respiratory illness, and although this effect was also present when ILI and laboratory-confirmed influenza were analysed separately, it was not found to be a significant difference for the latter two outcomes. Harms associated with physical interventions were under-investigated.

There is a need for large, well-designed RCTs addressing the effectiveness of many of these interventions in multiple settings and populations, as well as the impact of adherence on effectiveness, especially in those most at risk of ARIs.

PLAIN LANGUAGE SUMMARY

Do physical measures such as hand-washing or wearing masks stop or slow down the spread of respiratory viruses?

Key messages
We are uncertain whether wearing masks or N95/P2 respirators helps to slow the spread of respiratory viruses based on the studies we assessed.

Hand hygiene programmes may help to slow the spread of respiratory viruses.

How do respiratory viruses spread?

Fig. 1. An excerpt from the Cochrane Review's [33] 2-page plain language summary as of September 17, 2023.

2. "There is uncertainty about the effects of face masks. The low to moderate certainty of evidence means our confidence in the effect estimate is limited,..." [33]
3. "Compared with wearing no mask in the community studies only, wearing a mask may make little to no difference in how many people caught a flu-like illness/COVID-like illness..." [33]

3.2   Discussion of the Cochrane Review

The uncertainty stated in Cochrane Review's conclusions provided strong support for people questioning the effectiveness of mask mandates. The Cochrane Review attracted substantial attention beyond traditional scientific venues. As of December 26, 2023, the Cochrane Review was mentioned in 480 news stories from 240 outlets and 74,344 from X [previously Twitter] posts from 48,196 X users according to Altmetric.com, putting it in the top 5% of all research outputs scored by Altmetric.com.[1]

Cochrane responded to the news in a statement published on March 10, 2023 by Karla Soares-Weiser, Editor-in-Chief of the Cochrane Library [57]: "Many commentators have claimed that a recently-updated Cochrane Review shows that 'masks don't work', which is an inaccurate and misleading interpretation."

3.3   Evidentiary Standards of the Cochrane Review Series

Some aspects of the disagreement in the news concern what type of studies counts as evidence, as we will discuss in Sect. 5.2. For the 2023 Cochrane Review, the only acceptable evidence was Randomized Controlled Trials. Notably, in previous

---

[1] https://cochrane.altmetric.com/details/141934282

editions in the series, from the 2006 protocol through the third version of the review in 2011, evidence from other study designs, such as observational studies, was also reviewed.

The inclusion criteria for this series of Cochrane Reviews had changed to limit to Randomized Controlled Trials as of the immediately previous, November 2020 publication [31]: "For this 2020 update we only considered individual-level RCTs, or cluster-RCTs, or quasi-RCTs for inclusion. In previous versions of the review we also included observational studies (cohorts, case-controls, before-after, and time series studies). However, for this update there were sufficient randomised studies to address our study aims, so we excluded observational studies (which are known to be at a higher risk of bias)."

The November 2020 publication was accompanied by an editorial [58] noting "lack of evidence of effectiveness is not evidence that the interventions are ineffective. Rather, the details of these reviews show why there may never be strong evidence regarding the effectiveness of individual behavioural measures when deployed, often in combination, in a general population living in the complex, diverse circumstances of individuals' everyday lives."

These same considerations hold for the 2023 version of the review [33], which Cochrane did not mark as having an important change compared to the November 2020 review conclusions. In fact, the key messages are identical except for their placement: at the end of the plain language summary (November 2020) versus the top (January 2023; see Fig. 1).

4 Methodology

To analyze the news discussing the Cochrane Review, we first used Altmetric.com to retrieve news articles on the web, and selected a subset. Second, we extracted direct quotations. Third, we identified who was quoted and annotated the quotations. Finally, we analyzed the quotations. We managed the process using an Excel spreadsheet and MAXQDA version 22.7.0[2]; data supporting our analysis is available in the Illinois Databank [74].

Retrieve and Select the News Articles. To collect news articles on the web that discuss the Cochrane Review, we retrieved articles from Altmetric.com using their Altmetric Explorer on August 1, 2023. Overall, news articles we retrieved were published in January (1), February (193), March (108), April (53), May (31), June (8), and July (2). The selection criteria and process are depicted in Fig. 2. We selected all articles written in English, published in the United States with publication date prior to March 10, 2023 (according to Altmetric.com "Mention Date"), when Cochrane issued a statement about the "misleading interpretation" [57].

---

[2] https://www.maxqda.com/

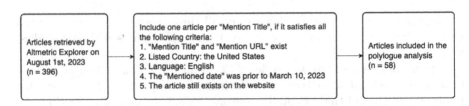

Fig. 2. Process of retrieving and selecting news articles on the web that discuss the Cochrane Review

Extract Direct Quotations Relating to the Cochrane Review. For each of the 58 news articles, we manually extracted direct quotations of reported speech that met any of the following criteria:

- The quotation mentioned words like "mask," "mask mandates," or "Cochrane Review"; or
- The paragraphs surrounding the quotation discussed masks or the issues closely related to masks; or
- The quotation or the paragraphs surrounding the quotation hyperlinked to a source that largely discusses mask effectiveness or mask mandates.

We focused on reported speech, hence we omitted and did not analyze technical terminology set off with quotation marks, such as "best" and "effect size" from [42]: 'this approach assumes (a) RCTs are the "best" evidence and (b) combining results from multiple RCTs will give you an average "effect size".' Our extraction included surrounding words and sentences, and in one case, a news agency's commentary, around direct quotations for context where needed. The quotations (with context) are the positions in our analysis.

Identify Who Was Quoted. We identified who was quoted; these are the players in our analysis. We grouped similar players. We excluded quotations when we could not identify who or what was being quoted.

Analyze Quotations. We analyzed quotations in two different ways. First we selected the most-quoted position that was not from the Cochrane Review and categorized how it was discussed in the news articles. Then we used polylogue analysis, filtered to the most-quoted players, to illustrate how players agreed and disagreed with each other.

To construct a specific polylogue diagram, our filtering process was:

1. Choose players who were quoted in at least four news articles.
2. Group the direct quotations that are sourced from the same news article or video together and choose a representative position.
3. When a player has multiple positions supporting or attacking the same player, we select a representative position for the diagram.

DEMASI: *Did you wear a mask?*

JEFFERSON: I follow the law. If the law says I need to wear one, then I wear one because I have to. I do not break the law. I obey the law of the country.

DEMASI: *Yeah, same. What would you say to people who still want to wear a mask?*

JEFFERSON: I think it's fair to say that if you want to wear a mask then you should have a choice, okay. But in the absence of evidence, you shouldn't be forcing anybody to do so.

DEMASI: *But people say, I'm not wearing a mask for me, I'm wearing it for you.*

JEFFERSON: I have never understood that difference. Have you?

DEMASI: *They say it's not to protect themselves, but to protect others, an act of altruism.*

JEFFERSON: Ah yes. Wonderful. They get the Albert Schweitzer prize for Humanitarianism. Here's what I think. Your overnight experts know nothing.

DEMASI *(laughs)*

JEFFERSON: There is just no evidence that they make any difference. Full stop. My job, our job as a review team, was to look at the evidence, we have done that. Not just for masks. We looked at hand washing, sterilisation, goggles etcetera...

Fig. 3. An excerpt from the Substack newsletter "Maryanne Demasi, reports" [13], showing Tom Jefferson's heavily quoted "full stop" position.

5   Results

We analyzed 58 news articles published from February 1, 2023 to March 9, 2023 (inclusive). Of these, 57 articles[3] linked to the Cochrane Review and used it in various ways; 41 quoted the Cochrane Review.

5.1   The Most Heavily Quoted Position that Is Not from the Cochrane Review

The Cochrane Review's first author, Tom Jefferson, was quoted in 19 articles, most often with the words: "There is just no evidence that they make any difference. Full stop." We further analyze the 12 articles that contained this comment, which Jefferson made during an interview with Maryanne Demasi posted on her Substack, a digital newsletter platform [13]; an excerpt is shown in Fig. 3.

It is difficult to determine whether "they" refers to masks or mask mandates. News authors seem to interpret Jefferson's "they" to mean "masks to prevent COVID-19" [60] or "mask mandates to prevent COVID-19" [28]. Yet in the interview, Demasi and Jefferson were turning at this point from current

---

[3] While selected for linking to the Cochrane Review, due to altmetric.com data errors, one [71] did not in fact link to the Cochrane Review.

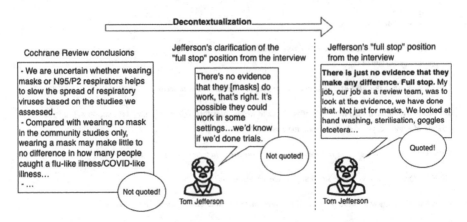

Fig. 4. Context is lost as we go from the Cochrane Review conclusions to statements in Jefferson's full interview with Demasi to his "full stop" position. In particular, the uncertainty stated in the Cochrane Review becomes "no evidence... Full stop..." [13].

events (presumably specific to COVID-19) back to the Cochrane Review, which concerns respiratory diseases in general.

The phrase "full stop" indicates certainty—the facts are in and the case is closed—and some news authors take such certainty to refer to "no evidence." However, "full stop" in Jefferson's reply is scoped: it must refer to evidence relevant for inclusion in the Cochrane Review, from words such as "... as a review team... we looked at" [13]. In the same interview, Jefferson made multiple statements about masks, mask mandates, and the related evidence base, at times with much more nuance. For example, after Demasi asked for a clarification about Jefferson's "full stop" position, Jefferson said [13], "there's no evidence that they do work, that's right. It's possible they could work in some settings... we'd know if we'd done trials." Compared to the "full stop" position, Jefferson's clarification provides more context by emphasizing what is missing in the current evidence base on mask effectiveness. However, perhaps due to its ambiguity, this more detailed statement was not mentioned in the 12 news articles that quoted Jefferson's "full stop" position.

Caveating the evidence considered is particularly important. The Cochrane Review indicates uncertainty about either effectiveness or ineffectiveness according to their evidence base [33]: "We are uncertain... based on the [Randomized Controlled Trial] studies... we assessed." Yet instead, Jefferson's "no evidence... full stop..." removed the uncertainty from the Cochrane Review conclusions, as shown in Fig. 4. Compared to the Cochrane Review conclusions, the "full stop" position does not emphasize the uncertainty about the evidence stressed in the Cochrane Review. Instead, Jefferson's language, especially "full stop," suggests that the evidence we currently have is conclusive. We call this decontextualization.

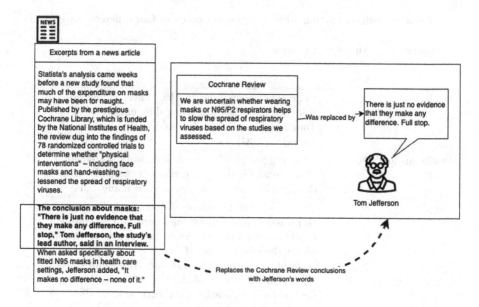

Fig. 5. A Fox News article [37] replaced the Cochrane Review conclusions with Jefferson's words from an interview with Maryanne Demasi [13].

Jefferson drew on his experience as first author of the 2006 protocol and five versions of the Cochrane Review since 2007, with particular specifications for the evidence to be considered (see Sect. 3.3). The absence of evidence was a continued point in the interview [13]: "I keep saying it repeatedly, it needs to be looked at by doing a huge, randomised study - masks haven't been given a proper trial." A particular challenge is distinguishing the absence of evidence from the evidence of absence; this is an important but little-covered distinction. Absence of evidence that "masks are effective" does not, in fact support the opposite conclusion, "masks are ineffective." While neither definitively excludes the conclusion that "masks don't work," the Cochrane Review's key message would be clearer to someone who understands that absence of evidence is not evidence of absence.

How the News Quoted Jefferson's "Full Stop" Position. The twelve articles quoting Jefferson's "full stop" position used it in four ways, as shown in Table 1: replacing, associating, distinguishing, and simplifying. Six articles replace the Cochrane Review; one example is shown in Fig. 5. In three articles, the Cochrane Review conclusions were not explicitly stated, but Jefferson's "full stop" position is distinguished from the review conclusions. For instance, according to the *Los Angeles Times* [44]: "The biggest problem with Jefferson's statement about masks is that it's profoundly at odds with the data in the very paper carrying his name." Another three articles use Jefferson's "full stop" position after presenting the Cochrane Review conclusion, to simplify it.

Table 1. Jefferson's "full stop" position is quoted in four different ways.

Category	Number of news articles	Example
Replacing	5	"The conclusion about masks: 'There is just no evidence that they make any difference. Full stop,' Tom Jefferson, the study's first author, said in an interview." [37]
Distinguishing	3	"The biggest problem with Jefferson's statement about masks is that it's profoundly at odds with the data in the very paper carrying his name." [44]
Simplifying	3	"The Cochrane Database of Systematic Reviews, a respected biomedical journal, surprised the public recently with a peer-reviewed article raising doubts about the effectiveness of wearing face masks and respirators during the pandemic. An author of the study, Tom Jefferson of the University of Oxford, declared of face masks in an interview..." [9]
Associating	1	"'There is just no evidence that they make any difference. Full stop,' Oxford epidemiologist Tom Jefferson concluded after he and 11 colleagues completed the most rigorous and extensive review of mask wearing to date." [12]

Finally, one article, from *The Hill*'s opinion section, associates the "full stop" position with the Cochrane Review, as what Jefferson "concluded after" [12] authoring the review without quite using Jefferson's statement to replace the Cochrane Review's conclusion. Associating or replacing the Cochrane Review conclusions aggravated the decontextualization process illustrated in Fig. 4 as we next describe.

Figure 5 illustrates how one news article [37] replaced the Cochrane Review conclusions ("The conclusion about masks") with Jefferson's "full stop" position, misstating the conclusions and obscuring the uncertainty of the evidence. Specifically, the article [37] presented Jefferson's "full stop position" as the Cochrane review's conclusion. They list Jefferson's words after "The conclusion about masks:" as though these words were directly quoted from the Cochrane Review, while in fact they were from its first author. The assertion "no evidence" is not caveated.

Decontextualization seems to explain how some news arrived at what Cochrane called an "inaccurate and misleading interpretation" [57]. This occurred 5 times in our sample, as shown in Table 1. Yet the uncertainty about the effectiveness of mask-wearing stated in the Cochrane Review left room for different interpretations of whether or not America needed mask mandates.

Table 2. The players quoted in the largest number of news articles. We show at least one player from 8 of the 9 player groups we identifed. The player group not shown is "other individuals."

Player name	Player group	Biography	News articles
The Cochrane Review	The Cochrane Review	A high-profile medical review	41
Tom Jefferson	Authors of the Cochrane Review	First author of the Cochrane Review	19
Bret Stephens	Journalists	A *New York Times* Op-Ed columnist	13
Robert Redfield	Government agency representatives	Former director of the US Centers for Disease Control and Prevention (CDC)	6
Anthony Fauci	Government agency representatives	Former chief medical advisor to the President of the US and the former director of the National Institute of Allergy and Infectious Diseases (NIAID)	4
Michael Osterholm	Scientists	Director of the Center for Infectious Disease Research and Policy (CIDRAP) and Regents Professor at University of Minnesota (UMN)	4
Lisa Brosseau	Scientists	Retired professor of environmental and occupational health sciences from the University of Illinois Chicago, and a research consultant with CIDRAP at UMN	4
Andrejko et al. 2022	Research publications[1]	A publication about the effectiveness of mask-wearing	4
Rochelle Walensky	Government agency representatives	Former director of the US CDC	3
US CDC	Government agencies	US Centers for Disease Control and Prevention	3
Health Feedback	Other groups	A fact-checking organization	2

[1] One legal statute also belongs to the research publications player group [74].

5.2   Polylogue Analysis of the Cochrane Review

We annotated 100 players and 337 positions from the 58 news articles in our sample. Table 2 shows example players from 8 of the 9 player groups we identified; "other individuals" (not shown) is the ninth player group.

The news brought together the words of multiple different players, including the Cochrane Review itself, as shown in our polylogue diagram, Fig. 6. Players' positions are connected with support (green solid arrows) and attack (red dashed lines ending in ×'s) relationships.

The news pointed out that not all studies were eligible for inclusion in the Cochrane Review. Figure 6 shows one such study [5].

Evidentiary standards were taken up in multiple ways. The observational study [5] mentioned by an outlet called *Reason* [64] was not acceptable according to the Cochrane Review's inclusion criteria (Sect. 3.3). The observational study determined that "people who reported always wearing a mask in indoor public settings were less likely to test positive for COVID-19 than people who didn't" [5], whereas the Cochrane Review concluded, "There is uncertainty about the effects of face masks" [33]. These two publications, shown as players in Fig. 6, have contradictory conclusions.

Michael Osterholm and his colleagues criticized the Cochrane Review in a commentary by arguing that "the Cochrane review authors incorrectly combined studies where people wore masks or respirators infrequently with those where they were worn all the time" [40].

Bret Stephens's *New York Times* opinion article [60] argued "mask mandates did nothing" by quoting the interview with Cochrane Review first author Jefferson analyzed above [13]. In that interview, Jefferson also criticized government agency representatives such as Fauci.

Government representatives and scientists showed different understandings of mask-wearing over time as the scientific evidence base changed, leading to contradictions in positions made at different stages of the COVID-19 pandemic, as shown in Fig. 6. In March 2020, before clear scientific evidence that mask-wearing for the public might be effective, and in the wake of mask shortages, Dr. Anthony Fauci stressed that masks cannot "provide the perfect protection that people think that it is" [1]. However, Redfield's position in September 2020 was [67]: "face masks are the most important powerful health tool we have." Both these positions were quoted in the news, suggesting that the epistemic uncertainty itself was newsworthy. The *Daily Mail* wrote "The debate around masks first turned sour in 2020 when health officials flip-flopped on their effectiveness." [66]. The *Daily Mail's* article, titled "Masks make 'little to no difference' to Covid infections, massive study finds," contrasted the "flip-flop" in governmental positions with an impression of newfound certainty from the Cochrane Review.

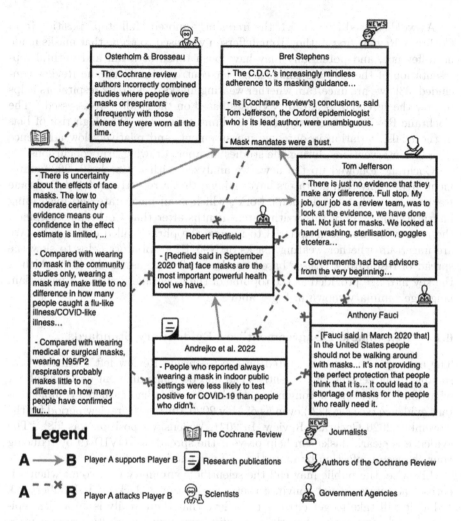

Fig. 6. Support (green solid arrows) and attack (red dashed lines ending in ×'s) relationships between players' positions. (Color figure online)

6   Discussion

The Cochrane Review we analyzed was salient for the news media reporting on the effectiveness of mask-wearing towards the end of the US federal COVID-19 Public Health Emergency. The news we analyzed quoted players with competing interpretations of the Cochrane Review as shown in Fig. 6. Polylogue analysis's capacity for handling quotations in a natural way is one of its strengths: summarizing how positions made by multiple players are discussed helps analyze news commentary about controversial scientific topics.

As we discussed in Sect. 5.1, the frequently-quoted "full stop" position from Cochrane Review first author Tom Jefferson was used to argue that masks made no difference, and potentially may have been taken as a full and faithful representation of the review's conclusions. By contrast, the Cochrane Review concluded [33] "we are uncertain whether wearing masks or N95/P2 respirators helps to slow the spread of respiratory viruses based on the studies we assessed." The Cochrane Review also clearly stated its limitations [33]: "The high risk of bias in the trials, variation in outcome measurement, and relatively low adherence with the interventions during the studies hampers drawing firm conclusions."

Cochrane followed up the news we analyzed with a March 10, 2023 statement [57]:"Many commentators have claimed that a recently-updated Cochrane Review shows that 'masks don't work', which is an inaccurate and misleading interpretation." As of this writing, ten months after that Cochrane statement, the review has not been updated to remove the phrase called out in [57]: "We are uncertain whether wearing masks or N95/P2 respirators helps to slow the spread of respiratory viruses based on the studies we assessed." [33], which is the key message provided as the top line of the Cochrane Review's 2-page plain language summary shown in Fig. 1 above.

6.1 "Reasonable Disagreement" on Evidentiary Standards

The epistemic uncertainty stated by the Cochrane Review left room for "reasonable disagreement" [6]. Scientists can and do make different decisions about what kind of evidence is convincing. Health scientists had gathered complementary evidence (see e.g. [22]) even as of May 2020, during the review period for the November 2020 Cochrane Review. In 2021, Walensky's position was [68], "The evidence is clear. Masks can help prevent the spread of COVID-19 by reducing your chance of infection by more than 80 percent."

Likewise, the public may call the scientific community to account when scientists' accounts do not convince them. For instance, Jackson & Lambert ask "what it will take to get citizens to believe that there really is no autism epidemic" [30], and argue that the scientific community needs to produce more convincing evidence to respond to reasonable concerns from citizens about possible environmental contributions to the growth in autism. They see open access, proliferation of information, and search engines as contributing to the vaccine controversy, noting that [30], "In the new media ecology, the public is equipped to demand a much more active role in getting science done on questions it considers important."

Experiments such as the "huge, randomised study" Jefferson suggested [13] could help convince scientists like him, and likely the public as well. In particular he wished we had "randomised half of the United Kingdom, or half of Italy, to masks and the other half to no masks" [13]. Aside from prioritizing evidence generation, further discussion of why specific evidence is or is not sufficiently convincing, to scientists or to the public, could further clarify differences in evidentiary standards.

6.2   Decontextualization of Information is Problematic

We traced how the news decontextualized the Cochrane Review and its conclusion. Statements made by Tom Jefferson, first author and the most heavily quoted player besides the Cochrane Review, were successively removed from context as we showed in Fig. 4. Jefferson's words "There is just no evidence that they make any difference. Full stop." [13] suggested certainty and allowed for multiple interpretations of "they." Among the twelve articles that quoted this position, five used it to replace the Cochrane Review conclusions, as we illustrated in Fig. 5.

Bekler et al. described "decontextualized truths" as a challenge of political information [7]. For epistemically uncertain science topics, "decontextualized scientific evidence" is more apt due to the inherent falsifiability of current scientific 'truths'. Decontextualization of information is an important aspect to consider in future studies of information disorder. It does not neatly fit into the current definition of information disorder: misinformation ("content that is false but not intended to harm"), disinformation ("content that is false and intended to harm"), and malinformation ("truthful information that is intended to harm") [70]. Even without intention to harm, such decontextualized information can be problematic.

When journalists try to simplify scientific information, they need to be wary of oversimplification, such as loss of context and caveats. This is challenging due to the "ambiguity of boundary between appropriate simplification and distortion" when science travels downstream from its producers [26, page 530]. However, special attention is essential since the decontextualization of scientific evidence may worsen scientific controversies.

6.3   Comparison to Information and Communication Research About COVID-19

Our work also contributes to the body of information and communication research about masks and COVID-19. Among the most similar research, Fernandes [17] focused on uncertainty and risk communication using an STS-infused qualitative discourse analysis; his data were three US, UK, and European news articles reporting the WHO's changes to COVID-19 advice on masks, smoking, and asymptomatic transmission. Bogomoletc et al. [10] analyzed how Twitter and news media cited six articles about mask efficacy to support both pro- and anti-mask positions at the beginning of the COVID-19 pandemic.

Our work complements existing international research about COVID-19 in the news by providing a late-pandemic, US perspective. O'Connor et al. [47] analyzed news articles related to COVID-19 and science from the island of Ireland early in the pandemic. Their qualitative analysis of 952 articles published between January and May 2020 identified three main themes: portrayal of the science process; positive and negative relationships with science; and the utility of science. Schultz and Ward [55] analyzed 670 news articles from France published between January and April 2020 relating to the drugs chloroquine or hydroxychloroquine, coding discussions about efficacy, prescribing, and the practice of science. While both O'Connor et al. and Schultz and Ward collected news from the first few months of the pandemic, our news data was US-associated news collected late in the pandemic, a few months before the end of the US Public Health Emergency. With our smaller dataset we conducted a fine-grained analysis of specific arguments by examining quotations.

6.4 Implications for Altmetrics Data Quality Analyses

In our case study, we observed at least three of the 14 specific altmetrics news data error types described by Yu et al. [73]:

1. Source news article has been deleted by the news platform
2. News link provided by Altmetric.com does not have attached hyperlink and specific news title is not provided
3. False positive news mention due to unknown reason

We also found two additional types of missing articles beyond the news almetrics errors described in Yu et al.'s analysis [73]: First, we found articles omitting the original version of a news article despite the inclusion of multiple versions from news aggregators. Second, we found missing articles that indirectly cited the Cochrane Review, such as Vox.com's "The new scientific review on masks and Covid isn't what you think" [51], which links to Cochrane's abstract-only page [32] for the Cochrane Review, rather than to the article itself.

6.5 Limitations

Our analysis mainly focused on two of the three concepts of polylogue analysis. The third concept, places, which concerns when and where arguments appear, was minimally used in selecting our data. Consideration of the temporal aspect of places would have helped better represent our data, particularly for government representatives whose positions changed over time.

We have only analyzed news published before March 10, 2023; we did not consider later news such as corrections or follow-up articles. When we collected articles on August 1, 2023, Altmetric.com identified 396 news articles as referring to the Cochrane Review; this number continues to increase and stands (as of December 26, 2023) at 480.

6.6 Future Work

Our future analysis will incorporate the polylogue analysis concept of places [39], including where and when the arguments appeared, and who was a bystander versus a ratified participant. The temporal aspect of places would be particular valuable for contextualizing crisis information and epistemic uncertainty in the future. Places could also incorporate the news venues, so we will combine our polylogue analysis with Ad Fontes[4] ratings of different news venues' reliability and left/right political bias to understand the extent to which positions correlated with partisanship of the venues in which they appeared.

We will examine the 16 news articles that linked to the Cochrane Review without directly quoting it to determine whether these articles decontexualized the Cochrane Review conclusions. Since the first author's words often replaced the review conclusions, we will also check how he was quoted in the 7 news articles that quoted him without quoting his "full stop" position.

Given the many choices for filtering quotations, we will experiment with the number of players and positions considered in our future polylogue analyses. For diagramming players and positions, automatic filtering tools would be particularly helpful for enabling exploratory analysis.

News about science has been shown to impact public health-related behavior [45]; future work should quantify the extent to which news about the effectiveness of mask-wearing impacted public behavior. In future work, we will analyze how the public responded to the Cochrane Review indirectly by referring, on social media, to news articles quoting it, using Alperin et al.'s concept of second-order citations [3]. We especially would like to understand what the public took from the review's conclusions and what policy actions the public thinks the Cochrane Review justified.

7   Conclusions

We presented a case study about how US news articles published discussed a controversial Cochrane Review about the effectiveness of mask-wearing late in the US federal COVID-19 Public Health Emergency. Epistemic uncertainty of the review conclusions was difficult to express in simple ways that wider public audiences could understand. In particular, due to epistemic uncertainty, multiple contradictory positions can coexist as credible. Future work on information disorder in science needs to consider not only the intention to harm, but also risks associated with oversimplification or decontextualization of current scientific evidence.

Acknowledgements. This project was made possible in part by the United States Institute of Museum and Library Services RE-250162-OLS-21. We thank Altmetric.com for data access. We thank Togzhan Seilkhanova for MAXQDA assistance. We thank Chris Bailey for advice on retrieving news articles. We thank Ian Brooks, Janaynne Carvalho do Amaral, Lev Frank, Yuanxi Fu, Kiel Gilleade, Liliana Giusti Serra, Bertram Ludäscher, Bart Verheij, and Emily Wegrzyn for providing feedback on a draft. Thanks to Sara Benson and Wendy Shelburne for copyright and licensing advice relating to our data deposit. Thanks to Jessica Hagman for advice on our MAXQDA data deposit and Hoa Luong for data curation assistance.

---

[4] https://adfontesmedia.com/

CRediT:

- Heng Zheng: Conceptualization, Data curation, Investigation, Methodology, Resources, Validation, Visualization, Writing - original draft, Writing - review & editing
- Theodore Dreyfus Ledford: Conceptualization, Writing - original draft, Writing - review & editing.
- Jodi Schneider: Conceptualization, Data curation, Funding acquisition, Methodology, Project administration, Resources, Supervision, Writing - original draft, Writing - review & editing.

Data Availability. Excerpts from the news articles used in our MAXQDA analysis and a spreadsheet of the data used from Altmetric.com are available in the following dataset:

Heng Zheng and Jodi Schneider (2023): Dataset for "Arguing about Controversial Science in the News: Does Epistemic Uncertainty Contribute to Information Disorder?". University of Illinois at Urbana-Champaign. https://doi.org/10.13012/B2IDB-4781172_V1

References

1. 60 Minutes: March 2020: Dr. Anthony Fauci talks with Dr Jon LaPook about Covid-19 (Mar 2020). https://www.youtube.com/watch?v=PRa6t_e7dgI
2. Aakhus, M., Lewiński, M.: Advancing polylogical analysis of large-scale argumentation: disagreement management in the fracking controversy. Argumentation **31**(1), 179–207 (Mar 2017). https://doi.org/10.1007/s10503-016-9403-9
3. Alperin, J.P., Fleerackers, A., Riedlinger, M., Haustein, S.: Second-order citations in altmetrics: a case study analyzing the audiences of COVID-19 research in the news and on social media (Apr 2023). https://doi.org/10.1101/2023.04.05.535734
4. Andone, C., Lomelí Hernández, J.A.: On arguments from ignorance in policy-making. In: Oswald, S., Lewiński, M., Greco, S., Villata, S. (eds.) The Pandemic of Argumentation, pp. 105–123. Springer International Publishing, Cham (2022). https://doi.org/10.1007/978-3-030-91017-4_6
5. Andrejko, K.L., et al.: California COVID-19 case-control study team: effectiveness of face mask or respirator use in indoor public settings for prevention of SARS-COV-2 infection - California, February-December 2021. Morb. Mortal. Wkly Rep. **71**(6), 212–216 (2022)
6. Antiochou, K., Psillos, S.: How to handle reasonable scientific disagreement: The case of COVID-19. In: Oswald, S., Lewiński, M., Greco, S., Villata, S. (eds.) The Pandemic of Argumentation, pp. 65–83. Springer International Publishing, Cham (2022). https://doi.org/10.1007/978-3-030-91017-4_4
7. Benkler, Y., Faris, R., Roberts, H., Zuckerman, E.: Study: Breitbart-led right-wing media ecosystem altered broader media agenda. Columbia Journalism Review (Mar 2017). https://www.cjr.org/analysis/breitbart-media-trump-harvard-study.php
8. van der Bles, A.M., et al.: Communicating uncertainty about facts, numbers and science. Royal Society Open Sci. **6**(5), 181870 (May 2019). https://doi.org/10.1098/rsos.181870
9. Board, E.: Opinion: In a crowded place, a face mask or respirator keeps the virus away. Washington Post (Mar 2023). https://www.washingtonpost.com/opinions/2023/03/03/face-masks-work-study/

10. Bogomoletc, E., Goodwin, J., Binder, A.R.: Masks don't work but you should get one: circulation of the science of masking during the COVID-19 pandemic. In: Berube, D.M. (ed.) Pandemic Communication and Resilience, pp. 213–244. Risk, Systems and Decisions, Springer International Publishing, Cham (2021). https://doi.org/10.1007/978-3-030-77344-1_14

11. Chung, M., Jones-Jang, S.M.: Red media, blue media, Trump briefings, and COVID-19: examining how information sources predict risk preventive behaviors via threat and efficacy. Health Commun. **37**(14), 1707–1714 (Dec 2022). https://doi.org/10.1080/10410236.2021.1914386

12. Concha, J.: The time has come for a 9/11-like commission on COVID-19. The Hill (Mar 2023). https://thehill.com/opinion/healthcare/3883819-the-time-has-come-for-a-9-11-like-commission-on-covid-19/

13. Demasi, M.: Exclusive: Lead author of new Cochrane review speaks out. Maryanne Demasi, reports [Substack newsletter] (Feb 2023). https://maryannedemasi.substack.com/p/exclusive-lead-author-of-new-cochrane

14. van Eemeren, F.H., Garssen, B., Krabbe, E.C.W., Snoeck Henkemans, A.F., Verheij, B., Wagemans, J.H.M.: Handbook of Argumentation Theory. Springer Reference, Dordrecht (2014)

15. Evans, R.: SAGE advice and political decision-making: 'Following the science' in times of epistemic uncertainty. Social Stud. Sci. **52**(1), 53–78 (Feb 2022). https://doi.org/10.1177/03063127211062586

16. Feinstein, N.W., Waddington, D.I.: Individual truth judgments or purposeful, collective sensemaking? Rethinking science education's response to the post-truth era. Educ. Psychol. **55**(3), 155–166 (2020). https://doi.org/10.1080/00461520.2020.1780130

17. Fernandes, A.: Communicating corrected risk assessments and uncertainty about COVID-19 in the post-truth era. Front. Commun. **6** (2021). https://doi.org/10.3389/fcomm.2021.646066

18. Fleerackers, A., Nehring, L., Maggio, L.A., Enkhbayar, A., Moorhead, L., Alperin, J.P.: Identifying science in the news: An assessment of the precision and recall of Altmetric.com news mention data. Scientometrics **127**(11), 6109–6123 (Nov 2022). https://doi.org/10.1007/s11192-022-04510-7

19. Fleerackers, A., Riedlinger, M., Moorhead, L., Ahmed, R., Alperin, J.P.: Communicating scientific uncertainty in an age of COVID-19: an investigation into the use of preprints by digital media outlets. Health Commun. **37**(6), 726–738 (May 2022). https://doi.org/10.1080/10410236.2020.1864892

20. van Gelder, T.: Enhancing deliberation through computer supported argument visualization. In: Kirschner, P.A., Buckingham Shum, S.J., Carr, C.S. (eds.) Visualizing Argumentation: Software Tools for Collaborative and Educational Sense-Making, pp. 97–115. Computer Supported Cooperative Work, Springer, London (2003). https://doi.org/10.1007/978-1-4471-0037-9_5

21. Goodwin, J., Bogomoletc, E.: Critical questions about scientific research publications in the online mask debate. In: Oswald, S., Lewiński, M., Greco, S., Villata, S. (eds.) The Pandemic of Argumentation, pp. 331–354. Argumentation Library, Springer International Publishing, Cham (2022). https://doi.org/10.1007/978-3-030-91017-4_17

22. Greenhalgh, T.: Face coverings for the public: Laying straw men to rest. J. Eval. Clin. Pract. **26**(4), 1070–1077 (2020). https://doi.org/10.1111/jep.13415

23. Guenther, L.: Science journalism. In: Oxford Research Encyclopedia of Communication. Oxford University Press (Mar 2019). https://doi.org/10.1093/acrefore/9780190228613.013.901

24. Hall Jamieson, K., Albarracín, D.: The relation between media consumption and misinformation at the outset of the SARS-COV-2 pandemic in the US. Harvard Kennedy School Misinformation Review (Apr 2020). https://misinforeview.hks.harvard.edu/article/the-relation-between-media-consumption-and-misinformation-at-the-outset-of-the-sars-cov-2-pandemic-in-the-us/

25. Hertzum, M.: How do journalists seek information from sources? A systematic review. Inform. Process. Manage. **59**(6), 103087 (Nov 2022). https://doi.org/10.1016/j.ipm.2022.103087

26. Hilgartner, S.: The dominant view of popularization: conceptual problems, political uses. Social Stud. Sci. **20**(3), 519-539 (Aug 1990). https://doi.org/10.1177/030631290020003006

27. Horn, R.E.: Infrastructure for navigating interdisciplinary debates: critical decisions for representing argumentation. In: Kirschner, P.A., Buckingham Shum, S.J., Carr, C.S. (eds.) Visualizing Argumentation: Software Tools for Collaborative and Educational Sense-Making, pp. 165–184. Computer Supported Cooperative Work, Springer, London (2003). https://doi.org/10.1007/978-1-4471-0037-9_8

28. Hsieh, P.: The unsettled science of Covid-19. Forbes (Feb 2023). https://www.forbes.com/sites/paulhsieh/2023/02/28/the-unsettled-science-of-covid-19/

29. Intemann, K., de Melo-Martín, I.: On masks and masking: epistemic harms and science communication. Synthese **202**(3), 93 (Sep 2023). https://doi.org/10.1007/s11229-023-04322-z

30. Jackson, S., Lambert, N.: A computational study of the vaccination controversy. In: Argumentation and Reasoned Action: Proceedings of the First European Conference on Argumentation, Lisbon, 9-12 June 2015, Vol.II, pp. 539-552. Studies in Logic and Argumentation, College Publications (2016)

31. Jefferson, T., et al.: [2020 version] Physical interventions to interrupt or reduce the spread of respiratory viruses. Cochrane Database of Systematic Reviews **2020**(11) (Nov 2020). https://doi.org/10.1002/14651858.CD006207.pub5

32. Jefferson, T., et al.: [Abstract for] Physical interventions to interrupt or reduce the spread of respiratory viruses (Jan 2023). https://www.cochrane.org/CD006207/ARI_do-physical-measures-such-hand-washing-or-wearing-masks-stop-or-slow-down-spread-respiratory-viruses

33. Jefferson, T., et al.: Physical interventions to interrupt or reduce the spread of respiratory viruses. Cochrane Database of Systematic Reviews (2023). https://doi.org/10.1002/14651858.CD006207.pub6

34. Jonsson, A., Brechensbauer, A., Grafström, M.: Communicating science through competing logics and a science-art lens. J. Sci. Commun. **21**(7), Y01 (Nov 2022). https://doi.org/10.22323/2.21070401

35. Kirschner, P.A., Buckingham Shum, S.J., Carr, C.S., Diaper, D., Sanger, C. (eds.): Visualizing Argumentation: Software Tools for Collaborative and Educational Sense-Making. Computer Supported Cooperative Work, Springer, London (2003). https://doi.org/10.1007/978-1-4471-0037-9

36. Kleijnen, J., Alderson, P., Aubin, J., Cairns, J., Crowe, S., Garner, P.: Evaluation of NIHR investment in Cochrane infrastructure and systematic reviews. Tech. rep., National Institute for Health and Care Research, UK (Feb 2017). https://archive.lstmed.ac.uk/7031/1/Evaluation%20of%20NIHR%20investment%20in%20Cochrane%20infrastructure%20and%20systematic%20reviews.pdf

37. Kliegman, A.: Nearly 1 trillion masks bought during pandemic despite new research suggesting no health benefits. Fox News (Mar 2023). https://www.foxnews.com/politics/nearly-1-trillion-masks-bought-pandemic

38. Lawrence, J., Visser, J., Reed, C.: Translational argument technology: engineering a step change in the Argument Web. J. Web Semantics **77**, 100786 (Jul 2023). https://doi.org/10.1016/j.websem.2023.100786

39. Lewiński, M., Aakhus, M.: Argumentation in Complex Communication: Managing Disagreement in a Polylogue. Cambridge University Press (Dec 2022)

40. Brosseau, L.M., MacIntyre, C.R., Ulrich, A., Osterholm, M.T.: Commentary: Wear a respirator, not a cloth or surgical mask, to protect against respiratory viruses (Feb 2023). https://www.cidrap.umn.edu/covid-19/commentary-wear-respirator-not-cloth-or-surgical-mask-protect-against-respiratory-viruses

41. Lurie, P., et al.: COVID-19 vaccine misinformation in English-language news media: retrospective cohort study. BMJ Open **12**(6), e058956 (Jun 2022). https://doi.org/10.1136/bmjopen-2021-058956

42. MacIntyre, C.R., Chughtai, A.A., Fisman, D., Greenhalgh, T.: Yes, masks reduce the risk of spreading COVID, despite a review saying they don't. The Conversation (2023). http://theconversation.com/yes-masks-reduce-the-risk-of-spreading-covid-despite-a-review-saying-they-dont-198992

43. Meltzer, G.Y., Chang, V.W., Lieff, S.A., Grivel, M.M., Yang, L.H., Des Jarlais, D.C.: Behavioral correlates of COVID-19 worry: Stigma, knowledge, and news source. Int. J. Environ. Res. Public Health **18**(21), 11436 (Jan 2021). https://doi.org/10.3390/ijerph182111436

44. Hiltzik, M.: Column: COVID deniers claim a new study says mask mandates don't work. They should try reading it. Los Angeles Times (Feb 2023). https://www.latimes.com/business/story/2023-02-24/covid-deniers-celebrate-a-study-that-claims-mask-mandates-dont-work-but-the-study-says-the-opposite

45. Motta, M., Stecula, D.: Quantifying the effect of Wakefield et al. (1998) on skepticism about MMR vaccine safety in the U.S. PLOS ONE **16**(8), e0256395 (Aug 2021). https://doi.org/10.1371/journal.pone.0256395

46. Musi, E., Carmi, E., Reed, C., Yates, S., O'Halloran, K.: Developing misinformation immunity: how to reason-check fallacious news in a human-computer interaction environment. Social Media + Society **9**(1), 20563051221150407 (Jan 2023). https://doi.org/10.1177/20563051221150407

47. O'Connor, C., et al.: Media representations of science during the first wave of the COVID-19 pandemic: a qualitative analysis of news and social media on the island of Ireland. Int. J. Environ. Res. Public Health **18**(18), 9542 (Sep 2021). https://doi.org/10.3390/ijerph18189542

48. Ortega, J.L.: Altmetrics data providers: a meta-analysis review of the coverage of metrics and publication. El Profesional de la Información **29**(1) (Jan 2020). https://doi.org/10.3145/epi.2020.ene.07

49. Park, H.W., Yoon, H.Y.: Global COVID-19 policy engagement with scientific research information: altmetric data study. J. Med. Internet Res. **25**(1), e46328 (2023). https://doi.org/10.2196/46328

50. Pinna, M., Picard, L., Goessmann, C.: Cable news and COVID-19 vaccine uptake. Sci. Reports **12**(1), 16804 (Oct 2022). https://doi.org/10.1038/s41598-022-20350-0

51. Piper, K.: The new scientific review on masks and Covid isn't what you think. Vox (Feb 2023). https://www.vox.com/future-perfect/2023/2/22/23609499/masks-covid-coronavirus-cochrane-review-pandemic-science-studies-infection

52. Priem, J., Taraborelli, D., Groth, P., Neylon, C.: altmetrics: a manifesto (Oct 2010). http://altmetrics.org/manifesto/

53. Reed, C., et al.: The Argument Web: an online ecosystem of tools, systems and services for argumentation. Philosophy & Technology **30**(2), 137–160 (Jun 2017). https://doi.org/10.1007/s13347-017-0260-8
54. Scheufele, D.A., Krause, N.M.: Science audiences, misinformation, and fake news. Proc. National Acad. Sci. **116**(16), 7662-7669 (Apr 2019). https://doi.org/10.1073/pnas.1805871115
55. Schultz, É., Ward, J.K.: Science under Covid-19's magnifying glass: Lessons from the first months of the chloroquine debate in the French press. J. Sociol. **58**(1), 76–94 (Mar 2022). https://doi.org/10.1177/1440783321999453
56. Smith, H., Morgoch, M.L.: Science & journalism: bridging the gaps through specialty training. J. Pract. **16**(5), 883–900 (May 2022). https://doi.org/10.1080/17512786.2020.1818608
57. Soares-Weiser, K.: Statement on 'Physical interventions to interrupt or reduce the spread of respiratory viruses' review (Mar 2023). https://www.cochrane.org/news/statement-physical-interventions-interrupt-or-reduce-spread-respiratory-viruses-review
58. Soares-Weiser, K., et al.: Policy makers must act on incomplete evidence in responding to COVID-19. The Cochrane Database Syst. Rev. **2020**(11), ED000149 (Nov 2020). https://doi.org/10.1002/14651858.ED000149
59. Spiteri, J.: Media bias exposure and the incidence of COVID-19 in the USA. BMJ Global Health **6**(9), e006798 (Sep 2021). https://doi.org/10.1136/bmjgh-2021-006798
60. Stephens, B.: Opinion: The mask mandates did nothing. Will any lessons be learned? The New York Times (Feb 2023). https://www.nytimes.com/2023/02/21/opinion/do-mask-mandates-work.html
61. Stocking, S.H., Holstein, L.W.: Constructing and reconstructing scientific ignorance: ignorance claims in science and journalism. Knowledge **15**(2), 186–210 (Dec 1993). https://doi.org/10.1177/107554709301500205
62. Stocking, S.H., Holstein, L.W.: Manufacturing doubt: journalists' roles and the construction of ignorance in a scientific controversy. Public Underst. Sci. **18**(1), 23–42 (2009). https://doi.org/10.1177/0963662507079373
63. Sugimoto, C.R., Larivière, V.: Measuring Research: What Everyone Needs to Know. Oxford University Press, Oxford, New York (Jan 2018)
64. Sullum, J.: A scientific review shows the CDC grossly exaggerated the evidence supporting mask mandates. Reason.com (Feb 2023). https://reason.com/2023/02/08/a-scientific-review-shows-the-cdc-grossly-exaggerated-the-evidence-supporting-mask-mandates/
65. Tabak, I., Dubovi, I.: What drives the public's use of data? The mediating role of trust in science and data literacy in functional scientific reasoning concerning COVID-19. Science Education **107**(5), 1071–1100 (2023). https://doi.org/10.1002/sce.21789
66. Tilley, C.: Masks make "little to no difference" to Covid infections or deaths. Daily Mail Online (Feb 2023). https://www.dailymail.co.uk/health/article-11702865/Masks-make-little-no-difference-Covid-infections-massive-cross-country-meta-analysis-finds.html
67. United States Senate Committee on Appropriations: Review of Coronavirus Response Efforts (Sep 2020). https://www.appropriations.senate.gov/hearings/review-of-coronavirus-response-efforts
68. U.S. Department of Health and Human Services: Ask Dr. Walensky: Why do I still need to wear a mask? (Archived 1/3/22) (Oct 2021). https://www.youtube.com/watch?v=MD8odL67F90

69. Van Witsen, A., Takahashi, B.: How science journalists verify numbers and statistics in news stories: towards a theory. J. Pract. 1–20 (Jul 2021). https://doi.org/10.1080/17512786.2021.1947152

70. Wardle, C.: The need for smarter definitions and practical, timely empirical research on information disorder. Digital J. **6**(8), 951-963 (Sep 2018). https://doi.org/10.1080/21670811.2018.1502047

71. Wen, L.S.: Opinion — the checkup with dr. wen: When will it be time for a second bivalent booster? Washington Post (Feb 2023). https://www.washingtonpost.com/opinions/2023/02/09/covid-bivalent-booster-vaccine-second-shot/

72. Wynne, B.: Misunderstood misunderstanding: social identities and public uptake of science. Public Understand. Sci. **1**(3), 281–304 (Jul 1992). https://doi.org/10.1088/0963-6625/1/3/004

73. Yu, H., Yu, X., Cao, X.: How accurate are news mentions of scholarly output? A content analysis. Scientometrics **127**(7), 4075–4096 (Jul 2022). https://doi.org/10.1007/s11192-022-04382-x

74. Zheng, H., Schneider, J.: Dataset for "Arguing about controversial science in the news: Does epistemic uncertainty contribute to information disorder?" (2024). https://doi.org/10.13012/B2IDB-4781172_V1

How Misinformation Manipulates Individuals: A Reflexive Thematic Analysis Based on 185 Cases

Yaning Cao[ID] and Qing Ke[✉][ID]

Nanjing University, Nanjing 210023, China
keqing@nju.edu.cn

Abstract. Exploring how misinformation manipulates individuals can reveal the logic of information manipulation and help better deal with the spread of different kinds of misinformation online including AIGC misinformation. To that end, this study conducted a reflexive thematic analysis based on 185 misinformation cases. The study found that there are 6 main manipulation mechanisms and 13 strategies behind misinformation. The 6 main mechanisms include providing clues to indicate credibility, reducing the psychological distance, expression of emotions to control the heuristic cognition, simplifying the difficulty of understanding, making content vivid to stimulate cognition and behavior manipulation. According to the result of reflexive thematic analysis, the misinformation manipulation model has been established. The results are helpful to fight misinformation online.

Keywords: Misinformation · Manipulate · Manipulation Mechanism

1 Introduction

Compared to the truth, misinformation spreads farther, faster, deeper, and more broadly [1]. It also has harmful effects on humanity. The rapid speed and harmful effects result from some special characteristics of misinformation, which induce social media users' perspectives and stimulate emotions. Thus, understanding how misinformation manipulates individuals' attitudes can help fight misinformation. Concerning this subject, prior work focused on the spread, detection, and mitigation of misinformation, or discussed how individuals perceive misinformation [2]. These studies have illustrated the negative impact of misinformation on social media users. Nevertheless, there has been little attention paid to the deceptive and luring features of misinformation, which implies that comprehension of manipulation mechanism behind misinformation remains incomplete.

Information manipulation reveals how deceptive content exerts influence on people [3]. In fact, misinformation is created and disseminated with the main purpose of manipulation [4]. Undoubtfully, misinformation has negative impacts. What is more, even short exposure to misinformation may result in unconscious change of behavior [5]. It is attributed to the fact that some features of misinformation stimulate users and manipulate them into believing false contents.

I. Sserwanga et al. (Eds.): iConference 2024, LNCS 14597, pp. 236–253, 2024.
https://doi.org/10.1007/978-3-031-57860-1_17

The purpose of this study is to reveal the manipulation mechanisms behind misinformation. We have conducted a reflexive thematic analysis based on 185 typical cases and analyzed manipulation mechanisms behind misinformation.

2 Theoretical Framework and Literature Review

2.1 Related Concepts and Theories

Concepts. Manipulation is defined as "controlling someone or something to one's own advantage, often unfairly or dishonestly" in Cambridge dictionary. Considering the dissemination process of information, manipulation is similar to persuasion. However, these two terms also have some differences. To begin with, information persuasion refers to human communication designed to influence the judgements and actions of others [6]. However, the term 'manipulation' denotes a process of control and regulation. Second, information manipulative intent has often been concealed. Elihu Katz held the view that the main difference of persuasion and manipulation is whether information receivers have known the possible influence [7]. Furthermore, in order to induce information receivers, manipulative information is often presented in a stimulative manner or intentional design, providing false or hidden information [8]. Conversely, persuasive information is designed to influence receivers by reason and argument. In brief, manipulation controls information receiver's position by concealing intention and luring design. Manipulation is a type of power abuse, and the receiver has been deprived of the option to receive information equally [9].

In summary, the term "manipulation" refers to an information dissemination process in which the sender presents information in concealing and guiding manners. The intention is to control information receivers' attitudes and behaviors. The process of manipulation can be interpreted by both senders of information and receivers. This process can be described as "manipulate" and "be manipulated." From the perspective of information senders, manipulation is intentional. Whereas from the perspective of receivers, it is the result of interpersonal communication.

Theories Related to Manipulation. In order to interpret deceptive behaviors within interpersonal communication, McCornack proposed Information Manipulation Theory in 1992 [10]. Information Manipulation Theory proposes that speakers manipulate listeners by violating four maxims, including quantity, quality, manner, and relevance of information [10]. Although this theory is used to interpret the process of deception, it can be applied to analyzing misinformation on social media [11]. Drawing on Information Manipulation Theory, this study interprets how does the manipulative features of information influence individuals.

In addition to Information Manipulation Theory, this study also incorporates persuasion theories into the theoretical framework to address the issue in a more scientific manner. The following outlines the reasons.

First of all, the persuasion model provides an analytical framework for this study. Based on Lasswell's model of communication, Carl Hovland's information persuasion theory interprets the process of persuasion as a linear model, including source, message, channel, and receiver [12]. We discussed the mentality in which individuals believe misinformation based on Carl Hovland's theories.

Secondly, persuasion theories can help explain some manipulative strategies of misinformation. For example, Aristotle's theory of rhetoric shows that there are three ways to persuade the audience in a speech, namely Ethos, Pathos and Logos [13]. Ethos means that information comes from a credible source; pathos refers to arousing listeners' emotions; logos includes logic arguments. These ways have been used to interpret the persuasive strategies of misinformation [14]. Considering the way of presentation, description of negative or positive consequences will result in different persuasive effects according to framing theory [15]. In addition, Persuasive Systems Design Model provides many principles to understand the interaction between information and humanity [16]. All theories above will help the explanation of manipulation strategies.

Finally, persuasion theories illustrate how certain misinformation influences. For example, the theory of fear appeals discusses the reaction when humans encounter threatening or frightening information [15]. Thus, this study also utilized fear appeal theory to analyze and interpret the manipulative features of misinformation.

In this study, we integrated manipulation theory and persuasion theories to conduct the research for the following reasons. On the one hand, Information Manipulation Theory neglects the arguments of information, while persuasion theories provide an in-depth analysis of the argument strategies. On the other hand, it is nearly impossible to use persuasion theories to describe some special language features of misinformation, such as simulative or emotional features. On account of the concealed intention and deceptive content, misinformation exerts influence in a manipulative manner instead of persuasive manner. **All in all, it is better to use the term "manipulation" to depict the influence of misinformation.** This study focuses on the manipulation mechanism behind misinformation.

2.2 The Manipulative Characteristics of Misinformation

Prior researchers have discussed factors that make misinformation more easily accepted by online users and indicated that misinformation has some special characteristics. First of all, some misinformation aligns with public information needs. Allport and Postman proposed the basic rumor formula [17], emphasizing that one of the essential characteristics of rumor is "importance". For instance, during COVID-19, the public focused on the virus and health. Hence, the outbreak of Corona Virus was accompanied by a tsunami of information, including misinformation, rumors, etc., namely "infodemic" [18]. Furthermore, misinformation is more emotional evocation than factual news [3]. Chuai [19] revealed that anger makes the fake news more contagious than real news on social media. Finally, some misinformation serves individuals' personal interests. As human society has entered into the 'post-truth' era, individuals are likely to adopt beliefs which align with their preferences and disregard the accuracy of information [20]. What is more, when individuals use 'motivated cognition' account, they are likely to trust misinformation which aligns with their ideas [21]. All these characteristics above can be attributed to manipulative characteristics. However, a systematic analysis on manipulative characteristics is lacking.

In fact, general characteristics of misinformation have caught researchers' attention. The conventional methods are mainly qualitative methods, including content analysis [22] or open coding methods [23]. Zhang [23] analyzed the surface features, semantic features, and source features of health misinformation, and designed a feature list [23]. In fact, health misinformation often exaggerates the effects, or lacks reliable arguments. For instance, Zheng [22] found that online health misinformation demonstrated higher certainty levels, using more declarative sentences, more emotional appeals, fewer exemplars, and credible sources than reliable information Khaja evaluated the truthfulness of 22 claims about drugs in Bahrain and recognized that the efficacy or safety has been exaggerated by drug misinformation [24]. Carrasco-Farré [3] pointed out that misinformation is easier to read, and more emotional Misinformation employs special writing styles in order to achieve manipulative goals, including maximizing reads, shares and virality [3]. Nevertheless, the studies above mostly focused on the writing styles or message features, failed to take psychological factors into consider, such as senders' intention or receivers' mentality. Besides, that research only provides a perspective from information senders or content, neglecting the concealed intention, luring content, or the dominated cognitive process.

2.3 Empirical Research Related to Manipulation of Misinformation

Existing studies have explored the features or themes of some specific types of false information, which have laid a stable foundation for this research. Dooheum et al. [25] used content analysis to explore the manipulative themes of misinformation in South Korea during COVID-19. Based on Information Manipulation Theory, Zhao et al. [26] discussed the content characteristics of COVID-19 misinformation, including information length and information specification. Apart from misinformation, deceptive information is also manipulative. Yoon [27] analyzed the e-commerce cases in South Korea and found that falsification, equivocation, and concealment are the most common deceptive manipulation techniques. These studies show that any content containing false information has a manipulative effect.

Past studies have also investigated the argument strategies or persuasion strategies behind misinformation or rumors. Based on Rumor Interaction Analysis System, Wood [28] proposed that conspiracy theories tend to appeal to supposedly knowledgeable authorities and ask rhetorical questions. From the perspective of persuasion, Chen [14] reported the persuasion strategies of misinformation-containing posts in Weibo, noting that "Pathos" is the most common acts of persuasion. Peng [29] discussed 12 common persuasion strategies of health misinformation through systematic literature review. Scannell et al. [30] identified the persuasion techniques of COVID-19 Anti-Discourse on Twitter.

The researches above has revealed some features of misinformation from the perspective of information receivers' mentality, and help understand the psychological behind misinformation preliminarily. However, just four maxims of Information Manipulation Theory cannot cover all features of misinformation online, and the persuasion theories also cannot interpret all the features related to individuals' psychology. Hence, this study uses open coding method and reflexive thematic analysis to analyze data, adopting both Information Manipulation Theory and persuasion theories to construct and interpret model. The study aims at revealing the manipulative strategies and mechanisms of misinformation.

3 Methodology

3.1 Data Collection and Preparing

Tencent Jiaozhen platform is affiliated with one of the best-known Chinese websites, Tencent. Jiaozhen platform is a fact-checking platform that devotes itself to refuting rumors, comparing, and telling the truth to the public. The topics of Jiaozhen platform involve health misinformation, popular science, society, and so on. In order to ensure the accuracy of the refutations, the content on Jiaozhen has been checked by professionals first, and then double-checked by professional fact checkers. Monthly rumor refutation list in Jiaozhen Platform selects the most concerning rumors this month which are representative and typical (Fig. 1).

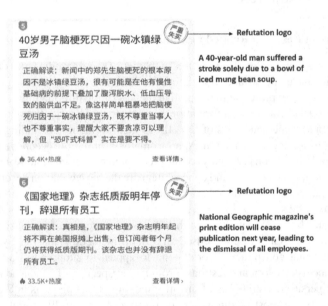

Fig. 1. Monthly rumor refutation lists in Jiaozhen Platform

Using web crawler, we gathered all refutations from Jiaozhen refutation lists between October 2022 and July 2023, and 185 cases were collected in total. These cases involve various topics, such as health, education and livelihood and so on. Each case contains the following elements:

1. The textual content of misinformation: including a popular version of misinformation.
2. Refutation: the fact-checker's individual introduction and the refutation of misinformation.

3. Pictures related to the rumor: including images related to the event, original forms of rumors, or text in images. (OCR technology was employed to recognize the text in images.)

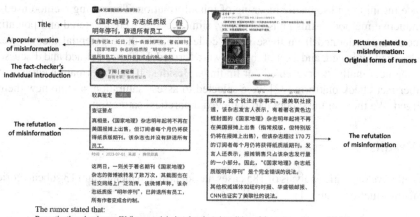

The rumor stated that:
Recently, there has been a Weibo post claiming that the print edition of the renowned journal "National Geographic" will "cease publication next year," leading to the dismissal of all employees, and all authors will transition to contractual agreements.

Fig. 2. A refutation case.

Each selected case contains both the textual content and refutation, namely (1) and (2). If the picture was missing, we would retrieve relating images from other fact-checking platforms in China and used the retrieved pictures to supplement the case. Moreover, we have only analyzed the textual content of misinformation and the pictures related to misinformation. The refutation text was only used for comprehension, not for coding or analysis (Fig. 2).

3.2 Data Analysis

This study employed reflexive thematic analysis [31] to code and analyze data for the following reasons. First, the coding method of RTA includes an open coding process and aims to sum up themes from codes. As the manipulation strategies and mechanisms of misinformation have not been revealed by previous studies, an open coding and inductive method is well-suited. Besides, RTA not only can be used to analyze the surface-level content, but also can capture the meanings from semantic to latent levels [31]. Because misinformation often conveys complex ideas using simple language, the coding method of reflexive thematic analysis is suitable. Furthermore, reflexive thematic analysis emphasizes the importance of reflexivity, which involves a disciplined practice of critically interrogating what we do, how and why we do it, and it means that the researchers' subjectivity is an essential resource for analysis [31]. In this study, reflexivity is conducive to understanding how information receivers are manipulated by misinformation, and this method is appropriate for exploring the mechanism of manipulation.

The total reflexive thematic analysis process of this study consists of six phases [32], including familiarizing, generating initial codes, searching for themes, reviewing, defining, and naming themes, and producing the report. At first, the researcher read and reread each case item, and identified the potential manipulation strategies of misinformation. Second, in order to generate initial codes, the researcher began to analyze the surface meaning and semantic meaning of misinformation. The coding method used is an inductive method in this phase. Thirdly, similar codes were clustered and potential themes were generated from these initial codes. Fourth, these potential themes were checked and reviewed, and a set of themes were formed. Fifth, we defined and discussed each theme. Finally, we presented our findings. Besides, 10 misinformation cases from another fact-check platform [33] were selected to assess saturation, and no new theme emerged. We thought the model had achieved theoretical saturation.

4 Results

The reflexive thematic analysis of 185 cases has identified 6 themes and 13 subcategories of misinformation (Table 1).

Table 1. Manipulation Strategies Categories of Misinformation.

Mechanisms or Strategies	Descriptions or Example	Theory or Source
1 Providing clues to indicate credibility	Using clues to imply reliable	
1.1 Source strategies	Presenting or suggesting source	Hovland's persuasion theory
1.1.1 Imitation	*from the date of the announcement, ...*	
1.1.2 Reliable source	*This event happened to my colleague's daughter* *Some authority papers have reported this event*	
1.2 Showing details	Presenting some related detailed	Aristotle's theory of rhetoric
Detail numbers/locations/date/contact numbers/descriptions	*On Oct 8th, in the early morning, a South China tiger appeared in Beijing-Zhuhai Expressway;*	
1.3 Visual contents	Presenting some images or videos	
1.4 Blending truth with falsehood	Using truth as arguments	

(continued)

Table 1. (*continued*)

Mechanisms or Strategies	Descriptions or Example	Theory or Source
2 Reducing the psychological distance	To narrow the psychological distance between information senders and receivers	Psychological distance
2.1 Closeness address	*Dear families* *Dear friends*	
3 Expression of emotions to control the heuristic cognition	Using emotional words to occupy individuals' cognition	[21]
3.1 Fear appeals	*Milk tea produced in xxx shop has cause fatalities*	Fear appeals
3.2 Other affection appeals	*…The whole scene was tragic and heart-wrenching*	
4 Simplifying the difficulty of understanding	To help individuals understand text	The least effort principle
4.1 Metaphor or comparison	*When pollutant leaks, it will become "toxic rain."*	
5 Making content vivid to stimulate cognition	Using vivid narration to attract and impress readers	Rhetorical Theory
5.1 Description and emphasis of degree	*Awesome news* *(It is an) Accurate information*	
5.2 Rhetoric strategies Hyperbole/contrast/rhetorical question or text that induces individuals' thoughts	Hyperbole: a *"Magic Medicine"* Contrast: *15 times more lethal than COVID-19* Rhetorical Question or Text that Induces Individuals' Thoughts: *You need 10,000 kilowatt-hours to run a kilometer. Why do we only need 43 kilowatt-hours?*	
5.3 Oddity strategy	*Ducks feed koi carp with their mouths at Beijing Aquarium*	
6 Behavior manipulation	Changing individuals' behaviors	
6.1 Reminding, proposing, or calling for sharing posts	*Please share this message and remind more people*	Aristotle's theory of rhetoric
6.2 Behavior generation or behavior avoidance	*Add me to your social media, and we will send a rice cooker to you*	Framing effect

4.1 Providing Clues to Indicate Credibility

Misinformation often provides clues to indicate credibility, and individuals use these clues to judge credibility. This cognitive process of human can be interpreted by Probabilistic Mental Model [34], which suggests that individuals can distinguish between fake and genuine information with a few clues while the complete description is no longer necessary. From the cases collected, it shows that there are four typical manipulation strategies related to this mechanism, including source, details, visual contents and blending truth with falsehood strategies.

Source Strategies. Source strategies refer to showing sources directly or implying that the source is reliable. Source credibility originated from Carl Hovland's persuasion research [12]. Hovland found that authority and trustworthiness are essential for perceived credibility. Especially, source strategies include imitation and reliable sources. Imitation refers to mimicking legitimate sources in an attempt to enhance its perceived credibility. Moreover, reliable sources can also increase the perceived credibility. The so-called "Reliable Source" may be authoritative or trustworthy sources. For instance, some misinformation declared that the message had been reported by CCTV (the most famous television channel in China). Actually, the message had never been reported. The so-called "reliable source" can also be a fabricated source. Another message proclaimed that it was sent by an important newspaper in Stockholm. However, the name of the newspaper was fictitious.

Apart from those authoritative sources, some misinformation asserts that the message originates from either themselves or individuals they know. When the speakers say that they have witnessed the case or participated in the incident in person, the event will appear less suspicious. Similarly, they also claim that the information comes from someone familiar. For example, a message mentioned: *This incident occurred at my younger brother's residence.* In this message, both the speaker's identity and younger brother's identity are unknown to individuals. Individuals are not even sure if this so-called brother really exists. Nevertheless, "younger brother" had increased the perceived credibility. In "Rumors: Uses, Interpretations, and Images," Jean-Noel Kapferer explained this strategy [35]. When the rumormongers find that their messages are not persuasive enough, they would mention that the message has come from a "seems certain and guaranteed" source. "That person" is in the known about the fact, and more authoritative. Interestingly, "that person" is near to individuals, but it is almost impossible to check.

Showing Details. Misinformation often includes specific details such as numbers, locations, dates, contact information and some detailed descriptions. This strategy can be explained by Aristotle's theory of rhetoric, namely "LOGOS." Compared to a vague writing style, the specific writing style increases the clarity of the text and makes it more logical. Consequently, individuals use these details to distinguish between misinformation and truth. Under these circumstances, individuals are likely to assume the misinformation post is accurate.

Visual Contents. Misinformation sometimes contains some visual contents, such as images or videos. Visual content enhances the perceived credibility of misinformation. In fact, the images or videos alleged from the scene are not necessarily true. A piece of misinformation states that a parent from Shandong province treated his or her child as a kite and flew the child in the sky. Regarding this topic, some online users have criticized irresponsible young parents in this era. However, the message was fabricated and adopted an incident picture from another province. Even if the visual content has been taken directly from the scene, the text may fabricate the truth. For example, a picture showed that a man was burning clothes. However, the description was distorted into *"families were burning bodies of the deceased on the street."*

Some misinformation presents images that are so-called related in order to enhance the communication effect. Despite the fact that the message does not state whether the image illustrates the scene or emphasizes the character as the protagonist, individuals will assume that the image is related to the text automatically.

Blending Truth with Falsehood. The strategy refers to some misinformation including half-truths [29]. Rumormongers often construct a piece of misinformation on the basis of common sense. For example, the rumor *"white strawberry is a genetically modified food"* was constructed on the basis of the following conventional views. Firstly, white strawberry is rare for most people. Secondly, using genetical modified techniques, human can produce new plant species. The rumor was created based on these two pieces of common sense.

Moreover, misinformation may be derived from genuine information. News reported that a famous company's senior executive suddenly died. Whereafter, some health misinformation, such as *"Long-distance running leads to sudden death,"* or *"Long-distance running will damage the heart and reduce life expectancy"* had derived from the event. The event has been processed repeatedly by the rich imagination of online users. Hence, some rumors have derived from genuine information with deliberate inducing design.

4.2 Reducing the Psychological Distance

The psychological distance means a cognitive separation between the self and others [36]. A close address can reduce the psychological distance between information senders and receivers. Some misinformation begins with words like *"dear families"* or *"dear friends."* In these contexts, the senders use a close address to imitate a friend or a family member. These words convey a sense of friendliness or closeness to individuals, and make individuals feel that it relates to themselves. As a result, the perceived importance of this message has been enhanced.

4.3 Expression of Emotions to Control the Heuristic Cognition

Intense feelings can cause individuals to make hasty judgments and hinder the gradual process of rational analysis, which is known as heuristic cognition [21]. When using heuristic cognition systems, individuals are susceptible to misinformation and are likely to be deceived. The strategies related to emotions include fear appeals, and other affection appeals like sympathy and anger.

Fear Appeals. The strategy "fear appeals" refers to arousing fear or emphasizing adverse consequence. Due to an instinct of focusing on the benefits and avoiding disadvantages, negative events receive more attention. In accordance with negativity dominance [37], the negative events have more persist influence on individuals. The consideration of risk aversion is the main reason of trust in misinformation which uses fear appeals strategies. What is more, some misinformation declares that the negative consequences result from some daily behavior, like *sudden death results from long-distance race,* or *fetal malformation results from daily use electronic products.* The contrast between these common daily behaviors and possible negative consequences has increased the perceived threat to individuals.

When a message uses fear appeals strategy, it not only describes the possible risk, but also presents "solutions." The event *"An old woman gave out masks to abduct children"* can interpret the process. The chat logs mentioned: *"The old woman is a wanted criminal. She wants to abduct children aged 8 to 12 years old. She will sell the organs."* In this message, *"abduct children"* and *"sell the organs"* have exaggerated the terrifying atmosphere. Hence, individuals, particularly those with children, experienced heightened fear. On this occasion, their cognitive resources were occupied with fear, thus there was a cut-off of the rational thinking process. Besides, the chat logs had reminded the individuals to *"keep an eye on the children, be carefully".* This solution is a means to reduce the perceived risk and help individuals avoid threats. Hovland's research has explained the cognitive process of the fear appeals. In an emotion-drive state, fear will prompt people to find some solutions that are conducive to reducing or dispelling fear [15]. The suggestion which helps reduce fears, such as *"keep an eye on children,"* will be integrated to information individuals' cognitive structure. Therefore, their attitudes will be changed. Although this kind of misinformation seems odd and absurd, it can arouse negative emotions and manipulate individuals.

Other Affection Appeals. Some messages emphasize familial responsibility with phrases like *"tell your family "Or "it's imperative to your families."* These statements are aimed at appealing affections of individuals and persuading them to share this message. A health rumor emphasized that a person who died of illness was *"just 38 years old".* The message expressed regret and aimed to evoke empathy in the readers. Similarly, some misinformation also uses irrational words to arouse great anger. All these strategies are intended to ignite the emotions. These emotions occupy individuals' cognitive resources [38]. The occupied cognitive resources result in irrational thinking process, namely intuitive thinking. In these circumstances, the experience of emotions takes precedence over truth.

4.4 Simplifying the Difficulty of Understanding

The greater the comprehensibility of the information, the better its communication effect will be, and more attention the information sender will receive. This mechanism can be treated as the reduction, the specific strategies including metaphor or comparison. For instance, a message *likened the 2019-nCov to Mini AIDS.* Whether individuals have high health information literacy, they will be threatened by AIDS. As a result, this strategy reduces the comprehension difficulty by comparing an abstract concept to a familiar concept.

4.5   Making Content Vivid to Stimulate Cognition

Vivid contents which use some rhetoric techniques can stimulate individuals' cognition and impress them. This kind strategies includes degree descriptions, emphasis, rhetoric and oddity.

Description and Emphasis of Degree. Descriptions of degree shows the powerful impact of events, and emphasis means stressing the importance of events. For example, a false message used the phrase *"a huge behavior in education"* stressed the reform would be significant. Meanwhile, the phrase used *"huge"* to emphasize that the event is relevant to a large number of people.

Misinformation text mentions the significant scale of the event repeatedly. It often uses phrases such as *"be sure to keep in mind"* or *"be sure to do something"* repeatedly. Research has found that repeat information can increase persuasive effect of text [39]. Furthermore, in order to reduce suspicion, the authenticity and effectiveness are also emphasized by misinformation.

Rhetoric Strategies. Rhetoric words enhance the vividness of the text. Some hyperbole words exaggerate the events or the effect, such as *"immediate elimination"* or *"fully eliminate."* Allport held the view that making the events seem important is the key of rumors, and rhetoric can impress individuals [17]. According to Information Manipulation Theory, hyperbole statements have violated the maxim of quantity [10]. The message *"per capita deposit of the young born in 1990s"* has exaggerated the per capita deposit of young people living in the three large cities in China to over one billion CNY. This message contradicts common sense, yet it has surprised individuals.

Another rhetoric strategy, contrast, can also be impressive and make events more vivid. A false message mentioned that *every kilometer of high-speed train running consumes 10,000 units of electricity in China.* The message compared high-speed train in China with Shinkansen, intending to mislead individuals that *China high-speed railway train uses much power.*

A rhetorical question or word that induces individuals' thoughts can be considered as a disclaimer to some extent. Such question or inducing word has not a clear statement, and wrong views will be originated from the individuals themselves [28]. This misleading feature reflects the manipulative characteristic of misinformation [28].

Oddity Strategy. To attract and draw attention, some misinformation events can be quite odd or dramatic. Abnormal events will be of interest to individuals and stimulate their cognitive processes. According to Truth Default Theory, unless there are too many doubts, individuals will assume that the message received is true [40]. When confronted with odd events or news, individuals lack the motivation to assess accuracy. Indeed, it does not matter to individuals if the message is accurate or not. For example, a photo showed that a cat was chasing a rat in the court and mentioned *"In order to certify that the cat bought cannot catch mice, it was taken to the court."* The event has been fairly dramatic and interesting, and it wasn't relevant to individuals. Besides, the photo can be treated as an evidence. As a result, individuals are likely to believe it.

Apart from odd events, anti-common-sense or unethical event also can be odd. These events can stimulate and catch individuals' attention immediately, such as *"Nicotine can help anti-aging, and smoking is good for health."*

4.6 Behavior Manipulation

Reminding, Proposing or Calling for Sharing Posts. This strategy refers to the altruism demonstrated in the text, such as a kindly reminder *"power prices would increase next month, and we suggest citizens to save energy."* Such a kind reminder is a persuasive strategy "ETHOS" of Aristotle's theory of rhetoric [13]. A kind reminder can reduce suspicion, and manipulate individuals to trust and share it without check. Even if the message will be refuted in future, it may not elicit the anger of being deceived.

Certain text suggests that sharing information is a beneficial practice and aims to encourage individuals to engage in it. Such as the phrase *"It is boundlessly beneficial to share this message"* has catered to the psychology of altruism [40]. Instant messaging software can be treated as an acquaintance circle, and the sharing behavior within the circle can show the reciprocity, trust, and concern of individuals.

Behavior Generation or Behavior Avoidance. According to Rumor Interaction Analysis System, much misinformation text persuades individuals to generate or avoid certain behaviors, namely directive rumor [28]. The description of behavior embodies the framing effect [41]. Information frame exerts persuasive influence through manipulating elaboration process. Considering risk aversion, negative frame has better persuasive effect than positive frame when individuals in highly motivated states [42].

The logic of behavior manipulation is shown in Fig. 3. At first, misinformation describes the possible negative consequences or positive consequences. Subsequently, advice mentioned will help avoid negative consequences in future (gain-loss frame, route 1) or mitigate current negative consequences (gain-loss frame, route 3). According to their statements, the negative consequences will happen or be exacerbated if the advice has not been adopted (loss frame, route 2 and route 4). For instance, a rumor advised that *the moles on the body should be removed through surgery*, and threatened that if individuals ignore their advice, *the moles may turn into cancer in future* (loss frame, route 2). According to prospect theory [43], people are likely to avoid risk when faced with certain returns. Besides, positive consequences are also mentioned frequently. Advice mentioned will lead to or reinforce positive consequences (route 5). A piece of misinformation stated that *removal of the uterus would make the abdomen flatter and relieve women of menstrual pain*. The statement used gain frame to attract individuals' attention. The rumor *"hysterectomy will relieve of menstrual pain."* has described how generating a certain behavior can lead to favorable outcomes (route 5). If the readers ignore their advice, the positive consequences will not happen (route 6).

Besides, some rumors disseminate instructions for people to engage in certain simple behaviors. For example, a health rumor stated that *the mixture of green tea and lemon water can kill COVID-19 virus*. In fact, individuals will weigh "the cost of not trusting the information" and "the benefit of trusting the information." After the judgement, individuals have discovered that the cost of behavior is relatively low, such as *preparing blended tea*. Therefore, individuals are likely to believe such kind rumors and practice false behaviors. However, mistrusting some information may lead to serious negative consequences.

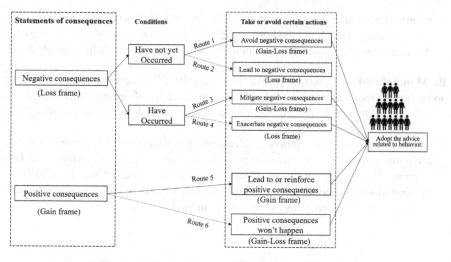

Fig. 3. The logic of behavior manipulation

5 Model

A framework has been developed according to the results of reflexive thematic analysis (Fig. 4). The manipulation process can be treated as an information dissemination process. Both manipulation and persuasion exert similar influences on individuals, which aim to change individuals' attitude and behaviors. Hence there are two routes, "information-attitude" and "information-attitude-behavior." We referred to McGuire's persuasion theory [44] to construct the theoretical model from the perspectives of misinformation (source and content) and individuals' reaction.

The elements of McGuire's six steps persuasive communication model are respectively denoted as presentation, attention, comprehension, yielding, retention, and behavior. According to this model, our model has been established, and it can be divided into two parts: "manipulation" and "be manipulated."

Manipulation. The first part is manipulation process of misinformation, including present, attention, and comprehension. During this phase, individuals are exposed to misinformation.

- **Present:** In order to convince users, misinformation posts present sources and contents in manipulative manners.
- **Attention:** When misinformation manipulates individuals, it acts on individuals' **attention**. For instance, the expression of emotions is aimed to control individuals' heuristic cognition, and individuals are likely to process information in a state of emotional arousal situation (theme 3). Furthermore, vivid description is aimed to impress individuals (theme 5). These two manners will stimulate human cognitive processes or attract individuals' attention.

- **Comprehension:** Misinformation also helps individuals to **understand** the contents, like providing some hints to show credibility (theme 1), drawing the psychological distance (theme 2), simplifying content (theme 4), or inducing behaviors (theme 6).

Be Manipulated. The second part is "be manipulated," including yielding, retention, and behavior. Individuals have comprehended the contents of misinformation, and false attitudes and behaviors have formed under the manipulative design in the previous phase.

- **Yield:** In order to change individuals' attitude, misinformation has manipulated their attention, controlled their cognition process, and made them agree or **yield** to the false contents. During this period, individuals' attitudes have been changed gradually.
- **Retention and Behavior:** In the **retention** process, individuals' false thoughts have been reinforced and they may change their **behavior**.

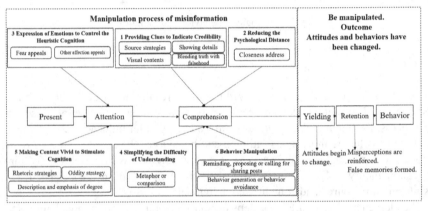

Fig. 4. The Manipulation mechanism model of misinformation.

6 Conclusion

This study analyzes manipulation strategies and mechanisms behind misinformation. The mechanisms include providing clues to indicate credibility, reducing the psychological distance, expression of emotions to control the heuristic cognition, simplifying the difficulty of understanding, making content vivid to stimulate cognition and behavior manipulation. Finally, this study develops a model to interpret the process of manipulation.

7 Implications, Limitations and Future Directions

The implications of this study are as follows. Firstly, our model can help understand the logic behind different types of misinformation, including AIGC (Artificial Intelligence Generated Contents) misinformation. Regardless of the types of misinformation, they all have similar manipulation mechanisms. Even if AIGC rumor or misinformation produced by Large Language Model, the logic is similar to rumors produced by humanity. Facing the potential challenges that Large Language Models may create information pollution problems, our model can help better understand the logic behind AIGC misinformation. Secondly, the outcome of this study may be viewed as a theoretical basis for predicting misinformation automatically. Thirdly, our model can be used as an information literacy educational material. If online users know the manipulative strategies and mechanisms of misinformation, they will process the information with a more rational manner.

There are some limitations. On the one hand, in order to select typical and representative cases, we just chose hot rumors from refutation lists. Those cases with less attention were neglected. On the other hand, as an exploratory study, we have not yet used the actual behavioral data of users.

References

1. Vosoughi, S., Roy, D., Aral, S.: The spread of true and false news online. Science **359**, 1146–1151 (2018)
2. Pal, A., Chua, A.Y.K.: Analysis of research on online rumors. In: 2019 5th International Conference on Information Management (ICIM), pp. 108–112 (2019). https://doi.org/10. 1109/INFOMAN.2019.8714707
3. Carrasco-Farré, C.: The fingerprints of misinformation: how deceptive content differs from reliable sources in terms of cognitive effort and appeal to emotions. Humanit. Soc. Sci. Commun. **9**, 162 (2022). https://doi.org/10.1057/s41599-022-01174-9
4. Muriel-Torrado, E., Pereira, D.B.: Correlations between the concepts of disinformation and Fogg's Behavior Model. Transinformação **32**, 1–15 (2020). https://doi.org/10.1590/2318-088 9202032e200026
5. Bastick, Z.: Would you notice if fake news changed your behavior? An experiment on the unconscious effects of disinformation. Comput. Hum. Behav. **116**, 106633 (2021)
6. Jones, J.G., Simons, H.W.: Persuasion in Society, 3rd edn. Routledge, Taylor & Francis Group, New York (2017)
7. Katz, E.: Rediscovering Gabriel Tarde∗. Polit. Commun. **23**, 263–270 (2006). https://doi.org/ 10.1080/10584600600808711
8. Oxman, A.D., et al.: Health communication in and out of public health emergencies: to persuade or to inform? Health Res Policy Sys. **20**, 28 (2022). https://doi.org/10.1186/s12961-022-00828-z
9. van Dijk, T.A.: Discourse and manipulation. Discourse Soc. **17**(3), 359–383 (2006)
10. McCornack, S.A.: Information manipulation theory. Commun. Monogr. **59**(1), 1–16 (1992)
11. Al-khateeb, S., Wigand, R.T., Agarwal, N.: Misinformation campaigns. Applying motivated reasoning and information manipulation theory to understand the role and impact of social media in the digital transformation. In: Alm, N., Murschetz, P.C., Weder, F., Friedrichsen, M. (eds.) Die digitale Transformation der Medien: Leitmedien im Wandel, pp. 387–401. Springer, Cham (2022). https://doi.org/10.1007/978-3-658-36276-8_18
12. Riley, M.W., Hovland, C.I., Janis, I.L., Kelley, H.H.: Communication and persuasion: psychological studies of opinion change. Am. Sociol. Rev. **19**(3), 355–357 (1953)
13. Lawsontancred, H.: The art of rhetoric. Penguin Classics; Reissue edition (1991)
14. Chen, S., Xiao, L., Mao, J.: Persuasion strategies of misinformation-containing posts in the social media. Inf. Process. Manage. **58**, 102665 (2021). https://doi.org/10.1016/j.ipm.2021. 102665

15. Dillard, J.P., Shen, L.: The SAGE Handbook of Persuasion, 2nd edn. SAGE, California (2012)
16. Oinas-Kukkonen, H., Harjumaa, M.: Persuasive systems design: key issues, process model, and system features. Commun. Assoc. Inf. Syst. **24**(1), 28 (2009)
17. Allport, G.W., Postman, L.: The Psychology of Rumor. Henry Holt, New York (1947)
18. Zarocostas, J.: How to fight an infodemic. The Lancet **395**(10225), 676 (2020)
19. Chuai, Y., Zhao, J.: Anger can make fake news viral online. Front. Phys. **10**, 970174 (2022)
20. Keyes, R.: The Post-Truth Era: Dishonesty and Deception in Contemporary Life, 1st edn. St. Martin's Press, New York (2004)
21. van der Linden, S.: Misinformation: susceptibility, spread, and interventions to immunize the public. Nat. Med. **28**, 460–467 (2022). https://doi.org/10.1038/s41591-022-01713-6
22. Zheng, X., Wu, S., Nie, D.: Online health misinformation and corrective messages in China: a comparison of message features. Commun. Stud. **72**(3), 474–489 (2021)
23. Zhang, S., Ma, F., Liu, Y., Pian, W.: Identifying features of health misinformation on social media sites: an exploratory analysis. Library Hi Tech. **40**(5), 1384–1401 (2022)
24. Al Khaja, K.A.J., AlKhaja, A.K., Sequeira, R.P.: Drug information, misinformation, and disinformation on social media: a content analysis study. J. Public Health Policy **39**(3), 343–357 (2018). https://doi.org/10.1057/s41271-018-0131-2
25. Dooheum, J., Jihye, P.: A content analysis of Covid-19 fake-news: pertaining to disinformation and its manipulative features. Locality Commun. **25**(4), 216–258 (2021)
26. Zhao, J., Fu, C., Kang, X.: Content characteristics predict the putative authenticity of COVID-19 rumors. Front. Public Health **10** (2022). https://doi.org/10.3389/fpubh.2022.920103
27. Yoon, J.S., Park, C.: A content analysis on consumer deception behaviors of internet shopping mall. J. Internet Electron. Commer. Res. **14**(3), 15–35 (2014)
28. Wood, M.J.: Propagating and debunking conspiracy theories on twitter during the 2015–2016 zika virus outbreak. Cyberpsychol. Behav. Soc. Netw. **21**(8), 485–490 (2018)
29. Peng, W., Lim, S., Meng, J.: Persuasive strategies in online health misinformation: a systematic review. Inf. Commun. Soc. **26**(11), 1–18 (2022). https://doi.org/10.1080/1369118X.2022.208 5615
30. Scannell, D., et al.: Covid-19 vaccine discourse on twitter: a content analysis of persuasion techniques, sentiment and mis/disinformation. J. Health Commun. **26**(7), 443–459 (2021)
31. Braun, V., Clarke, V.: Thematic Analysis: A Practical Guide. SAGE Publications Ltd., Los Angeles (2022)
32. Braun, V., Clarke, V.: Thematic analysis. In: Maggino, F. (ed.) Encyclopedia of Quality of Life and Well-Being Research, pp. 1–7. Springer, Cham (2020). https://doi.org/10.1007/978-3-319-69909-7_3470-2
33. WEIBO FACT-CHECK@sina weibo. https://weibo.com/u/1866405545. Accessed 17 Sept 2023
34. Gigerenzer, G., Hoffrage, U., Kleinbölting, H.: Probabilistic mental models: a Brunswikian theory of confidence. Psychol. Rev. **98**, 506–528 (1991)
35. Kapferer, J.-N.: Rumors: Uses, Interpretations, and Images, 1st edn. Routledge, New York (2013)
36. Baltatescu, S.: Psychological distance. In: Michalos, A.C. (ed.) Encyclopedia of Quality of Life and Well-Being Research, pp. 5145–5146. Springer, Cham (2014). https://doi.org/10.1007/978-94-007-0753-5_2306
37. Rozin, P., Royzman, E.B.: Negativity bias, negativity dominance, and contagion. Pers. Soc. Psychol. Rev. **5**(4), 296–320 (2001)
38. Eysenck, M.W., Derakshan, N., Santos, R., Calvo, M.G.: Anxiety and cognitive performance: the attentional control theory. Emotion **7**(2), 336–353 (2007)
39. Caccioppo, J.T., Petty, R.E.: Effects of message repetition and position on cognitive response, recall, and persuasion. J. Pers. Soc. Psychol. **37**(1), 97–109 (1979)

40. Bordia, P., Difonzo, N.: Problem solving in social interactions on the internet: rumor as social cognition. Soc. Psychol. Q. **67**(1), 33–49 (2004)
41. Jou, J., Shanteau, J., Harris, R.J.: An information processing view of framing effects: the role of causal schemas in decision making. Mem. Cognit. **24**(1), 1–15 (1996). https://doi.org/10.3758/BF03197268
42. Jin, J., Zhang, W., Chen, M.: How consumers are affected by product descriptions in online shopping: event-related potentials evidence of the attribute framing effect. Neurosci. Res. **125**, 21–28 (2017)
43. Kahneman, D., Tversky, A.: Prospect theory: an analysis of decision under risk. In: Gärdenfors, P., Sahlin, N.-E. (eds.), Decision, Probability, and Utility: Selected Readings, pp. 183–214. (Reprinted from "Econometrica", vol. 47, pp. 263–291 (1979)). Cambridge University Press (1988)
44. Mc Guire, W.J.: Personality and attitude change: an information-processing theory. In: Psychological Foundations of Attitudes, pp. 171–196. Elsevier (1968). https://doi.org/10.1016/B978-1-4832-3071-9.50013-1

Detecting the Rumor Patterns Integrating Features of User, Content, and the Spreading Structure

Pengwei Yan[1], Guo Yu[1,2], Zhuoren Jiang[1(✉)], Tianqianjin Lin[1],
Weikang Yuan[1], and Xiaozhong Liu[3]

[1] Department of Information Resources Management, Zhejiang University,
Hangzhou 310058, China
{yanpw,jiangzhuoren,lintqj,yuanwk}@zju.edu.cn
[2] Department of Big Data Security and Secrecy, Wuhan University, Wuhan 430072,
China
yg3282@whu.edu.cn
[3] Computer Science Department, Worcester Polytechnic Institute,
Worcester 01609-2280, MA, USA
xliu14@wpi.edu

Abstract. The openness characteristic of social networks facilitates the rapid spread of rumors, necessitating effective methods for detecting and managing the abundance of rumors on social media. Existing studies have primarily focused on improving the accuracy of rumor detection, but often overlook the vital aspects of interpretability and explanation of rumor patterns, limiting their credibility and real-world usability. Additionally, previous works have typically examined only a subset of user features, content, and spreading structure, neglecting the analysis of compound rules. To address these limitations, we propose a novel framework for detecting rumor patterns that emphasize comprehensive feature construction and the explanation of compound rules. Our framework incorporates multi-dimensional features, including user characteristics, post content, and the structure of information propagation. Advanced techniques, including large language models (such as ChatGPT) and graph motif discovery algorithms, are employed for feature construction. By leveraging diverse features, crucial integrated rules identified by Rulefit can investigate the contextually dependent associations among various interrelated rumor factors. We consolidate and analyze seven distinct rumor patterns based on the Credible Early Detection Dataset, deriving valuable insights into the inherent characteristics of rumors. The recognition of rumor patterns empowers social media platforms and fact-checking organizations to develop targeted and explainable interventions that effectively mitigate the spread of rumors and safeguard the integrity of information. These interventions greatly enhance the transparency and trustworthiness of rumor management, fostering a more reliable information ecosystem.

Keywords: Social Media · Rumor Detection · Explainable AI · Integrated Rule

I. Sserwanga et al. (Eds.): iConference 2024, LNCS 14597, pp. 254–267, 2024.
https://doi.org/10.1007/978-3-031-57860-1_18

1   Introduction

Online rumors are unverified information that is spread on online platforms and are often rife with deceit and falsehood [8]. The openness characteristic of social media allows rumors to spread rapidly and widely, potentially disrupting social order and public security [17]. Hence, the pervasive spread of rumors and misinformation has become a significant concern for individuals, organizations, and society at large in recent years.

To effectively combat the spread of rumors, researchers have developed automated methods for distinguishing between rumors and reliable information. Early research in this field focused on training machine learning models using manually extracted features, which achieved a relatively high level of accuracy in identifying rumors in social media datasets [7,33]. Subsequent studies have further expanded on these ideas and focused on refining feature extraction methods and designing more advanced models [26]. For instance, an approach [20] captured the temporal features based on the time series of a rumor's lifecycle to recognize rumors. A bi-directional graph model [4] was designed to explore both characteristics by operating on both top-down and bottom-up propagation of rumors.

However, existing research efforts still face the following challenges: **Neglecting Interpretability**. Many studies have focused solely on improving the prediction performance of the models while neglecting the interpretation of the rumor detection process. The black-box nature of these algorithms can reduce the credibility [1]. Interpretable analysis of machine learning models [22] sheds light on distilling the key factors and mechanisms for identifying rumors. By combining interpretable analysis with rumor detection models, it is possible to enhance transparency and trust, reduce misjudgments and biases, and improve the model's adaptability in various scenarios. **Incomplete Rumor Features**. One of the challenges to discovering rule-based rumor patterns is that comprehensive rumor data is rather complicated, consisting of features of users, contents, and spreading structures. Rumor patterns considering diverse features lead to sophisticated results and unveil the intricate nature of rumors. Nevertheless, acquiring the multiple semantic features of content and spreading structure poses significant challenges. **Lack of Compound Rules and Consolidated Patterns**. Some existing studies have explored the potential for interpreting rumor characteristics according to rumor detection models [3,9]. However, these studies primarily emphasized the assessment of isolated features, neglecting the analysis of compound decision rules and categorized patterns crucial for effective rumor detection. While the factors or mechanisms critical to effective rumor detection tasks tend to manifest as combinations of features [23]. Besides, rules that capture associations among multiple correlated factors are also more readily accepted by people due to their resemblance to human decision-making processes [10].

To address the above challenges, we proposed a rumor pattern detection framework based on systematic feature construction and integrated rule explanation. First, rumor features from three perspectives, including user attribute, post content, and spreading structure, are mined by advanced methods like Chat-GPT [5] and gSpan [32]. Then, Rulefit algorithm [11] analyzes variable connections from a holistic perspective, generating rules that combine cross-dimensional features. Due to the characteristics of Rulefit's hybrid model, a variety of rules can be extracted and important rules for prediction can be identified through sparse linear regression. These rules are subsequently categorized and interpreted as high-level rumor patterns. Based on the Credible Early Detection (CED) Dataset [24], we discovered seven rumor patterns such as "Highly interactive but with few likes or reposts imply rumors", and "Propagation dominated by deep structural factors increase the probability of being rumors", which are summarized and categorized based on rules generated according to constructed 25 features.

This paper makes the following contributions to the field of rumor detection:

1. Integration of Multi-dimensional Features: We systematically construct features of users, post contents, and spreading structures to investigate the contextually dependent associations among various interrelated factors. Multiple sophisticated approaches, including large-scale language models (such as ChatGPT) and graph motif discovery algorithm, are employed in the feature construction.
2. Pattern Discovery: We employ the hybrid algorithm Rulefit to discover important rules and categorize them into high-order rumor patterns. These patterns provide valuable insights into the inherent characteristics of rumors, which can serve as discriminative indicators for diminishing misjudgments and biases.
3. Practical Implications: The insights gained from this study can increase transparency and trustworthiness, and facilitate in shaping more effective strategies to combat rumors and misinformation. By identifying patterns that are characteristic of false narratives, social media platforms and fact-checking organizations can develop targeted interventions to mitigate the spread of rumors and protect the integrity of information.

2   Methodology

The goal of the proposed framework is to discover integrated rules combining comprehensive features and investigate the contextually dependent associations among these factors. For the feature determination, we refer to current rumor-related research [17,25,26,30] and include features of posts, users, and propagation structures. As shown in Fig. 1, the proposed framework consists of two parts: features construction, rules generation & patterns interpretation. By leveraging the power of advanced methods, the framework first extracts multiple-dimensional rumor-related features. Then the Rulefit, a tree-based hybrid algorithm, is used to explore and filter out crucial rules for recognizing rumors. Finally, these rules are then categorized and interpreted into meaningful rumor patterns.

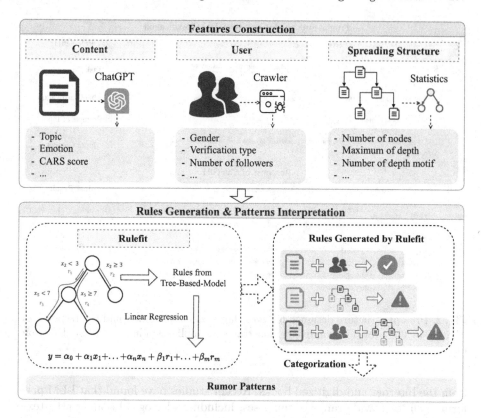

Fig. 1. Research Framework. The framework mainly consists of two parts: *Features Construction* and *Rules Generation & Patterns Interpretation*. The elements under-colored by ▨ are features, rules, and patterns learned with the proposed framework. In Features Construction part, features of content, user, and spreading structure are explored. In Rules Generation & Patterns Interpretation, the hybrid model *Rulefit* is utilized to generate and filter out rules composed of multiple features, which are further categorized and analyzed as rumor patterns. The different colors or shapes of 🗎, 👥, ⬚ in Rules Generated by Rulefit represent different values of corresponding features.

2.1 Features Construction

To explore the context-dependent connections among multiple correlated factors, we mine the features of the post content, the user who posts, and the propagation structures of the post.

Post Content. Firstly, explicit semantic features like text length, whether contains links or pictures are included. Meanwhile, we utilize the powerful *ChatGPT* to extract implicit semantic features such as topic and emotion. ChatGPT [5] is a pre-trained large language model (LLM) based on a massive neural network with billions of parameters and trained on hundreds of billions of words of text

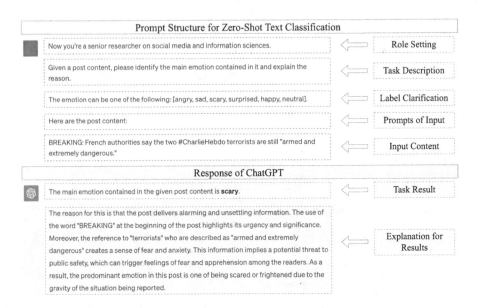

Fig. 2. Prompt structure designed for zero-shot text classification and the response of ChatGPT. The provided example demonstrates its application in an emotion detection task.

from the Internet and digitized books. Recent studies have found that LLM performs well for a wide range of purposes, including ideological scaling [31], text annotation tasks [12,14], and simulating samples for survey research [2]. Specifically, semantic features *credibility*, *accuracy*, *reasonableness*, and *support*, are included based on the CARS framework [15] for assessing information quality.

Figure 1 illustrates the utilization of ChatGPT in our framework for extracting semantic features. To fully leverage the powerful comprehension capability of LLMs, we have designed customized prompts. An example of prompts tailored for zero-shot labeling is depicted in Fig. 2. The adoption of zero-shot text classification with ChatGPT effectively overcomes the dependency on labeled data and model training encountered in traditional feature mining approaches. Furthermore, we have performed manual checking to validate the annotations generated by ChatGPT, ensuring their accuracy and reliability.

User Attributes. Moreover, previous studies [18,28] have shown that specific characteristics differentiate rumor-related people from rumor-irrelevant people like the number of followers usually implies the social influence of individuals and the authority of their posts. As individual characteristics can affect content credibility, they are also considered key features in the proposed framework.

Spreading Structures. Lastly, the propagation structures formed by individual interactions, such as likes, comments, and reposts, are also informative for identifying rumors [18]. Regarding the spreading structure as a propagation tree [27], the motif discovery algorithm gSpan [32] is utilized to detect the spreading structures. Figure 3 shows the motif examples that gSpan can learn. We take the number of depth motifs, the number of breadth motifs, and the maximum depth of the tree to measure the topological characteristics of interaction behaviors in rumors.

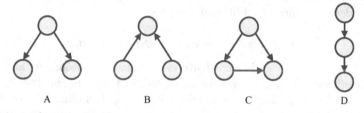

Fig. 3. Motifs examples detected by gSpan for graph data. For a rumor propagation tree, nodes represent the posted content, while edges represent reposting or commenting, and the direction of edges aligns with the spreading. For example, if a post p received a comment, marked as q, then we have an edge from node p to q. Motif A and D are regarded as the breadth spreading structure and depth spreading structure, while motif B and C describe different structures of information receiver.

2.2   Rules Generation and Patterns Interpretation

Based on explored multiple dimensional features, Rulefit [11] is used to identify informative rules that capture the intricate relationships among features.

RuleFit is an explainable algorithm that combines decision rules with a linear model to create a hybrid model. In general, it consists of two steps, the first is generating rules by tree-based model, and the second is taking the generated rules as categorical variables into linear regression. It is employed as a way to capture both the interpretability of decision rules and the explainable coefficient in linear models.

For the first step, RuleFit works by generating a large number of decision rules using a tree-based model, such as Decision Tree or Random Forest. Each rule includes measurements *Support*, *Importance*, and *Coefficient*. The *Support* of a rule in RuleFit refers to the percentage of instances in the training data that satisfy the conditions of that rule. A rule with high support indicates that it applies to a significant portion of the data. The *Importance* of a rule measures its relevance or contribution to the overall predictive performance of the RuleFit model. A higher importance value indicates that a rule plays a more influential role in making predictions. The *Coefficient* of a rule in RuleFit indicates the weight or effect assigned to that rule in the linear regression component of the hybrid model. Let $x_1, x_2, ...x_n$ are variables learned in feature construction, the first step can be represented as follows:

$$\mathcal{R} = \{r_1, r_2, ..., r_m\} \tag{1}$$
$$= \text{Tree-Based-Model}(x_1, x_2, ..., x_n). \tag{2}$$

for r_i are rules, i.e. paths from the root node to the leaf node of generated trees by Tree-Based-Model, composed by $\{x_1, x_2, ...x_n\}$

Then, a linear model is fitted using both the original input features and the generated decision rules as additional features.

$$y = \alpha_0 + \alpha_1 x_1 + ... + \alpha_n x_n + \beta_1 r_1 + ... + \beta_m r_m \tag{3}$$

for $r_i \in \mathcal{R}$ are rules as additional features in linear regression, α_i and β_i are learned coefficients of origin variables and generated rules in the first step. The algorithm has been applied in various domains [6,30], including finance, healthcare, and marketing, where interpretability and accuracy are both important. Based on the generated rules with corresponding importance, crucial rules are filtered and interpreted into more explainable patterns, providing insights into the formation mechanism of rumors.

3   Experiments and Analysis

3.1   Data Preparation and Rules Generation

To validate the effectiveness of the proposed framework, we conduct the rumor patterns analysis based on a publicly available rumor dataset, Credible Early Detection (CED) Dataset [24]. CED Dataset is a Chinese rumor dataset crawled from the Sina Weibo Information Reporting Platform, including a total of 1,538 rumor posts and 1,849 non-rumor posts from September 2009 to June 2017. The dataset contains forwarding and commenting information related to the original posts and has been widely used in rumor detection research [25,35]. According to the proposed framework, we extracted the rumor-related features from the content of the post, the user attributes, and the propagation structure. Specifically, the derived features for rumor pattern discovery are shown in Table 1.

Table 1. Features constructed for CED Dataset according to the proposed framework.

Category of features	Features
Content	topic, emotion, length, has URL, the number of pics, credibility, accuracy, reasonableness, support, agitated propagation.
User	gender, verified type, description, the number of followers, the number of posts, the number of friends.
Spreading Structure	the number of reposts, the number of likes, the number of comments, the maximum depth, the number of depth spreading motif, the number of breadth spreading motif, the ratio of questioning, the ratio of denying

The diverse features make a solid foundation for finding more meaningful compound rules. In our experiment, the Gradient Boosting Tree, a popular and powerful tree-based model, is deployed as the rule generator for Rulefit. The maximum depth of trees is set to 5 to ensure the rules are well-interpretable and complex enough to comprehensively consider various factors. Figure 4 shows the distribution of 145 rules generated by Rulefit.

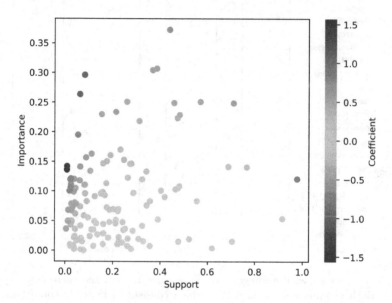

Fig. 4. Summary of Rules Generated from the CED Dataset. The points represent the generated 145 rules, with *support* by the x-axis, *importance* by the y-axis, and *coefficient* by color.

3.2 Analysis of Integrated Rumor Patterns

As a large number of rules were generated, we selected the rules with high contribution to rumor detection to analyze. In particular, 12 rules with support larger than 0.20 and importance larger than 0.20 are further analyzed and interpreted. As shown in Fig. 5, we categorized the 12 rules into seven patterns and analyzed them as follows:

Patterns		A		B	C		D	E			F		G
	Rules	R1	R2	R3	R4	R5	R6	R7	R8	R9	R10	R11	R12
User	num_posts						75						
	num_followers	50	75				25	50		50			
	num_friends						25						
	gender												
Content	topic			○							○	○	
	emotion			○									
	credibility	50											
	accuracy											50	
	reasonableness		25										50
	support											50	75
	agitated_propagation						○		○				
	length												75
	has_url			○									○
	num_pics									50	25		
Spreading Structure	num_nodes				50	50	75		25				
	num_likes				25								25
	num_comments				50								
	num_reposts					25			25				
	max_depth							75	25				
	num_depth_motif							50					
	num_breadth_motif									50			
	ratio_deny										50		
	ratio_question											50	

○ Categorical variable   ☐ Continuous variable   25 50 75 25th, 50th, 75th percentile   ▨ < ▨ >

Fig. 5. This figure shows the categorized rumor patterns A-G and corresponding rules R1-R12. Each column represents a rule which consists of multiple conditions with variables listed in rows. For rules, colored green indicates non-rumorous, while orange represents rumors. For variables, ○ (Color figure online) represents categorical variable while ☐ represents a continuous variable. Numbers 25, 50, and 75 in rectangles represent the 25th, 50th, and 75th percentile of each variable. For continuous variables, red means ">" and blue means "<". For example, R1 represents "num_followers > 50% percentile number of num_followers & credibility > 50% percentile number of credibility".

Pattern A: High Authority Accounts and Credible Content Implies Non-rumors. Pattern A consists of rules R1 and R2, both considering the number of followers and credibility or reasonableness of the posted content. For R1, if a user has more followers than half of the users (approximately 240,000 followers in the CED Dataset) and a credibility score not below the median (around 7 out of 10 in the CED Dataset), the social media post is likely to be a non-rumor. Additionally, R2 suggests that links found in the content of high authority users, serving as sources or evidence, further support the truthfulness of the content. This pattern relies on the recognition of high authority as a reliable indicator of whether a post is a rumor [18]. On social media platforms, accounts with a large following often include those endorsed by official institutions, key opinion leaders, and some profit-driven self-media accounts. These accounts are strongly incentivized to maintain their credibility and commercial value in a monitored environment where spreading rumors can cause reputational damage [19]. Therefore, accounts with a substantial number of followers generally represent high authority due to the backing of official institutions and their proactive information review processes.

Pattern B: Negative Emotional Expression on Human Security Often Implies Rumor. In Pattern B, R3 focuses on features derived from content, including the topic and emotions. Specifically, R3 states that if a post expresses anger, fear, or sorrow and the topic relates to human security and social order, it is highly likely to be a rumor. Sentiment and emotions play a significant role in the spread of information, particularly through emotional contagion, as noted by [21]. When a rumor contains provocative or emotionally impactful content, it tends to trigger strong emotional reactions in individuals who come across it [34]. Furthermore, topics related to social order, which directly affect people's daily lives and safety, tend to attract widespread attention and contribute to the dissemination of rumors. Rumor spreaders often incorporate fear, anger, and other intense sentiments into discussions about social order and security. By evoking strong emotions, they aim to elicit empathy from the public, leading to increased attention, engagement, and sharing of the rumor, thereby facilitating its spread.

Pattern C: High Interaction but Few Likes or Reposts Imply Rumors. In Pattern C, two rules, R4 and R5, focus on features derived from the spreading structure. They share a common pattern: the propagation structure has a relatively large number of nodes, surpassing the median, but the number of likes or reposts is significantly low, falling below the 25th percentile. Likes and reposts are forms of user behavior that serve as endorsements for the credibility of content [16]. These actions are publicly visible, appearing on users' profiles or timelines and potentially reaching their network of followers. Thus receiving likes or reposts enhances the credibility of post content. Additionally, if the main form of interaction is comments, it suggests the content is controversial.

Pattern D: Agitated Propagation Content Published by Dubious Accounts Implies Rumors. R6 in Pattern D identifies rumors by considering features from users, content, and the spreading structure. The number of followers usually increases as a social media user continuously engages on the platform. For users in Pattern D who are active but abnormally have low influence, content showing agitated propagation from them becomes even more suspicious to be a rumor.

Pattern E: Propagation with Deep Dissemination Chains Increases the Probability of Being Rumors. Rules R7, R8, and R9 in Pattern E are all dominated by deep structures in the propagation tree. Social media platforms, known for their broadcasting nature, facilitate the dissemination of information primarily in terms of breadth rather than depth [13]. Taking R7 as an example, if a user's post exhibits a significant maximum depth and number of depth motifs, it suggests the presence of deep dissemination chains. In social media, long-chain structures often emerge when the content lacks value or credibility, relying on close relationships and high trust for dissemination [29]. Due to strong interpersonal ties and tightly shared values, rumors may face challenges in reaching a broader audience outside the group. This creates an enhancement mechanism that drives the diffusion of information into deep structures rather than broad ones.

Pattern F: Content Receiving Numerous Negative Responses on Health or Social Order Tend to Be Rumor. R10 and R11 show that the rumor contents receive a significant proportion of negative responses. Negative responses, such as questioning and denial, are strong indicators of the dubious veracity of content. The nature of negative expressions varies based on the content topic. Health-related content may be directly refuted with concrete evidence due to its basis in objective knowledge, whereas social order-related content presents different challenges.

Pattern G: Content Tells a Long Story but with Low Reasonableness and Few Positive Responses Implies Rumors. R12 considers both the content features and the spreading structure. In this pattern, a lengthy expression accompanied by links may attempt to persuade the audience through a captivating story. However, the low reasonableness of the content raises suspicions about the claims made in the narrative. Additionally, the lack of engagement in terms of likes for this seemingly "good story" further suggests its dubious nature.

4   Conclusion and Future Work

This research addresses the widespread dissemination of rumors on social media platforms through the recognition of rule-based rumor patterns. We propose a discovery framework utilizing the explainable hybrid linear model Rulefit. The framework incorporates features from users, posts, and spreading structures, enabling a comprehensive analysis and capturing contextual associations among multiple correlated factors. We analyze seven rumor patterns using the Chinese CED Dataset, providing valuable insights into the characteristics of rumors. Our findings have practical implications for combatting misinformation and offer a foundation for future research directions.

Nonetheless, the capacity to explore various and practical rumor patterns within the proposed framework hinges upon the richness and pertinence of the input features. Therefore, scalability and generalizability testing of the proposed framework on larger and more diverse datasets should be conducted. This will allow us to assess the framework's performance in different contexts and ensure its applicability on a broader scale.

Acknowledgement. This work is supported by the National Natural Science Foundation of China (72104212, 72134007), the Natural Science Foundation of Zhejiang Province (LY22G030002), and the Fundamental Research Funds for the Central Universities.

References

1. Adadi, A., Berrada, M.: Peeking inside the black-box: a survey on explainable artificial intelligence (xai). IEEE access **6**, 52138–52160 (2018)
2. Argyle, L.P., Busby, E.C., Fulda, N., Gubler, J.R., Rytting, C., Wingate, D.: Out of one, many: Using language models to simulate human samples. Polit. Anal. **31**(3), 337–351 (2023)
3. Ayoub, J., Yang, X.J., Zhou, F.: Combat covid-19 infodemic using explainable natural language processing models. Inform. Process. Manage. **58**(4), 102569 (2021)
4. Bian, T., et al.: Rumor detection on social media with bi-directional graph convolutional networks. In: Proceedings of the AAAI Conference on Artificial Intelligence. vol. 34, pp. 549–556 (2020)
5. Brown, T., et al.: Language models are few-shot learners. Adv. Neural. Inf. Process. Syst. **33**, 1877–1901 (2020)
6. Burkart, N., Huber, M.F.: A survey on the explainability of supervised machine learning. J. Artif. Intell. Res. **70**, 245–317 (2021)
7. Castillo, C., Mendoza, M., Poblete, B.: Information credibility on twitter. In: Proceedings of the 20th International Conference On World Wide Web, pp. 675–684 (2011)
8. Chami, G.F., Ahnert, S.E., Kabatereine, N.B., Tukahebwa, E.M.: Social network fragmentation and community health. Proc. Natl. Acad. Sci. **114**(36), E7425–E7431 (2017)
9. Chien, S.Y., Yang, C.J., Yu, F.: Xflag: explainable fake news detection model on social media. Int. J. Human-Comput. Interact. **38**(18–20), 1808–1827 (2022)
10. Davidson, A.D., Hamilton, M.J., Boyer, A.G., Brown, J.H., Ceballos, G.: Multiple ecological pathways to extinction in mammals. Proc. Natl. Acad. Sci. **106**(26), 10702–10705 (2009)
11. Friedman, J.H., Popescu, B.E.: Predictive learning via rule ensembles (2008)
12. Gilardi, F., Alizadeh, M., Kubli, M.: Chatgpt outperforms crowd-workers for text-annotation tasks. arXiv preprint arXiv:2303.15056 (2023)
13. Goel, S., Anderson, A., Hofman, J., Watts, D.J.: The structural virality of online diffusion. Manage. Sci. **62**(1), 180–196 (2016)
14. Kojima, T., Gu, S.S., Reid, M., Matsuo, Y., Iwasawa, Y.: Large language models are zero-shot reasoners. Adv. Neural. Inf. Process. Syst. **35**, 22199–22213 (2022)
15. Li, Y., Fan, Z., Yuan, X., Zhang, X.: Recognizing fake information through a developed feature scheme: a user study of health misinformation on social media in china. Inform. Process. Manage. **59**(1), 102769 (2022)
16. Li, Z., Zhang, Q., Du, X., Ma, Y., Wang, S.: Social media rumor refutation effectiveness: evaluation, modelling and enhancement. Inform. Process. Manage. **58**(1), 102420 (2021)

17. Li, Z., Zhao, Y., Duan, T., Dai, J.: Configurational patterns for covid-19 related social media rumor refutation effectiveness enhancement based on machine learning and fsqca. Inform. Process. Manage. **60**(3), 103303 (2023)

18. Liang, G., He, W., Xu, C., Chen, L., Zeng, J.: Rumor identification in microblogging systems based on users' behavior. IEEE Trans. Comput. Social Syst. **2**(3), 99–108 (2015)

19. Lou, C., Yuan, S.: Influencer marketing: how message value and credibility affect consumer trust of branded content on social media. J. Interact. Advert. **19**(1), 58–73 (2019)

20. Ma, J., Gao, W., Wei, Z., Lu, Y., Wong, K.F.: Detect rumors using time series of social context information on microblogging websites. In: Proceedings of the 24th ACM International on Conference on Information and Knowledge Management, pp. 1751–1754 (2015)

21. Paz, L.V., et al.: Contagious depression: automatic mimicry and the mirror neuron system-a review. Neurosci. Biobehav. Rev. **134**, 104509 (2022)

22. Reis, J.C., Correia, A., Murai, F., Veloso, A., Benevenuto, F.: Explainable machine learning for fake news detection. In: Proceedings of the 10th ACM Conference on Web Science, pp. 17–26 (2019)

23. Ribeiro, M.T., Singh, S., Guestrin, C.: Anchors: High-precision model-agnostic explanations. In: Proceedings of the AAAI Conference on Artificial Intelligence, vol. 32 (2018)

24. Song, C., Tu, C., Yang, C., Liu, Z., Sun, M.: Ced: credible early detection of social media rumors. arXiv preprint arXiv:1811.04175 (2018)

25. Song, C., Shu, K., Wu, B.: Temporally evolving graph neural network for fake news detection. Inform. Process. Manage. **58**(6), 102712 (2021)

26. Sun, T., Qian, Z., Dong, S., Li, P., Zhu, Q.: Rumor detection on social media with graph adversarial contrastive learning. In: Proceedings of the ACM Web Conference 2022, pp. 2789–2797 (2022)

27. Wang, S., Terano, T.: Detecting rumor patterns in streaming social media. In: 2015 IEEE International Conference on Big Data (big data), pp. 2709–2715. IEEE (2015)

28. Wang, Y., Zheng, L., Zuo, J.: Online rumor propagation of social media on nimby conflict: temporal patterns, frameworks and rumor-mongers. Environ. Impact Assess. Rev. **91**, 106647 (2021)

29. Wang, Z., Yan, P., Jiang, Z.: Interpretable graph neural network for social media rumor detection. J. China Society for Sci. Technical Inform. **42**(11), 1369–1381 (2023)

30. Whiting, D.G., Hansen, J.V., McDonald, J.B., Albrecht, C., Albrecht, W.S.: Machine learning methods for detecting patterns of management fraud. Comput. Intell. **28**(4), 505–527 (2012)

31. Wu, P.Y., Tucker, J.A., Nagler, J., Messing, S.: Large language models can be used to estimate the ideologies of politicians in a zero-shot learning setting. arXiv preprint arXiv:2303.12057 (2023)

32. Yan, X., Han, J.: gspan: Graph-based substructure pattern mining. In: 2002 IEEE International Conference on Data Mining, 2002. Proceedings, pp. 721–724. IEEE (2002)

33. Yang, F., Liu, Y., Yu, X., Yang, M.: Automatic detection of rumor on sina weibo. In: Proceedings of the ACM SIGKDD Workshop on Mining Data Semantics, pp. 1–7 (2012)

34. Yin, F., Xia, X., Pan, Y., She, Y., Feng, X., Wu, J.: Sentiment mutation and negative emotion contagion dynamics in social media: A case study on the chinese sina microblog. Inf. Sci. **594**, 118–135 (2022)
35. Yuan, C., Ma, Q., Zhou, W., Han, J., Hu, S.: Jointly embedding the local and global relations of heterogeneous graph for rumor detection. In: 2019 IEEE International Conference on Data Mining (ICDM), pp. 796–805. IEEE (2019)

Nudging Away Health Misinformation on Social Media: The Roles of Social Influences and Power Distance

Xinyue Li[1] ⓘ, Mandie Liu[2,3] ⓘ, Jingwen Lian[1] ⓘ, and Qinghua Zhu[1(✉)] ⓘ

[1] Nanjing University, Nanjing 210023, China
qhzhu@nju.edu.cn
[2] City University of Hong Kong, Hong Kong 999077, China
[3] Southern University of Science and Technology, Shenzhen 518055, China

Abstract. Nudges are considered as potential and promising approaches to combat misinformation on social media, yet they often overlooked the influence of other users. This study aims to explore the impact of social influence on people's attitudes toward health misinformation by utilizing nudges on social media. We conducted a 2 * 3 between-subject web-based experiment to test the effectiveness of informational and normative social influences and obtained data from 247 participants. The preliminary results show that both social influences reduce sharing likelihood of misinformation, by decreasing perceived credibility. Informational social influence increases individuals' perceived threat while normative social influence decreases it. Power distance significantly moderates the relationship between normative social influence and perceived threat. This study contributes to nudging away misinformation by revealing the roles of two distinctive social influences, and also furnishes practical implications for the misinformation governance on social media.

Keywords: Social Nudges · Social Influence · Health Misinformation · Power Distance · Social Media

1 Introduction

The rapid rise of social media has turned it into a breeding ground for the production and spread of health misinformation [1]. Such misinformation confuses individuals, erodes their trust in science, and lead to irrational health behaviors [2]. Hence, health misinformation governance is imperative. One proposed solution is the nudge, designed to gently guide behaviors toward desired outcomes [3]. Caraban et al. [4] divided the nudge into three types: signal, facilitator, and spark. Existing studies often focus on the first two approaches [5, 6], aiming to remind individuals or reduce their efforts in countering misinformation. In China, social media platforms like Weibo and RED have started using red/white flags as warning signals for inoculation of misinformation. However, these studies overlook the potential of other user's effect on social media in sparking users' motivations.

I. Sserwanga et al. (Eds.): iConference 2024, LNCS 14597, pp. 268–279, 2024.
https://doi.org/10.1007/978-3-031-57860-1_19

Social nudges, which provide references to individual's behaviors or guidelines [7], assume a pivotal role in the decision-making process given the propensity of individuals to adhere to social norms, embrace collective behaviors, and cultivate group identities [8]. Different approaches of social nudge may lead to different social influences. Deutsch and Gerard once categorized social influence into two types: informational social influence and normative social influence [9]. The former involves the acceptance of certain knowledge and evidence while the latter is related to self-maintenance and compliance. Nevertheless, it remains unclear whether both social influences can effectively contribute to combatting health misinformation. It also worth noting that the role of social influence may be influenced by information characteristics like source credibility [10] and individual characteristics like power distance [11]. Therefore, this study seeks to address health misinformation on social media by leveraging nudges and social influence theory. Two research questions are posed:

RQ1: How can informational and normative social influence impact individual's attitudes toward health misinformation through nudges on social media?

RQ2: How do the source credibility and power distance moderate the relationship of social influence with individual's attitudes toward health misinformation?

2 Literature Review

2.1 Nudging Away Misinformation

Misinformation denotes information that is objectively inaccurate or factually incorrect [12]. Nudges have emerged as a relatively psychological intervention to counter misinformation [13]. When used in digital environments, this is called digital nudging, a new concept in Human-Computer Interaction that uses UI elements to influence choices [14]. Currently, some studies have begun to explore the role of digital nudging in addressing misinformation, with a primary focus on signal and facilitator one [15]. However, prior studies have disregarded the significant role played by others on social media.

Social nudges, as one of the sparks, guide users' behaviors by using others' behaviors as a reference. Social influence theory posits that individual's attitudes, beliefs, and subsequent actions can be influenced by others [16]. Based on social nudges principles, Bhuiyan created a tool named NudgeCred to utilize others' opinions to diminish the credibility and sharing likelihood of misinformation [17]. However, previous research on social nudges in the field of misinformation has remained at a rudimentary exploratory stage, lacking more in-depth and meticulous investigations. For example, it has not considered the differences between various types of social nudges, nor has it taken into account the potential impact of individual characteristics.

2.2 Social Influence

Social influence encompasses how individuals or groups impact others' thoughts, feelings, and behaviors [18], categorized as informational and normative social influence [9]. Its efficacy in molding individual behaviors has been extensively demonstrated in various domains, including knowledge adoption in virtual communities [19] and e-shopping intention [20]. According to Thaler and Sunstein's [3] viewpoints, social influence can be employed through social nudges. Informational social influence means to accept information obtained from another as evidence about reality. Information source holds a pivotal role in this influence [21]. Normative social influence leads an individual to conform to the expectations of another one or a group. Notably, socially normative cues tend to be readily accessible in online settings, such as virtual community [19]. People often accept normative social influence to avoid isolation or potential risks [22], especially in collectivist groups [9, 23]. Previous studies mainly focused on commercial decision-making, ignoring more persuasive scenarios like misinformation. Additionally, few studies have explored these two forms of social influence as nudges, particularly on social media.

2.3 Power Distance

Power distance refers to the extent to which differences in power are expected and accepted [24]. Prior research primarily explored power distance between nations, considering it as a cultural factor [25, 26]. Those with higher power distance people prioritize the authority opinions, while those with lower power distance value statistical evidence over expert opinions [27]. Consequently, power distance additionally reinforces an individual's predisposition to information from credible sources [28]. Nowadays, the emergence and proliferation of social media provide a channel for higher power distance individuals to foster their cognitive orientation to exert influence upon others [29]. It becomes imperative to investigate the role of power distance in addressing misinformation on social media which is flooded with a large amount of health misinformation.

3 Research Model and Hypotheses

3.1 Effects of Informational and Normative Social Influence

Regarding informational social influence, on one hand, enhanced access to more information empowers individuals to make judicious and comprehensive judgements. Gimpel et al. [6] decreased the credibility of misinformation by unveiling related articles on social media. On the other hand, individuals tend to defer to the authority and expertise of a presenter when evaluating information on a particular issue [19]. Informational social influence on social media occurs when an individual regards the information provided by others as evidence of truth, thereby facilitating the formulation of more accurate judgements. Consequently, this diminishes the sharing likelihood associated with misinformation.

H1: Informational social influence will inhibit individual's likelihood of sharing.

Regarding normative social influence, it guides individuals toward conformity with the expectations of others [9]. Flanagin and Metzger [30] suggested that consensus of others can enhance trust in online sources and significantly influence people's attitudes, opinions and behaviors [31]. When individuals encounter health information on social media, they often conform to the choices of their surroundings to harmonize their attitudes and behaviors. Kwahk and Kim suggested that normative social influence exerts a substantial impact on social media, particularly due to the expansive social circles [32]. Therefore, when users find other people are skeptical of this information, they are less likely to share this information.

H2: Normative social influence will inhibit individual's likelihood of sharing.

3.2 Mediating Roles of Perceived Threat and Credibility

Perceived threat is a psychological response that arises when an individual becomes aware of an impending threat or potential attack [33]. In previous studies, perceived threat has been identified as a significant motivator prompting individuals to adopt protective health behaviors [34]. Williams discovered that perceived threat could elevate the likelihood of users sharing misinformation [35]. In this study, social influences through nudges offer individuals information or behaviors exhibited by others, helping reduce their threat when encountering uncertain information. This contributes to improving their irrational health information behaviors.

H3: Perceived threat mediated the relationship of informational (a)/normative social influence (b) with individuals' likelihood of sharing misinformation.

Perceived credibility is the comprehensive evaluation judgement made by information recipients [36]. When social influence offers the opposite information or opinions for the misinformation, the perceived credibility of the misinformation will be reduced based on the trust beliefs in social information. Perceived credibility plays a pivotal role in people's decisions to share information [37, 38]. When user perceive health information as credible, they are more inclined to share it with their friends or family [39].

H4: Perceived credibility mediated the relationship of informational (a)/normative social influence (b) with individuals' likelihood of sharing misinformation.

3.3 Moderating Roles of Source Credibility and Power Distance

Source credibility denotes a communicator's positive attributes that impact the recipients' willingness to accept the conveyed content [40]. It is not only one of three elements of informational social influence but is also considered a crucial factor in the social influencing process [10]. In accordance with social comparison theory, people always engage in upward comparisons, meaning they select superior benchmarks within a certain domain to enhance their choice making [41]. Social nudges with strong source credibility foster trust in the information they provide [17], reducing the perceived threat and credibility of misinformation.

H5: The effect of informational(a)/normative(b) social influence on perceived threat (a/b-1) and credibility (a/b-2) of misinformation is stronger when source credibility is higher.

As a significant personal characteristic that influences behaviors, power distance means the degree to which disparities in power are anticipated and accepted [24]. De Meulenaer et al. [28] believed that power distance reinforces individuals' tendency towards information from credible sources. In regions with high power distance, expert evidence may be particularly persuasive [42]. Hence, when authoritative figures are present, individuals with high power distance may be more susceptible to the influence of social nudges, thereby reducing their perceived threat and credibility of misinformation.

H6: The effect of informational(a)/normative(b) social influence on perceived threat (a/b-1) and credibility (a/b-2) of misinformation is stronger when power distance is higher.

Figure 1 illustrates the included constructs and hypotheses.

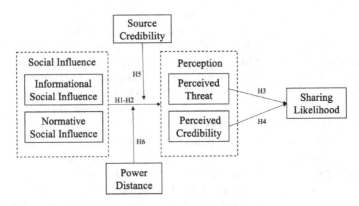

Fig. 1. Research model

4 Methodology

4.1 Pre-test: Experiment and Measures

To investigate the impact of informational and normative social influences, acting as social nudges, on individuals' attitudes towards health misinformation disseminated on social media, we conducted a web-based experiment. We adopted a 2 * 3 between-subject design, as illustrated in Table 1, and subjects were randomly assigned to five groups. After excluding samples that did not pass the attention check, we finally included a total of 247 participants (38.5% male; 85.4% received a bachelor's degree or higher; 61.5% reported good health status; almost 74% showed high e-Health literacy) through Chinese online questionnaire website (wjx.cn) and personal contacts.

Table 1. Overview of the experiment design

Source	Social Influence		
	Absent	Informational social influence	Normative social influence
Expert	Group1 (N = 50)	Group2 (N = 51)	Group4 (N = 46)
Friend		Group3 (N = 48)	Group5 (N = 52)

Participants first received general instructions about the study and answered questions about their demographics, social media usage, eHealth literacy, and power distance. Next, they were told to simulate a scenario created using prototyping tool (modao.cc) in which they encounter health information on Weibo (Chinese social media platform). In the control group, participants were furnished with a piece of health misinformation "Strawberries are the dirtiest fruit," drawing inspirations from the prevalent online health misinformation on a government-sponsored platform (piyao.org.cn). In the experimental group, participants were presented with digital nudging information before encountering health misinformation. Informational social influence nudges aimed to spread other's scientific knowledge and accurate information regarding this subject, while normative social influence nudges endeavor to instill skepticism in others about the information (Fig. 2). Friend (your friend in Weibo) and expert (Chinese Institute of Food Science and Technology, CIFST) are two categorize of sources.

After reading these materials, participants completed the final part of the survey including misinformation credibility, their perceived threat and sharing likelihood. A manipulation check was integrated into the concluding survey to gauge whether participants discerned disparities in social influences [43].

Fig. 2. Example slides of social nudges

To measure the variables, we employed established measures from previous literature, as shown in Table 2. All these items are measured on a 5-point Likert scale.

Table 2. Measurement items

Construct	Sampled measurement items	Source
eHealth literacy	I possess the ability to differentiate between high-quality and low-quality health information sources on the Internet	Norman and Skinner [44]
Power distance	People in higher positions should make most decisions without consulting people in lower positions	Yoo et al. [45]
Perceived threat	After I read this health information, I felt threatened	Pfau et al. [46]
Perceived credibility	I think this health information is accurate	Vraga et al. [47]
Sharing likelihood	I will share this health information	Nekmat [15]

4.2 Data Analysis and Preliminary Results

First, we examined the reliability and validity of these constructs. All variables demonstrated acceptable levels (Cronbach $\alpha > 0.9$), and they also passed the discriminant validity check by calculating average variance extracted (AVE). Then, we checked the experimental manipulations regarding informational and normative social influence. Participants in group 2 and 3 perceived higher informational social influence (mean difference = 0.890, $p < 0.001$), and those in group 4 and 5 demonstrated higher perception of normative social influence (mean difference = 0.490, $p < 0.001$), compared to the test value of 3.00 (i.e., the scale midpoint). We conducted ANCOVA with perceived threat, perceived credibility and sharing likelihood of misinformation as dependent variables and considering control variables like gender, age, e-Health literacy to explore the impact of two social influences on mitigating health misinformation. Table 3 illustrated that comparing to control group, informational social influence heightened individuals' perceived threat (mean difference = 0.247, $p < 0.05$), decreased the perceived credibility (mean difference = -0.596, $p < 0.01$) and reduced sharing likelihood of misinformation (mean difference = -0.248, $p < 0.05$). In contrast, normative social influence diminished individuals' perceived threat (mean difference = -0.45, $p < 0.01$), and also reduced perceived credibility (mean difference = -0.75, $p < 0.05$) and the likelihood of sharing misinformation (mean difference = -0.419, $p < 0.05$). Therefore, H1-H2 are supported.

Table 3. Results of ANCOVAs

Source	Type III sum of squares	d.f.	Mean square	F	p-value
Dep. var: Perceived Threat of Misinformation					
Informational social influence	1.999	1	1.999	4.443	**<0.05**
Normative social influence	6.482	1	6.482	10.414	**<0.01**
Power distance * Informational social influence	7.150	15	0.477	1.032	0.428
Power distance * Normative social influence	8.118	7	1.160	2.909	**<0.01**
Dep. var: Perceived Credibility of Misinformation					
Informational social influence	9.099	1	9.099	7.096	**<0.01**
Normative social influence	5.851	1	5.851	5.105	**<0.05**
Power distance * Informational social influence	9.799	15	0.653	0.594	0.875
Power distance * Normative social influence	2.635	7	0.376	0.446	0.870
Dep. var: Sharing Likelihood of Misinformation					
Informational social influence	7.456	1	7.456	4.869	**<0.05**
Normative social influence	5.020	1	5.020	3.996	**<0.05**

We further conducted mediating analysis to examine the roles of perceived threat and credibility by applying PROCESS for SPSS 27.0 [48]. Figure 3 illustrates that perceived threat (indirect effect $= -0.215$; CI $= -0.36, -0.09$) and credibility (indirect effect $= -0.340$; CI $= -0.59, -0.08$) fully mediated the relationship between normative social influence and individuals' likelihood to share, thereby supporting H3b and H4b. Furthermore, the results indicate that the mediating role of perceived threat between informational social influence and sharing likelihood is not significant (not support H3a), whereas perceived credibility plays a mediating role in this relationship (indirect effect $= -0.426$; CI $= -0.69, -0.14$), thus supporting H4a. We finally tested the moderating roles of power distance using Hayes' Process. The results demonstrate that power distance significantly negatively influences the relationship between normative social influence and perceived threat (Coeff $= 0.343$, $p < 0.01$), suggesting that when power distance was higher, this relationship was weaker. However, the moderating effects of power distance on the relationship between informational social influence and perceived credibility and threat (H6a), and the relationship between normative social influence and perceived credibility (H6b-2) are not significant. In addition, source credibility shows no significant moderating effect in the relationship between social influence and individuals' attitudes toward health misinformation (not support H5).

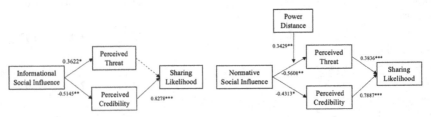

Fig. 3. Effects of Informational and Normative Social Influence on Perceived Threat, Credibility and Sharing Likelihood.

5   Initial Conclusions and Remaining Work

Our initial findings support the ascertains that both informational and normative social influence decrease the sharing likelihood of health misinformation, consistent with previous studies [7]. When individuals learn about others' opinions on health information, it can change their initial misperceptions. Besides, two forms of social influence operate through different mechanisms. Informational one primarily decreases the sharing likelihood by undermining the credibility of information. Interestingly, this is accompanied by an increase in perceived threat, which contradicts our initial hypothesis. We guess that this phenomenon may result from an excess of information, leading to high cognitive load [49]. Conflicting and more information heighten individuals' threat and panic, prompting them to share their intensified emotional response. Conversely, normative one reduced the sharing likelihood of misinformation through the decreases of perceived threat and credibility, which supports our hypothesis [30]. Individuals often find it more comfortable to make judgements when they conform to established social norms. Furthermore, power distance weakens the impact of normative social influence, and source credibility does not serve as a moderator in the influence of social influence. This suggests that friends and experts on social media wield a leveling or equaling influence over individuals' perspective on health misinformation [50], where people tend to be less aware of social hierarchies, potentially yielding outcomes that differ from real-life contexts [51].

This paper also offers some practical insights for addressing health misinformation on social media. It suggests using tailored recommendation and similarity algorithms to offer more pertinent health truth as factual arguments; employing digital nudging to highlight attitudes and behaviors of others, no matter who they are; and encouraging esteemed medical institutions to blog more popularly while prompting regular users to engage in misinformation correction for a democratized sharing of health knowledge. However, this ongoing study still has limitations. The sample size is quite small, and duration of the nudge may affect its effectiveness. Gathering data from a larger sample over a longer time is crucial to thoroughly test these hypotheses and deeply uncover the underlying mechanisms of how social influence works in fighting health misinformation.

Acknowledgement. This research has been made possible through the financial support of the National Science Foundation of China under Grant No. 72174083.

References

1. Suarez-Lledo, V., Alvarez-Galvez, J.: Prevalence of health misinformation on social media: systematic review. J. Med. Internet Res. **23**(1), e17187 (2021)
2. Borges do Nascimento, I.J., et al.: Infodemics and health misinformation: a systematic review of reviews. Bull. World Health Organ. **100**(9), 544–561 (2022)
3. Thaler, R.H., Sunstein, C.R.: Nudge: Improving Decisions About Health, Wealth, and Happiness, Penguin, New York (2009)
4. Caraban, A., Karapanos, E., Gonçalves, D., Daniel, C.: 23 ways to nudge: a review of technology-mediated nudging in human-computer interaction. In: Proceedings of the 2019 CHI Conference on Human Factors in Computing Systems, pp. 1–15. Association for Computing Machinery, New York, USA (2019)
5. Clayton, K., et al.: Real solutions for fake news? Measuring the effectiveness of general warnings and fact-check tags in reducing belief in false stories on social media. Polit. Behav. **42**, 1073–1095 (2020)
6. Gimpel, H., Heger, S., Kasper, J., Schäfer, R.: The power of related articles - improving fake news detection on social media platforms. In: Hawaii International Conference on System Sciences, pp. 1–10, Hawaii, USA (2020)
7. Andı, S., Akesson, J.: Nudging away false news: evidence from a social norms experiment. Digit. J. **9**(1), 106–125 (2020)
8. Kahneman, D., Slovic, P., Tversky, A.: Judgment Under Uncertainty: Heuristics and Biases. Science, vol. 185, pp. 106–125. Cambridge University Press, Cambridge (1974)
9. Deutsch, M., Gerard, H.B.: A study of normative and informational social influences upon individual judgment. Psychol. Sci. Public Interest **51**(3), 629–636 (1955)
10. Hu, X., Chen, X., Davison, R.M.: Social support, source credibility, social influence, and impulsive purchase behavior in social commerce. Int. J. Electron. Commer. **23**(3), 297–327 (2019)
11. Li, K.K., Chan, M.W.H., Lee, S.S., Kwok, K.O.: The mediating roles of social benefits and social influence on the relationships between collectivism, power distance, and influenza vaccination among Hong Kong nurses: a cross-sectional study. Int. J. Nurs. Stud. **99**, 103359 (2019)
12. Bode, L., Vraga, E.: In related news, that was wrong: the correction of misinformation through related stories functionality in social media. J. Commun. **65**(4), 619–638 (2015)
13. Gwiaździński, P., et al.: Psychological interventions countering misinformation in social media: a scoping review. Front. Psych. **13**, 974782 (2023)
14. Mirsch, T., Lehrer, C., Jung, R.: Digital nudging: altering user behavior in digital environments. In: International Conference on Wirtschaftsinformatik, pp. 634–648, Switzerland (2017)

15. Nekmat, E.: Nudge effect of fact-check alerts: source influence and media skepticism on sharing of news misinformation in social media. Soc. Media + Soc. **6**(1), 205630511989732 (2020)

16. Kelman, H.C.: Compliance, identification, and internalization three processes of attitude change. J. Conflict Resolut. **2**(1), 51–60 (1958)

17. Bhuiyan, M.M., Michael, L., Sang-Won, M.: NudgeCred: supporting news credibility assessment on social media through nudges. Proc. ACM Human-Computer Interact. **5**, 1–30 (2021)

18. Rashotte, L.: Social Influence. The Blackwell Encyclopedia of Sociology. Blackwell, Malden (2007)

19. Chou, C.-H., Wang, Y.-S., Tang, T.I.: Exploring the determinants of knowledge adoption in virtual communities: a social influence perspective. Int. J. Inf. Manage. **35**(3), 364–376 (2015)

20. Zhu, S., Chen, J.: E-commerce use in urbanising China: the role of normative social influence. Behav. Inf. Technol. **35**(5), 357–367 (2016)

21. Hovland, C.I., Janis, I.L., Kelley, H.H.: Communication, and Persuasion, England (1953)

22. Fu, J.-R., Lu, I.-W., Chen, J.H.F., Farn, C.-K.: Investigating consumers' online social shopping intention: an information processing perspective. Int. J. Inf. Manag. **54**, 102189 (2020)

23. Huang, C.Y., Tzou, P.J., Sun, C.T.: Collective opinion and attitude dynamics dependency on informational and normative social influences. Simul.-Trans. Soc. Model. Simul. Int. **87**(10), 875–892 (2011)

24. Hofstede, G.: Cultures and Organizations: Software of the Mind, McGraw-Hill, New York (1997)

25. Yang, Z., Floyd, K., Tanner, J.F., Jr.: Effects of antismoking messages from media on adolescent smoking: the roles of family, school, and culture. J. Bus. Res. **103**, 222–231 (2019)

26. Perea, A., Slater, M.D.: Power distance and collectivist/individualist strategies in alcohol warnings: effects by gender and ethnicity. J. Health Commun. **4**(4), 295–310 (1999)

27. Jung, J.M., Kellaris, J.J.: Responsiveness to authority appeals among young French and American consumers. J. Bus. Res. **59**(6), 735–744 (2006)

28. De Meulenaer, S., De Pelsmacker, P., Dens, N.: Power distance, uncertainty avoidance, and the effects of source credibility on health risk message compliance. Health Commun. **33**(3), 291–298 (2018)

29. Dadgar, M., Vithayathil, J., Osiri, J.K.: Social media usage and cultural dimensions: an empirical investigation. In: Hawaii International Conference on System Sciences, pp. 2243–2252, Hawaii, USA (2017)

30. Metzger, M.J., Flanagin, A.J.: Credibility and trust of information in online environments: the use of cognitive heuristics. J. Pragmat. **59**, 210–220 (2013)

31. Waardenburg, T., Winkel, R., Lamers, M.H.: Normative social influence in persuasive technology: intensity versus effectiveness. In: Persuasive Technology. Design for Health and Safety. In Proceedings of the 7th International Conference, pp. 145–156, Linköping, Sweden (2012)

32. Kwahk, K.Y., Kim, B.: Effects of social media on consumers' purchase decisions: evidence from Taobao. Serv. Bus. **11**, 803–829 (2017)

33. Compton, J., Ivanov, B.: Untangling threat during inoculation-conferred resistance to influence. Commun. Rep. **25**(1), 1–13 (2012)

34. Chen, L., Tang, H.: Intention of health experts to counter health misinformation in social media: effects of perceived threat to online users, correction efficacy, and self-affirmation. Public Underst. Sci. **32**(3), 284–303 (2022)

35. Williams Kirkpatrick, A.: The spread of fake science: lexical concreteness, proximity, misinformation sharing, and the moderating role of subjective knowledge. Public Underst. Sci. **30**(1), 55–74 (2020)

36. Choi, W., Stvilia, B.: Web credibility assessment: conceptualization, operationalization, variability, and models. J. Am. Soc. Inf. Sci. **66**(12), 2399–2414 (2015)

37. Lu, C., Hu, B., Li, Q., Bi, C., Ju, X.D.: Psychological inoculation for credibility assessment, sharing intention, and discernment of misinformation: systematic review and meta-analysis. J. Med. Internet Res. **25**, e49255 (2023)
38. Ali, K., Li, C., Zain-ul-abdin, K., Ali, S.: The effects of emotions, individual attitudes towards vaccination, and social endorsements on perceived fake news credibility and sharing motivations. Comput. Hum. Behav. **134**, 107307 (2022)
39. Liu, M., Yang, Y., Sun, Y.: Exploring health information sharing behavior among Chinese older adults: a social support perspective. Health Commun. **34**(14), 1824–1832 (2019)
40. Ohanian, R.: Construction and validation of a scale to measure celebrity endorsers' perceived expertise, trustworthiness, and attractiveness. J. Advert. **19**(3), 39–52 (1990)
41. Shen, Y.C., Huang, C.Y., Chu, C.H., Liao, H.C.: Virtual community loyalty: an interpersonal-interaction perspective. Int. J. Electron. Commer. **15**(1), 49–74 (2010)
42. Hornikx, J., Hoeken, H.: Cultural differences in the persuasiveness of evidence types and evidence quality. Commun. Monogr. **74**(4), 443–463 (2007)
43. Sun, Y., He, H.: Understanding consumers' purchase intentions of single-use plastic products. Front. Psychol. **14**, 1105959 (2023)
44. Norman, C.D., Skinner, H.A.: EHealth literacy: essential skills for consumer health in a networked world. J. Med. Internet Res. **8**(2), e9 (2006)
45. Yoo, B., Donthu, N., Lenartowicz, T.: Measuring Hofstede's five dimensions of cultural values at the individual level: development and validation of CVSCALE. J. Int. Consum. Mark. **23**, 193–210 (2011)
46. Pfau, M., et al.: The traditional explanation for resistance versus attitude accessibility. Hum. Commun. Res. **30**, 329–360 (2004)
47. Vraga, E.K., Kim, S.C., Cook, J., Bode, L.: Testing the effectiveness of correction placement and type on Instagram. Int. J. Press/Politics **25**(4), 632–652 (2020)
48. Hayes, A.F.: PROCESS: a versatile computational tool for observed variable mediation, moderation, and conditional process modeling. University of Kansas, KS (2012)
49. Bawden, D., Robinson, L.: The dark side of information: overload, anxiety and other paradoxes and pathologies. J. Inf. Sci. **35**, 180–191 (2009)
50. Straub, D., Keil, M., Brenner, W.: Testing the technology acceptance model across cultures: a three country study. Inf. Manag. **33**(1), 1–11 (1997)
51. Huang, L., Lu, M.-T., Wong, B.K.: The impact of power distance on email acceptance: evidence from the PRC. J. Comput. Inf. Syst. **44**(1), 93–101 (2003)

Multidimensional Information Literacy and Fact-Checking Behavior: A Person-Centered Approach Using Latent Profile Analysis

Xiao-Liang Shen[1](✉) ⓘ and You Wu[2] ⓘ

[1] School of Information Management, Wuhan University, Wuhan 430072, China
xlshen@whu.edu.cn
[2] Economics and Management School, Wuhan University, Wuhan 430072, China

Abstract. Information literacy plays a crucial role in empowering social media users to effectively engage in fact-checking behaviors, thereby shielding them from becoming victims of rumors and misinformation. However, existing research predominantly treats users as a homogeneous group, neglecting potentially distinct user profiles based on their levels of information literacy. Such profiles may exhibit significant variations in users' fact-checking behaviors, and these differences could also change over time. To bridge this research gap, the present study adopted a person-centered approach and conducted a two-wave longitudinal investigation. Using latent profile analysis, this study identified three distinct latent profiles: the information literacy proficient profile, the information literacy competent profile, and the information literacy novice profile. Additionally, based on longitudinal data analysis, this study further revealed that, in the short term, the fact-checking behavior of the information literacy competent profile exhibits no significant difference compared to that of the information literacy proficient profile, and significantly outperforms the information literacy novice profile. However, in the long term, the fact-checking behavior of the information literacy competent profile and the information literacy novice profile no longer displays significant differences. This study offers valuable insights for social media platform managers to design targeted strategies tailored to distinct user profiles.

Keywords: Person-centered · Information Literacy · Fact-checking Behavior · Latent Profile Analysis · Longitudinal Study

1 Introduction

In today's digital age, the proliferation of rumors across social media and the internet has become a widespread concern. A rumor is a statement whose truth value has not been unverified or is intentionally false [1]. Social media rumors not only incite panic and unnecessary anxiety but also possess the potential to inflict serious negative consequences on individuals, organizations, and society [2]. Amidst this age of

I. Sserwanga et al. (Eds.): iConference 2024, LNCS 14597, pp. 280–297, 2024.
https://doi.org/10.1007/978-3-031-57860-1_20

information explosion, the fact-checking behaviors of users concerning rumors play a pivotal role. By actively verifying the authenticity and credibility of information, users can effectively discern rumors and misinformation and prevent their dissemination [3]. Information literacy among users has been identified as a significant determinant of their fact-checking behaviors [4]. A high level of information literacy empowers users to approach rumors more rationally and accurately verify them, thus avoiding being misled by false information [5]. However, despite endeavors by social media platforms to encourage fact-checking behaviors, these initiatives often treat users as a homogeneous group, ignoring the fact that users exhibit varying levels of information literacy. For instance, individuals with high information literacy may actively seek and critically evaluate fact-checking information [6], while those with low information literacy may struggle to navigate through the vast amount of misinformation and are more susceptible to believing and spreading rumors. Neglecting the heterogeneity in users' information literacy levels may hinder the efficacy of interventions aimed at curtailing the spread of rumors and misinformation. Therefore, identifying latent user profiles is of immense significance, as it not only provides insights into the nuanced ways individuals engage with and respond to rumors but also allows for an examination of potential disparities in fact-checking behaviors across different user profiles. By unveiling these distinctions, researchers and platform managers can gain valuable insights into how information literacy shapes users' approach to fact-checking behaviors. This, in turn, facilitates the development of targeted interventions and educational initiatives aimed at enhancing users' fact-checking behaviors to counter the spread of rumors on social media. Consequently, it is crucial to explore diverse user profiles based on their information literacy levels and to understand how these profiles impact and differ in social media users' fact-checking behaviors.

However, previous studies investigating information literacy and fact-checking behaviors exhibit several notable limitations. Firstly, previous research has predominantly adopted a traditional variable-centered approach [6, 7], neglecting potential variations in the combined responses of user profiles (or subpopulations) across diverse dimensions of information literacy. Consequently, the heterogeneous nature of individuals with distinct information literacy levels has been disregarded, impeding a comprehensive understanding of users' characteristics and inherent traits. In light of this, it is imperative to delve into the simultaneous interaction of multidimensional information literacy indicators within an individual and their influence on the formation of diverse user profiles that may manifest varying degrees of information literacy. Secondly, previous research has lacked systematic empirical investigations aimed at discerning the differential impacts of diverse user profiles on fact-checking behaviors, and how these impacts may evolve over time. Despite theoretical support for the link between information literacy and fact-checking behaviors [4, 6], behavioral disparities among distinct user profiles and their temporal dynamics remain unclear. Addressing this research gap is significant as it allows researchers to compare information consumption patterns (i.e., fact-checking behavior) of different user profiles from both short-term and long-term perspectives. This, in turn, can furnish platform managers with valuable insights for developing short-term and long-term intervention strategies to counteract the spread of rumors and misinformation in the digital age.

To address these gaps, this study employs a person-centered approach, specifically latent profile analysis (LPA), which classifies individuals based on their responses across multiple dimensions of information literacy. LPA is a statistical technique used to identify latent subgroups within a larger population based on their response across multiple variables. Unlike traditional variable-centered approaches that focus on relationships between variables, LPA is a person-centered method that aims to identify distinct profiles of individuals who share similar response patterns. By considering the intraindividual variation across multiple dimensions of information literacy, LPA enables the identification of distinct user profiles within the information literacy dataset [8]. This study thus transcends the traditional variable-centered approach, providing a more comprehensive perspective on the disparities in fact-checking behaviors among diverse user profiles. Furthermore, to gain deeper insights into how these disparities evolve over time, this study utilizes a longitudinal two-wave design to examine and compare fact-checking behaviors among the identified user profiles in both short-term and long-term contexts. Consequently, this study aims to achieve two main research objectives:

(1) To identify distinct latent user profiles by classifying individuals based on their response to various dimensions of information literacy.
(2) To compare the differences in fact-checking behaviors among these latent user profiles by conducting a two-wave longitudinal investigation.

This study is expected to make several theoretical contributions. Firstly, unlike conventional approaches that treat users as a homogeneous group, this study recognizes user heterogeneity, unveiling various latent user profiles characterized by diverse combinations of information literacy dimensions. This introduces a fresh perspective to information literacy-related studies. Secondly, this study furnishes empirical evidence and establishes connections between different user profiles and their fact-checking behaviors, as well as the evolution of these disparities over time. This enhances our understanding of fact-checking performance among diverse profiles in both short-term and long-term contexts. Thirdly, departing from the conventional variable-centered approaches like correlation and regression analysis, this research employs a person-centered method, specifically LPA, offering a more comprehensive and quantitatively intricate depiction of information literacy dimensions. Consequently, this study introduces a novel research perspective and provides methodological inspiration for future research. In addition, the practical implications highlight the necessity for tailored interventions and educational strategies catering to diverse user profiles based on their information literacy levels, fostering a more effective and targeted approach to mitigating the impact of rumors on social media.

2   Literature Review

2.1   Information Literacy

Information literacy entails a combination of comprehension, learning, and proficiency in managing information, and the awareness of when and what type of information is needed, along with competencies encompassing the discovery, assessment, and ethical utilization of information for the purpose of learning [7]. In light of the complex and dynamic nature of information within social media, research evidence indicates that adopting a multidimensional perspective is useful for comprehensively capturing the broad concept of information literacy [9, 10]. In this regard, Ahmad et al. [7] have proposed a comprehensive framework for information literacy comprising six distinct dimensions:

(1) Information Acquisition: the capacity to proficiently locate and obtain relevant and credible information from diverse sources and formats;

(2) Information Evaluation: the skills to critically assess the quality, credibility, and relevance of information, considering factors such as source credibility, accuracy, objectivity, and timeliness;

(3) Information Use: the capacity to employ acquired information effectively and appropriately for specific tasks or objectives, involving the synthesis, integration, and application of information;

(4)Awareness of Information Environment: recognizing and understanding of the broader information landscape, including diverse information sources, formats, and dissemination channels;

(5) Learning from Information Experience: the capacity to reflect on and extract meaningful insights from the process of seeking, using, and interacting with information to continuously develop and improve information literacy skills;

(6) Information Ethics: the awareness and adherence to ethical principles and values associated with information access, use, and dissemination, encompassing considerations such as intellectual property rights, privacy, and responsible information sharing.

Previous studies on information literacy have predominantly utilized traditional variable-centered methodologies, treating participants as a homogeneous group without delving into their individual distinctions [6, 9, 11]. While variable-centered approaches, such as regression and ANOVA, have merits in establishing relationships between specific predictors and outcomes, they might not capture the nuanced interactions of variables within individuals. In contrast, person-centered analytic methodologies offer a distinct perspective by enabling researchers to explore how variables operate conjointly within individuals. In this sense, the conventional variable-centered approach may overlook the possibility that individuals with varying levels of information literacy form distinct subgroups with unique traits and behavioral patterns. To address this gap, our study adopts a person-centered latent profile analysis (LPA) methodology. By doing so, we aim to uncover diverse user profiles based on individuals' responses to multidimensional information literacy indicators. The LPA approach allows for a more nuanced understanding of information literacy, identifying and analyzing specific subgroups within the larger population. This facilitates the discernment of significant differences among these distinct profiles. By considering the heterogeneity of information literacy, our study contributes to a more comprehensive and accurate portrayal of social media users. This nuanced understanding informs the development of tailored interventions and educational strategies for these different user profiles.

2.2 Information Literacy and Fact-Checking Behaviors

Fact-checking behaviors refer to the actions taken by social media users to verify the accuracy and veracity of online content [12]. In the age of information explosion where an abundance of information swiftly circulates across various social media platforms, fact-checking behaviors play a pivotal role in fighting the spread of misinformation and fake news. Distinguishing truth from falsehood within the vast ocean of information has become increasingly challenging, underscoring the necessity for users to possess the information literacy to critically assess and fact-check the information they encounter. Prior investigations have underscored the significance of information literacy in promoting fact-checking behaviors and combating the dissemination of rumors and fake news [10, 13]. Information literacy fosters the development of critical thinking skills, which are essential for effective fact-checking. It encourages individuals to question information, evaluate arguments, and seek multiple perspectives, thus empowering them to make informed judgments and reduce the likelihood of falling victim to false or misleading information. For example, in a case study by Delellis & Rubin [10], where 18 educators were interviewed, qualitative findings identified a significant overlap between skills related to information literacy, including traits such as skepticism and the capacity to synthesize diverse perspectives, and the detection of fake news, underscoring the inherent connection between information literacy and the truth discernment. Additionally, Jones-Jang et al. [6] empirically investigated whether individuals exhibiting higher levels of literacy, including media literacy, information literacy, news literacy, and digital literacy, demonstrate greater competence in discerning fake news. Their findings suggested that among various literacies, it is information literacy that significantly increases the likelihood of discerning fake news. Besides, Wu et al. [14] employed a combination of qualitative and quantitative methods to establish a typology of rumor-combating behaviors. The results emphasized that users' efforts to enhance their information and media literacy constitute an important approach to combating the spread of rumors.

Nonetheless, despite evidence from these studies supporting a significant link between user information literacy and fact-checking behavior, a substantial gap remains in understanding how different user profiles, characterized by varying levels of information literacy, contribute to fact-checking behavior. This knowledge gap hinders our ability to ascertain discernible distinctions in fact-checking behaviors among distinct user profiles and whether these distinctions persist over time. To bridge this gap, the current study employs a two-wave longitudinal study to scrutinize variations in fact-checking behaviors across different user profiles and how these variations evolve over time. In other words, this study aims to identify whether certain profiles exhibit a higher inclination towards engaging in fact-checking behaviors compared to others. Furthermore, it endeavors to determine whether these differences consistently endure over time or whether specific user profiles are more susceptible to a decline in fact-checking behaviors from a long-term perspective. By investigating these aspects, this study seeks to enrich our understanding of the intricate dynamics of fact-checking behaviors and their sustainability within diverse user profiles on social media platforms.

3   Methods

3.1   Participants and Procedure

We recruited participants through Credamo, a professional data platform in China, which offers functionality similar to that of Amazon Mechanical Turk. This platform ensures reliable data aligned with top-tier academic standards, enhancing the credibility of the findings. A two-wave longitudinal study with a time lag of one month was conducted, and informed consent was obtained from all participants. The informed consent form comprised three key elements: (1) Providing participants with all relevant information that may influence their decisions to participate; (2) Ensuring participants fully understood the provided information; (3) Emphasizing the voluntary nature of participation and participants' freedom to withdraw at any time.

To maintain data quality, attention-check questions and trap questions were included in both Time 1 (April 2023) and 2 (May 2023). At Time 1, participants were asked to respond to measurements related to six information literacy dimensions, fact-checking behaviors, and demographic questions, resulting in 632 responses. After excluding invalid responses due to short completion times, a large number of consecutive identical values, or failure to pass the attention checks and trap questions, we retained 501 valid responses. One month later, at Time 2, we invited the same 501 respondents to complete a follow-up investigation focusing on measuring fact-checking behaviors, resulting in 356 submitted responses. Using the same evaluation criteria as in Time 1, we excluded six invalid responses, leaving 350 valid responses that could be matched to Time 1 data. The demographic distribution of these final 350 participants is presented in Table 1.

Table 1. The demographic distribution of participants

Variable	Category	Participants (N = 350)	
		Frequency	Percent
Gender	Male	185	52.9
	Female	165	47.1
Age	≤ 20	13	3.7
	21–25	97	27.7
	26–30	88	25.1
	31–40	105	30
	41–50	31	8.9
	>50	16	4.6
Monthly income (¥)	<5000	133	38
	5000–10000	141	40.3
	10001–15000	38	10.9
	>15000	38	10.9
Education	≤ High school	33	9.4
	Junior college	73	20.9
	Bachelor	196	56
	Master's or Ph.D	48	13.7

3.2 Measurements

Information Literacy. To ensure the reliability and validity of the survey instrument, we adopted the established scales for measuring information literacy and modified the item wording to align with the specific context of this study. We utilized twenty items adapted from Ahmad et al. [7] to capture the six dimensions of information literacy. These items were evaluated using a 7-point Likert scale. To assess the content validity of these measurement items, we invited two master's students and two doctoral students to independently evaluate the 20 items. They were asked to assess the items for potential issues such as semantic ambiguity, comprehension difficulties, and lack of logical clarity. Synthesizing their insights, we made necessary adjustments to the measurement. Subsequently, we conducted a pretest with 30 social media users using the Credamo platform. Participants were instructed to assess the items according to the aforementioned criteria. Based on the feedback received, we further refined the measurement. The final measurement items are presented in Table 2.

Actual Fact-checking Behavior. To mitigate potential inflation of self-reported intention due to social desirability bias, this study measures users' actual fact-checking behavior rather than relying on self-reported fact-checking intention. The assessment process of actual fact-checking behavior involves presenting participants with fact-checking content links, and their engagement with these links serves as an indicator of genuine fact-checking behavior during two distinct time periods, denoted as Time 1 (T1) and Time 2 (T2). At both T1 and T2, participants were presented with four rumor headlines, each accompanied by corresponding fact-checking links.

To ensure the selection of unbiased information materials for assessing participants' fact-checking behaviors, the following steps were undertaken. Firstly, to avoid potential bias from concentrating on a single topic, this study included rumors spanning four distinct and popular topics: health, social welfare, technology, and nature. A total of 32 rumors, with eight rumors for each topic, were gathered from the official platform "https://www.piyao.org.cn," sponsored by the Cyberspace Administration of China, which is dedicated to debunking false rumors and misinformation.

Subsequently, to refine the choice of rumor materials, our primary criterion was to assess their level of misleadingness. This was necessary because false rumors with low misleadingness might prompt participants to rely on their own cognitive judgment and experiences rather than engaging in fact-checking. Such cases could potentially fail to accurately reflect and distinguish the fact-checking habits of the participants. To maximize perplexity and judgment difficulty, we recruited 30 social media users to assess the veracity of the 32 rumors (True/False). Based on the accuracy of the participants' truth discernment, we identified the two rumors with the highest error rates among the eight rumors for each topic. These final eight false rumors, comprising the two most misleading rumors from the four different topics, were selected as the information materials for T1 and T2.

Furthermore, fact-checking messages associated with each of the eight rumors were crafted based on official truth statements obtained from "https://www.piyao.org.cn." An example of such fact-checking content is provided in Fig. 1. Participants were given the option to click on these fact-checking content links. If they chose to fact-check, they could click on the link below the rumor headlines to access the corresponding rebuttals. The cumulative count of links clicked at both T1 and T2 served as a quantitative measure to assess the extent of participants' actual fact-checking behaviors.

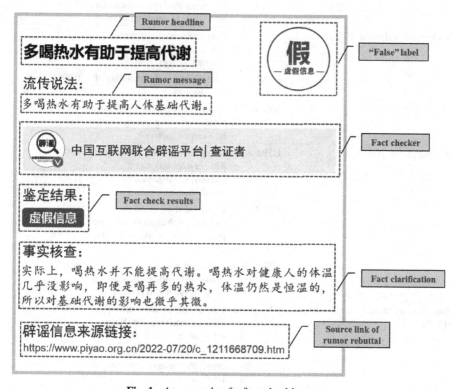

Fig. 1. An example of a fact-checking page

Table 2. The measurements and factor loadings

Construct	Factors	Measurement items	Factor loadings
Information acquisition (ACQ)	ACQ1	1. I can easily get my hands on right information when needed	0.898
	ACQ2	2. When looking for information I can easily identify the right information sources	0.877
	ACQ3	3. I often get involved in discussions with others to get information	0.704
Information evaluation (EVA)	EVA1	1. I can spot inaccuracy, errors, etc. in information acquired from different sources	0.890
	EVA2	2. I can determine the reliability of the information	0.896
	EVA3	3. I can identify points of agreement and disagreement among information sources	0.923
Information use (USE)	USE1	1. I am good at putting information into personal action (e.g., problem-solving, informed decisions, etc.)	0.889
	USE2	2. I am good at using information for positive changes in individual practices (e.g., work, study, life, etc.)	0.911
	USE3	3. I am good at using information to challenge traditional mindsets to see things in different ways	0.860
Awareness of information environment (ENV)	ENV1	1. I understand online platforms' rules for receiving and sharing information	0.887
	ENV2	2. I know how online platforms enable their users to get needed information	0.859
	ENV3	3. I understand online platforms' acceptable ways of information sharing	0.828
	ENV4	4. I am aware of the organization of information on online platforms	0.787

(continued)

Table 2. (*continued*)

Construct	Factors	Measurement items	Factor loadings
Learning from information experience (LEA)	LEA1	1. I can identify what sources and processes will be helpful for finding and using information in the future	0.818
	LEA2	2. When I find new information, I try to find out how I can use it in new ways	0.764
	LEA3	3. I revise my thinking as a result of group discussions or information collected	0.795
	LEA4	4. Information makes me think or act beyond the boundary of my own experiences	0.697
Information ethics (ETH)	ETH1	1. I always pay attention to information privacy protection in online environments	0.845
	ETH2	2. I obtain, store, and disseminate information according to laws and regulations	0.875
	ETH3	3. I understand when to give credit or hide my information sources	0.825

3.3 Analytic Approach

Latent Profile Analysis (LPA) categorizes individuals into distinct classes based on their response patterns to a continuous dependent variable. It uses maximum likelihood estimation to determine the probability of accurate classification for each person and identifies the overall best-fitting class. The modeling process iteratively adds classes to find the optimal fit to the data. Various fit indices were used to determine the optimal number of profiles, including log-likelihood (LL), Akaike information criteria (AIC), Bayesian information criterion (BIC), sample-size adjusted BIC (SSA-BIC), Lo–Mendell–Rubin likelihood ratio test (LMR), bootstrap likelihood test (BLRT), and entropy [15]. Specifically, lower values for LL, AIC, BIC, and SSA-BIC indicate a better-fitting model. A significant p-value for LMR and BLRT suggests that the k-1–class model should be rejected in favor of a k–class model (k = number of profiles) [16]. While no consensus exists regarding a specific cut-off value for entropy, higher values approaching 1.0 signify fewer classification errors within the model. Additionally, it was ensured that the smallest profile in the final solution should contain at least five percent of the sample [16]. Moreover, the interpretability and distinctive characteristics of each profile played a crucial role in determining the ultimate solution.

4 Results

4.1 Reliability and Validity of Measurements

As depicted in Table 3, both alpha and composite reliability (CR) meet the recommended threshold of 0.7, while the average variance extracted (AVE) surpasses the suggested level of 0.5, thereby affirming sufficient reliability [17]. In addition, the factor loadings for the measurement items range from 0.697 to 0.923, as detailed in Table 2, signifying a strong convergent validity. To evaluate the discriminant validity of the constructs, we compared the correlations between constructs with the square root of the AVE for each construct. Our findings revealed that the square root of the AVE for each construct surpasses the correlations with other constructs, providing robust evidence of discriminant validity [17]. Consequently, the measurements exhibit satisfactory reliability and validity.

Table 3. The reliability and validity of measurements

Construct	Mean	SD	Alpha	CR	AVE
ACQ	5.280	1.039	0.770	0.869	0.691
EVA	5.143	1.154	0.888	0.930	0.815
USE	5.279	1.165	0.864	0.917	0.787
ENV	5.545	0.994	0.863	0.906	0.707
LEA	5.409	0.897	0.771	0.853	0.593
ETH	5.891	0.945	0.808	0.885	0.720

4.2 LPA Results

Profile Analyses. To explore information literacy profiles, we conducted a latent profile analysis (LPA). The six dimensions of information literacy were used as latent profile indicators. LPA is an abductive approach, particularly suitable for investigating phenomena lacking substantial theoretical guidance for a *priori* classification, as is the case in this study [15]. In line with established practices, we initiated the modeling process by specifying two latent profiles and subsequently increased the number of profiles until the model fit was no longer satisfactory [18]. According to the results presented in Table 4, the three-profile solution best fits the dataset. This solution demonstrated lower metrics for LL, AIC, BIC, and SSA-BIC compared to the two-profile solution, thus indicating a better-fitting model. Besides, it demonstrated a relatively high entropy exceeding 0.80, yielded significant results for both LMR and BLRT, and encompassed more than five percent of the sample within the smallest profile, all while maintaining theoretically meaningful profiles.

During the subsequent phase of the latent profile analysis, we examined the overarching trends within the profiles. To achieve this, we analyzed the mean values and standard deviations (SD) of the study variables within the latent profiles. As depicted in Table 5,

Table 4. Fit statistics for profile structures

Model	Log -likelihood	AIC	BIC	SSA-BIC	Entropy	LMR p-value	BLRT p-value	Number	Smallest profile (%)
Class 2	−2429.762	4897.523	4970.824	4910.549	0.982	0.013	0.000	44/306	12.571
Class 3	−2183.374	4418.749	4519.055	4436.574	0.889	0.003	0.000	142/29/179	8.286
Class 4	−2074.240	4214.480	4341.792	4237.104	0.914	0.065	0.000	32/153/14/151	4
Class 5	−2002.797	4085.595	4239.912	4113.018	0.896	0.023	0.000	7/22/41/157/123	2

these latent profiles exhibited distinct characteristics across six dimensions of information literacy. Specifically, Profile 1 comprised individuals with low levels of information acquisition (ACQ), information evaluation (EVA), information use (USE), awareness of information environment (AIE), learning from information experience (LIE), and information ethics (ETH). Therefore, it was labeled "the information literacy novice profile" and included 29 users, constituting 8.286% of the total participants. Profile 2 contained individuals displaying moderate levels of ACQ, EVA, USE, AIE, LIE, and ETH. This cluster was labeled "the information literacy competent profile" and consisted of 142 users, accounting for 40.571% of the participants. Profile 3 comprised individuals exhibiting high levels of ACQ, EVA, USE, AIE, LIE, and ETH. It was labeled "the information literacy proficient profile" and included 179 users, representing 51.143% of the participants. Figure 2 provides a graphical representation of latent profiles using estimated means.

Table 5. Three latent profiles across six information literacy indicators

	Profile 1	Profile 2	Profile 3
Sample Size (% of Sample)	N = 29 (8.286%)	N = 142 (40.571%)	N = 179 (51.143%)
	Mean		
Information acquisition (ACQ)	3.136	4.941	5.894
Information evaluation (EVA)	2.566	4.753	5.868
Information use (USE)	2.567	4.905	6.014
Awareness of information environment (AIE)	3.045	5.277	6.161
Learning from information experience (LIE)	3.519	5.132	5.933
Information ethics (ETH)	3.6	5.736	6.385

Profile Comparisons on the Outcome of Fact-checking Behavior. After identifying three sets of latent user profiles through the optimal LPA solution, our focus turned

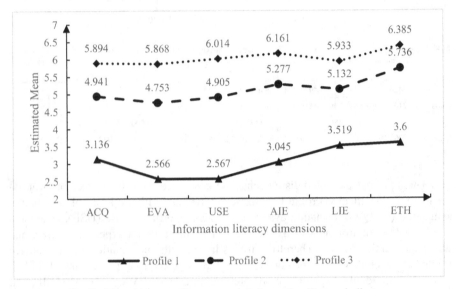

Fig. 2. Three latent profiles across six information literacy indicators

to assess the statistical significance of the connections between the derived latent user profiles and the distal outcome variable (i.e., fact-checking behavior). This involved conducting a series of pairwise chi-square difference tests to gauge the significance of variations in fact-checking behaviors across distinct user profiles. To conduct these tests, we employed the Bolck-Croon-Hagenaars (BCH) method, which is recognized as a robust approach for comparing distal continuous outcome variables like fact-checking behaviors [16]. This method evaluates means for continuous distal outcomes across latent profiles to identify differences between information literacy profiles. Specifically, we employed the BCH procedure to examine the disparities among the three profiles concerning fact-checking behaviors at Time 1 (T1). As detailed in Table 6, the BCH test results demonstrated significant distinctions among the profiles in relation to this measure. Pairwise comparisons revealed significant differences between all three profiles. However, it is worth noting an exception in the comparison between Profile 2 (the information literacy competent profile) ($M = 2.653, SE = 0.095$) and Profile 3 (the information literacy proficient profile) ($M = 2.812, SE = 0.091$) for fact-checking behaviors (difference = -0.159, p > 0.05). A similar analysis was conducted to assess differences among the three profiles regarding fact-checking behaviors at Time 2 (T2). The BCH test results also indicated significant differences among the profiles in relation to this validity measure. Pairwise comparisons again revealed significant differences between all three profiles. Nonetheless, a notable exception was observed in the comparison between Profile 1 (Information novice) ($M = 2.138, SE = 0.206$) and Profile 2 (Information competent) ($M = 2.252, SE = 0.116$) for fact-checking behaviors (difference = $-0.114, p > 0.05$).

Table 6. Distal outcome (BCH) results comparing fact-checking behaviors among the three information literacy profiles.

T1: Fact-checking behavior			T2: Fact-checking behavior		
	Mean	S.E		Mean	S.E
Profile 1	1.861	0.228	Profile 1	2.138	0.206
Profile 2	2.653	0.095	Profile 2	2.252	0.116
Profile 3	2.812	0.091	Profile 3	2.615	0.097
	Chi-square	P-value		Chi-square	P-value
Overall test	15.087	0.001	Overall test	7.410	0.025
Profile 1 vs. 2	10.290	0.001	Profile 1 vs. 2	0.235	0.628
Profile 2 vs. 3	1.326	0.250	Profile 2 vs. 3	5.167	0.023
Profile 1 vs. 3	15.075	0.000	Profile 1 vs. 3	4.403	0.036

5 Discussion and Conclusion

5.1 Discussion of Key Findings

The present study employed a person-centered LPA approach to identify three user profiles based on individuals' multidimensional information literacy: The information literacy proficient profile, the information literacy competent profile, and the information literacy novice profile. This study further investigated the relationship between these three profiles and social media users' fact-checking behaviors. The results indicated significant differences in fact-checking behaviors among the three user profiles in the short term (T1). Specifically, the proficient and competent profiles engaged in fact-checking more frequently than the novice profile, while no significant difference was found between the proficient and competent profiles. In the long term (T2), there were overall significant differences in fact-checking behavior among these user profiles, but the pairwise comparisons yielded different results compared to the short-term differences. Specifically, the proficient profile engaged in fact-checking more frequently than both the competent and novice profiles, while no significant difference was observed between the competent and novice profiles. It is worth noting that comparing the results between these two periods revealed that the proficient profile consistently exhibits frequent fact-checking behavior in both the short and long term, whereas the frequency of fact-checking behavior decreased gradually over time for the competent profile. These findings shed light on the variations in fact-checking behaviors among different user profiles and how these variations change over time.

5.2 Theoretical Implications

This study holds three significant theoretical implications. Firstly, in contrast to previous research that treated users as a homogeneous group, this study delineates three distinct user profiles based on their levels of information literacy. The identified user profiles shed light on the interplay among different dimensions of information literacy, indicating that diverse subpopulations exhibit varying combinations of these dimensions. By scrutinizing the heterogeneity within social media users, this study validates the necessity of transcending a homogeneous interpretation of information literacy, highlights the coexistence and comparability of various information literacy dimensions within individuals, and underscores the variations among distinct user subgroups. Therefore, by exploring the multifaceted nature of information literacy and its diverse manifestations among different user profiles, this study contributes to the current understanding of subpopulations with differing information literacy levels.

Secondly, this study investigates the relationship between user profiles and social media users' fact-checking behavior, not only revealing behavioral disparities among distinct user subgroups but also elucidating how these disparities change over time. The findings demonstrate that, whether in the short or long term, Profile 3 (the information literacy proficient profile) consistently outperforms Profile 1 (the information literacy novice profile) in fact-checking behaviors. Additionally, in the long term, the fact-checking performance of Profile 2 (the information literacy competent profile) gradually decreases to the point where there is no significant difference compared to that of Profile 1 (the information literacy novice profile). These results shed light on how the relationship between information literacy and fact-checking behaviors differ across distinct user profiles, providing a novel and unique theoretical perspective to understand and explain fact-checking behaviors. By employing a longitudinal research design, this study further examines the evolving trajectories of behavioral differences among distinct user profiles across different time spans, thus developing a more comprehensive understanding of the connection between user profiles and fact-checking behaviors.

Thirdly, unlike previous studies that heavily relied on the traditional variable-centered approach, this study made a noteworthy contribution by adopting a person-centered approach, specifically utilizing latent profile analysis (LPA). While this analytical strategy has gained increased attention in organizational science in recent years, its implementation within the library and information science (LIS) discipline remains limited. Through the LPA approach, this study successfully identified three distinct user profiles and revealed significant differences among subgroups in terms of their fact-checking behaviors. This methodological shift offers a fresh perspective for future research, indicating that individuals can be classified into different subgroups characterized by different configurable profiles of attributes, and enabling the identification of latent user subgroups within a larger population based on a certain set of variables. We also call for greater attention from LIS scholars towards the person-centered approach and LPA analytical strategy.

5.3 Practical Implications

From a practical perspective, this study inspires social media platforms to adopt a user-centric approach, offering tailored interventions for specific user profiles. To begin with, users falling into the category of information literacy novice profile exhibit lower frequencies of fact-checking behavior in both the short and long term. Consequently, platforms should prioritize ongoing efforts to support this group and implement more frequent intervention strategies. For example, platforms could organize regular social media information literacy training and educational programs designed specifically for the information literacy novice profile. These initiatives aim to enhance their information literacy levels and foster a culture of actively verifying the authenticity of information within this group. By delivering accessible and engaging educational content, platforms can effectively empower the information literacy novice subgroup to critically evaluate the information they encounter on social media.

Secondly, it is also important to pay attention to users falling within the information literacy competent profile, as their fact-checking behavior tends to decline over time, gradually resembling that of individuals in the information literacy novice profile. Therefore, platforms should maintain continuous vigilance with regard to the behavioral shifts within the information literacy competent profile and engage in long-term intervention to prevent the shift towards behavior patterns of the information literacy novice profile. For instance, platforms can implement personalized notifications and reminders to encourage individuals in the information literacy competent profile to fact-check information before sharing it within their social networks. Additionally, platforms can establish collaborative initiatives that involve individuals in the information literacy competent profile in the process of identifying and flagging misinformation. This approach can help reinforce their fact-checking habits, thereby sustaining their critical thinking skills and maintaining a relatively high level of information literacy.

5.4 Limitations and Future Research

This study has certain limitations that should be acknowledged. Firstly, this research was conducted within the Chinese context, possibly leading to notable disparities in the levels of information literacy among social media users across different countries. This could result in variations in user profile classification. Therefore, it would be advantageous to assess the information literacy of social media users in other countries in order to ascertain the generalizability of our findings. Secondly, this research solely focuses on behavioral changes over time among various information literacy profiles, without exploring the underlying reasons and mechanisms driving such changes. Future studies may delve deeper into the intermediate processes to gain a more comprehensive understanding of the behavioral evolution within information literacy profiles. Third, future research could incorporate objective measures to assess information literacy and investigate the impact of different user profiles on other rumor response behaviors, as well as track the evolving trends of these impacts over time.

6 Conclusions

This study confirms that social media users can be categorized into three different user profiles based on their information literacy levels: The information literacy proficient profile, the information literacy competent profile, and the information literacy novice profile. Moreover, this study highlights the significant disparities in fact-checking behaviors among these three user profiles both in the short and long term. Specifically, the proficient profile, whether in the short term or long term, consistently exhibits a higher frequency of fact-checking behavior compared to the novice profile. However, although the competent profile initially outperforms the novice profile in fact-checking behavior, the behavioral frequency gradually declines over time, eventually becoming indistinguishable from that of the novice profile. To summarize, this study sheds light on the differentiated fact-checking behaviors associated with distinct information literacy profiles, emphasizing the evolving and dynamic nature of these behaviors over time.

Acknowledgements. The work described in this paper was partially supported by the grants from the National Natural Science Foundation of China (Project No. 72274144, 72311540158), and the Humanities and Social Sciences Foundation of the Ministry of Education, China (Project No. 22YJA870013).

Disclosure of Interests. The authors have no competing interests to declare that are relevant to the content of this article.

References

1. Dong, W., Liao, S., Zhang, Z.: Leveraging financial social media data for corporate fraud detection. J. Manag. Inf. Syst.Manag. Inf. Syst. **35**(2), 461–487 (2018)
2. Alkhodair, S.A., Ding, S.H., Fung, B.C., Liu, J.: Detecting breaking news rumors of emerging topics in social media. Inf. Process. Manage. **57**(2), 102018 (2020)
3. Moon, W.K., Chung, M., Jones-Jang, S.M.: How can we fight partisan biases in the COVID-19 pandemic? AI source labels on fact-checking messages reduce motivated reasoning. Mass Commun. Soc.Commun. Soc. **26**(4), 646–670 (2023)
4. Çömlekçi, M.F.: Why do fact-checking organizations go beyond fact-checking? a Leap toward media and information literacy education. Int. J. Commun.Commun. **16**, 4563–4583 (2022)
5. De Paor, S., Heravi, B.: Information literacy and fake news: How the field of librarianship can help combat the epidemic of fake news. J. Acad. Librariansh.Librariansh. **46**(5), 102218 (2020)
6. Jones-Jang, S.M., Mortensen, T., Liu, J.: Does media literacy help identification of fake news? Information literacy helps, but other literacies don't. Am. Behav. Sci.Behav. Sci. **65**(2), 371–388 (2021)
7. Ahmad, F., Widén, G., Huvila, I.: The impact of workplace information literacy on organizational innovation: an empirical study. Int. J. Inf. Manage. **51**, 102041 (2020)
8. Qahri-Saremi, H., Turel, O.: Ambivalence and coping responses in post-adoptive information systems use. J. Manag. Inf. Syst.Manag. Inf. Syst. **37**(3), 820–848 (2020)
9. Çoklar, A.N., Yaman, N.D., Yurdakul, I.K.: Information literacy and digital nativity as determinants of online information search strategies. Comput. Hum. Behav.. Hum. Behav. **70**, 1–9 (2017)
10. Delellis, N.S., Rubin, V.L.: Educators' perceptions of information literacy and skills required to spot 'fake news.' Proc. Assoc. Inform. Sci. Technol. **55**(1), 785–787 (2018)
11. Wu, D., Zhou, C., Li, Y., Chen, M.: Factors associated with teachers' competence to develop students' information literacy: a multilevel approach. Comput. Educ.. Educ. **176**, 104360 (2022)
12. Jiang, S.: The roles of worry, social media information overload, and social media fatigue in hindering health fact-checking. Social Media+ Society **8**(3), 20563051221113070 (2022)
13. Durodolu, O.O., Ibenne, S.K.: The fake news infodemic vs information literacy. Library Hi Tech News **37**(7), 13–14 (2020)

14. Wu, Y., Shen, X.L., Sun, Y.: Establishing the typology and the underlying structure of rumor-combating behaviors: a multidimensional scaling approach. Inf. Technol. People **36**(7), 2661–2686 (2023)
15. Campion, E.D., Csillag, B.: Multiple jobholding motivations and experiences: a typology and latent profile analysis. J. Appl. Psychol. **107**(8), 1261–1287 (2022)
16. Tian, A.W., Meyer, J.P., Ilic-Balas, T., Espinoza, J.A., Pepper, S.: In search of the pseudo-transformational leader: a person-centered approach. J. Bus. Res. **158**, 113675 (2023)
17. Fornell, C., Larcker, D.F.: Structural equation models with unobservable variables and measurement error: algebra and statistics. J. Mark. Res. **18**(3), 382–388 (1981)
18. Nylund, K.L., Asparouhov, T., Muthén, B.O.: Deciding on the number of classes in latent class analysis and growth mixture modeling: a Monte Carlo simulation study. Struct. Equ. Modeling. Equ. Modeling **14**(4), 535–569 (2007)

Libraries, Bibliometrics and Metadata

What Research Skills Do Scholars Excel at?—Based on Individual Contribution and External Recognition

Aoxia Xiao[1]($\boxtimes$) (iD), Siluo Yang[1] (iD), Mingliang Yue[2] (iD), and Minshu Jin[1]

[1] School of Information Management, Wuhan University, Wuhan, People's Republic of China
xax_929@whu.edu.cn
[2] Wuhan Library, Chinese Academy of Sciences, Wuhan, People's Republic of China

Abstract. Diverse research skills are used by scholars in their studies, such as methods design, data investigation, and writing, which significantly influence their research quality and subsequent scientific reputation. Existing scholar evaluation programs focus on providing a composite indicator for ranking scholars and lack specific analysis of scholars' research skill performance. This study proposes a practical framework that characterizes research skill performance from two perspectives: individual contribution and external recognition. Individual contribution is assessed through the author's contribution statement, while external recognition is evaluated through citations and altmetrics. Based on these two perspectives, the framework measures scholars' skill performance in three dimensions: proficiency, academic reputation, and social impact. These dimensions provide a detailed and specific evaluation of individual scholar performance and allow for the advancement of successful research collaborations. The application of this framework to a specific scholar, Smith GD, who has published the most articles in the open-access journal *PLOS Medicine*, demonstrates its effectiveness in portraying scholars' academic performance. The results show that Smith GD shows strong research skills in methodology, results analysis and validation, and manuscript writing, but could benefit from collaborating with colleagues who excel in practical operations and external support.

Keywords: Scholar Evaluation · Research Skills · Academic Performance · Author Contribution

1 Introduction

Academic success is strongly influenced by reputation [1], which is built through a researcher's publication performance and authorship claims [2]. This reputation is vital for obtaining positions, funding, tenure, and recognition through prizes. Scholars are evaluated throughout their careers, and scientific output is the main source of reputation accumulation and academic recognition [3].

Traditionally, bibliometric indicators are based on mathematical foundations, which rely on the publications as a measure of individual contribution, and on the citations

I. Sserwanga et al. (Eds.): iConference 2024, LNCS 14597, pp. 301–321, 2024.
https://doi.org/10.1007/978-3-031-57860-1_21

as a measure of external recognition, regardless of whether simple or complex calculations are used [2]. There are three ways to calculate author-level impact [4]: count the publications(Number of publications, Academic age, Authors-per-paper), count the citations(Number of Citations, Citations per paper, Age-Weighted Citation Rate [5]), or combine the publication and citation counts to create a "hybrid indicator"(h-index [6], g-index [7], h2 [8], e-Index [9]). Additionally, some more complex metrics may adjust models for different subject areas, the number of authors, and author age or career length. To conclude, their ultimate goal is to construct a comprehensive metric to measure the academic performance of scholars and form researcher rankings used in career evaluations, funding, and tenure decisions. However, the evaluation of scholars cannot rely on only one indicator, which makes it difficult to obtain a complete characterization of scholars' academic personalities and evaluate the performance of specific research skills.

For a long time, the research skills cultivation of graduate students or specific personnel (especially medical talents) has been attached great importance [10–14], but the evaluation of scholars has neglected the examination of the performance of research skills. However, the existing macro-level evaluation of researchers cannot reflect the performance of individuals in specific skills, which may affect the accuracy of the results when used to solve practical problems such as finding collaborators [15]. Meanwhile, interdisciplinary collaboration in science is becoming increasingly common, and quantifying the competence and influence of individuals is a key point in facilitating team building, evaluation, and refinement [15, 16]. Currently, some studies identify scholars' skills through the terms extracted from scholarly outputs and calculate skill levels based on the similarity between scholars [17–19]. However, on the one hand, the skills identified through terminology extraction do not cover the full range of skills required in scientific research and reflect only specific skills in particular research areas rather than describing the generic skills of academic research. On the other hand, such studies focus more on the skill sets of researchers in academic teams, and there is still a lack of research on the measurement of author-level skill.

The introduction of author contribution lists in scholarly publishing allows researchers to list all research elements and contributors involved in a study. A standardized "taxonomy" enables researchers to assign contributor roles in a structured format through manuscript submission software [20], promoting collaboration by clearly delineating each contributor's expertise [16]. Contribution information has been used in credit allocation and author ranking [21–23]. While the existing studies have put forward ideas on the evaluation of researchers based on the author's contribution, like traditional author-level metrics, they mainly focus on comprehensive evaluation and lack characterization of scholars' research skills. Using author contribution information, Kong et al. [15] proposed a hypergraph-based model for assessing scientific research skills, which assumes that an author's skill performance is determined by their engagement within a specific area. However, this study focused only on individual contributions and ignored external recognition.

In this study, we analyze the categories of research skills and the dimensions of scholars' skill performance and design a scheme for portraying research skills that incorporates both scholars' self-contribution and external recognition. Research skills refer to the professional skills possessed by researchers that can directly affect the output of research achievements. This study used the author's contribution statement to identify research skill categories while classifying scholars' skill performance into proficiency, academic reputation, and social impact.

2 Research Objective

The measurement of scholars' research skills wants to address the questions of "what researchers are doing" and "how well they are doing." This study is based on the following logic: (1) To reflect the proficiency of scholars' research skills by calculating the participation and contribution of the scholar to the research project. Specifically, it is assumed that the fewer the participating authors and the higher the authorship order of the scholar, the greater the scholar's proficiency in the corresponding skill. (2) To reflect the academic reputation accumulated by scholars through their research work, citation content analysis can be used. By analyzing the context of citations, the higher the citation strength of the content involved in the relevant skill and the higher the contribution of the evaluated author in the skill, the higher the academic reputation of the author in this skill accumulated through this achievement. (3) To reflect the social impact of research work that scholars have participated in, altmetrics indicators can be used. The higher the altmetrics indicators score of the research outcome and the higher the contribution of the evaluated author in the skill, the greater the social impact of the author in this skill accumulated through this outcome. It should be noted that this study does not perform a content analysis of altmetrics as the citation. Citations have richer content than altmetrics as they are part of scholarly discourse, making content analysis feasible. Altmetrics, on the other hand, are mainly based on social media and online activity, such as likes and shares, which lack the necessary depth and context for content analysis.

Therefore, we propose a quantitative approach to characterize researchers' academic expertise. The major contributions of this research are that the academic performance of scholars is evaluated from different research skills (e.g., conceptualization, methodology, investigation, formal analysis, visualization funding acquisition, and writing), and described from three dimensions: proficiency, academic reputation, and social impact (Fig. 1). This approach provides a more nuanced understanding of a scholar's strengths and weaknesses across different research skills and dimensions, thus enabling a more comprehensive view of their academic performance. In addition, valuable insights into the distribution of skills and expertise within a research team can be provided. Besides, the approach allows for comparisons of performance across different stages of a scholar's career, as well as within the same skill across different research topics. This is important as academic performance is often influenced by various factors, such as changes in research interests or research positions.

Then the method proposed in this study can solve the following problems: (1) measuring the gap between the different academic skills of the same scholar and identifying any tendencies for scholars to excel in certain skills, (2) examining the variations in academic skills demonstrated by the same scholar at different stages of their academic career, and (3) comparing the academic performance of scholars in the same skill across different research fields.

Fig. 1. The performance of research skills in different dimensions

3 Methods

In this study, scholars' proficiency in research skills is evaluated by calculating their author contributions based on the contribution statement, while academic reputation and social impact are assessed using citation and altmetrics indicators (Fig. 2). However, it is important to consider scholars' actual participation and contribution share when calculating their academic reputation and social impact, thus the final results should take into account both the author's contribution and the citation or altmetrics indicators.

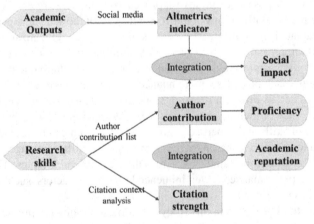

Fig. 2. Indicator Construction Logic

3.1 Author Contribution-Based Proficiency of Scholars' Research Skills

This study uses two steps to calculate research skill proficiency: (1) Classification of research skills categories. This study uses Contributor Roles Taxonomy (CRediT) as the basis for identifying research skills involving various aspects of scientific research such as research conception, methodological design, practical operation, analysis of results, manuscript writing, and external support. (2) Calculation of proficiency indicators. This study uses Harmonic Counting [24–26], which calculates the weighting of researchers' participation and contribution, to reflect scholars' research skills proficiency.

CRediT Standards and Skill Categories. The contributorship model of authorship has been proposed by the scientific community to address the limitation of only allowing manuscript participants to be listed as authors [27]. In 2014, the international standards body CASRAI proposed the Contributor Roles Taxonomy (CRediT), based on the work of Allen et al.[20]. The CRediT laid the foundation for quantitative analysis of author contributions and became an ANSI/NISO standard in February 2022 (https://credit.niso.org/). CRediT has been used in over 120 journals until 2019 and its use is still growing substantially [28].

This study uses the CRediT criteria as a basis for classifying research skills. The 14 roles in CRediT are divided into 6 categories according to the research process, including conceptualization, methodology, practical operation, results analysis and validation, external support, and manuscript writing (see Table 1). The six categories of research skills essentially encompass the steps involved in a complete research process and the competencies required.

Table 1. Classification of research skills and their meanings

Research skill	Meaning	CRediT role included
Conceptualization	Ideas: formulation or evolution of overarching research goals and aims	Conceptualization
Methodology	Development or design of methodology; creation of models	Methodology
Practical operation	Implement specific operations in the research process	Investigation, Data curation, Software, Visualization
Results analysis and validation	Analysis and validation of the findings and conclusion of the study	Formal analysis, Validation
External support	Provide or obtain external research support	Funding acquisition, Resources, Project administration, Supervision
Manuscript writing	Write or revise the manuscript	Writing – original draft, Writing – review & editing

Contribution-Based Proficiency Calculation. The calculation of proficiency includes two important weights: the weight of authors in the same contributor role, and the weight of the contributor role in the whole study. Generally, the more often a skill is used by the scholar, the higher their proficiency is. For the specific research skill, the higher the authorship order of the scholar and the more important the skill in the study, the more proficient the scholar is in this skill. We assume that the article has a total of m authors and n contributor roles. P_{ij} is the participation ratio of the j-th author to the i-th contributor role ($i = 1, 2,..., n; j = 1, 2,..., m$), and W_i is the weight of the i-th contributor role in a study. Then the proficiency $Proj$ obtained by the j-th author from a research skill containing k contributor roles in a study can be expressed by Eq. (1).

$$Proj = \frac{\sum_{i=1}^{k} P_{ij} W_i}{k} \tag{1}$$

Each contributor role can include multiple co-authors [21], which makes determining P_{ij} an important issue. Every paper has an authorship order and more and more studies are ranking authorship in terms of the agreed contribution size among authors [29]. Furthermore, the authorship order within contributor roles is highly consistent with the order of article bylines [30]. In addition, the authors with the higher order of authorship tend to participate in more contributor roles and contribute more to the studies [31]–[33]. Therefore, we divide the author weights in the same contributor role according to the order of the author's signature, i.e., P_{ij} depends on the author's ranking r in the contributor role, and this order is based on the authorship order of the whole article. Harmonic Counting [26] has shown good adaptability and fairness among all existing order-based weight assignment methods [34, 35], so we use Harmonic Counting to calculate the weights of authors in the contributor role. Then the scholarly contribution of the r-th author in a contributor role containing M authors can be expressed by Eq. (2).

$$P_{ij} = \frac{\frac{1}{r}}{\left(1 + \frac{1}{2} + \frac{1}{3} + \ldots + \frac{1}{M}\right)} \tag{2}$$

Besides, since the skills valued vary across subject areas and outcome types, the weighting of skills is obtained by calculating the ranking of skills in the field (see Eq. (3)). In a previous study, Kong et al.[15] calculated the weights of the edges in the hypergraph consisting of authors, skills, and research fields based on this logic.

$$R_i = 1 - \frac{\gamma - 1}{L} \tag{3}$$

R_i denotes the percentile ranking of the i-th contributor role. γ denotes the ranking of the role i that is used in the particular field, which is calculated by ranking roles according to the times they are used in the field. L is the number of roles that are used in the field. But R_i is not the weight of contributor roles in specific academic outcomes, as not all roles involved in the field will appear in every outcome. The weight of a contributor role in a specific outcome is determined by the roles that appear in that outcome. Thus, in an academic outcome containing n contributor roles, the weight W_i of the i-th contributor role is represented by Eq. (4).

$$W_i = \frac{R_i}{\sum_{i=1}^{n} R_i} \tag{4}$$

3.2 The Citation-Based Academic Reputation of Scholars' Research Skills

Scholars' academic reputations are built up from the recognition of research output by the academic community, often in the form of citations [36]. Traditional citation analysis methods treat all citations equally, disregarding their specific contribution to the literature. Small [37] proposed the concept of citation context, which examines the textual content surrounding a reference to identify its subject and motivation. By analyzing citation context, the citation strength, or the number of times a cited paper is mentioned in the citing paper, can be determined [38, 39]. This approach is more reliable in academic evaluation and can differentiate coauthors' citation credit in a study [40, 41].

Yang et al.[23] proposed the CAC (Context-based Author Credit) model, which identifies contributor roles in citations by analysis of citation context and calculates the citation strength instead of citing papers. This study analyzes the academic reputation of scholars in each skill based on the CAC model by combining author contributions and the content of citations.

Assuming that the j-th author participates in n contributor roles in research, then the academic credit C_{ij} of the j-th author in the i-th contributor role can be expressed by Eq. (5). Then the academic reputation Rep_j obtained by the j-th author from a research skill containing k contributor roles in this article can be expressed by Eq. (6).

$$C_{ij} = \alpha P_{ij} S_i + (1 - \alpha) H_j \times \frac{\sum S_i}{n} \tag{5}$$

$$Rep_j = \sum_{i=1}^{k} C_{ij} \tag{6}$$

S_i is the citation strength of the i-th contributor role, which is calculated by identifying the citation through the analysis of the citation context. The identification standard was proposed by Yang et al.[23] (see Table 2). H_j is the weight of the j-th author in a study containing H authors based on harmonic counts: $H_j = \frac{\frac{1}{j}}{\left(1 + \frac{1}{2} + \frac{1}{3} + ... + \frac{1}{H}\right)}$. Alpha ($\alpha$) is a coefficient in the CAC model used to partition citation strength. The citations-based credit calculation method focuses on the contributor role that is closely related to the content of the citation. However, in practice, different contributor roles are often interrelated and mutually supportive. To address this, α is set to a specific role, and the ratio of the whole coauthors is set to 1-α, allowing for the adjustment of credit allocation per citation. This study assumes that when a contributor role is recognized (cited), half of the credit should be attributed to the mutual support of others. In Eq. (5), α is set to 0.5. Practically, α can be adjusted accordingly. Therefore, Eq. (5) demonstrates that $\alpha P_{ij} S_i$ represents academic credit obtained directly from citations of the j-th author's contributor roles, and $(1 - \alpha) H_j \times \frac{\sum S_i}{n}$ represents academic credit obtained from the mutual support of the entire study.

Table 2. Identification standard of contributor roles related to the content [23]

Contributor roles	Classification basis
Conceptualization	(1) Citations in the Introduction or Background part of the citing paper, especially the summary citation (2) Citations that point out the research scope or research angle of the cited paper
Data curation	(1) Citations that use the dataset from the cited paper directly
Formal analysis	(1) Citations that cite data processing results of the cited paper (2) Citations that cite analysis results/ main conclusions of the cited paper (3) Citations that perform statistical descriptions of data from cited paper
Investigation	(1) Citations that cite data from cited paper directly (2) Citations that describe the investigation behavior of the cited paper. If there is no Investigation in the contributor list of cited paper, consider classifying to Methodology
Methodology	(1) Citations that cite research methods directly from cited paper
Software	(1) Citations that cite algorithms from cited paper. If there is no Software in the contributor list of cited paper, consider classifying to Methodology
Visualization	(1) Citation of the table/figure from the cited paper

3.3 Altmetrics-Based Social Impact of Scholars' Research Skills

Altmetrics provides a complementary perspective to traditional citation-based metrics by measuring the online attention and impact of scholarly articles [42]. Altmetrics considers a broad range of sources, including social media, news articles, blogs, policy documents, and online reference managers, to capture the diverse ways in which research is being disseminated and used [43]. Altmetrics has been shown to correlate with traditional citation-based metrics, but also provides additional insights into the broader social impact of research achievements [44–46].

Altmetric.com is a renowned commercial provider of altmetrics with a focus on academic publishing. It adopts an open policy regarding the scientific use of its altmetric data [47], and generates alternative metrics or "altmetrics" for various research outputs. The Altmetric Attention Score (AAs), a metric indicating the extent of attention a research output has received, is produced by Altmetric.com by gathering data from a vast array of online sources. The AAs is widely employed by scholars as a means of making informal judgments and in support of research impact evaluation [48–50].

This study uses AAs to calculate the social impact of each skill of scholars. For a paper with known AAs, the social impact Imp_j of the j-th author's research skills of the paper can be expressed by Eq. (7).

$$Imp_j = AAs \times Pro_j \qquad (7)$$

4 Data Analysis

4.1 Data Collection

Considering the usage of the author contribution statement in different journals, *PLOS Medicine* was chosen as the data source, which has adopted CRediT since 2017. A dataset comprising 1386 articles was constructed by searching for papers published in *PLOS Medicine* on Web of Science Core Collection within the period of 2017-01-01 to 2022-12-31 using the 'article' type filter. The scholar with the highest number of publications, Smith GD, was selected for an empirical object (21 publications and their 812 citing papers included). The data was acquired on April 6, 2023. Due to the shortcomings in data access - (1) not all publishers require author contributions to be listed or coded up to now; (2) many large academic publishers do not provide open access to their data, making access to data limited; and (3) the actual use of author contributions is still short, and the period covered by the data is limited - the empirical results of this study are only used to demonstrate the validity and feasibility of the method proposed in this study and provide clues to the characterization of scholar's academic competence.

   This study's data processing involves four main steps. Firstly, obtaining the frequency of contributor roles in 1386 articles for calculating their percentile rankings and skill weights. Secondly, obtaining author bylines and author contribution lists of 21 articles by Smith GD to determine Smith GD's participation in each contributor role. Thirdly, obtaining AAs for the 21 publications to calculate Smith GD's social impact of various skills in these studies. Fourthly, manually identifying the citation context of 812 citing papers for 21 publications by Smith GD to calculate the actual citation strength of various contributor roles. The proficiency, social impact, and academic reputation of each skill of Smith GD can be calculated by using the data obtained with these steps as well as the proposed method from the previous section. In addition, part of the code for data processing in this study was generated with the assistance of the Large Language Models (LLMs): ChatGPT.

4.2 Proficiency

This study searched *PLOS Medicine* on the Web of Science for articles published between 2017 and 2022, resulting in a dataset of 1282 articles after excluding 104 articles with missing contribution lists. The contribution lists at the end of articles were analyzed to determine the frequency and percentile ranking of contributor roles and R_i was calculated using Eq. (3). The results are shown in Table 3.

Table 3. Contributor Roles Ranking and R_i Values in *PLOS Medicine* Articles from 2017–2022

Contributor role	Count	Ranking γ	R_i
Conceptualization	1277	2	0.929
Methodology	1235	5	0.714
Investigation	1048	8	0.500
Data curation	1136	6	0.643
Software	514	14	0.071
Visualization	724	11	0.286
Formal analysis	1267	4	0.786
Validation	665	12	0.214
Funding acquisition	965	9	0.429
Resources	645	13	0.143
Project administration	929	10	0.357
Supervision	1125	7	0.571
Writing – original draft	1280	1	1.000
Writing – review & editing	1277	3	0.857

By analyzing the author's bylines and contributions listed in each article, the study employed Eq. (1), Eq. (2), and Eq. (4) to calculate Smith GD's proficiency scores in various research skills. The results of the analysis are presented in Table 4. Table 4 summarizes Smith GD's proficiency scores in various research skills based on his authorship order and contribution patterns in the 21 articles. The scores range from 0 to 1 in a study, with higher scores indicating greater proficiency the scholar gets from the research in a particular skill. The results show that Smith GD was more proficient in several research skills, including results analysis and validation, and manuscript writing, with proficiency scores above 0.7. However, his proficiency scores for other skills, such as practical operation and External support, were relatively low, both in the low 0.2 range.

Table 4. Smith GD's proficiency scores in various research skills

Article record	Conceptualization	Methodology	Practical operation	Results analysis and validation	External support	Manuscript writing
e1002221	0.0231	0	0	0	0.0040	0.0070
e1002314	0	0.0080	0.0011	0	0	0.0073
e1002376	0	0.0966	0.0025	0.0797	0	0.0730
e1002476	0.0085	0.0833	0.0077	0.0688	0	0.0923
e1002634	0.0310	0.0102	0.0048	0.0099	0	0.0088
e1002641	0.0299	0.0070	0.0135	0.0696	0.0084	0.0916
e1002649	0.0147	0.0113	0	0.0917	0	0.1235
e1002724	0.0032	0.0002	0.0107	0.0023	0.0203	0.0031
e1002739	0	0.0397	0.0015	0.0045	0	0.0108
e1002868	0.0499	0.1409	0.0106	0.0258	0.0070	0.0750
e1002893	0.0204	0.0157	0.0103	0	0	0.1093
e1003062	0.0234	0.0123	0.0200	0.0618	0.0150	0.0568
e1003183	0.0118	0.0047	0.0183	0.0545	0.0095	0.0708
e1003234	0.0237	0.0077	0.0022	0.0125	0.0302	0.0899
e1003305	0	0.0152	0.0093	0.0372	0.0003	0.0177
e1003410	0.0381	0.0293	0.0134	0.0591	0	0.0894
e1003452	0.0279	0.01	0.0180	0.0157	0.0282	0.0726
e1003536	0.0724	0.0089	0.0063	0.0586	0.0250	0.0745
e1003555	0.0366	0.0113	0.0412	0.0189	0.0302	0.0789
e1003751	0.1646	0.0058	0.0137	0.0696	0.0253	0.0921
e1003897	0	0	0	0	0	0.0010
SUM	0.5794	0.5182	0.2051	0.7401	0.2034	1.2455

4.3 Academic Reputation

Smith GD's 21 publications were cited by 812 research articles in the WoS core collection, among which 23 were not accessible in full text, resulting in a dataset of 789 citing articles. Context analysis and the identification of contributor roles were conducted based on the standard (see Table 2) proposed by Yang et al.[23] to obtain the citation strength of the 21 publications and their contributor roles. The 21 publications were cited 1167 times by 789 citing papers, with a total citation strength of 1167. Based on Eq. (5) and Eq. (6), Smith GD's academic reputation scores for different research skills in each publication can be calculated (similar to proficiency in Table 4). And the total academic reputation scores for each skill accumulated from this set of studies are shown in Table 5, which demonstrates that Smith GD's work in results analysis and validation consistently generated the highest academic reputation scores across all skills and came in a distant second, followed by practical operation and methodology, while his work in conceptualization, manuscript writing, and external support had a relatively lower academic reputation score.

Table 5. Smith GD's academic reputation scores in various research skills

Article record	Conceptualization	Methodology	Practical operation	Results analysis and validation	External support	Manuscript writing
e1002221	1.6578	0	0	0	0.6481	0.6481
e1002314	0	2.6383	0.6978	0	0	0.6765
e1002376	0	4.0039	0.4916	15.8373	0	0.6746
e1002476	0.4074	2.0042	0.3072	11.9208	0	0.3417
e1002634	0.6448	0.3059	0.3575	1.6748	0	0.1695
e1002641	1.1092	0.3980	0.4239	19.0713	0.1547	0.3093
e1002649	1.0748	0.7177	0	18.1786	0	0.8571
e1002724	0.1352	0.0101	0.0259	0.9216	0.0168	0.0084
e1002739	0	1.5172	0.4260	2.7139	0	0.2011
e1002868	0.1095	2.6095	0.6095	1.1095	0.1095	0.2190
e1002893	0.6806	0.5276	1.0211	0	0	0.1878
e1003062	2.1923	2.0844	13.5012	89.0923	0.9256	1.8512
e1003183	0.0041	0.0278	0.2074	0.5041	0.0164	0.0082
e1003234	0.0143	0.0143	0.0143	0.7416	0.0430	0.0286
e1003305	0	0.1767	0.1128	3.5334	0.0167	0.0334
e1003410	1.8361	2.1770	1.6267	17.8134	0	1.6267
e1003452	0.1250	0.1176	0.3644	0.1674	0.0466	0.0310
e1003536	1.8407	0.4402	0.2039	10.1360	0.2719	0.1360
e1003555	0.0597	0.1692	0.1194	1.7264	0.2389	0.1194
e1003751	0.0058	0.0058	0.0115	1.0058	0.0058	0.0115
e1003897	0	0	0	0	0	0.0378
SUM	11.8973	19.9452	20.5220	196.1480	2.4938	8.1770

4.4 Social Impact

The study retrieved the Altmetric Attention Scores (AAs) of the 21 articles authored by Smith GD from Altmetric.com with the statistical deadline of April 10, 2023. With knowledge of the AAs for each article and Smith GD's proficiency scores in various research skills, the study calculated Smith GD's social impact in each skill for each article using Eq. (7). Table 6 presents the Smith GD's total social impact scores for each skill accumulated from this set of studies, which demonstrate that Smith GD's work in manuscript writing, results analysis and validation, and methodology generated the highest social impact scores across all skills, while his work in conceptualization, practical operation, and external support had a relatively lower social impact.

Table 6. Smith GD's social impact scores in various research skills

Article record	Conceptualization	Methodology	Practical operation	Results analysis and validation	External support	Manuscript writing
e1002221	5.1602	0	0	0	0.8931	1.5733
e1002314	0	0.5300	0.0719	0	0	0.4828
e1002376	0	11.0147	0.2867	9.0869	0	8.3180
e1002476	6.1232	59.7476	5.4994	49.2938	0	66.1934
e1002634	0.3104	0.1015	0.0475	0.0985	0	0.0884
e1002641	0.8378	0.1952	0.3788	1.9494	0.2363	2.5647
e1002649	1.5330	1.1794	0	9.5332	0	12.8409
e1002724	0.2527	0.0172	0.8352	0.1825	1.5795	0.2379
e1002739	0	2.7379	0.1011	0.3074	0	0.7445
e1002868	1.2485	3.5213	0.2641	0.6455	0.1761	1.8746
e1002893	0.1429	0.1099	0.0724	0	0	0.7654
e1003062	1.1919	0.6273	1.0196	3.1518	0.7641	2.8953
e1003183	0.0947	0.0374	0.1465	0.4356	0.0757	0.5662
e1003234	0.0474	0.0153	0.0045	0.025	0.0604	0.1798
e1003305	0	0.1372	0.0835	0.3349	0.0024	0.1592
e1003410	0.9149	0.7039	0.3226	1.4194	0	2.1456
e1003452	0.3628	0.13	0.2336	0.2042	0.3669	0.9443
e1003536	6.5848	0.8135	0.5765	5.3299	2.2748	6.7813
e1003555	4.1667	1.2871	4.7008	2.1546	3.4457	8.9992
e1003751	13.3294	0.4714	1.1079	5.6392	2.0507	7.4605
e1003897	0	0	0	0	0	0.0201
SUM	42.3012	83.3777	15.7524	89.7917	11.9256	125.8353

5 Results

The approach proposed in this study allows for a more comprehensive evaluation of scholarly output beyond the traditional metrics of citations and publications, by identifying and characterizing research skills.

Using 21 postings by Smith GD, this study demonstrates the usefulness of the proposed framework from the next two perspectives: variations in performance across research skills of the same scholar and skill performance variations across stages of the same scholar's career. Due to the limitations of data collection, this study did not conduct a comparative analysis of scholars' research skills performance in different research areas.

5.1 Variations in Performance Across Research Skills of the Same Scholar

The results of Smith GD's research skills characterization as demonstrated in the 21 papers selected for this study are summarized. Equation (8), the feature scaling formula, was used to get the normalization of indicators. The results can be seen in Table 7, and the radar chart based on it is shown in Fig. 3. Besides, a parallel coordinates chart was drawn to show the differences across the proposed three dimensions of the same skill (see Fig. 4).

$$X' = \frac{X - X_{min}}{X_{max} - X_{min}} \tag{8}$$

Table 7. The results of Smith GD's research skills characterization and their normalization data

Research skills	Proficiency		Academic reputation		Social impact	
	X	X'	X	X'	X	X'
Conceptualization	0.5794	0.3608	11.8973	0.0486	42.3012	0.2667
Methodology	0.5182	0.3020	19.9452	0.0901	83.3777	0.6273
Practical operation	0.2051	0.0016	20.5220	0.0931	15.7524	0.0336
Results analysis and validation	0.7401	0.5150	196.148	1	89.7917	0.6836
External support	0.2034	0	2.4938	0	11.9256	0
Manuscript writing	1.2455	1	8.1770	0.0293	125.8353	1

Smith GD performs well in skills such as methodology, results analysis and validation, and manuscript writing. Due to the fundamental nature of manuscript writing, which is necessary for all research publications, the frequency and weight of this skill are high, leading to a higher proficiency score. Besides, Altmetrics are not subjected to specific content analysis, and social impact is calculated based on the score of the publication's AAs and the author's contributions to a particular skill. As a result, the

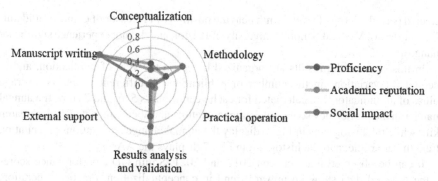

Fig. 3. The radar chart of the normalization data of Smith GD's research skills characterization

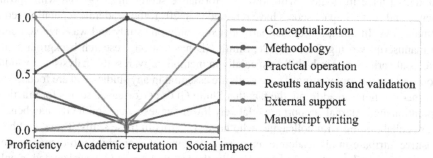

Fig. 4. The parallel coordinates chart of Smith GD's research skills characterization

distribution of social impact scores across different skills is consistent with proficiency scores. However, the academic reputation scores for Smith GD in various skills are markedly different from other dimensions, with results analysis and validation having a significant lead due to a large number of citations of research findings, indicating the greater importance attached to the value and credibility of research results in the medicine field.

Overall, except for manuscript writing, Smith GD has focused more on skills related to results analysis and validation, conceptualization, and methodology in the past six years, resulting in higher performance scores in these skills. However, practical operation and external support receive lower scores, which may be carried out more by Smith GD's collaborators.

5.2 Skill Performance Variations Across Stages of the Same Scholar's Career

We aim to reflect scholars' development of academic skills and scholarly identity transformation through changes in their performance in various academic skills over time. Due to limitations in data availability, this study only covers the past six years and cannot analyze the entire academic career of the selected subject, Smith GD. Therefore, our analysis is limited to his performance during this period. Furthermore, during the selected period, George Davey Smith held the position of Professor of Clinical Epidemiology at Bristol Medical School, University of Bristol, and did not experience significant changes.

In this section, the results are organized based on the year of publication, and to account for variations in the number of publications in different years, the average values of all indicators are calculated for each year. Figures 5, 6, and 7 show the annual changes in the proficiency score, academic reputation, and social impact of each research skill, while the histograms in Fig. 6 display the annual changes in citations and citation strength per article, and the histogram in Fig. 7 displays the AAs.

It can be observed that between 2017 and 2021, Smith GD's performance scores in the selected data show an upward trend in conceptualization, practical operation, and external support, while methodology shows a declining trend. Results analysis and validation have fluctuated, with lower performance scores in 2019, and while proficiency and social impact scores have rebounded in 2021, the academic reputation score remains low. In 2022, Smith GD participated in only one study and was involved only in manuscript writing. To conclude, Smith GD has a strong research background and excels at various research skills, especially in methodology, results analysis and validation, and manuscript writing. These skills are essential in any studies that are focused on the medical field. In addition, the fact that Smith GD's performance scores for practical operation and external support are relatively lower suggests that Smith GD may benefit from collaborating with colleagues who have strengths in these skills. This could be a positive attribute in an academic team, as it demonstrates an ability to recognize and work with complementary skill sets. Finally, the fact that Smith GD participated in only one study in 2022, and was involved only in manuscript writing, may indicate that the focus of his work may have shifted or that he has fewer opportunities to participate in research. Additionally, the lower academic reputation score in 2021 suggests that there may be areas for improvement in Smith GD's research performance.

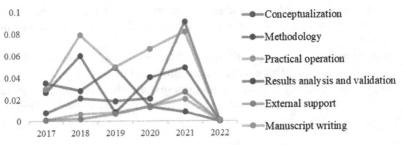

Fig. 5. Average proficiency score for each skill by year

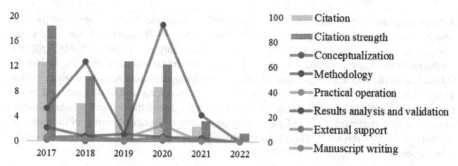

Fig. 6. Average academic reputation score for each skill by year

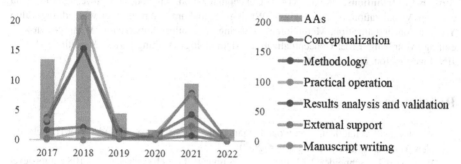

Fig. 7. Average social impact score for each skill by year

6 Conclusions

This study proposes a detailed framework for characterizing scholars' research skill performance based on two distinct perspectives: individual contribution and external recognition. The assessment of individual contribution is based on the author contribution list, while external recognition is measured using citations and altmetrics. The framework quantifies scholars' skill performance in three dimensions: proficiency, academic reputation, and social impact, thus extending the evaluation of scholars' academic competence to the specific dimensions of their research skills. This approach distinguishes itself from existing evaluation schemes that rely on composite indicators to reflect scholars' academic performance. Rather, this study specifically analyzes the roles played by scholars in research. Specifically, this study extracts a list of research skills that are involved in a complete research process from the contribution list. It then proposes an actionable quantification plan for scholars' skill performance based on their contributions, citation content analysis, and altmetrics. The effectiveness of this approach is demonstrated through its application to characterizing the research skills of a specific scholar, Smith GD. This research can be useful in various aspects, such as scholar evaluation, academic team building, research project involvement, and research skill training. Overall, the proposed approach contributes to a comprehensive understanding of scholars' research skills and provides a useful tool for assessing and developing scholars' research competence and promoting successful research collaboration.

Acknowledgments. This research was made possible through the financial support of the Chinese National Social Science Fund for the Post-Funding Project "Research on Knowledge Communication Systems Based on Full-Text Scientometrics Analysis" (Project ID: 22FTQB003). Furthermore, our sincere appreciation goes to Dr. Nicolas Robinson-Garcia from the University of Granada for his valuable insights and suggestions, which significantly contributed to the refinement of this research. We would also like to express our gratitude to all colleagues and expert reviewers who provided valuable feedback and suggestions during the research process. Finally, a special acknowledgment is due to ChatGPT for generating a substantial portion of the data processing code used in this study. This contribution has been instrumental in advancing the progress of our research.

Author Contributions. Aoxia XIAO: Conceptualization, Methodology, Investigation, Data curation, Visualization, Formal analysis, Writing-original draft, Writing-review & editing; Siluo YANG: Conceptualization, Methodology, Funding acquisition, Supervision, Writing-review & editing; Mingliang YUE: Conceptualization, Methodology, Writing-review & editing; Minshu JIN: Investigation, Data curation.

References

1. Whitley, R.: The intellectual and social organization of the sciences, 2nd ed. Oxford [England]; New York: Oxford University Press (2000)

2. Wildgaard, L., Schneider, J.W., Larsen, B.: A review of the characteristics of 108 author-level bibliometric indicators. Scientometrics **101**(1), 125–158 (2014). https://doi.org/10.1007/s11 192-014-1423-3

3. Cole, S., Cole, J.R.: Scientific output and recognition: a study in the operation of the reward system in science. Am. Sociol. Rev. **32**(3), 377 (1967). https://doi.org/10.2307/2091085

4. Wildgaard, L.: A comparison of 17 author-level bibliometric indicators for researchers in astronomy, environmental science, philosophy and public health in web of science and google scholar. Scientometrics **104**(3), 873–906 (2015). https://doi.org/10.1007/s11192-015-1608-4

5. Harzing, A.-W.: Publish or Perish, Harzing.com, Feb. 06, 2016. https://harzing.com/resour ces/publish-or-perish (Accessed 01 Mar 2023)

6. Hirsch, J.E.: An index to quantify an individual's scientific research output. Proc. Natl. Acad. Sci. **102**(46), 16569–16572 (2005). https://doi.org/10.1073/pnas.0507655102

7. Egghe, L.: Theory and practise of the g-index. Scientometrics **69**(1), 131–152 (2006). https://doi.org/10.1007/s11192-006-0144-7

8. Kosmulski, M.: A new Hirsch-type index saves time and works equally well as the original h-index. ISSI Newsl. **2**(3), 4–6 (2006)

9. Zhang, C.-T.: The e-index, complementing the h-index for excess citations. PLoS ONE **4**(5), e5429 (2009). https://doi.org/10.1371/journal.pone.0005429

10. Mabrouk, P.A.: Research skills and ethics—a graduate course empowering graduate students for productive research careers in graduate school and beyond. J. Chem. Educ. **78**(12), 1628 (2001). https://doi.org/10.1021/ed078p1628

11. Tractenberg, R.E., Umans, J.G., McCarter, R.J.: A mastery rubric: guiding curriculum design, admissions and development of course objectives. Assess. Eval. High. Educ. **35**(1), 15–32 (2010). https://doi.org/10.1080/02602930802474169

12. Kersnik, J., Ungan, M., Klemenc-Ketis, Z.: Why does teaching research skills to family medicine trainees make sense? Eur. J. Gen. Pract. **21**(4), 253–256 (2015). https://doi.org/10.3109/13814788.2015.1057813

13. Beuning, P.J.: Research skills and ethics: the 20-year evolution of a professional development graduate course. Anal. Bioanal. Chem. **409**(4), 859–862 (2017). https://doi.org/10.1007/s00 216-016-9989-7
14. Uebel, K., Iqbal, M.P., Barbara-Ann Adelstein: A pragmatic approach to promoting research skills in all medical students. Med. Educ. **54**(5), 445–446 (2020). https://doi.org/10.1111/ medu.14097
15. Kong, X., Liu, L., Yu, S., Yang, A., Bai, X., Xu, B.: Skill ranking of researchers via hypergraph. PeerJ Comput. Sci. **5**, e182 (2019). https://doi.org/10.7717/peerj-cs.182
16. Dalmeet Singh Chawla: Digital badges aim to clear up politics of authorship. Nature **526**(7571), 145–146 (2015). https://doi.org/10.1038/526145a
17. Farhadi, F., Sorkhi, M., Hashemi, S., Hamzeh, A.: An effective expert team formation in social networks based on skill grading. In: 2011 IEEE 11th International Conference on Data Mining Workshops, Vancouver, BC, Canada: IEEE, Dec. 2011, pp. 366–372. https://doi.org/ 10.1109/ICDMW.2011.28
18. Kong, X., Jiang, H., Yang, Z., Xu, Z., Xia, F., Tolba, A.: Exploiting publication contents and collaboration networks for collaborator recommendation. PLoS ONE **11**(2), e0148492 (2016). https://doi.org/10.1371/journal.pone.0148492
19. Li, L., Tong, H., Cao, N., Ehrlich, K., Lin, Y.-R., Buchler, N.: Enhancing team composition in professional networks: problem definitions and fast solutions. IEEE Trans. Knowl. Data Eng. **29**(3), 613–626 (2017). https://doi.org/10.1109/TKDE.2016.2633464
20. Allen, L., Scott, J., Brand, A., Hlava, M., Altman, M.: Publishing: credit where credit is due. Nat. News **508**(7496), 312 (2014). https://doi.org/10.1038/508312a
21. Ding, J., Liu, C., Zheng, Q., Cai, W.: A new method of co-author credit allocation based on contributor roles taxonomy: proof of concept and evaluation using papers published in PLOS ONE. Scientometrics **126**(9), 7561–7581 (2021). https://doi.org/10.1007/s11192-021-04075-x
22. Rahman, M.T., Regenstein, J.M., Kassim, N.L.A., Haque, N.: The need to quantify authors' relative intellectual contributions in a multi-author paper. J. Informetr. **11**(1), 275–281 (2017). https://doi.org/10.1016/j.joi.2017.01.002
23. Yang, S., Xiao, A., Nie, Y., Dong, J.: Measuring coauthors' credit in medicine field — Based on author contribution statement and citation context analysis. Inf. Process. Manag. **59**(3), 102924 (2022). https://doi.org/10.1016/j.ipm.2022.102924
24. Hagen, N.T.: Harmonic allocation of authorship credit: source-level correction of bibliometric bias assures accurate publication and citation analysis. PLoS ONE **3**(12), e4021 (2008). https://doi.org/10.1371/journal.pone.0004021
25. Hagen, N.T.: Harmonic publication and citation counting sharing authorship credit equitably – not equally, geometrically or arithmetically. Scientometrics **84**(3), 785–793 (2010). https:// doi.org/10.1007/s11192-009-0129-4
26. Hagen, N.T.: Harmonic coauthor credit: a parsimonious quantification of the byline hierarchy. J. Informetr. **7**(4), 784–791 (2013). https://doi.org/10.1016/j.joi.2013.06.005
27. Holcombe, A.O.: Contributorship, not authorship: use credit to indicate who did what. Publications **7**(3), 48 (2019). https://doi.org/10.3390/publications7030048
28. Allen, L., O'Connell, A., Kiermer, V.: How can we ensure visibility and diversity in research contributions? hHow the contributor role taxonomy (CRediT) is helping the shift from authorship to contributorship. Learn. Publ. **32**(1), 71–74 (2019). https://doi.org/10.1002/leap. 1210
29. Waltman, L.: An empirical analysis of the use of alphabetical authorship in scientific publishing. J. Informetr. **6**(4), 700–711 (2012). https://doi.org/10.1016/j.joi.2012.07.008
30. Yang, S., Wolfram, D., Wang, F.: The relationship between the author byline and contribution lists: a comparison of three general medical journals. Scientometrics **110**(3), 1273–1296 (2017). https://doi.org/10.1007/s11192-016-2239-0

31. Larivière, V., Desrochers, N., Macaluso, B., Mongeon, P., Paul-Hus, A., Sugimoto, C.R.: Contributorship and division of labor in knowledge production. Soc. Stud. Sci. **46**(3), 417–435 (2016). https://doi.org/10.1177/0306312716650046

32. Corrêa Jr, E.A., Silva, F.N., da Luciano, F., Costa, D.R., Amancio,: Patterns of authors contribution in scientific manuscripts. J. Informet. **11**(2), 498–510 (2017). https://doi.org/10.1016/j.joi.2017.03.003

33. Lu, C., Zhang, C., Xiao, C., Ding, Y.: Contributorship in scientific collaborations: the perspective of contribution-based byline orders. Inf. Process. Manag. **59**(3), 102944 (2022). https://doi.org/10.1016/j.ipm.2022.102944

34. Kim, J., Kim, J.: Rethinking the comparison of coauthorship credit allocation schemes. J. Informetr. **9**(3), 667–673 (2015). https://doi.org/10.1016/j.joi.2015.07.005

35. Donner, P.: A validation of coauthorship credit models with empirical data from the contributions of PhD candidates. Quant. Sci. Stud. **1**(2), 551–564 (2020). https://doi.org/10.1162/qss_a_00048

36. Ding, Y.: Applying weighted PageRank to author citation networks. J. Am. Soc. Inf. Sci. Technol. **62**(2), 236–245 (2011). https://doi.org/10.1002/asi.21452

37. Small, H.: Citation context analysis. Prog. Commun. Sci. **3**, 287–310 (1982)

38. Sombatsompop, N., Kositchaiyong, A., Markpin, T., Inrit, S.: Scientific evaluations of citation quality of international research articles in the SCI database: Thailand case study. Scientometrics **66**(3), 521–535 (2006). https://doi.org/10.1007/s11192-006-0038-8

39. Hu, Z., Lin, G., Sun, T., Hou, H.: Understanding multiply mentioned references. J. Informetr. **11**(4), 948–958 (2017). https://doi.org/10.1016/j.joi.2017.08.004

40. Pak, C., Yu, G., Wang, W.: A study on the citation situation within the citing paper: citation distribution of references according to mention frequency. Scientometrics **114**(3), 905–918 (2018). https://doi.org/10.1007/s11192-017-2627-0

41. Wang, M., Ren, J., Li, S., Chen, G.: Quantifying a paper's academic impact by distinguishing the unequal intensities and contributions of citations. IEEE Access **7**, 96198–96214 (2019). https://doi.org/10.1109/ACCESS.2019.2927016

42. Priem, J., Taraborelli, D., Groth, P., Neylon, C.: Altmetrics: A manifesto Oct 26, (2010). https://altmetrics.org/manifesto/ (Accessed Apr. 06, 2023)

43. Galligan, F., Dyas-Correia, S.: Altmetrics: rethinking the way we measure. Ser. Rev. **39**(1), 56–61 (2013). https://doi.org/10.1080/00987913.2013.10765486

44. Eysenbach, G.: Can tweets predict citations? metrics of social impact based on twitter and correlation with traditional metrics of scientific impact. J. Med. Internet Res. **13**(4), e2012 (2011). https://doi.org/10.2196/jmir.2012

45. Thelwall, M., Haustein, S., Larivière, V., Sugimoto, C.R.: Do altmetrics work? twitter and ten other social web services. PLoS ONE **8**(5), e64841 (2013). https://doi.org/10.1371/journal.pone.0064841

46. Zahedi, Z., Costas, R., Wouters, P.: How well developed are altmetrics? a cross-disciplinary analysis of the presence of 'alternative metrics' in scientific publications. Scientometrics **101**(2), 1491–1513 (2014). https://doi.org/10.1007/s11192-014-1264-0

47. Ortega, J.L.: Blogs and news sources coverage in altmetrics data providers: a comparative analysis by country, language, and subject. Scientometrics **122**(1), 555–572 (2020). https://doi.org/10.1007/s11192-019-03299-2

48. Gumpenberger, C., Glänzel, W., Gorraiz, J.: The ecstasy and the agony of the altmetric score. Scientometrics **108**(2), 977–982 (2016). https://doi.org/10.1007/s11192-016-1991-5

49. Thelwall, M., Nevill, T.: Could scientists use Altmetric.com scores to predict longer term citation counts? J. Informetr. **12**(1), 237–248 (2018). https://doi.org/10.1016/j.joi.2018.01.008
50. Yang, S., Zheng, M., Yonghao, Yu., Wolfram, D.: Are altmetric.com scores effective for research impact evaluation in the social sciences and humanities? J. Informet. **15**(1), 101120 (2021). https://doi.org/10.1016/j.joi.2020.101120

Community Members' Perspective on Public Libraries as Places to Overcome Social Divisions: A Case Study in Oslo

Tomoya Igarashi[1](✉) [iD], Jamie Johnston[2] [iD], and Masanori Koizumi[1] [iD]

[1] University of Tsukuba, Kasuga 1-2, Tsukuba, Ibaraki, Japan
igarashi@klis.tsukuba.ac.jp

[2] Oslo Metropolitan University, St. Olavs Plass, P.O. Box 4, NO-0130 Oslo, Norway

Abstract. Public libraries are expanding their role with a growing emphasis on their potential to address a prominent contemporary social issue: overcoming social divisions. However, the perceptions of community members concerning libraries' expanded role remain largely unknown. This study aimed to elucidate the experiences and perceptions of local community residents regarding public libraries' role in mitigating social disparities. A case study was conducted at Deichman, a public library system in Oslo, using an online questionnaire focused on exploring the motivations behind library visits and identifying the library services deemed essential by residents. Based on 501 responses, the findings suggest that they predominantly associate libraries with their traditional roles of book lending and information provision, both in terms of their personal usage and the importance they attribute to various library services. In contrast, services aimed at bridging social divisions were not frequently deemed significant. Nevertheless, there were instances where respondents highlighted unique experiences facilitated by the library, including the connecting of diverse communities. These interactions are essential for reducing gaps in experiences and promoting mutual understanding among residents. It is anticipated that as more individuals encounter such transformative experiences, the overarching perception of public libraries will evolve accordingly.

Keywords: Social division · Community Perspective · Public Library · Questionnaire · Norway

1 Introduction

1.1 The Role of Public Libraries in Overcoming Social Divisions

Public libraries have historically played a pivotal role in diverse aspects of societal development. Beyond their traditional roles of lending books and disseminating information, contemporary public libraries are increasingly recognised for their broad range of activities and community initiatives. These include promoting digital inclusion [1], facilitating social inclusion [2], aiding in the integration of immigrants [3], orchestrating events and programmes [4], serving as a nexus for community meetings and exchanges [5], and fostering a vibrant and robust public sphere [6], amongst others. These activities attest to the expanding role and underscore the potential of public libraries in bridging societal divides stemming from economic, ethnic and gender differences [7]. These differences often manifest in misunderstandings and conflicts among individual people and groups, giving rise to tensions that contribute to social instability and fuel democratic dysfunction [8, 9] In contemporary times, marked increases in economic disparities are evident. As underlying mechanisms of social differentiation and alienation continuously alter societal structures, the urgency to address these resulting divisions becomes increasingly paramount.

Public libraries, traditionally perceived as institutions grounded in a philosophy of equality and universality, are envisioned to play a pivotal role in mitigating social divisions. To this end, they proactively address challenges such as the digital divide, economic disparities, and demographic segregation [10]. Addressing economic divisions often involves providing services like job search assistance, referral services from support agencies, and furnishing diverse experimental opportunities. This ensures equitable access to knowledge gained from practical, hands-on experience, thereby curtailing the perpetuation of social inequalities.

Furthermore, public libraries are expanding their offerings to include a wide variety of events focused on creativity, technology, and games [11], which now play a central role in their service provisions. These events, along with the carefully curated hands-on experiences they offer, provide library users with encounters that they often do not have in their daily settings. Addressing social divides is realised through these events by providing opportunities for interaction with individuals of diverse backgrounds, be it in terms of ethnicity, age, or values. These interactions foster mutual understanding, which, in turn, can reduce prejudices and the misunderstandings stemming from them. As a result of their expanding array of activities and initiatives, public libraries show great potential for overcoming social divisions.

1.2 Literature Review

Several studies have explored librarians' perspectives on the evolving range of library services. For instance, Johnston et al. conducted a questionnaire across seven countries to discern public librarians' views on their professional role in fostering the formation of the public sphere [12]. While this study primarily focused on the context of the formation of the public sphere, it unequivocally showed that public libraries have broadened their service offerings in response to societal changes. Furthermore, librarians deem these augmented functions as integral, complementing their conventional role of facilitating information access. Audunson and Tóth, based on a separate analysis from the same study, highlighted that public librarians consider services related to new technologies to be of paramount importance [13]. Hence, while public libraries are extending their service gamut beyond traditional roles, librarians unarguably perceive these new functions as significant. Nevertheless, there remains ambiguity regarding the extent to which local community members avail these services and how they compare the importance of these novel offerings with traditional ones.

Exploring how libraries are experienced and perceived, some studies specifically focus on users of various types of services. Lakind and colleagues argue that libraries play a crucial role in bridging significant gaps in learning and experience, particularly with makerspaces facilitating unique encounters, tools, creative pursuits, and community interactions [14]. Koizumi and Larsen illuminate how public libraries elevate library users' awareness of societal issues and stimulate deliberation through reading circles and exhibitions centred on pressing social concerns [15]. Johnston's research delineates that dialogues held in language cafés within Norwegian libraries have engendered mutual cultural appreciation, mitigated biases, amplified interactions between Norwegian and immigrants, and bolstered friendships amongst participants [16]. While these case-specific insights indicate that public libraries can be instrumental in ameliorating social divisions, considering the magnitude of social divisions as a contemporary issue, the overarching perception and utilisation of public libraries by local community members remain somewhat nebulous.

1.3 About Deichman (Public Library System in Oslo)

This study focused on Oslo, Norway, where distinct socioeconomic divisions are evident. There is a pronounced division between the affluent western part of Oslo and its eastern counterpart, which is less affluent and has a higher concentration of residents with immigrant backgrounds. Statistics indicate that the eastern area faced challenges such as lower education and literacy rates, reduced life expectancy, and elevated poverty levels [17].

Deichman is the official name of Oslo's public library system. Established as Norway's inaugural public library, Deichman now has 22 branches spread across Oslo, including its main library. In 2020, the new central library, known as Deichman Bjørvika, opened its doors to the public. Recognised for its architectural brilliance and multifunctional spaces, it was awarded the title of "Public Library of the Year 2021" by the International Federation of Library Associations (IFLA) [18].

Furthermore, the Public Libraries Act, as amended in Norway in 2014, mandates that libraries are independent meeting places and arenas for discussion and debate, in addition to providing information, education, and promoting cultural activities by guaranteeing free access to books and other media [19]. The primary vision of the law is to engender environments conducive to enriching experiences and exchanges, ultimately bridging societal divisions. Norwegian libraries have responded to the changes in the law by offering a broader spectrum of activities that facilitate and promote social meetings and interactions [20]. Consequently, the Deichman library system is well-positioned to address the central issue examined in this study.

1.4 Research Purpose

The overarching aim of this study is to determine local community members' experiences and perceptions regarding the role of public libraries in overcoming social divisions, with a specific focus on the Deichman library as a case study. This is explored through the following research questions:

RQ1: How have local community members experienced the library's activities and events aimed at addressing social divisions?

RQ2: How do local community members, encompassing both users and non-users of Deichman, perceive the library's role in overcoming social divisions?

In this context, social division refers to the stratification of society resulting from inequalities stemming from aspects such as economic background, ethnicity, and gender, leading to misunderstandings and conflicts between social groups. Importantly, determining how local community residents perceive the traditional and newly proposed functions of the library is important for the positioning of the new services. As these services become more mainstream, it is anticipated that public perceptions may shift. Nevertheless, it remains essential to discern the present sentiment as it holds significance for both organisational strategy goals and public communication. A deeper exploration into how libraries, through their varied activities and events, help bridge societal gaps will offer a tangible glimpse into their societal impact.

The terms 'resident(s),' 'local resident(s),' and/or 'community member(s)' will be used interchangeably to refer to the surveyed population or individuals from the sample— essentially, those residing in Oslo.

2 Methodology

An online questionnaire was administered to a representative sample of approximately 500 individuals aged 17 and above residing in Oslo. The questionnaire's design was based on previous research and developed collaboratively by the involved researchers. Primarily, it sought to understand the respondents' motivations for using the library and their perceptions of the library's distinct functions. Moreover, open-ended questions delved into the 'positive impacts of library usage and event attendance' and 'experiences within the library'. These open-ended questions were framed to elicit detailed insights into library users' experiences and their views on the library's role in overcoming social divisions. The descriptive responses were analysed upon careful reading by the authors.

Previous research has suggested that public libraries can play a pivotal role in addressing social divisions by providing access to knowledge, experiential opportunities, and fostering social interaction. These previously identified ways in which libraries address social divisions were used as response options because respondents might not fully understand the concept of social division. For instance, in the section querying the purpose of library visits, options such as 'Using the Internet' and 'Meeting friends' were included. This facilitated the identification of how library services designed to address social divisions are perceived and utilised, juxtaposed against other standard library offerings.

Sentio Research, a prominent research entity in Norway specializing in social science research, handled the dissemination and collection of the questionnaires. The questionnaire was distributed online to respondents and responses completed online. This strategy enabled the garnering of feedback from a broader response base, inclusive of those who might not frequent libraries. Since the questions in the survey included actual library experience, the respondents were screened to ensure that at least 400 respondents had used a library. The questionnaire was distributed between 30 August and 6 September 2022. Conducted in Norwegian, the option selections and open-ended responses highlighted in this chapter have been translated by the authors.

Of the 501 responses collected, 409 respondents had prior experience with public libraries, while 92 had not. Table 1 shows the age distribution of respondents. It was reasonably balanced across various age brackets. Table 2 shows the gender of respondents. There is also no significant bias. In terms of origin, a significant majority identified as native Norwegians. Considering Oslo's demographic composition, it is important to note the underrepresentation of immigrant respondents and the overrepresentation of those born in Norway.

Table 1. Age distribution of respondents

Age groups	Number of respondents
10s	20
20s	99
30s	102
40s	87
50s	76
60s	53
70s	50
Over 80s	14

Table 2. Gender of respondents

Gender	Number of respondents
Male	217
Female	284

3   Results and Analysis

3.1   Purposes of Visiting Deichman

Table 3 presents the responses from the 409 respondents who have reported using public libraries. Respondents were asked about their 'main (primary) purpose' of using the library and for 'other (additional) purposes'. Respondents were permitted to select up to three options for 'other (additional) purposes. The rightmost column displays the total number of selections for either 'main (primary) purpose' or 'other (additional) purposes. Percentages in Table represent the proportion of the total respondents (409 in this instance) who selected an option for one of these two categories. For example, 'borrowing books' was chosen by 310 out of the 409 respondents as either their 'main (primary) purpose' or 'other (additional) purpose'. This translates to 75.8% of respondents identifying 'borrowing books' as one of their reasons for using the library.

Each Deichman branch tailors events and programmes to resonate with the unique characteristics of the neighbourhood or area it serves. It is conceivable that patterns of library usage differ based on these localised characteristics. To analyse this, we categorised the functions and services offered by each branch. Three branches were specifically spotlighted in this analysis: Deichman Bjorvika (the main library), Deichman Stovner, and Deichman Holmlia. Deichman Stovner is situated in a district characterised by the highest immigrant population and the lowest average income in Oslo. Deichman Holmia lies in a district where Pakistani immigrants—one of the first immigrant groups—initially settled, and it remains a profoundly multicultural area today. This region, akin to Furuset, also exhibits a significant immigrant population coupled with lower average incomes. Both areas serve as examples of communities contending with the complexities of social division. Table 4 delineates the purposes identified by patrons of each branch, whether as their main or other purposes. The listed percentages indicate the fraction of each branch's users who selected a particular purpose.

Table 3. Main and other purposes for visiting Deichman library system (n = 409)

	Main purpose	Other purposes	Total
Borrowing books	235	75	310 [75.8%]
Borrowing CDs or DVDs	7	54	61 [14.9%]
Reading by yourself in the library	37	87	124 [30.3%]
Reading with several people (e.g. reading groups, social reading)	3	20	23 [5.6%]
Using the PCs in the library	6	8	14 [3.4%]
Participating in events and programme	12	55	67 [16.4%]
Using the Internet	0	13	13 [3.2%]
Using digital equipment (e.g., 3D printer)	10	33	43 [10.5%]
Survey and research	8	23	31 [7.6%]
Asking questions to the librarian (reference service)	2	22	24 [5.9%]
Studying	29	47	76 [18.6%]
Working	14	42	56 [13.7%]
Meeting with friends	18	45	63 [15.4%]
Playing games	0	6	6 [1.5%]
Others	20	15	35 [8.6%]
Nothing	8	-	-

Table 4. Purpose for visiting each Deichman library

	Bjørvika		Furuset		Holmlia	
Borrowing books	142	75.5%	8	61.5%	10	83.3%
Borrowing CDs or DVDs	27	14.4%	1	7.7%	4	33.3%
Reading by yourself in the library	77	41.0%	6	46.2%	2	16.7%
Reading with several people (e.g. reading groups, social reading)	14	7.5%	2	15.4%	0	0.0%
Using the PCs in the library	4	2.1%	1	7.7%	1	8.3%
Participating in events and programme	38	20.2%	5	38.5%	4	33.3%
Using the Internet	6	3.2%	3	23.1%	0	0.0%
Using digital equipment (e.g., 3D printer)	22	11.7%	2	15.4%	1	8.3%
Survey and research	12	6.4%	1	7.7%	1	8.3%
Asking questions to the librarian (reference service)	5	2.7%	0	0.0%	1	8.3%
Studying	44	23.4%	5	38.5%	1	8.3%
Working	37	19.7%	1	7.7%	1	8.3%
Meeting with friends	51	27.1%	2	15.4%	0	0.0%
Playing games	3	1.6%	0	0.0%	0	0.0%
Others	19	10.1%	1	7.7%	1	8.3%
Nothing	29	15.4%	1	7.7%	4	33.3%

The predominant reason cited for using public libraries was 'Borrowing books'. Over half (235 respondents) identified this as their primary reason, and this figure rose to approximately 75.8% when other purposes were considered. 'Reading by yourself in the library' emerged as the next most frequently chosen reason. Promoting reading is an activity that public libraries have championed for many years, and it remains the chief reason people frequent these establishments. Another traditional service is 'Asking questions to the librarian (reference service)', though only about 5.6% of respondents selected this, making it less popular than other options. The third most popular choice was 'Studying'. Public libraries also serve as quiet, focused spaces, and this environment supports various learning activities. This tranquil nature is another hallmark of the traditional public library.

After studying, 'Participating in events and programmes' emerged as another main reason for library visits. Such events and programmes offer diverse experiential opportunities in creative workshops, enable individuals to familiarise themselves with diverse perspectives through discussions, and foster social interaction. This is important because disparities in people's experiences due to economic circumstances and access to resources can influence interactions between residents of diverse social classes. For instance, engaging in video editing demands both equipment and proficiency, and those without access to such resources or knowledge are less likely to engage in experience-based conversations. Additionally, acquiring programming skills through practical experience can open doors to more well-prepared employment opportunities. Ultimately, creating chances for people to have experiences they might not otherwise have due to economic constraints can encourage interaction across different social classes, potentially reshaping social stratification. Thus, promoting participation in events can be pivotal in bridging social divisions. One facet of public libraries that aids in addressing social divisions is their role in narrowing the digital gap. This is evident in options like 'Using the PCs in the library' and 'Internet using', although these were chosen by only a few respondents. It is worth noting that these results might be influenced by the survey's online format. Given that it was an online survey, respondents likely have decent access to local networks, such as home Wi-Fi or mobile data. They would also possess a device to respond to the survey, making it conceivable that there were fewer mentions of PC or network use as primary reason. Amongst the feedback provided in open-ended questions about positive library experiences, comments included "I was able to use equipment I did not have at home for free" and "I was able to access experiences that I could not access for financial reasons".

In the highly diverse yet economically less affluent neighborhoods of Deichman Stovner and Deichman Holmlia, activities like 'Using the Internet' and 'Participating in events and programs'—which provide diverse experiences and/or practical, hands-on opportunities—were more frequently mentioned compared to the main library. This highlights the importance of providing such services in areas marked by diversity but potentially lacking some of the resources found in more prosperous communities. However, the limited number of respondents indicating their attendance at these activities at Deichman Stovner suggests that further in-depth research may be necessary in the future.

3.2 Anecdotes About Meeting and Interacting at Deichman

Public libraries have been posited as spaces for meeting and interaction. Gatherings and engagements that foster dialogue and mutual understanding play a crucial role in bridging societal divides, especially those stemming from demographic differences. In response to whether library visits led to new interactions, 54 respondents—approximately 13.2% of library users—confirmed that they had made new connections. Although not an overwhelming percentage, it underscores the evolving role of libraries as meeting places and spaces for social interaction.

To gain deeper insights into the nature of these interactions, respondents were asked to describe instances of when they made new connections at the library. Some responded that they connected around similar interests, for example one indicated that that they "met people with similar interests/backgrounds" and another said that they "made new friends in the creative workshops". Respondents also noted that they connected with people of diverse backgrounds, as one respondent said, "I met people from different countries in the language café who are now my friends" and another reported that "I discuss social issues in debates and lectures with people of different ages and backgrounds and say hello to them. Interesting to get to know other types of people." The role of the library in facilitating these interactions was not overlooked. One respondent reflected that "a cross-cultural community has emerged from conversations about common interests. It is a community/conversation that would not have been created without the library".

These testimonies suggest that public libraries are facilitating interactions amongst residents whose paths might not have crossed otherwise. Thus, conversations facilitated by events like language cafés and lectures, or shared interests, can be seen as catalysts for residents meeting and connecting with others. The frequency of respondents indicating that they made new social connections, and even friends, during these gatherings is promising as these types of activities and events gain momentum. Furthermore, some respondents indicated that their interactions with other library patrons facilitated interpersonal reflection and enriched their lives, as one said, "the opportunity to understand other people's opinions helped to promote interpersonal understanding and remove intercultural barriers" and another stated that "encounters with others have enriched my life".

3.3 Roles of Public Libraries Perceived Important by Oslo Residents

To gain an understanding of local community residents' perceptions, respondents were asked about the roles of public libraries that they considered to be important. Responses were collected from current library users, former library users, and individuals unfamiliar with libraries. Respondents were asked to specify the primary role they considered to be of the upmost importance (Most important) and three subsequent roles that they regarded to be of relative importance (Important). The results are presented in Table 5.

Table 5. Roles of public libraries perceived important by residents (n = 501)

	Most important	Important	Total
Provision of book collection and lending	240	183	423 [84.4%]
Provision of information for daily life	3	79	82 [16.4%]
Access to knowledge and information	163	220	383 [76.4%]
Cultural dissemination	34	173	207 [41.3%]
Public discussion arena	0	36	36 [7.2%]
Meeting place	13	142	155 [30.9%]
Place for learning	16	116	132 [26.3%]
Support for learning	15	109	124 [24.8%]
Support for creative activities	1	36	37[7.4%]
Support digital equality	4	46	50 [10.0%]
Immigrant inclusion and integration	6	67	73 [14.6%]
Others	6	5	11 [2.2%]

The role identified to be of primary importance was 'Provision of book collection and lending', chosen by an overwhelming majority of the respondents. Following closely behind was 'Access to knowledge and information'. These findings indicate that respondents deem the library's role in providing access to information through literature as being of central importance. However, education-related roles, such as 'place for learning' and 'support for learning', received more moderate rankings, primarily as roles of secondary importance. As might be anticipated, and as will be discussed, these last two roles may be of greater relevance to a younger cohort of library users.

In contrast, roles connected to the expanded social role of libraries, such as 'Cultural dissemination' and 'Meeting place', ranked highly as roles of secondary importance. However, only a little over a third nominated 'Public discussion arena' and "Support for creative activities" as roles of secondary importance, with almost no one indicating them to be of primary importance. These findings are noteworthy considering the most recent revisions to the Norwegian Library Act, which came into effect in 2014 [19]. The act tasks libraries with active dissemination in relation to their primary role of promoting enlightenment, education, and other cultural activities. It also mandates them to serve as independent meeting places and arenas for discussion and debate. The findings from this study clearly suggest that these roles are still seen by the respondents as secondary in importance to the more traditional role of providing access to literature and information, though support for and recognition of these roles may be increasing. Another nuanced interpretation is that these roles may be experienced as functions or activities facilitating the realization of knowledge and understanding found in collection resources and/or as part of the overarching objective of learning promotion. As such, respondents may perceive them as secondary.

As previously discussed, 'Support for digital equality' is seen as a vital role of public libraries in bridging societal divides. However, it received a relatively low ranking, and primarily as a role of secondary importance. This aligns with the findings of a multi-country study by Johnston et al. on librarians' perceptions of the library's role. 'Promoting equality by evening out the digital divide' ranked low across the surveyed librarians [12]. However, it is important to consider that in Norway the proportion of households with internet access is around 99% [21]. Consequently, achieving digital equality in Norway may be less about the provision of access and more about skill development related to ICT use and digital literacy. These factors may have influenced the respondents' perception of the importance of this role.

As noted above, the perceived importance of public library roles may be influenced by various factors, such as age. In particular, age is predicted to have a significant impact at a time when the functions of public libraries are changing rapidly along with social conditions. Age groups that have enjoyed traditional functions for a long time may perceive those functions as more important. Therefore, the correlation between respondents' age and their perceptions of the library's roles was further explored. Table 6 presents responses according to age group.

Table 6. Public library functions that residents perceived as important by age group.

	Under 20s		30s-50s		Over 60s	
Provision of book collection and lending	96	80.7%	225	84.9%	102	87.2%
Providing information for daily life	16	13.4%	50	18.9%	16	13.7%
Access to knowledge and information	82	68.9%	208	78.5%	93	79.5%
Cultural dissemination	40	33.6%	107	40.4%	60	51.3%
Public discussion arena	13	10.9%	20	7.5%	3	2.6%
Meeting place	49	41.2%	76	28.7%	30	25.6%
Place for learning	44	37.0%	74	27.9%	14	12.0%
Support for learning	36	30.3%	61	23.0%	27	23.1%
Support for creative activities	14	11.8%	17	6.4%	6	5.1%
Guaranteeing digital equality	10	8.4%	32	12.1%	8	6.8%
Immigrant inclusion and integration	15	12.6%	39	14.7%	19	16.2%
Others	1	0.8%	7	2.6%	3	2.6%

The association between age and the functions that people consider important in libraries was investigated on the data. The null hypotheses are as follows: H_0: no link between the perceived significance of library functions and age. A chi-square test was performed, and the p-value was 0.0036. The null hypothesis was rejected at a 5% significance level, suggesting a pronounced bias between perceived library function importance and age. Subsequent chi-square tests for age groups—under 20s with 30−50s, under 20s with over 60s, and 30−50s with over 60s—yielded p-values of 0.086, 0.00017, and 0.080, respectively. Utilising the Bonferroni correction method, a significant bias was observed at the 5% level between the under 20s and over 60s.

'Provision of book collection and lending' garnered importance across all age demographics, underscoring its timeless value. Conversely, the adjusted standardised residuals for 'Cultural dissemination', 'Public discussion arena' and 'places for learning' were 2.61, 2.35 and 3.75, respectively, indicates that those aged 60 and above viewed 'Cultural dissemination' a more pivotal, while the 'Place for learning' was favoured by the under 20s. Notably, the role of 'cultural dissemination' in public libraries has been acknowledged for its importance across all three age groups but increases with age. This view of 'Cultural dissemination' as more pivotal by the older generations may be a result of cultural policies from the latter part of the 20th century, which, according to Audunson et al. [22] aimed to democratise culture by ensuring accessibility to the entire population, irrespective of social background or geographical location. This welfare-oriented cultural policy vision, aimed at fostering democracy and promoting ordinary people's quality of life, manifested not only in the establishment of numerous new libraries but also in the proliferation of new media and a diverse array of cultural activities within libraries. These activities included, for instance, children's theatre, film screenings, and exhibitions. The older respondents view of the library's role may simply reflect these policies and libraries' activities in fulfilling them.

The younger cohort, those under 20, exhibited a greater inclination towards the 'Public discussion arena' compared to their senior counterparts, possibly because this aspect has been a central focus of libraries for a significant portion of their lives, since the amendment to the Norwegian library law that took effect in 2014. The subsequent increase in activities in this area may have contributed to shaping their perspectives regarding the role of libraries. Although the difference was not substantial, younger respondents also prioritised 'Meeting place' and 'Support for creative activities' more than their older counterparts, reflecting a shift towards the expanded social role of the library. The sample size across age groups was limited, necessitating further research to explore the extent to which this expanded view of the library's role has been adopted by younger residents in order to draw any definitive conclusions.

The older demographic demonstrated a pronounced appreciation for the 'Immigrant inclusion and integration'. The preponderance of events like language cafés, where native Norwegian speakers—often older volunteers—facilitate integration, likely influences this perspective. Greater participation in such events increases the likelihood of older residents recognising this as a pivotal library function. Intriguingly, younger participants placed a lower premium on 'Access to knowledge and information'. With the ubiquity of the internet and digital devices, they seemingly value contemporary functions like 'meeting places' and 'support for creative activities' over traditional informational access.

4 Discussion

The questionnaire revealed that the primary reason for visiting public libraries remains reading. Alongside this primary use, book borrowing and accessing knowledge and information emerged as pivotal library functions. A significant majority highlighted book borrowing as an essential service, reinforcing that even in contemporary times, reading remains a chief library offering, enriching lives in the process. Libraries as hubs for learning, especially for the younger demographic, was also prominent. This is in alignment with the Public Library Plan of Oslo for 2014–2018, which underscored the library's role in this aspect, stating, "Libraries play a central role as places of learning and knowledge for children and young people" [23]. Consequently, their stature as learning centres is continuing to grow.

The findings also suggest that the broader cultural policies may have influenced the way different generations perceive and use the library. Older respondents indicate the library's role in cultural dissemination to be more pivotal, while younger generations highlight the meeting place role and more participatory activities as being more pivotal. While these findings appear to represent broad tendencies, they clearly align with the shift in cultural policy over the last 60 or so years. There has been a transition from a focus on the democratization of culture, ensuring accessibility of culture and cultural offerings for all, to a greater emphasis on participation, meeting places, and discussion. Both approaches to cultural policy share the common goal of diminishing social inequalities and fostering democracy, though they place slightly different emphasis on these objectives. These findings suggest that broader cultural policies, as well as library-specific strategies and policies, are reflected in the ways community members perceive and use libraries. This is a significant insight pertaining to libraries' effectiveness in legitimizing their operations and overall images within the communities they serve.

The provision of ICT and other equipment and facilities appears to offer opportunities for hands-on learning and exploration that may not be accessible elsewhere, thereby aiding in bridging social inequalities. First, the role of libraries in bridging the digital gap is noteworthy. While only a limited number of respondents used libraries for digital services such as internet access or PC usage, this can be of immense importance for inclusion and participation in a highly connected society, as is the case in Norway with internet connectivity nearing 100%. Findings from a recent report by Statistics Norway reveal that factors such as advanced age, a limited level of education, retirement, or staying at home, and residing in regions with low population density, elevate the chances of falling behind digitally. Notably, young students were shown to have a higher probability of digital exclusion, as well as poorly integrated immigrant women. [24]. Conversely, and of great relevance to libraries, the report also indicates that living in municipalities that provide innovative digital services diminishes the likelihood of falling behind digitally. Second, another aspect relevant to the risk of young students experiencing digital exclusion falls under the umbrella of tackling societal divisions, and it involves the library's role in providing diverse experiences. Younger visitors find the support for creative activities, such as the provision of makerspaces, pivotal. As awareness of these offerings grows, so too may their popularity and utilization, potentially countering the higher risk of digital exclusion faced by young students or youth.

Events and programmes, aimed at enhancing the library experience, were not as popular as activities related to reading. Nonetheless, about 40% of library visitors participated in an event. With an increased variety of events and diversified content, participation rates may rise in the future. Yet, for those attending library events and programmes, the potential benefits can be significant. Some respondents in the questionnaire highlighted that public libraries play a role beyond serving as mere experience centres, noting that the libraries facilitate interactions and the establishment of social connections that bridge societal divides. They described encounters at language cafés and other gatherings over shared interests that led to friendships and even the formation of communities bridging age, ethnicity, or cultural differences. These interactions, while not always resulting in close friendships, appeared to foster familiarity, and understanding. This can be seen as a significant outcome in the effort to create a stronger sense of community and reduce social divisions, which is an overarching role for libraries set forth in Norway's National Library Strategy 2020–2023 [25].

In summary, Deichman library branches are popular destinations, particularly among non-Western immigrants [26]. As Norwegians and immigrants utilise these spaces together, it seems that mutual recognition, and perhaps even deeper connections, are developing. Younger respondents often emphasised the library's role as a hub for community gatherings. If this perception persists, it might soon become a cornerstone of the library's ethos. Some respondents highlighted events as catalysts for interaction, and with the continued popularity of such library events, they may increasingly play a central role in fostering social connections and reducing social divisions.

5   Conclusion

This study aimed to explore residents' perspectives on public libraries, focusing on the Deichman Library system in Oslo and its role in addressing societal divisions. Through an online questionnaire, the research addressed two main questions. Firstly, regarding residents' experiences at Deichman libraries, traditional roles such as book borrowing and solitary reading remained prominent, especially for older library users, while younger users saw the library as a place for learning. Although libraries are expanding services, including digital tools and events, the transformative impact of these experiences is still emerging. The study envisions a future where diverse events become commonplace, providing a broader range of enriching experiences. Secondly, examining residents' perceptions of libraries as catalysts for overcoming social divisions, findings indicated respondents' perceptions aligned with the more traditional library roles, such as reading and learning. Newer initiatives to reduce societal disparities, while not currently paramount for most respondents, show potential acceptance, particularly among younger participants. The evolving role of modern libraries as tech hubs and community spaces is recognised, but public opinion still emphasises their traditional roles. The study suggests a need for concerted efforts to raise awareness and encourage participation in innovative services and activities to fulfil policy aims to promote democracy, through increased inclusion and participation, and thereby, reduce social divisions and create an increased sense of community.

The study acknowledges its limitation in predominantly native Norwegian respondents, highlighting the importance of future research from immigrants' perspectives. Nevertheless, it provides valuable insights into current perspectives on public libraries, offering guidance for future developments and stimulating discussions on their evolving role in addressing societal divisions.

Acknowledgments. This work was supported by JSPS KAKENHI Grant Numbers JP20H04479, JP21J10661.

Disclosure of Interests. The authors have no competing interests to declare that are relevant to the content of this article.

References

1. Kinney, B.: The internet, public libraries, and the digital divide. Public Libr. Quart. **29**(2), 104–161 (2010). https://doi.org/10.1080/01616841003779718
2. Birdi, B., Wilson, K., Cocker, J.: The public library, exclusion, and empathy: a literature review. Libr. Rev. **57**(8), 576–592 (2008). https://doi.org/10.1108/00242530810899568
3. Audunson, R., Essmat, S., Aabø, S.: Public libraries: a meeting place for immigrant women? Libr. Inform. Sci. Res. **33**(3), 220–227 (2011). https://doi.org/10.1016/j.lisr.2011.01.003

4. Mathiasson, M.H., Jochumsen, H.: Between collections and connections: analyzing public library programs in terms of format, content, and role and function. Libr. Quart. **90**(3), 364–379 (2020). https://doi.org/10.1086/708963

5. Audunson, R.: The public library as a meeting-place in a multicultural and digital context: The necessity of low-intensive meeting-places. J. Document. **61**(3), 429–441 (2005). https://doi.org/10.1108/00220410510598562

6. Larsen, H.: Archives, libraries, and museums in the Nordic model of the public sphere. J. Document. **74**(1), 187–194 (2018). https://doi.org/10.1108/JD-12-2016-0148

7. Anthias, F.: The concept of 'social division' and theorising social stratification: looking at ethnicity and class. Sociology **35**(4), 835–854 (2001). https://doi.org/10.1177/0038038501035004003

8. Itten, A.V.: Overcoming social division: Conflict resolution in times of polarization and democratic disconnection. Routledge, New York (2018)

9. Diamond, L.: Democratic regression in comparative perspective: scope, methods, and causes. Democratization **28**(1), 22–42 (2020). https://doi.org/10.1080/13510347.2020.1807517

10. Igarashi, T., Koizumi, M., Widdersheim, M.M.: Overcoming social divisions with the public library. J. Document. **79**(1), 52–65 (2023). https://doi.org/10.1108/JD-12-2021-0244

11. Igarashi, T., Watanabe, M., Tomita, Y., Sugeno, Y., Yamagishi, M., Koizumi, M.: Public library events with spaces and collections: case analysis of the Helsinki Central Library Oodi. J. Librarianship Inform. Sci. **55**(3), 681–693 (2023). https://doi.org/10.1177/09610006221097405

12. Johnston, J., et al.: Public librarians' perception of their professional role and the library's role in supporting the public sphere: a multi-country comparison. J. Document. **78**(5), 1109–1130 (2022). https://doi.org/10.1108/JD-09-2021-0178

13. Audunson, R., Tóth, M.: The legitimacy of public library services: do the general public and librarians agree? In: Proceedings of the XXVII Bobcatsss Symposium, pp. 366–376 (2019)

14. Lakind, A., Willett, R., Halverson, E.R.: Democratizing the maker movement: a case study of one public library system's makerspace program. Reference User Serv. Quart. **58**(4), 234–245 (2019). https://doi.org/10.5860/rusq.58.4.7150

15. Koizumi, M., Larsen, H.: Democratic librarianship in the Nordic model. J. Librarianship Inform. Sci. **55**(1), 208–217 (2023). https://doi.org/10.1177/09610006211069673

16. Johnston, J.: Friendship potential: Conversation-based programming and immigrant integration. J. Librarianship Inform. Sci. **51**(3), 670–688 (2019). https://doi.org/10.1177/0961000617742459

17. Wessel, T.: Economic segregation in Oslo: Polarisation as a contingent outcome. In: Tammaru, T., van Ham, M., Marcińczak, S., Musterd, S. (eds.) Socio-economic segregation in European capital cities: East meets west, pp. 132–155. Routledge, London (2016)

18. IFLA: New public library world champion named, https://www.ifla.org/news/new-public-library-world-champion-named/. Accessed 06 Mar 2022

19. Folkebibliotekloven: Lov om folkebibliotek (folkebibliotekloven), https://lovdata.no/dokument/NL/lov/1985-12-20-108. Accessed 20 Mar 2023

20. Audunson, R., Evjen, S.: The public library: an arena for an enlightened and rational public sphere? the case of Norway. Information Research. **22**(1), CoLIS paper 1641 (2017)

21. Eurostat Statistics Explained: Digital economy and society statistics - households and individuals, https://ec.europa.eu/eurostat/statistics-explained/index.php?title=Digital_economy_and_society_statistics_-_households_and_individuals. Accessed 14 Sep 2023

22. Audunson, R., Jochumsen, H., Rydbeck, K.: Library history of the Scandinavian countries. In: Libraries. Archives, and Museums in Transition, pp. 17–30. Routledge, London (2022)

23. The Norwegian Ministry of Culture: National strategy for libraries 2015–2018. Norwegian Ministry of Culture, Oslo (2015)
24. Statistics Norway, https://www.ssb.no/en/teknologi-og-innovasjon/informasjons-og-kommunikasjonsteknologi-ikt/artikler/digital-exclusion-who-has-a-risk-to-fall-outside. Accessed 05 Jan 2024
25. The Norwegian Ministry of Culture: The Norwegian Ministry of Education and Research: A space for democracy andself-cultivation: National strategy for libraries 2020–2023. Norwegian Government Security and Service Organisation, Oslo (2019)
26. Oslo Kommune: Oslotrender 2019. https://www.oslo.kommune.no/getfile.php/13346363-1572856400/Tjenester og tilbud/Politikk og administrasjon/Politikk/Oslotrender 2019.pdf. Accessed 14 Sep 2023

Unpacking Research Contributions: Investigation from Contextual and Processual Perspectives

Zhe Cao[1,2] , Yuanyuan Shang[3] , Lin Zhang[1,2,4(✉)] , and Ying Huang[1,2,4]

[1] School of Information Management, Wuhan University, Wuhan, China
linzhang1117@whu.edu.cn

[2] Center for Science, Technology & Education Assessment (CSTEA), Wuhan University, Wuhan, China

[3] Chinese Academy of Social Sciences Evaluation Studies, Beijing, China

[4] Centre for R&D Monitoring (ECOOM) and Department MSI, KU Leuven, Louvain, Belgium

Abstract. Traditionally, scientific evaluation leaning on quantity and citation metrics rarely places a study within a specific context or a particular historical process for examination, making it difficult to fully reveal its substantial contributions. In a specific scientific field, each study focuses on a certain topic and corresponds to a certain evolutionary stage of the topic. However, few studies analyze research contributions from context-oriented and process-oriented perspectives. This study investigates the contributions of research under several representative topics in the field of quantitative science studies, using articles published in the international journal *Scientometrics* as samples. BERTopic model is employed for topic clustering, and four research topics are selected for in-depth analysis. In order to unveil research contributions to knowledge production and to different audiences, various metrics including disruptiveness, citation impact and altmetrics are combined for indicator-level analysis, and articles are classified into different categories according to the knowledge contribution types and research orientations for content-level analysis. Results reveal that representative research topics exhibit greater disruptiveness and research impact compared to the overall sample. However, as research topics develop, there is a declining trend in introducing new knowledge and producing impact within academia. Simultaneously, there is a certain degree of enhancement in their impact beyond academia, and also a shift in knowledge contribution types and research orientations. Our findings contribute to a contextual and processual understanding of diverse research contributions, serving as a reference for the evaluation practices of research outcomes oriented towards contribution assessment.

Keywords: Research Contribution · Knowledge Contribution Type · Research Orientation · Scientometrics · BERTopic

I. Sserwanga et al. (Eds.): iConference 2024, LNCS 14597, pp. 338–355, 2024.
https://doi.org/10.1007/978-3-031-57860-1_23

1 Introduction

At the beginning of 2023, the publication of a breakthrough study in *Nature* has drawn significant attention from both academia and society at large. The research has found a gradual reduction in groundbreaking original innovations, suggesting a potential slowdown in the pace of scientific advancement [1]. Presently, there has been an exponential increase in the scale of research output on a global scale. Particularly in a specific scientific field, there are continuous influxes, growths, and declines of studies about different research topics. These research waves seemingly enrich the knowledge base of the field. However, the exact contributions yielded by the studies under these research waves remain to be scrutinized and comprehensively evaluated.

The scientific knowledge framework is structured hierarchically, employing a series of terms such as *discipline, field* and *topic* to describe distinct levels of knowledge structure [2–4]. This study focuses on the research contributions concerning representative research topics within a specific scientific field. A scientific field is perceived as an aggregation of various research topics, possessing a defined research scope, a certain scale of research and relatively independent knowledge systems. The formation and development of individual research topics propel the overall advancement of the scientific field. In this way, situating a study within the evolutionary trajectory of a certain topic, its contribution can be characterized from both a contextual and processual perspective. As for the contextual perspective, each study is scrutinized within the framework of its specific topic. We hold the belief that analyzing the contributions of a study should take into account the topic it focuses on, comparing it with research focusing on similar topics, in order to better reflect its significance. As for the processual perspective, studies on different thematic evolutionary stages are compared. We make a bold assumption that regarding a research topic, pioneering achievements in its early stages, substantial mid-term accumulations, and the latest findings display divergent contributor characteristics. Comprehending the evolutionary patterns of research contributions aids in a deeper understanding of the past and in shaping future endeavors.

This study aims to initially identify representative topics within a specific scientific field, analyzing their overall characteristics and developmental trends. Subsequently, this study investigates the contributions of research under these representative topics to the advancement of their respective topics. In terms of case selection, this study focuses on research within the field of scientometrics, a research field that employs quantitative methods to study the patterns of science. Over a significant period, this field has accumulated a rich array of research topics, established a comprehensive methodological framework, and developed a widespread scholarly community [5]. The objective of this study is to reveal the multidimensional contributions of research outcomes based on an analysis from the thematic evolutionary angle, providing a contextual and processual view to better assess the value of research achievements.

2 Research Framework

The research framework of this study is shown in Fig. 1. By integrating theories of knowledge production and the interaction between science and society, this study analyzes the contributory characteristics of research from two dimensions – contribution to knowledge production and contribution to different audiences. At the indicator level, this study investigates the degree of introducing new knowledge and the impact within and outside academia of research under identified topics. At the content level, this study delves into the knowledge contribution types of academic papers and their research orientations.

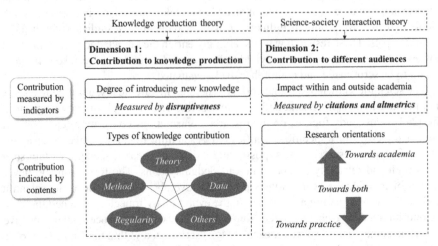

Fig. 1. Research framework

Knowledge production is closely related to research and development activities, and deeply embedded in the innovation system [6], which can be regarded as the core of science [7]. The theory of knowledge production focuses on issues concerning how knowledge is created, disseminated, and applied, becoming increasingly prominent in both theoretical value and practical significance within contemporary knowledge societies. In a certain sense, scientific research constitutes a process of knowledge production, wherein the introduction of new ideas, methods, perspectives, etc., is a crucial aspect in assessing its actual contribution. This study, on one hand, addresses the degree to which scientific research introduces new knowledge and, on the other, focuses on its specific type of knowledge contribution. In terms of introducing new knowledge, previous research has developed novelty indices to capture the origin of creative ideas in combinatorial processes, and also disruptiveness indices to capture not just the origin, but also the impact of new ideas [8]. The latter is employed in this study. In terms of knowledge contribution types, some scholars have proposed several classification schemes [9, 10]. For example, the annotation scheme proposed by Chen et al. includes types of contributions such as dataset/resources creation, theory proposal, and so forth. Nevertheless, these schemes are primarily rooted in methodological approaches, based on samples from disciplines like computer science, which do not entirely align with our samples. Thereby, this study will establish its own classification scheme for knowledge contributions based on existing research and the characteristics of the data used (see details in Sect. 3.3).

From a historical evolutionary perspective, academia has not held a unified under-standing of the relationship between science and society for an extended period. British scientist John D. Bernal, in his work *The Social Function of Science*, delineated two contrasting perspectives on science during its early development – idealism and realism. The former emphasized the purity of science and the value of unfettered exploration, considering the societal function of science as relatively secondary and subservient. The latter underscored the practical application of science and its societal impact, advocating for science to address real-world issues and meet societal needs [11]. Since the 20th cen-tury, science, technology, and society have progressively intertwined. Scientific research increasingly emphasizes being driven by societal needs, effectively serving the resolution of practical issues in various domains such as policy support, technological innovation, economic development, social progress, and cultural dissemination. Regarding the inter-action between science and society, the role of scientific research in both academia and society stands as a crucial perspective in measuring its tangible contributions. This study not only focuses on the research impact within and outside academia but also delves into the divergent research orientations towards academic and practical scenarios, which will expand the understanding of research contributions to a considerable extent.

3   Data and Method

3.1   Research Data

In a certain sense, the research published in specialized journals within a scientific field reflects the development of that particular field. Some studies have characterized the development of academic fields based on analysis of papers published in professional journals [12, 13]. *Scientometrics* stands as a representative international journal in the field of quantitative science studies, characterized by a longstanding history, a relatively substantial volume of publications, and a comprehensive coverage of topics. This study regards the articles published in this journal as representative of scientometric research. A comprehensive dataset was compiled by retrieving all articles (totaling 6562 pieces) published in *Scientometrics* up to October 28, 2023, from the Web of Science database.

Through cross-platform data integration based on digital object identifiers (DOIs) of articles, three aspects of data were retrieved to measure disruptiveness, citation impact and impact outside academia respectively:

(1) The indicator of category normalized citation impact (CNCI) was obtained from the InCites platform to measure impact within the academic community. This indicator eliminates various interferences brought by document type, year of publication and subject area, serving as a useful index of academic impact.

(2) Altmetrics are a way of tracking and measuring the online engagement of research beyond traditional bibliometrics, which can partly reflect the research impact outside academia. The Altmetric score of each article can be collected from the journal's official website.

(3) Citation data for both references and citations were retrieved from the open data platform OpenAlex, which can be used to calculate disruptiveness. The study utilizes an enhanced version of the disruptive index proposed by Wu et al. in 2019, which

is called *Rela_Dz* [14, 15], to measure the degree of introducing new knowledge of articles, reflecting their disruptive nature. The calculation process is depicted in Figure 2, with detailed derivation available in the original text. A higher index indicates a stronger disruptive nature of the paper, whereas a lower index suggests a greater continuity with existing research. Some studies suggest that computing the disruptive index requires a citation window of at least three years [16]. This study focuses on analyzing research published before 2020 after identifying representative topics to meet this requirement.

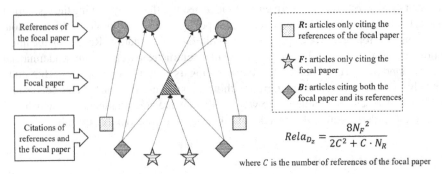

where C is the number of references of the focal paper

Fig. 2. Calculation process of the disruptiveness indicator

3.2 Topic Identification Based on BERTopic Model

BERTopic is a topic modeling technique that derives from BERT [17]. BERT is an acronym for Bidirectional Encoder Representations from Transformers which was developed in 2018 as transformer-based machine learning model [18]. It has been pre-trained in massive amounts of corpus data and thus performs very well in various NLP tasks. BERTopic is devised as a family member of BERT specifically for the purpose of topic modeling. BERTopic operates via the following few steps: (1) Documents are represented as embeddings using BERT model. (2) Employ the UMAP algorithm for dimensionality reduction of text vectors and utilize the HDBSCAN algorithm for topic clustering of the reduced document vectors. (3) Utilize the class-based TF-IDF (c-TF-IDF) algorithm to compute the importance of vocabulary within clusters, assigning a topic to each cluster and establishing dynamic topic representations. (4) Optimize the terms using the Maximal Marginal Relevance (MMR) algorithm, which improves the coherence among the terms for the same topic and the topic representation.

BERTopic demonstrates notable advantages over other topic modeling methods, particularly in pre-trained embeddings, the c-TF-IDF process, and automatic reduction of topic numbers [19]. The clustering results exhibit higher levels of topic coherence, diversity, and interpretability [20] and have been widely employed in discovering themes within complex short-text datasets [21, 22]. Considering the intended thematic clustering of academic paper abstracts in this study, given their concise and complex content, as well as semantic richness, the BERTopic model is employed to cluster 6003 articles that contain abstract information.

3.3 Article Classification Based on Manual Labeling

In this section, we aim to categorize abstracts of articles according to the types of knowledge contribution and the research orientations. Two classification schemes reflect, at the content level, distinct underlying features of two dimensions of research contributions – to knowledge production and to different audiences.

Types of knowledge contribution seek to differentiate the characteristics of research content, focusing on whether it emphasizes theoretical, methodological, empirical, or other types of investigations. Specifically, it is divided into five types including *theory, method, data, regularity,* and *others.* Research contributing to theory primarily involves proposing new theories or exploring and refining existing theories, often holding significant implications for the development of a scientific field. Research contributing to method encompasses the proposal, evaluation, or enhancement of new or existing methodologies. Noted that the term "method" covers a range of instrumental contents such as indicators, algorithms, models, software, among others. Research contributing to data involves constructing new datasets or analyzing and comparing existing data sources, representing a distinctive and foundational aspect within the field of scientometrics. Research contributing to regularity involves utilizing data analysis to reveal phenomena, identify correlations, extract patterns, and recognize trends, constituting a commonly observed category within the field of scientometrics. Research that does not fall into the aforementioned four categories is classified as "others."

Research orientations aim to distinguish the contributory characteristics of research objectives, delineating whether they primarily serve the academic community or have a broader application beyond academia. In this regard, this study refers to research conducted by Zhang et al. [23] which has made a distinction between different research purposes – advancing scientific progress versus advancing societal progress, to distinguish different research orientations. Specifically, the research orientation is categorized into three types including *towards academia, towards practice,* and *towards both.* Research oriented towards academic scenarios aims to address scientific problems and generate academic values, primarily contributing within the academic community. Research oriented towards practical scenarios aims to address societal issues and produce diverse values, with its primary contributions lying outside the academic community. Research that combines both aspects caters to academic and practical scenarios to a certain extent, balancing both academic and societal values. Whereas the identification of knowledge contribution types relies more on statements in the abstract that describe the content of the research, the identification of research orientations depends more on statements in the abstract that describe the research objectives or significance.

For the articles to be classified, we produced a "blinded" data file with linkable publication ID to the original dataset and no other information than the title, abstract, and DOI for link to full text if needed. Two coauthors of this study read all abstracts independently and coded them according to the definitions above. In this way, each article can be labeled with a type of knowledge contribution and research orientation. After the phase of independent blinded reading, the agreement in coding is checked. Still using blinded data, the two readers discussed the articles with inconsistent labeling results together and concluded with only one coding alternative.

4 Results

4.1 Identification of Representative Research Topics

After applying the BERTopic model for clustering, 50 research topics in the field of scientometrics are identified. The total output of articles for different years and the proportional distribution of research within each topic are illustrated in Fig. 3(a). Considering the emphasis of this study on the contributions of representative research topics within the field, a comprehensive evaluation is conducted, taking into account various factors such as the number of articles in each topic, the presence of discernible evolutionary trends, and the representativeness of the topic. In this paper, the four most representative topics are selected for a pilot study. The following analysis will be based on these four topics (see keywords for each topic in Fig. 3(b)).

Topic 1: h-index and Related Metrics. This topic corresponds to cluster 3_index_citation_hirsch_number. Keywords include index, citation, hirsch, number, ranking, scientific, g-index, awardees, measure, harmonic, etc. 165 pieces of articles (2.7%) have been classified into this topic. In 2005, Jorge Hirsch, a physicist from the University of California, San Diego, proposed the h-index in an article published in the *Proceedings of the National Academy of Sciences* (PNAS) [24]. This metric serves as a hybrid quantitative indicator to assess both the quantity and quality of academic output by researchers. Its introduction has triggered an unprecedented response within the academic community, leading to not only a series of subsequent improved metrics but also widespread adoption in the evaluation practices of researchers, academic institutions, and related scholarly groups.

Topic 2: Gender Difference in Academia. This topic corresponds to cluster 5_gender_productivity_gap_researcher. Keywords include gender, productivity, gap, researcher, bias, academic, Swedish, participation, doctoral, proportion, etc. 149 pieces of articles (2.5%) have been classified into this topic. Since the peak of the first wave of feminism around the time of World War I, society has traversed over a century seeking gender equality. With the gradual integration of science into society, the gender differences within the scientific community have garnered increased attention [25–27]. For an extended period, women have held a relatively disadvantaged position in the realm of science and technology. Despite two waves of feminism in the 20th century fostering women's involvement in the public sphere, their participation and representation in scientific activities remain low. The challenges faced by women in gaining acknowledgment and acclaim within the scientific community far outweigh those encountered by men [28]. Consequently, gender differences in science have drawn the attention of scholars in related fields, who have gradually explored and elucidated the phenomena and underlying reasons of this phenomenon, making it one of the classic topics in the field of scientometrics.

Topic 3: Altmetrics. This topic corresponds to cluster 6_twitter_altmetric_altmetrics_social. Keywords include twitter, altmetrics, social, scholarly, research, impact, metric, blog, etc. 132 pieces of articles (2.2%) have been classified into this topic. In 2010, Jason Priem and Heather Piwowar first proposed and explored the concept of altmetrics, advocating a novel approach distinct from traditional citation metrics to measuring research impact [29]. They emphasized the significance of non-traditional channels such as social media, blogs, and news coverage in evaluating research impact, suggesting their inclusion within the scope of assessing scholarly output. Subsequently, altmetrics have emerged as a pivotal topic within the field of scientometrics, stimulating broader discussions on evaluating the multifaceted impact of research outputs. With the widespread adoption of social media and online communication modes, the concept, and methodologies of altmetrics have continuously evolved and been actively explored within academia.

Topic 4: University Ranking and Academic Quality. This topic corresponds to cluster 7_university_ranking_higher_academic. Keywords include university, ranking, higher, academic, arwu, weight, shanghai, faculty, scholarship, institutional, etc. 130 pieces of articles (2.17%) have been classified into this topic. Universities constitute vital origins for scientific advancements and stand as crucial forces within national innovation systems. Evaluating academic research within universities contributes to fostering research innovation, nurturing talent, and implementing national strategies for scientific and technological development. This evaluation holds significant importance in propelling advancements within the scientific domain and the overall development of a nation. Scholars in the field of scientometrics initially focused on research output and its quantifiable indicators. Universities, as primary hubs for scientific research, serve as

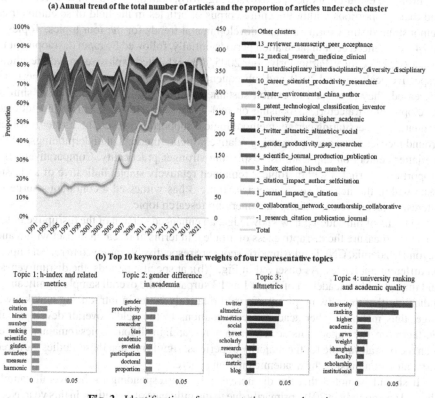

(a) Annual trend of the total number of articles and the proportion of articles under each cluster

(b) Top 10 keywords and their weights of four representative topics

Fig. 3. Identification of representative research topics

essential arenas for the application of quantitative science studies, generating impactful avenues for societal and policy influences through relevant research. Consequently, an increasing number of scholars are paying attention to issues related to university rankings and the academic standards of institutions, providing a scientific foundation for the assessment and enhancement of research quality within universities.

As this study aims to uncover the contributions of representative thematic research through an in-depth investigation with a relatively narrow focus, only the aforementioned four research topics are selected. Topics of smaller publishing volumes or conventional issues in scientometrics such as the journal evaluation and citation analysis are not included in our analysis. Throughout the subsequent analysis, a series of studies emerging alongside the evolution of these four representative topics will be referred to as *research waves*.

4.2   General Trends and Overall Characteristics of Research Waves

This section delineates the developmental trends of four representative topics, and their relative levels of disruptiveness and research impact within the overall sample. Its aim is to offer an overarching perspective on the progression of four research waves in the development of the scientific field.

From the evolutionary perspective (see Fig. 4(a)), both the number of research output and their proportions within the entire corpus of articles in the field of scientometrics demonstrate distinct formation and developmental trends for the four topics. Topics 1 and 4 experienced certain incubation periods initially, followed by rapid development in the early 21st century. Particularly after 2005, they exhibited explosive growth, reaching respective peaks around 2010, and subsequently stabilizing. Although their proportions decreased, they continued to exhibit sustained output. These two topics share similar developmental trajectories, focusing on real-world scenarios of talent or institutional evaluation, necessitating certain methodological support. However, the former revolves around metrics as its core, possessing relatively higher theoretical underpinnings, while the latter centers on applications, displaying stronger practicality. Comparatively, the proportion of articles within Topic 2 remained relatively stable, indicative of a classic issue within the field of scientometrics. Topic 3 has witnessed a continuous surge in interest in recent years, which is an emerging research topic.

In terms of introducing new knowledge, an enhanced version of the disruptive index is used to measure the disruptiveness of articles. In terms of research impact within and beyond academia, CNCI and Altmetric score are respectively employed to reflect impact on different audiences. As observed in Fig. 4(b), at specific periods, the disruptiveness and impact within academia of Topic 1 and 3 surpassed the overall sample significantly, indicating that these two topics performed relatively better in introducing new knowledge, thus making higher academic contributions to the field's overall development. Furthermore, the impact outside academia of research in all four topics remained higher than the overall sample for the majority of periods, signifying that these studies garnered more attention outside the academic citation sphere.

It should be noted that the disruptive index corresponding to the overall sample showed an anomaly in 2010, primarily due to the influence of an outlier. In this year, Nees Jan van Eck and Ludo Waltman published an article to present VOSviewer, a computer program for bibliometric mapping [30]. The tool has gained widespread attention and usage among researchers, representing a groundbreaking achievement. It may explain the extremely high disruptiveness value of approximately 2998. While the mean value is affected by outliers, articles with extremely high indicator values are found to be rare by manual checking. Thereby, the above results can generally reflect the characteristics of research under representative topics.

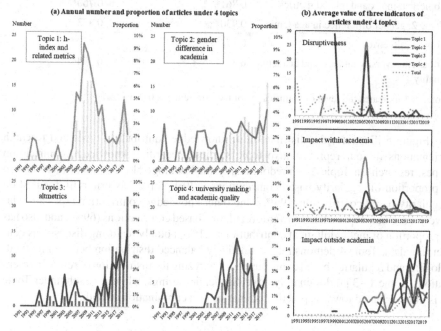

Fig. 4. General trends and features of articles under 4 representative topics

4.3   Research Contribution on Different Evolutionary Stages of Research Waves

Classification of Knowledge Contribution Types and Research Orientations. In order to delve deeper into research contributions beyond indicator-based analysis, this section dissects the specific types of knowledge contribution and their research orientations in representative topic studies, laying the groundwork for subsequent analysis.

Given that the dual classification work is independently performed by two coauthors of this study, the kappa statistic is employed to test the reliability of the classification results. The kappa is one of the most commonly used statistics to test interrater reliability, which ranges from −1 to 1 [31]. The closer the kappa value is to 1, the higher the consistency between the classification results of two annotators. As observed in Table 1, studies under four representative topics are categorized into different knowledge contribution types and research orientations respectively, with kappa values all above 0.7 and statistically significant at the 0.001 level. The statistics indicate that the classification results exhibit a high level of reliability.

Table 1. Kappa statistics

	Knowledge contribution type	Research orientation
Topic 1: h-index and related metrics	0.861***	0.760***
Topic 2: gender difference in academia	0.930***	0.853***
Topic 1: almetrics	0.878***	0.840***
Topic 1: university ranking and academic quality	0.841***	0.794***

Note: *** indicates the level of significance of the difference is 0.001

Figure 5 illustrates the distribution of knowledge contribution types and research orientations in four representative topic studies. Regarding knowledge contribution types, research on Topic 1 is predominantly methodological (83%), and there is also a proportion of regularity-based contributions (17%). Topic 2 is primarily focused on regularity-based contributions (94%), and other knowledge contribution types are relatively marginal. Topic 3 leans towards regularity-based contributions (69%), and also has a proportion of methodological contributions (21%), notably featuring discussions concerning data. Topic 4 demonstrates a relatively balanced distribution between methodological and regularity-based contributions. Analyzing the distribution of research orientations, Topic 1−3 predominantly target academic settings, while research under Topic 4 is more oriented towards practical scenarios or a combination of both.

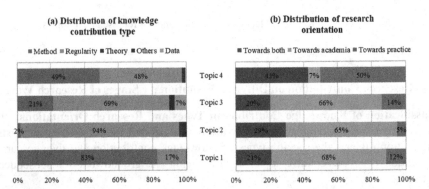

Fig. 5. Reliability assessment of article classification and the distribution of knowledge contribution types and research orientations of four topics.

Trends of the Distribution of Articles with Different Types. Figure 6 depicts the annual proportion of articles with different knowledge contribution types (a) and research orientations (b) under four representative topics. Our first observation is that as time goes by, the distribution of knowledge contribution types becomes increasingly diverse, except for Topic 2, where research contributing to regularity dominate in most times. Our second observation is that the research orientations change over time, and there is an increasing trend to conduct both academia- and practice- oriented research. Regarding the relative proportions of specific types of research, there are variations on account of the different topics. In the following part, we will combine the above two classification dimensions with disruptiveness and impact indicators to conduct a more in-depth analysis.

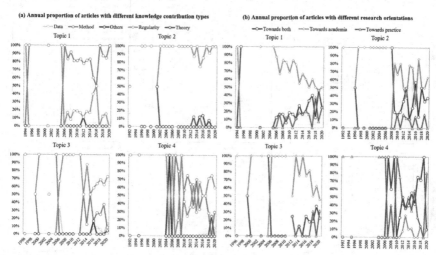

Fig. 6. Annual trends of proportion of articles with different knowledge contribution types and research orientations.

Hybrid Analysis of Research Contributions on Indicator and Content Levels. Drawing upon the aforementioned classification schemes and resultant outcomes, this section further integrates relevant metrics to make a comparison among research across different stages of thematic evolution, aiming to investigate the evolutionary patterns of research contributions. Figure 7 illustrates the temporal variations in disruptiveness, impact within academia, and impact outside academia of studies under four representative topics. Simultaneously, it considers the types of knowledge contribution (differentiated by color) and research orientations (differentiated by shape).

In terms of disruptiveness, there appears to be a decreasing trend in the disruptive indicator of research across the four topics over time, suggesting a diminishing generation of novel knowledge as the research waves progress. However, a closer examination of the types of knowledge contribution within these topics reveals a certain transformation as the topics evolve. For instance, Topic 1 was initially aimed at fostering innovation in methodologies, yet as the topic progressed, there emerged an increasing number of studies focused on revealing patterns. These studies effectively applied indicators, to some extent propelling the practical implementation of related research. Similarly, Topic 4, which primarily concentrated on methods such as constructing evaluation metric systems in its early stages, gradually shifted towards more explorations of patterns using these methods. In actual, previous research has found that new methods are positively associated with disruption scores, whereas new theories and new results are negatively associated with disruption scores [32]. This finding may partly explain the decreasing disruptiveness of studies under the above two topics. Additionally, although Topic 3 predominantly revolves around instrumental aspects, its origins lie in the interaction between

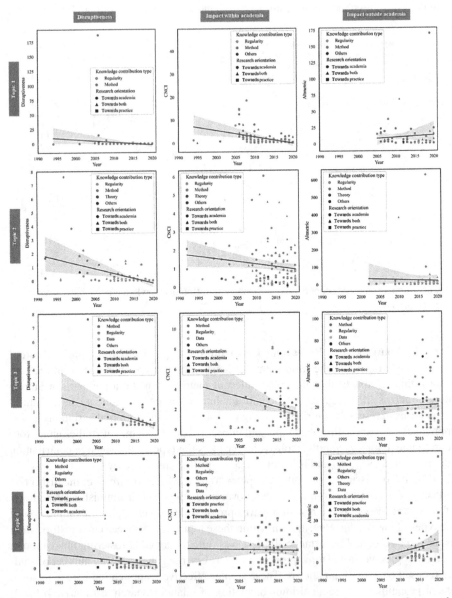

Fig. 7. Annual trends of indicator performances, knowledge contribution types and research orientations of research under four topics.

science and society. Consequently, in its early stages, the focus predominantly rested on studies of regularities. However, as the topic progressed, it prompted a proliferation of methodological discussions, and even explorations into altmetric data. This progression facilitated the transition of altmetric studies from conceptualization to operationalization.

In terms of research impact, there is a notable decreasing trend in the impact within academia of the majority of topics studied, while their impact beyond academia shows a slight upward trend. Though the enhancement of Altmetric score might be associated with the prevalence of social media, our finding may still partially indicate a shift in the contributions of related research from within the academic realm to outside it. Hence, further exploration is warranted regarding the evolving research orientation. Overall, there is an increasing emphasis across various topics on contributions that cater to both academic and practical settings. Specifically, Topics 1 to 3 initially focused predominantly on academic contexts in earlier research stages but progressively moved towards a societal orientation as they developed. For instance, Topics 1 and 3 increasingly concentrated on the practical application of h-index-related indicators and altmetrics, while Topic 2 increasingly focused on the impact of gender equality in science on economic, social, and cultural aspects. Topic 4 stemmed from higher education evaluation practices. Hence, its early research primarily targeted practical settings. However, effective practical development necessitates theoretical and methodological support, leading to a subsequent emergence of more research with academic merit in later stages.

4.4 Case Analysis of Representative Articles

In this section, we aim to conduct a case study to introduce several representative articles, so as to intuitively elucidate the research contributions of these articles within the thematic evolutionary trajectory.

As for Topic 1, two cases are selected to show how a research topic derived from method innovation produces impact within and outside the academic community. The article with the highest CNCI value under this topic is identified as from Leo Egghe, in which he proposed the g-index [33]. This new index is an improvement of the h-index, which inherits the good properties of the h-index, and better takes into account the citation scores of the top articles. This article contributes to methodological innovation and orients towards the academia, which was published in the early stage of this topic and produced considerable impact within academia. The article with the highest Altmetric score is also identified as methodological contribution and academic orientation [34]. However, this article has proposed a novel definition of α-author, based on which a new index h_α is developed. By making a bibliometric concept more attractive and communicable, this article has won high impact on the social media, shared by over 260 tweeter users until the end of 2023. Notably, this article is authored by Hirsh, who originally created h-index and continued to bring something new to this topic.

As for Topic 2, we'd like to introduce an article with the highest Altmetric score under this topic [35], so as to reflect the distinctive contribution of research with a strong topical relevance. Oriented towards academic scenario, this article analyzes three types of lack of objectivity of gender studies (bias, normativity, political activism), and seeks different explanations for the behaviors or phenomena under study (biology/genetics, individual/group differences, environment/culture, societal institutions). Although this article may contribute less to theory or methodology for quantitative science studies, it bridges issues in scientometric research with the public concerns, capable of triggering people sharing, discussion and reflection about the phenomena of gender differences. To a certain degree, this article has its unique contribution to the field of scientometrics and also the public.

The thematic essence of Topic 3 bears resemblance to Topic 1 to a certain degree, yet it leans towards emerging aspects and does not exhibit markedly prominent performance indicators. Given space limitations, this section excludes the cases related to this topic. We would like to use the remaining space to introduce an article with high disruptiveness under Topic 4, so as to illustrate how a piece of research focused on an application-driven topic contributes to academia. As the topic develops to be more mature, a study compares five existing university rankings to unveil the value and limits of different ranking systems [36]. Although oriented towards application scenarios, due to its systematic and in-depth comparative analysis, this article has a higher level of introducing new knowledge compared to previous research, generating greater academic value.

In summary, the aforementioned articles demonstrate differentiated characteristics across various indicators. Only through a multidimensional contribution analysis from contextual and processual perspectives can their true significances be understood.

5　Conclusions and Discussion

This study centers on the field of scientometrics, aiming to explore the contributory characteristics of representative research topics within this field. Its objective is to contextualize individual studies within a situational framework, seeking to comprehend their different roles as the topics develop.

Taking all articles published in *Scientometrics* as the research sample, this study employs BERTopic to conduct topic clustering, and selects four representative research topics, namely h-index and related metrics, gender difference in academia, altmetrics, as well as university ranking and academic quality. Comparisons of the disruptiveness and impact metrics between research under these topics and the entire samples reveal varying degrees of prominence across different indicators for distinct topics. This suggests that research waves have to some extent facilitated the knowledge production and the diffusion of research impact within and beyond the academic community. From the evolutionary perspective of individual topics, comparative analysis of research across different developmental stages of topics indicates a gradual decrease in the introduction of new knowledge and a decline in academic impact alongside the evolution of research waves. However, there have been certain shifts in the type of knowledge contribution and research orientation, along with a degree of enhancement in impact outside academia. This implies that subsequent research plays a facilitating role in the continuous deepening and expansion of these topics.

Our findings may provide following two aspects of implications on future research and policymaking:

(1) Revealing the multidimensional contributions of research waves in a certain scientific field with a combination of indicators and content analysis aids in advancing the comprehension of the value that individual studies contribute to their respective topics and fields. Presently, scholarly understanding of research contributions heavily relies on quantitative metrics, often employing citation indices, novelty metrics, altmetrics, among others, to gauge the value of a study. This paper refers to theories of knowledge production and interaction between science and society, and delineates types of knowledge contribution and research orientations on the basis of indicator analysis. It discerns a shift across various thematic studies in the knowledge contribution types and research orientations whereas certain indicators go down. To some extent, this research facilitates the analysis and interpretation of the underlying causes behind indicator performance and sheds light on content aspects that indicators struggle to reflect, thereby aiding in transcending from indicators to indicating.

(2) Considering the multidimensional contributions of academic papers in a process-oriented and contextualized manner holds significant policy implications for the scientific evaluation of research outcomes. In the international context, representative documents pertaining to the reform of research evaluation such as *San Francisco Declaration on Research Assessment* (2012) and *Bibliometrics: the Leiden Manifesto for research metrics* (2015) highlight the necessity of transcending traditional citation-based metrics in academic evaluation of entities such as researchers and research institutions. Instead, emphasis is placed on assessing their actual value generated across multiple dimensions. In the domestic sphere, since the release of the *Opinions of Deepening the Reform of Project Review, Talent Evaluation, and Institutional Assessment* (the "Sanping Opinions") in 2018, there has been systematic progress in the reform of scientific research evaluation. In 2021, the *Guiding Opinions of the General Office of the State Council on Improving the Evaluation Mechanism of Scientific and Technological Achievements* explicitly proposed an evaluation orientation centered on innovation, performance, and actual contributions. This study endeavors to place academic papers within the contexts of historical progression and disciplinary advancement, examining their multidimensional contributions. It represents a positive exploration to engage in multifaceted scientific evaluation practices from various perspectives.

Indeed, this study bears limitations that warrant further expansion and deepening. Regarding sample selection, this research delves into the field of scientometrics as an illustrative case, and only selects four representative topics in this field for a pilot study. However, there exists potential for future inclusion of comparative analysis across other disciplinary domains and among different types of research topics, so as to uncover more universally applicable and far-reaching patterns. In terms of methodological design, this study primarily classifies knowledge contribution types and research orientations in academic papers through manual annotation. Future exploration could involve a semi-automated annotation approach integrating human and machine capabilities, thereby allowing for the analysis of larger-scale datasets.

Acknowledgements. This work was supported by the National Natural Science Foundation of China (grant no. 71974150, 72374160), and the National Laboratory Center for Library and information Science in Wuhan University.

References

1. Park, M., Leahey, E., Funk, R.J.: Papers and patents are becoming less disruptive over time. Nature **613**(7942), 138–144 (2023)
2. Zitt, M., Ramanana-Rahary, S., Bassecoulard, E.: Relativity of citation performance and excellence measures: from cross-field to cross-scale effects of field-normalisation. Scientometrics **63**(2), 373–401 (2005)
3. Sugimoto, C.R., Weingart, S.: The kaleidoscope of disciplinarity. Journal of Documentation **71**(4), 775–794 (2015)
4. Waltman L., Van Eck N.J.: Field Normalization of Scientometric Indicators. In: GLäNZEL W, MOED H F, SCHMOCH U, et al. Springer Handbook of Science and Technology Indicators. Cham; Springer International Publishing, pp. 281–300 (2019)
5. Ivancheva, L.: Scientometrics today: a methodological overview. COLLNET J. Scientometrics Inform. Manage. **2**(2), 47–56 (2008)
6. Carayannis, E.G., Campbell, D.F.J.: Definition of Key Terms: Knowledge, Knowledge Production, Innovation, Democracy, and Governance [M]. In: CARAYANNIS, E.G., CAMPBELL, D.F.J., Smart Quintuple Helix Innovation Systems: How Social Ecology and Environmental Protection are Driving Innovation, Sustainable Development and Economic Growth. Cham; Springer International Publishing, pp. 5–15 (2019)
7. Kuhn, T.S.: The Structure of Scientific Revolutions, 2nd edn. [M]. Chicago: University of Chicago Press (1970)
8. Leibel, C., Bornmann, L.: What do we know about the disruption index in scientometrics? An overview of the literature. Scientometrics (2023)
9. Chao, W., Chen, M., Zhou, X., et al.: A joint framework for identifying the type and arguments of scientific contribution. Scientometrics **128**(6), 3347–3376 (2023)
10. Chen, H., Nguyen, H., Alghamdi, A.: Constructing a high-quality dataset for automated creation of summaries of fundamental contributions of research articles. Scientometrics **127**(12), 7061–7075 (2022)
11. Bernal, J.D.: The social function of science [M]. Hertford: Stephen Austin and Son (1938)
12. Vakkari, P., Järvelin, K., Chang, Y.-W.: The association of disciplinary background with the evolution of topics and methods in library and information science research 1995–2015. J. Am. Soc. Inf. Sci. **74**(7), 811–827 (2023)
13. Lund, B.D.: Who really contributes to information science research? an analysis of disciplinarity and nationality of contributors to ten top journals. Malays. J. Libr. Inf. Sci. **25**(3), 15–29 (2020)
14. Wu, L., Wang, D., Evans, J.A.: Large teams develop and small teams disrupt science and technology. Nature **566**(7744), 378–382 (2019)
15. Liu, X., Shen, Z., Liao, Y., et al.: The research about the improved disruption index and its influencing factors (in Chinese). Libr. Inform. Serv. **64**(24), 84–91 (2020)
16. Bornmann, L., Tekles, A.: Disruption index depends on length of citation window. Profesional de la información **28**(2), e280207 (2019)
17. Grootendorst, M.: BERTopic: neural topic modeling with a class-based TF-IDF procedure. arXiv preprint arXiv:220305794 (2022)
18. Devlin, J., Chang, M.-W., Lee, K., et al.: Bert: Pre-training of deep bidirectional transformers for language understanding. arXiv preprint arXiv:181004805 (2018)

19. Egger, R., Yu, J.: A topic modeling comparison between LDA, NMF, Top2Vec, and BERTopic to Demystify Twitter Posts. Frontiers in Sociology 7(2022)

20. Contreras, K., Verbel, G., Sanchez, J., et al.: Using topic modelling for analyzing panamanian parliamentary proceedings with neural and statistical methods. In: proceedings of the 2022 IEEE 40th Central America and Panama Convention (CONCAPAN), F 9–12 Nov. 2022 (2022)

21. Hristova, G., Netov, N.: Media coverage and public perception of distance learning during the COVID-19 pandemic: a topic modeling approach based on BERTopic. In: Proceedings of the 2022 IEEE International Conference on Big Data (Big Data), F 17–20 Dec 2022 (2022)

22. Wang, Z., Chen, J., Chen, J., et al.: Identifying interdisciplinary topics and their evolution based on BERTopic. Scientometrics (2023)

23. Zhang, L., Sivertsen, G., Du, H., et al.: Gender differences in the aims and impacts of research. Scientometrics 126(11), 8861–8886 (2021)

24. Hirsch, J.E.: An index to quantify an individual's scientific research output. Proc. Natl. Acad. Sci. 102(46), 16569–16572 (2005)

25. Fox, M.F., Faver, C.A.: Men, women, and publication productivity: patterns among social work academics. Sociol. Q. 26(4), 537–549 (1985)

26. Long, J.S.: The origins of sex differences in science. Soc. Forces 68(4), 1297–1316 (1990)

27. Zuckerman, H., Cole, J.R.: Women in American science. Minerva 13(1), 82–102 (1975)

28. Ross, M.B., Glennon, B.M., Murciano-Goroff, R., et al.: Women are credited less in science than men. Nature 608(7921), 135–145 (2022)

29. Priem, J., Hemminger, B.H.: Scientometrics 2.0: New metrics of scholarly impact on the social Web. First Monday 15(7) (2010)

30. Van Eck, N.J., Waltman, L.: Software survey: VOSviewer, a computer program for bibliometric mapping. Scientometrics 84(2), 523–538 (2010)

31. Mchugh, M.L.: Interrater reliability: the kappa statistic. Biochemia medica 22(3), 276–282 (2012)

32. Leahey, E., Lee, J., Funk, R.J.: What types of novelty are most disruptive? Am. Sociol. Rev. 88(3), 562–597 (2023)

33. Egghe, L.: Theory and practise of the g-index. Scientometrics 69(1), 131–152 (2006)

34. Hirsch, J.E.: $H\alpha$: An index to quantify an individual's scientific leadership. Scientometrics 118(2), 673–686 (2019)

35. Söderlund, T., Madison, G.: Objectivity and realms of explanation in academic journal articles concerning sex/gender: a comparison of Gender studies and the other social sciences. Scientometrics 112(2), 1093–1109 (2017)

36. Moed, H.F.: A critical comparative analysis of five world university rankings. Scientometrics 110(2), 967–990 (2017)

Micro Citation Importance Identification and Its Application to Literature Evaluation

Weimin Nie and Shiyan Ou(✉)

School of Information Management, Nanjing University, Nanjing, China
nieweimin@smail.nju.edu.cn, oushiyan@nju.edu.cn

Abstract. We present our approach for identifying the importance of citing sentences, where the importance of citing sentences is termed "micro citation importance" in our research. This approach characterizes a regression method based on the pretrained language model SciBERT, where the citation function is incorporated into the citing sentence as its input. Remarkably, our approach demonstrates superior performance on the 3C Citation Context Classification Shared Task corpus, suggesting that both regarding micro citation importance identification as a regression problem and integrating the citation function contribute to enhanced performance. Furthermore, we extend our investigation to literature evaluation, introducing a novel metric coined "micro citation frequency" derived from micro citation importance acquired by our proposed regression method. Notably, it is observed that micro citation frequency outperforms the established metric of citation frequency in terms of evaluating high-quality papers, further validating our proposed regression method. Our work not only enriches citation content analysis, but also holds implications for optimizing literature evaluation.

Keywords: Citation Importance · Pretrained Language Model · Citation Function · Literature Evaluation · Citation Content Analysis

1 Introduction

In recent years, Citation Content Analysis (CCA), the next generation of citation analysis [1], has attracted substantial attention. Specifically, CCA consists of various tasks such as citation content extraction, citation classification, citation topic modeling, citation entity extraction and cited span identification, among others.

Among these tasks, citation classification categorizes citations from various perspectives [2], including citation function and citation sentiment. Recently, citation importance has emerged as a novel viewpoint of citation classification, designed to measure the extent of intellect support provided by cited papers to their citing papers [3]. As a result, papers can be discriminated based on their respective citation importance, which has substantial applications, such as scientific paper retrieval, research achievement evaluation and research trend tracking.

Currently, most studies of identifying citation importance regard it as a binary classification problem, categorizing citations as either "influential" or "incidental" [4]. And

I. Sserwanga et al. (Eds.): iConference 2024, LNCS 14597, pp. 356–375, 2024.
https://doi.org/10.1007/978-3-031-57860-1_24

traditional machine learning methods are predominantly used to develop citation importance classifiers, utilizing features such as the individual mention count, paper metadata, and cue phrases within the citation content. However, as the research focus on citation importance identification shifts from the coarse-grained paper to the fine-grained citation content, traditional machine learning methods have exposed limitations in extracting textual semantics. Consequently, deep learning methods have gained more attention due to their superior ability in this regard.

Despite considerable advancements, several issues remain underexplored in citation importance identification. Firstly, most studies have relied on traditional machine learning methods, with limited exploration of deep learning techniques. Secondly, inadequate attention has been dedicated to the role of citation function in identifying citation importance. Lastly, constraining citation importance identification within a classification framework impedes its subsequent application, such as precise literature evaluation.

In view of these issues, this study proposes a regression method based on the pretrained language model SciBERT, where the citation function and the citing sentence are integrated as its input. Our method demonstrates superior performance on the 3C Citation Context Classification Shared Task corpus. Furthermore, acknowledging the significance of literature evaluation, we expand our investigation by introducing an innovative metric termed "micro citation frequency" to the process. This metric proves its superiority in evaluating high-quality paper when compared with the well-established metric of citation frequency, thus providing additional validation for the proposed regression method.

The remaining part of the paper proceeds as follows: Sect. 2 reviews related work regarding citation importance and literature evaluation. And Sect. 3 elaborates the proposed regression method. The experimental process and the discussion of results obtained are presented in Sect. 4. Section 5 delves into preliminary research on literature evaluation. Finally, Sect. 6 summarizes the entire paper.

2 Related Work

2.1 Citation Importance

Citation classification is one of the main tasks in CCA, with the aim to distinguish citations from diverse perspectives. Existing studies mainly focus on citation function and citation sentiment. Specially, in the citation function task, citations are categorized into 4 to 6 distinct groups [5–8] according to the roles played by cited papers in their corresponding citing papers. On the other hand, the citation sentiment task typically classifies citations into three groups based on the stance adopted by authors when referencing the cited papers [9, 10].

Recently, citation importance has attracted increasing attention. In 2015, Zhu et al. [11] administered a web questionnaire to enquire researchers about cited papers that were significant to their studies, hence classifying cited papers into two categories: "influential" and "incidental". Moreover, Valenzuela et al. [12] deemed that citation importance is closely related to citation function and introduced rules to classify cited papers as "influential" or "incidental" based on their respective citation functions. These seminal studies have collectively initiated research on the binary citation importance.

Subsequently, most of recent research on citation importance identification categorizes citations into either "influential" or "incidental."

The methods for the binary citation importance can be divided into two groups: traditional machine learning methods and deep learning methods. Among these, traditional machine learning methods have predominantly been utilized in relevant studies, which typically consist of classifiers and feature engineering. Common classifiers include Support Vector Machines, Logistic Regression, Random Forest and so on. Notably, Random Forest and Support Vector Machines have consistently demonstrated preferable performance across various studies [4, 13, 14]. And feature engineering aims to convert specific problem-related information into numerical representations [15]. Hou et al. [16] pointed out that the number of times a cited paper is mentioned in the content of one of its citing papers, namely the individual mention count, reflects the cited paper's contribution to the citing paper. As a consequence, the individual mention count has been utilized in citation importance identification. For instance, Nazir et al. [17] segmented the content of papers into four sections: Introduction, Literature Review, Methodology, and Results & Discussion. They recorded the individual mention count of a cited paper in each section of the citing paper, considering these counts as features. In addition, researchers have taken paper metadata into consideration. For example, Hassan et al. [18] calculated the textual similarity between the abstracts of citing and cited papers in citation importance identification.

It is noteworthy that the citation content provides contextual information on how a paper is cited [19]. However, the aforementioned studies didn't delve into it, resulting in limited performance [1, 20]. Yang et al. [21] utilized the citation content to generate paper summarizations. Subsequently, increased attention has been directed towards the citation content in identifying citation importance [22]. Qayyum et al. [23] probed cue phrases within the citation content, while An et al. [24] collected "influential" and "incidental" cue phrases. They determined the importance of a cited paper to its citing paper by analyzing the occurrence of these cue phrases in the citation content.

In 2020, Kunnath et al. [25, 26] conducted a shared task of identifying the importance of citing sentences instead of entire papers. They released an annotated corpus, which have advanced citation importance identification from the paper level to the citation content level. In this shared task, Mishra et al. [27] assessed the performance of two distinct feature sets. The first set consisted solely of citing sentences, while the second one included citing sentences along with titles of both citing papers and cited papers. Interestingly, the first feature set consistently outperformed the second one when coupled with different classifiers. However, it is formidable for traditional machine learning methods to comprehensively extract textual semantics, while deep learning methods are more preferable in this regard. Consequently, a few studies have attempted to exploit deep learning methods within the shared task [28]. To differentiate between citation importance at the paper level and at the citation content level, this study will henceforth use the terms "macro citation importance" for the former and "micro citation importance" for the latter. The primary focus of this study lies in micro citation importance.

It is noteworthy that the citation importance is intricately connected to both the citation function and the citation sentiment. As early as 1975, Moravcsik and Murugesan [29] manually annotated cited papers from viewpoints such as the citation importance, the citation function and the citation sentiment. Then, Valenzuela et al. [12] categorized cited papers into two importance groups based on four citation functions. Given the relatedness among the citation importance, the citation function and the citation sentiment, researchers have incorporated relevant features into citation importance identification. For instance, Aljuaid et al. [30] introduced the sentiment feature of citation content when identifying macro citation importance. In addition to sentiment, Wang et al. [20] considered the section location of citation content. Similarly, Nazir et al. [31] simultaneously took the sentiment and section location features of citation content into account. Noteworthily, these studies essentially regarded the section location of a citation as a proxy for its corresponding citation function. Indeed, the section location can offer partial insights into a citation's function within the citing paper [32, 33]. For example, citations in "Method" sections typically provide data and methods for citing papers, while those in "Literature Review" sections generally present background information related to citing papers. However, it is essential to emphasize that the section location alone can't fully substitute for the citation function [34]. Therefore, a direct examination of the citation function is crucial in identifying citation importance.

While most prior studies treated citation importance identification as a classification problem, confining it within such a framework has impeded further applications [35]. For instance, cited papers within the same category cannot be further compared in terms of their importance degree. In response, researchers have attempted to leverage continuous values [36], instead of discrete labels, to represent the importance of cited papers to their citing papers. Wang et al. [37] considered factors such as the length of citation content, the individual mention count and the section location to measure the importance of cited papers. The resulting continuous values were subsequently utilized to improve the PageRank algorithm for literature evaluation. Likewise, Xia et al. [38] derived continuous importance values based on the individual mention count and the section location. Then they constructed a weighted citation network using these continuous values and performed the main path analysis within the network. Nevertheless, these methods for generating citation importance values were in essence unsupervised, making it challenging to directly validate their credibility. Whereas Wan and Liu [35] employed a regression method to identify macro citation importance, which generated continuous values representing the importance of cited papers to citing papers. This methodology further facilitated more convenient evaluation of both papers and authors. Specifically, the features applied within their traditional machine learning method consisted of the individual mention count, the section location, the time interval, the length of citing sentence and so on. However, their regression approach differed from current research on micro citation importance identification in terms of the analysis object and the number of categories. And the traditional machine learning method they utilized constrained overall performance. Despite these issues, their regression approach sheds light on micro citation importance identification.

2.2 Literature Evaluation

Scientific evaluation is integral to relevant realms, with literature evaluation forming its cornerstone [39]. Extensive research on literature evaluation has yielded fruitful outcomes. Here, we sketch a concise overview of literature evaluation.

Methods for literature evaluation can be broadly categorized into two groups: qualitative methods and quantitative methods [40, 41]. Peer review stands out as a typical qualitative method, characterizing expert scholars within similar fields assessing the quality of papers [42]. Despite being widely acknowledged as the "gold standard" in literature evaluation and extensively utilized, it is vital to recognize its intrinsic flaws [43], such as resource-intensive procedures [44], subjective and arbitrary evaluation processes [45], and susceptibility to social influences [46]. Consequently, numerous modifications have been suggested to improve peer review, including optional compensated peer review [47], modified reviewer recommendation [48, 49], open peer review [50] and peer review assessment [51], among others.

In addition to qualitative methods, quantitative methods have been utilized in literature evaluation, offering the potential to alleviate certain flaws associated with peer review. Among these, citation frequency denotes the number of times a specific paper is referenced by other papers, serving as a longstanding metric that often acts as a benchmark against which other metrics can be assessed [52].

With advancements in full-text databases and open science, researchers now have access not only to the bibliographic data but also to the full-text data of papers, thereby expanding the range of data sources for literature evaluation [53]. Initially, researchers examined the number of times a specific paper is mentioned in the content of other papers, namely the mention count [54]. And the mention count of a paper can be calculated by summing up the individual mention counts from all its citing papers. Ding et al. [55] revealed a moderate correlation between the mention count and the citation frequency. As technologies develop, researchers can now automatically analyze the citation content of a specific paper, going beyond the mere acquisition of its mention count, leading to the inclusion of citation content in literature evaluation. Xu et al. [56] discovered notable disparities in the distribution of citation sentiment when researchers referenced awarded papers compared to those citing non-awarded papers. Thus, they concluded that the citation sentiment holds the potential to enhance literature evaluation. Furthermore, Geng and Yang [57] classified citations to a specific paper into three categories: positive, negative and neutral. They assigned weights to these different types of citations using the analytic hierarchy process and calculated the weighted citation frequency accordingly. Ma et al.[58] focused on citations from reputable experts, scoring citations based on cue phrases in their content, allowing for adjustments to the citation frequency. Their proposed method demonstrated superior performance in reprehensive work selection compared to both the citation frequency and the journal impact factor.

3   Methods

In this study, we approach the task of identifying micro citation importance as a regression problem rather than a classification challenge. Our method is designed to comprehensively extract semantic features from the citation content and generate continuous values ranging from 0 to 1. These values serve as a quantitative measure of the citation content's importance.

Given the superior performance demonstrated by pretrained language models (PLMs) across various tasks [59] and the intrinsic link between the citation importance and the citation function, we propose a regression method based on SciBERT, one of prominent PLMs. Furthermore, the citation function is integrated to augment performance. As depicted in Fig. 1, our framework consists of three key components: an input layer, a semantics extraction layer, and an output layer.

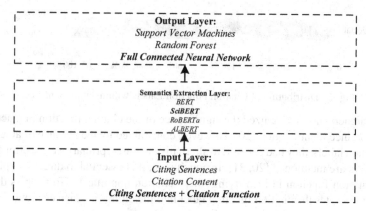

Fig. 1. Framework of the Proposed Method

The input layer functions as the recipient of input, such as a citing sentence, initialing the entire process. Subsequently, the semantics extraction layer is designed to comprehensively extract semantic features from the input and convert them into a vector representation. Finally, the output layer receives the vector representation from the semantics extraction layer and generates a continuous prediction value representing the importance degree of the input.

3.1 Input Layer

Note that the citation content typically encompasses the citing sentence containing the citation marker as well as its surrounding context in the citing paper. However, our study primarily concentrates on the citing sentence alone, omitting its surrounding context, which is supported by the experimental results obtained in Sect. 4.2.

Moreover, micro citation importance can be regarded as a holistic assessment of the citing sentence. The citation function not only constitutes a substantial part of the citing sentence but is also closely associated with the citation importance [12]. Therefore, the citation function is supposed to be taken into account in identifying micro citation importance.

In addition, we analyzed the distribution of citation function labels within both "influential" and "incidental" citing sentences, as depicted in Fig. 2, within our experimental corpus (Sect. 4.1). Obviously, significant disparities were observed in the distribution of citation function labels between these two categories. For example, in "incidental" citing sentences, the "background" label accounted for as much as 67.46%, whereas in "influential" citing sentences, the proportion of the "background" label decreased to 41.36%. These findings further highlight the imperative of integrating the citation function when identifying micro citation importance.

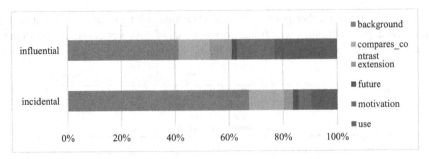

Fig. 2. Distribution of Citation Function Labels within Citing Sentences

Researchers have recognized the significance of the citation function in macro citation importance identification [20]. However, constrained by the absence of actual citation function labels, they had to resort to alternative features, primarily the sections where
cited papers are mentioned [20, 31]. In conclusion, it is essential to directly explore the
role of citation function in identifying micro citation importance. To address this, our
study incorporates the citation function label into the citing sentence as input.

3.2 Semantics Extraction Layer and Output Layer

Considering the exceptional performance of PLMs across various tasks [59], we have
opted for PLMs over traditional techniques like the Bag-of-Words model for semantic
feature extraction. Moreover, among the available PLMs, we have specifically chosen
SciBERT, primarily due to its exclusive pretrained corpus consisting of scientific papers,
aligning seamlessly with our research. This choice is further supported by the results
obtained in Sect. 4.2.

The citation function label and the citing sentence are reorganized to form a processed
text sequence denoted as X_{cs} as follows.

$$X_{cs} = [[CLS], label_{function}, [SEP], token_1, token_2, \cdots, token_i, \cdots, token_n] \qquad (1)$$

where $label_{function}$ denotes the corresponding citation function label, and $token_i$ represents the ith token within the citing sentence. n is the total number of tokens in the citing
sentence. Moreover, both [CLS] and [SEP] are special tokens, utilized by SciBERT to
understand the structure of text sequence. [CLS] marks the beginning of the entire text
sequence, while [SEP] serves as a delimiter between the citation function label and the
citing sentence.

The processed text sequence X_{cs} then undergoes 12 stacked Transformer encoders.
These encoders are designed to extract semantic features from X_{cs}. In the final Transformer encoder, the vector corresponding to [CLS] serves as a unified representation
encapsulating the semantic meaning of both the citation function and the citing sentence.

Next, the [CLS] vector is fed into a fully connected neural network, which produces
a continuous prediction value ranging from 0 to 1, leveraging the sigmoid activation
function. Noteworthily, a fully connected neural network employing the softmax activation function is commonly known as a softmax classifier. Similarly, a fully connected
neural network applying the sigmoid activation function is termed a sigmoid regressor
in our research.

Moreover, during the training phase, the overall loss is computed using the mean square error function, which is subsequently utilized for backpropagation to fine-tune the network's weights.

Furthermore, it is essential to establish mechanisms for mutual conversion between discrete labels in the experimental corpus and the continuous prediction values generated by our regression method. In the training phase, citing sentences labeled as "influential" receive a value of 1, whereas those labeled as "incidental" are assigned a value of 0. Subsequently, during the testing phase, a mapping function (Formula (2)) is utilized to convert prediction values into citation importance labels.

$$f(p) = \begin{cases} 0 & p < t \\ 1 & p \geq t \end{cases} \tag{2}$$

where p represents the prediction value of a citing sentence, and t is a specific threshold or cutoff point. Essentially, the mapping function classifies a citing sentence as either "incidental" or "influential" based on its prediction value. The citing sentence is categorized as "incidental" if its prediction value falls below t. Conversely, if the prediction value is equal to or greater than t, the citing sentence is classified as "influential." Thus, t serves as a crucial hyperparameter within the proposed regression method, which was determined by the validation set. Following the methodology outlined in [60], the algorithm for determining the threshold t is depicted in Fig. 3.

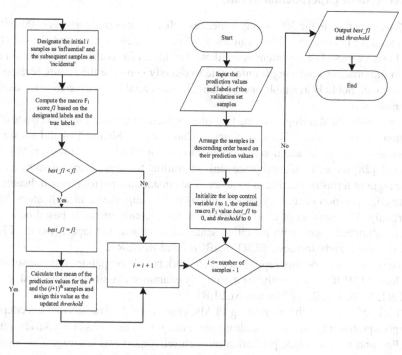

Fig. 3. Threshold Determination Algorithm

4   Experimental Process and Results

4.1   Experimental Process

This study utilized the 3C Citation Context Classification Shared Task corpus [25, 26], comprising 3000 citing sentences from diverse disciplines. Every citing sentence is meticulously annotated for both citation function and citation importance. Consequently, the task is divided into two sub-tasks: citation function classification and citation importance identification. In the former sub-task, citing sentences are assigned to categories such as "background", "compares_contrast", "extension", "future", "motivation" and "use" [6]. The latter sub-task involves classifying citing sentences as either "influential" or "incidental," which is essentially micro citation importance identification.

Adhering to the methodology outlined by Maheshwari et al. [28], a subset of 500 citing sentences was randomly selected from the pool of 3000 to constitute the testing set. Furthermore, another 300 sentences were chosen from the remaining 2500 sentences to form the validation set. The training set was ultimately comprised of the remaining 2200 sentences.

What is more, this study leverages the macro F_1 as its primary evaluation metric, in alignment with the 3C Citation Context Classification Shared Task. Additionally, the micro F_1 scores are reported.

4.2   Analysis of Experimental Results

Baseline. Apart from the 3000 citing sentences utilized in this study, another 1000 citing sentences have been reserved for evaluation within the 3c citation context classification shared task corpus. These sentences are devoid of labels for both citation function and citation importance, rendering it unfeasible to directly compare the results obtained in our study with publicly available ones [61]. So, it is essential for us to establish a baseline for comparison.

Regrettably, the developers of the first-place system in the citation importance identification sub-task of the 3C Citation Context Classification Shared Task did not submit a paper, depriving us of additional insights into their methodology. However, Maheshwari et al. [28] secured a second-place ranking, trailing the first-place system by a mere 0.01 margin in terms of the macro F_1 score. The outstanding performance indicates the cutting-edge position of their system in micro citation importance identification. More importantly, Maheshwari et al. detailed their classification methods based on PLMs in their submitted paper, with the citing sentence serving as the input. And the PLMs utilized in their study included BERT, SciBERT and RoBERTa.

In our study, we not only reproduced their work but also expanded our investigation to include ALBERT. As a result, we thoroughly examined classification methods based on BERT, SciBERT, RoBERTa and ALBERT.

BERT [59], one of the pioneering PLMs, consists of 12 Transformer encoders. It undergoes pretraining on a large-scale corpus, engaging in the tasks of masked language modeling and next sentence prediction through self-supervised learning. This enables it to capture language nuances without the need for manual corpus annotation. Since the debut of BERT, researchers have iteratively refined it, giving rise to various PLMs.

Notable examples include SciBERT, RoBERTa and ALBERT [62]. SciBERT's corpus consists of papers from both the computer science and biomedical domains [63], a desirable feature for our research. RoBERTa [64] adjusts the training data size and critical hyperparameters of BERT, while ALBERT [65] enhances BERT's computational efficiency through parameter reduction techniques.

Table 1. Performance of Classification Methods Based on PLMs

PLM	Micro F_1	Macro F_1	Macro F_1 from [28]
BERT	**0.7020**	**0.7010**	0.6611
SciBERT	0.6900	0.6892	**0.6778**
RoBERTa	0.5900	0.5857	0.6636
ALBERT	0.6500	0.6481	\

Table 1 displays the performance of classification methods based on PLMs. The second and third columns of the table represent the micro F1 scores and the macro F1 scores, respectively, acquired by these methods on our study's testing set. Among them, the BERT-based classification method achieved the highest macro F1 score of 0.7010, outperforming the SciBERT-based, ALBERT-based, and RoBERTa-based classification methods in descending order.

In the last column in Table 1, we present the macro F_1 scores retrieved from Maheshwari et al.'s study [28]. Their SciBERT-based classification method achieved a macro F_1 score of 0.6778, which is close to our study's result of 0.6892. Additionally, their RoBERTa-based classification method outperformed ours, exhibiting a higher macro F_1 score of 0.6636 compared to our observed score of 0.5857. Conversely, their BERT-based classification method showed a lower macro F_1 score of 0.6611, in contrast to our study's performance of 0.7010. Considering these findings, we have selected the BERT-based classification method as the strong baseline, given its superior performance on our study's testing set.

Citing Sentences and Relevant Information. After establishing the strong baseline, we proceed to investigate the impact of inputs on performance. The citing sentence serves as the annotation unit within our experimental corpus, offering an intuitive starting point for exploring its role in identifying micro citation importance. Notably, the aforementioned strong baseline also employed the citing sentence as its input. In addition, researchers have incorporated other relevant information [28, 66, 67] to enhance performance. In alignment with these endeavors, the citation function and the citation content are taken into account in our study. As elaborated in Sect. 3.1, the citation function is intricately connected with the citation importance and can contribute to performance enhancement. Furthermore, the citation content encompasses the contextual content surrounding the citing sentence, providing deeper insights into how a paper is cited. Therefore, extending our analysis beyond the citing sentence to include the citation content also has the potential to improve performance. Given that the citation content was not manually annotated within our experimental corpus, we employed a state-of-the-art system developed by Pride et al. [68] to automatically identify the citation content.

To facilitate a comprehensive comparison encompassing citing sentences, citation content, and citation function, we separately provided the classification methods with distinct inputs, including the citing sentence, the citation content, and the combination of citation function and citing sentence. This methodology attempts to strike a balance between efficacy and resource consumption.

Figure 4 depicts the macro F_1 scores acquired by classification methods employing these three distinct inputs: the citing sentence, the citation content and the combination of citation function and citing sentence. Noteworthily, the data represented by the line labeled "Citing Sentence" corresponds to the values presented in Table 1.

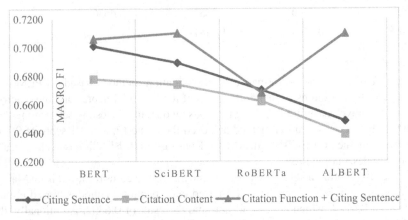

Fig. 4. Macro F_1 Scores of Classification Methods with Different Inputs

The performance of these classification methods reveals a relatively uniform pattern across various PLMs. In general, the combination of citation function and citing sentence consistently demonstrates the highest performance. Following closely is the citing sentence alone, while the citation content yields the lowest macro F1 score. Consequently, we have opted to use the combination of citation function and citing sentence as the preferred input. Besides, the inferior performance of the citation content may be attributed to the introduction of unnecessary noise during the citation content identification process.

Comparison Between Regression Methods and Classification Methods. So far, our analysis has exclusively concentrated on classification methods based on PLMs. Furthermore, we have expanded our investigation to include regression methods, conducting a comparative analysis between regression methods with classification methods. In this comparison, the combination of citation function and citing sentence serves as the input for both types of methods.

Table 2 reports the performance of classification methods based on PLMs, which is identical to the data represented by the "Citation Function + Citing Sentence" line in Fig. 4.

Table 2. Performance of Classification Methods Based on PLMs (Citation Function + Citing Sentence)

PLM	Micro F_1	Macro F_1
BERT	0.7060	0.7060
SciBERT	**0.7100**	**0.7100**
RoBERTa	0.6680	0.6680
ALBERT	**0.7100**	0.7098

And Table 3 reports the performance of regression methods based on PLMs, in which the "Threshold" column represents the threshold defined in Formula (2).

Table 3. Performance of Regression Methods Based on PLMs

PLM	Threshold	Micro F_1	Macro F_1
BERT	0.5199	0.7060	0.7050
SciBERT	0.7995	**0.7380**	**0.7366**
RoBERTa	0.0821	0.6840	0.6825
ALBERT	0.4609	0.7160	0.7160

To commence, Table 3 reveals that the SciBERT-based regression method obtained the highest macro F_1 score of 0.7366, exhibiting a notable improvement of 0.0356 over the strong baseline. Moreover, as indicated in Table 2 and Table 3, with the exception of the BERT-based regression method, all other regression methods outperformed their respective classification methods. This observation also indicates that treating micro citation importance identification as a regression task contributes to enhanced performance.

It is noteworthy that the output layers in both classification and regression methods based on PLMs essentially function as fully connected neural networks with distinct activation functions. Specifically, the former is commonly recognized as the softmax classifier, while the latter is termed the sigmoid regressor in our study. To facilitate a more extensive comparison between regression and classification methods, we additionally examined the performance of various classifiers and regressors within the output layer, in addition to the softmax classifier and the sigmoid regressor. Prior research has consistently shown the superiority of the Support Vector Classifier and the Random Forest Classifier over others [4, 13, 14]. Consequently, we leveraged the Support Vector Classifier (SVC) and Random Forest Classifier (RFC), along with their regression counterparts: Support Vector Regressor (SVR), and Random Forest Regressor (RFR). Table 4 and 5 present their respective performances.

Table 4. Performance of SVC and SVR

| | SVC | | SVR | | |
	Micro F_1	Macro F_1	Threshold	Micro F_1	Macro F_1
BERT	0.6320	0.6315	0.4118	0.7140	0.7135
SciBERT	0.6480	0.6479	0.3947	0.7140	0.7126
RoBERTa	0.6480	0.6462	0.5454	0.6800	0.6794
ALBERT	0.6700	0.6690	0.5033	0.6940	0.6940

Table 5. Performance of RFC and RFR

| | RFC | | RFR | | |
	Micro F_1	Macro F_1	Threshold	Micro F_1	Macro F_1
BERT	0.6460	0.6460	0.4039	0.6760	0.6760
SciBERT	0.7040	0.7040	0.5909	0.6820	0.6812
RoBERTa	0.6440	0.6421	0.6003	0.6860	0.6848
ALBERT	0.6620	0.6616	0.5370	0.6920	0.6915

Upon analyzing both Table 4 and Table 5, it becomes evident that, with the exception of the inferior performance of SciBERT-RFR compared to SciBERT-RFC, all other regressors coupled with PLMs outperform their corresponding classifiers. These results further underscore that micro citation importance identification should be treated as a regression task rather than a classification task. Furthermore, when coupled with various PLMs, SVR attained a mean macro F_1 score of 0.6999, surpassing the average macro F_1 score of 0.6834 achieved by RFR. Noteworthily, both the 0.6999 achieved by SVR and the 0.6834 achieved by RFR still fell short of the 0.7100 acquired by the sigmoid regressor (as calculated in Table 3), highlighting the effectiveness of the sigmoid regressor.

5   Preliminary Study on Micro Citation Importance's Application to Literature Evaluation

Recognizing the significance of literature evaluation and striving for a more thorough analysis of the proposed regression method for micro citation importance identification, we have initiated preliminary investigations into the potential application of micro citation importance generated by our proposed regression method in the context of literature evaluation.

Noteworthily, citation frequency stands as a foundational metric in literature evaluation, quantifying the number of times a specific paper is cited by others. Nevertheless, when assessing a paper, citation frequency fails to distinguish among its citing papers. In contrast, micro citation importance delves into the fine-grained citation content beyond the coarse-grained paper, offering the potential for a more nuanced evaluation of the impact of cited papers on their respective citing papers. With this in mind, we attempt to utilize micro citation importance, acquired through our proposed regression method, to augment citation frequency, introducing a novel metric termed "micro citation frequency" to literature evaluation.

Assume a paper is cited by m other papers, and the number of its corresponding citing sentences in the ith citing paper is denoted as n_i. The citation frequency and the micro citation frequency of the specific paper, represented as cf and mcf, respectively, are calculated using Formula (3) and (4).

$$cf = \sum_{i}^{m} 1 = m \tag{3}$$

$$mcf = \sum_{i=1}^{m} \sum_{j=1}^{n^i} 1 \times w_{ij} \tag{4}$$

where w_{ij} represents the micro citation importance value for the jth citing sentence in the corresponding i^{th} citing paper.

We have curated our tailored application corpus using the ACL Anthology Corpus with Full Text [69], which encompasses the full text of papers presented at the Association for Computational Linguistics conferences. Within this corpus, we have identified 552383 citation relations between papers and gathered 789961 citing sentences.

Our process commenced with a citation frequency analysis, capturing the citation frequencies of papers. Subsequently, the proposed regression method was applied to identify the importance values of citing sentences extracted from our application corpus. Next, we computed the micro citation frequencies of papers. Finally, we delved into the capabilities of both citation frequency and micro citation frequency to assess high-quality papers. It is essential to explain the high-quality paper selection process in advance.

Among the conferences organized by the Association for Computational Linguistics, the Annual Meeting of the Association for Computational Linguistics (ACL), the Conference on Empirical Methods in Natural Language Processing (EMNLP) and the Annual Meeting of the North American Chapter of the Association for Computational Linguistics (NAACL) are widely recognized as the foremost platforms for scholarly communication in the realm of computational linguistics and natural language processing [70]. Consequently, papers honored at these conferences hold significant prestige and are regarded of high quality. And a total of 76 awarded papers from ACL, EMNLP, and NAACL were collected, all of which were considered high-quality.

In this preliminary research, we approached the assessment of high-quality papers as a literature retrieval problem. Specifically, we examined the count of high-quality papers within the top k papers, ranked by citation frequency and micro citation frequency. Notably, the variable k ranged from 5 to 50, incremented in steps of 5.

As depicted in Fig. 5, the count of high-quality papers within the top k papers, ranked by micro citation frequency, consistently exceeded that of citation frequency, regardless of the value of k. These findings imply that micro citation frequency demonstrates a superior capacity to identify high-quality papers compared to citation frequency.

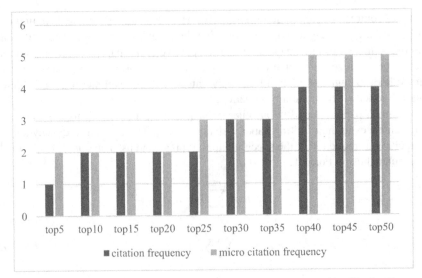

Fig. 5. Counts of High-Quality Papers Among the Top *k* Papers, Ranked by Citation Frequency and Micro Citation Frequency.

6 Conclusions

We have proposed an innovative approach for identifying micro citation importance, involving a regression method based on SciBERT. This method is designed to generate continuous values that represent the importance of citing sentences. Additionally, the citation function has been incorporated into the citing sentence to enhance performance. As a result, our proposed regression method obtained a macro F_1 score of 0.7366, demonstrating a notable improvement of 0.0356 over the strong baseline. These outcomes affirm that both treating micro citation importance identification as a regression task and integrating the citation function contribute to overall performance enhancement.

Furthermore, recognizing the significance of literature evaluation, we have delved into the application of micro citation importance acquired by our proposed regression method to this process. In this context, we have introduced a novel metric termed "micro citation frequency," derived from micro citation importance. In this preliminary research, micro citation frequency demonstrates superior capabilities of evaluating high-quality papers compared to the established metric of citation frequency, providing additional validation for our proposed regression method.

Our work addresses certain limitations associated with traditional citation frequency, which primarily stem from the reliance on coarse-grained information within papers. Instead, we attempt to differentiate papers based on the fine-grained information derived from their corresponding citing sentences, enabling a more precise literature evaluation. In conclusion, our work not only enriches citation content analysis but also holds implications for improving practices in literature evaluation.

However, several issues need to be addressed in relation to this study. Firstly, although we have considered citation content and citation function, it is crucial to further explore the impact of other relevant factors on micro citation importance identification in future endeavors. Secondly, despite our preliminary exploration, the current findings fall short of a comprehensive examination of the proposed metric of micro citation frequency. Besides, we did not exclude the influence of other factors, such as publication time, on micro citation frequency. Lastly, it is essential to delve deeper into additional potential applications of micro citation importance.

Acknowledgement. This research was supported by the National Social Science Foundation of China (17ATQ001).

References

1. Ding, Y., Zhang, G., Chambers, T., Song, M., Wang, X., Zhai, C.: Content-based citation analysis: the next generation of citation analysis. J. Am. Soc. Inf. Sci. **65**, 1820–1833 (2014). https://doi.org/10.1002/asi.23256
2. Wang, W., Ma, J., Chen, C., Zhang, L.: A review of citation context classifications and implementation methods. Libr. Inform. Serv. **60**, 118–127 (2016). https://doi.org/10.13266/j.issn.0252-3116.2016.06.018
3. Lu, W., Meng, R., Liu, X.: A deep scientific literature mining-oriented framework for citation content annotation. J. Libr. Sci. China. **40**, 93–104 (2014). https://doi.org/10.13530/j.cnki.jlis.140029
4. Kunnath, S.N., Herrmannova, D., Pride, D., Knoth, P.: A meta-analysis of semantic classification of citations. Quant. Sci. Stud. **2**, 1170–1215 (2022). https://doi.org/10.1162/qss_a_0 0159
5. Abu-Jbara, A., Ezra, J., Radev, D.: Purpose and polarity of citation: towards NLP-based Bibliometrics. In: Proceedings of the 2013 Conference of the North American Chapter of the Association for Computational Linguistics: Human Language Technologies, pp. 596–606. Association for Computational Linguistics, Atlanta, Georgia (2013)
6. Jurgens, D., Kumar, S., Hoover, R., McFarland, D., Jurafsky, D.: Measuring the evolution of a scientific field through citation frames. Trans. Assoc. Comput. Linguist. **6**, 391–406 (2018). https://doi.org/10.1162/tacl_a_00028
7. Dong, C., Schäfer, U.: Ensemble-style self-training on citation classification. In: Proceedings of 5th International Joint Conference on Natural Language Processing, pp. 623–631. Asian Federation of Natural Language Processing, Chiang Mai, Thailand (2011)
8. Ou, S., Lin, H.: A study of automatic classification of citation texts and its application. Libr. Inform. Serv. **66**, 125–136 (2022). https://doi.org/10.13266/j.issn.0252-3116.2022.16.012
9. Athar, A.: Sentiment analysis of citations using sentence structure-based features. In: Proceedings of the ACL 2011 Student Session, pp. 81–87. Association for Computational Linguistics, USA (2011)
10. Piao, S.S., Ananiadou, S., Tsuruoka, Y., Sasaki, Y., McNaught, J.: Mining opinion polarity relations of citations. In: International Workshop on Computational Semantics, pp. 366–371 (2007)
11. Zhu, X., Turney, P., Lemire, D., Vellino, A.: Measuring academic influence: not all citations are equal. J. Am. Soc. Inf. Sci. **66**, 408–427 (2015). https://doi.org/10.1002/asi.23179
12. Valenzuela, M., Ha, V., Etzioni, O.: Identifying meaningful citations. In: Workshops at the Twenty-Ninth AAAI Conference on Artificial Intelligence (2015)
13. Hassan, S.-U., Akram, A., Haddawy, P.: Identifying important citations using contextual information from full text. In: 2017 ACM/IEEE Joint Conference on Digital Libraries (JCDL), pp. 1–8 (2017). https://doi.org/10.1109/JCDL.2017.7991558

14. Pride, D., Knoth, P.: Incidental or Influential? - Challenges in Automatically Detecting Citation Importance Using Publication Full Texts. In: Kamps, J., Tsakonas, G., Manolopoulos, Y., Iliadis, L., Karydis, I. (eds.) Research and Advanced Technology for Digital Libraries: 21st International Conference on Theory and Practice of Digital Libraries, TPDL 2017, Thessaloniki, Greece, September 18-21, 2017, Proceedings, pp. 572–578. Springer International Publishing, Cham (2017). https://doi.org/10.1007/978-3-319-67008-9_48

15. Jake VanderPlas: Python Data Science Handbook, https://jakevdp.github.io/PythonDataScienceHandbook/. Accessed Sept 16 2023

16. Hou, W.-R., Li, M., Niu, D.-K.: Counting citations in texts rather than reference lists to improve the accuracy of assessing scientific contribution. BioEssays 33, 724–727 (2011). https://doi.org/10.1002/bies.201100067

17. Nazir, S., Asif, M., Ahmad, S., Bukhari, F., Afzal, M.T., Aljuaid, H.: Important citation identification by exploiting content and section-wise in-text citation count. PLoS ONE 15, e0228885 (2020). https://doi.org/10.1371/journal.pone.0228885

18. Hassan, S.-U., Safder, I., Akram, A., Kamiran, F.: A novel machine-learning approach to measuring scientific knowledge flows using citation context analysis. Scientometrics 116, 973–996 (2018). https://doi.org/10.1007/s11192-018-2767-x

19. Jha, R., Jbara, A.-A., Qazvinian, V., Radev, D.R.: NLP-driven citation analysis for scientometrics. Nat. Lang. Eng. 23, 93–130 (2017). https://doi.org/10.1017/S1351324915000443

20. Wang, M., Zhang, J., Jiao, S., Zhang, X., Zhu, N., Chen, G.: Important citation identification by exploiting the syntactic and contextual information of citations. Scientometrics 125, 2109–2129 (2020). https://doi.org/10.1007/s11192-020-03677-1

21. Yang, S., Lu, W., Zhang, Z., Wei, B., An, W.: Amplifying scientific paper's abstract by leveraging data-weighted reconstruction. Inf. Process. Manage. 52, 698–719 (2016). https://doi.org/10.1016/j.ipm.2015.12.014

22. Aljohani, N.R., Fayoumi, A., Hassan, S.-U.: An in-text citation classification predictive model for a scholarly search system. Scientometrics 126, 5509–5529 (2021). https://doi.org/10.1007/s11192-021-03986-z

23. Qayyum, F., Afzal, M.T.: Identification of important citations by exploiting research articles' metadata and cue-terms from content. Scientometrics 118, 21–43 (2019). https://doi.org/10.1007/s11192-018-2961-x

24. An, X., Sun, X., Xu, S., Hao, L., Li, J.: Important citations identification by exploiting generative model into discriminative model. J. Inf. Sci. 49, 107–121 (2023). https://doi.org/10.1177/0165551521991034

25. Kunnath, S.N., Pride, D., Gyawali, B., Knoth, P.: Overview of the 2020 WOSP 3C citation context classification task. In: Proceedings of the 8th International Workshop on Mining Scientific Publications, pp. 75–83. Association for Computational Linguistics, Wuhan, China (2020)

26. Kunnath, S.N., Pride, D., Herrmannova, D., Knoth, P.: Overview of the 2021 SDP 3C Citation Context Classification Shared Task. In: Presented at the Second Workshop on Scholarly Document Processing , Stroudsburg, PA June 10 (2021)

27. Mishra, S., Mishra, S.: Scubed at 3c Task B - a simple baseline for citation context influence classification. In: Proceedings of the 8th International Workshop on Mining Scientific Publications, pp. 65–70. Association for Computational Linguistics, Wuhan, China (2020)

28. Maheshwari, H., Singh, B., Varma, V.: SciBERT sentence representation for citation context classification. In: Proceedings of the Second Workshop on Scholarly Document Processing, pp. 130–133. Association for Computational Linguistics, Online (2021)

29. Moravcsik, M.J., Murugesan, P.: Some results on the function and quality of citations. Soc. Stud. Sci. 5, 86–92 (1975). https://doi.org/10.1177/030631277500500106

30. Aljuaid, H., Iftikhar, R., Ahmad, S., Asif, M., Tanvir Afzal, M.: Important citation identification using sentiment analysis of in-text citations. Telematics Inform. **56**, 101492 (2021). https://doi.org/10.1016/j.tele.2020.101492

31. Nazir, S., et al.: Important citation identification by exploding the sentiment analysis and section-wise in-text citation weights. IEEE Access. **10**, 87990–88000 (2022). https://doi.org/10.1109/ACCESS.2022.3199420

32. Huth, E.J.: Structured abstracts for papers reporting clinical trials. Ann. Intern. Med. **106**, 626–627 (1987). https://doi.org/10.7326/0003-4819-106-4-626

33. Sollaci, L.B., Pereira, M.G.: The introduction, methods, results, and discussion (IMRAD) structure: a fifty-year survey. J. Med. Libr. Assoc. **92**, 364–371 (2004)

34. Xue J., Ou S.: Research progress on discourse structure modelling and discourse parsing of scientific articles. library & information, pp. 120–132 (2019). https://doi.org/10.11968/tsyqb.1003-6938.2019034

35. Wan, X., Liu, F.: Are all literature citations equally important? automatic citation strength estimation and its applications. J. Am. Soc. Inf. Sci. **65**, 1929–1938 (2014). https://doi.org/10.1002/asi.23083

36. Rachatasumrit, N., Bragg, J., Zhang, A.X., Weld, D.S.: CiteRead: integrating localized citation contexts into scientific paper reading. In: 27th International Conference on Intelligent User Interfaces, pp. 707–719. Association for Computing Machinery, New York, NY, USA (2022). https://doi.org/10.1145/3490099.3511162

37. Wang, R., Li, S., Yin, Q., Zhang, J., Yao, R., Wu, O.: Improved pagerank and new indices for academic impact evaluation using AI papers as case studies. J. Inform. Sci. 01655515221105038 (2022). https://doi.org/10.1177/01655515221105038

38. Xia, H., Hu, Q., Wang, Z.: Tracing the knowledge flow main path based on important citations. J. China Society Sci. Tech. Inform. **41**, 451–462 (2022). https://doi.org/10.3772/j.issn.1000-0135.2022.05.002

39. Lou, W., Cai, Z.: The nature and methods of scientific evaluation on scientific articles. J. Intell. **40**, 171–177 (2021). https://doi.org/10.3969/j.issn.1002-1965.2021.05.024

40. Bu, Y., Xu, J., Huang, W.: Citation-based quantitative evaluations on scientific publications: a literature review on citation-based impact indicators. Document., Inform. Knowl. **38**, 47–59+46 (2021). https://doi.org/10.13366/j.dik.2021.06.047

41. Bai, R., Yang, J., Wang, X.: Research status and development trend of single academic paper evaluation. Inform. Stud.: Theory Appl. **38**, 11–17 (2015). https://doi.org/10.16353/j.cnki.1000-7490.2015.11.003

42. Vitanov, N.K.: Science Dynamics and Research Production. Springer International Publishing, Cham (2016)

43. Wang, P., Song, Z.: The inherent drawbacks and limitations of the peer review system. Science and Technology Management Research. 22–26+13 (1994)

44. Garfield, E.: The agony and the ecstasy—the history and meaning of the journal impact factor. J. Biol. Chem. **295**, 1–22 (2005)

45. Geng, Y., Guo, Y., Fang, Y., Zhang, G., Tian, W., Wang, X.: Are the results of the elite peer evaluation consistent with the public peer evaluation?——an analysis on reprinted newspapers and periodicals of RUC. J. Intell. **41**, 156–162+146 (2022). https://doi.org/10.3969/j.issn.1002-1965.2022.10.022

46. National Natural Science Foundation of China: List of Prohibited Requesting for Peer Review for National Natural Science Foundation of China Projects, https://www.nsfc.gov.cn/publish/portal0/tab442/info89394.htm. Accessed 27 Dec 2023

47. García, J.A., Rodriguez-Sánchez, R., Fdez-Valdivia, J.: Can a paid model for peer review be sustainable when the author can decide whether to pay or not? Scientometrics **127**, 1491–1514 (2022). https://doi.org/10.1007/s11192-021-04248-8

48. Liu, X., Wang, X., Zhu, D.: Reviewer recommendation method for scientific research proposals: a case for NSFC. Scientometrics **127**, 3343–3366 (2022). https://doi.org/10.1007/s11192-022-04389-4

49. Zhao, X., Zhang, Y.: Reviewer assignment algorithms for peer review automation: a survey. Inf. Process. Manage. **59**, 103028 (2022). https://doi.org/10.1016/j.ipm.2022.103028

50. Wei, C., Zhao, J., Ni, J., Li, J.: What does open peer review bring to scientific articles? Evid. PLoS J. Sci. **128**, 2763–2776 (2023). https://doi.org/10.1007/s11192-023-04683-9

51. Meng, J.: Assessing and predicting the quality of peer reviews: a text mining approach. Electron. Libr. **41**, 186–203 (2023). https://doi.org/10.1108/EL-06-2022-0139

52. Garfield, E.: Citation indexes for science: a new dimension in documentation through association of ideas. Science **122**, 108–111 (1955). https://doi.org/10.1126/science.122.3159.108

53. Waltman, L.: A review of the literature on citation impact indicators. J. Informet. **10**, 365–391 (2016). https://doi.org/10.1016/j.joi.2016.02.007

54. Hu, Z., Chen, C., Liu, Z., Hou, H.: From counting references to counting citations: a new way to calculate the total cited times of references. Libr. Inform. Serv. **57**, 5 (2013). https://doi.org/10.7536/j.issn.0252-3116.2013.21.001

55. Ding, Y., Liu, X., Guo, C., Cronin, B.: The distribution of references across texts: some implications for citation analysis. J. Informet. **7**, 583–592 (2013). https://doi.org/10.1016/j.joi.2013.03.003

56. Xu, L., Ding, K., Lin, Y., Zhang, C.: Does citation polarity help evaluate the quality of academic papers? Scientometrics **128**, 4065–4087 (2023). https://doi.org/10.1007/s11192-023-04734-1

57. Geng, S., Yang, J.: A method to evaluate the academic influence of papers based on citation sentiment. Inform. Stud.: Theory Appl. **41**, 93–98 (2018). https://doi.org/10.16353/j.cnki.1000-7490.2018.12.017

58. Ma, R., Liu, Z., Lyu, Y., Feng, Y.: Representative paper selection based on citation comment weighing. J. China Society Sci. Tech. Inform. **42**, 279–288. https://doi.org/10.3772/j.issn.1000-0135.2023.03.003

59. Kenton, D., Chang, M.-W., Lee, K., Toutanova, K.: BERT: pre-training of deep bidirectional transformers for language understanding. In: Presented at the Proceedings of the 2019 Conference of the North American Chapter of the Association for Computational Linguistics: Human Language Technologies , Stroudsburg, PA, USA (2019)

60. Ubiquitous Knowledge Processing Lab: Sentence Transformers: Multilingual Sentence, Paragraph, and Image Embeddings using BERT & Co., https://github.com/UKPLab/sentence-transformers/blob/3e1929fddef16df94f8bc6e3b10598a98f46e62d/sentence_transformers/evaluation/BinaryClassificationEvaluator.py. Accessed 07 Apr 2023

61. 3C Shared Task (2021) Citation Context Classification based on Influence. https://www.kaggle.com/competitions/3c-shared-task-influence-v2/leaderboard. Accessed 06 Apr 2023

62. Qiu, X., Sun, T., Xu, Y., Shao, Y., Dai, N., Huang, X.: Pre-trained models for natural language processing: a survey. Sci.China Technol. Sci. **63**, 1872–1897 (2020). https://doi.org/10.1007/s11431-020-1647-3

63. Beltagy, I., Lo, K., Cohan, A.: SciBERT: a pretrained language model for scientific text. In: Presented at the Proceedings of the 2019 Conference on Empirical Methods in Natural Language Processing and the 9th International Joint Conference on Natural Language Processing (EMNLP-IJCNLP) , Stroudsburg, PA, USA (2019)

64. Liu, Y., et al.: RoBERTa: A Robustly Optimized BERT Pretraining Approach, http://arxiv.org/abs/1907.11692. Accessed 21 May 2022

65. Lan, Z., Chen, M., Goodman, S., Gimpel, K., Sharma, P., Soricut, R.: ALBERT: A Lite BERT for self-supervised learning of language representations. In: Presented at the 8th International Conference on Learning Representations (2020)

66. Varanasi, K.K., Ghosal, T., Tiwary, P., Singh, M.: IITP-CUNI@3C: supervised approaches for citation classification (Task A) and citation significance detection (Task B). In: Proceedings of the Second Workshop on Scholarly Document Processing, pp. 140–145. Association for Computational Linguistics, Online (2021)

67. B, P., S, I.I., Kumar, K.S., Karthikeyan, L., Kp, S.: Amrita_CEN_NLP@SDP2021 Task A and B. In: Proceedings of the Second Workshop on Scholarly Document Processing, pp. 146–149. Association for Computational Linguistics, Online (2021)

68. Nambanoor Kunnath, S., Pride, D., Knoth, P.: Dynamic context extraction for citation classification. In: Proceedings of the 2nd Conference of the Asia-Pacific Chapter of the Association for Computational Linguistics and the 12th International Joint Conference on Natural Language Processing (Volume 1: Long Papers), pp. 539–549. Association for Computational Linguistics, Online only (2022)

69. Rohatgi, S.: ACL anthology corpus with full text. https://github.com/shauryr/ACL-anthology-corpus. Accessed 29 Nov 2022

70. China Computer Federation: Recommended International Academic Conference and Journal Catalog of the China Computer Federation (2022) (2023)

Exploring the Citation Lag in LIS: Trends and Correlations

Hanqin Yang[1]([✉]), Jingrui Hou[2], Qibiao Hu[1], and Ping Wang[1]

[1] School of Information Management, Wuhan University, Wuhan, Hubei, China
hanqin@whu.edu.cn

[2] Department of Computer Science, School of Science, Loughborough University, Loughborough, UK

Abstract. Interdisciplinary collaboration has emerged as a pivotal driver of academic progress and innovation. As researchers work across disciplinary boundaries, it becomes imperative to identify and examine the factors that affect the pace of scientific knowledge dissemination. This study introduces citation lag as a metric to gauge the knowledge diffusion speed in Library and Information Science research. It further explores the factors associated with citation lag from both disciplinary and publication perspectives. Our results indicate that an article is less likely to be cited if it remains uncited within 24 months after publication. Both the disciplinary attribute and the Open access mechanism were found to have a significant impact on citation lag. Furthermore, the result reveals a negative correlation between publication lag and citation lag, implying that rigorous editorial review processes may ensure article quality and accelerate knowledge diffusion. Drawing on these insights, this paper endeavors to provide valuable guidance for crafting scholarly articles and facilitating knowledge diffusion.

Keywords: Citation Lag · Knowledge Diffusion · Disciplinary Attribute · OA Mechanism · Publication Lag

1 Introduction

Scientific advancement is a cumulative process, with new studies building upon antecedent research findings. The publication and citation of scientific literature is a crucial way for disseminating and sharing innovative accomplishments in the realm of scientific research [1]. As authors craft their scientific manuscripts, they cite preceding work to illustrate the intrinsic connections between existing and new knowledge. This practice establishes a conduit for researchers to exchange ideas and contribute to the generation of knowledge in subsequent studies.

Pioneering advancements within the academic sphere have increasingly necessitated collaborations across disciplinary boundaries [2]. As the path and extent of knowledge diffusion are not directly observable, citations are commonly employed as a proxy for knowledge diffusion [3]. The utilization of citation analysis in knowledge diffusion research has offered valuable insights for understanding the exchange of scientific discoveries [4] and evaluating the performance of interdisciplinary connections [5, 6]. The

I. Sserwanga et al. (Eds.): iConference 2024, LNCS 14597, pp. 376–391, 2024.
https://doi.org/10.1007/978-3-031-57860-1_25

temporal dimension constitutes a critical perspective of these studies, which has garnered attention due to its capacity to characterize the rate of knowledge diffusion. Previous research has examined the citations of scientific literature from the temporal perspective, tracing the evolution of a publication's value [7–9]. However, limited attention has been paid to the concept of citation lag concerning individual articles. The manner in which scientific publications are recognized can be quite diverse [7]. Some articles receive immediate citations, while others may be overlooked for an extended period before being discovered or rediscovered. Furthermore, certain articles may remain uncited for years subsequent to their publication.

Citation lag (CL), defined as the duration between an article's publication and its first citation [9], reflecting the time required for a publication to be recognized and utilized by other scholars. To some extent, CL may function as an indicator of an article's immediate value and possesses the potential to quantify the velocity of knowledge diffusion. Despite this potential, existing studies have not fully investigated the utility of CL in measuring knowledge diffusion rates. Consequently, it is necessary to calculate the CL at the article level to further explore the performance of scientific knowledge diffusion.

Given the significance of CL as a potential indicator of knowledge diffusion performance, it is crucial to investigate the various factors that may affect this metric. Prior research has revealed that disciplinary attributes can impact citation performance, as the degree of connectedness among disciplines varies [10]. Moreover, publishing mechanisms, such as open access (OA) mechanism, have been shown to impact knowledge transfer and its speed [11]. Additionally, the publication lag has been found to be associated with the half-life of research articles [12], which is calculated based on citation frequency and the time required for citations to occur. However, few studies have examined the relationship between CL and the factors affecting knowledge diffusion performance. This gap necessitates further exploration to enhance our understanding of the complex interplay between CL and these factors. To bridge this research gap, this paper endeavors to investigate the CL within a specific discipline, obtaining valuable insights into the dynamics of knowledge dissemination in a given discipline. Specifically, a literature review was conducted to identify the crucial factors affecting CL. Then, this study examined the association between CL and these factors through statistical methods, aiming to gain more comprehensive understanding of the influential factors about knowledge diffusion performance and the underlying mechanism.

The remainder of this paper is organized as follows. Section 2 comprehensively reviews current research on knowledge diffusion to identify pivotal factors that may be associated with CL. Section 3 delineates the dataset collection, selection and extraction. Section 4 presents the data analysis and results. In Sect. 5, we discuss the main findings and the implications. Finally, Sect. 6 concludes this study.

2 Related Work

2.1 Citation Lag in Scientific Research

Lag is an inherent aspect of the knowledge exchange and diffusion process [12]. Knowledge diffusion can be observed through the citation of technology patents and scientific articles, with a delay between the generation of scientific knowledge and its subsequent citation. In terms of technology patents, prior research posits that CL represents the time it takes for a patent to receive its first citation after publication, directly reflecting the rate at which the technical knowledge is adopted by subsequent inventions and indicating the patent's value [13]. According to [14], patents cited earlier were likely to be cited more rapidly and possess higher value. A time delay also exists in citations from scientific articles to patents [15], reflecting the pace of knowledge communication from academia to industry. Specifically, as [16] proposed, the shorter lag signifies accelerated knowledge diffusion, suggesting that more recent scientific knowledge informs technology patents. [17] employed CL to assess the novelty of scientific knowledge in patents. Consequently, CL holds the potential for assessing both the speed of knowledge diffusion and the novelty of scientific knowledge.

Citations from scientific articles to other articles serve to characterize knowledge diffusion within academia [18]. The age distribution of an article cited follows discernible patterns rather than a random curve [12]. CL, defined as the duration between an article's publication and its citation, can be leveraged as a crucial indicator for evaluating knowledge diffusion performance [8]. Recent studies have endeavored to measure CL by examining the time gap between the year in which the citation peaks and the year of initial publication [19]. However, individual articles may exhibit no citation peak or multiple peaks. [9] defined CL as the time elapsed before an article receives its first citation following publication and utilized CL to reveal the value of patents in the supply chain field. This paper adopts the definition from [9] owing to the following reasons: Firstly, it ensures that each article has a unique publication time and first citation time, resulting in an accurate CL. Secondly, the research unit is focused on individual articles, enabling a fine-grained understanding of scientific knowledge diffusion at the article level.

Existing research reveals that the age of an article can be used to measure the performance of interdisciplinary knowledge diffusion. According to [20], the time required for an article to transition from an "unused" to a "used" status, it is discovered that the sooner an article is cited after publication, the more significant it is within scientific communities. Comparatively, [21] observed that articles accepted for publication exhibited a faster citation speed than those published in other journals after rejection. However, these studies primarily employed CL as an indicator for scientific evaluation, neglecting its potential for measuring knowledge diffusion at the article level. Moreover, the relationship between CL and other relevant factors influencing the speed of knowledge diffusion has not been fully examined.

2.2 Factors Affecting Knowledge Diffusion Speed

Disciplinary Attribute. Interdisciplinary collaboration has become an increasingly frequent and significant phenomenon globally [2, 22]. Current research reveals that cooperation beyond disciplinary boundaries fosters interdisciplinary knowledge integration and provides a more diverse array of perspectives [10] and methodologies [23] for problem-solving. In a context characterized by continuous exchange and integration between disciplines, it is recognized that disciplinary aspects can influence citations. The time and speed of knowledge exchange and diffusion vary across different disciplines [10]. CL of articles within a discipline was discovered to be shorter than that of external disciplines [24]. Moreover, significant differences in citation speed among disciplinary clusters was observed [25]. According to [9], the inter- and intra-cluster CL derived from citation networks was utilized as a novel metric to characterize the speed of knowledge spread across subfields within a research area. These findings indicate that an article's disciplinarity significantly influences its CL. Moreover, previous studies have demonstrated that the disciplinary attribute of the journal in which an article is published affects its citation rate [10]. The pronounced specialization within a journal may limit the visibility of an article published therein, subsequently impacting its citation frequency, irrespective of the article's scientific value [26]. Building upon this premise, this paper assumes that the disciplinary attributes of a journal exert an influence on the first citation time of an article.

Open Access Mechanism. Open access to scientific publications has emerged as a countermeasure to publishers' monopolies on academic outputs [27], and it has since been widely embraced as a novel publication mechanism. OA literature, which is digital, online, free of charge, and largely free from most copyright and licensing restrictions [28], facilitates the efficient publication and dissemination of scientific findings [29]. Previous studies have underscored the citation advantage associated with OA mechanisms. For instance, [30] demonstrated that OA mechanisms increase the likelihood of an article being read, although they found no significant difference in the number of citations within the first year after publication [30]. Other research has revealed that literature published in most OA journals exhibits distinct citation patterns and speeds compared to literature published through traditional manners [11]. Articles published in OA journals circumvent offline editing, printing, and other technical processes, resulting in time savings and more rapid exposure to the scientific community [11]. Drawing on these findings, this study assumes that there is an association between OA mechanism and CL.

Publication Lag. The publication lag of an article refers to the time elapsed between submission to the editorial office and acceptance or publication [31]. Several studies have identified a negative correlation between publication lag and journal impact factor [32–34] observed a substantial negative relationship between publication lag and the number of citations. However, the correlation between publication lag and CL remains unexplored.

Given these considerations, CL has been utilized to assess the scientific impact of articles and the performance of knowledge diffusion [35]. Nevertheless, few studies have examined the association between CL and other factors influencing the knowledge diffusion speed. This paper endeavors to explore the general trend of CL at the article level. Subsequently, we attempt to uncover the correlation between CL and the disciplinary attribute, OA mechanism, and publication lag.

3 Dataset

3.1 Data Collection

Our research investigates the CL at the article level by collecting temporal data from official journal publications. Previous studies have assumed that articles published in journals categorized multiple subjects by the Web of Science (WoS) or Scopus are multidisciplinary, while others are monodisciplinary [23, 36]. This assumption, albeit oversimplified, holds some validity as multi-assigned journals inherently possess a more interdisciplinary nature than single-assigned journals, indicating a higher likelihood of encompassing interdisciplinary research. The disciplinary attribute is one of the indices assigned to each article and the journal in which it is published by the WoS Core Collection. In addition, the WoS Core Collection provides important metadata for the article indexed, such as the journal name, publication time, and the citation frequency. The Journal Citation Reports (JCR) annually provide a ranked list of journals indexed by WoS Core Collection. Analyzing citation-related data from these two resources informs our comprehension of the knowledge diffusion performance through scientific articles. Therefore, this study collected citation data from the WoS Core Collection and the JCR.

3.2 Data Selection and Extraction

Journal Impact Factor (JIF) from JCR, quantifies as the average number of citations of the article published in a journal, has been adopted to evaluate the scientific merit of articles published [37]. Although several other types of citation-based measures (e.g., SCImago Journal Rank, Eigenfactor) have been proposed, JIF is still a prominent and most frequently used bibliometric measures for scientific research evaluation [38]. It is noted that citations of articles across disciplines should not be compared with each other, as the citation density varies across disciplines [39]. However, field-normalized metrics, such as the JIF quartile, mitigate this concern. The JIF quartile rankings are calculated for each journal within a specific subject category, based on the quartile position of the journal's impact factor distribution within that subject category. A journal is classified as a Q1 journals if its impact factor ranks within the top 25% of the impact factors for journals in its subject category. Previous research reveals the crucial role of Q1 indicators in evaluating the scientific impact [40, 41]. Therefore, this study focuses on articles published on Q1 journals reported in JCR 2019, within a specific subject category: Library and Information Science (LIS).

We obtained original articles published in these selected journals from 2010–2019, and their metadata provided by WoS, such as the authors, journal name, publication time, WoS category, and citation frequency. To accurately examine the "article-article" relationship within journal publications, we collected bibliometric data of both original articles and their citations, limiting the document type to "article". Data collection was completed in mid-October 2020, resulting in a harvest of 13,817 original articles published between 2010–2019 from 21 journals ranked in the top quartile of LIS according to JCR 2019.

In this study, we utilized "month" as the smallest time unit for calculating CL. From the 13,817 original articles, we identified 7,638 articles with both publication time and first citation time (including year and month) for CL calculation. For articles devoid of publication time, we sourced the publication time from the journal's official website or publisher. In cases where only a few issues of a journal lacked publication time, we extrapolated from the publication time of other issues. For instances where only publication years were available but no months, we referred to the periodical publication cycle for guidance. For example, for monthly publications (journals that publish 12 issues a year) such as the *International Journal of Geographical Information Science* and the *Journal of the Association for Information Systems*, we used the issue number per year to supplement the publication month. For bimonthly publications (journals that publish 6 issues a year) such as the *Journal of Knowledge Management*, we completed missing publication months using February, April, June, August, October, and December. For quarterly publications (journals that publish 4 issues a year) such as the *Journal of Management Information Systems*, we substituted the abbreviation of seasons with March, June, September, and December, respectively.

By employing these strategies, we manually completed publication time and first citation time for 583 articles. Consequently, we were able to analyze the CL of 8,221 articles. For the 8,221 articles selected, we differentiated OA articles from Non-OA articles using filters provided by the WoS Core Collection. The publishing process of an article typically includes several stages, such as submission, revision, acceptance, and publication. In this study, the publication lag is calculated as the duration between an article's acceptance and its public presentation. A majority of the selected journals have provided detail temporal information of the publishing process since 2015. These journals are primarily published by Elsevier, Wiley, Taylor & Francis, and Springer. Consequently, to analyze the association between publication lag and CL, we obtained the temporal publication information for 3,005 articles published between 2015 and 2019 from the websites of these journals. Based on this information, we calculated the publication lag for 3,005 articles. Figure 1 shows the process of data selection and extraction.

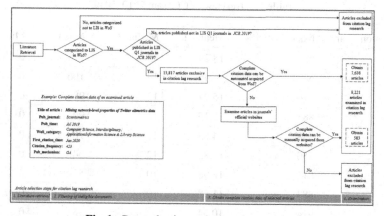

Fig. 1. Data selection and extraction process.

4 Data Analysis and Results

4.1 Citation Lag in LIS

Overview. Table 1 presents an overview of the CL for 8,221 articles. The average CL is 13.65 months, indicating that articles were cited for the first time between 13 and 14 months after publication (SD = 12). Moreover, the average CL exhibits an annal decrease, with the exception of publication year 2013, when the average CL is marginally longer than that of 2012. A more detailed examination of the data reveals that the CL for a small number of articles was exceptionally lengthy, which influenced the average CL in 2013.

The median CL stands at 11 months, with the maximum and minimum CL being 115 months and 0 months, respectively. Regarding the maximum CL for each year, there is a noticeable decrease from 2010 to 2019, indicating that the time required for a scientific article published in LIS Q1 journals to be discovered and recognized by the scientific community is getting shorter and shorter.

Out of the 8,221 articles, 329 (4%) have a CL of 0 months, indicating that these articles were cited in the month of publication. However, for most articles, the processes of review, revision, and typesetting before publication are the time needed. Moreover, it takes time for an article to be read, recognized, and cited. Therefore, the CL for 7,892 articles (96%) exceeds 0 months. Furthermore, the CL for 92 articles (1.12%) is longer than 60 months, suggesting that these articles were not noticed or recognized within 5 years after publication and were potentially not cited until similar research appeared. One article's CL reached 115 months, as it was published in August 2010 and first cited in March 2020, nearly a decade after publication. Changes over the years illustrate that, with the progression of time and technological advancements, the time required for a scientific article to be discovered and recognized by the scientific community has been

Table 1. Overview of CL from 2010–2019

Publication Year	No. of Articles	Mean CL	Median CL	Max CL	Min CL
2010	633	18.29	13	115	0
2011	687	16.96	13	106	0
2012	776	15.94	12	98	0
2013	883	16.15	13	90	0
2014	948	14.83	12	76	0
2015	850	13.85	12	64	0
2016	813	12.98	10	55	0
2017	883	11.58	10	43	0
2018	914	10.34	9	35	0
2019	834	7.54	7	20	0
Sum	8221	13.65	11	115	0

diminishing. However, it remains ambiguous as to what influences the CL. Therefore, this study aims to explore the factors that affect CL.

Distribution of Citation Lag. Figure 2 displays the CL distribution for each article, with the horizontal axis denoting the publication year and the vertical axis signifying the date when the article is cited for the first time. A conspicuous linear concentration can be observed in Fig. 2, with the trend line's slope being 0.9102 and the R-square value being 0.8709. It is evident from Fig. 2 that the majority of articles receive their first citation within 2 years after their publication, a trend that is further confirmed in Fig. 3.

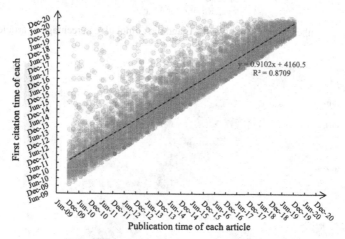

Fig. 2. Distribution of CL from 2010–2019.

Figure 3 depicts the number of articles corresponding to a specific value of CL and the cumulative percentage of cited articles. Approximately 90% of the articles were cited within 24 months after publication, while over 50% were cited within 12 months. Merely about 10% of the samples had their first citation more than 24 months after publication. For articles published in journals ranked in the top quartile of the LIS discipline, the results indicate that if an article is not cited within 2 years of its publication, it is less likely to be cited within the subsequent 8 years.

To examine the above-mentioned indication, we visualize the CL for each half-year subsequent to publication. The heatmap depicted in Fig. 4 illustrates the proportion of articles, with the vertical axis denoting the time of publication and the horizontal axis denoting the time when the first citation occurred. Assuming that N represents the number of articles published at time T_a, if there are n articles being cited for the first time at time T_b, the color of each cell reflects the proportion of articles published at time T_a that have been cited at time T_b, calculated by n/N. The scale of the proportion, ranging from 0.00 to 0.60, can be found on the right. The brighter the color, the more articles are cited for the first time at that time. Figure 4 indicates that most articles are cited within two years after publication.

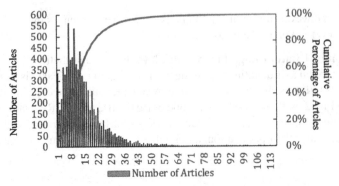

Fig. 3. The number of articles of given CL and the cumulative percentage of articles cited.

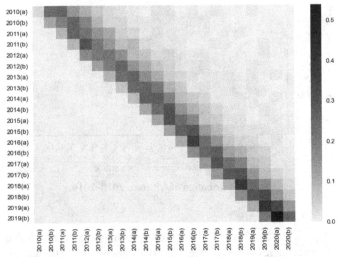

Fig. 4. The CL Distribution for Each Half-year After Publication, (a) Stands for the First Half of the Year While (b) Denotes the Second Half of the Year.

This study further explored the CL of each article with varying citation frequencies. Scientific articles grouped into the top 5% in terms of their citation frequency are recognized as highly-cited articles [42]. Out of the 8,221 articles, 411 were cited in the top 5%, with a minimum citation frequency of 71. This implies that articles with a citation frequency of no less than 71 were considered highly-cited in this study, and the remaining articles were classified as non-highly cited group. Figure 5 shows that the CL of highly-cited articles is generally shorter than that of non-highly cited articles, and the CL distribution of highly-cited articles is more concentrated. The results indicate that highly-cited articles received their first citations in a relatively short period of time after publication and accumulated higher citations during the rest of the observation period, which is consistent with the adaptive mechanism of literature citation. On the contrary, the distribution of CL in non-highly cited group has no obvious concentration pattern, reflecting that if an article does not attract citations quickly after publication, it will adversely affect its subsequent citation performance.

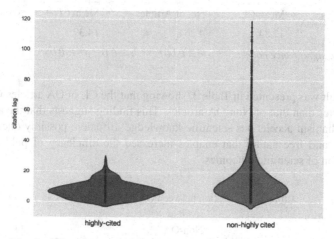

Fig. 5. CL of Highly-cited Articles and Non-highly Cited Articles.

4.2 Correlation Between Citation Lag and Disciplinary Attribute, OA Mechanism, and Publication Lag

Disciplinary Attribute. Previous research discovered that disciplinary attributes impact the citation performance of articles [26]. Drawing on the identification of inter-disciplinarity from [23], this study explored the impact of citations' interdisciplinarity on CL of each article. Specifically, WoS Core Collection provides subject category for articles indexed, which can be used as the disciplinary attribute of each article. For 8,221 articles published in LIS Q1 journals, this study classified the first citation articles of them into "LIS" group and "Non-LIS" group. We classified citation articles categorized with Library Science and Information Science into the "LIS" group, and the other articles were classified into "Non-LIS" group. Then, the Mann-Whitney U test was conducted to explore the differences in CL between LIS and Non-LIS citations.

The results revealed a significant difference in CL between LIS citations and Non-LIS citations. The mean CL of LIS citations was 12.85 months, which was shorter than that of Non-LIS citations (14.39 months). This indicates that knowledge diffusion within a discipline is relatively faster than knowledge diffusion across disciplines (Table 2).

OA Mechanism. WoS Core Collection provides a filter in the search result page to distinguish the articles published through OA mechanism. Therefore, we can classify articles into "OA" group and "Non-OA" group according to their publication mechanism. Specifically, regarding the 8,221 articles obtained initially, those filtered by through OA were labeled as "OA" group and the others were classified as "Non-OA" group. Then, the Mann-Whitney U test was employed to investigate whether there is a significant difference in CL between these two groups.

Table 2. Correlation between Disciplinary Attribute and CL.

LIS		Non-LIS		P-value
No. of Articles	Mean CL	No. of Articles	Mean CL	0.000***
3,957	12.84	4,264	14.39	

*Note: P-value significance codes: *** p <= 0.001, ** <= 0.01, p* < 0.05*

The result was presented in Table 3, showing that the CL of OA articles was significantly shorter than that of Non-OA articles. This finding suggests that the application of OA mechanism accelerates scientific knowledge diffusion, possibly due to its digital, online, and free nature that enables increased the efficiency of publication and dissemination of scientific outcomes.

Table 3. Correlation between OA Mechanism and CL.

OA		Non-OA		P-value
No. of Articles	Mean CL	No. of Articles	Mean CL	0.000***
2,115	12.29	6,106	14.09	

*Note: P-value significance codes: *** p <= 0.001, ** <= 0.01, p* < 0.05*

Publication Lag. The publication lag is commonly defined as the duration between an article's acceptance and its publication [31]. In this study, we quantified the publication lag of articles based on publication data obtained from the WoS Core Collection and the official websites of journals. Neither the CL nor the publication lag followed a normal distribution, so we used the Spearman correlation coefficient to examine their relationship. The result was shown in Table 4. It indicates a significant negative correlation between CL and publication lag, suggesting that a longer publication lag may lead to a faster first citation of an article.

Table 4. Spearman Correlation between Publication Lag and CL.

No. of Articles	Mean publication lag	Mean CL	Spearman
3,005	4.45	10.00	−0.09**

*Note: P-value significance codes: *** p <= 0.001, ** <= 0.01, p* < 0.05*

5   Discussion

5.1   Decreasing Citation Lag and Concentration Trend

In this paper, we undertake an empirical analysis of CL for articles published in Q1 journals within the LIS discipline over the past decade, as well as the correlation between CL and other factors influencing the speed of knowledge diffusion. Our findings present a combination of variability and consistency.

Our analysis reveals a declining trend in the annual average CL, suggesting that newly published articles are being discovered more rapidly by the scientific community. This indicates that newer knowledge from LIS disciplines fosters scientific knowledge exchange and innovation [16]. Additionally, we identify a trend toward concentration in the distribution of CL at the article level. This significant concentration discloses that half of the articles are cited within 12 months after publication, and 90% of articles are cited for the first time within 24 months after publication. It implies that most articles published in LIS journals ranked within the first quartile will receive recognition from scientific communities within 2 years.

5.2   Citation Lag Variability Among Different Citation Frequencies

In this study, we reveal a significant decline in the maximum value of CL for each year. For articles published prior to 2019, the average citation rate reaches 96% overall, while the maximum value of CL decreases from 115 months in 2010 to 35 months in 2018. However, the minimum value of CL remains constant at 0 months, indicating that every year there is an article cited for the first time in its publication month. Previous studies demonstrate that it takes time for a publication to be recognized and cited [13]. Moreover, the self-citation phenomenon raises attention from researchers [43, 44]. Further exploration of the short CL phenomenon is indeed warranted. Furthermore, we discern differences in the distribution of CL for articles with varying citation frequencies. Highly-cited articles exhibit a concentrated distribution of CL on the left side of the axis, indicating that they receive their first citation in a relatively short period and accumulate more citations over time. In contrast, the CL of non-highly cited articles shows an even distribution along the axes, with no clear concentration. Moreover, we discover that articles not cited within two years of publication are less likely to be cited within the subsequent eight years.

5.3   Impact of Disciplinary Attribute, OA Mechanism, and Publication Lag on Citation Lag

Impact of Disciplinary Attribute on Citation Lag. This study investigates the relationship between CL and the disciplinary categories assigned to first citation of each article by the WoS Core Collection. Our findings indicate that the CL of citations from LIS disciplines is shorter than that from non-LIS disciplines, aligning with previous research [24]. Specifically, we observe a higher citation counts and relatively shorter CL within the LIS discipline, indicative of accelerated knowledge diffusion. Conversely, citations from non-LIS disciplines exhibit longer CL, signifying a slower knowledge diffusion rate across disciplines. However, longer CL does not necessarily convey negative implications, as it takes time to recognize the value of scientific work [7]. Moreover, although multiple disciplinary attributes may increase the possibility of an article being exposed [26, 45], this does not necessarily denote faster knowledge diffusion. The time it takes for an article to be noticed and recognized by the scientific community fundamentally depends on the intrinsic value of the article.

Impact of OA Mechanism on Citation Lag. From the perspective of publication mechanisms, we primarily examine the correlation between OA mechanisms and CL. The OA filter provided by the WoS Core Collection enables us to differentiate OA articles from Non-OA articles. Our study unveils a significant difference in CL between OA and Non-OA articles. The implementation of OA mechanisms facilitates easier access to research articles for the public, thereby accelerating knowledge diffusion. This underscores the importance of innovative publishing mechanisms in overcoming the limitations of traditional publishing and fostering scholarly communication.

Correlation between Publication Lag and Citation Lag. This study reveals a negative correlation between publication lag and CL. Prior studies identified a negative correlation between CL and both citation frequency and journal impact factor [33]. We extended this investigation to explore the relationship between CL and publication lag. Our findings suggest that the speed at which an article is cited is negatively correlated with the time required for the editorial review process. The possible explanation may be that a rigorous editorial review and proofreading process ensures the normalization and preciseness of academic articles [33], leading to rapid citation rates. Conversely, a relatively undemanding editorial review system may fill submission gaps in journals but may not contribute to long-term improvements in article quality and citation strength.

6　Conclusion

This study introduced CL as an indicator for the evaluation of knowledge diffusion speed. Through an empirical analysis of bibliometric data collected from the WoS Core Collection and the JCR 2019, this study depicted the distribution of CL within the LIS discipline and investigated the factors associated with CL from both disciplinary and publication perspectives. Specifically, by conducting a comprehensive review of studies on knowledge diffusion, this study identified the factors affecting knowledge diffusion performance, including the disciplinary attribute, OA mechanism, and publication lag. To examine the associations between CL and these identified factors, this study employed classical statistical methods including the Mann-Whitney U test and Spearman correlation analysis. The results show that both the disciplinary attribute and OA mechanism have a significant impact on the CL through the Mann-Whitney U test. Moreover, this study demonstrates a negative correlation between the CL and the publication lag via the Spearman Correlation Coefficient. These findings support that knowledge diffusion within a discipline is faster than that across disciplines. The accumulation of citation priority is not solely influenced by whether the literature is published in interdisciplinary journals or highly specialized journals. The intrinsic appeal of the research for citation should be taken into consideration. Furthermore, this study underscores the importance of new publication mechanisms, such as OA mechanism, in facilitating scientific knowledge diffusion. In addition, our findings suggest that a demanding editorial review process may contribute to the accelerated knowledge diffusion through journal articles. Therefore, both the choice of journals for publication and the adoption of appropriate publication mechanisms should be carefully considered.

Despite these valuable insights, there are some limitations that should be acknowledged. Firstly, the data collected in this study was mainly from the WoS Core Collection, a common platform for the collection of citation data. Future studies should collect data from other scientific databases such as Scopus or Google Scholar, as well as explore citations from non-traditional sources, such as social media or blog posts, to provide a more comprehensive understanding of citation dynamics. Secondly, this study focuses on the analysis of data from LIS discipline, which may limit the generalizability of our findings to other disciplines. Future research could expand this investigation to include a broader range of disciplines, allowing for comparisons and further exploration of the factors influencing CL. Thirdly, this study investigates the impact of the disciplinary attribute, OA mechanism, and publication lag on the CL, the differences in these impacts deserve further exploration.

In conclusion, while this study has provided valuable insights into the factors influencing CL in the LIS discipline, there is ample opportunity for further exploration and research. Addressing these limitations and expanding the scope of future work will contribute to a more comprehensive understanding of knowledge diffusion dynamics and the factors that shape the speed and impact of scholarly research.

References

1. Zeng, A., et al.: The science of science: from the perspective of complex systems. Phys. Rep. **714**, 1–73 (2017)
2. Xu, H., Guo, T., Yue, Z., Ru, L., Fang, S.: Interdisciplinary topics of information science: a study based on the terms interdisciplinarity index series. Scientometrics **106**(2), 583–601 (2016)
3. Yan, E., Zhu, Y.: Adding the dimension of knowledge trading to source impact assessment: approaches, indicators, and implications. J. Am. Soc. Inf. Sci. **68**(5), 1090–1104 (2017)
4. Bornmann, L., Daniel, H.D.: What do citation counts measure? a review of studies on citing behavior. J. Document. **64**(1), 45–80 (2008)
5. Wang, M., Zhang, J., Jiao, S., Zhang, T.: Evaluating the impact of citations of articles based on knowledge flow patterns hidden in the citations. PLoS ONE **14**(11), e0225276 (2019)
6. Liu, Y., Rousseau, R.: Knowledge diffusion through publications and citations: a case study using ESI fields as unit of diffusions. J. Am. Soc. Inf. Sci. **61**(2), 340–351 (2010)
7. Van Calster, B.: It takes time: a remarkable example of delayed recognition. J. Am. Soc. Inf. Sci. Technol. **63**(11), 2341–2344 (2012)
8. Bornmann, L., Daniel, H.D.: The citation speed index: a useful bibliometric indicator to add to the h index. J. Informet. **4**(3), 444–446 (2010)
9. Nakamura, H., Suzuki, S., Hironori, T., Kajikawa, Y., Sakata, I.: Citation lag analysis in supply chain research. Scientometrics **87**(2), 221–232 (2011)
10. Levitt, J.M., Thelwall, M.: Is multidisciplinary research more highly cited? a macrolevel study. J. Am. Soc. Inf. Sci. Technol. **59**(12), 1973–1984 (2008)
11. Harzing, A.W., Adler, N.J.: Disseminating knowledge: from potential to reality-new open-access journals collide with convention. Acad. Manag. Learn. Educ. **15**(1), 140–156 (2016)

12. Egghe, L., Rousseau, R.: The influence of publication delays on the observed aging distribution of scientific literature. J. Am. Soc. Inf. Sci. **51**(2), 158–165 (2000)
13. Gay, C., Le Bas, C., Patel, P., Touach, K.: The determinants of patent citations: an empirical analysis of French and British patents in the US. Econ. Innov. New Technol. **14**(5), 339–350 (2005)
14. Lee, J., Sohn, S.Y.: What makes the first forward citation of a patent occur earlier? Scientometrics **113**, 279–298 (2017)
15. Finardi, U.: Time relations between scientific production and patenting of knowledge: the case of nanotechnologies. Scientometrics **89**(1), 37–50 (2011)
16. Zhao, Z., Lei, X.: Empirical analysis of the relationship between technology innovation and basic research. Curr. Sci. **104**(6), 714–720 (2013)
17. Park, H.W., Kang, J.: Patterns of scientific and technological knowledge flows based on scientific papers and patents. Scientometrics **81**(3), 811–820 (2009)
18. Sun, F., Zhu, L.: Citation genetic genealogy: a novel insight for citation analysis in scientific literature. Scientometrics **91**, 577–589 (2012)
19. Wu, R., Yang, H., Shi, W., Ng, S.: The knowledge import and export of LIS: the destinations, citation peak lag, and changes. In: Proceedings of the ACM/IEEE Joint Conference on Digital Libraries in 2020, pp. 197–206. ACM (2020)
20. Egghe, L.: A heuristic study of the first-citation distribution. Scientometrics **48**(3), 345–359 (2000)
21. Bornmann, L., Daniel, H.D.: Citation speed as a measure to predict the attention an article receives: an investigation of the validity of editorial decisions at Angewandte Chemie International Edition. J. Informetr. **4**(1), 83–88 (2010)
22. Stephens, N., Khan, I., Errington, R.: Analysing the role of virtualisation and visualisation on interdisciplinary knowledge exchange in stem cell research processes. Palgrave Commun. **4**(1), 1–13 (2018)
23. Morillo, F., Bordons, M., Gomez, I.: Interdisciplinarity in science: a tentative typology of disciplines and research areas. J. Am. Soc. Inf. Sci. Technol. **54**(13), 1237–1249 (2003)
24. Rinia, E.D., Van Leeuwen, T., Bruins, E., Van Vuren, H., Van Raan, A.: Citation delay in interdisciplinary knowledge exchange. Scientometrics **51**(1), 293–309 (2001)
25. Abramo, G., Cicero, T., D'Angelo, C.A.: A sensitivity analysis of researchers' productivity rankings to the time of citation observation. J. Informet. **6**(2), 192–201 (2012)
26. Slyder, J.B., et al.: Citation pattern and lifespan: a comparison of discipline, institution, and individual. Scientometrics **89**(3), 955–966 (2011)
27. Sotudeh, H., Estakhr, Z.: Sustainability of open access citation advantage: the case of Elsevier's author-pays hybrid open access journals. Scientometrics **115**, 563–576 (2018)
28. Wang, M., Zhang, J., Chen, G., Chai, K.H.: Examining the influence of open access on journals' citation obsolescence by modeling the actual citation process. Scientometrics **119**, 1621–1641 (2019)
29. Borrego, A., Barrios, M., Villarroya, A., Ollé, C.: Scientific output and impact of postdoctoral scientists: a gender perspective. Scientometrics **83**(1), 93–101 (2010)
30. Davis, P.M., Lewenstein, B.V., Simon, D.H., Booth, J.G., Connolly, M.J.: Open access publishing, article downloads, and citations: randomised controlled trial. BMJ **337**(7665), 343–345 (2008)
31. Yegros, A., Amat, C.B.: Editorial delay of food research papers is influenced by authors' experience but not by country of origin of the manuscripts. Scientometrics **81**(2), 367–380 (2009)
32. Ray, J., Berkwits, M., Davidoff, F.: The fate of manuscripts rejected by a general medical journal. Am. J. Med. **109**(2), 131–135 (2000)
33. De Marchi, M., Rocchi, M.: The editorial policies of scientific journals: testing an impact factor model. Scientometrics **51**(2), 395–404 (2001)

34. Shen, S., Rousseau, R., Wang, D., Zhu, D., Liu, H., Liu, R.: Editorial delay and its relation to subsequent citations: the journals nature, science and cell. Scientometrics **105**, 1867–1873 (2015)

35. Yin, Y., Wang, D.: The time dimension of science: connecting the past to the future. J. Informet. **11**(2), 608–621 (2017)

36. Levitt, J., Thelwall, M.: The most highly cited Library and Information Science articles: interdisciplinarity, first authors and citation patterns. Scientometrics **78**(1), 45–67 (2009)

37. Brito, R., Rodríguez-Navarro, A.: Evaluating research and researchers by the journal impact factor: is it better than coin flipping? J. Informet. **13**(1), 314–324 (2019)

38. Miranda, R., Garcia-Carpintero, E.: Comparison of the share of documents and citations from different quartile journals in 25 research areas. Scientometrics **121**(1), 479–501 (2019)

39. Waltman, L.: A review of the literature on citation impact indicators. J. Informet. **10**(2), 365–391 (2016)

40. Bornmann, L., de Moya Anegón, F., Mutz, R.: Do universities or research institutions with a specific subject profile have an advantage or a disadvantage in institutional rankings? a latent class analysis with data from the SCImago ranking. J. Am. Soc. Inf. Sci. Technol. **64**(11), 2310–2316 (2013)

41. Bornmann, L., Williams, R.: Can the journal impact factor be used as a criterion for the selection of junior researchers? a large-scale empirical study based on ResearcherID data. J. Informet. **11**(3), 788–799 (2017)

42. Bornmann, L., Mutz, R.: Further steps towards an ideal method of measuring citation performance: the avoidance of citation (ratio) averages in field-normalization. J. Informet. **5**(1), 228–230 (2011)

43. Hyland, K.: Self-citation and self-reference: credibility and promotion in academic publication. J. Am. Soc. Inf. Sci. Technol. **54**(3), 251–259 (2003)

44. Szomszor, M., Pendlebury, D.A., Adams, J.: How much is too much? the difference between research influence and self-citation excess. Scientometrics **123**(2), 1119–1147 (2020)

45. Ackerson, L.G., Chapman, K.: Identifying the role of multidisciplinary journals in scientific research. Coll. Res. Libr. **64**(6), 468–478 (2003)

Customer Service, Hard Work, and Normativity: Identity Standards Encoded into Public Library Routines

Darin Freeburg[✉] ⓘ and Katie Klein

University of South Carolina, Columbia, SC 29208, USA
darinf@mailbox.sc.edu

Abstract. Routines are a defining feature of the library workplace. While these routines can improve efficiency and keep libraries from needing to constantly reinvent the wheel, they can also introduce inequities that negatively impact library staff based on components of their identity. In this study, ten staff members from public libraries in America recorded a total of 50 audio diaries about their experiences in routine work. Analysis revealed the nature and source of identity standards encoded into library routines, how discrepancies in these standards are introduced, and what staff do to work around those discrepancies. Findings suggest that certain staff are more susceptible to these challenges, including staff of color, LGBTQIA+ staff, staff with mental illnesses, and staff with chronic pain. Yet, staff also employed their creative agency as they devised ways to work around problematic routines. This study contributes to research on routine dynamics and has implications for the continued promotion of equity, diversity, and inclusion in public libraries.

Keywords: Routine dynamics · Public Library Staff · Identity Control Theory

1 Introduction

Though the workplace can represent a source of fulfillment and rewards, it can also represent a potential *nexus point* for social oppression, introducing more barriers for certain workers than others [3, p. 231]. Simply because of who they are, many workers face barriers that make it difficult to enter, stay, succeed, and advance in the workplace, and their skills and expertise are often severely underutilized [14]. Libraries, in particular, continue to be "deeply racialized spaces where race-conscious motives, practices, and policies are inevitably enacted" [22, p. 197]. As a result, staff who do not meet certain white, middle-class, heterosexual, cisgender, or hyper-able criteria can face significant barriers [23].

Many of these barriers are hidden within library routines and the expectations placed on staff who engage in these routines—expectations that are often grounded in simplistic and normative evaluations of a staff member's individual and group identities based on visual and immediately accessible characteristics [21]. This means that, while routines

© The Author(s), under exclusive license to Springer Nature Switzerland AG 2024
I. Sserwanga et al. (Eds.): iConference 2024, LNCS 14597, pp. 392–406, 2024.
https://doi.org/10.1007/978-3-031-57860-1_26

suggest what library staff should *do* during a routine, they also suggest who library staff should *be*. This can be seen when routines are more rigidly prescribed for BIPOC staff Ossom-Williamson et al. [34], leading to a devaluation of their skills that can cause them to doubt their professional worth [35]. It can be seen in the microaggressions encoded into routines that subject staff to constant questioning about where they are really from Mody et al.[31], assume lower levels of intelligence by spelling out simple words for Black staff Hall [22], or define the work of a staff member by visual elements of their identity, e.g., the expectation to work like a *gay librarian* [38]. It can also be seen when routines lack necessary accommodation for staff with disabilities, suggesting that they need to complete the routine as if they had no disability. The resulting frustration and burnout are contributing to high rates of attrition among minoritized staff [23].

To uncover more about the identity standards encoded into routines, the effects of these standards, and what staff do in response, the current study asked ten public library staff to maintain an audio diary based on their experiences in routine work. While the findings suggest the presence of multiple problematic routines, they also reveal the creative agency of staff as they develop and implement workarounds. This study represents an important contribution to equity, diversity, and inclusion (EDI) research within libraries, because while routines are often perceived as immovable and immutable, they can also function as a significant source of change [16].

2   Literature Review

2.1   Routine Dynamics

The current study is grounded in practice theory and the study of routine dynamics. Practice theory considers what people do, how what they do creates and recreates institutional and social structures, and how those structures go on to influence future action [18]. Rather than seeing agency and structure as separate, practice theory sees them as mutually constituted such that "some of the key properties of each [are] effects of the other" [50, p. 339]. In practice, this means that people have opportunities to push back against and change the structure. The study of routine dynamics considers routines as one particular type of practice, distinct from other practices because they represent task-oriented behaviors that occur in particular sequences [18]. This sequence becomes familiar to people as the routine is repeated, and there are often attempts to improve the sequence to achieve certain outcomes. Routines can help to simplify complex work, avoid reinventing the wheel each time an action is performed, and circumvent continuous infighting about how work should proceed [16]. Yet, Feldman and Pentland [17, p. 849] note that routines can also work to "perpetuate privilege and oppression."

Routines are comprised of ostensive and performative elements. The ostensive elements of a routine outline the abstract blueprints, recipes, or templates for work behavior [2, 19]. This represents the structure of a routine, or its *patterning* D'Adderio [11], which consists of a worker's embodied and cognitive understanding of "abstract regularities and expectations" in the workplace [36, p. 241]. But, while the ostensive elements outline the general blueprints, they are never detailed enough to specify exact behavior [16]. Instead, these details are worked out in the performance of a routine. Workers express their agency as they interpret and apply the ostensive elements through routine performance, always introducing some variation from those ostensive elements. In this way, the performance of a routine is like a musical performance [16]. While the musical score outlines how the music should be played, there is always some variability in each musician's performance of that score.

The performative element of routine work suggests that workers do not mindlessly and robotically follow ostensive routines. Rather, routine performance represents an "effortful" activity [37, p. 488]. When routine performance fails to produce the intended outcome, creates new problems, enables new opportunities, or suggests the need for improvements Feldman [15], workers have an opportunity to change their performance of the routine in response: "Repetition introduces opportunities for changes that overcome minor or temporary obstacles but also introduces opportunities to do the routine differently or better" [16, p. 7]. These workarounds are "goal-driven adaptations, improvisations, or other activities that attempt to bypass or overcome obstacles or exceptions" in a routine [1, p. 5]. Over time, these variations in performance can change the ostensive blueprints themselves, i.e., change the musical score.

2.2 Identity and Routines

The current study seeks to provide a framework researchers can use to more fully consider issues of identity, power, privilege, and oppression embedded in routines. Identity has become a staple concern in the study of organizations [6]. In the context of routines, standards for a worker's identity are encoded into a routine's ostensive elements. This means that routines establish expectations, not only for what a worker should do but also for who they should be as they perform the routine. Identity control theory (ICT) suggests three main identity types that can be encoded into these routines [44]. The group standard references who a worker is as a member of a social group. The role standard references who a worker is as someone in a specific role or with a certain job description. Personal standards reference who a worker is as a "biographically and existentially separate and perhaps even unique human being" [24, p. 189].

These standards mean different things to different actors in the work system. Meanings originating from the self-represent *ideal* standards that a person aspires to maintain, while meanings originating from others represent *ought* standards a person feels obligated to maintain [25, 44]. According to ICT, a worker compares the salient identity standard with the identities they perceive in a routine's performance. Something in the performance of a worker or other actor can invalidate either an ought or ideal standard. For instance, a worker's mistakes can invalidate management standards for quality, or rule enforcement from management can invalidate a worker's own standards for autonomy. These discrepancies trigger "an error signal that both generates emotion and produces meaningful behavior or activity that changes meanings in the situation so that the error is reduced, and the perceptions match the standard" [44, p. 3].

Workers attempt to resolve discrepancies in identity standards using workarounds, which function as a type of identity work "the range of activities individuals engage in to create, present, and sustain personal identities that are congruent with and supportive of the self-concept" [43, p. 1348]. The goal of identity work is typically to secure a positive, valuable, good, or beneficial self-image, and behaviors range from accepting or complying with how one is perceived by others to resisting or redefining those perceptions to be more in line with one's self-perception [6]. For instance, Lutgen-Sandvik [28] found that workers experiencing bullying engaged in identity work to account for disruptions to their sense of identity. Behaviors included changing how they work, efforts to repair reputational damage, and attempts to convince others of the truthfulness of their story. Brown & Lewis [7] found that lawyers engaged in timekeeping and billing routines could realize their ideal identities as productive legal professionals by accepting the influence of disciplinary processes on their performance.

Informed by this research in routine dynamics and identity, the current research asks the following research questions:

- RQ1: What identity standards for staff are encoded into the ostensive element of public library routines?
- RQ2: How does the routine performance of a system actor introduce perceived discrepancies in identity standards?
- RQ3: What do library staff do to resolve perceived discrepancies in identity standards?
- RQ4: What effect do the workarounds of staff have on perceived discrepancies?

3   Methods

3.1   Study Design

A defining feature of routine dynamics is the assertion that workers are active and intentional in constructing their work environments *in situ* [27]. Yet, traditional organizational research methods, like retrospective surveys and interviews, tend to situate the research outside of this construction by asking participants to reflect on a past event. As a result, a participant's construction of meaning is often based on plausible rather than accurate remembering [42]. Diary methods have increasingly been adopted in organizational research to counteract these challenges Ohly, et al. [33]; van Eerde, Holman, & Totterdell [46], because they place data collection closer to the phenomenon under study, i.e., to "life as it is lived" [4, p. 597]. In an audio diary, participants are asked to record themselves speaking rather than writing journal entries. Recording enables a more immediate and fluid response that is better equipped than written diaries to capture a participant's thoughts on stressful experiences [10]. Audio diaries have several other advantages over traditional written diaries, including richer insight into a participant's sense-making process [32] and reduced burden on participants [29].

3.2   Sample

Public library staff were recruited from libraries in the Southeastern United States. To recruit, researchers asked libraries to distribute a flyer about the research and attended staff meetings in person at several sites. Participants who expressed interest through an online form then met with the researchers through Zoom for a more in-depth overview of the study and its requirements. This was done to increase informed consent and decrease attrition, with the assumption that knowing more about the expectations would make participants more likely to stay for the duration of the study. The sample population included ten staff, who each completed a demographics survey to capture elements of their self-described identity (Table 1). Participants were full-time staff representing 9 different libraries, and they worked in customer service, children and youth librarianship, circulation, and technical services.

Table 1. Self-described identities of study participants, aggregated.

Race	Sexuality	Gender	Job Category	Disability	Mental or Other Disorder
White (N = 6)	Heterosexual or straight (N = 4)	Woman (N = 8)	Professional (N = 6) Paraprofessional (N = 4)	Chronic pain (N = 2)	Anxiety (N = 4)
Black (N = 4)	Queer (N = 2)	Man (N = 1)		Seizure disorder (N = 1)	Depression (N = 2)
	Gay (N = 1)	Nonbinary (N = 1)		Heart condition (N = 1)	Obsessive-compulsive disorder (N = 1)
	Bisexual (N = 2)			Scoliosis (N = 1)	Autism (N = 1)
	Biromantic asexual (N = 1)			Asthma (N = 1)	
	Pansexual (N = 1)				

3.3 Process

Following a detailed set of prompts, each participant recorded five separate diaries of their routine experiences over the course of five different days. Participants recorded diaries between May 2023 and September 2023, and each participant typically completed their diaries within two weeks. Participants were encouraged to record entries immediately after engaging in a routine task, but since participants may not have the time or space to record these at work, they were given the option of recording them at the end of the day. Recordings were completed on the participant's cell phone, and each participant was provided with their own cloud-based folder to submit recordings to the research team. Participants were informed that they were in complete control of the diary entries, including the specific things they talk about and whether they would send certain diaries to the research team. Diaries were transcribed and uploaded to Nvivo for analysis.

3.4 Analysis

A total of 50 audio diaries were included in the analysis, representing a total of 476.6 min ($M = 9.5$, $Mdn = 7.9$). Each diary described one routine, and the units of analysis were the 50 individual routines. Template analysis was used to group these routines into types. Template analysis is commonly used in organizational research, and in diary research in particular Pilbeam et al. [39]; Poppleton, Briner, & Kiefer [40], and involves the creation of a list of hierarchically ordered codes that account for themes emerging from a detailed reading of transcripts [26]. Participants discussed their experiences in several common library routines (Table 2). These routines were then grouped according to the system actor depicted as the source of the identity standard and the system actor whose performance was perceived as introducing a discrepancy with the standard. Once the routines were grouped according to type, a secondary analysis was conducted to identify patterns in the type of identity standard, the nature of the performance discrepancy, what participants did to work around those discrepancies, and the extent to which those workarounds resolved the discrepancies.

Table 2. Routines described by participants.

Type	Examples
Collections maintenance	Shelf reading, weeding materials, processing book deliveries
Customer service	"Working the floor" and responding to patron inquiries and requests, reader's advisory, drive-through, front desk, enforcing code of conduct
Programming	Designing and implementing programs for specific patron groups, e.g., storytime, summer reading
Displays	Selecting and arranging materials for display, book bundling
Administrative	Clerical work, e.g., balancing the cash drawer, HR paperwork, purchasing and budgeting, library statistics
Opening/closing	Opening and closing the library to the public

4 Findings

4.1 Identity Standards (RQ1)

Customer Service Role. The most common standard concerned a participant's role as a member of library staff and working in a library meant providing excellent customer service. Kayla noted the standards of older patrons as they worked with library technology: "I know that someone's getting frustrated at me when they end up, like, snapping their fingers to get my attention." Riley suggested that patrons could base this standard on their own political beliefs, noting a patron's comments during his floor routine: "[The patron] just looked at me and was like, 'Y'all are really pushing that LGBTQ-whatever agenda, huh? With all these books?'... And she said, 'Well, it just all over [and] I just don't appreciate y'all indoctrinating my children.'" Ashley noted that management standards for customer service extended even to her behavior outside of work: "I feel like our expectation is to be good representatives of the library even when we're not on work hours at that point." So, the customer service standard typically represented an ought standard imposed on participants from other system actors, and these standards were well-defined and seemingly clear. Yet, customer service could also be part of a participant's ideal standards, suggesting an internalization of the ought standard. For instance, Megan's ideal role standard centered around a sense of obligation to younger patrons: "While these kids are not my biological children, they're still my kids... it feels really personal to me when something is going on with them and I feel sort of an obligation to try and fix it."

Hard Worker. Personal standards often meant that a participant was a uniquely hard worker, going beyond the requirements of their specific role. In yearly self-evaluations, management asked Marie to prove how she went above and beyond her role standards: "It was, like, oh, you can only be outstanding by going way, way above and beyond your job duties, which doesn't really make a lot of sense to me... I think if you're doing your work at a hundred percent, then that should be the top rating and you shouldn't necessarily have to go above and beyond your workload." Colleagues expected Riley to help them with their work, in addition to his own: "I had people coming into the workroom saying, 'Hey, can you come help us with this?' Or I would be getting some awkward looks from my coworkers who were checking in a whole bunch of books."

Similar to customer service standards, while hard work standards often originated from other system actors, participants also internalized them. For instance, Megan's ideal standard meant perfection: "I had meant to get to the library at 7:30 just so I could make sure that everything was perfect."

Normal. Patrons were depicted as having few personal standards for participants, instead expecting participants to cover their unique personal identities with normativity as defined by their role standards. Lexi noted a patron's expectations for her physical appearance: "He kept being like, 'I can't understand you because you're wearing that mask.' And then he said something along the lines of like, 'the mask, the hair, the dress. Are you just trying to stand out?'" Similarly, a patron appeared to question Jasmin's professionalism because of the clothes they wore: "I think I'm allowed to wear what I wanna wear and still be as competent as I was in a dress or in jeans." This depersonalization, centered around a participant's appearance, represents an overly simplistic evaluation of staff that may form the basis of other stereotypical expectations [21].

Advocate. Group standards could mean being an advocate for that group. Riley, a gay man, noted this about his own ideal standard: "[I wear] so much paraphernalia that basically says, 'I am here to support any of the gay people.'" Clara, who identifies as queer, noted the expectation of management and colleagues that she works on the library's display for PRIDE month: "I also felt like if I said no, it would be hypocritical… Like, everyone knows what I stand for at the library, so what would it look like if I said no to doing a PRIDE display?".

Punching Bag. Patrons seemed to justify their abusive behavior based on a participant's group identity. Jasmin felt that a patron's abusive behavior was due to the perception that they were a woman: "At no point did [the patron] get loud and belligerent with safety, but whenever he spoke to me and my partner who were short women, he immediately got louder." Amanda noted that male patrons could see female staff as accepting of their advances: "My manager, for example, does not have to worry about that happening to him when he gets the book drop. He's a man, so random men are not gonna come up to him and follow him around and hit on him."

4.2 Discrepancies (RQ2)

Bodies. Elements of a participant's physical body could introduce performance discrepancies, suggesting that overly simplistic standards built around visual features of identity can introduce actual barriers in routine work. Jasmin's visible Black identity seemed to invalidate a patron's standard for library staff: "After I had given the customer the information, she looked at me and just immediately sidestepped over to speak with my partner who… Just happened to be a white male… And then asked him the exact same question [laugh]." Riley's visible identity as a gay man disconfirmed patron standards for librarians:

"I have to be defensive around families, especially some of our homeschooled kids or more conservative families. I got this weird feeling of, like, because I am male in an improperly stereotypically female position, and also because I am gay, there's a lot of assumptions or looks that I get in this profession."

Megan's chronic pain from endometriosis made it difficult to meet colleague standards for a *peppy* children's librarian: "To put it gently, I felt like I was being stabbed while I was standing up."

Anxiety. While most discrepancies stemmed from the performance of other actors, participants also acknowledged that their own anxiety could lead to performance discrepancies. Although Stephanie knew how to fulfill her role in making room reservations for patrons, her anxiety made her doubt her ability: "I get nervous that I don't know how to do it, like, fully or the best." This led to a discrepancy with her ideal standard: "Although I knew what to do, for whatever reason I was just like, 'What do I do?' And so, I immediately just defer to [a manager]." Marie's anxiety made it difficult for her to enforce the library's code of conduct, which meant difficulty fulfilling management standards: "I do have a little bit of anxiety. I have a hard time, you know, talking to customers about things that they're doing wrong [laugh]."

Ostensive Design. Participants felt that the design of a routine could introduce discrepancies, suggesting that the ostensive elements of a routine can directly introduce barriers to performance. Management's design of the workload made it difficult for Ashley to fulfill a patron's customer service standard:

"The way that things are set up here is that all of these tasks get shifted to the.

person in the drive-through . . . Something as simple as putting books on hold for a customer shouldn't take that much time or shouldn't take long, but [it does] because I'm doing three or four things at a time."

The library board's new and cumbersome processes for the display routine made it difficult for Clara to meet management and colleague standards for completing the PRIDE display: "They have never been that interested in what we do for displays until now. All they've done lately is just make it harder for us to do displays."

Overreliance. The reliance of management and colleagues on participants could introduce a discrepancy. The expectation from management and colleagues that Clara would work on the PRIDE display introduced a discrepancy with Clara's ideal standard:

"I like this job. I don't want to get fired . . . I'm [also] not out to my family because they're homophobic. So, the thought goes through my mind like, what if I do this display request and somehow either it's rejected, or it's not rejected, and I do the display and that ends up in the news with my name attached to it."

A colleague interrupted Ashley's front desk routine: "I was still helping [a customer] with [scanning], but [my colleague] saw me at the desk. So, she tried to grab my attention and said, 'Well, hey, since you're back at the desk, I don't know what I'm doing. Can you help me on my computer?'" This overreliance is likely influenced by a colleague's hard work standard.

Disrespectful Behavior. When patrons behaved in a way participants felt was inappropriate, it forced participants to choose between invalidating patron or ideal standards. A patron asked Stephanie if she was married: "For context, he is 62 years old, and I am 22 years old. I am not married; however, I felt very uncomfortable when he asked me that question." Although Jasmin's physical appearance made it "obvious that I am some flavor of queer," a patron asked them for help finding a group for men against gay aggression: "I am a non-binary person. My partner who was on the desk at the time is also queer, and it was very weird... This one felt kind of gross." It is likely that a patron's depersonalization of staff and ridged customer service expectations contribute to this behavior.

4.3 Workarounds (RQ3)

Subtractive. In subtractive workarounds, participants removed, restricted, or hid something about their own performance in an effort to resolve a discrepancy. Riley concealed his gay identity to avoid disconfirming patron standards: "I feel myself putting more of a mask on and trying not to help or be as enthusiastic... I have to kind of diminish myself to do a lot of work with families." Megan hid her physical pain to meet colleague and management standards for being a *peppy* children's librarian: "I had to keep my face from twisting in pain... I call it putting on my second face."

Outcomes. Subtractive workarounds typically validated the standards of others, while invalidating a participant's own standards—eliciting negative emotions. Though Riley wanted to "be an example of queer joy," his masking of that identity made him feel small: "I feel myself, like, shrink a bit to try and let them have a space in the library. I feel a little defeated talking to them... I get depressed [laugh]." Megan's masking led to exhaustion: "While I was successful in making it through the patron interactions, it really kind of took a toll on me throughout the day." Yet, subtractive workarounds aligned with Marie's ideal standard: "I will put myself out, you know, kind of relinquish what I need sometimes for other people... I don't have a problem with that."

Additive. In additive workarounds, participants added to their performance in an effort to resolve a discrepancy. This could mean increased effort, as noted by Tara's efforts to avoid invalidating patron customer service standards: "I just try to fit in those additional responsibilities. I just have to kind of turn on the gears in my brain that allow me to do that task successfully." When management behavior threatened her ability to meet management's own standards, Ashley prepared herself for a heavier workload: "I just need to mentally prepare myself that I might have a little bit extra work left behind." Participants also added resolve, as noted by Amanda's attempts to *muddle through* a discrepancy in her ideal standards rather than directly resolve it: "I've never heard of any other staff members having an issue with it, so I've always just put up with it and figured it was just me."

Outcomes. While additive workarounds could resolve discrepancies in one standard, they could also introduce new discrepancies in another. For instance, Kayla's decision to push through resource limitations and continue helping older patrons invalidated patron standards for her availability: "I know a lot of people who need [help] and they don't ask, because they feel like they'd be inconveniencing us." Tara invalidated patron customer service standards despite her increased effort: "Some of the books came out a day or two after they were supposed to be released."

Reframing. In reframing workarounds, participants shifted their focus from resolving a discrepancy to resolving the cognitive dissonance caused by the discrepancy. Jasmin tried to rationalize a patron's rude behavior: "I also kind of feel like this was a circumstance where someone was trying to get a job and jobs are important." When Megan's anxiety threatened her ideal standard, she shifted her temporal focus to the present: "I did take a 15-min break just to recenter myself, you know, use some mindfulness tactics, because as much as I think they sound really lame [laugh], they do work." Tara shifted her temporal focus to future performances: "I just had to use it as a learning opportunity... I've definitely kind of taken some time to think about how things could have been done differently."

Outcomes. While reframing typically did not resolve the discrepancy, it did help participants resolve the dissonance the discrepancy caused. For instance, it could suggest that the discrepancy was not caused by a participant's own inability to meet a standard, but rather by some other external factor. By planning for the future, participants were able to continue seeing themselves as high performers. Yet, focusing on the present did improve Megan's performance in a way that removed the discrepancy: "This was a lot more successful than I had thought it would be, because I was able to sort of reorient myself and, you know, gather my social battery a little bit more."

Outward Change. In outward change workarounds, participants directed their change efforts at other system actors. When a patron's uncomfortable questions threatened her ideal standard, Clara told the patron to stop: "I told him multiple times, like, 'Oh, I'm sorry I don't answer personal questions at work, but I am happy to help you with your library business.'" Tara asked a colleague to stop their work to help her: "It was extremely helpful for another staff member to step in and offer to give the new employee a tour of the building." Lexi pushed back against the routine itself: "The way I handled the obstacle was to just put it away and to stop doing the task."

Outcomes. Outward change workarounds were limited because successful resolution depended on another system actor's performance. For instance, the patron simply ignored Stephanie's efforts: "He said, 'I want to apologize for asking if you were married the other day'... And then he said, 'I would've asked you out, but you probably are married or something.' And again, this made me very uncomfortable." When a patron followed Jasmin to their car, colleagues ignored their looks for help: "I felt a little abandoned by my coworkers, because they kept going to their cars... They just kinda looked and went to their own vehicles while someone verbally accosted me." Trying to change other actors could also introduce new discrepancies, as Kayla noted with her efforts to get colleagues to adopt a new system that better fit her processing disorder: "It seems no matter how often I try to explain to people that it's not me having OCD, that it's not me being super controlling, that I literally need it put this way to efficiently function, [I can't]."

5 Discussion

5.1 Theoretical Takeaways

The current study contributes to the study of routine dynamics by answering Feldman and Pentland [17, p.846]'s call to move beyond a routine's ability to produce goods and services to a consideration of the ways in which routines "reproduce[s] patterns of social equality and inequality". Findings suggest that the inequality in routines is due, in part, to the tendency of a routine's ostensive components to center around standards for a worker's identity. Failure to conform to these standards can represent significant challenges and discomfort for library staff Cooke [8] and may help explain why library staff often feel it necessary to "hide parts of themselves to remain viable in their careers" [34]. Yet, the findings also suggest that these inequities are hidden within ostensive expectations for customer service and hard work. Because these expectations are not explicitly based on identity, it can make it seem like the routine is equitable—even when inequities are revealed in performance. These findings support Diamond and Lewis [12]'s findings about racial discrimination embedded in school disciplinary routines. Although the routine was discriminatory in practice, the ostensive components of the routine were not explicitly discriminatory, hiding the routine's actual discriminatory effects.

5.2 Practical Takeaways

Customer Service. The presence of customer service standards in the current study aligns with the reality that librarianship is a customer-facing service profession [9, 30]. Libraries are facing increasing competitive pressure to adopt a *customer value mandate* that distinguishes them from other information organizations [49]. Many libraries have even shifted from a focus on *patrons* to a focus on *customers* [41]. LiQUAL+, a customer satisfaction instrument used in academic libraries, is underpinned by the assumption that "only customers judge quality; all other judgments are essentially irrelevant" Zeithami, Parasuraman, & Berry [51], cited in Thompson, Kyrillidou, & Cook [45]. Yet, the findings suggest the need to consider more fully the impact of a customer-centric focus on library staff. For instance, the finding that patrons appeared to define staff, not as unique people, but as workers there to serve their interests, is indicative of an *entitlement* attitude. Here, a patron expects that they are inherently deserving of "special treatment and automatic compliance with his or her expectations" without doing anything to earn it [5, p. 274]. The behaviors of these entitled patrons can lead to negative affect, burnout, and feelings of dehumanization [20]. The tendency of management to also define staff by their service to customers highlights the role of management in conferring a "social legitimacy and a sense of inevitability" to a patron's abuse of staff [47, p. 270].

Vocational Awe. Hard work featured prominently in the current study's findings, as participants were defined as hard workers and often engaged in workarounds that increased the intensity of their work e.g., masking, muddling through, increasing effort. And while this may be seen as a necessary expectation in any workplace, hard work in libraries must be considered through the lens of vocational awe. Vocational awe refers to a belief among library workers that, because of the commendable things a library does, libraries are "inherently good and sacred, and therefore beyond critique" [13]. A participant's acceptance of customer service standards, often at the expense of their own, may be influenced by a belief that librarians are *priests* and *saviors* whose self-sacrifice supports the communities in which they work [13]. Staff may feel the need to push down their personal identities to meet the standards of *the calling*. One potential consequence of vocational awe is that it can suggest to staff that efforts to prioritize their ideal standards—e.g., abandoning the routine, taking a break, looking to someone else for help—are selfish and represent an abandonment of the call. This can lead to burnout, acceptance of less pay, job creep, and a privilege of the status quo [13].

Contextual Supports. Findings also suggest opportunities for libraries to better support staff through the proactive development of contextual supports. These supports include formal policies and practices that support equality and signal "the types of behaviors that are acceptable and expected;" a supportive climate that affords psychological safety, positive social interactions, and freedom to express one's true self; and relationships that offer empathy and support [48, p. 195]. In the context of the current study, supports may involve eliminating the need for certain workarounds. For instance, a policy on mandatory mental health days may shift a worker's reliance on merely pushing through after experiencing traumatic discrepancies. Changes to workplace culture that increase opportunities for a staff member's cultural and self-expression can reduce reliance on masking. Inviting patrons to get to know staff as unique individuals could decrease entitlement, as it is likely easier for patrons to feel entitled to a faceless job role than to a unique person. Supports may also involve supporting staff efforts to engage in certain workarounds. For instance, libraries can provide staff with tools for resolving cognitive discrepancies in healthy ways. Libraries can also help staff build skills for effectively pushing back and prioritizing their ideal standards, while also giving them opportunities to validate those standards.

6 Conclusion

Routines are a defining feature of the library workplace. And while these routines can improve efficiency and keep libraries from needing to constantly reinvent the wheel, they can also introduce inequities that negatively impact workers based on components of their identity. Through an analysis of 50 audio diaries from ten public library staff, the current study considered the presence of identity standards in the routine work of public library staff. Findings show that staff are expected to be service-oriented, hard-working, and advocates for their group, while also hiding their unique personal identity and being accepting of patron abuse. And while a staff member's own performance in a routine often invalidated these standards, both the performance and the standards they invalidated were often based on identity-based standards of normativity. The efforts of staff to work around these discrepancies are leading to added stress, frustration, and depersonalization. Findings suggest that certain staff are more susceptible to these challenges, including staff of color, LGBTQIA+ staff, staff with mental illnesses, and staff with chronic pain. Yet, the findings also suggest opportunities for library management and decision-makers to introduce contextual supports that work to eliminate problematic routines or help staff work around them.

Acknowledgment. This research was funded by the Institute of Museum and Library Services, USA.

References

1. Alter, S.: Theory of workarounds. Commun. Assoc. Inf. Syst. **34**(55), 1041–1066 (2014)
2. Becker, M.C.: Organizational routines: a review of the literature. Ind. Corp. Chang. **13**(4), 643–678 (2004)
3. Blustein, D.L.: The role of work in psychological health and well-being: a conceptual, historical, and public policy perspective. Am. Psychol. **63**(4), 228–240 (2008)
4. Bolger, N., Davis, A., Rafaeli, E.: Diary methods: capturing life as it is lived. Annu. Rev. Psychol. **54**, 579–616 (2003). https://doi.org/10.1146/annurev.psych.54.101601.145030
5. Boyd, H.C., Helms, J.E.: Customer entitlement theory and measurement. Psychol. Mark. **22**(3), 271–286 (2005)
6. Brown, A.D.: Identities in organization studies. Organ. Stud. **40**(1), 7–22 (2019). https://doi.org/10.1177/0170840618765014
7. Brown, A.D., Lewis, M.A.: Identities, discipline and routines. Organ. Stud. **32**(7), 871–895 (2011)
8. Cooke, N.A.: Information services to diverse populations: Developing culturally competent library professionals. Libraries Unlimited (2017)
9. Cronin, B., Martin, I.: Social skills training in librarianship. J. Librariansh. **15**(2), 105–122 (1983)
10. Crozier, S.E., Cassell, C.M.: Methodological considerations in the use of audio diaries in work psychology: adding to the qualitative toolkit. J. Occup. Organ. Psychol. **89**(2), 396–419 (2016)
11. D'Adderio, L.: The replication dilemma unravelled: how organizations enact multiple goals in routine transfer. Organ. Sci. **25**(5), 1325–1350 (2014). https://doi.org/10.1287/orsc.2014.0913
12. Diamond, J.B., Lewis, A.E.: Race and discipline at a racially mixed high school: status, capital, and the practice of organizational routines. Urban Education **54**(6), 831–859 (2019)
13. Ettarh, F. (2018, Jan.). Vocational awe and librarianship: The lies we tell ourselves. *In the Library with the Lead Pipe.* https://www.inthelibrarywiththeleadpipe.org/2018/vocational-awe/
14. Fassinger, R.E.: Workplace diversity and public policy: challenges and opportunities for psychology. Am. Psychol. **63**(4), 252–268 (2008)
15. Feldman, M.S.: Organizational routines as a source of continuous change. Organ. Sci. **11**(6), 611–629 (2000). https://doi.org/10.1287/orsc.11.6.611.12529
16. Feldman, M.S., Pentland, B.T.: Reconceptualizing organizational routines as a source of flexibility and change. Adm. Sci. Q. **48**(1), 94–118 (2003)
17. Feldman, M.S., Pentland, B.T.: Routine dynamics: toward a critical conversation. Strateg. Organ. **20**(4), 846–859 (2022). https://doi.org/10.1177/14761270221130876
18. Feldman, M.S., Pentland, B.T., D'Adderio, L., Dittrich, K., Rerup, C., Seidl, D.: What is routine dynamics? In: Feldman, M.S., Pentland, B.T., D'Adderio, L., Dittrich, K., Rerup, C., Seidl, D. (eds.) Cambridge Handbook of Routine Dynamics, pp. 1–18. Cambridge University Press, Cambridge (2021)
19. Felin, T., Foss, N.: Organizational routines and capabilities: historical drift and a course-correction toward microfoundations. Scand. J. Manag. **25**(2), 157–167 (2009)

20. Fisk, G.M., Neville, L.B.: Effects of customer entitlement on service workers' physical and psychological well-being: a study of waitstaff employees. J. Occup. Health Psychol. **16**(4), 391–405 (2011)
21. Fiske, S.T.: Social cognition and social perception. Annu. Rev. Psychol. **44**, 155–194 (1993)
22. Hall, T.D.: The 21st-century Black librarian in America. The Black body at the reference desk: Critical race theory and Black librarianship. In: Jackson, A.P., Jefferson, Jr., J.C., Nosakhere, A.S. (eds.) The 21st-Century Black librarian in America, pp. 197–202. The Scarecrow Press (2012)
23. Hathcock, A.: White librarianship in Blackface: Diversity initiatives in LIS. In the Library with the Lead Pipe (2015). https://www.inthelibrarywiththeleadpipe.org/2015/lis-diversity/
24. Hewitt, J.P.: Dilemmas of the American self. Temple University Press, Philadelphia (1989)
25. Higgins, E.T.: Self-discrepancy: a theory relating self and affect. Psychol. Rev. **94**, 319–340 (1987)
26. King, N.: Doing template analysis. In: Symon, G., Cassell, C. (eds.) Qualitative Organizational Research: Core Methods and Current Challenges, pp. 426–450. Sage, Thousand Oaks (2012)
27. Lopez-Cotarelo, J.: Ethnomethodology and routine dynamics. In: Feldman, M.S., Pentland, B.T., D'Adderio, L., Dittrich, K., Rerup, C., Seidl, D. (eds.) Cambridge Handbook of Routine Dynamics, pp. 49–61. Cambridge University Press, Cambridge (2021)
28. Lutgen-Sandvik, P.: Intensive remedial identity work: responses to workplace bullying trauma and stigmatization. Organization **15**(1), 97–119 (2008)
29. Markham, T., Couldry, N.: Tracking the reflexivity of the (dis)engaged citizen: some methodological reflections. Qual. Inq. **13**, 675–695 (2007). https://doi.org/10.1177/1077800407301182
30. Miao, H., Bassham, M.W.: Embracing customer service in libraries. Libr. Manag. **28**(1/2), 53–61 (2007)
31. Mody, N., Natarzaj, L., Singh, G., Worcester, A.: The other Asian: reflections of South Asian Americans in libraryland. In: Chou, R.L., Pho, A. (eds.) Pushing the Margins: Women of Color and Intersectionality in LIS. Library Juice Press, Sacramento (2018)
32. Monrouxe, L.V.: Solicited audio diaries in longitudinal narrative research: a view from inside. Qual. Res. **9**(1), 81–103 (2009). https://doi.org/10.1177/1468794108098032
33. Ohly, S., Sonnentag, S., Niessen, C., Zapf, D.: Diary studies in organizational research: an introduction and some practical recommendations. J. Pers. Psychol. **9**(2), 79–93 (2010)
34. Ossom-Williamson, P., Williams, J., Goodman, X., Minter, C.I.J., Logan, A.: Starting with I: combating anti-blackness in libraries. Med. Ref. Serv. Q. **40**(2), 139–150 (2021)
35. Owuamalam, C.K., Zagefka, H.: On the psychological barriers to the workplace: when and why metastereotyping undermines employability beliefs of women and ethnic minorities. Cultur. Divers. Ethnic Minor. Psychol. **20**(4), 521–528 (2014)
36. Pentland, B.T., Feldman, M.S.: Issues in empirical field studies of organizational routines. In: Becker, M.C. (ed.) Handbook of Organizational Routines, pp. 281–300. Edward Elgar, Cheltenham (2008)
37. Pentland, B.T., Reuter, H.H.: Organizational routines as grammars of action. Adm. Sci. Q. **39**, 484–510 (1994)
38. Phillips, J.D.: It's okay to be gay . . . a librarian's journey to acceptance and activism. In: Nectoux, T.M. (ed.) Out Behind the Desk: Workplace Issues for LGBTQ Librarians. Library Juice Press, Sacramento (2011)
39. Pilbeam, C., Davidson, R., Doherty, N., Denyer, D.: What learning happens? using audio diaries to capture learning in response to safety-related events within retail and logistics organizations. Saf. Sci. **81**, 59–67 (2016)
40. Poppleton, S., Briner, R.B., Kiefer, T.: The roles of context and everyday experience in understanding work-non-work relationships: a qualitative diary study of white- and blue-collar workers. J. Occup. Organ. Psychol. **81**(3), 481–502 (2008)

41. Pundsack, K.: Customers or patrons? How you look at your library's users affects customer service. Public Libraries Online (2015). https://publiclibrariesonline.org/2015/03/customers-or-patrons-how-you-look-at-your-librarys-users-affects-customer-service/

42. Rausch, A.: Task characteristics and learning potentials—empirical results of three diary studies on workplace learning. Vocat. Learn. **6**(1), 55–79 (2013). https://doi.org/10.1007/s12186-012-9086-9

43. Snow, D.A., Anderson, L.: Identity work among the homeless: the verbal construction and avowal of personal identities. Am. J. Sociol. **92**, 1336–1371 (1987)

44. Stets, J.E., Burke, P.J.: New directions in identity control theory. Adv. Group Process. **22**, 43–64 (2005)

45. Thompson, B., Cook, C., Heath, F.: Two short forms of the LibQUAL+ survey: assessing users' perceptions of library service quality. Libr. Q. Inf. Commun. Policy **73**(4), 453–465 (2003)

46. van Eerde, W., Holman, D., Totterdell, P.: Editorial: special section: diary studies in work psychology. J. Occup. Organ. Psychol. **78**(2), 151–154 (2005). https://doi.org/10.1348/096317905X40826

47. Wang, L.: When the customer is king: employment discrimination as customer service. Virginia J. Social Policy Law **249** (2016)

48. Webster, J., Adams, G.A., Maranto, C.L., Sawyer, K., Thoroughgood, C.: Workplace contextual supports for LGBT employees: a review, meta-analysis, and agenda for future research. Hum. Res. Manag. **57**, 193–210 (2018)

49. Weinstein, A.T., McFarlane, D.A.: How libraries can enhance customer service by implementing a customer value mindset. Int. J. Nonprofit Volunt. Sect. Mark. **22**(e1571), 1–7 (2016)

50. Wendt, A.E.: The agent-structure problem in international relations theory. Int. Organ. **41**(3), 335–370 (1987)

51. Zeithaml, V.A., Parasuraman, A., Berry, L.L.: Delivering Quality service: Balancing Customer Perceptions and Expectations. The Free Press, Los Angeles (1990)

Will Affiliation Diversity Promote the Disruptiveness of Papers in Artificial Intelligence?

Xuli Tang[1] , Xin Li[2](✉) , and Ming Yi[1]

[1] School of Information Management, Central China Normal University, Wuhan, China
{xltang,yiming0415}@ccnu.edu.cn
[2] School of Medicine and Health Management, Tongji Medical College, Huazhong University of Science and Technology, Wuhan, China
xl60@hust.edu.cn

Abstract. This study investigates the causal relationship between affiliation diversity and the disruptiveness of papers in the field of Artificial Intelligence (AI). We obtained 646,100 AI-related papers with complete affiliation information between 1950 and 2019 from the Microsoft Academic Graph. Descriptive analysis and Propensity Score Matching (PSM) methods are employed in this study. The results show that homophily (over 70%) has still been prevalent over the past 70 years among multi-affiliation collaborations in AI, despite the average affiliation diversity exhibiting startling upward trends when AI steps into the deep learning stage. Affiliation diversity cannot promote the disruptiveness of AI papers. On the contrary, AI papers with affiliation diversity can be 1.75% less disruptive compared to AI papers that collaborated by similar affiliations.

Keywords: Affiliation Diversity · Artificial Intelligence · Disruptiveness of Papers

1 Introduction

Disruptiveness is broadly acknowledged as the key to breaking down the barriers of old science and creating new technologies, methods, and theories [1, 2]. However, just as the preeminent journal Nature declares, disruptive science and technology have dramatically and mysteriously dropped since 1945 despite the skyrocket in scientific publications [3, 4]. Researchers have been endeavoring to figure out the reasons behind this phenomenon. For example, Sheng et al. [5] explored the relationship between the prior knowledge underlying research and the disruptiveness of papers in medicine and biomedical sciences. Yang et al. [6] studied the quality of government-funded papers from the perspective of knowledge integration and disruptiveness in both PubMed and Microsoft Academic Graph (MAG). Liu et al. [2] investigated the relationship between interdisciplinary collaboration and disruptiveness in six interdisciplinary journals. Notwithstanding, few studies have examined disruptive shifts in papers from the perspective of multi-affiliation collaborations.

© The Author(s), under exclusive license to Springer Nature Switzerland AG 2024
I. Sserwanga et al. (Eds.): iConference 2024, LNCS 14597, pp. 407–415, 2024.
https://doi.org/10.1007/978-3-031-57860-1_27

With the increase in team sizes and co-authored papers, the importance of multi-affiliation collaborations (e.g., international collaborations, university-industry collaborations, inter-affiliation collaborations) has been emphasized in scientific innovation [7, 8]. Collaboration with diverse institutions can effectively promote the exchange of ideas, knowledge, and resources and improve production creativity [9, 10]. Abramo et al. [11] found that international collaboration has a positive effect on the quantity and quality of publications. Dong et al. [12] demonstrated that papers produced by smaller teams with affiliation diversity are more innovative than papers published by larger teams within unique institutions. It is worth mentioning that affiliation diversity may also hinder effective communication by increasing the geographical distance of co-authors [13]. Despite the affiliation diversity mentions, to our best knowledge, the causal effect of affiliation diversity on the disruptiveness of papers remain unexplored. Besides, the disparity among affiliations, which indicates the manner and degree in which the affiliations may be distinguished, is broadly ignored in the calculation of affiliation diversity.

In this preliminary study, we will fill this gap by examining the causal relationship between multi-affiliation diversity and the disruptiveness of papers in Artificial Intelligence using descriptive analysis and Propensity Score Matching. Meanwhile, we will propose an improved affiliation diversity indicator to measure the distribution of affiliation differences in multiple-affiliation collaboration by taking disparity into account. As an emerging field, Artificial Intelligence has achieved a qualitative leap from theory to application in the past 70 years, completely changing our lives. Hence, it is meaningful to explore the disruptiveness of papers in the field of Artificial Intelligence.

Our primary research questions are as follows:

(1) Is there a causal relationship between affiliation diversity and the disruptiveness of AI papers? If so, to what extent does affiliation diversity influence the disruptiveness of AI papers?
(2) How to measure affiliation diversity by taking disparity into account?

2   Methods

2.1   Data and Processing

The dataset employed in this study has been derived from Microsoft Academic Graph (MAG). We referred to [14] and used both conference papers and journal papers published in Artificial Intelligence, computer vision, machine learning, nature language processing, and pattern recognition to represent AI research from 1950 to 2019. Bibliographic data for each paper, like title, year, author, author affiliation, and abstract, were extracted from Microsoft Azure Server. After removing records with a single author or missing affiliation information, we obtained around 646,100 AI papers with 1,008,548 authors belonging to 9,627 affiliations.

To better reflect the semantic relationships among different affiliations, we mapped the AI author affiliation into Wikidata based on its name and then extracted the embedding vector for each affiliation using pre-training results of Wikidata by [15]. Figure 1 shows a two-dimensional projection of the affiliation space through t-SNE (t-distributed Stochastic Neighbor Embedding) algorithm, with an emphasis on affiliation types, such as educational organization (red), enterprise (yellow), etc. Enterprises (in yellow) are clustered into a single cluster, while educational affiliations (in red) include six dispersed cluster structures. Other types of affiliations are relatively dispersed and do not form a significant cluster phenomenon. This indicates that classifying affiliations solely based on affiliation types does not reflect the similarity between affiliations well, and the graph embeddings can better measure the degree of correlation between affiliations.

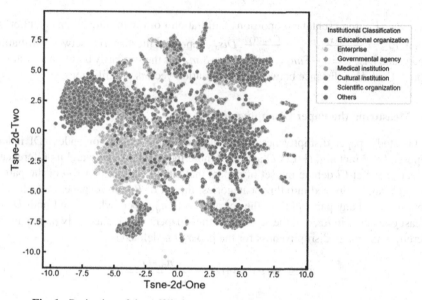

Fig. 1. Projection of the Affiliation onto two-dimensional space using t-SNE

To decrease the influence of the confounders, for each paper, we obtained the following information: (1) the embedding vectors for the abstract of each paper were calculated by the Doc2vec technique. (2) whether or not it belongs to high-impact conferences or journals. In our study, the top 5% of journals in the JCR ranking report were defined as high-impact journals, while the top 10 conferences published in AMiner were defined as high-impact conferences. (3) other external features like published year, publication impact, reference numbers, and citation numbers were also collected from the MAG. (4) team size was counted and collected. (5) The individual's leadership is calculated by h_α pointed out by [16], and the largest h_α in an author-team was defined as leadership (Ldrshp). Then, the max-min normalization was used for the standardization of raw feature data, such as year, reference count, citation count, team size, and so on.

2.2 Measuring the Affiliation Diversity

In this study, diversity is measured with the well-known Integration Score proposed by [17]. We define co-authors in a paper as a team and represent a team A of an AI paper D with m co-authors as $A = \{a_1, a_2, \ldots, a_m\}$. Now, for any given author $a_i \in A$, let $I(a_i)$ denote the affiliation of a_i. Note that for each paper D, set

$I = \{I(a_1), I(a_2), \ldots, I(a_m), a_i \in A\}$ is a multi-set. We define $under(I)$ with $n(n \leq m)$ non-duplicate elements as the underlying set of I. Therefore, the affiliation diversity of a team A of an AI paper D is defined as:

$$d_I(A) = \sum_{\substack{x, y \in under(I) \\ x \neq y}}^{n} Dis_{x,y}{}^{\alpha} \cdot (Pr_x \cdot Pr_y)^{\beta}, \tag{1}$$

where Pr_x, Pr_y represent the proportion of affiliation x or y to the number of coauthors in a team, $Pr_x = \frac{Count(x)}{m}$, $Pr_y = \frac{Count(y)}{m}$. $Dis_{x,y}$ represent the disparity between affiliation x and y, and $Dis_{x,y} = 1 - Sim_{x,y}$, we measure $Sim_{x,y}$ as the similarity between affiliations through Euclidean distance between representation vectors of affiliations.

2.3 Measuring the Paper Disruptiveness

In this study, paper disruptiveness is calculated by the Disruption Index (DI index) proposed by Wu et al. [1]. Let D and Re denote the focal AI paper and its references, respectively. Let Ci denote the set of papers that cited the focal paper D or the papers in Re. Ci can be divided into three categories: the set of P with n_p papers which cited D but not cited any papers in Re, the set of Q with n_q papers which cited both D and at least one paper in Re, and the set of K with n_k papers which cited only papers in Re. Therefore, the paper disruptiveness for the paper D is defined as:

$$DI = \Pr(P) - \Pr(Q) = \frac{n_p - n_q}{n_p + n_q + n_k}, \tag{2}$$

Further, we ranked the DI index in ascending order and binned the data by choosing the top 0.1%, top 0.2%, top 0.3%, ..., and 100% data. Then, all DI indexes will be assigned to the interval between 0 and 100.

2.4 Propensity Score Matching

To explore the causal relationships between affiliation diversity and the paper disruptiveness in the field of AI, we adopted Propensity Score Matching (PSM), which is one of the most popular matching methods for estimating treatment effects when randomized trials are not available [18].

The PSM analysis involves three primary steps: covariate selection, matching and balancing checks, and causal effect estimation [19]. Covariates affect treatment assignments and outcomes simultaneously and should be controlled in causal inference. We usually select covariates based on previous research, experience, or pre-experiment [19].

Then, we need to divide the experiment object (AI papers) into treated group ($d_I(A) > 0$) and control group ($d_I(A) \leq 0$) and mapped multidimensional observed covariates into a propensity score through the probit model, logistic regression, or other machine learning models [19]. By matching the propensity score of subjects in both the treated group and the control group, we can generate a covariate balance between the two groups, as in a successful randomized experiment.

The Average Treatment Effect (ATE) is used to estimate the causal effect. Let X and $ps(X_i)$ denote the observed covariates and the propensity score of i-th paper of X_i. Then, we perform PSM between the control and each treatment group and obtain m matching paper pairs as M. After matching, Let Y_{1j}, Y_{0j} ($j \in M$) as the outcome (paper disruptiveness) of j-th paper pair in the treatment group and control group respectively. Therefore, the ATE can be estimated as follows.

$$ATE = \frac{1}{m} \sum\nolimits_{j \in M} \{E(Y_{1j}|ps(X_j), T_j = 1) - E(Y_{0j}|ps(X_j), T_j = 1)\}, \qquad (3)$$

3 Results

3.1 Overview of Affiliation Diversity and Paper Disruptiveness in AI

Figure 2a shows the Cumulative Distribution Function (CDF) of affiliation diversity of AI papers over the past 70 years. The CDF is a step function that accumulates the probabilities of affiliation diversity (d_I) taking values less than or equal to x ($x \in [0, 1]$). More than 70% of scientific collaboration happened within a similar affiliation, and the maximum value of the diversity index is around 30%. This indicates that homophily is still prevalent among affiliation collaborations in the field of Artificial Intelligence.

To obtain a detailed understanding of the changes in affiliation diversity and paper disruptiveness during the development of AI, we investigate the trends of average affiliation diversity and average disruptiveness percentile over time, respectively. As Fig. 2b indicates, in the decade of 1950–2014, the average affiliation diversity and the average disruptiveness percentile of AI papers show opposite trends. The average affiliation diversity generally showed an upward trend with apparent fluctuations. In contrast, the average disruptiveness percentile of AI papers significantly and monotonically declines, consistent with the slowed canonical phenomenon in science during this period demonstrated by [4]. Note, since 2014, when AI steps into the deep learning stage [20], the average affiliation diversity and the average disruptiveness percentile both exhibit startling upward trends.

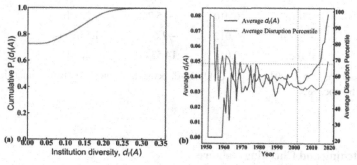

Fig. 2. (a) The Cumulative Distribution Function (CDF) of affiliation diversity of AI papers. (b) the change of average affiliation diversity and average disruptiveness percentile over time

3.2 Covariate Selection

In this study, we carefully select observed candidate covariates such as paper topics (Topic1, Topic2, ...Topic10), publication year (pubYear), publication impact (pubCore), team size (tsize), leadership distance (Ldrshp) number of references (refNum), number of 5-year citations(5YearCi) based on previous studies.

We examined the relationship between the treatments and the observed candidate covariates. The results of the logistic regression before matching are displayed in Table 1. Except for the variables of "Topic1", "Topic4", and "Topic6", all the other covariates affect the affiliation diversity significantly. Hence, "Topic1", "Topic4", and "Topic6" were removed from covariates, and the others were applied in the matching process.

Table 1. Result of regression between the covariates and the treatment before matching

variable	estimate	SE	Z value	pr(>|z|)	Sig
(Intercept)	−2.546	0.036	−71.283	<2.00E−16	***
pubYear	1.006	0.040	25.003	<2.00E−16	***
pubCore	0.170	0.013	12.712	<2.00E−16	***
refNum	11.818	0.206	57.295	<2.00E−16	***
tsize	3.426	0.025	135.136	<2.00E−16	***
Ldrshp	0.248	0.056	4.469	7.85E−06	***
5YearCi	3.839	0.829	4.632	3.61E−06	***
Topic1	0.007	0.017	0.401	0.6887	
Topic2	0.105	0.012	9.014	<2e−16	***
Topic3	0.182	0.012	15.655	<2e−16	***
Topic4	−0.014	0.010	−1.353	0.1761	
Topic5	0.021	0.010	2.119	0.0341	*
Topic6	0.002	0.013	0.160	0.8725	
Topic7	−0.066	0.010	−6.678	2.42E−11	***
Topic8	−0.155	0.010	−15.708	<2e−16	***
Topic9	−0.094	0.012	−7.683	1.55E−14	***
Topic10	0.165	0.011	14.534	<2e−16	***

Note: * p < 0.05, ** p < 0.01, *** p < 0.001.10-dimensions Topics refer to 10 dimensions topics generated by doc2vec.

3.3 Matching and Checking Balance

In pre-matching experiments, nearest neighbor matching, optimal full matching [21] and generalized full matching [22] with respect to the observed confounding factors are tested on our datasets. Generalized full matching resembles optimal full matching, but performs better on our large datasets, allowing for faster and more efficient dataset balancing. Hence, we selected generalized full matching with probit regression model for propensity score in this study and set the caliper to 0.05 to minimize the error and improve the quality of matching. The comparison of covariate balance before and after matching are shown in Table 2, the standardized mean difference (SMD) of publication year (pubYear) is less than 0.1 after matching, and the SMDs of other covariates is less than 0.05 after matching. That indicates that the good balance and the successful matches.

Table 2. Comparison of the covariates of the sample before and after PSM

	Before matching			After matching		
	Means Treated	Means Control	SMD	Means Treated	Means Control	SMD
distance	0.363	0.275	0.641	0.301	0.301	0.000
pubYear	0.898	0.873	0.234	0.875	0.881	-0.052
pubCore	0.108	0.093	0.052	0.095	0.097	-0.008
refNum	0.028	0.022	0.298	0.024	0.024	0.010
tsize	0.207	0.119	0.551	0.147	0.145	0.009
Ldrshp	0.033	0.028	0.062	0.029	0.029	-0.002
5YearCi	0.002	0.002	0.096	0.002	0.002	0.008
Topic2	0.257	0.247	0.024	0.247	0.250	-0.007
Topic3	-0.627	-0.665	0.084	-0.649	-0.653	0.009
Topic5	0.708	0.693	0.032	0.692	0.698	-0.013
Topic7	-1.117	-1.103	-0.026	-1.100	-1.107	0.012
Topic8	-0.439	-0.403	-0.086	-0.411	-0.414	0.009
Topic9	0.501	0.503	-0.005	0.500	0.502	-0.004
Topic10	-0.286	-0.313	0.070	-0.310	-0.305	-0.012

3.4 Estimating the Causal Effect

The average treatment effects are estimated after matching. The *marginaleffects* package in R is applied to this task. As shown in Table 3, the ATE of AI papers with affiliation diversity is -1.75 (p < 0.000) relative to those with no affiliation diversity. That suggests a negative causal relationship between affiliation diversity and paper disruptiveness in AI. AI papers with affiliation diversity can be 1.75% less disruptive than those collaborated by the resemble affiliation.

Table 3. The treatment effects.

Matching methods	ATE	SE	Sig.
Generalized full matching	−1.75	0.134	***

4 Conclusion and Limitation

In this study, we explore the causal relationship between affiliation diversity and paper disruptiveness in the field of AI based on Propensity Score Matching (PSM). As for indicators, affiliation diversity was measured by the Integration Score, with the embedding vector for each affiliation extracted from the pre-training results of Wikidata. The DI index measures the disruptiveness of AI papers. Other sixteen-relevant candidate covariates were also considered.

We find that homophily (over 70%) is still prevalent over the past 70 years among multi-affiliation collaborations in the field of Artificial Intelligence, despite the average affiliation diversity exhibiting startling upward trends when AI steps into the deep learning stage. Overall, the average affiliation diversity and the average disruptiveness percentile of AI papers show opposite directions from 1950 to 2013 and maintain the same significant growth trend since 2014.

It is worth mentioning that affiliation diversity cannot promote paper disruptiveness in Artificial Intelligence. On the contrary, AI papers with affiliation diversity can be 1.75% less disruptive compared to AI papers that collaborated by the resemble affiliation. Our conclusions can be used to guide policymaking or innovation forecasting.

The limitations of the current study should be acknowledged. First, we have only split papers into groups with- and without- affiliation diversity, leaving the distinction between high- and low- affiliation diversity unexamined. In the future work, we will set multiple treatment groups with different levels of affiliation diversity to verify the robustness of our conclusions. Second, the datasets used in this study are limited to AI conference papers and journal papers collected from Microsoft Academic Graph (MAG), we will take into account other type resources like code in Github, AI preprints and AI patents. Third, there are many potential diversity factors, such as gender diversity and disciplinary diversity. Our future research will examine the causal effect of these factors on the disruptiveness of papers in AI.

Acknowledgment. This work was supported by Science Foundation of the Ministry of Education of China (Grant No. 22YJC870014), National Natural Science Foundation of China (Grant No.72204090).

References

1. Wu, L., Wang, D., Evans, J.A.: Large teams develop and small teams disrupt science and technology. Nature **566**(7744), 378–382 (2019)
2. Liu, X., Yi, B., Li, M., Li, J.: Is interdisciplinary collaboration research more disruptive than monodisciplinary research? Proc. Assoc. Inf. Sci. Technol. **58**(1), 264–272 (2021)

3. Park, M., Leahey, E., Funk, R.J.: Papers and patents are becoming less disruptive over time. Nature **613**, 138–144 (2023)
4. Chu, J.S., Evans, J.A.: Slowed canonical progress in large fields of science. Proc. Natl. Acad. Sci. **118**(41), e2021636118 (2021)
5. Sheng, L., Lyu, D., Ruan, X., Shen, H., Cheng, Y.: The association between prior knowledge and the disruption of an article. Scientometrics 1–21 (2023)
6. Yang, S., Kim, S.Y.: Knowledge-integrated research is more disruptive when supported by homogeneous funding sources: a case of US federally funded research in biomedical and life sciences. Scientometrics **128**, 3257–3282 (2023)
7. Wuchty, S., Jones, B.F., Uzzi, B.: The increasing dominance of teams in production of knowledge. Science **316**(5827), 1036–1039 (2007)
8. Jones, B., Wuchty, S., Uzzi, B.: Multi-university research teams: Shifting impact, geography, and stratification in science. Science **322**, 1259–1262 (2008)
9. Hottenrott, H., Lawson, C.: A first look at multiple institutional affiliations: a study of authors in Germany, Japan and the UK. Scientometrics **111**, 285–295 (2017)
10. Shao, Z., Yuan, S., Wang, Y.: Institutional collaboration and competition in artificial intelligence. IEEE Access **8**, 69734–69741 (2020)
11. Abramo, G., D'Angelo, C.A., Solazzi, M.: The relationship between scientists' research performance and the degree of internationalization of their research. Scientometrics **86**(3), 629–643 (2011)
12. Dong, Y., Ma, H., Tang, J., Wang, K.: Collaboration diversity and scientific impact. arXiv preprint arXiv:1806.03694 (2018)
13. Tang, X., Li, X., Ma, F.: Internationalizing AI: evolution and impact of distance factors. Scientometrics **127**(1), 181–205 (2022)
14. Frank, M.R., Wang, D., Cebrian, M., Rahwan, I.: The evolution of citation graphs in artificial intelligence research. Na. Mach. Intell. **1**(2), 79–85 (2019)
15. Lerer, A., Wu, L., Shen, J., et al. Pytorch-biggraph: a large-scale graph embedding system. arXiv preprint arXiv:1903.12287 (2019)
16. Hirsch, J.E.: An index to quantify an individual's scientific research output. Proc. Natl. Acad. Sci. **102**(46), 16569–16572 (2005)
17. Stirling, A.: A general framework for analysing diversity in science, technology and society. J. R. Soc. Interface **4**(15), 707–719 (2007)
18. Liu, M., Hu, X.: Will collaborators make scientists move? a generalized propensity score analysis. J. Informet. **15**(1), 101113 (2021)
19. Fan, L., Guo, L., Wang, X., Xu, L., Liu, F.: Does the author's collaboration mode lead to papers' different citation impacts? an empirical analysis based on propensity score matching. J. Informet. **16**(4), 101350 (2022)
20. Tang, X., Li, X., Ding, Y., Song, M., Bu, Y.: The pace of artificial intelligence innovations: speed, talent, and trial-and-error. J. Informet. **14**(4), 101094 (2020)
21. Stuart, E.A., Green, K.M.: Using full matching to estimate causal effects in nonexperimental studies: examining the relationship between adolescent marijuana use and adult outcomes. Dev. Psychol. **44**(2), 395–406 (2008)
22. Sävje, F., Higgins, M.J., Sekhon, J.S.: Generalized full matching. Polit. Anal. **29**(4), 423–447 (2021)

Platform, Visuals, and Sound: Webtoon's Immersive Romance Reading Engagement

Hyerim Cho(✉) [iD], Denice Adkins [iD], Diogenes da Silva Santos [iD],
and Alicia K. Long [iD]

University of Missouri, Columbia, MO 65211, USA
hyerimcho@missouri.edu

Abstract. The current research investigates Webtoon, an emerging visual narrative reading platform that has received global attention for its fast growth and adaptations to different media. The research team particularly focuses on the Webtoon romance genre and its readers to see how Webtoon's unique sensory elements embedded in reading support romance readers' reading engagement. With an exploratory approach, 16 avid Webtoon romance readers were interviewed. Findings show that Webtoon romance readers appreciated the immersive reading experience supported by Webtoon's format, visual presentations, and audio effects, which helped heighten the overall atmosphere and emotions of the romance works they read. However, the unintentional use of multimedia effects or technical asynchronicity distracted their reading engagement.

Keywords: New Media · Reader Engagement · Webtoon · Romance Readers

1 Introduction

Romance is a widely read fiction genre with a diverse reader base [1]. In 2022, more than 52% of all print book sales in the United States were fiction books. Among them, romance was the biggest category, generating over $1.44 billion in revenue [2].

While readers have widely loved this genre, understanding romance readers' needs and appeals has been challenging for researchers and library practitioners. As Saricks [3, p. 202] states, "Defining a genre so large and diverse that it accounts for approximately 50% of all paperback fiction sales is not an easy task," and "in any genre in which the appeal is primarily to the emotions and thus difficult to verbalize, readers and librarians have more difficulty working together."

Noting this challenge, the research team focuses on the emerging multimedia reading platform, Webtoon, and its romance narrative. Webtoon is a type of graphic narrative medium like comic books and graphic novels but provided primarily on the web and via mobile applications in a weekly, sequential manner. With its convenient and mostly free access, Webtoon's international readership has grown considerably recently. The trend of genre popularity is similar to the print books' sales records; in 2019, of the most-read webcomic series on Webtoon, ten works were categorized as romance, with several other slice-of-life genre works closely associated with romance themes [4]. Despite the fast growth and demand for Webtoon and its romance genre, studies that understand this newly emerged reading platform and its readers are lacking; what are the distinguishable characteristics of Webtoon romance materials, and do Webtoon romance readers have unique reading experiences due to those characteristics?

The current manuscript presents an emerging theme from a larger, ongoing research project where the research team investigates and compares different reading engagement and experiences between traditional romance novels and romance Webtoon. In this short paper, the research team highlights how multimedia elements embedded in Webtoon romance works influence readers' engagement and immersive experiences, focusing on its platform characteristics, artistic styles and visual presentations, and sound/audio effects. In doing so, this manuscript aims to contribute to reader engagement and genre studies, as well as Readers' Advisory (RA) studies. Particularly, the following research question will be answered:

RQ: How do the multimedia elements in Webtoon influence romance readers' reading engagement and experiences?

2 Literature Review

As a hybrid form of comic books, graphic novels, and digital media, Webtoon offers a distinct and immersive reading experience [5]. This literature review synthesizes existing research focused on Webtoon's unique platform attributes, the visual elements, and the audio facets in the context of reader engagement and experiences.

Ease of access is one of Webtoon's strongest features, contributing to its rapidly growing global readership. Spector [6] highlighted how mobile optimization and accessibility had made Webtoon a go-to platform for diverse readers, a point that holds particular significance for the romance genre, where readers cherish convenience and emotional immersion [7]. Another crucial aspect of Webtoon's popularity is its design consistency. Tidwell [8] expounded on the role of consistent design patterns in enhancing user experiences across digital platforms. This consistency is even more critical in serialized narratives like romance, which require sustained engagement over time. Additionally, Quach et al. [9] emphasized the role of privacy and sustainability in digital platforms. Romance readers, who often delve into emotionally charged narratives, are likely to be attracted to a platform that offers a discreet reading environment, strengthening the importance of privacy features within Webtoon.

The visual aspects of Webtoons provide an additional layer of reader engagement. Shao [10] examined how artistic choices could significantly enhance a reader's immersion, while Loaiza Alamo [11] addressed the Korean webtoon from a graphic perspective, describing how visual codes contribute to the cross-media narrative of Korean webtoons. This research highlighted that visual elements could evoke specific emotional responses, reinforcing the genre's fundamental appeal to emotions [12]. Spalter and Van Dam [13] further discussed the rising importance of visual literacy in the digital age. Since Webtoon often employs visual cues to supplement or replace textual narratives, the ability to 'read' these cues becomes crucial for an emotionally fulfilling experience, especially in the romance genre [14].

Webtoon takes the immersive experience a step further by incorporating audio elements. These elements may be isolated sound effects, a musical overlay for certain parts of the episode, or background music throughout the entire episode. Sound de-sign, as discussed by DeWitt and Bresin [15], can dramatically elevate a digital experience. In Webtoon, ambient sounds and background scores often deepen reader engagement, particularly in a genre where the emotional atmosphere is paramount. Mayer and Moreno [16] provided insights into how audio could assist in reducing cognitive load, thus making it easier for the reader to engage both emotionally and cognitively with the narrative.

Despite a wealth of related research, a glaring gap exists in the literature focusing on the combined influence of platform features, visual elements, and audio aspects on romance reader engagement within Webtoon. Previous studies have either considered Webtoon as a broad platform without a genre-specific lens [17] or concentrated on other types of digital platforms [18, 19]. This study aims to fill this gap by offering nuanced insights into how the multimedia elements of Webtoon contribute to the romance genre's appeal, thus enriching our understanding of this massively popular yet academically uncharted medium.

3 Methods

This qualitative, exploratory study analyzed reader engagement with romance storylines within the Webtoon format. Traditional text-based romance novels typically engage with only one sense vision when reading print or e-books or hearing when listening to audiobooks. However, Webtoon uses multiple media (text and images) and often multiple types of sensory input (seeing and hearing).

Participants included those people who had read both formats. Recruitment first began through an online appeal directed toward students at two universities; later, recruitment was done through snowball sampling. Three members of the research team conducted interviews with 18 participants via Zoom, between April and August 2023. Two interviews were excluded due to lack of fit with the participation criteria, leaving a total of 16 participants. Ten participants used she/her pronouns, three participants used they/them, two participants used she/they, and one participant used any. Three indicated an Asian cultural background, two identified as Latinx, and three identified as Black. No claim is made about the representativeness of the participant sample to the general population due to the small sample size and the focused nature of participant selection. As yet, insufficient research has been done on Webtoon romance readers to accurately describe their population characteristics.

The interview protocol contained questions designed to elicit reading experiences with each format, as well as a comparison between formats. Questions asked about readers' experiences with the formats and their engagement, but also elicited data about elements of the formats that influenced the selection. The average interview time was 28 min, and the interviewers kept notes to indicate their reflections on the interviews. Interviews were recorded, transcribed, and anonymized.

Data analysis used a split coding model, with members of the research team dividing the transcripts and engaging in open coding of those transcripts to identify primary themes. Prior to this, the principal investigator led a discussion of potential themes and elements based on previous research in Webtoon and romance genres. During and after open coding, the research group met weekly to discuss results and compare emerging themes. Finally, a final scheme of emergent themes was created through a consensus model. In areas of disagreement, a resolution was reached by discussing the rationales for a particular theme, revising verbiage, and expanding or creating new themes as needed. In this paper, the theme of reader engagement will be highlighted.

4 Findings and Discussion

4.1 Webtoon's Platform and Format Characteristics

Most participants appreciated Webtoon's consistency and accessibility. Webtoon's short and digestible episodes are updated weekly, providing a reading routine for many readers. Knowing when the next episodes will be added and catching up with them provided comfortable regularity to readers. In addition, Webtoon provides easy access. The majority of Webtoon readers use smartphone applications to read Webtoon, so they can easily enjoy the pleasure of reading anytime and anywhere without needing to carry a physical book.

> "It's so hard to bring back up a book sometimes just because books can be a little heavy and a little inconvenient to take out, and everyone's on their phone all the time, so you can just do a quick few swipes and you will finish a chapter of a Webtoon by then when it comes to romance." [Participant 15]

Most Webtoon works are free to read as long as one has online access. This free access is a notable feature of Webtoon compared to other entertainment media or graphic mediums such as movies and comic books. However, several participants also shared their concerns about some of the Webtoon sources being more commercialized and paywalled recently, moving in the opposite direction from the easy access that Webtoon has been able to provide.

Lois and Gregson [20, p. 465] state that romance narratives are "despite its immense popularity with readers, as well as its wide range of writing styles, plot complexities, and degrees of sensuality," the least respected genre. In the current study, too, participants talked about privacy regarding reading romance Webtoon in public and the potentially negative perceptions toward it. While Participant 18 shared their perspectives that reading Webtoon romance could be a more private experience due to the platform, Participant 14 shared that they tend to be more careful about reading Webtoon romance in public in case certain scenes might include more "spicy" visuals.

4.2 Visual Elements and Reading Engagement

Visual elements strongly contribute to readers' engagement with Webtoon romance stories. For example, the illustration style engages readers through visual appeal and realism: "They're really aesthetically appealing and not just the characters, the character designs, but also the settings and minor things like the clothing designs." [Participant 3] The artistic style, use of colors, and other visual cues helped create the mood for the story and convey emotions.

"I really like when people describe feelings through colors and different shapes that you wouldn't maybe necessarily think about, but it sets the mood where you just know there's heightened feeling." [Participant 17]

The romance reading experience in Webtoon is also distinctive regarding the effort needed to visualize characters or settings. In Webtoon, the illustrations portray the characters' physical appearances, body language, and the setting's cultural elements with a more instantaneous delivery than when those characteristics are described primarily in text or black and white colors only, allowing readers to concentrate more on the story:

"I don't have to use my imagination for what the characters look like or what the settings look like. It's easier for me to become more engaged in the story a little bit more. Again, the art helps too with that more immersive experience, and I find myself being engaged more with webtoons overall in that way." [Participant 3]

In addition, engaging with Webtoon by scrolling down contributes to immersive romance reading experiences. Actively interacting with the platform by scrolling, combined with artistic expressions and visual cues, helps signify changes or set up scenes. Participant 8 highlighted the importance of a "good scene setting," stating that it "overall builds kind of the ambiance without it being a movie playing on a screen." Most Webtoon romance readers in this study mentioned that this immersive feeling they enjoyed while reading Webtoon was why they preferred reading on Webtoon to other reading platforms.

Nonetheless, in some cases, visual elements can also detract from reader engagement. Participants emphasized that visual art, decorative elements, colors, and settings need to support the progression of the story in a consistent and intentional way. If the visual elements are disconnected from the mood, setting, or plot, the result subtracts from the reading experience. As stated by Participant 9: "as long as the illustration seems to fit with the story, so a really dark post-apocalyptic, two lovers finding each other and they get *chibi*, cute, extra colorful, it might send me away."

4.3 Audio Elements and Reading Engagement

While the visual elements of Webtoon are necessary and expected for the format, the sound element is less typical. Nonetheless, the inclusion of sound in Webtoon also affects reader engagement, both positively and negatively.

For many readers, the inclusion of the sound element heightens their immersion into the storyline, with some sound effects indicating critical plot points and music evoking mood for specific episodes. Many participants noted their enjoyment of audio elements in Webtoon. One participant mentioned the value of sound effects: "It kind of signals, 'This is important,' or 'Something really big is going to happen.'" [Participant 18] In addition to sound effects, participants enjoyed the inclusion of music, and two participants were able to discuss the Webtoon series with a particularly effective use of music.

"[Music] can add to special episodes, maybe the actual love confession or things like that. Having the music in the background can help to set the mood, and it creates a more immersive environment." [Participant 10]

In keeping with Participant 9's desire that the visual illustration fit the story, some Webtoon readers want sound and music that is consistent with the storyline they are following. Participant 8 noted that "some Webtoons have better audio than others," while Participant 5 said, "If it's a soft chapter and it's like them being romantic, I don't want to hear battle music in the background." Incongruency in the mood evoked by the storyline versus the mood evoked by the music negatively affected reader immersion.

Another reader indicated that immersion was negatively affected when the sound effects or music were inconsistent with where they were in the narrative.

"I don't think Webtoon has a way of tracking at which point you're reading. They know that you're on the page, but they don't know at which point on the page that you are. So, the music might not be on par with your reading. Sometimes, I might be way beyond where the sound effect is at." [Participant 15]

Nonetheless, some readers did not find audio effects particularly engaging, with sound detracting from their reading experience. A participant who read Webtoon before bed indicated turning the audio off to not disturb their roommate, and another noted not finding audio effects meaningful and not listening to them. Other respondents cited the note about turning on sound for particular episodes in terms that suggest that audio is unexpected. One referred to the sound feature advisory as a "warning" [Participant 17], and another said the note was "helpful to know it's coming so it doesn't just scare you." [Participant 5].

5 Conclusion

The current short paper explored the emerging theme of romance Webtoon reading engagement supported (or distracted) by embedded multimedia elements and format characteristics of Webtoon. Based on the semi-structured interviews with 16 avid Webtoon romance readers, the research team found that the newly emerged reading platform, Webtoon, has provided new reading experiences to readers. It has provided easier accessibility to the entertainment media that is convenient to enjoy, and the illustrated storytelling with artistic expressions, along with timely sound effects or background music, provided immersive romantic reading experiences to readers.

However, some sensory media elements and how they were placed within Webtoon could sometimes distract readers' engagement with the story, such as artistic styles that conflict with the overall atmosphere/tone of the work or narratives and the use of music or sound effects that do not synchronize well with particular scenes. Thus, while the intentional and thoughtful placement of sensory elements on the reading platform can support readers' engagement, it might also ruin the immersive reading engagement when not executed correctly.

While this manuscript looked at romance Webtoon readers' experiences only, the research team envisions that reading platforms, in general, will diversify further with different technologies and platforms. Based on the findings from the current study, the research team suggests that the careful consideration of 1) the mood of narratives and scenes and 2) the technical synchronicity of sensory elements would be critical when designing an immersive reading experience.

Lastly, romance fiction has been defined as narratives with two basic elements: "a central love story and an emotionally satisfying and optimistic ending" [1]. However, a romance Webtoon is a serialized narrative. Also, several romance Webtoon works were completed on a sad note, conflicting with North America's traditional definition of romance genre. Future studies should investigate how the definition of the evolving genre should be revisited, considering the various formats and cultural sentiments. In addition, noting the uniqueness of its platform and genre, further analysis of the Webtoon romance elements, such as the narrative structure, social reading and reader interactions, and diverse characters, may provide a better understanding of the platform and readers' engagement.

Acknowledgments. This project has been funded by the *Romance Writers of America (RWA) Academic Grant*. Our research team shares our gratitude for this opportunity.

References

1. Romance Writers of America: About the romance genre. https://www.rwa.org/Online/Romance_Genre/About_Romance_Genre.aspx. Accessed 14 Sept 2023
2. Curcic, D.: Fiction books sales statistics. Wordsrated. https://wordsrated.com/book-sales-statistics. Accessed 14 Sept 2023
3. Saricks, J.G.: The Readers' Advisory Guide to Genre Fiction. American Library Association, Chicago (2001)
4. Puc, S.: Webtoon: Why so many of the most popular webcomics are romance (2022). https://www.cbr.com/romance-webcomics-most-popular-webtoon-tapas/. Accessed 14 Sept 2023
5. Cho, H., Adkins, D., Pham, N.M.: "I only wish that I had had that growing up": understanding Webtoon's appeals and characteristics as an emerging reading platform. Proc. Assoc. Inf. Sci. Technol. **59**(1), 44–54 (2022)
6. Spector, N.A.: How mobile webcomics are working to save reading. Publishers Weekly (2022). https://www.publishersweekly.com/pw/by-topic/industry-news/comics/article/90614-how-mobile-webcomics-are-working-to-save-reading.html
7. Saricks, J.G.: The Readers' Advisory Guide to Genre Fiction. American Library Association, Chicago (2001)
8. Tidwell, J.: Designing Interfaces: Patterns for Effective Interaction Design. O'Reilly Media, Newton (2010)
9. Quach, S., Thaichon, P., Martin, K.D., Weaven, S., Palmatier, R.W.: Digital technologies: tensions in privacy and data. J. Acad. Mark. Sci. **50**(6), 1299–1323 (2022)
10. Shao, K.: Comic narrative expression and aesthetics: From print to webtoons [Master's thesis, Long Island University]. Digital Commons LIU (2021). https://digitalcommons.liu.edu/brooklyn_fulltext_master_theses/26/
11. Loaiza Alamo, R.: El papel de los códigos visuales en la narrativa transmedia del webtoon coreano [Undergraduate thesis, Universidad Peruana de Ciencias Aplicadas]. Repositorio Académico UPC (2021). https://repositorioacademico.upc.edu.pe/handle/10757/658749
12. Saricks, J.G.: The readers' advisory guide to genre fiction. United Kingdom, American Library Association (2021)
13. Spalter, A.M., Van Dam, A.: Digital visual literacy. Theory Pract. **47**(2), 93–101 (2008)
14. Mende, M., Scott, M.L., Garvey, A.M., Bolton, L.E.: The marketing of love: how attachment styles affect romantic consumption journeys. J. Acad. Mark. Sci. **47**, 255–273 (2019)

15. DeWitt, A., Bresin, R.: Sound design for affective interaction. In: International Conference on Affective Computing and Intelligent Interaction, pp. 523–533. Springer, Heidelberg (2007)
16. Mayer, R.E., Moreno, R.: Nine ways to reduce cognitive load in multimedia learning. Educ. Psychol. **38**(1), 43–52 (2003)
17. Jang, W., Song, J.E.: Webtoon as a new Korean Wave in the process of glocalization. Kritika Kultura **29** (2017)
18. Kakderi, C., Psaltoglou, A., Fellnhofer, K.: Digital platforms and online applications for user engagement and collaborative innovation. In: The 20th Conference of the Greek Society of Regional Scientists (2018)
19. De Reuver, M., Sørensen, C., Basole, R.C.: The digital platform: a research agenda. J. Inf. Technol. **33**(2), 124–135 (2018)
20. Lois, J., Gregson, J.: Sneers and leers: romance writers and gendered sexual stigma. Gend. Soc. **29**(4), 459–483 (2015)

Correction to: Arguing About Controversial Science in the News: Does Epistemic Uncertainty Contribute to Information Disorder?

Heng Zheng⬤, Theodore Dreyfus Ledford⬤, and Jodi Schneider⬤

Correction to:
Chapter 16 in: I. Sserwanga et al. (Eds.): *Wisdom, Well-Being, Win-Win*, LNCS 14597,
https://doi.org/10.1007/978-3-031-57860-1_16

The original version of this paper, the third author was not labelled as corresponding author. In addition, there were a number of minor mistakes in the text and the references. These have been corrected.

The updated version of this chapter can be found at
https://doi.org/10.1007/978-3-031-57860-1_16

Author Index

I. Sserwanga et al. (Eds.): iConference 2024, LNCS 14597, pp. 425–428, 2024.
https://doi.org/10.1007/978-3-031-57860-1

Printed in the United States
by Baker & Taylor Publisher Services